FIFTH

ETHICS AND TECHNOLOGY

Controversies, Questions, and Strategies for Ethical Computing

HERMAN T. TAVANI
Rivier University

WILEY

VP AND EXECUTIVE PUBLISHER Donald Fowley
SENIOR ACQUISITIONS EDITOR Bryan Gambrel
ASSOCIATE DEVELOPMENT EDITOR Jennifer Lartz
MARKET SOLUTIONS ASSISTANT Jessy Moor
PROJECT MANAGER Gladys Soto
PROJECT SPECIALIST Nichole Urban
PROJECT ASSISTANT Emily Meussner
MARKETING MANAGER Daniel Sayre
ASSISTANT MARKETING MANAGER Puja Katariwala
ASSOCIATE DIRECTOR Kevin Holm
PRODUCTION EDITOR Loganathan Kandan
PHOTO RESEARCHER Nicholas Olin
COVER PHOTO CREDIT © agsandrew/Getty Images, Inc.

This book was set in 10/12 Times Ten LT Std Roman by SPi Global and printed and bound by Lightning Source, Inc.

Founded in 1807, John Wiley & Sons, Inc. has been a valued source of knowledge and understanding for more than 200 years, helping people around the world meet their needs and fulfill their aspirations. Our company is built on a foundation of principles that include responsibility to the communities we serve and where we live and work. In 2008, we launched a Corporate Citizenship Initiative, a global effort to address the environmental, social, economic, and ethical challenges we face in our business. Among the issues we are addressing are carbon impact, paper specifications and procurement, ethical conduct within our business and among our vendors, and community and charitable support. For more information, please visit our website: www.wiley.com/go/citizenship.

ISBN: 978-1-119-23975-8 (PBK)
ISBN: 978-1-119-22415-0 (EVALC)

Library of Congress Cataloging-in-Publication Data:

Tavani, Herman T., author.
Ethics and technology : controversies, questions, and strategies for ethical computing / Herman T. Tavani, Rivier University.—Fifth edition.
pages cm
Includes bibliographical references and index.
ISBN 978-1-119-23975-8 (pbk.)
1. Computer networks—Moral and ethical aspects. I. Title.
TK5105.5.T385 2016
174' 9004678—dc23

2015031994

Printing identification and country of origin will either be included on this page and/or the end of the book. In addition, if the ISBN on this page and the back cover do not match, the ISBN on the back cover should be considered the correct ISBN.

Printed in the United States of America

10 9 8 7 6 5 4 3 2 1

For Regina and Joe

CONTENTS AT A GLANCE

PREFACE xvii

FOREWORD xxvii

CHAPTER 1. INTRODUCTION TO CYBERETHICS: CONCEPTS, PERSPECTIVES, AND METHODOLOGICAL FRAMEWORKS 1

CHAPTER 2. ETHICAL CONCEPTS AND ETHICAL THEORIES: FRAMEWORKS FOR ANALYZING MORAL ISSUES 27

CHAPTER 3. CRITICAL REASONING SKILLS FOR EVALUATING DISPUTES IN CYBERETHICS 63

CHAPTER 4. PROFESSIONAL ETHICS, CODES OF CONDUCT, AND MORAL RESPONSIBILITY 87

CHAPTER 5. PRIVACY AND CYBERSPACE 113

CHAPTER 6. SECURITY IN CYBERSPACE 151

CHAPTER 7. CYBERCRIME AND CYBER-RELATED CRIMES 175

CHAPTER 8. INTELLECTUAL PROPERTY DISPUTES IN CYBERSPACE 201

CHAPTER 9. REGULATING COMMERCE AND SPEECH IN CYBERSPACE 236

CHAPTER 10. THE DIGITAL DIVIDE, DEMOCRACY, AND WORK 263

CHAPTER 11. ONLINE COMMUNITIES, VIRTUAL REALITY, AND ARTIFICIAL INTELLIGENCE 292

CHAPTER 12. ETHICAL ASPECTS OF EMERGING AND CONVERGING TECHNOLOGIES 317

GLOSSARY 347

INDEX 353

TABLE OF CONTENTS

PREFACE xvii

New to the *Fifth Edition* xviii
Audience and Scope xix
Organization and Structure of the Book xx
The Web Site for *Ethics and Technology* xxii
A Note to Students xxiii
Note to Instructors: A Roadmap for Using This Book xxiii
A Note to Computer Science Instructors xxiv
Acknowledgments xxv

FOREWORD xxvii

CHAPTER 1

INTRODUCTION TO CYBERETHICS: CONCEPTS, PERSPECTIVES, AND METHODOLOGICAL FRAMEWORKS 1

Scenario 1–1: Hacking into the Mobile Phones of Celebrities 1
1.1 Defining Key Terms: Cyberethics and Cybertechnology 2
1.1.1 What Is Cybertechnology? 3
1.1.2 Why the Term Cyberethics? 3
1.2 The Cyberethics Evolution: Four Developmental Phases in Cybertechnology 4
1.3 Are Cyberethics Issues Unique Ethical Issues? 7
Scenario 1–2: Developing the Code for a Computerized Weapon System 8
Scenario 1–3: Digital Piracy 8
1.3.1 Distinguishing between Unique Technological Features and Unique Ethical Issues 9
1.3.2 An Alternative Strategy for Analyzing the Debate about the Uniqueness of Cyberethics Issues 10
1.3.3 A Policy Vacuum in Duplicating Computer Software 10
1.4 Cyberethics as a Branch of Applied Ethics: Three Distinct Perspectives 12
1.4.1 Perspective #1: Cyberethics as a Field of Professional Ethics 12
1.4.2 Perspective #2: Cyberethics as a Field of Philosophical Ethics 14
1.4.3 Perspective #3: Cyberethics as a Field of Sociological/Descriptive Ethics 16
Scenario 1–4: The Impact of Technology X on the Pleasantville Community 17
1.5 A Comprehensive Cyberethics Methodology 19
1.5.1 A "Disclosive" Method for Cyberethics 19
1.5.2 An Interdisciplinary and Multilevel Method for Analyzing Cyberethics Issues 21
1.6 A Comprehensive Strategy for Approaching Cyberethics Issues 21
1.7 Chapter Summary 22
Review Questions 23
Discussion Questions 23
Scenarios for Analysis 23
Endnotes 24
References 25
Further Readings 26
Online Resources 26

▶ **CHAPTER 2**

ETHICAL CONCEPTS AND ETHICAL THEORIES: FRAMEWORKS FOR ANALYZING MORAL ISSUES 27

Scenario 2–1: The Case of the "Runaway Trolley": A Classic Moral Dilemma 27
2.1 Ethics and Morality 29
2.1.1 What Is Morality? 29
2.1.2 The Study of Morality: Three Distinct Approaches for Evaluating and Justifying the Rules Comprising a Moral System 32
2.2 Discussion Stoppers as Roadblocks to Moral Discourse 35
2.2.1 Discussion Stopper #1: People Disagree on Solutions to Moral Issues 36
2.2.2 Discussion Stopper #2: Who Am I to Judge Others? 37
2.2.3 Discussion Stopper #3: Morality Is Simply a Private Matter 39
2.2.4 Discussion Stopper #4: Morality Is Simply a Matter for Individual Cultures to Decide 40
Scenario 2–2: The Price of Defending Moral Relativism 41
2.3 Why Do We Need Ethical Theories? 43
2.4 Consequence-Based Ethical Theories 44
2.4.1 Act Utilitarianism 46
Scenario 2–3: A Controversial Policy in Newmerica 46
2.4.2 Rule Utilitarianism 46
2.5 Duty-Based Ethical Theories 47
2.5.1 Rule Deontology 48
Scenario 2–4: Making an Exception for Oneself 48
2.5.2 Act Deontology 49
Scenario 2–5: A Dilemma Involving Conflicting Duties 50
2.6 Contract-Based Ethical Theories 51
2.6.1 Some Criticisms of Contract-Based Theories 52
2.6.2 Rights-Based Contract Theories 53
2.7 Character-Based Ethical Theories 54
2.7.1 Being a Moral Person vs. Following Moral Rules 54
2.7.2 Acquiring the "Correct" Habits 55
2.8 Integrating Aspects of Classical Ethical Theories into a Single Comprehensive Theory 56
2.8.1 Moor's Just-Consequentialist Theory and Its Application to Cybertechnology 57
2.8.2 Key Elements in Moor's Just-Consequentialist Framework 58
2.9 Chapter Summary 59
Review Questions 59
Discussion Questions 60
Scenarios for Analysis 60
Endnotes 61
References 61
Further Readings 62

▶ **CHAPTER 3**

CRITICAL REASONING SKILLS FOR EVALUATING DISPUTES IN CYBERETHICS 63

SCENARIO 3–1: Reasoning About Whether to Download Software from "Sharester" 63
3.1 What Is Critical Reasoning? 64
3.1.1 Some Basic Concepts: (Logical) Arguments and Claims 64
3.1.2 The Role of Arguments 65
3.1.3 The Basic Structure of an Argument 65
3.2 Constructing an Argument 67
3.3 Valid Arguments 68
3.4 Sound Arguments 71
3.5 Invalid Arguments 73
3.6 Inductive Arguments 74
3.7 Fallacious Arguments 75

3.8 A Seven-Step Strategy for Evaluating Arguments 77
3.9 Identifying Some Common Fallacies 79
3.9.1 Ad Hominem Argument 79
3.9.2 Slippery Slope Argument 80
3.9.3 Fallacy of Appeal to Authority 80
3.9.4 False Cause Fallacy 81
3.9.5 Fallacy of Composition/Fallacy of Division 81
3.9.6 Fallacy of Ambiguity/Equivocation 82
3.9.7 The False Dichotomy/Either–Or Fallacy/All-or-Nothing Fallacy 82
3.9.8 The Virtuality Fallacy 83
3.10 Chapter Summary 84
Review Questions 84
Discussion Questions 85
Scenarios for Analysis 85
Endnotes 85
References 86
Further Readings 86

▶ **CHAPTER 4**
PROFESSIONAL ETHICS, CODES OF CONDUCT, AND MORAL RESPONSIBILITY 87

Scenario 4–1: Fatalities Involving the Oerlikon GDF-005 Robotic Cannon 87
4.1 What Is *Professional Ethics?* 88
4.1.1 What Is a Profession? 89
4.1.2 Who Is a Professional? 89
4.1.3 Who Is a Computer/IT Professional? 90
4.2 Do Computer/IT Professionals Have Any Special Moral Responsibilities? 90
4.3 Professional Codes of Ethics and Codes of Conduct 91
4.3.1 The Purpose of Professional Codes 92
4.3.2 Some Criticisms of Professional Codes 93
4.3.3 Defending Professional Codes 94
4.3.4 The IEEE-CS/ACM Software Engineering Code of Ethics and Professional Practice 95
4.4 Conflicts of Professional Responsibility: Employee Loyalty and Whistle-Blowing 97
4.4.1 Do Employees Have an Obligation of Loyalty to Employers? 97
4.4.2 Whistle-Blowing 98
Scenario 4–2: NSA Surveillance and the Case of Edward Snowden 101
4.5 Moral Responsibility, Legal Liability, and Accountability 103
4.5.1 Distinguishing Responsibility from Liability and Accountability 104
4.5.2 Accountability and the Problem of "Many Hands" 105
Scenario 4–3: The Case of the *Therac-25 Machine 105*
4.5.3 Legal Liability and Moral Accountability 106
4.6 Do Some Computer Corporations Have Special Moral Obligations? 107
4.7 Chapter Summary 108
Review Questions 109
Discussion Questions 109
Scenarios for Analysis 110
Endnotes 110
References 111
Further Readings 112

▶ **CHAPTER 5**
PRIVACY AND CYBERSPACE 113

Scenario 5–1: A New NSA Data Center 113
5.1 Privacy in the Digital Age: *Who* Is Affected and Why Should We Worry? 114
5.1.1 Whose Privacy Is Threatened by Cybertechnology? 115
5.1.2 Are Any Privacy Concerns Generated by Cybertechnology Unique or Special? 115

5.2 What Is Personal Privacy? 117
5.2.1 Accessibility Privacy: Freedom from Unwarranted Intrusion 118
5.2.2 Decisional Privacy: Freedom from Interference in One's Personal Affairs 118
5.2.3 Informational Privacy: Control over the Flow of Personal Information 118
5.2.4 A Comprehensive Account of Privacy 119
Scenario 5–2: Descriptive Privacy 119
Scenario 5–3: Normative Privacy 120
5.2.5 Privacy as "Contextual Integrity" 120
Scenario 5–4: Preserving Contextual Integrity in a University Seminar 121
5.3 Why Is Privacy Important? 121
5.3.1 Is Privacy an Intrinsic Value? 122
5.3.2 Privacy as a Social Value 123
5.4 Gathering Personal Data: Surveillance, Recording, and Tracking Techniques 123
5.4.1 "Dataveillance" Techniques 124
5.4.2 Internet Cookies 124
5.4.3 RFID Technology 125
5.4.4 Cybertechnology and Government Surveillance 126
5.5 Analyzing Personal Data: Big Data, Data Mining, and Web Mining 127
5.5.1 Big Data: What, Exactly, Is It, and Why Does It Threaten Privacy? 128
5.5.2 Data Mining and Personal Privacy 128
Scenario 5–5: Data Mining at the XYZ Credit Union 129
5.5.3 Web Mining: Analyzing Personal Data Acquired from Our Interactions Online 132
5.6 Protecting Personal Privacy in Public Space 132
5.6.1 PPI vs. NPI 133
Scenario 5–6: Shopping at SuperMart 133
Scenario 5–7: Shopping at Nile.com 134
5.6.2 Search Engines and the Disclosure of Personal Information 135
5.7 Privacy Legislation and Industry Self-Regulation 137
5.7.1 Industry Self-Regulation and Privacy-Enhancing Tools 137
5.7.2 Privacy Laws and Data Protection Principles 139
5.8 A Right to "Be Forgotten" (or to "Erasure") in the Digital Age 140
Scenario 5–8: An Arrest for an Underage Drinking Incident 20 Years Ago 141
5.8.1 Arguments Opposing RTBF 142
5.8.2 Arguments Defending RTBF 143
5.8.3 Establishing "Appropriate" Criteria 144
5.9 Chapter Summary 146
Review Questions 146
Discussion Questions 147
Scenarios for Analysis 148
Endnotes 148
References 149
Further Readings 150

▶ **CHAPTER 6**
SECURITY IN CYBERSPACE 151

Scenario 6–1: The "Olympic Games" Operation and the Stuxnet Worm 151
6.1 Security in the Context of Cybertechnology 152
6.1.1 Cybersecurity as Related to Cybercrime 153
6.1.2 Security and Privacy: Some Similarities and Some Differences 153
6.2 Three Categories of Cybersecurity 154
6.2.1 Data Security: Confidentiality, Integrity, and Availability of Information 155
6.2.2 System Security: Viruses, Worms, and Malware 156
6.2.3 Network Security: Protecting our Infrastructure 156
Scenario 6–2: The "GhostNet" Controversy 157

6.3 Cloud Computing and Security 158
6.3.1 Deployment and Service/Delivery Models for the Cloud 158
6.3.2 Securing User Data Residing in the Cloud 159
6.3.3 Assessing Risk in the Cloud and in the Context of Cybersecurity 160
6.4 Hacking and "The Hacker Ethic" 160
6.4.1 What Is "The Hacker Ethic"? 161
6.4.2 Are Computer Break-ins Ever Ethically Justifiable? 163
6.5 Cyberterrorism 164
6.5.1 Cyberterrorism vs. Hacktivism 165
Scenario 6–3: *Anonymous* and the "Operation Payback" Attack 166
6.5.2 Cybertechnology and Terrorist Organizations 167
6.6 Information Warfare (IW) 167
6.6.1 Information Warfare vs. Conventional Warfare 167
6.6.2 Potential Consequences for Nations that Engage in IW 168
6.7 Chapter Summary 170
Review Questions 170
Discussion Questions 171
Scenarios for Analysis 171
Endnotes 171
References 172
Further Readings 174

▶ **CHAPTER 7**
CYBERCRIME AND CYBER-RELATED CRIMES 175

Scenario 7–1: Creating a Fake Facebook Account to Catch Criminals 175
7.1 Cybercrimes and Cybercriminals 177
7.1.1 Background Events: A Brief Sketch 177
7.1.2 A Typical Cybercriminal 178
7.2 Hacking, Cracking, and Counter Hacking 178
7.2.1 Hacking vs. Cracking 179
7.2.2 Active Defense Hacking: Can Acts of "Hacking Back" or Counter Hacking Ever Be Morally Justified? 179
7.3 Defining Cybercrime 180
7.3.1 Determining the Criteria 181
7.3.2 A Preliminary Definition of Cybercrime 181
7.3.3 Framing a Coherent and Comprehensive Definition of Cybercrime 182
7.4 Three Categories of Cybercrime: Piracy, Trespass, and Vandalism in Cyberspace 183
7.5 Cyber-Related Crimes 184
7.5.1 Some Examples of Cyber-Exacerbated vs. Cyber-Assisted Crimes 184
7.5.2 Identity Theft 185
7.6 Technologies and Tools for Combating Cybercrime 187
7.6.1 Biometric Technologies 187
7.6.2 Keystroke-Monitoring Software and Packet-Sniffing Programs 188
7.7 Programs and Techniques Designed to Combat Cybercrime in the United States 189
7.7.1 Entrapment and "Sting" Operations to Catch Internet Pedophiles 189
Scenario 7–2: Entrapment on the Internet 189
7.7.2 Enhanced Government Surveillance Techniques and the Patriot Act 189
7.8 National and International Laws to Combat Cybercrime 190
7.8.1 The Problem of Jurisdiction in Cyberspace 190
Scenario 7–3: A Virtual Casino 191
Scenario 7–4: Prosecuting a Computer Corporation in Multiple Countries 192
7.8.2 Some International Laws and Conventions Affecting Cybercrime 192
Scenario 7–5: The Pirate Bay Web Site 193
7.9 Cybercrime and the Free Press: The Wikileaks Controversy 193

7.9.1 Are WikiLeaks' Practices Ethical? 194
7.9.2 Are WikiLeaks' Practices Criminal? 194
7.9.3 WikiLeaks and the Free Press 195
7.10 Chapter Summary 196
Review Questions 197
Discussion Questions 197
Scenarios for Analysis 198
Endnotes 199
References 199
Further Readings 200

▶ **CHAPTER 8**
INTELLECTUAL PROPERTY DISPUTES IN CYBERSPACE 201

Scenario 8–1: Streaming Music Online 201
8.1 What Is Intellectual Property? 202
8.1.1 Intellectual Objects 203
8.1.2 Why Protect Intellectual Objects? 203
8.1.3 Software as Intellectual Property 204
8.1.4 Evaluating a Popular Argument Used by the Software Industry to Show Why It Is Morally Wrong to Copy Proprietary Software 205
8.2 Copyright Law and Digital Media 206
8.2.1 The Evolution of Copyright Law in the United States 206
8.2.2 The Fair-Use and First-Sale Provisions of Copyright Law 207
8.2.3 Software Piracy as Copyright Infringement 208
8.2.4 Napster and the Ongoing Battles over Sharing Digital Music 209
8.3 Patents, Trademarks, and Trade Secrets 212
8.3.1 Patent Protections 212
8.3.2 Trademarks 213
8.3.3 Trade Secrets 214
8.4 Jurisdictional Issues Involving Intellectual Property Laws 214
8.5 Philosophical Foundations for Intellectual Property Rights 215
8.5.1 The Labor Theory of Property 215
Scenario 8–2: DEF Corporation vs. XYZ Inc. 216
8.5.2 The Utilitarian Theory of Property 216
Scenario 8–3: Sam's e-Book Reader Add-on Device 217
8.5.3 The Personality Theory of Property 217
Scenario 8–4: Angela's B++ Programming Tool 218
8.6 The "Free Software" and "Open Source" Movements 219
8.6.1 GNU and the Free Software Foundation 219
8.6.2 The "Open Source Software" Movement: OSS vs. FSF 220
8.7 The "Common Good" Approach: An Alternative Framework for Analyzing the Intellectual Property Debate 221
8.7.1 Information Wants to be Shared vs. Information Wants to be Free 223
8.7.2 Preserving the Information Commons 225
8.7.3 The Fate of the Information Commons: Could the Public Domain of Ideas Eventually Disappear? 226
8.74 The Creative Commons 227
8.8 PIPA, SOPA, and RWA Legislation: Current Battlegrounds in the Intellectual Property War 228
8.8.1 The PIPA and SOPA Battles 228
8.8.2 RWA and Public Access to Health-Related Information 229
Scenario 8–5: Elsevier Press and "The Cost of Knowledge" Boycott 229
8.8.3 Intellectual Property Battles in the Near Future 231
8.9 Chapter Summary 231
Review Questions 231

Discussion Questions 232
Scenarios for Analysis 232
Endnotes 233
References 234
Further Readings 235

▶ CHAPTER 9
REGULATING COMMERCE AND SPEECH IN CYBERSPACE 236

Scenario 9–1: *Anonymous* and the Ku Klux Klan 236
9.1 Introduction and Background Issues: Some Key Questions and Critical Distinctions Affecting Internet Regulation 237
9.1.1 Is Cyberspace a Medium or a Place? 238
9.1.2 Two Categories of Cyberspace Regulation: Regulating Content and Regulating Process 239
9.1.3 Four Modes of Regulation: The Lessig Model 240
9.2 Digital Rights Management (DRM) 242
9.2.1 Some Implications of DRM for Public Policy Debates Affecting Copyright Law 242
9.2.2 DRM and the Music Industry 243
Scenario 9–2: The Sony Rootkit Controversy 243
9.3 E-Mail Spam 244
9.3.1 Defining Spam 244
9.3.2 Why Is Spam Morally Objectionable? 245
9.4 Free Speech vs. Censorship and Content Control in Cyberspace 246
9.4.1 Protecting Free Speech 247
9.4.2 Defining Censorship 247
9.5 Pornography in Cyberspace 248
9.5.1 Interpreting "Community Standards" in Cyberspace 248
9.5.2 Internet Pornography Laws and Protecting Children Online 249
9.5.3 Virtual Child Pornography 250
9.5.4 Sexting *and Its Implications for Current Child Pornography Laws 252*
Scenario 9–3: A Sexting Incident Involving Greensburg Salem High School 252
9.6 Hate Speech and Speech that Can Cause Physical Harm to Others 254
9.6.1 Hate Speech on the Web 254
9.6.2 Online "Speech" that Can Cause Physical Harm to Others 255
9.7 "Network Neutrality" and the Future of Internet Regulation 256
9.7.1 Defining Network Neutrality 256
9.7.2 Some Arguments Advanced by Net Neutrality's Proponents and Opponents 257
9.7.3 Future Implications for the Net Neutrality Debate 257
9.8 Chapter Summary 258
Review Questions 259
Discussion Questions 259
Scenarios for Analysis 260
Endnotes 260
References 261
Further Readings 262

▶ CHAPTER 10
THE DIGITAL DIVIDE, DEMOCRACY, AND WORK 263

Scenario 10–1: Digital Devices, Social Media, Democracy, and the "Arab Spring" 264
10.1 The Digital Divide 265
10.1.1 The Global Digital Divide 265
10.1.2 The Digital Divide within Nations 266
Scenario 10–2: Providing In-Home Internet Service for Public School Students 267
10.1.3 Is the Digital Divide an Ethical Issue? 268
10.2 Cybertechnology and the Disabled 270

10.3 Cybertechnology and Race 271
10.3.1 Internet Usage Patterns 272
10.3.2 Racism and the Internet 272
10.4 Cybertechnology and Gender 273
10.4.1 Access to High-Technology Jobs 274
10.4.2 Gender Bias in Software Design and Video Games 275
10.5 Cybertechnology, Democracy, and Demotratic Ideals 276
10.5.1 Has Cybertechnology Enhanced or Threatened Democracy? 276
10.5.2 How has Cybertechnology Affected Political Elections in Democratic Nations? 279
10.6 The Transformation and the Quality of Work 280
10.6.1 Job Displacement and the Transformed Workplace 281
10.6.2 The Quality of Work Life in the Digital Era 283
Scenario 10–3: Employee Monitoring and the Case of *Ontario vs. Quon* *284*
10.7 Chapter Summary 287
Review Questions 287
Discussion Questions 288
Scenarios for Analysis 288
Endnotes 289
References 289
Further Readings 291

▶ **CHAPTER 11**
ONLINE COMMUNITIES, VIRTUAL REALITY, AND ARTIFICIAL INTELLIGENCE 292

Scenario 11–1: Ralph's Online Friends and Artificial Companions 292
11.1 Online Communities and Social Networking Services 293
11.1.1 Online Communities vs. Traditional Communities 294
11.1.2 Blogs and Some Controversial Aspects of the Bogosphere 295
Scenario 11–2: "The Washingtonienne" Blogger 295
11.1.3 Some Pros and Cons of SNSs (and Other Online Communities) 296
Scenario 11–3: A Suicide Resulting from Deception on MySpace 298
11.2 Virtual Environments and Virtual Reality 299
11.2.1 What Is Virtual Reality (VR)? 300
11.2.2 Ethical Aspects of VR Applications 301
11.3 Artificial Intelligence (AI) 305
11.3.1 What Is AI? A Brief Overview 305
11.3.2 The Turing Test and John Searle's "Chinese Room" Argument 306
11.3.3 Cyborgs and Human–Machine Relationships 307
11.4 Extending Moral Consideration to AI Entities 310
Scenario 11–4: Artificial Children 310
11.4.1 Determining Which Kinds of Beings/Entities Deserve Moral Consideration 310
11.4.2 Moral Patients vs. Moral Agents 311
11.5 Chapter Summary 312
Review Questions 313
Discussion Questions 313
Scenarios for Analysis 313
Endnotes 314
References 315
Further Readings 316

▶ **CHAPTER 12**
ETHICAL ASPECTS OF EMERGING AND CONVERGING TECHNOLOGIES 317

Scenario 12–1: When "Things" Communicate with One Another 317
12.1 Converging Technologies and Technological Convergence 318
12.2 Ambient Intelligence (AmI) and Ubiquitous Computing 319

12.2.1 Pervasive Computing, Ubiquitous Communication, and Intelligent User Interfaces 320
12.2.2 Ethical and Social Aspects of AmI 321
Scenario 12–2: E. M. Forster's "(Pre)Cautionary Tale" 322
Scenario 12–3: Jeremy Bentham's "Panopticon/Inspection House" (Thought Experiment) 323
12.3 Nanotechnology and Nanocomputing 324
12.3.1 Nanotechnology: A Brief Overview 324
12.3.2 Ethical Issues in Nanotechnology and Nanocomputing 326
12.4 Autonomous Machines 329
12.4.1 What Is an AM? 329
12.4.2 Some Ethical and Philosophical Questions Pertaining to AMs 332
12.5 Machine Ethics and *Moral Machines* 336
12.5.1 What Is Machine Ethics? 336
12.5.2 Designing Moral Machines 337
12.6 A "Dynamic" Ethical Framework for Guiding Research in New and Emerging Technologies 340
12.6.1 Is an ELSI-Like Model Adequate for New/Emerging Technologies? 340
12.6.2 A "Dynamic Ethics" Model 341
12.7 Chapter Summary 341
Review Questions 342
Discussion Questions 342
Scenarios for Analysis 343
Endnotes 343
References 344
Further Readings 346

GLOSSARY 347

INDEX 353

PREFACE

Since the publication of the fourth edition of *Ethics and Technology* in late 2012, the digital landscape has continued to evolve, resulting in new variations of moral, legal, and social concerns. For example, ongoing unease about personal privacy has been further exacerbated by Big Data (sometimes also referred to as Big Data Analytics), as well as by the "Internet of Things." Surveillance-related privacy concerns have also intensified, especially in the aftermath of revelations that the National Security Agency (NSA) allegedly snooped on American citizens. And the intentional leaking of classified NSA information by Edward Snowden has generated renewed interest in the topic of whistle-blowing.

Other recent ethical/social concerns arise in connection with hacking-related activities carried out by various nation-states. In late 2014, for example, the government of North Korea admitted responsibility for a series of break-ins at Sony Corporation, in which the government threatened to commit 9/11-like terrorist threats if Sony released a controversial movie. A different kind of hacking-related activity has significantly impacted the commercial sphere, where major retail stores in the United States, including Target and Home Depot, have been embarrassed by break-ins compromising their customer databases. A third kind of hacking-related activity targeted select (high-profile) female celebrities, whose social media accounts and mobile devices were hacked; in some cases, nude photos of these celebrities were also made available on selected Web sites.

It is not only celebrities, however, who are vulnerable to having their devices and accounts hacked or to having unauthorized content (including embarrassing photos) displayed on the Internet. Ordinary users are also at risk in this regard mainly because of the myriad ways in which one's digitized personal data can now be so easily compromised and made accessible on the Web. Consider, for example, a relatively recent controversy involving "revenge porn sites," where people can post nude and other kinds of embarrassing photos of their ex-romantic partners. Because it is difficult to have content permanently deleted from the Internet, users often struggle in vain to have embarrassing online personal information removed. And concerns about the indefinite period of time in which one's digitized personal information can persist on the Internet have influenced countries in the European Union to adopt a privacy principle called the "Right to Be Forgotten," where citizens in those countries have the right to have certain kinds of online personal information about them "erased." However, we will see that this principle, sometimes also referred to as the "Right to Erasure," has been controversial and has not been adopted by most countries, including the United States.

Other relatively recent ethics-related concerns arise in connection with technologies such as *3D printing* and *augmented reality* (AR); whereas the former makes possible the "printing" of controversial objects such as guns, the latter introduces concerns generated by "wearable" (computing) technologies such as Google Glass. Additionally, "smart cars," such as those currently produced by Google, raise concerns about moral/legal responsibility issues for vehicle-related accidents and injuries. Also in the context of transportation-related controversies, we can ask what effect the relatively new shuttle/taxi-related services such as Uber, made possible by apps designed for digital devices, will likely have for the future of the (more traditional) taxicab industry.

Although new technologies emerge and existing technologies continue to mature and evolve, many of the ethical issues associated with them are basically variations of existing ethical problems. At bottom, these issues illustrate (contemporary examples of) traditional ethical concerns having to do with fairness, obligations to assist others in need, and so forth. So, we should not infer that the moral landscape itself has been altered because of behaviors made possible by these technologies. We will see that, for the most part, the new issues examined in this edition of *Ethics and Technology* are similar in relevant respects to the kinds of ethical issues we examined in the book's previous editions. However, many emerging technologies present us with challenges that, initially at least, do not seem to fit easily into our conventional ethical categories. So, a major objective of this textbook is to show how those controversies can be analyzed from the perspective of standard ethical concepts and theories.

The purpose of *Ethics and Technology*, as stated in the prefaces to the four previous editions of this book, is to introduce students to issues and controversies that comprise the relatively new field of cyberethics. The term "cyberethics" is used to refer to the field of study that examines moral, legal, and social issues involving cybertechnology. Cybertechnology, in turn, refers to a broad spectrum of computing/information and communication technologies that range from stand-alone computers to the current cluster of networked devices and applications.

This textbook examines a wide range of cyberethics issues—from specific issues of moral responsibility that directly affect computer and information technology (IT) professionals to broader social and ethical concerns that affect each of us in our day-to-day lives. Questions about the roles and responsibilities of computer/IT professionals in developing safe and reliable computer systems are examined under the category of professional ethics. Broader social and ethical concerns associated with cybertechnology are examined under topics such as privacy, security, crime, intellectual property, Internet regulation, and so forth.

▶ NEW TO THE *FIFTH EDITION*

New pedagogical material includes:

- *Learning objectives,* highlighted at the beginning of each chapter, describing the principal student outcomes intended for that chapter
- *Beginning-of-chapter scenarios*, designed to illustrate one or more of the key themes/issues/controversies examined in that chapter
- Some new *in-chapter scenarios* (comprising both actual cases and hypothetical situations), which enable students to apply methodological concepts/frameworks and ethical theories introduced in Chapters 1 and 2
- Some new *sample arguments*, which encourage students to apply the tools for argument analysis introduced in Chapter 3
- Some new end-of-chapter *review questions* and *discussion questions*
- Some new end-of-chapter "Scenarios for Analysis," which can be used either for in-class analysis and group projects or outside-class assignments

New issues examined and analyzed include:

- State-sponsored cyberattacks and their implications for (inter)national security
- Whistle-blowing controversies generated by the leaking of highly sensitive (governmental) information in digital form
- NSA surveillance-related leaks and their implications for both personal privacy and national security

- Privacy threats posed by Big Data
- Challenges posed to the recording industry/artists by the online services that stream digital music
- Ethical and social aspects of the "Internet of things"
- Disruptions made possible by international "hacktivist" groups such as *Anonymous*.
- Controversies associated with a person's "right" to have some kinds of personal information about them "erased" from the Internet

In revising the book, I have eliminated some older, now out-of-date, material. In some instances, I have also streamlined the discussion of topics that were examined in greater detail in previous editions of the book; in these cases, a condensed version of that material, which is still highly relevant, has been carried over to the present edition.

▶ AUDIENCE AND SCOPE

Because cyberethics is an interdisciplinary field, this textbook aims at reaching several audiences and thus easily runs the risk of failing to meet the needs of any one audience. I have nonetheless attempted to compose a textbook that addresses the needs of computer science, philosophy, social/behavioral science, and library/information science students. Computer science students need a clear understanding of the ethical challenges they will face as computer professionals when they enter the workforce. Philosophy students, on the contrary, should understand how moral issues affecting cybertechnology can be situated in the field of applied ethics in general and then analyzed from the perspective of ethical theory. Social science and behavioral science students will likely want to assess the sociological impact of cybertechnology on our social and political institutions (government, commerce, and education) and sociodemographic groups (affecting gender, race, ethnicity, and social class). And library/information science students should be aware of the complexities and nuances of current intellectual property laws that threaten unfettered access to electronic information and should be informed about recent regulatory schemes that threaten to censor certain forms of electronic speech.

Students from other academic disciplines should also find many issues covered in this textbook pertinent to their personal and professional lives; some undergraduates may elect to take a course in social and ethical aspects of technology to satisfy one of their general education requirements. Although *Ethics and Technology* is intended mainly for undergraduate students, it could be used, in conjunction with other texts, in graduate courses as well.

We examine ethical controversies using *scenarios* that include both actual cases and hypothetical examples, wherever appropriate. In some instances, I have deliberately constructed provocative scenarios and selected controversial cases to convey the severity of the ethical issues we consider. Some readers may be uncomfortable with, and possibly even offended by, these scenarios and cases—for example, those illustrating unethical practices that negatively affect children and minorities. Although it might have been politically expedient to skip over issues and scenarios that could unintentionally offend certain individuals, I believe that no textbook in applied ethics would do justice to its topic if it failed to expose and examine issues that adversely affect vulnerable groups in society.

Also included in most chapters are *sample arguments* that are intended to illustrate some of the rationales that have been put forth by various interest groups to defend policies and laws affecting privacy, security, property, and so forth in cyberspace. Instructors and students can evaluate these arguments via the rules and criteria established in Chapter 3 to see how well, or how poorly, the premises in these arguments succeed in establishing their conclusions.

Exercise questions are included at the end of each chapter. First, basic "review questions" quiz the reader's comprehension of key concepts, themes, issues, and scenarios covered in that chapter. These are followed by higher-level "discussion questions" designed to encourage students to reflect more deeply on some of the controversial issues examined in the chapter. Building on the higher-level nature of the discussion questions, "Scenarios for Analysis" are also included at the end of each chapter. These "unanalyzed scenarios" provide students and instructors with additional resources for analyzing important controversies introduced in the various chapters. For example, these scenarios can be used as in-class resources for group projects.

Some discussion questions and end-of-chapter scenarios ask students to compare and contrast arguments and topics that span multiple chapters; for instance, students are asked to relate arguments used to defend intellectual property rights, considered in Chapter 8, to arguments for protecting privacy rights, examined in Chapter 5. Other questions and scenarios ask students to apply foundational concepts and frameworks, such as ethical theories and critical reasoning techniques introduced in Chapters 2 and 3, to the analysis of specific cyberethics issues examined in subsequent chapters. In some cases, these end-of-chapter questions and scenarios may generate lively debate in the classroom; in other cases, they can serve as a point of departure for various class assignments and group projects. Although no final "solutions" to the issues and dilemmas raised in these questions and scenarios are provided in the text, some "strategies" for analyzing them are included in the section of the book's Web site (www.wiley.com/college/tavani) titled "Strategies for Discussion Questions."

▶ ORGANIZATION AND STRUCTURE OF THE BOOK

Ethics and Technology is organized into 12 chapters. Chapter 1, "Introduction to Cyberethics: Concepts, Perspectives, and Methodological Frameworks," defines key concepts and terms that will appear throughout the book. For example, definitions of terms such as *cyberethics* and *cybertechnology* are introduced in this chapter. We then consider the question of whether any ethical issues involving cybertechnology are unique ethical issues. Next, we show how cyberethics issues can be approached from three different perspectives: professional ethics, philosophical ethics, and sociological/descriptive ethics, each of which represents the approach generally taken by a computer scientist, a philosopher, and a social/behavioral scientist. Chapter 1 concludes with a proposal for a comprehensive and interdisciplinary methodological scheme for analyzing cyberethics issues from these perspectives.

In Chapter 2, "Ethical Concepts and Ethical Theories: Frameworks for Analyzing Moral Issues," we examine some of the basic concepts that make up a moral system. We draw a distinction between *ethics* and *morality* by defining ethics as "the study of morality." "Morality," or a moral system, is defined as an informal, public system comprising rules of conduct and principles for evaluating those rules. We then examine consequence-based, duty-based, character-based, and contract-based ethical theories. Chapter 2 concludes with a model that integrates elements of competing ethical theories into one comprehensive and unified theory.

Chapter 3, "Critical Reasoning Skills for Evaluating Disputes in Cyberethics," includes an overview of basic concepts and strategies that are essential for debating moral issues in a structured and rational manner. We begin by describing the structure of a logical *argument* and show how arguments can be constructed and analyzed. Next, we examine a technique for distinguishing between arguments that are valid and invalid, sound and unsound, and inductive and fallacious. We illustrate examples of each type with topics affecting cybertechnology and cyberethics. Finally, we identify some strategies for spotting and labeling "informal logical fallacies" that frequently occur in everyday discourse.

Chapter 4, "Professional Ethics, Codes of Conduct, and Moral Responsibility," examines issues related to professional responsibility for computer/IT professionals. We consider whether there are any special moral responsibilities that computer/IT professionals have as professionals. We then examine some professional codes of conduct that have been adopted by computer organizations. We also ask: To what extent are software engineers responsible for the reliability of the computer systems they design and develop, especially applications that include "life-critical" and "safety-critical" software? We then ask whether computer/IT professionals are permitted, or perhaps even required, to "blow the whistle" when they have reasonable evidence to suggest that a computer system is unreliable. Finally, we consider whether some computer corporations might have special moral responsibilities because of the nature of the products they develop or services they provide.

We discuss privacy issues involving cybertechnology in Chapter 5. First, we examine the concept of privacy as well as some arguments for why privacy is considered an important human value. We then look at how personal privacy is threatened by the kinds of surveillance techniques and data-collection schemes made possible by cybertechnology. Specific data-gathering and data-analysis techniques are examined in detail. We next consider some challenges that "big data," data mining, and Web mining pose for protecting personal privacy in public space. In Chapter 5, we also consider whether stronger privacy legislation is needed to protect online consumers or whether industry self-regulation techniques in conjunction with privacy enhancing tools can provide an adequate alternative. We conclude this chapter with an analysis of the European Union's "Right to Be Forgotten" principle and identify some challenges it poses for major search engine companies operating in Europe.

Chapter 6, "Security in Cyberspace," examines security threats in the context of computing and cybertechnology. We begin by differentiating three distinct senses of *security*: data security, system security, and network security. Next, we examine some challenges that cloud-computing services pose for cybersecurity. We then analyze the concepts of "hacker" and "hacker ethic," and we ask whether computer break-ins can ever be morally justified. In the final section of this chapter, we differentiate acts of "hacktivism," cyberterrorism, and information warfare, and we examine some impacts that each has had thus far.

We begin our analysis of cybercrime, in Chapter 7, by asking if it is possible to construct a profile of a "typical" cybercriminal. We then propose a definition of cybercrime that enables us to distinguish between "cyberspecific" and "cyber-related" crimes and show how this distinction can help in formulating more coherent cybercrime laws. We also consider the notion of legal jurisdiction in cyberspace and examine some of the challenges it poses in prosecuting cybercrimes that involve interstate and international venues. In addition, we examine some technological efforts used to combat cybercrime, such as controversial uses of biometric technologies. Chapter 7 concludes with an analysis of the WikiLeaks controversy from the perspective of cybercrime.

One objective of Chapter 8, "Intellectual Property Disputes in Cyberspace," is to show why understanding the concept of intellectual property (IP) is important in an era of digital information. We examine three philosophical/legal theories of property rights and then draw some key distinctions affecting four legal concepts pertaining to IP: copyrights, patents, trademarks, and trade secrets. We also examine some alternative frameworks such as the Free Software Foundation (FSF), Open Source Software (OSS), and Creative Commons (CC) initiatives, and we conclude our analysis of IP issues by arguing for a principle that presumes in favor of sharing digital information while also acknowledging the legitimate interests of rights holders.

In Chapter 9, "Regulating Commerce and Speech in Cyberspace," we draw distinctions between two different senses of "regulation" as it applies to the Internet: regulating commerce and regulating speech. We then examine controversies surrounding e-mail spam, which some believe can be viewed as a form of "speech" in cyberspace. We all consider whether all forms of online speech should be granted legal protection; for example, should child pornography, hate speech, and speech that can cause physical harm to others be tolerated in online forums? We conclude our examination of Internet-regulation issues in Chapter 9 with an analysis of the "net neutrality" controversy.

Chapter 10 examines a wide range of equity and access issues from the perspective of cybertechnology's impact for *sociodemographic groups* (affecting class, race, and gender), as well as for *social/political institutions* (such as the government) and *social sectors* (such as the workplace). The chapter begins with an analysis of the "digital divide." We then examine specific equity and access issues affecting disabled persons, racial minorities, and women. Next, we explore the relationship between cybertechnology and democracy, and we consider whether the Internet enhances democracy or threatens it. The final section of this chapter examines some of the social and ethical impacts that cybertechnology has had thus far for employment in the contemporary workplace.

In Chapter 11, we examine a wide range of ethical issues pertaining to online communities, virtual reality (VR) environments, and artificial intelligence (AI) developments. We begin by analyzing the impact that cybertechnology has for our traditional understanding of the concept of community; in particular, we ask whether online communities, such as Facebook and Twitter, raise any special ethical or social issues. Next, we examine some ethical implications of behavior made possible by virtual environments and VR/augmented reality applications. We then describe the impact that recent developments in AI have for our sense of self and for what it means to be human. The final section of Chapter 11 questions whether certain kinds of (highly sophisticated) AI entities may ultimately deserve some degree of moral consideration and thus might cause us to expand our conventional framework of moral obligation to include those entities.

Chapter 12, the final chapter of *Ethics and Technology*, examines some ethical challenges that arise in connection with emerging and converging technologies such as ambient intelligence (AmI) and nanocomputing. This chapter also examines some issues in the emerging (sub)field of *machine ethics*. Among the questions considered are whether we should develop autonomous machines that are capable of making moral decisions and whether we could trust those machines to always act in our best interests. Chapter 12 concludes with the introduction and brief analysis a comprehensive ("dynamic") ethical framework designed to guide researchers and inform policy makers in the development of new and emerging technologies.

A glossary that defines terms commonly used in the context of computer ethics and cyberethics is also included. However, the glossary is by no means intended as an exhaustive list of such terms. Additional material for this text is available on the book's Web site: www.wiley.com/college/tavani.

▶ THE WEB SITE FOR *ETHICS AND TECHNOLOGY*

Seven appendices for *Ethics and Technology* are available only in online format. Appendices A to E include the full text of five professional codes of ethics: the ACM Code of Ethics and Professional Conduct, the Australian Computer Society Code of Ethics, the British Computer Society Code of Conduct, the IEEE Code of Ethics, and the IEEE-CS/ACM Software Engineering Code of Ethics and Professional Practice, respectively. Specific sections of these codes are included in hardcopy format as well, in relevant sections of Chapter 4. Two appendices, F and G, are also available online. Appendix F contains the section of the *IEEE-CS/ACM Computing Curricula 2001 Final Report* that describes the social, professional, and ethical units of instruction mandated in their CS curriculum. Appendix G provides some additional critical reasoning techniques that expand on the strategies introduced in Chapter 3.

The Web site for *Ethics and Technology* also contains additional resources for instructors and students. Presentation slides in PowerPoint format for Chapters 1–12 are available in the "Instructor" sections of the site. As noted earlier, a section on "Strategies," which includes some techniques for answering the discussion questions and unanalyzed scenarios included at the end of each of the book's 12 chapters, is also included on this site.

▶ A NOTE TO STUDENTS

If you are taking an ethics course for the first time, you might feel uncomfortable with the prospect of embarking on a study of moral issues and controversial topics. For example, discussions involving ethical questions are sometimes perceived as "preachy" and judgmental, and the subject matter of ethics is sometimes viewed as essentially personal and private in nature. Because these are common concerns, I address them early in the textbook. First, I draw a distinction between an *ethicist*, who studies morality or a "moral system," and a *moralist* who may assume to have the correct answers to all of the questions; note that a primary objective of this book is to *examine and analyze ethical issues*, not to presume that any of us already have the correct answer to any of the questions we consider.

To accomplish this objective, I introduce three types of conceptual frameworks early in the textbook. Chapter 1 provides a methodological scheme that enables you to identify controversial problems and issues involving cybertechnology that are ethical in nature. The conceptual scheme included in Chapter 2, employing ethical theories, provides some general principles that guide your analysis of specific cases as well as your deliberations about which kinds of solutions to problems should be proposed. A third, and final, conceptual framework is introduced in Chapter 3 in the form of critical reasoning techniques, which provide rules and standards that you can use for evaluating the strengths of competing arguments and for defending a particular position that you reach on a certain issue.

This textbook was designed and written for you, the student! Whether or not it succeeds in helping you to meet the objectives of a course in cyberethics is very important to me. So I welcome your feedback on this textbook, and I would sincerely appreciate hearing your ideas on how this textbook could be improved. Please feel free to email me at htavani@rivier.edu with your suggestions and comments. I look forward to hearing from you!

▶ NOTE TO INSTRUCTORS: A ROADMAP FOR USING THIS BOOK

The chapters that make up *Ethics and Technology* are sequenced so that readers are exposed to foundational issues and conceptual frameworks before they examine specific problems in cyberethics. In some cases, it may not be possible for instructors to cover all of the material in Chapters 1–3. It is strongly recommended, however, that before students are assigned materials in Chapters 4–12, they at least read Sections 1.1, 1.4, 1.5, and 2.4. Instructors using this textbook can determine which chapters best accommodate their specific course objectives.

CS instructors, for example, will likely want to assign Chapter 4, on professional ethics and responsibility, early in the term. Philosophy instructors, on the other hand, may wish to begin their courses with a thorough examination of the materials on ethical theories and critical reasoning skills included in Chapters 2 and 3. Whereas library/information science instructors may wish to begin their classes by examining issues in Chapters 8 and 9, on intellectual property and Internet regulation, social science instructors will likely want to examine issues discussed in Chapters 10 and 11 at an early period in their course. Issues discussed in Chapter 12 may be of particular interest to instructors teaching advanced undergraduate courses, as well as graduate-level courses.

Many textbooks in applied ethics include a requisite chapter on ethical concepts/theories at the beginning of the book. Unfortunately, they often treat them in a cursory manner; furthermore, these ethical concepts and theories are seldom developed and reinforced in the remaining chapters. Thus, readers often experience a "disconnect" between the material included in the book's opening chapter and the content of the specific cases and issues discussed in subsequent chapters. By incorporating relevant aspects of ethical theory into our analysis of the specific cyberethics issues that we examine in this book, I believe that I have succeeded in avoiding the "disconnect" between theory and practice that is commonplace in many applied ethics textbooks.

▶ A NOTE TO COMPUTER SCIENCE INSTRUCTORS

Ethics and Technology can be used as the main text in a course dedicated to ethical and social issues in computing, or it can be used as a supplementary textbook for computer science courses in which one or more ethics modules are included. As I suggested in the preceding section, instructors may find it difficult to cover all of the material included in this book in the course of a single semester. And as I also previously suggested, computer science instructors will likely want to ensure that they allocate sufficient course time to the professional ethical issues discussed in Chapter 4. Also of special interest to computer science instructors and their students will be the sections on open-source code and intellectual property issues in Chapter 8 and regulatory issues affecting software code in Chapter 9.

Because computer science instructors may need to limit the amount of class time they devote to covering foundational concepts included in the earlier chapters, I recommend covering at least the critical sections of Chapters 1–3 described previously. This should provide computer science students with some of the tools they will need as professionals to deliberate on ethical issues and to justify the positions they reach.

In designing this textbook, I took into account the guidelines on ethical instruction included in the *Computing Curricula 2001 Final Report*, issued in December 2001 by the IEEE-CS/ACM Joint Task Force on Computing Curricula, which recommends the inclusion of 16 core hours of instruction on social, ethical, and professional topics in the curriculum for undergraduate computer science students. (See the online Appendix F at www.wiley.com/college/tavani for detailed information about the social/professional (SP) units in the *Computing Curricula 2001*.) Each topic, prefaced with an SP designation, defines one "knowledge area" or a CS "body of knowledge." They are distributed among the following 10 units:

SP1: History of computing (e.g., history of computer hardware, software, and networking)

SP2: Social context of computing (e.g., social implications of networked computing, gender-related issues, and international issues)

SP3: Methods and tools of analysis (e.g., identifying assumptions and values, making and evaluating ethical arguments)

SP4: Professional and ethical responsibilities (e.g., the nature of professionalism, codes of ethics, ethical dissent, and whistle-blowing)

SP5: Risks and liabilities of computer-based systems (e.g., historical examples of software risks)

SP6: Intellectual property (e.g., foundations of intellectual property, copyrights, patents, and software piracy)

SP7: Privacy and civil liberties (e.g., ethical and legal basis for privacy protection, technological strategies for privacy protection)

SP8: Computer crime (e.g., history and examples of computer crime, hacking, viruses, and crime prevention strategies)

SP9: Economic issues in computing (e.g., monopolies and their economic implications; effect of skilled labor supply)

SP10: Philosophical frameworks (e.g., ethical theory, utilitarianism, relativism)

All 10 SP units are covered in this textbook. Topics described in SP1 are examined in Chapters 1 and 10, and topics included in SP2 are discussed in Chapters 1 and 11. The methods and analytical tools mentioned in SP3 are discussed at length in Chapters 2 and 3, whereas professional issues involving codes of conduct and professional responsibility described in SP4 are included in Chapters 4 and 12. Also discussed in Chapter 4, as well as in Chapter 6, are issues involving risks and liabilities (SP5). Intellectual property issues (SP6) are discussed in detail in Chapter 8 and in certain sections of Chapter 9, whereas privacy and civil liberty concerns (SP7) are discussed mainly in Chapters 5 and 12. Chapters 6 and 7 examine topics described in SP8. Economic issues (SP9) are considered in Chapters 9 and 10. And philosophical frameworks of ethics, including ethical theory (SP10), are discussed in Chapters 1 and 2.

Table 1 illustrates the corresponding connection between SP units and the chapters of this book.

TABLE 1 SP ("Knowledge") Units and Corresponding Book Chapters

SP unit	1	2	3	4	5	6	7	8	9	10
Chapter(s)	1, 9	1, 10	2, 3	4	6	8, 9	5, 12	6, 7	9, 10	1, 2

▶ ACKNOWLEDGMENTS

In revising *Ethics and Technology* for a fifth edition, I have once again drawn from some concepts, distinctions, and arguments introduced in several of my previously published works. Where appropriate, these works are acknowledged in the various chapters in which they are cited.

The fifth edition of this book has benefited from suggestions and comments I received from many anonymous reviewers, as well as from Maria Bottis, Jeff Buechner, Lloyd Carr, Frances Grodzinsky, and Regina Tavani. I am especially grateful to Fran Grodzinsky (Sacred Heart University), with whom I have coauthored several papers, for permitting me to incorporate elements of our joint research into relevant sections of this book. I am also grateful to the numerous reviewers and colleagues who have commented on the previous editions of this book; many of their helpful suggestions have been carried over to the present edition. I also wish to acknowledge many former students whose helpful comments and suggestions on previous editions of the text have benefited the present edition.

I also wish to thank the editorial/production staff at John Wiley & Sons, especially Bryan Gambrell, Beth Golub, Loganathan Kandan, Gladys Soto, Mary Sullivan, and Nichole Urban for their support during the various stages of the revision process for the fifth edition of *Ethics and Technology*.

Finally, I must once again thank the most important person in my life: my wife, Joanne. Without her continued support and extraordinary patience, the fifth edition of this book could not have been completed. This edition of *Ethics and Technology* is dedicated to my daughter Regina, and son-in-law Joe.

Herman T. Tavani
Nashua, NH

FOREWORD

The computer/information revolution is shaping our world in ways it has been difficult to predict and to appreciate. When mainframe computers were developed in the 1940s and 1950s, some thought only a few computers would ever be needed in society. When personal computers were introduced in the 1980s, they were considered fascinating toys for hobbyists but not something serious businesses would ever use. When Web tools were initially created in the 1990s to enhance the Internet, they were a curiosity. Using the Web to observe the level of a coffee pot across an ocean was intriguing, at least for a few moments, but not of much practical use. Today, armed with the wisdom of hindsight, the impact of such computing advancements seems obvious, if not inevitable, to all of us. What government claims that it does not need computers? What major business does not have a Web address? How many people, even in the poorest of countries, are not aware of the use of cell phones?

The computer/information revolution has changed our lives and has brought with it significant ethical, social, and professional issues; consider the area of privacy as but one example. Today, surveillance cameras are abundant, and facial recognition systems are effective even under less than ideal observing conditions. Information about buying habits, medical conditions, and human movements can be mined and correlated relentlessly using powerful computers. Individuals' DNA information can easily be collected, stored, and transmitted throughout the world in seconds. This computer/information revolution has brought about unexpected capabilities and possibilities. The revolution is not only technological but also ethical, social, and professional. Our computerized world is perhaps not the world we expected, and, even to the extent that we expected it, it is not a world for which we have well-analyzed policies about how to behave. Now more than ever, we need to take cyberethics seriously.

Herman Tavani has written an excellent introduction to the field of cyberethics. His text differs from others in at least three important respects: First, the book is extraordinarily comprehensive and up to date in its subject matter. The text covers all of the standard topics such as codes of conduct, privacy, security, crime, intellectual property, and free speech and also discusses sometimes overlooked subjects such as democracy, employment, access, and the digital divide. Tavani more than anyone else has tracked and published the bibliographical development of cyberethics over many years, and his expertise with this vast literature shines through in this volume. Second, the book approaches the subject matter of cyberethics from diverse points of view. Tavani examines issues from a social science perspective, from a philosophical perspective, and from a computing professional perspective, and then he suggests ways to integrate these diverse approaches. If the task of cyberethics is multidisciplinary, as many of us believe, then such a diverse but integrated methodology is crucial to accomplishing the task. His book is one of the few that constructs such a methodology. Third, the book is unusually helpful to students and teachers because it contains an entire chapter discussing critical thinking skills and is filled with review and discussion questions.

The cyberage is going to evolve. The future details and applications are, as always, difficult to predict. But it is likely that computing power and bandwidth will continue to grow while computing devices themselves will shrink in size to the nanometer scale. More and more information devices will be inserted into our environment, our cars, our houses, our clothing, and us.

Computers will become smarter. They will be made out of new materials, possibly biological. They will operate in new ways, possibly using quantum properties. The distinction between the virtual world and the real world will blur more and more. We need a good book in cyberethics to deal with the present and prepare us for this uncertain future. Tavani's *Ethics and Technology* is such a book.

James H. Moor
Dartmouth College

CHAPTER

1

Introduction to Cyberethics: Concepts, Perspectives, and Methodological Frameworks

LEARNING OBJECTIVES

Upon completing this chapter, you will successfully be able to:

- Define *cybertechnology* and identify a wide range of technologies and devices that fall under that category,
- Define *cyberethics* and describe a cluster of moral, social, and legal issues that can be analyzed within that branch of applied ethics,
- Articulate key aspects of four distinct *phases* in the historical development and evolution of cybertechnology and cyberethics,
- Determine whether any of the ethical issues generated by cybertechnology are genuinely *unique* ethical issues, or whether they are simply new variations of traditional ethical issues,
- Differentiate among three distinct *applied ethics perspectives*—professional ethics, philosophical ethics, and sociological/descriptive ethics—that can be used to analyze the wide range of cyberethics issues examined in this book,
- Explain the components of a *comprehensive methodological framework* that we will use in our analysis of cyberethics issues in later chapters of this book.

Our primary objective in Chapter 1 is to introduce some foundational concepts and methodological frameworks that we will use to evaluate specific cyberethics issues examined in detail in subsequent chapters. We begin by reflecting on a scenario that briefly illustrates a cluster of ethical issues that arise in a recent controversy involving the use of cybertechnology.

▶ **SCENARIO 1–1:** Hacking into the Mobile Phones of Celebrities

In September 2014, one or more anonymous intruders hacked into the online accounts of the mobile phones of more than 100 celebrities, including actress Jennifer Lawrence and model Kate Upton. Nude photos of some of these celebrities were subsequently leaked to the Internet via the 4Chan Web site. The hacker(s) had allegedly broken into Apple Corporation's iCloud (a file-sharing service that enables users to store their data) gaining access to controversial pictures. Some of the celebrities whose accounts were hacked had previously deleted the photos on their physical devices and thus assumed that these pictures no longer existed.

Whereas some of the affected celebrities claimed that the nude photos of them were fake images, others admitted that the controversial pictures were authentic. Some of these celebrities threatened to bring legal action against anyone who posted nude photos of them on the Internet; for example, Jennifer Lawrence, through her spokesperson, warned that she would pursue criminal prosecution against those individuals.

In response to the intense media coverage generated by the hacking and leaking of the celebrities' photos, spokespersons for both Apple and the Federal Bureau of Investigation (FBI) announced that investigations into this incident were underway.[1] ▪

This scenario raises a number of ethical, legal, and social issues affecting digital technology and cyberspace. One major concern involves privacy; in fact, Lawrence's attorney described the hacking incident as a "flagrant violation" of his client's privacy. Other issues that arise in this scenario involve property rights—for example, are the leaked photos in question solely the property of the celebrities (as in the case of the physical electronic devices these celebrities own)? Or does the fact that those photos also reside in the cloud alter their status as the sole property of an individual? Also, at issue in this scenario are questions concerning (cyber)security—how secure is the personal data stored on our devices or in a storage service space such as the cloud? Other aspects of this controversial incident can be analyzed from the perspective of (cyber)crime; for example, some have suggested that this kind of cyber intrusion is not simply a hacking incident, or merely an instance of online harassment, but is also a serious "sex crime."

The hacking scenario involving the celebrities' photos provides us with a context in which we can begin to think about a cluster of ethical issues—privacy, property, security, crime, harassment, and so forth—affecting the use of electronic devices, in particular, and cybertechnology in general. A number of alternative scenarios and examples could also have been used to illustrate many of the same moral and legal concerns that arise in connection with digital technology. In fact, examples abound. One has only to read a daily newspaper or view regular television news programs to be informed about controversial issues involving electronic devices and the Internet, including questions that pertain to property rights, privacy violations, security, anonymity, and crime. Ethical aspects of these and other issues are examined in the 12 chapters comprising this textbook. In the remainder of Chapter 1, however, we identify and examine some key foundational concepts and methodological frameworks that can better help us to analyze issues in cyberethics.

▶ 1.1 DEFINING KEY TERMS: CYBERETHICS AND CYBERTECHNOLOGY

Before we propose a definition of cyberethics, it is important to note that the field of cyberethics can be viewed as a branch of (applied) ethics. In Chapter 2, where we define ethics as "the study of morality," we provide a detailed account of what is meant by morality and a moral system, and we also focus on some important aspects of theoretical, as opposed to, applied ethics. For example, both ethical concepts and ethical theories are also examined in detail in that chapter. There, we also include a "Getting Started" section on how to engage in ethical reasoning in general, as well as reasoning in the case of some specific moral dilemmas. In Chapter 1, however, our main focus is on clarifying some key cyber and cyber-related terms that will be used throughout the remaining chapters of this textbook.

For our purpose, *cyberethics* can be defined as the study of moral, legal, and social issues involving cybertechnology. Cyberethics examines the impact of cybertechnology on our social, legal, and moral systems, and it evaluates the social policies and laws that have been framed in response to issues generated by its development and use. To grasp the significance of these reciprocal relationships, it is important to understand what is meant by the term *cybertechnology*.

1.1.1 What Is Cybertechnology?

Cybertechnology, as used throughout this textbook, refers to a wide range of computing and communication devices, from stand-alone computers to connected, or networked, computing and communication technologies. These technologies include, but need not be limited to, devices such as "smart" phones, iPods, (electronic) tablets, personal computers (desktops and laptops), and large mainframe computers. Networked devices can be connected directly to the Internet, or they can be connected to other devices through one or more privately owned computer networks. Privately owned networks, in turn, include local-area networks (LANs) and wide-area networks (WANs). A LAN is a privately owned network of computers that span a limited geographical area, such as an office building or a small college campus. WANs, on the other hand, are privately owned networks of computers that are interconnected throughout a much broader geographic region.

How exactly are LANs and WANs different from the Internet? In one sense, the Internet can be understood as *the network of interconnected computer networks*. A synthesis of contemporary information and communications technologies, the Internet evolved from an earlier U.S. Defense Department initiative (in the 1960s) known as the ARPANET. Unlike WANs and LANs, which are privately owned computer networks, the Internet is generally considered to be a public network, in the sense that much of the information available on the Internet resides in "public space" and is thus available to anyone. The Internet, which should be differentiated from the World Wide Web, includes several applications. The Web, based on Hypertext Transfer Protocol (HTTP), is one application; other applications include File Transfer Protocol (FTP), Telnet, and e-mail. Because many users navigate the Internet by way of the Web, and because the majority of users conduct their online activities almost exclusively on the Web portion of the Internet, it is very easy to confuse the Web with the Internet.

The Internet and privately owned computer networks, such as WANs and LANs, are perhaps the most common and well-known examples of cybertechnology. However, "cybertechnology" is used in this book to represent the entire range of computing and communication systems, from stand-alone computers to privately owned networks and to the Internet itself. "Cyberethics" refers to the study of moral, legal, and social issues involving those technologies.

1.1.2 Why the Term Cyberethics?

Many authors have used the term "computer ethics" to describe the field that examines moral issues pertaining to computing and information technologies (see, e.g., Barger 2008; Johnson 2010). Others use the expression "information ethics" (e.g., Capurro 2007) to refer to a cluster of ethical concerns regarding the flow of information that is either enhanced or restricted by computer technology.[2] And because of concerns about ethical issues involving the Internet in particular, some have also used the term "Internet ethics" (see, e.g., Langford 2000). As we shall see, however, there are some disadvantages to using each of these expressions, especially insofar as each fails to capture the wide range of moral issues involving cybertechnology.[3]

For our purposes, "cyberethics" is more appropriate and more accurate than "computer ethics" for two reasons. First, the term "computer ethics" can connote ethical issues associated with computing *machines* and thus could be construed as pertaining to stand-alone or "unconnected computers." Because computing technologies and communication technologies have converged in recent years, resulting in networked systems, a computer system may now be thought of more accurately as a new kind of *medium* than as a machine. Second, the term "computer ethics" might also suggest a field of study that is concerned exclusively with ethical issues affecting computer/information technology (IT) professionals. Although these issues are very important and are examined in detail in Chapter 4 as well as in relevant sections of Chapters 6 and 12, we should note that the field of cyberethics is not limited to an analysis of moral issues that affect only professionals.

"Cyberethics" is also more accurate, for our purposes, than "information ethics." For one thing, the latter expression is ambiguous because it can mean a specific methodological framework *Information Ethics (IE)* for analyzing issues in cyberethics (Floridi 2007).[4] Also, it can connote a cluster of ethical issues of particular interest to professionals in the fields of library science and information science (Buchanan and Henderson 2009). In the latter sense, "information ethics" refers to ethical concerns affecting the free flow of, and unfettered access to, information, which include issues such as library censorship and intellectual freedom. (These issues are examined in Chapter 9.) Our analysis of cyberethics issues in this text, however, is not limited to controversies generally considered under the heading "information ethics."

We will also see why "cyberethics" is preferable to "Internet ethics." For one thing, the ethical issues examined in this textbook are not limited to the Internet; they also include privately owned computer networks and interconnected communication technologies—that is, technologies that we refer to collectively as cybertechnology. Although most of the issues considered under the heading cyberethics pertain to the Internet or the Web, some issues examined in this textbook do not involve networks per se; for example, issues associated with computerized monitoring in the workplace, with professional responsibility for designing reliable computer hardware and software systems, and with the implications of cybertechnology for gender and race need not involve networked computers and devices. In light of the wide range of moral issues examined in this book—ethical issues that cut across the spectrum of devices and communication systems (comprising cybertechnology), from stand-alone computers to networked systems—the term "cyberethics" is more comprehensive, and thus more appropriate, than "Internet ethics."[5]

Finally, we should note that some issues in the emerging fields of "agent ethics," "bot ethics," "robo-ethics," or what Wallach and Allen (2009) call "machine ethics" overlap with a cluster of concerns examined under the heading of cyberethics. Wallach and Allen define machine ethics as a field that expands upon traditional computer ethics because it shifts the main area of focus away from "what people do with computers to questions about what machines do by themselves." It also focuses on questions having to do with whether computers can be autonomous agents capable of making good moral decisions. Research in machine ethics overlaps with the work of interdisciplinary researchers in the field of artificial intelligence (AI).[6] We examine some aspects of this emerging field (or subfield of cyberethics) in Chapters 11 and 12.

▶ 1.2 THE CYBERETHICS EVOLUTION: FOUR DEVELOPMENTAL PHASES IN CYBERTECHNOLOGY

In describing the key evolutionary phases of cybertechnology and cyberethics, we begin by noting that the meaning of "computer" has evolved significantly since the 1940s. If you were to look up the meaning of that word in a dictionary written before World War II, you would most likely discover that a computer was defined as a person who calculated numbers. In the time period immediately following World War II, the term "computer" came to be identified with a (calculating) machine as opposed to a person (who calculated).[7] By the 1980s, however, computers had shrunk in size considerably and they were beginning to be understood more in terms of desktop machines (that manipulated symbols as well as numbers), or as a new kind of medium for communication, rather than simply as machines that crunch numbers. As computers became increasingly connected to one another, they came to be associated with metaphors such as the "information superhighway" and cyberspace; today, many ordinary users tend to think about computers in terms of various Internet- and Web-based applications made possible by cybertechnology.

In response to some social and ethical issues that were anticipated in connection with the use of electronic computers, the field that we now call cyberethics had its informal and humble beginnings in the late 1940s. It is interesting to note that during this period—when ENIAC (Electronic Numerical Integrator and Computer), the first electronic computer, developed at the University of Pennsylvania, became operational in 1946—some analysts confidently predicted that no more than five or six computers would ever need to be built. It is also interesting to point out that during this same period, a few insightful thinkers had already begun to describe some social and ethical concerns that would likely arise in connection with computing and cybertechnology.[8] Although still a relatively young academic field, cyberethics has now matured to a point where several articles about its historical development have appeared in books and scholarly journals. For our purposes, the evolution of cyberethics can be summarized in four distinct *technological phases*.[9]

Phase 1 (1950s and 1960s): Large (Stand-Alone) Mainframe Computers

In *Phase 1*, computing technology consisted mainly of huge mainframe computers, such as ENIAC, that were "unconnected" and thus existed as stand-alone machines. One set of ethical and social questions raised during this phase had to do with the impact of computing machines as "giant brains." Today, we might associate these kinds of questions with the field of artificial intelligence (AI). The following kinds of questions were introduced in Phase 1: Can machines think? If so, should we invent thinking machines? If machines can be intelligent entities, what does this mean for our sense of self? What does it mean to be human?

Another set of ethical and social concerns that arose during Phase 1 could be catalogued under the heading of privacy threats and the fear of Big Brother. For example, some people in the United States feared that the federal government would set up a national database in which extensive amounts of personal information about its citizens would be stored as electronic records. A strong centralized government could then use that information to monitor and control the actions of ordinary citizens. Although networked computers had not yet come on to the scene, work on the ARPANET—the Internet's predecessor, which was funded by an agency in the U.S. Defense Department—began during this phase, in the 1960s.

Phase 2 (1970s and 1980s): Minicomputers and Privately Owned Networks

In *Phase 2*, computing machines and communication devices in the commercial sector began to converge. This convergence, in turn, introduced an era of computer/communications networks. Mainframe computers, minicomputers, microcomputers, and personal computers could now be linked together by way of one or more privately owned computer networks such as LANs and WANs (see Section 1.1.1), and information could readily be exchanged between and among databases accessible to networked computers.

Ethical issues associated with this phase of computing included concerns about personal privacy, intellectual property (IP), and computer crime. Privacy concerns, which had emerged during Phase 1 because of worries about the amount of personal information that could be collected by government agencies and stored in a centralized government-owned database, were exacerbated because electronic records containing personal and confidential information could now also easily be exchanged between two or more commercial databases in the private sector. Concerns affecting IP and proprietary information also emerged during this phase because personal (desktop) computers could be used to duplicate proprietary software programs. And concerns associated with computer crime appeared during this phase because individuals could now use computing devices, including remote computer terminals, to break into and disrupt the computer systems of large organizations.

Phase 3 (1990–Present): The Internet and World Wide Web

During *Phase 3*, the Internet era, availability of Internet access to the general public has increased significantly. This was facilitated, in no small part, by the development and phenomenal growth of the World Wide Web in the 1990s. The proliferation of Internet- and Web-based technologies has contributed to some additional ethical concerns involving computing technology; for example, issues of free speech, anonymity, jurisdiction, and trust have been hotly disputed during this phase. Should Internet users be free to post any messages they wish on publicly accessible Web sites or even on their own personal Web pages—in other words, is that a "right" that is protected by free speech or freedom of expression? Should users be permitted to post anonymous messages on Web pages or even be allowed to navigate the Web anonymously or under the cover of a pseudonym?

Issues of jurisdiction also arose because there are no clear national or geographical boundaries in cyberspace; if a crime occurs on the Internet, it is not always clear where—that is, in which legal jurisdiction—it took place and thus it is unclear where it should be prosecuted. And as e-commerce emerged during this phase, potential consumers initially had concerns about trusting online businesses with their financial and personal information. Other ethical and social concerns that arose during Phase 3 include disputes about the public vs. private aspects of personal information that has become increasingly available on the Internet. Concerns of this type have been exacerbated by the amount of personal information included on social networking sites, such as Facebook and Twitter, and on other kinds of interactive Web-based forums made possible by "Web 2.0" technology (described in Chapter 11).

We should note that during Phase 3, both the interfaces used to interact with computer technology and the devices used to "house" it were still much the same as in Phases 1 and 2. A computer was still essentially a "box," that is, a CPU, with one or more peripheral devices, such as a video screen, keyboard, and mouse, serving as interfaces to that box. And computers were still viewed as devices essentially external to humans, as things or objects "out there." As cybertechnology continues to evolve, however, it may no longer make sense to try to understand computers simply in terms of objects or devices that are necessarily external to us. Instead, computers will likely become more and more a part of who or what we are as human beings. For example, Moor (2005) notes that computing devices will soon be a part of our clothing and even our bodies. This brings us to Phase 4.

Phase 4 (Present–Near Future): Converging and Emerging Technologies

Presently, we are on the threshold of *Phase 4*, a point at which we have begun to experience an unprecedented level of convergence of technologies. We have already witnessed aspects of technological convergence beginning in Phase 2, where the integration of computing and communication devices resulted in privately owned networked systems, as we noted previously. And in Phase 3, the Internet era, we briefly described the convergence of text, video, and sound technologies on the Web, and we noted how the computer began to be viewed much more as a new kind of medium than as a conventional type of machine. The convergence of information technology and biotechnology in recent years has resulted in the emerging fields of bioinformatics and computational genomics; this has also caused some analysts to question whether computers of the future will still be silicon based or whether some may also possibly be made of biological materials. Additionally, biochip implant technology, which has been enhanced by developments in AI research (described in Chapter 11), has led some to predict that in the not-too-distant future it may become difficult for us to separate certain aspects of our biology from our technology.

Today, computers are also ubiquitous or pervasive; that is, they are "everywhere" and they permeate both our workplace and our recreational environments. Many of the objects that we encounter in these environments are also beginning to exhibit what Brey (2005) and others call "ambient intelligence," which enables "smart objects" to be connected to one another via

TABLE 1-1 Summary of Four Phases of Cyberethics

Phase	Time Period	Technological Features	Associated Issues
1	1950s–1960s	Stand-alone machines (large mainframe computers)	Artificial intelligence (AI), database privacy ("Big Brother")
2	1970s–1980s	Minicomputers and the ARPANET; desktop computers interconnected via privately owned networks; not yet widely accessible to the general public	Issues from Phase 1 plus concerns involving intellectual property and software piracy, computer crime, and communications privacy
3	1990s–present	Internet, World Wide Web, and early "Web 2.0" applications, environments, and forums; became accessible to ordinary people	Issues from Phases 1 and 2 plus concerns about free speech, anonymity, legal jurisdiction, behavioral norms in virtual communities
4	Present to near future	Convergence of information and communications technologies with nanotechnology and biotechnology, in addition to developments in emerging technologies such as AmI, augmented reality, and 3D printing	Issues from Phases 1–3 plus concerns about artificial electronic agents ("bots") with decision-making capabilities, AI-induced bionic chip implants, nanocomputing, pervasive computing, Big Data, IoT, etc.

wireless technology. Some consider radio-frequency identification (RFID) technology (described in detail in Chapter 5) to be the first step in what is now referred to as the Internet of Things (IoT), as well as *pervasive* or *ubiquitous computing* (described in detail in Chapter 12).

What other kinds of technological changes should we anticipate as research and development continue in Phase 4? For one thing, computing devices will likely continue to become more and more indistinguishable from many kinds of noncomputing devices. For another thing, a computer may no longer typically be conceived of as a distinct device or object with which users interact via an explicit interface such as a keyboard, mouse, and video display. We are now beginning to conceive of computers and cybertechnology in drastically different ways. Consider also that computers are becoming less visible—as computers and electronic devices continue to be miniaturized and integrated/embedded in objects, they are also beginning to "disappear" or to become "invisible" as distinct entities.

Many analysts predict that computers and other electronic devices will become increasingly smaller in size, ultimately achieving the nanoscale. (We examine some ethical implications of nanotechnology and nanocomputing in Chapter 12.) Many also predict that aspects of nanotechnology, biotechnology, and information technology will continue to converge. However, we will not speculate any further in this chapter about either the future of cybertechnology or the future of cyberethics. The purpose of our brief description of the four phases of cybertechnology mentioned here is to provide a historical context for understanding the origin and evolution of at least some of the ethical concerns affecting cybertechnology that we will examine in this book.

Table 1-1 summarizes key aspects of each phase in the development of cyberethics as a field of applied ethics.

▶ 1.3 ARE CYBERETHICS ISSUES UNIQUE ETHICAL ISSUES?

Few would dispute the claim that the use of cybertechnology has had a significant impact on our moral, legal, and social systems. Some also believe, however, that cybertechnology has introduced new and unique moral problems. Are any of these problems genuinely unique moral issues? There are two schools of thought regarding this question.

Consider once again Scenario 1–1, in the chapter's opening section. Have any new ethical issues been introduced in the hacking incident described in that scenario? Or are the issues that arise here merely examples of existing ethical issues that may have been exacerbated in some sense by new technologies, including new storage systems to archive personal data? Also, consider some factors having to do with *scope* and *scale*: The hacked photos of the celebrities can be seen by millions of people around the world, as opposed to previous cases where one might have to go to an "adult" store to acquire copies of the nude photos. Also, consider that harassment-related activities of the kind described in Scenario 1–1 can now occur on a scale or order of magnitude that could not have been realized in the pre-Internet era.

But do these factors support the claim that cybertechnology has introduced some new and unique ethical issues? Maner (2004) argues that computer use has generated a series of ethical issues that (i) did not exist before the advent of computing and (ii) could not have existed if computer technology had not been invented.[10] Is there any evidence to support Maner's claim? Next, we consider two scenarios that, initially at least, might suggest that some new ethical issues have been generated by the use of cybertechnology.

▶ SCENARIO 1–2: Developing the Code for a Computerized Weapon System

Sally Bright, a recent graduate from Technical University, has accepted a position as a software engineer for a company called Cyber Defense, Inc. This company has a contract with the U.S. Defense Department to develop and deliver applications for the U.S. military. When Sally reports to work on her first day, she is assigned to a controversial project that is developing the software for a computer system designed to deliver chemical weapons to and from remote locations. Sally is conflicted about whether she can, given her personal values, agree to work on this kind of weapon delivery system, which would not have been possible without computer technology. ■

Is the conflict that Sally faces in this particular scenario one that is new or unique because of computers and cybertechnology? One might argue that the ethical concerns surrounding Sally's choices are unique because they never would have arisen had it not been for the invention of computer technology. In one sense, it is true that ethical concerns having to do with whether or not one should participate in developing a certain kind of computer system did not exist before the advent of computing technology. However, it is true only in a trivial sense. Consider that long before computing technologies were available, engineers were confronted with ethical choices involving whether or not to participate in the design and development of certain kinds of controversial technological systems. Prior to the computer era, for example, they had to make decisions involving the design of aircraft intended to deliver conventional as well as nuclear bombs. So is the fact that certain technological systems happen to include the use of computer software or computer hardware components morally relevant in this scenario? Have any new or unique ethical issues, in a nontrivial sense of "unique," been generated here? Based on our brief analysis of this scenario, there does not seem to be sufficient evidence to substantiate the claim that one or more new ethical issues have been introduced.

▶ SCENARIO 1–3: Digital Piracy

Harry Flick is an undergraduate student at Pleasantville State College. In many ways, Harry's interests are similar to those of typical students who attend his college. But Harry is also very fond of classic movies, especially films that were made before 1950. DVD copies of these movies are difficult to find; those that are available tend to be expensive to purchase, and very few are available for loan at libraries. One day, Harry discovers a Web site that has several classic films (in digital form) freely available for downloading. Since the movies are still protected by copyright, however, Harry has some concerns about whether it would be permissible for him to download any of these films (even if only for private use). ■

Is Harry's ethical conflict one that is unique to computers and cybertechnology? Are the ethical issues surrounding Harry's situation new and thus unique to cybertechnology, because the practice of downloading digital media from the Internet—a practice that many in the movie and recording industries call "digital piracy"—would not have been possible if computer technology had not been invented in the first place? If so, this claim would, once again, seem to be true only in a trivial sense. The issue of piracy itself as a moral concern existed before the widespread use of computer technology. For example, people were able to "pirate" audio cassette tapes simply by using two or more analog tape recorders to make unauthorized copies of proprietary material. The important point to note here is that moral issues surrounding the pirating of audio cassette tapes are, at bottom, the same issues underlying the pirating of digital media. They arise in each case because, fundamentally, the behavior associated with unauthorized copying raises moral concerns about property, fairness, rights, and so forth. So, as in Scenario 1–2, there seems to be insufficient evidence to suggest that the ethical issues associated with digital piracy are either new or unique in some nontrivial sense.

1.3.1 Distinguishing between Unique Technological Features and Unique Ethical Issues

Based on our analysis of the two scenarios in the preceding section, we might conclude that there is nothing new or special about the kinds of moral issues associated with cybertechnology. In fact, some philosophers have argued that we have the same old ethical issues reappearing in a new guise. But is such a view accurate?

If we focus primarily on the moral issues themselves *as moral issues*, it would seem that perhaps there is nothing new. Cyber-related concerns involving privacy, property, free speech, and so forth can be understood as specific expressions of core (traditional) moral notions, such as autonomy, fairness, justice, responsibility, and respect for persons. However, if instead we focus more closely on cybertechnology itself, we see that there are some interesting and possibly unique features that distinguish this technology from earlier technologies. Maner has argued that computing technology is "uniquely fast," "uniquely complex," and "uniquely coded." But even if cybertechnology has these unique features, does it necessarily follow that any of the moral questions associated with that technology must also be unique? One would commit a logical fallacy if he or she concluded that cyberethics issues must be unique simply because certain features or aspects of cybertechnology are unique. The fallacy can be expressed in the following way:

PREMISE 1. Cybertechnology has some unique technological features.

PREMISE 2. Cybertechnology has generated some ethical concerns.

CONCLUSION. At least some ethical concerns generated by cybertechnology must be unique ethical concerns.

As we will see in Chapter 3, this reasoning is fallacious because it assumes that characteristics that apply to a certain technology must also apply to ethical issues generated by that technology.[11]

1.3.2 An Alternative Strategy for Analyzing the Debate about the Uniqueness of Cyberethics Issues

Although it may be difficult to prove conclusively whether or not cybertechnology has generated any new or unique ethical issues, we must not rule out the possibility that many of the controversies associated with this technology warrant special consideration from an ethical perspective. But what, exactly, is so different about issues involving computers and cybertechnology that make them deserving of special moral consideration? Moor (2007) points out that computer technology, unlike most previous technologies, is "logically malleable"; it can be shaped and molded to perform a variety of functions. Because noncomputer technologies are typically designed to perform some particular function or task, they lack the universal or general-purpose characteristics that computing technologies possess. For example, microwave ovens and DVD players are technological devices that have been designed to perform specific tasks. Microwave ovens cannot be used to view DVDs, and DVD players cannot be used to defrost, cook, or reheat food. However, a computer, depending on the software used, can perform a range of diverse tasks: it can be instructed to behave as a video game, a word processor, a spreadsheet, a medium to send and receive e-mail messages, or an interface to Web sites. Hence, cybertechnology is extremely malleable.

Moor points out that because of its logical malleability, cybertechnology can generate "new possibilities for human action" that appear to be limitless. Some of these possibilities for action generate what Moor calls "policy vacuums," because we have no explicit policies or laws to guide new choices made possible by computer technology. These vacuums, in turn, need to be filled with either new or revised policies. But what, exactly, does Moor mean by "policy"? Moor (2004) defines policies as "rules of conduct, ranging from formal laws to informal, implicit guidelines for actions."[12] Viewing computer ethics issues in terms of policies is useful, Moor believes, because policies have the right level of generality to consider when we evaluate the morality of conduct. As noted, policies can range from formal laws to informal guidelines. Moor also notes that policies can have "justified exemptions" because they are not absolute; yet policies usually imply a certain "level of obligation" within their contexts.

What action is required to resolve a policy vacuum when it is discovered? Initially, a solution to this problem might seem quite simple and straightforward. We might assume that all we need to do is identify the vacuums that have been generated and then fill them with policies and laws. However, this will not always work, because sometimes the new possibilities for human action generated by cybertechnology also introduce "conceptual vacuums," or what Moor calls "conceptual muddles." In these cases, we must first eliminate the muddles by clearing up certain conceptual confusions before we can frame coherent policies and laws.

1.3.3 A Policy Vacuum in Duplicating Computer Software

A critical policy vacuum, which also involved a conceptual muddle, emerged with the advent of personal desktop computers (henceforth referred to generically as PCs). The particular vacuum arose because of the controversy surrounding the copying of software. When PCs became commercially available, many users discovered that they could easily duplicate software programs. They found that they could use their PCs to make copies of proprietary computer programs such as word processing programs, spreadsheets, and video games. Some users assumed that in making copies of these programs they were doing nothing wrong. At that time, there were no explicit laws to regulate the subsequent use and distribution of software programs once they had been legally purchased by an individual or by an institution. Although it might be difficult to imagine today, at one time software was not clearly protected by either copyright law or the patent process.

Of course, there were clear laws and policies regarding the theft of physical property. Such laws and policies protected against the theft of personal computers as well as against the theft of a physical disk drive residing in a PC on which the proprietary software programs could easily be duplicated. However, this was not the case with laws and policies regarding the "theft," or unauthorized copying, of software programs that run on computers. Although there were IP laws in place, it had not been determined that software was or should be protected by IP law: it was unclear whether software should be understood as an idea (which is not protected by IP law), as a form of writing protected by copyright law, or as a set of machine instructions protected by patents. Consequently, many entrepreneurs who designed and manufactured software programs argued for explicit legal protection for their products. A policy vacuum arose with respect to duplicating software: Could a user make a backup copy of a program for herself? Could she share it with a friend? Could she give the original program to a friend? A clear policy was needed to fill this vacuum.

Before we can fill the vacuum regarding software duplication with a coherent policy or law, we first have to resolve a certain conceptual muddle by answering the question: what, exactly, is computer software? Until we can clarify the concept of software itself, we cannot frame a coherent policy as to whether or not we should allow the free duplication of software. Currently, there is still much confusion, as well as considerable controversy, as to how laws concerning the exchange (and, in effect, duplication) of proprietary software over the Internet should be framed.

In Moor's scheme, how one resolves the conceptual muddle (or decides the conceptual issue) can have a significant effect on which kinds of policies are acceptable. Getting clear about the conceptual issues is an important first step, but it is not a sufficient condition for being able to formulate a policy. Finally, the justification of a policy requires much factual knowledge, as well as an understanding of normative and ethical principles.

Consider the controversies surrounding the original Napster Web site and the Recording Industry Association of America (RIAA), in the late 1990s, regarding the free exchange of music over the Internet. Proponents on both sides of this dispute experienced difficulties in making convincing arguments for their respective positions due, in no small part, to confusion regarding the nature and the status of information (digitized music in the form of MP3 files) being exchanged between Internet users and the technology (P2P systems) that facilitated this exchange. Although cybertechnology has made it possible to exchange MP3 files, there is still debate, and arguably a great deal of confusion as well, about whether doing so should necessarily be illegal. Until the conceptual confusions or muddles underlying arguments used in the Napster vs. RIAA case in particular, and about the nature of P2P file-sharing systems in general, are resolved, it is difficult to frame an adequate policy regarding the exchange of MP3 files in P2P transactions.

How does Moor's insight that cyberethics issues need to be analyzed in terms of potential policy vacuums and conceptual muddles contribute to our earlier question as to whether there is anything unique or special about cyberethics? First, we should note that Moor takes no explicit stance on the question as to whether any cyberethics issues are unique. However, he does argue that cyberethics issues deserve special consideration because of the nature of cybertechnology itself, which is significantly different from alternative technologies in terms of the vast number of policy vacuums it generates (Moor 2001). So, even though the ethical issues associated with cybertechnology—that is, issues involving privacy, IP, and so forth—might not be new or unique, they nonetheless can put significant pressure on our conceptual frameworks and normative reasoning to a degree not found in other areas of applied ethics. Thus, it would seem to follow, on Moor's line of reasoning, that an independent field of applied ethics that focuses on ethical aspects of cybertechnology is indeed justified.

► 1.4 CYBERETHICS AS A BRANCH OF APPLIED ETHICS: THREE DISTINCT PERSPECTIVES

Cyberethics, as a field of study, can be understood as a branch of *applied ethics*. Applied ethics, as opposed to theoretical ethics, examines practical ethical issues. It does so by analyzing those issues from the vantage point of one or more ethical theories. Whereas ethical theory is concerned with establishing logically coherent and consistent criteria in the form of standards and rules for evaluating moral problems, the principal aim of applied ethics is to analyze specific moral problems themselves through the application of ethical theory. As such, those working in fields of applied ethics, or practical ethics, are not inclined to debate some of the finer points of individual ethical theories. Instead, their interest in ethical theory is primarily with how one or more theories can be successfully applied to the analysis of specific moral problems that they happen to be investigating.

For an example of a practical ethics issue involving cybertechnology, consider again the original Napster controversy. Recall that at the heart of this dispute is the question: should proprietary information, in a digital format known as MP3 files, be allowed to be exchanged freely over the Internet? Those advocating the free exchange of MP3 files could appeal to one or more ethical theories to support their position. For example, they might appeal to utilitarianism, an ethical theory that is based on the principle that our policies and laws should be such that they produce the greatest good (happiness) for the greatest number of people. A utilitarian might argue that MP3 files should be distributed freely over the Internet because the consequences of allowing such a practice would make the majority of users happy and would thus contribute to the greatest good for the greatest number of persons affected.

Others might argue that allowing proprietary material to be exchanged freely over the Internet would violate the rights of those who created, and who legally own, the material. Proponents of this view could appeal to a nonutilitarian principle or theory that is grounded in the notion of respecting the rights of individuals. According to this view, an important consideration for an ethical policy is that it protects the rights of individuals—in this case, the rights of those who legally own the proprietary material in question—irrespective of the happiness that might or might not result for the majority of Internet users.

Notice that in our analysis of the dispute over the exchange of MP3 files on the Internet (in the Napster case), the application of two different ethical theories yielded two very different answers to the question of which policy or course of action ought to be adopted. Sometimes, however, the application of different ethical theories to a particular problem will yield similar solutions. We will examine in detail some standard ethical theories, including utilitarianism, in Chapter 2. Our main concern in this textbook is with applied, or practical, ethics issues and not with ethical theory per se. Wherever appropriate, however, ethical theory will be used to inform our analysis of moral issues involving cybertechnology.

Understanding cyberethics as a field of applied ethics that examines moral issues pertaining to cybertechnology is an important first step. But much more needs to be said about the perspectives that interdisciplinary researchers bring to their analysis of the issues that make up this relatively new field. Most scholars and professionals conducting research in this field of applied ethics have proceeded from one of three different perspectives—professional ethics, philosophical ethics, or sociological/descriptive ethics. Gaining a clearer understanding of what is meant by each perspective is useful at this point.

1.4.1 Perspective #1: Cyberethics as a Field of Professional Ethics

According to those who view cyberethics primarily as a branch of *professional ethics*, the field can best be understood as identifying and analyzing issues of ethical responsibility for computer and IT professionals. Among the cyberethics issues considered from this perspective are those having to do with the computer/IT professional's role in designing, developing, and maintaining computer hardware and software systems. For example, suppose a programmer discovers that a software product she has been working on is about to be released for sale to the public even though that product is unreliable because it contains "buggy" software. Should she blow the whistle?

Those who see cyberethics essentially as a branch of professional ethics would likely draw on analogies from other professional fields, such as medicine and law. They would point out that in medical ethics and legal ethics, the principal focus of analysis is on issues of moral responsibility that affect individuals as members of these *professions*. By analogy, they would go on to argue that the same rationale should apply to the field of cyberethics—that is, the primary, and possibly even exclusive, focus of cyberethics should be on issues of moral responsibility that affect computer/IT professionals. Gotterbarn (1995) can be interpreted as defending a version of this position when he asserts

> The only way to make sense of 'Computer Ethics' is to narrow its focus to those actions that are within the control of the individual *moral* computer professional.[13] [Italics Gotterbarn]

So, in this passage, Gotterbarn suggests that the principal focus of computer ethics should be on issues of professional responsibility and not on the broader moral and social implications of that technology.

The analogies Gotterbarn uses to defend his argument are instructive. He notes, for example, that in the past, certain technologies have profoundly altered our lives, especially in the ways that many of us conduct our day-to-day affairs. Consider three such technologies: the printing press, the automobile, and the airplane. Despite the significant and perhaps revolutionary effects of each of these technologies, we do not have "printing press ethics," "automobile ethics," or "airplane ethics." So why, Gotterbarn asks, should we have a field of computer ethics apart from the study of those ethical issues that affect the professionals responsible for the design, development, and delivery of computer systems? In other words, Gotterbarn suggests that it is not the business of computer ethics to examine ethical issues other than those that affect computer professionals.

Professional Ethics and the Computer Science Practitioner

Gotterbarn's view about what the proper focus of computer ethics research and inquiry should be is shared by other practitioners in the field of computer science. However, some of those practitioners, as well as many philosophers and social scientists, believe that Gotterbarn's conception of computer ethics as simply a field of professional ethics is too narrow. In fact, some who identify themselves as computer professionals or as "information professionals," and who are otherwise sympathetic to Gotterbarn's overall attention to professional ethics issues, believe that a broader model is needed. For example, Buchanan (2004), in describing the importance of analyzing ethical issues in the "information professions," suggests that some nonprofessional ethics issues must also be examined because of the significant impact they have on noninformation professionals, including ordinary computer users. Consider that these issues can also affect people who have never used a computer.

Of course, Buchanan's category of "information professional" is considerably broader in scope than Gotterbarn's notion of computer professional. But the central point of her argument still holds, especially in the era of the Internet and the World Wide Web. In the computing era preceding the Web, Gotterbarn's conception of computer ethics as a field limited to the study of ethical issues affecting computer professionals seemed plausible. Now, computers are virtually everywhere, and the ethical issues generated by certain uses of computers and cybertechnology affect virtually everyone, professional and nonprofessional alike.

Despite the critiques leveled against Gotterbarn's conception of the field, his position may turn out to be the most plausible of the three models we consider. Because of the social impact that computer and Internet technologies have had during the past three decades, we have tended to identify many of the ethical issues associated with these technologies, especially concerns affecting privacy and IP, as computer ethics issues. But Johnson (2000) believes that in the future, computer-related ethical issues, such as privacy and property (that are currently associated with the field of computer ethics), may become part of what she calls "ordinary ethics." In fact, Johnson has suggested that computer ethics, as a separate field of applied ethics, may eventually "go away." However, even if Johnson's prediction turns out to be correct, computer ethics as a field that examines ethical issues affecting responsibility for computer professionals will, in all likelihood, still be needed. In this sense, then, Gotterbarn's original model of computer ethics might turn out to be the correct one in the long term.

Applying the Professional Ethics Model to Specific Scenarios

It is fairly easy to see how the professional ethics model can be used to analyze issues involving professional responsibility that directly impact computer/IT professionals. For example, issues concerned with the development and implementation of critical software would fit closely with the professional model. But can that model be extended to include cases that may only affect computer professionals indirectly? Consider again Scenario 1–1, where celebrities' photos were hacked and subsequently leaked to the Internet. While the unauthorized break-ins into one's property and the posting/displaying nude photos of celebrities are both illegal and immoral acts, are they also examples of a computer ethics issue that affects computer/IT professionals and the computer profession? Arguably, computer corporations such as Apple are responsible for securing the data that resides in their storage systems, such as the iCloud, from cyberattacks of this kind. One could also argue that if the software engineers employed by these corporations had written more effective code, the hackers might have been prevented from accessing the controversial photos. So it would seem that there are at least some indirect ways that the professional ethics perspective can be brought to bear on this scenario. Of course, there are many other ethically controversial aspects of Scenario 1–1 that do not pertain directly to computer professionals and software engineers.

Many of the ethical issues discussed in this book have implications for computer/IT professionals, either directly or indirectly. Issues that have a direct impact on computer professionals in general, and software engineers in particular, are examined in Chapter 4, which is dedicated to professional ethics. Computer science students and computer professionals will likely also want to assess some of the indirect implications that issues examined in Chapters 5 through 12 also have for the computing profession.

1.4.2 Perspective #2: Cyberethics as a Field of Philosophical Ethics

What, exactly, is *philosophical ethics* and how is it different from professional ethics? Since philosophical methods and tools are also used to analyze issues involving professional ethics, any attempt to distinguish between the two might seem arbitrary, perhaps even odd. For our purposes, however, a useful distinction can be drawn between the two fields because of the approach each takes in addressing ethical issues. Whereas professional ethics issues typically involve concerns of responsibility and obligation affecting individuals as members of a certain profession, philosophical ethics issues include broader concerns—social policies as well as individual behavior—that affect virtually everyone in society. Cybertechnology-related moral issues involving privacy, security, property, and free speech can affect everyone, including individuals who have never even used a computer.

To appreciate the perspective of cyberethics as a branch of philosophical ethics, consider James Moor's classic definition of the field. According to Moor (2007), cyberethics, or what he calls "computer ethics," is the analysis of the nature and social impact of computer technology and the corresponding formulation and justification of policies for the ethical use of such technology.[14]

Two points in Moor's definition are worth examining more closely. First, computer ethics (i.e., what we call "cyberethics") is concerned with the social impact of computers and cybertechnology in a broad sense and not merely the impact of that technology for computer professionals. Secondly, this definition challenges us to reflect on the social impact of cybertechnology in a way that also requires a justification for our social policies.

Why is cyberethics as a field of philosophical ethics dedicated to the study of ethical issues involving cybertechnology, warranted when there aren't similar fields of applied ethics for other technologies? Recall our earlier discussion of Gotterbarn's observation that we do not have fields of applied ethics called "automobile ethics" or "airplane ethics," even though automobile and airplane technologies have significantly affected our day-to-day lives. Moor could respond to Gotterbarn's point by noting that the introduction of automobile and airplane technologies did not affect our social policies and norms in the same kinds of fundamental ways that computer technology has. Of course, we have had to modify and significantly revise certain laws and policies to accommodate the implementation of new kinds of transportation technologies. In the case of automobile technology, we had to extend, and in some cases modify, certain policies and laws previously used to regulate the flow of horse-drawn modes of transportation. And clearly, automobile and airplane technologies have revolutionized transportation, resulting in our ability to travel faster and farther than was possible in previous eras.

What has made the impact of computer technology significantly different from that of other modern technologies? We have already seen that for Moor, three factors contribute to this impact: logical malleability, policy vacuums, and conceptual muddles. Because cybertechnology is logically malleable, its uses often generate policy vacuums and conceptual muddles. In Section 1.3.2, we saw how certain kinds of conceptual muddles contributed to some of the confusion surrounding software piracy issues in general and the Napster controversy in particular. What implications do these factors have for the standard methodology used by philosophers in the analysis of applied ethics issues?

Methodology and Philosophical Ethics

Brey (2004) notes that the standard methodology used by philosophers to conduct research in applied ethics has three distinct stages in that an ethicist must:

1. Identify a particular controversial practice as a moral problem.
2. Describe and analyze the problem by clarifying concepts and examining the factual data associated with that problem.
3. Apply moral theories and principles in the deliberative process in order to reach a position about the particular moral issue.[15]

We have already noted (in Section 1.3) how the first two stages in this methodology can be applied to an analysis of ethical issues associated with digital piracy. We saw that, first, a practice involving the use of cybertechnology to "pirate" or make unauthorized copies of proprietary information was *identified* as morally controversial. At the second stage, the problem was *analyzed* in descriptive and contextual terms to clarify the practice and to situate it in a particular context. In the case of digital piracy, we saw that the concept of piracy could be analyzed in terms of moral issues involving theft and IP theory. When we describe and analyze problems at this stage, we will want to be aware of and address any policy vacuums and conceptual muddles that are relevant.

At the third and final stage, the problem must be *deliberated* over in terms of moral principles (or theories) and logical arguments. Brey describes this stage in the method as the "deliberative process." Here, various arguments are used to justify the application of particular moral principles to the issue under consideration. For example, issues involving digital piracy can be deliberated upon in terms of one or more standard ethical theories, such as utilitarianism (defined in Chapter 2).

Applying the Method of Philosophical Ethics to Specific Scenarios

To see how the philosophical ethics perspective of cyberethics can help us to analyze a cluster of moral issues affecting cybertechnology, we once again revisit Scenario 1–1. In applying the philosophical ethics model to this scenario, our first task is to identify one or more moral issues that arise in that context; we have already seen that this scenario illustrates a wide range of ethical issues. For example, we saw that the range of ethical issues include privacy and anonymity, security and crime, property rights and free speech, and so forth.

We can now ask, what kinds of policy vacuums and conceptual muddles, if any, also arise in this scenario? For one thing, questions affecting property rights here might seem a bit stretched and strained and thus challenge some of our received notions affecting property. However, policy vacuums concerning IP in the digital era are by no means new. For example, we noted earlier that the original Napster scenario introduced controversies with respect to sharing copyrighted information, in the form of proprietary MP3 files, online. Scenario 1–1, however, introduces a property-related issue that goes beyond that kind of concern. Here, we have a question about one's claim to the sole ownership of a digital image that resides in a company's storage facility, that is, in addition to, or in place of, residing on a person's electronic device.

1.4.3 Perspective #3: Cyberethics as a Field of Sociological/Descriptive Ethics

The two perspectives on cyberethics that we have examined thus far—professional ethics and philosophical ethics—can both be understood as *normative* inquiries into applied ethics issues. Normative inquiries or studies, which focus on evaluating and prescribing moral systems, can be contrasted with *descriptive* inquiries or studies. Descriptive ethics is, or aims to be, nonevaluative in approach; typically, it describes particular moral systems and sometimes also reports how members of various groups and cultures view particular moral issues. This kind of analysis of ethical and social issues is often used by sociologists and social scientists—hence, our use of the expression "sociological/descriptive perspective" to analyze this methodological framework.

Descriptive vs. Normative Inquiries

Whereas descriptive investigations provide us with information about what *is* the case, normative inquiries evaluate situations from the vantage point of questions having to do with what *ought to be* the case. Those who approach cyberethics from the perspective of descriptive ethics often describe sociological aspects of a particular moral issue, such as the social impact of a specific technology on a particular community or social group. For example, one way of analyzing moral issues surrounding the "digital divide" (examined in Chapter 10) is first to describe the problem in terms of its impact on various sociodemographic groups involving social class, race, and gender. We can investigate whether, in fact, fewer poor people, nonwhites, and women have access to cybertechnology than wealthy and middle-class persons, whites, and men. In this case, the investigation is one that is basically descriptive in character. If we were then to inquire whether the lack of access to technology for some groups relative to others was unfair, we would be engaging in a normative inquiry. For example, a normative investigation of this issue would question whether certain groups *should* have more access to cybertechnology than they currently have. The following scenario illustrates an approach to a particular cyberethics issue via the perspective of sociological/descriptive ethics.

▶ **SCENARIO 1–4:** The Impact of Technology X on the Pleasantville Community

AEC Corporation, a company that employs 8,000 workers in Pleasantville, has decided to purchase and implement a new kind of digital technology, Technology X. The implementation of Technology X will likely have a significant impact for AEC's employees in particular, as well as for Pleasantville in general. It is estimated that 3,000 jobs at AEC will be eliminated when the new technology is implemented during the next six months. ■

Does the decision to implement Technology X pose a normative ethical problem for the AEC Corporation, as well as for Pleasantville? If we analyze the impact that Technology X has with respect to the number of jobs that are gained or lost, our investigation is essentially descriptive in nature. In reporting this phenomenon, we are simply describing or stating what *is/is not* at issue in this case. If, however, we argue that AEC either should or should not implement this new technology, then we make a claim that is normative (i.e., a claim about what *ought/ought not* to be the case). For example, one might argue that the new technology should not be implemented because it would displace workers and thus possibly violate certain contractual obligations that may exist between AEC and its employees. Alternatively, one might argue that implementing Technology X would be acceptable provided that certain factors are taken into consideration in determining which workers would lose their jobs. For example, suppose that in the process of eliminating jobs, older workers and minority employees would stand to be disproportionately affected. In this case, critics might argue that a fairer system should be used.

Our initial account of the impact of Technology X's implementation for Pleasantville simply reported some descriptive information about the number of jobs that would likely be lost by employees at AEC Corporation, which has sociological implications. As our analysis of this scenario continued, however, we did much more than merely describe what the impact was; we also evaluated the impact for AEC's employees in terms of what we believed *ought* to have been done. In doing so, we shifted from an analysis based on claims that were merely descriptive to an analysis in which some claims were also normative.

Some Benefits of Using the Sociological/Descriptive Approach to Analyze Cyberethics Issues

Why is the examination of cyberethics issues from the sociological/descriptive ethics perspective useful? Huff and Finholt (1994) suggest that focusing on descriptive aspects of social issues can help us to better understand many of the normative features and implications. In other words, when we understand the descriptive features of the social effects of a particular technology, the normative ethical questions become clearer. So Huff and Finholt believe that analyzing the social impact of cybertechnology from a sociological/descriptive perspective can better prepare us for our subsequent analysis of practical ethical issues affecting our system of policies and laws.

We have already noted that virtually all of our social institutions, from work to education to government to finance, have been affected by cybertechnology. This technology has also had significant impacts on different sociodemographic sectors and segments of our population. The descriptive information that we gather about these groups can provide important information that, in turn, can inform legislators and policy makers who are drafting and revising laws in response to the effects of cybertechnology.

From the perspective of sociological/descriptive ethics, we can also better examine the impact that cybertechnology has on our understanding of concepts such as community and individuality. We can ask, for instance, whether certain developments in social networking technologies used in Twitter and Facebook have affected the way that we conceive traditional notions such as "community" and "neighbor." Is a community essentially a group of individuals with similar interests, or perhaps a similar ideology, irrespective of geographical limitations? Is national identity something that is, or may soon become, anachronistic? While these kinds of questions and issues in and of themselves are more correctly conceived as descriptive rather than normative concerns, they can have significant normative implications for our moral and legal systems as well. Much more will be said about the relationship between descriptive and normative approaches to analyzing ethical issues in Chapters 10 and 11, where we examine the impact of cybertechnology on sociodemographic groups and on some of our social and political institutions.

Applying the Sociological/Descriptive Ethics Approach to Specific Scenarios

Consider how someone approaching cyberethics issues from the perspective of sociological/descriptive ethics might analyze the scenario involving the hacked photos of celebrities described in Scenario 1–1. In this case, the focus might be on gathering sociodemographic and socioeconomic data pertaining to the kinds of individuals who are likely to hack into a celebrity's cell phone or electronic device. For example, some social scientists might consider the income and educational levels of hackers, as compared to individuals who engage in alternative kinds of online activities or who do not use the Internet at all. Others might further inquire into why some individuals seem to display little-to-no concern about posting nude photos of people that could be viewed, potentially at least, by millions of people. Still others engaged in research from the point of view of sociological/descriptive ethics might inquire into whether there has been an increase in the number of hacking incidents in recent years. And if the answer to this question is "yes," the researcher might next question whether such an increase is linked to the widespread availability of hacking tools that are now available on the Internet.

Also, the researcher might consider whether certain groups in the population are now more at risk than others with respect to being hacked. That researcher could further inquire whether there are any statistical patterns to suggest that female celebrities are more likely to be hacked than are individuals in other groups. The researcher could also ask if women in general are typically more vulnerable than men to the kinds of harassment associated with this form of online behavior.

Also, a researcher approaching this scenario from the sociological/descriptive ethics perspective might set out to determine whether an individual who never would have thought of physically harassing a person in geographical space might now be inclined to do so because of the relative ease of doing so with cybertechnology. Or is it the case that some of those same individuals might now be tempted to do so because they believe that they will not likely get caught? Also, has the fact that a potential hacker realizes that he or she can harass a person on the Internet under the cloak of relative anonymity/pseudonymity contributed to the increase in harassment online? These are a few of the kinds of questions that could be examined from the sociological/descriptive perspective of cyberethics.

Table 1-2 summarizes some key characteristics that differentiate the three main perspectives for approaching cyberethics issues.

TABLE 1-2 Summary of Cyberethics Perspectives

Type of Perspective	Associated Disciplines	Issues Examined
Professional	Computer Science	Professional responsibility
	Engineering	System reliability/safety
	Library/Information Science	Codes of conduct
Philosophical	Philosophy	Privacy and anonymity
	Law	Intellectual property
		Free speech
Sociological/descriptive	Sociology/behavioral sciences	Impact of cybertechnology on governmental/financial/ educational institutions and sociodemographic groups

In Chapters 4–12, we examine specific cyberethics questions from the vantage points of our three perspectives. Issues considered from the perspective of professional ethics are examined in Chapters 4 and 12. Cyberethics issues considered from the perspective of philosophical ethics, such as those involving privacy, security, IP, and free speech, are examined in Chapters 5–9. And several of the issues considered in Chapters 10 and 11 are examined from the perspective of sociological/descriptive ethics.

▶ 1.5 A COMPREHENSIVE CYBERETHICS METHODOLOGY

The three different perspectives of cyberethics described in the preceding section might suggest that three different kinds of methodologies are needed to analyze the range of issues examined in this textbook. The goal of this section, however, is to show that a single, comprehensive method can be constructed and that this method will be adequate in guiding us in our analysis of cyberethics issues.

Recall the standard model used in applied ethics, which we briefly examined in Section 1.4.2. There, we saw that the standard model includes three stages, that is, where a researcher must (i) identify an ethical problem, (ii) describe and analyze the problem in conceptual and factual terms, and (iii) apply ethical theories and principles in the deliberative process. We also saw that Moor argued that the conventional model was not adequate for an analysis of at least some cyberethics issues. Moor believed that additional steps, which address concerns affecting "policy vacuums" and "conceptual muddles," are sometimes needed before we can move from the second to the third stage of the methodological scheme. We must now consider whether the standard model, with Moor's additional steps included, is complete. Brey (2004) suggests that it is not.

Brey believes that while the (revised) standard model might work well in many fields of applied ethics, such as medical ethics, business ethics, and bioethics, it does not always fare well in cyberethics. Brey argues that the standard method, when used to identify ethical aspects of cybertechnology, tends to focus almost exclusively on the *uses* of that technology. As such, the standard method fails to pay sufficient attention to certain features that may be embedded in the technology itself, such as design features that may also have moral implications.

We might be inclined to assume that technology itself is neutral and that only the *uses* to which a particular technology is put are morally controversial. However, Brey and others believe that it is a mistake to conceive of technology, independent of its uses, as something that is value-free, or unbiased. Instead, they argue, moral values are often embedded or implicit in features built into technologies at the design stage. For example, critics, including some feminists, have pointed out that in the past the ergonomic systems designed for drivers of automobiles were biased toward men and gave virtually no consideration to women. That is, considerations having to do with the average height and typical body dimensions of men were implicitly built into the design specification. These critics also note that decisions about how the ergonomic systems would be designed were all made by men, which likely account for the bias embedded in that particular technological system.

1.5.1 A "Disclosive" Method for Cyberethics

As noted earlier, Brey believes that the standard, or what he calls "mainstream," applied ethics methodology is not always adequate for identifying moral issues involving cybertechnology. Brey worries that using the standard model we might fail to notice certain features embedded in the design of cybertechnology. He also worries about the standard method of applied ethics because it tends to focus on known moral controversies, and because it fails to identify certain practices involving the use of cybertechnology that have moral import but that are not yet known. Brey refers to such practices as having "morally opaque" (or morally nontransparent) features, which he contrasts with "morally transparent" features.

According to Brey, morally controversial features that are transparent tend to be easily recognized as morally problematic. For example, many people are aware that the practice of placing closed circuit video surveillance cameras in undisclosed locations is controversial from a moral point of view. Brey notes that it is, however, generally much more difficult to discern morally opaque features in technology. These features can be morally opaque for one of two reasons: either they are unknown or they are known but perceived to be morally neutral.[16]

Consider an example of each type of morally opaque (or morally nontransparent) feature. Computerized practices involving data mining (defined in Chapter 5) would be unknown to those who have never heard of the concept of data mining and who are unfamiliar with data mining technology. However, this technology should not be assumed to be morally neutral merely because data mining techniques are unknown to nontechnical people, including some ethicists as well. Even if such techniques are opaque to many users, data mining practices raise certain moral issues pertaining to personal privacy.

Next, consider an example of a morally opaque feature in which a technology is well known. Most Internet users are familiar with search engine technology. What users might fail to recognize, however, is that certain uses of search engines can be morally controversial with respect to personal privacy. Consequently, one of the features of search engine technology can be morally controversial in a sense that it is not obvious or transparent to many people, including those who are very familiar with and who use search engine technology. So, while a well-known technology, such as search engine programs, might appear to be morally neutral, a closer analysis of practices involving this technology will disclose that it has moral implications.

Figure 1-1 illustrates some differences between morally opaque and morally transparent features.

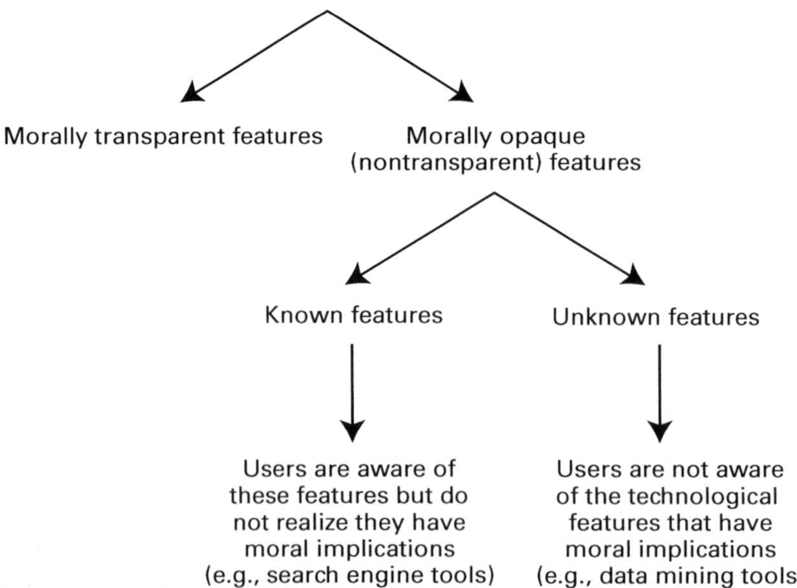

Figure 1-1 Embedded technological features having moral implications.

Brey argues that an adequate methodology for computer ethics must first identify, or "disclose," features that, without proper probing and analysis, would go unnoticed as having moral implications. Thus, an extremely important first step in Brey's "disclosive method" is to reveal moral values embedded in the various features and practices associated with cybertechnology itself.

1.5.2 An Interdisciplinary and Multilevel Method for Analyzing Cyberethics Issues

Brey's disclosive model is *interdisciplinary* because it requires that computer scientists, philosophers, and social scientists collaborate. It is also *multilevel* because conducting computer ethics research requires three levels of analysis:

- Disclosure level
- Theoretical level
- Application level

First of all, the moral values embedded in the design of computer systems must be disclosed. To do this, we need computer scientists because they understand computer technology much better than philosophers and social scientists do. However, social scientists are also needed to evaluate system design and make it more user-friendly. Then philosophers can determine whether existing ethical theories are adequate to test the newly disclosed moral issues or whether more theory is needed. Finally, computer scientists, philosophers, and social scientists must cooperate by applying ethical theory in deliberations about moral issues.[17] In Chapter 2, we examine a range of ethical theories that can be used.

In the deliberations involved in applying ethical theory to a particular moral problem, one remaining methodological step also needs to be resolved. Van den Hoven (2000) has noted that methodological schemes must also address the "problem of justification of moral judgments." For our purposes, we use the strategies of logical analysis included in Chapter 3 to justify the moral theories we apply to particular issues.

Table 1-3 summarizes the three levels, academic disciplines, and corresponding tasks and functions involved in Brey's disclosive model.

It is in the interdisciplinary spirit of the disclosive methodology proposed by Brey that we will examine the range of cyberethics issues described in Chapter 12.

▶ 1.6 A COMPREHENSIVE STRATEGY FOR APPROACHING CYBERETHICS ISSUES

The following methodological scheme, which expands on the original three-step scheme introduced in Section 1.4.2, is intended as a strategy to assist you in identifying and analyzing the specific cyberethics issues examined in this book. Note, however, that this procedure is

TABLE 1-3 Brey's Disclosive Model

Level	Disciplines Involved	Task/Function
Disclosure	Computer Science, Social Science (optional)	Disclose embedded features in computer technology that have moral import
Theoretical	Philosophy	Test newly disclosed features against standard ethical theories
Application	Computer Science, Philosophy, Social Science	Apply standard or newly revised/formulated ethical theories to the issues

not intended as a precise algorithm for resolving those issues in some definitive manner. Rather, its purpose is to guide you in the identification, analysis, and deliberation processes by summarizing key points that we have examined in Chapter 1.

Step 1. *Identify* a practice involving cybertechnology, or a feature of that technology, that is controversial from a moral perspective:

- **1a.** Disclose any hidden or opaque features.
- **1b.** Assess any descriptive components of the ethical issue via the sociological implications it has for relevant social institutions and sociodemographic groups.
- **1c.** In analyzing the normative elements of that issue, determine whether there are any specific guidelines, that is, social policies or ethical codes, that can help resolve the issue (e.g., see the relevant professional codes of conduct described in Chapter 4 as well as in Appendices A–E, available at www.wiley.com/college/tavani).
- **1d.** If the normative ethical issue cannot be resolved through the application of existing policies, codes of conduct, and so on, go to Step 2.

Step 2. *Analyze* the ethical issue by clarifying concepts and situating it in a context:

- **2a.** If a policy vacuums exists, go to Step 2b; otherwise, go to Step 3.
- **2b.** Clear up any conceptual muddles involving the policy vacuum and go to Step 3.

Step 3. *Deliberate* on the ethical issue. The deliberation process requires two stages:

- **3a.** Apply one or more ethical theories (see Chapter 2) to the analysis of the moral issue, and then, go to Step 3b.
- **3b.** Justify the position you reached by evaluating it via the standards and criteria for successful logic argumentation (see Chapter 3).

Note that you are now in a position to carry out much of the work required in the first two steps of this methodological scheme. In order to satisfy the requirements in Step 1d, a step that is required in cases involving professional ethics issues, you will need to consult the relevant sections of Chapter 4. Upon completing Chapter 2, you will be able to execute Step 3a; and after completing Chapter 3, you will be able to satisfy the requirements for Step 3b.

▶ 1.7 CHAPTER SUMMARY

In this introductory chapter, we defined several key terms, including *cyberethics* and *cybertechnology*, used throughout this textbook. We also briefly described four evolutionary phases of cyberethics, from its origins as a loosely configured and informal field concerned with ethical and social issues involving stand-alone (mainframe) computers to a more fully developed field that is today concerned with ethical aspects of ubiquitous, networked computers and devices. We then briefly considered whether any cyberethics issues are unique or special in a nontrivial sense. We next examined three different perspectives on cyberethics, showing how computer scientists, philosophers, and social scientists each tend to view the field and approach the issues that comprise it. Within that discussion, we also examined some ways in which embedded values and biases affecting cybertechnology can be disclosed and thus made explicit. Finally, we introduced a comprehensive methodological scheme that incorporates the expertise of computer scientists, philosophers, and social scientists who work in the field of cyberethics.

▶ REVIEW QUESTIONS

1. What, exactly, is *cyberethics*? How is it different from and similar to computer ethics, information ethics, and Internet ethics?
2. What is meant by the term *cybertechnology*? How is it similar to and different from computer technology?
3. Describe in detail each of the "four phases" involving the evolution of cybertechnology. What are the key technological developments in each phase?
4. Describe in detail each of the four phases comprising the development of cyberethics as a field of applied ethics. What are the key ethical issues that arise in each phase?
5. Why does Walter Maner believe that at least some cyberethics issues are unique? What arguments does he provide to support his view?
6. Why is it important to distinguish between unique technological features and unique ethical issues when evaluating the question, Are cyberethics issues unique?
7. What alternative strategy does James Moor use to analyze the question whether cyberethics issues are unique ethical issues?
8. Why does Moor believe that cybertechnology poses special problems for identifying and analyzing ethical issues?
9. Explain what Moor means by the expression "logical malleability," and why he believes that this technological feature of computers is significant.
10. What does Moor mean by the phrase "policy vacuum," and what role do these vacuums play in understanding cyberethics?
11. Explain what Moor means by a "conceptual muddle". How can these muddles sometimes complicate matters when trying to resolve policy vacuums?
12. Summarize the principal aspects of the perspective of cyberethics as a field of *professional* ethics.
13. Describe the principal aspects of the perspective of cyberethics as a field of *philosophical* ethics.
14. Summarize the key elements of the perspective of cyberethics as a field of *sociological/descriptive* ethics.
15. Describe the kinds of criteria used to distinguish normative ethical inquiries from those that are essentially descriptive.
16. What are the three elements of the standard, or "mainstream," method for conducting applied ethics research?
17. How is Philip Brey's "disclosive method of computer ethics" different from what Brey calls "mainstream computer ethics"?
18. What does Brey mean by "morally opaque" or "morally nontransparent" features embedded in computer technology?
19. In which ways is Brey's disclosive method "multilevel"? Briefly describe each level in his methodology.
20. In which ways is that method also "multidisciplinary" or interdisciplinary? Which disciplines does it take into consideration?

▶ DISCUSSION QUESTIONS

21. Assess Don Gotterbarn's arguments for the claim that computer ethics is, at bottom, a field whose primary concern should focus on moral responsibility issues for computer professionals. Do you agree with his position?
22. Think of a controversial issue or practice involving cybertechnology that has not yet been identified as an ethical issue, but which might eventually be recognized as one that has moral implications. Apply Brey's "disclosive method" to see whether you can isolate any embedded values or biases affecting that practice. Also, be sure to separate any "morally opaque features" from those that are "morally transparent" (or nonopaque).
23. We identified three main perspectives from which cyberethics issues can be examined. Can you think of any additional perspectives from which cyberethics issues might also be analyzed?
24. Identify a current ethical issue involving the use of a recent or emerging technology. Apply the three-step process in the "comprehensive framework" (or strategy for Approaching Moral Issues in Cybertechnology) that we articulated in Section 1.6.

Scenarios for Analysis

1. We briefly considered the question whether some cyberethics issues are new or unique ethical issues. In the following scenario, which could be titled "Contesting the Ownership of a Twitter Account," (i) identify the ethical issues that arise and (ii) determine whether any of them are unique to cybertechnology.

Noah Kravitz was employed by PhoneDog Media, a mobile phone company, for nearly four years. PhoneDog had two divisions: an e-commerce site (phonedog.com) that sold mobile phones and a blog that enabled customers to interact with the company. Kravitz created a blog on Twitter (called Phonedog_Noah) while employed at PhoneDog, and his blog attracted 17,000 followers by the time he left the company in October 2010. However, Kravitz informed PhoneDog that he wanted to keep his Twitter blog, with all of his followers; in return, Kravitz agreed that he would still "tweet" occasionally on behalf of his former company, under a new (Twitter) "handle," or account name, NoahKravitz. Initially, PhoneDog seemed to have no problem with this arrangement. In July 2011, however, PhoneDog sued Kravitz, arguing that his list of Twitter followers was, in fact, a company list. PhoneDog also argued that it had invested a substantial amount of money in growing its customer list, which it considered to be the property of PhoneDog Media. The company has sought $340,000 in damages—the amount that PhoneDog estimated it had lost based on 17,000 customers at $2.50 per customer over an eight-month period (following Kravitz's departure from the company).[18]

2. Identify and evaluate the ethical issues that arise in the following scenario from the three main perspectives of cyberethics that we examined in Chapter 1.3. Explain.

In April 2014, Donald Sterling, then owner of the National Basketball Association (NBA)'s San Diego Clippers, was accused of making racist remarks about African Americans. It turns out that Sterling's then (girl)friend, V. Stiviano, had recorded those remarks on an electronic device and then later decided to make them available to a wider audience. This incident received extensive media coverage in the United States and beyond. Many people were appalled by Sterling's remarks, and some also pointed out the irony in this incident, given that the majority of the players on his basketball team (who were largely responsible for generating income for Sterling) were African Americans. Shortly following the fallout from this controversy, Sterling was forced by the NBA to sell his team to a new owner. While most people agreed that Sterling should resign and be required to relinquish his NBA franchise, some were nevertheless troubled by the manner in which his remarks, which were made in confidence to a close friend, were secretly recorded via a digital device and then (eventually) made available to the public.[19]

The practice of secretly recording someone's private conversations is not exactly new; after all, law enforcement authorities have used "wiring" devices to trap suspected criminals into disclosing information that can lead to their arrests. But the idea that ordinary people, especially those in intimate relationships, can now so easily record conversations in deceptive ways via their tiny digital devices can seem chilling. For example, would this practice influence what intimate friends would be willing (or not willing) to say to each other in (supposed) confidence? Would it also alter our privacy expectations in the future with respect to conversations with romantic partners?

▶ ENDNOTES

1. See, for example, Dan Kedmey, "Hackers Leak Explicit Photos of More than 100 Celebrities," *Time Magazine*, September 1, 2014. Available at http://time.com/3246562/hackers-jennifer-lawrence-cloud-data/. Accessed 9/5/14.
2. Some have used a combination of these two expressions. For example, Ess (2014) uses "information and computer ethics" (ICE) to refer to ethical issues affecting "digital media." And Capurro (2007) uses the expression "Intercultural Information Ethics" (IIE).
3. We should note that others have used the expression ICT (information and communications technology) ethics to describe the field that we refer to as cyberethics, whereas Ess (2014) has recently proposed the expression "digital media ethics." But as in the case of the other competing expressions we have critiqued, these two also fail to capture the breadth of the wide range of topics we cover under the expression "cyberethics."
4. Floridi (2007, p. 63) contrasts Information Ethics (IE) with computer ethics (CE), by noting that the former is the "philosophical foundational counterpart of CE."
5. It is worth noting that some authors have used the term "cyberethics" in ways that are different from the definition proposed here. See, for example, Baird, Ramsower, and Rosenbaum (2000).
6. Anderson and Anderson (2011) also use the term "machine ethics" to refer to this new field, which they describe as one "concerned with giving machines ethical principles." They contrast the development of ethics for people who use machines with the development of ethics for machines. Others, however, such as Lin, Abney, and Bekey (2012), use the expression "robot ethics" to describe this emerging field.
7. See the interview conducted with Paul Ceruzzi in the BBC/PBS video series, *The Machine That Changed the World* (1990).

8. For example, Bynum (2008) notes that Norbert Weiner, in his writings on cybernetics in the late 1940s, anticipated some of these concerns.
9. My analysis of the "four phases" in this section draws from and expands upon some concepts and distinctions introduced in Tavani (2001). Note that what I am calling a "technological phase" is not to be confused with something as precise as the expression "computer generation," which is often used to describe specific stages in the evolution of computer hardware systems.
10. Maner (2004, p. 41) argues that computers have generated "entirely new ethical issues, unique to computing, that do not surface in other areas."
11. My description and analysis of the "uniqueness debate" in this section draws from and expands upon some concepts and distinctions introduced in Tavani (2001); for a more extended analysis of this debate, see Tavani (2002a).
12. Moor (2004), p. 107.
13. Gotterbarn (1995), p. 21.
14. Moor (2007), p. 31.
15. Brey (2004), pp. 55–6.
16. For more details regarding this distinction, see Brey (2004), pp. 56–7.
17. See Brey, pp. 64–5. For a discussion of how Brey's interdisciplinary model can also be applied to computer ethics instruction, see Tavani (2002b).
18. See J. Biggs, "A Dispute Over Who Owns a Twitter Account Goes to Court." *New York Times*, December 25, 2011. Available at http://www.nytimes.com/2011/12/26/technology/lawsuit-may-determine-who-owns-a-twitter-account.html?_r=3.
19. See, for example, the account of this incident in http://www.huffingtonpost.com/2014/04/26/donald-sterling-racist_n_5218572.html

▶ REFERENCES

Anderson, Michael, and Susan Leigh Anderson, eds. 2011. *Machine Ethics*. New York: Cambridge University press.

Baird, Robert M., Reagan Ramsower, and Stuart E. Rosenbaum, eds. 2000. *Cyberethics: Moral, Social, and Legal Issues in the Computer Age*. Amherst, NY: Prometheus Books.

Barger, Robert N. 2008. *Computer Ethics: A Case-Based Approach*. New York: Cambridge University Press.

Brey, Philip. 2004. "Disclosive Computer Ethics." In R. A. Spinello and H. T. Tavani, eds. *Readings in CyberEthics*. 2nd ed. Sudbury, MA: Jones and Bartlett Publishers, pp. 55–66. Reprinted from *Computers and Society* 30, no. 4 (2000): 10–16.

Brey, Philip. 2005. "Freedom and Privacy in Ambient Intelligence," *Ethics and Information Technology* 7, no. 4: 157–66.

Buchanan, Elizabeth A. 2004. "Ethical Considerations for the Information Professions." In R. A. Spinello and H. T. Tavani, eds. In *Readings in CyberEthics*. 2nd ed. Sudbury, MA: Jones and Bartlett Publishers, pp. 613–24.

Buchanan, Elizabeth A. and Kathrine A. Henderson. 2009. *Case Studies in Library and Information Science Ethics*. Jefferson, NC: McFarland.

Bynum, Terrell Ward. 2008. "Milestones in the History of Information and Computer Ethics." In K. E. Himma and H. T. Tavani, eds. *The Handbook of Information and Computer Ethics*. Hoboken, NJ: John Wiley and Sons, pp. 25–48.

Capurro, Rafael. 2007. "Intercultural Information Ethics." In R. Capurro, J. Freübrauer, and T. Hausmanninger, eds. *Localizing the Internet: Ethical Aspects in Intercultural Perspective*. Munich: Fink Verlag, pp. 21–38.

Ess, Charles. 2014. *Digital Media Ethics*. 2nd ed. London, UK: Polity Press.

Floridi, Luciano. 2007. "Information Ethics: On the Philosophical Foundations of Computer Ethics." In J. Weckert, ed. *Computer Ethics*. Aldershot, UK: Ashgate, pp. 63–82. Reprinted from *Ethics and Information Technology* 1, no. 1 (1999): pp. 37–56.

Gotterbarn, Don. 1995. "Computer Ethics: Responsibility Regained." In D. G. Johnson and H. Nissenbaum, eds. *Computing, Ethics, and Social Values*. Upper Saddle River, NJ: Prentice Hall.

Huff, Chuck and Thomas Finholt, eds. 1994. *Social Issues in Computing: Putting Computing in its Place*. New York: McGraw Hill.

Johnson, Deborah G. 2000. "The Future of Computer Ethics." In G. Collste, ed. *Ethics in the Age of Information Technology*. Linköping, Sweden: Centre for Applied Ethics, pp. 17–31.

Johnson, Deborah G. 2010. *Computer Ethics*. 4th ed. Upper Saddle River, NJ: Prentice Hall.

Langford, Duncan, ed. 2000. *Internet Ethics*. New York: St. Martin's Press.

Lin, Patrick, Keith Abney, and George A. Bekey, eds. 2012. *Robot Ethics: The Ethical and Social Implications of Robotics*. Cambridge, MA: MIT Press.

Maner, Walter. 2004. "Unique Ethical Problems in Information Technology." In T. W. Bynum and S. Rogerson, eds. *Computer Ethics and Professional Responsibility*. Malden, MA: Blackwell, pp. 39–59. Reprinted from *Science and Engineering Ethics* 2, no. 2 (1996): 137–54.

Moor, James H. 2001. "The Future of Computer Ethics: You Ain't Seen Nothing Yet." *Ethics and Information Technology* 3, no. 2: 89–91.

Moor, James H. 2004. "Just Consequentialism and Computing." In R. A. Spinello and H. T. Tavani, eds. *Readings in CyberEthics*. 2nd ed. Sudbury, MA: Jones and Bartlett Publishers, pp. 407–17. Reprinted from *Ethics and Information Technology* 1, no. 1 (1999): 65–69.

Moor, James H. 2005. "Should We Let Computers Get Under Our Skin?" In R. Cavalier ed. *The Impact of the Internet on Our Moral Lives*. Albany, NY: State University of New York Press, pp. 121–38.

Moor, James H. 2007. "What Is Computer Ethics?" In J. Weckert, ed. *Computer Ethics*. Aldershot, UK: Ashgate, pp. 31–40. Reprinted from *Metaphilosophy* 16, no. 4 (1985): 266–75.

Tavani, Herman T. 2001. "The State of Computer Ethics as a Philosophical Field of Inquiry." *Ethics and Information Technology* 3, no. 2: 97–108.

Tavani, Herman T. 2002a. "The Uniqueness Debate in Computer Ethics: What Exactly Is at Issue, and Why Does it Matter?" *Ethics and Information Technology*, 4, no. 1: 37–54.

Tavani, Herman T. 2002b. "Applying an Interdisciplinary Approach to Teaching Computer Ethics." *IEEE Technology and Society Magazine* 21, no. 3: 32–38.

van den Hoven, Jeroen. 2000. "Computer Ethics and Moral Methodology." In R. Baird, R. Ramsower, and S. Rosenbaum, eds. *Cyberethics: Social and Moral Issues in the Computer Age*. Amherst, NY: Prometheus Books, pp. 80–94. Reprinted from *Metaphilosophy*, 28, no. 3 (1997): 234–48.

Wallach, Wendell and Colin Allen. 2009. *Moral Machines: Teaching Robots Right from Wrong*. New York: Oxford University Press.

▶ FURTHER READINGS

Brey, Philip, Adam Briggle, and Edward Spence. 2012. *The Good Life in a Technological Age*. New York: Routledge.

Floridi, Luciano, ed. 2010. *The Cambridge Handbook of Information and Computer Ethics*. Cambridge, MA: MIT Press.

Floridi, Luciano. 2013. *The Ethics of Information*. Oxford University Press.

Heikkero, Topi. 2012. *Ethics in Technology: A Philosophical Study*. Lanham, MD: Lexington Books.

Holbrook, J. Britt and Carl Mitcham, eds. *Ethics, Science, Technology, and Engineering: A Global Resource*. 2nd ed. 2015. 4 Vols. Farmington Hills, MI: Macmillan Reference,.

Mittleman, Daniel, ed. 2014. *Annual Editions: Technologies, Social Media, and Society*. 20th ed. New York: McGraw Hill.

Moor, James H. 2008. "Why We Need Better Ethics for Emerging Technologies." In J. van den Hoven and J. Weckert, eds. *Information Technology and Moral Philosophy*. New York: Cambridge University Press, pp. 26–39.

Sandler, Ronald L., ed. 2014. *Ethics and Emerging Technologies*. New York: Palgrave Macmillan/St. Martin's.

van den Hoven, Jeroen. 2008. "Moral Methodology and Information Technology." In K. E. Himma and H. T. Tavani, eds. *The Handbook of Information and Computer Ethics*. Hoboken, NJ: John Wiley and Sons, pp. 49–67.

Wallach, Wendell. 2015. *A Dangerous Master: How to Keep Technology from Slipping Beyond Our Control*. New York: Basic Books.

▶ ONLINE RESOURCES

Association for Computing—Special Interest Group on Computers and Society. http://www.sigcas.org/

Ethical Issues in the Online World (Santa Clara University). http://www.scu.edu/ethics-center/ethicsblog/internet-ethics.cfm

Heuristic Methods for Computer Ethics. http://csweb.cs.bgsu.edu/maner/heuristics/maner.pdf

ICT Ethics Bibliography. Annotated bibliographies in ICT (information and Communications Technology) Ethics are included in a series of ten installments (published between 1999 and 2013) in the *Journal Ethics and Information Technology* (http://www.springer.com/computer/swe/journal/10676).

International Center for Information Ethics (ICIE). http://icie.zkm.de/

International Society for Ethics and Information Technology. http://inseit.net/

Research Center for Computing and Society. http://www.southernct.edu/organizations/rccs/

Stanford Encyclopedia of Philosophy. http://plato.stanford.edu/ Includes several articles on topics pertaining to issues in computer/information ethics.

CHAPTER

2

Ethical Concepts and Ethical Theories: Frameworks for Analyzing Moral Issues

LEARNING OBJECTIVES

Upon completing this chapter, you will successfully be able to:

- Distinguish between the notions of *ethics* and *morality*, and show why it is useful to differentiate these two concepts,
- Articulate the key elements comprising a system of morality, or *moral system*,
- Identify four distinct kinds of "discussion stoppers" that often serve as roadblocks to meaningful debates involving ethical disputes,
- Describe why morality is not simply *personal*, *subjective*, or *relative* to a particular culture,
- Explain the need for and role of *ethical theory* in analyzing cyberethics issues,
- Articulate four classic/traditional ethical theories—consequence-based, duty-based, contract-based, and character-based theories—and apply them to specific cyberethics issues,
- Describe the components of a single, comprehensive framework that incorporates key aspects of each of the four standard ethical theories.

In Chapter 1, we defined cyberethics as the study of moral issues involving cybertechnology. However, we have not yet defined what is meant by *ethics*, *morality*, and *moral system*. In this chapter, we define these terms as well as other foundational concepts, and we examine a set of ethical theories that will guide us in our deliberation on the specific cyberethics issues we confront in Chapters 4–12. We begin by reflecting on a scenario that illustrates some of the difficulties involved in the reasoning process one might typically encounter when trying to resolve a moral dilemma.

▶ SCENARIO 2–1: The Case of the "Runaway Trolley": A Classic Moral Dilemma

Imagine that you are driving a trolley and that all of a sudden you realize that the trolley's brake system has failed. Further imagine that approximately 100 meters ahead of you are five crew men working on a section of the track on which your trolley is traveling. You realize that you cannot stop the trolley and that you will probably not be able to prevent the deaths of the five workers. But then, you suddenly realize that you could "throw a switch" that would cause the trolley to go on to a different track. You also happen to notice that one person is working on that track. You realize that if you do nothing, five people will likely die, whereas if you engage the switch to change tracks, only one person would likely die.[1] ■

What would you do in this situation—let the trolley take its "natural" course, expecting that five people will likely die, or would you intentionally change the direction of the trolley, likely causing the death of one person who otherwise would have lived? If you use what some call a "cost-benefits" approach in this particular situation, you might reason in the following way: throwing the switch will have a better outcome, overall, because more human lives would be saved than lost. So, in this case, you conclude that throwing the switch is the right thing to do because the net result is that four more people will live. If the reasoning process that you used in this particular case is extended to a general principle, you have embraced a type of consequentialist or utilitarian ethical theory (described later in this chapter). But can this principle/theory be consistently extended to cover similar cases?

Next, consider a variation of this dilemma, which also involves a runaway trolley, but this time you are a spectator. Imagine that you are standing on a bridge overlooking the track on which a runaway trolley is traveling. You observe that the trolley is heading for the station where there are many people gathered outside. Standing next to you on the bridge is a very large and obese person (weighing approximately 500 pounds), who is leaning forward over the rail of the bridge to view the runaway trolley. You realize that if you gently pushed the obese person forward as the trolley approaches, he would fall off the bridge and land in front of the trolley; the impact would be sufficient to stop the trolley. Thus, you could save the lives of many people who otherwise would die.

Would you be willing to push the obese person off the bridge? If not, why not? What has changed in the two scenarios? After all, if you are reasoning from the standpoint of a utilitarian/consequentialist theory, the same outcome would be realized—one person dies, while many others live. But you may find it far more difficult to push (intentionally) one person to his death, even though doing so would mean that several persons will live as a result. However, in this case, you might reason that intentionally causing someone's death (especially by having a "direct hand" in it) is morally wrong. You may also reason that actively and deliberately causing one person's death (as opposed to another's) is unjust and unfair and that it would be a dangerous moral principle to generalize. In this case, your reasoning would be nonutilitarian or nonconsequentialist.

Perhaps you see the inconsistency in the means used to make decisions in the two similar scenarios. However, you might react initially by saying that it is permissible to flip-flop on moral principles, depending on the particular circumstances you face. But we will see that it is difficult to have a coherent moral system where the ethical theories used to frame policies are inherently inconsistent. Fortunately, there is no need for us to resolve these questions at this point in the chapter. Rather, the purpose of posing this dilemma now is to get us to begin thinking about how we can respond to moral dilemmas and moral issues that we will invariably face in our professional as well as personal lives.

Moral Dilemmas vs. Moral Issues

It is important to note that the phrase "moral dilemma" is often misused to describe a "moral issue" that need not involve a true dilemma. We will see that not every moral issue is a moral dilemma and not every dilemma is necessarily moral in nature. For example, the unauthorized duplication of copyrighted material is a moral issue, but it need not involve a moral dilemma, or for that matter, a dilemma of any kind. Conversely, I may face a dilemma involving whether to meet my sister, who lives in a different country but happens to be traveling near my home town today, or keep an urgent medical appointment today with my physician who has drastically rearranged his schedule to be able to see me. In this case, I have to choose either to (i) see my sister and cancel a very important medical appointment or (ii) keep my appointment and miss a rare opportunity to see my sister; but we should note that this dilemma is not necessarily moral in nature.

The term *dilemma* refers a situation where one is confronted with having to make a choice between two options, both of which can entail an undesirable or unpleasant outcome. Often times, a dilemma involves one's having to choose an option that he or she perceives to be the lesser of two evils. However, our primary interest in this chapter is not so much with the specific choices one makes in these kinds of situations; instead, it is with (i) the principle that one uses in making his or her choice and (ii) whether that principle can be applied systematically and consistently in making moral decisions in similar kinds of cases. To that end, the (now) classic "runaway trolley" scenario illustrates the difficulties one can face in using such principles to reason through a moral dilemma.

Later in this chapter, we revisit the "trolley dilemma" and we complicate it somewhat by replacing the trolley's human driver with an autonomous computer system. We then examine in detail some specific ethical theories that can be applied in our analyses of this and other moral dilemmas, as well as moral issues in general. First, however, we examine some basic concepts that comprise morality and a moral system.

▶ 2.1 ETHICS AND MORALITY

What differences, if any, are there between the notions of ethics and morality? Whereas *ethics* is derived from the Greek *ethos*, the term *morality* has its roots in the Latin *mores*. Both the Greek and the Latin terms refer to notions of custom, habit, behavior, and character. Although "ethics" and "morality" are often used interchangeably in everyday discourse, we draw some important distinctions between the two terms as we will use them in this textbook. First, we define ethics as the study of morality.[2] This definition, of course, raises two further questions:

a. What is *morality*?

b. What is *the study of morality*?

We had begun to answer question (b) in Chapter 1, where we described three approaches to cyberethics issues. You may want to review Section 1.4, which describes how moral issues can be studied from the perspectives of professional ethics, philosophical ethics, and sociological/descriptive ethics. We will say more about "the study of morality," especially from a philosophical perspective, in Section 2.1.2.

2.1.1 What Is Morality?

As noted earlier, we defined ethics as the study of morality. However, there is no universally agreed-upon definition of "morality" among ethicists and philosophers. For our purposes, however, *morality* can be defined as a system of rules for guiding human conduct and principles for evaluating those rules. Note that (i) morality is a *system* and (ii) it is a system comprised of *moral rules*. These rules can be understood as *rules of conduct*, which are very similar to the notion of policies, described in Chapter 1. There, "policies" were defined as rules of conduct that have a wide range of application. According to Moor (2004), policies range from formal laws to informal, implicit guidelines for actions.

There are two kinds of rules of conduct:

1. *Directives* that guide our conduct as individuals (at the microlevel)

2. *Social policies* framed at the macrolevel

Directives are rules that guide our individual actions and direct us in our moral choices at the "microethical" level (i.e., the level of individual behavior). "Do not steal" and "Do not harm others" are examples of directives. Other kinds of rules guide our conduct at the "macrolevel" (i.e., at the level of social policies and social norms).

Rules of conduct that operate at the macroethical level guide us in both framing and adhering to social policies. For example, rules such as "Proprietary software should not be duplicated without proper authorization" or "Software that can be used to invade the privacy of users should not be developed" are instances of social policies. Notice the correlation between the directive "Do not steal" (a rule of conduct at the microlevel) and the social policy "Unauthorized duplication of software should not be allowed" (a rule of conduct at the macrolevel).

Figure 2-1 illustrates the different kinds of rules that comprise a moral system.

What Kind of a System Is a Moral System?

According to Gert (2005, 2007), morality is a "system whose purpose is to prevent harm and evils." In addition to preventing harm, a moral system aims at promoting human flourishing. Although there is some disagreement regarding the extent to which the promotion of human flourishing is required of a moral system, virtually all ethicists believe that, at a minimum, the fundamental purpose of a moral system is to prevent or alleviate harm and suffering. We have already seen that at the heart of a moral system are rules of conduct and principles of evaluation. We next consider some other characteristics that define a moral system.

Gert describes a moral system as one that is both public and informal. The system is *public*, he argues, because everyone must know what the rules are that define it. Gert uses the analogy of a game, which has a goal and a corresponding set of rules. The rules are understood by all of the players, and the players use the rules to guide their behavior in legitimately achieving the goal of the

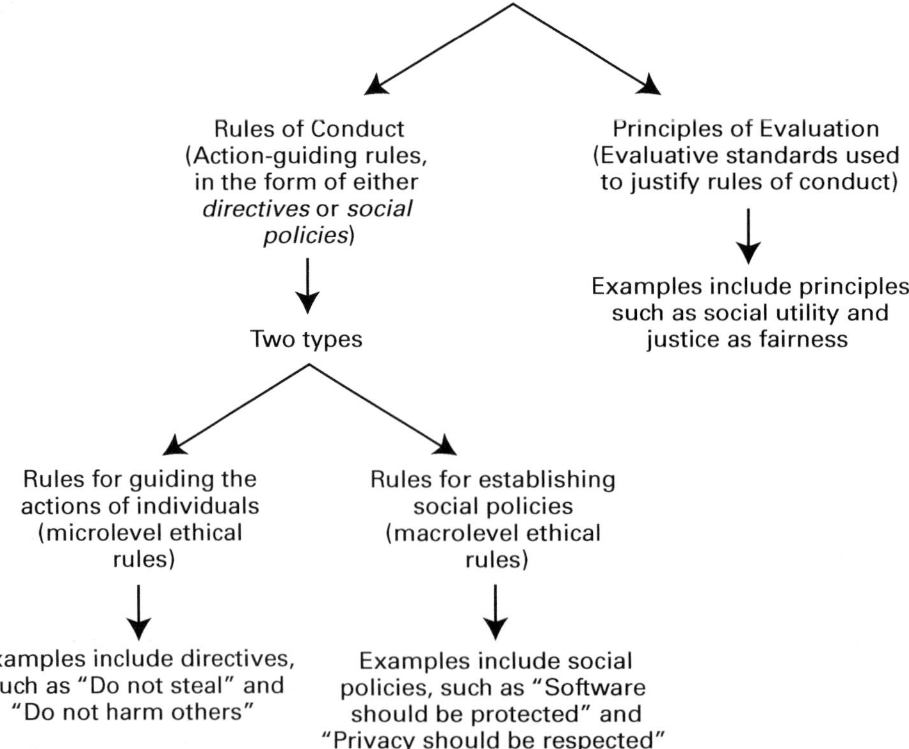

Figure 2-1 Basic components of a moral system.

game. The players can also use the rules to evaluate or judge the behavior of other players in the game. However, there is one important difference between a moral system and a game: Not everyone is required to participate in a game, but we are all obligated to participate in a moral system.

Morality is also *informal* because, Gert notes, a moral system has no formal authoritative judges presiding over it. Unlike games in professional sports that have rules enforced by referees in a manner that approaches a legal system, morality is less formal. A moral system is more like a game of cards or a "pickup game" in baseball or basketball. Here, the players are aware of the rules, but even in the absence of a formal official or referee to enforce the game's rules, players generally adhere to them.

Gert's model of a moral system includes two additional features: *rationality* and *impartiality*. A moral system is rational in that it is based on principles of logical reason accessible to ordinary persons. Morality cannot involve special knowledge that can be understood only by privileged individuals or groups. The rules in a moral system must be available to all rational persons who, in turn, are (what ethicists call) *moral agents*, bound by the system of moral rules. We do not hold nonmoral agents (such as young children, mentally challenged persons, and pets) morally responsible for their own actions, but moral agents often have responsibilities to nonmoral agents. (We examine the concepts of "agency" and "moral agency" in detail in Chapter 12.)

A moral system is *impartial* in the sense that the moral rules are ideally designed to apply equitably to all participants in the system. In an ideal moral system, all rational persons are willing to accept the rules of the system, even if they do not know in advance what their particular place in that system will be. To ensure that impartiality will be built into a moral system and that its members will be treated as fairly as possible, Gert invokes his "blindfold of justice" principle. Imagine that you are blindfolded while deciding what the rules of a moral system will be. Since you do not know in advance what position you will occupy in that system, it is in your own best interest to design a system in which everyone will be treated fairly. As an impartial observer who is also rational, you will want to ensure against the prospect of ending up in a group that is treated unfairly.[3]

Table 2-1 summarizes four key features in Gert's model of a moral system.

Core Values and Their Role in a Moral System

So far, we have defined morality as a system that is public, informal, rational, and impartial. We have also seen that at the heart of a moral system are two kinds of rules for guiding conduct. But where, exactly, do these (moral) rules come from? Some philosophers suggest that the moral rules are ultimately derived from a society's framework of values.[4] The term *value* comes from the Latin *valere*, which means having worth or being of worth. Values are objects of our desires or interests; examples include happiness, love, and freedom.

Philosophers often distinguish between two types of values, *intrinsic* and *instrumental*. Any value that serves some further end or good is called an instrumental value because it is tied to some external standard. Automobiles, computers, and money are examples of goods that have instrumental value. Values such as life and happiness, on the other hand, are *intrinsic* because they are valued for their own sake. Later in this chapter, we will see that a group called *utilitarians* argue that happiness is an intrinsic value. And in Chapter 5, we will see that some ethicists believe personal privacy is a value that has both intrinsic and instrumental attributes.

TABLE 2-1 Four Features of Gert's Moral System

Public	Informal	Rational	Impartial
The rules are known to all of the members	The rules are informal, not like formal laws in a legal system	The system is based on principles of logical reason accessible to all its members	The system is not partial to any one group or individual

Another approach to cataloguing values is to distinguish *core values*, some of which may or may not also be intrinsic values, from other kinds of values. Moor (2004), for example, believes that life, happiness, and autonomy are core values because they are basic to a society's thriving and perhaps even to its survival. Autonomy, Moor argues, is essentially a cluster of values that includes ability, security, knowledge, freedom, opportunity, and resources. Although core values might be basic to a society's flourishing and possibly to that society's survival, it does not follow that each core value is also a moral value.

Sometimes, descriptions of morals and values suggest that morals are identical to values. Values, however, can be either moral or nonmoral, and moral values need to be distinguished from the broader set of nonmoral values. Consider again the roles that rationality and impartiality play in a moral system. Rationality informs us that it is in our interest to promote values consistent with our own survival, happiness, and flourishing as individuals. When used to further only our own self-interests, these values are not necessarily moral values (e.g., they can be nonmoral or amoral; so, they need not be either moral or immoral). Once we bring in the notion of impartiality, however, we begin to take the moral point of view. When we frame the rules of conduct in a moral system, we articulate one or more core moral values, such as autonomy, fairness, and justice. For example, the rule of conduct "Treat people fairly" is derived from the moral value of impartiality.

Although we have answered the question concerning the basis for a society's moral rules, noting that they are derived from that society's system of core values, we have not yet considered another key question: How are these rules ultimately evaluated and justified? Typically, the moral rules are justified by a set of evaluative standards, or *principles*. For example, the principle of social utility, which is concerned with promoting the greatest good for the greatest number, can be used as a kind of "litmus test" for determining whether the policy "Proprietary software should not be copied without permission" can be justified on moral grounds. In this case, the policy in question could be justified by showing that not allowing the unauthorized copying of software will produce more overall social good than will a policy that permits software to be duplicated freely.

Similarly, the policy "Users should not have their privacy violated" might be justified by appealing to the same principle of social utility. Alternatively, a different principle such as "respect for persons," or possibly a principle based on the notion of fairness, might be used to justify the social policy in question. A society's principles for evaluating and justifying its moral rules tended to be grounded in one of three kinds of frameworks or sources: religion, law, or (philosophical) ethics. To see how this applies, we next turn to the second of the two main questions posed at the beginning of this section: What is the study of morality?

2.1.2 The Study of Morality: Three Distinct Approaches for Evaluating and Justifying the Rules Comprising a Moral System

Consider the rule (of conduct) "Do not steal," which underpins many cyberethics controversies involving software piracy and intellectual property disputes. Virtually every moral system includes at least one rule that explicitly condemns stealing. But why, exactly, is stealing morally wrong? The answer we give typically depends on whether we take the religious, the legal, or the philosophical/ethical point of view.

Approach #1: Grounding Moral Principles in a Religious System

Why is stealing morally wrong? Consider the following rationale:

> Stealing is wrong because it offends God or because it violates one of God's Ten Commandments.

Here, the "moral wrongness" in the act of stealing is grounded in religion; stealing, in the Judeo-Christian tradition, for example, is explicitly forbidden by 1 of the 10 Commandments. From the point of view of this and other institutionalized religions, then, stealing is wrong because it offends God or because it violates the commands of a divine authority. Furthermore, Christians generally believe that those who steal will be punished in the next life even if they are not caught and punished for their sins in the present life.

One difficulty in applying this rationale in a nation such as the United States is that American society is pluralistic. While the United States was once a relatively homogeneous culture with roots in the Judeo-Christian tradition, American culture has in recent years become increasingly heterogeneous. So people with different religious beliefs, or with no religious beliefs at all, can disagree with those whose moral beliefs are grounded solely on religious convictions that are Judeo-Christian based. Because of these differences, many argue that we need to ground the rules and principles of a moral system on criteria other than those provided by any particular organized religion. Some suggest that civil law can provide the foundation needed for a moral system to work.

Approach #2: Grounding Moral Principles in a Legal System

An alternative rationale to the one proposed in the preceding section is as follows:

> Stealing is wrong because it violates the law.

One advantage of using law instead of religion as the ground for determining why stealing is wrong is that it eliminates certain kinds of disputes between religious and nonreligious persons and groups. If stealing violates the law of a particular jurisdiction, then the act of stealing can be declared wrong independent of any religious beliefs or disbeliefs—Christian, Muslim, or even agnostic or atheist. And since legal enforcement of rules can be carried out independent of religious beliefs, there is a pragmatic advantage to grounding moral principles (and their corresponding rules) in law rather than in religion: Those breaking a civil law can be punished, for example, by either a fine or imprisonment, or both.

But laws are not uniform across political boundaries: Laws vary from nation to nation and state to state within a given nation. In the United States, the unauthorized copying and distribution of proprietary software is explicitly illegal. However, in certain Asian countries, the practice of copying proprietary software is not considered criminal (or even if it is technically viewed as a crime, actual cases of piracy may not be criminally prosecuted). So there can be a diversity of legal systems just as there is a diversity of religious systems.

Perhaps a more serious flaw in using a legal approach is that history has shown that certain laws, although widely accepted, institutionalized, and practiced within a society, have nonetheless been morally wrong. For example, slavery was legally valid in the United States until 1865. And in South Africa, apartheid was legally valid until 1991. So if we attempt to ground moral principles in law, we are still faced with serious challenges. Also, we can ask whether it is possible, or even desirable, to institutionalize morality such that we require specific laws for every possible moral issue?

Approach #3: Grounding Moral Principles in a Philosophical System of Ethics

A third way to approach the problem of how to ground moral systems is to say:

> Stealing is wrong because it is wrong.

Notice what this statement implies. The moral rightness or wrongness of stealing is not grounded in any external authority, theological or legal. So regardless of whether God condemns stealing or whether stealing violates existing civil laws, stealing is held to be wrong in itself. On what grounds can such a claim be made? Many philosophers and ethicists argue that reason alone is sufficient to show that stealing is wrong—reason informs us that there is something either in the very act of stealing or in the consequences of the act that makes stealing morally wrong.

In the case of both religion and law, sanctions in the form of punishments can be applied to deter individuals from stealing. In the first case, punishment for immoral behavior is relegated to the afterlife. And in the second case, punishment can be meted out here and now. In the case of philosophical ethics, sanctions take the form of social disapprobation (disapproval) and, possibly, social ostracism, but there is no punishment in a formal sense.

According to the system of philosophical ethics, stealing is morally wrong by criteria that reason alone is sufficient to determine. Of course, we need to specify what these criteria are; we will do this in Sections 2.4–2.7, where we discuss four kinds of ethical theories.

The Method of Philosophical Ethics: Logical Argumentation and Ethical Theory

In Chapter 1, we briefly described the philosophical method and saw how it could be used to analyze cyberethics issues. We also saw that the method philosophers use to analyze moral issues is normative, in contrast to the descriptive method that is used by many social scientists. We saw that sociological and anthropological studies are descriptive because they describe or report how people in various cultures and groups behave with respect to the rules of a moral system. For example, a sociologist might report that people who live in nations along the Pacific Rim believe that it is morally permissible to make copies of proprietary software for personal use. However, it is one thing simply to report or describe what the members of a particular culture believe about a practice such as duplicating proprietary software, and it is something altogether different to say that people ought to be permitted to make copies of that proprietary material. When we inquire into moral issues from the latter perspective, we engage in a normative investigation.

We have seen that normative analyses of morality can involve religion and law as well as philosophy. We have also seen, however, that what separates philosophy from the other two perspectives of normative analysis is the methodology used to study the moral issues. To approach these issues from the perspective of philosophical ethics is, in effect, to engage in a philosophical study of morality.

If you are taking a course in ethics for the first time, you might wonder what is meant by the phrase "philosophical study." We have already described what is meant by a descriptive study, which is essentially a type of scientific study. Philosophical studies and scientific studies are similar in that they both require that a consistent methodological scheme be used to verify hypotheses and theories; and these verification schemes must satisfy the criteria of rationality and impartiality. But philosophical studies differ from scientific studies in one important respect: Whereas scientists typically conduct experiments in a laboratory to confirm or refute one or more hypotheses, philosophers do not have a physical laboratory to test ethical theories and claims. Instead, philosophers confirm or reject the plausibility of the evidence for a certain claim or thesis via the rules of logical argumentation (which we will examine in Chapter 3); these rules are both rational and impartial. Another important feature that distinguishes a philosophical study of morality from other kinds of normative investigation into morality is the use of ethical theory in the analysis and deliberation of the issues.

Figure 2-2 illustrates how the rules that comprise a moral system are both derived from core values and evaluated/justified on grounds that tend to be religious, legal, or philosophical in nature.

Ethicists vs. Moralists

We note that ethicists who study morality from the perspective of philosophical methodology, and who thus appeal to logical arguments to justify claims and positions involving morality, are very different from a group that we can call *moralists*. Moralists often claim to have all of the answers regarding moral questions and issues, and many of them have also been described as "preachy" and "judgmental." We should note that some moralists may also have a particular moral agenda to advance. Ethicists, on the other hand, use the philosophical method in analyzing and attempting to resolve moral issues; they must remain open to different sides of

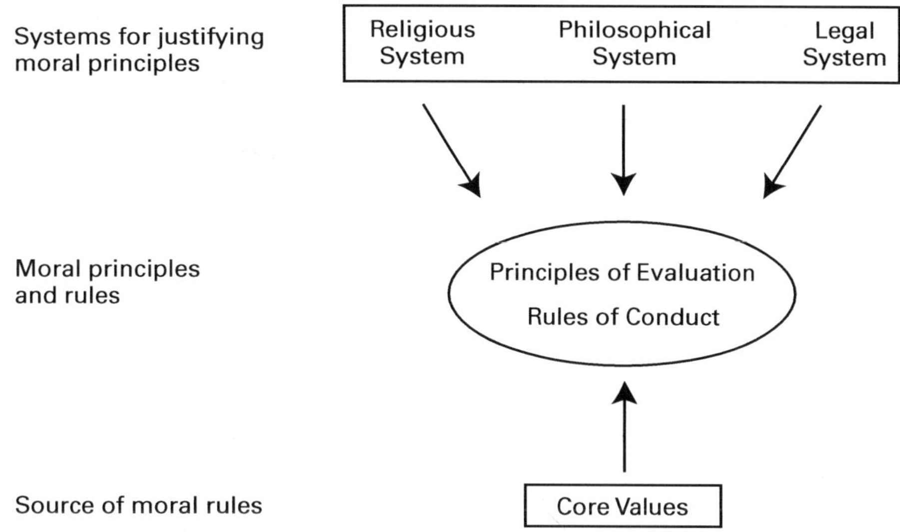

Figure 2-2 Components 2-2 of a moral system.

a dispute, and their primary focus is on the study of morality and the application of moral theories. As such, ethicists approach moral issues and controversies by way of standards that are both rational (based on logic) and impartial (open to others to verify). Some of these important distinctions are examined later in this chapter, that is, in our analysis of key differences between moral absolutism and moral objectivism.

▶ 2.2 DISCUSSION STOPPERS AS ROADBLOCKS TO MORAL DISCOURSE

We have suggested that impartial and objective standards, such as those provided by ethical theory and the rules of logical argumentation, can be used in our analysis of moral issues. However, many people might be surprised that tests and standards of any kind can be applied to disputes about morality and moral issues. So before beginning our examination of the ethical theory, perhaps we should first acknowledge and try to address some concerns that many people frequently encounter when either they willingly engage in or find themselves involuntarily drawn into discussions involving moral issues. We will see why these concerns are often based on some conceptual confusions about the nature of morality itself.

Have you ever been engaged in a serious conversation about a moral issue when, all of a sudden, one party in the discussion interjects with a remark to the effect, "But who's to say what is right or wrong anyway?" Or perhaps someone might interject, "Who are we to impose our values and ideas on others?" Clichès such as these are just two examples of the kinds of simplistic or nonreflective questions that we are likely to hear in discussions involving moral issues. I call remarks of this type "discussion stoppers" because often they close down prematurely what otherwise might be a useful discussion. These stoppers can take many different forms, and some are more common than others, but we can analyze them in terms of four distinct questions:

1. People disagree about morality, so how can we reach an agreement on moral issues?
2. Who am I/who are we to judge others and to impose my/our values on them?
3. Isn't morality simply a private matter?
4. Isn't morality simply a matter that different cultures and groups should determine for themselves?

2.2.1 Discussion Stopper #1: People Disagree on Solutions to Moral Issues

Because different people often have different beliefs as to the correct answer to many moral questions, some infer that there is no hope of reaching any kind of agreement on answers to *any* moral question. And from this inference, some conclude that any meaningful discourse about morality is impossible. Three crucial points that people who draw these and similar inferences about morality fail to recognize, however, are as follows:

I. Experts in other fields of study, such as science and mathematics, also disagree as to the correct answers to certain questions.

II. There is common agreement as to answers to some moral questions.

III. People do not always distinguish between disagreements about general principles and disagreements about factual matters in disputes involving morality.

We briefly examine each of these points.

Experts in Many Fields Disagree on Fundamental Issues

First, we should note that morality is not the only area in which intelligent people have disagreements. Scientists and mathematicians disagree among themselves about core issues in their disciplines, yet we do not dismiss the possibility of meaningful discourse in science and mathematics merely because there is some disagreement among experts in those fields. Consider also that computer scientists disagree among themselves whether open-source code is better than proprietary code, whether Linux is a better operating system than Windows 10, or whether C++ is a better programming language than Java.

One example of how natural scientists can disagree among themselves is apparent in the classic and contemporary debate in physics regarding the nature of light. Some physicists argue that light is ultimately composed of particles, whereas others claim that light is essentially composed of waves. Because physicists can disagree with each other, should we conclude that physics itself must be a totally arbitrary enterprise? Or, alternatively, is it not possible that certain kinds of disagreements among scientists might indeed be healthy for science? The debate about the nature of light has actually contributed to moving the field of physics forward in ways that it otherwise might not progress. In this sense, then, a certain level of disagreement and dispute among scientists is a positive and constructive function in the overall enterprise of scientific discovery. Similarly, why not assume that certain kinds of disagreements in ethics—that is, those that are based on points aimed at achieving constructive resolutions—actually contribute to progress in the field of ethics?

Also note that disagreement exists among contemporary mathematicians as to whether or not numbers are constructed (as opposed to having an independent existence). Because mathematicians disagree about the truth of certain claims pertaining to foundational issues in mathematics, does it follow that the field of mathematics itself is arbitrary? Does it also follow that we should give up any hope of eventually reaching an agreement about basic truths in mathematics? And should we dismiss as arbitrary the theories of mathematics as well as the theories of physics, simply because there is some level of disagreement among scholars in both academic fields? Would it be reasonable to do so? If not, then why should one dismiss ethics merely because there is some disagreement among ethicists and among ordinary persons as to the correct answers to some moral issues?

Note that certain conditions (parameters, rules, etc.) must be satisfied in order for a particular claim or a particular theory to qualify as acceptable in debates among scientists and among mathematicians. We will see that certain rules and parameters must also be satisfied in order for a particular claim or theory to qualify as acceptable in debates among ethicists. Just as there are claims and theories in physics and in mathematics that are not considered plausible by the scientific and mathematical communities, similarly, not every claim or theory involving morality is considered reasonable by ethicists. Like mathematicians and scientists, ethicists continue to disagree with one another; for example, they will likely continue to debate about which ethical theories should be applied in the case of cloning and genomic research. But like scientists and mathematicians, ethicists will continue to work within the constraints of certain acceptable rules and parameters in advancing their various theories.

Common Agreement on Some Moral Issues

We can now turn to our second point: People have demonstrated considerable agreement on answers to some moral questions, at least with respect to moral principles. We might be inclined to overlook the significant level of agreement regarding ethical principles, however, because, as Gert (2005, 2007) notes, we tend to associate moral issues with highly controversial concerns such as the death penalty, euthanasia, abortion, and cloning, all involving life-and-death decisions. We tend to forget that there are also many basic moral principles on which we do agree; for instance, nearly everyone believes that people should tell the truth, keep promises, respect their parents, and refrain from activities involving stealing and cheating. And most people agree that willful murder is wrong. It would be prudent for us to pay closer attention to our beliefs regarding these core moral principles in order to find out why there is such agreement.

So if we agree on many basic moral principles, such as our commonly held beliefs that murder is wrong and stealing is wrong, then why do many people also believe that disputes about moral issues are impossible to resolve? Beliefs and assumptions regarding morality may be based on certain conceptual confusions, and one source of confusion may be our failure to distinguish between the alleged factual matters and the general principles that constitute moral issues. This brings us to our third point.

Disagreements about Principles vs. Disagreements about Facts

De George (2010) has pointed out that in analyzing moral issues, we need to be very careful in distinguishing our disagreements about moral principles from our disagreements about certain facts, or empirical data, associated with a particular moral issue. For example, in the current debate over intellectual property rights in cyberspace, the dispute is not so much about whether we should accept the moral principle that stealing is wrong, for parties on both sides of the debate would acknowledge that stealing is indeed morally wrong. What they disagree about is whether an activity that involves either the unauthorized copying of proprietary software or the unauthorized exchange of proprietary information over a computer network is itself a form of stealing. In other words, the debate is not about a moral principle, but rather has to do with certain empirical matters, or factual claims.

Recall our discussion of the original Napster controversy in Chapter 1. It might turn out that this particular controversy is not a moral dispute but rather a debate over factual claims. And once the factual questions are resolved, the Napster controversy might be understood as one that is, at bottom, nonmoral in nature. Being able to recognize these distinctions will help us to eliminate some of the confusion surrounding issues that initially are perceived to be moral but ultimately may turn out to be nonmoral, or descriptive.

2.2.2 Discussion Stopper #2: Who Am I to Judge Others?

People are often uncomfortable with the prospect of having to evaluate the moral beliefs and practices of others. We generally feel that it is appropriate to *describe* the different moral beliefs that others have but that it is inappropriate to make *judgments* about the moral beliefs held by others. This assumption is problematic at two levels: First, as a matter of descriptive fact, we constantly judge others in the sense that we make certain evaluations about them. And second, from a normative perspective, in certain cases, we *should* make judgments (evaluations) about the beliefs and actions of others. We briefly examine both points.

Persons Making Judgments vs. Persons Being Judgmental

First, we need to make an important distinction between "making a judgment" about someone or something and "being a judgmental person." Because someone makes a judgment, or evaluation, about X, it does not follow that he or she is also necessarily being a judgmental person. For example, a person can make the judgment "Linux is a better operating system than Windows" and yet not be a judgmental person. One can also judge that "Mary is a better computer programmer than Harry" without necessarily being judgmental about either Mary or Harry. Being judgmental is a behavioral trait that is sometimes exhibited by those who are strongly opinionated or who tend to speak disparagingly of anyone who holds a position on some topic that is different from their own. "Judging" in the sense of evaluating something, however, does not require that the person making the judgment be a judgmental person.

We routinely judge, or evaluate, others. We judge others whenever we decide whom we will pursue as friends, as lovers, or as colleagues. Judging is an integral part of social interaction. Without judgment at this level, we would not be able to form close friendships, which we distinguish from mere acquaintances. And it would be difficult for us to make meaningful decisions about where we wish to live, work, recreate, and so forth.

Judgments Involving Condemnations vs. Judgments Involving Evaluations

Why do we tend to be so uncomfortable with the notion of judging others? Part of our discomfort may have to do with how we currently understand the term "judge." As we saw earlier, we need to be careful to separate the cognitive act of judging (i.e., making judgments about someone or something) from the behavioral trait of "being judgmental." Consider the biblical injunction that instructs us to refrain from judging others in the sense of condemning them. In that sense of "judge" there would seem to be much wisdom in the biblical command.

However, there is also another sense of "judge" that means "evaluate," which is something we are often required to do in our everyday lives. Consider some of the routine judgments, or evaluations, you make when deciding between competing options available to you in your day-to-day life. When you change jobs or purchase a house or an automobile, you make a judgment about which job, house, or automobile you believe is best for your purposes. When you chose the particular college or university that you are attending, you evaluated that particular institution relative to others.

There are also people employed in professions that require them to make judgments. For example, professional sporting associations employ referees and field judges who make decisions or judgments concerning controversial plays. Judges evaluate contest entries to determine which entries are better than others. Think, for example, about the judging that typically occurs in selecting the winning photographs in a camera club contest. Or consider that when a supervisor writes a performance review for an employee, she is making a judgment about the employee's performance.

Are We Ever Required to Make Judgments about Others?

It could be argued that just because we happen to make judgments about others, it doesn't necessarily follow that we ought to judge persons. However, there are certain occasions when we are not only justified in making judgments about others, but we are also morally obligated to do so. Consider, for instance, that in many societies, an individual selects the person that he or she will marry, judging (evaluating) whether the person he or she is considering will be a suitable lifelong partner in terms of plans, goals, aspirations, etc. In this case, failing to make such a judgment would be not only imprudent but also, arguably, immoral. It would be immoral because, in failing to make the appropriate judgments, one would not be granting his or her prospective spouse the kind of consideration that he or she deserves.

Next, consider an example involving child abuse. If you see an adult physically abusing a child in a public place by repeatedly kicking the child, can you not at least judge that the adult's behavior is morally wrong even if you are uncomfortable with making a negative judgment about that particular adult?

Also consider a basic human rights violation. If you witness members of a community being denied basic human rights, should you not judge that community's practice as morally wrong? For example, if women in Afghanistan are denied education, medical treatment, and jobs solely on the grounds that they are women, is it wrong to make the judgment that such practices, as well as the system that permits those practices, are immoral?

So it would seem that some serious confusions exist with respect to two distinct situations: (1) someone making a judgment about X, and (2) someone being a judgmental person. With that distinction in mind, we can avoid being judgmental and yet still make moral judgments when appropriate, and especially when we are obligated to do so.

2.2.3 Discussion Stopper #3: Morality Is Simply a Private Matter

Many people assume that morality is essentially personal in nature and must, therefore, be simply a private matter. Initially, such a view might seem reasonable, but it is actually both confused and problematic. In fact, "private morality" is essentially an oxymoron, or contradictory notion. For one thing, morality is a *public* phenomenon—recall our discussion of Gert's account of morality as a "public system" in Section 2.1.1, where we saw that a moral system includes a set of public rules that apply to all of the members of that system. Thus, morality cannot be reduced to something that is simply private or personal.

We have already seen that morality is a system of normative rules and standards whose content is studied by ethicists in the same way that mathematicians study the content of the field of mathematics. Would it make sense to speak of personal mathematics, personal chemistry, or personal biology? Such notions sound absurd because each discipline has a content area and a set of standards and criteria, all of which are open and available to all to examine. Since public rules make up the content of a moral system, which itself can be studied, we can reasonably ask how it would make sense to speak of private morality.

If morality were simply a private matter, then it would follow that a study of morality could be reduced to a series of descriptive reports about the personal preferences or personal tastes of individuals and groups. But is such an account of morality adequate? Are the moral choices that we make nothing more than mere personal choices? If you happen to prefer chocolate ice cream and I prefer vanilla or if you prefer to own a laptop computer and I prefer to own a desktop computer, we will probably not choose to debate these preferences. You may have strong personal beliefs as to why chocolate ice cream is better than vanilla and why laptop computers are superior to desktop computers; however, you will most likely respect my preferences for vanilla ice cream and desktop computers, and, in turn, I will respect your preferences.

Do moral choices fit this same kind of model? Suppose you happen to believe that stealing is morally wrong, but I believe that stealing is okay (i.e., morally permissible). One day, I decide to steal your laptop computer. Do you have a right to complain? You would not, if morality is simply a private matter that reflects an individual's personal choices. Your personal preference may be not to steal, whereas my personal preference is for stealing. If morality is grounded simply in terms of the preferences that individuals happen to have, then it would follow that stealing *is* morally permissible for me but *is not* for you. But why stop with stealing? What if I happen to believe that killing human beings is okay? So, you can probably see the dangerous implications for a system in which moral rules and standards are reducible to personal preferences and personal beliefs.

The view that morality is private and personal can quickly lead to a position that some ethicists describe as *moral subjectivism.* According to this position, what is morally right or wrong can be determined by individuals themselves, so that morality would seem to be in the "eye of the beholder." Moral subjectivism makes pointless any attempt to engage in meaningful ethical dialogue.

2.2.4 Discussion Stopper #4: Morality Is Simply a Matter for Individual Cultures to Decide

Some might assume that morality can best be understood not so much as a private or a personal matter but as something for individual cultures or specific groups to determine. According to this view, a moral system is dependent on, or relative to, a particular culture or group. Again, this view might initially seem quite reasonable; it is a position that many social scientists have found attractive. To understand some of the serious problems inherent in this position, it is useful to distinguish between *cultural relativism* and *moral relativism.*

Cultural Relativism

Cultures play a crucial role in the transmission of the values and principles that constitute a moral system. It is through culture that initial beliefs involving morality are transmitted to an individual. In this sense, cultures provide their members with what ethicists often refer to as "customary morality," or conventional morality, where one's moral beliefs are typically nonreflective (or perhaps prereflective). For example, if asked whether you believe that acts such as pirating software or invading someone's privacy are wrong, you might simply reply that both kinds of behavior are wrong because your society taught you that they are wrong. However, is it sufficient for one to believe that these actions are morally wrong merely *because* his or her culture says they are wrong? Imagine, for example, a culture in which the principle "Murder is wrong" is not transmitted to its members. Does it follow that murdering people would be morally permissible for the members of that culture?

The belief that morality is simply a matter for individual cultures to decide is widespread in our contemporary popular culture. This view is often referred to as *cultural relativism*, and at its base is the following assumption:

A. Different cultures have different beliefs about what constitutes morally right and wrong behavior.

Note that this assumption is essentially descriptive in nature, because it makes no normative judgment about either the belief systems of cultures or the behavior of people in those cultures. Although it is generally accepted that different cultures have different conceptions about what is morally right and morally wrong behavior, this position has been challenged by some social scientists who argue that some of the reported differences between cultures have been greatly exaggerated. Other social scientists suggest that all cultures may possess some universal core moral values.[5]

However, let us assume that claim (A) is true and next ask whether it logically implies (B).

B. We should not morally evaluate the behavior of people in cultures other than our own (because different cultures have different belief systems about what constitutes morally right and wrong behavior).

Note that (B) is a different kind of claim than (A). Also note that to move from (A) to (B) is to move from cultural relativism to *moral relativism.*

Moral Relativism

What are the differences between the two forms of relativism? We saw that cultural relativism is essentially a descriptive thesis, merely reporting that people's moral beliefs vary from culture to culture. Moral relativism, on the contrary, is a normative thesis because it asserts that one *should not* make moral judgments about the behavior of people who live in cultures other than one's own. However, critics point out that if moral relativists are correct, then any kind of behavior can be morally acceptable—provided that such behavior is approved by the majority of people in a particular culture.

Critics also note that the moral relativist's reasoning is flawed. For example, they point out that sometimes it is appropriate for people to question certain kinds of behavioral practices, regardless of where those practices are carried out. Consider a specific case involving a practice in some cultures and tribes in West Africa, where a ritual of female circumcision is performed. Is it wrong for those living outside these cultures to question this practice from the perspective of morality or human rights? Although this practice has been a tradition for generations, some females living in tribes that still perform it on teenage girls have objected. Let us assume, however, that the majority of members of cultures that practice female circumcision approve it. Would it be inappropriate for those who lived outside of West Africa to question whether it is morally wrong to force some women to experience this ritual against their wishes? And if so, is it inappropriate (perhaps even morally wrong) to question the practice simply because the persons raising such questions are not members of the particular culture?

If we embrace that line of reasoning used by the moral relativist, does it follow that a culture can devise any moral scheme it wishes as long as the majority of its members approve it? If so, is moral relativism a plausible thesis? Perhaps the following scenario can help us to understand further the flawed reasoning in moral relativism.

▶ **SCENARIO 2–2:** The Price of Defending Moral Relativism

Two ethnic groups whose values are very different—Cultures A and B—share a common geographical border. The residents of Culture A are fairly peaceful people, tolerant of the diverse beliefs found in all other cultures. And they believe that all cultures should essentially mind their own business when it comes to matters involving morality. Those in Culture B, on the contrary, dislike and are hostile to those outside their culture. Culture B has recently developed a new computer system for delivering chemical weapons that it plans to use in military attacks on other cultures, including Culture A. Since Culture A subscribes to the view of moral relativism, and thus must respect the views of all cultures with regard to their various systems of moral beliefs, can it condemn, in a logically consistent manner, Culture B's actions as immoral? ■

Because Culture A embraces moral relativism, it must be tolerant of all of Culture B's practices and actions, as it would in the case of all cultures. Furthermore, Culture A cannot condemn the actions of Culture B, since, in the relativist's view, moral judgments about Culture B can be made only by those who reside in that culture. So, Culture A cannot say that Culture B's actions are morally wrong.

Moral relativists can only say that Cultures A and B are different. They cannot say that one is better than another or that the behavior in one is morally permissible, while the other is morally impermissible. Consider that while the systems for treating Jews used by the Nazis and by the British in the 1940s were clearly different, moral relativists could not say, with any sense of logical consistency, that one system was morally superior to the other. In the same way, Culture B cannot be judged by Culture A to be engaging in morally wrong conduct even though Culture B wishes to destroy A and to kill all of its members. Perhaps you can see that there is a price to pay for being a moral relativist. Is that price worth paying?

Although moral relativism might initially seem attractive as an ethical position, we can now see why it is conceptually flawed. To debate moral issues, we need a conceptual and methodological framework that can provide us with impartial and objective criteria to guide us in our deliberations. Otherwise, ethical debate might quickly reduce to a shouting match in which those with the loudest voices or, perhaps worse yet, those with the "biggest sticks" win the day.

Moral Absolutism and Moral Objectivism

Why is moral relativism so attractive to so many people, despite its logical flaws? Pojman (2006) notes that many people tend to assume that if they reject moral relativism, they must automatically endorse some form of *moral absolutism*. But do they necessarily need to make an either/or choice here? Pojman and others believe that it is possible to hold a view called *ethical objectivism*, which is between the two extremes.[6] Recall our earlier distinction between ethicists and moralists at the end of Section 2.1.2; the group that we identified there as moralists are similar to moral absolutists in that both believe they have all of the correct answers for every moral question. Whereas absolutists argue that there is only one uniquely correct answer to every moral question, moral relativists assume that there are no universally correct answers to any moral questions. Moral objectivists disagree with both positions; they disagree with absolutists by pointing out that there can be more than one acceptable answer to some moral questions, despite the fact that most cultures agree on the answers to many moral issues. For example, we saw that there is considerable agreement across cultures on principles such as "murder is morally wrong" and that "stealing is morally wrong." However, objectivists also acknowledge that reasonable people can nonetheless disagree on what the correct answers are to some moral questions.

Objectivists also differ from relativists in at least one important respect. Relativists suggest that *any* answer to a moral question can be appropriate, as long the majority in a culture hold that view. Objectivists such as Gert (2005, 2007) counter by arguing that even if there is no uniquely correct answer to every moral question, there are nonetheless many incorrect answers to some of these questions.[7] To illustrate this point, consider an analogy involving a normative dispute that happens to be nonmoral in nature—namely, a debate about who was the greatest baseball player of all time. Reasonable people could disagree on the correct answer to this normative question. For example, some might argue that it was Babe Ruth or Hank Aaron; others could reasonably claim that it was Ty Cobb or Joe DiMaggio. All four answers are objectively plausible. But someone could not reasonably defend the claim that the best baseball player was Danny Ainge or Stan Papi, since those answers are clearly unacceptable (even if we, as individuals, happen to like these former baseball players). So, there are definitely some wrong answers to this normative question, and thus we cannot endorse the "anything goes" view of relativists in defending a rational answer to the question concerning the greatest baseball player of all time. The rationale used in this scenario can be extended to the analysis of normative questions that are moral in nature.

We can now see how moral objectivism offers an alternative to the extreme views of moral relativism and moral absolutism. Unlike moral absolutism, objectivism allows for a plurality of plausible answers to some controversial moral questions, provided that certain rational criteria are satisfied. But unlike relativists, objectivists would not find every answer acceptable, because some answers would fall outside the criteria of (rationally defensible) moral behavior, in the same way that some answers fell outside the criteria for rationally acceptable answers to the normative question about the greatest baseball player. Because moral objectivism allows for the possibility that there may be more than one (rationally) acceptable answer to at least some moral questions, it is compatible with a view that some call "ethical pluralism" (Ess 2006, 2014). Although objectivism and pluralism do not entail moral relativism, they allow for multiple ethical theories—provided, of course, that those theories satisfy objective criteria. Because relativism fails to satisfy such criteria, however, it cannot be included in the list of "objective" ethical theories we will examine (such as utilitarianism, deontology, etc.) in the remaining sections of this chapter.

Fortunately, ethical theory can provide us with criteria for objectively analyzing moral issues so that we can avoid the problems of moral relativism without having to endorse moral absolutism. Before proceeding directly to our discussion of ethical theories, however, it would be useful to summarize some of the key points in our analysis of the four discussion stoppers. Table 2-2 summarizes these points.

TABLE 2-2 Summary of Logical Flaws in the Discussion Stoppers

Stopper #1	Stopper #2	Stopper #3	Stopper #4
People disagree on solutions to moral issues	*Who am I to judge others?*	*Ethics is simply a private matter*	*Morality is simply a matter for individual cultures to decide*
1. Fails to recognize that experts in many areas disagree on key issues in their fields	1. Fails to distinguish between the act of judging and being a judgmental person	1. Fails to recognize that morality is essentially a public system	1. Fails to distinguish between descriptive and normative claims about morality
2. Fails to recognize that there are many moral issues on which people agree	2. Fails to distinguish between judging as condemning and judging as evaluating	2. Fails to note that personally based morality can cause major harm to others	2. Assumes that people can never reach common agreement on some moral principles
3. Fails to distinguish between disagreements about principles and disagreements about facts	3. Fails to recognize that sometimes we are required to make judgments	3. Confuses moral choices with individual or personal preferences	3. Assumes that a system is moral because a majority in a culture decides it is moral

▶ 2.3 WHY DO WE NEED ETHICAL THEORIES?

In our analysis of the four discussion stoppers, we saw some of the obstacles that we encounter when we debate moral issues. Fortunately, there are ethical theories that can guide us in our analysis of moral issues involving cybertechnology. But why do we need something as formal as ethical theory? An essential feature of theories in general is that they guide us in our investigations and analyses. Science uses theory to provide us with general principles and structures with which we can analyze our data. Ethical theory, like scientific theory, provides us with a framework for analyzing moral issues via a scheme that is internally coherent and consistent as well as comprehensive and systematic. To be coherent, a theory's individual elements must fit together to form a unified whole. To be consistent, a theory's component parts cannot contradict each other. To be comprehensive, a theory must be able to be applied broadly to a wide range of actions. And to be systematic, a theory cannot simply address individual symptoms peculiar to specific cases while ignoring general principles that would apply in similar cases.

Recall our brief analysis of the moral dilemma involving the runaway trolley (Scenario 2–1) in the opening section of this chapter. There we saw how easy it might be for a person to use two different, and seemingly inconsistent, forms of reasoning in resolving the dilemma, depending on whether that person was driving the trolley or merely observing it as a bystander on a bridge. Of course, we might be inclined to think that it is fine to flip-flop on moral decisions, since many people seem to do this much of the time. But philosophers and logicians in general, and ethicists in particular, point out many of the problems that can arise with inconsistent reasoning about moral issues.

Some critics, however, might be inclined to respond that philosophers and ethicists often dream up preposterous moral dilemmas, such as the trolley case, to complicate our decision-making process. Yet, the trolley scenario may not be as farfetched as some critics might assume. Consider that classic dilemmas involving humans in general, and human drivers of vehicles in particular, will likely take on even more significance in the near future when human drivers of commercial vehicles are replaced by computer systems, which are typically referred to as "autonomous systems." In fact, the transport systems connecting terminal buildings in some large airports are now operated by ("driverless") autonomous systems. (In Chapter 12, we examine some specific challenges we will need to face as autonomous systems replace more and more humans who currently drive commercial vehicles.)

Next, consider a slight variation or twist in Scenario 2–1. Imagine that a "driverless" trolley—that is, a trolley being "driven" by an autonomous computer system—is in the same predicament as the one facing the human driver described in that scenario.[8] If you were a software engineer or a member of the team developing the computer system designed to "drive" this trolley, what kind of "ethical-decision-making" instructions would you recommend be built into the autonomous system? Should the autonomous computer system be instructed (i.e., programmed) to reason in a way that it would likely reach a decision to "throw the switch" to save five humans who otherwise would die (as a result of the failed braking system), thus steering the trolley instead in a direction that will intentionally kill one human? In other words, should the "computerized driver" be embedded mainly (or perhaps even exclusively) with a programming code that would influence (what we earlier called) consequentialist- or utilitarian-like moral decision making? Alternatively, should programming code that would support nonconsequentialist decision-making considerations also be built into this autonomous system. We postpone our analysis of these kinds of questions (involving "machine ethics") until Chapter 12; for now, we focus on challenges that ordinary humans have in determining how to apply ethical theories in their deliberations.

Next, imagine that as a result of an accident (involving a runaway trolley), five people are rushed to the hospital. Each patient, whose condition is "critical," is in need of a vital human organ to live, and there is not sufficient time to get these organs from a transplant donor bank located outside the hospital. Also, the hospital happens to be understaffed with surgeons at the time the accident victims are admitted to the emergency ward. So a medical physician (Dr Smith) on duty at the hospital, who is administering a postsurgery physical exam to a patient in one room, is suddenly called into the emergency room. Dr Smith determines that one patient needs a heart and another a kidney; a third, a liver; a fourth, a pancreas; and a fifth, a pair of lungs. Smith also determines that unless the victims receive the organ transplants immediately, each will die. Then it suddenly occurs to Dr Smith that the hospital patient on whom he had been conducting the physical exam is in excellent health. If the healthy patient's organs were removed and immediately given to each accident victim, all five would live. Of course, the healthy patient would die as a result. But the net effect would be that four more humans would live. What should Smith do in this case? What would you do if you were in the doctor's shoes?

As you have probably determined at this point, it is helpful to have in place a systematic, comprehensive, coherent, and consistent set of principles or rules to guide us in our moral decisions. To that end, various kinds of ethical theories have been developed. We next examine four standard types of ethical theories: consequence based, duty based, contract based, and character based.

▶ 2.4 CONSEQUENCE-BASED ETHICAL THEORIES

Some have argued that the primary goal of a moral system is to produce desirable consequences or outcomes for its members. For these ethicists, the consequences (i.e., the ends achieved) of actions and policies provide the ultimate standard against which moral decisions must be evaluated. So if one must choose between two courses of action—that is, either "Act A" or "Act B"—the morally correct action will be the one that produces the most desirable outcome. Of course, we can further ask the question, "Whose outcome" (i.e., "the most desirable outcome for whom")? Utilitarians argue that the outcome or consequences for the greatest number of individuals, or the majority, in a given society is paramount in moral deliberation. According to the utilitarian theory,

> An individual act (X) or a social policy (Y) is morally permissible if the consequences that result from (X) or (Y) produce the greatest amount of good for the greatest number of persons affected by the act or policy.

Utilitarians stress the "social utility" or social usefulness of particular actions and policies by focusing on the consequences that result from those actions and policies. Jeremy Bentham (1748–1832), who was among the first philosophers to formulate utilitarian ethical theory in a systematic manner, defended this theory via two claims:

I. Social utility is superior to alternative criteria for evaluating moral systems.

II. Social utility can be measured by the amount of happiness produced.

According to (I), the moral value of actions and policies ought to be measured in terms of their social usefulness (rather than via abstract criteria such as individual rights or social justice). The more utility that specific actions and policies have, the more they can be defended as morally permissible actions and policies. In other words, if Policy Y encourages the development of a certain kind of computer software, which in turn would produce more jobs and higher incomes for those living in Community X, then Policy Y would be considered more socially useful and thus the morally correct policy. But how do we measure overall social utility? That is, which criterion can we use to determine the social usefulness of an act or a policy? The answer to this question can be found in (II), which has to do with happiness.

Bentham argued that nature has placed us under two masters, or sovereigns: pleasure and pain. We naturally desire to avoid pain and to seek pleasure or happiness. However, Bentham believed that it is not the maximization of individual pleasure or happiness that is important, but rather generating the greatest amount of happiness for society in general. Since it is assumed that all humans, as individuals, desire happiness, it would follow on utilitarian grounds that those actions and policies that generate the most happiness for the most people are most desirable. Of course, this reasoning assumes:

a. All people desire happiness.

b. Happiness is an intrinsic good that is desired for its own sake.

We can ask utilitarians what proof they have for either (a) or (b). John Stuart Mill (1806–1873) offered the following argument for (a):

> The only possible proof showing that something is audible is that people actually hear it; the only possible proof that something is visible is that people actually see it; and the only possible proof that something is desirable is that people actually desire it.

From the fact that people desire happiness, Mill inferred that promoting happiness ought to be the criterion for justifying a moral system. Unlike other goods that humans desire as means to one or more ends, Mill argued that people desire happiness for its own sake. Thus, he concluded that happiness is an intrinsic good. (Recall our earlier discussion of intrinsic values in Section 2.1.2.)

You might consider applying Mill's line of reasoning to some of your own goals and desires. For example, if someone asked why you are taking a particular college course (such as a course in cyberethics), you might respond that you need to satisfy three credit hours of coursework in your major field of study or in your general education requirements. If you were then asked why you need to satisfy those credit hours, you might respond that you would like to earn a college degree. If next someone asks you why you wish to graduate from college, you might reply that you wish to get a good-paying job. If you are then asked why you want a good-paying job, your response might be that you wish to purchase a home and that you would like to be able to save some money. If asked why again, you might reply that saving money would contribute to your long-term financial and emotional security. And if further asked why you want to be financially and emotionally secure, you might respond that ultimately you want to be happy. So, following this line of reasoning, utilitarians conclude that happiness is an intrinsic good—that is, something that is good in and of itself, for its own sake, and not merely a means to some further end or ends.

2.4.1 Act Utilitarianism

We noted previously that utilitarians look at the expected outcomes or consequences of an act to determine whether or not that act is morally permissible. However, some critics point out that because utilitarianism tends to focus simply on the roles that individual acts and policies play in producing the overall social good (the greatest good for the greatest number), it is conceptually flawed. Consider a hypothetical scenario in which a new controversial policy is being debated.

▶ **SCENARIO 2–3:** A Controversial Policy in Newmerica

A policy is under consideration in a legislative body in the nation of Newmerica, where 1% of the population would be forced to work as slave laborers in a manufacturing facility to produce inexpensive computer chips. Proponents of this policy argue that, if enacted into law, it would result in lower prices for electronic devices for consumers in Newmerica. They argue that it would also likely result in more overall happiness for the nation's citizens because the remaining 99% of the population, who are not enslaved, would be able to purchase electronic devices and other computer-based products at a much lower price. Hence, 99% of Newmerica's population benefit at the expense of the remaining 1%. This policy clearly seems consistent with the principle of producing the greatest good for the greatest number of Newmerica's population, but should it be enacted into law? ■

The above scenario illustrates a major flaw in at least one version of utilitarianism, namely, *act utilitarianism*. According to act utilitarians,

> An act, X, is morally permissible if the consequences produced by doing X result in the greatest good for the greatest number of persons affected by Act X.

All things being equal, actions that produce the greatest good (happiness) for the greatest number of people seem desirable. However, policies and practices based solely on this principle can also have significant negative implications for those who are not in the majority (i.e., the greatest number). Consider the plight of the unfortunate few who are enslaved in the computer chip processing plant in the above scenario. Because of the possibility that such bizarre cases could occur, some critics who embrace the goals of utilitarianism in general reject act utilitarianism.

Critics who reject the emphasis on the consequences of individual acts point out that in our day-to-day activities, we tend not to deliberate on each individual action as if that action were unique. Rather, we are inclined to deliberate on the basis of certain principles or general rules that guide our behavior. For example, consider some principles that may guide your behavior as a consumer. Each time that you enter a computer store, do you ask yourself, "Shall I steal this particular software game in this particular store at this particular time?" Or have you already formulated certain general principles that guide your individual actions, such as, "It is never morally permissible to steal"? In the latter case, you are operating at the level of a rule or principle rather than deliberating at the level of individual actions.

2.4.2 Rule Utilitarianism

Some utilitarians argue that the consequences that result from following *rules* or principles, not the consequences of individual acts, ultimately matter in determining whether or not a certain practice is morally permissible. This version of utilitarian theory, called *rule utilitarianism*, can be formulated in the following way:

> An act, X, is morally permissible if the consequences of following the general rule, Y, of which act X is an instance, would bring about the greatest good for the greatest number.

Note that here we are looking at the consequences that result from following certain kinds of rules as opposed to consequences resulting from performing individual acts. Rule utilitarianism eliminates as morally permissible those cases in which 1% of the population is enslaved so that the majority (the remaining 99%) can prosper. Rule utilitarians believe that policies that permit the unjust exploitation of the minority by the majority will also likely have overall negative social consequences and thus will not be consistent with the principal criterion of utilitarian ethical theory.

How would a rule utilitarian reason in the case of the trolley accident involving five victims (described in the preceding section), each of whom needs an organ transplant to survive? For an (extreme) act utilitarian, the decision might be quite simple: Remove the five organs from the one healthy patient (even though he will die) so that five humans who otherwise would die could now live. But would a rule utilitarian see this particular action as justifiable on rule-utilitarian grounds—that is, could it form the basis for an acceptable policy (in general) for hospitals and medical facilities?

Imagine a society in which it is possible for a person to report to a medical center for a routine physical exam only to discover that his or her vital organs could be removed in order to save a greater number of people. Would anyone be willing to submit to a routine physical exam in such a society? Of course, a rule utilitarian could easily reject such a practice on the following grounds: Policies that can intentionally cause the death of an innocent individual ought not to be allowed, even if the net result of following such policies meant that more human lives would be saved. For one thing, such a policy would seem unfair to all who are adversely affected. But perhaps more importantly from a rule utilitarian's perspective, adopting such a policy would not result in the greatest good for society.

Rule utilitarianism would seem to be a more plausible ethical theory than act utilitarianism. However, some critics reject all versions of utilitarianism because they believe that no matter how this theory is expressed, utilitarianism is fundamentally flawed. These critics tend to attack one or both of the following aspects of utilitarian theory:

I. Morality is basically tied to the production of happiness or pleasure.

II. Morality can ultimately be decided by consequences (of either acts or policies).

Critics of utilitarianism argue that morality can be grounded neither in consequences nor in happiness. Hence, they argue that some alternative criterion or standard is needed.

▶ 2.5 DUTY-BASED ETHICAL THEORIES

Immanuel Kant (1724–1804) argued that morality must ultimately be grounded in the concept of duty, or obligations that humans have to one another, and never in the consequences of human actions. As such, morality has nothing to do with the promotion of happiness or the achievement of desirable consequences. Thus, Kant rejects utilitarianism in particular and all consequentialist ethical theories in general. He points out that, in some instances, performing our duties may result in our being unhappy and may not necessarily lead to consequences that are considered desirable. Theories in which the notion of duty, or obligation, serves as the foundation for morality are called *deontological* theories because they derive their meaning from the Greek root *deon*, which means duty. How can a deontological theory avoid the problems that plague consequentialist theories such as utilitarianism? Kant provides two answers to this question, one based on our nature as rational creatures and the other based on the notion that human beings are ends in themselves. We briefly consider each of Kant's arguments.

What does Kant mean when he says that humans have a rational nature? Kant argues that what separates us from other kinds of creatures and what binds us morally is our rational capacity. Unlike animals who may be motivated only by sensory pleasure, humans have the ability to reason and deliberate. So Kant reasons that if our primary nature were such that we merely seek happiness or pleasure, as utilitarians suggest, then we would not be distinguishable from other creatures in morally relevant ways. But because we have a rational capacity, we are able to reflect upon situations and make moral choices in a way that other kinds of (nonrational) creatures cannot. Kant argues that our rational nature reveals to us that we have certain duties or obligations to each other as "rational beings" in a moral community.

We can next examine Kant's second argument, which concerns the roles of human beings as ends in themselves. We have seen that in focusing on criteria involving the happiness of the majority, utilitarians allow, even if unintentionally, that the interests and well-being of some humans can be sacrificed for the ends of the greatest number. Kant argues that a genuinely moral system would never permit some humans to be treated simply as means to the ends of others. He also believes that if we are willing to use a standard based on consequences (such as social utility) to ground our moral system, then that system will ultimately fail to be a moral system. Kant argues that each individual, regardless of his or her wealth, intelligence, privilege, or circumstance, has the same moral worth. From this, Kant infers that each individual is an end in himself or herself and, therefore, should never be treated merely as a means to some end. Thus, we have a duty to treat fellow humans as ends.

2.5.1 Rule Deontology

Is there a rule or principle that can be used in an objective and impartial way to determine the basis for our moral obligations? For Kant, there is such a standard or objective test which can be formulated in a principle that he calls the *categorical imperative*. Kant's imperative has a number of variations, and we will briefly examine two of them. One variation of his imperative directs us to:

> Act always on that maxim or principle (or rule) that ensures that all individuals will be treated as ends-in-themselves and never merely as a means to an end.

Another variation of the categorical imperative can be expressed in the following way:

> Act always on that maxim or principle (or rule) that can be universally binding, without exception, for all human beings.[9]

Kant believed that if everyone followed the categorical imperative, we would have a genuinely moral system. It would be a system based on two essential principles: universality and impartiality. In such a system, every individual would be treated fairly since the same rules would apply universally to all persons. And because Kant's imperative observes the principle of impartiality, it does not allow for one individual or group to be privileged or favored over another. In other words, if it is morally wrong for you to engage in a certain action, then it is also morally wrong for all persons like you—that is, all rational creatures (or moral agents)—to engage in that action. And if you are obligated to perform a certain action, then every moral agent is likewise obligated to perform that action. To illustrate Kant's points about the role that universal principles play in a moral system, consider the following scenario.

▶ **SCENARIO 2–4:** Making an Exception for Oneself

Bill, a student at Technical University, approaches his philosophy instructor, Professor Kanting, after class one day to turn in a paper that is past due. Professor Kanting informs Bill that since the paper is late, he is not sure that he will accept it. But Bill replies to Kanting in a way that suggests that he is actually doing his professor a favor by turning in the paper late. Bill reasons that if he had turned in the paper when it was due, Kanting would have been swamped with papers. Now, however, Kanting will be able to read Bill's paper in a much more leisurely manner, without having the stress of so many papers to grade at once. Kanting then tells Bill that he appreciates his concern about his professor's well-being, but he asks Bill to reflect a bit on his rationale in this incident. Specifically, Kanting asks Bill to imagine a case in which all of the students in his class, fearing that their professor would be overwhelmed with papers arriving at the same time, decided to turn their papers in one week late. ■

On deontological grounds, Bill can only make an exception for himself if everyone else (in this case, every other student in Bill's class) had the right to make exceptions for himself or herself as well. But if everyone did that, then what would happen to the very notion of following rules in a society? Kant believed that if everyone decided that he or she could make an exception for himself or herself whenever it was convenient to do so, we couldn't even have practices such as promise keeping and truth telling. For those practices to work, they must be universalizable (i.e., apply to all persons equally) and impartial. When we make exceptions for ourselves, we violate the principle of impartiality, and we treat others as means to our ends.

In Kant's deontological scheme, we do not consider the potential consequences of a certain action or of a certain rule to determine whether that act is morally permissible. Rather, the objective rule to be followed—that is, the litmus test for determining when an action will have moral worth—is whether the act complies with the categorical imperative.

For a deontologist such as Kant, enslaving humans would always be immoral, regardless of whether the practice of having slaves might result in greater social utility for the majority (e.g., being able to purchase consumer products at a lower price) than the practice of not allowing slavery. The practice of slavery is immoral, not because it might have negative social consequences in the long term but because (i) it allows some humans to be used only as a means to an end and (ii) a practice such as slavery could not be consistently applied in an objective, impartial, and universally binding way.

Kant would ask, for example, whether we could consistently impose a universal maxim that would allow slavery. He believed that we could not consistently (in a logically coherent sense) formulate such a principle that would apply to all humans, unless we also were willing to be subject to slavery. If we allow for the practice that some individuals can be enslaved but not others, then we would be allowing for exceptions to the moral rule. We would also allow some individuals to be used merely as a means to the ends of others rather than having a system in which all humans are treated as ends in themselves.

Although Kant's version of deontological ethics avoids many of the difficulties of utilitarianism, it, too, has been criticized as an inadequate ethical theory. Critics point out, for example, that even if Kant's categorical imperative provides us with the ultimate test for determining when some particular course of action is our duty, it will not help us in cases where we have two or more conflicting duties. Consider that, in Kant's system, we have duties both to keep promises and tell the truth. Thus, acts such as telling a lie or breaking a promise can never be morally permissible. However, Kant's critics point out that sometimes we encounter situations in which we are required *either* to tell the truth and break a promise *or* to keep a promise and tell a lie. In these cases, we encounter genuine moral dilemmas. Kant's deontological theory does not provide us with a mechanism for resolving such conflicts.

2.5.2 Act Deontology

Although Kant's version of deontology has at least one significant flaw, some philosophers believe that a deontological account of morality is nonetheless the correct kind of ethical theory. They also believe that a deontological ethical theory can be formulated in a way that avoids the charges of Kant's critics. One attempt at reformulating this theory was made by David Ross (1877–1971). Ross rejected utilitarianism for many of the same reasons that Kant did. However, Ross also believed that Kant's version of deontology is not fully adequate.

Ross argues that when two or more moral duties clash, we have to look at individual situations in order to determine which duty will override another. Like act utilitarians, then Ross stresses the importance of analyzing individual situations to determine the morally appropriate course of action to take. Unlike utilitarians, however, Ross believes that we must not consider the consequences of those actions in deliberating over which course of action morally trumps, or outweighs, another. Like Kant, Ross believes that the notion of duty is the ultimate criterion for determining morality. But unlike Kant, Ross does not believe that blind adherence to certain maxims or rules can work in every case for determining which duties we must ultimately carry out.

Ross believes that we have certain *prima facie* (or self-evident) *duties*, which, all things being equal, we must follow. He provides a list of prima facie duties such as honesty, benevolence, justice, and so forth. For example, each of us has a prima facie duty not to lie and a prima facie duty to keep a promise. And if there are no conflicts in a given situation, then each prima facie duty is also what he calls an *actual duty*. But how are we to determine what our actual duty is in situations where two or more prima facie duties conflict with one another? Ross believes that our ability to determine what our actual duty will be in a particular situation is made possible through a process of "rational intuitionism" (similar to the one used in mathematics).[10]

We saw that for Kant, every *prima facie* duty is, in effect, an absolute duty because it applies to every human being without exception. We also saw that Kant's scheme does not provide a procedure for deciding what we should do when two or more duties conflict. However, Ross believes that we can determine what our overriding duty is in such situations by using a deliberative process that requires two steps:

a. Reflect on the competing *prima facie* duties.

b. Weigh the evidence at hand to determine which course of action would be required in a particular circumstance.

The following scenario illustrates how Ross's procedure can be carried out.

▶ **SCENARIO 2–5:** A Dilemma Involving Conflicting Duties

You have promised to meet a classmate this evening at 7:00 in the college library to study together for a midterm exam for a computer science course you are taking. While driving in your car to the library, you receive a call on your cell phone informing you that your grandmother has been taken to the hospital and that you should go immediately to the hospital. You consider calling your classmate from your car, but you realize that you don't have his phone number. You also realize that you don't have time to try to reach your classmate by e-mail. What should you do in this case? ■

All things being equal, you have a moral obligation to keep your promise to your friend. You also have a moral obligation to visit your grandmother in the hospital. On both counts, Kant and Ross are in agreement. But what should we do when the two obligations conflict? For a rule deontologist like Kant, the answer is unclear as to what you should do in this scenario, since you have two absolute duties. For Ross, however, the following procedure for deliberation is used. You would have to weigh between the two prima facie duties in question to determine which will be your actual duty in this particular circumstance. In weighing between the two conflicting duties, your actual duty in this situation would be to visit your grandmother, which means, of course, that you would have to break your promise to your friend. However, in a different kind of situation involving a conflict of the same two duties, your actual duty might be to keep the promise made to your friend and not visit your grandmother in the hospital.

Notice that in cases of weighing between conflicting duties, Ross places the emphasis of deliberation on certain aspects of the particular situation or context rather than on mere deliberation about the general rules themselves. Unlike utilitarians, however, Ross does not appeal to the consequences of either actions or rules in determining whether a particular course of action is morally acceptable. For one thing, Ross argues that he would have to be omniscient to know what consequences would result from his actions. So, like all deontologists, Ross rejects the criteria of consequences as a viable one for resolving ethical dilemmas.

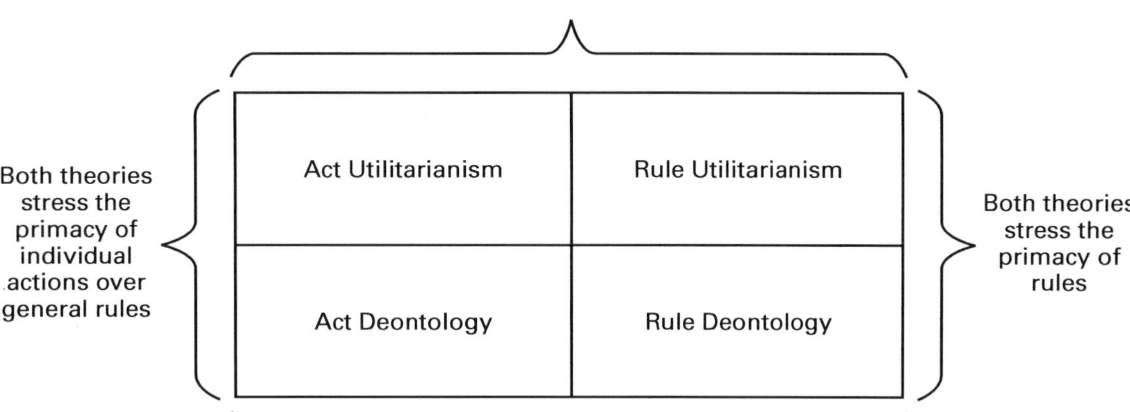

Figure 2-3 Acts vs. rules and consequences vs. duties.

One difficulty for Ross's position is that, as noted earlier, it uses a process called "rational intuitionism." Appealing to the intuitive process used in mathematics to justify certain basic mathematical concepts and axioms, Ross believes that the same process can be used in morality. However, his position on moral intuitionism is controversial and has not been widely accepted by contemporary ethicists. And since intuitionism is an important component in Ross's theory of act deontology, many ethicists who otherwise might be inclined to adopt Ross's theory have been skeptical of it. Nevertheless, variations of that theory have been adopted by contemporary deontologists.

Figure 2-3 summarizes key features that differentiate act and rule utilitarianism and act and rule deontology.

▶ 2.6 CONTRACT-BASED ETHICAL THEORIES

During the past two centuries, consequence-based and duty-based ethical theories have tended to receive the most attention from philosophers and ethicists. However, other kinds of ethical theories, such as those that emphasize criteria involving social contracts and individual rights, have recently begun to receive some serious attention as well.

From the perspective of some social contract theories, a moral system comes into being by virtue of certain contractual agreements between individuals. One of the earliest formal versions of a contract-based ethical theory can be found in the writings of Thomas Hobbes (1588–1679). In his classic work *Leviathan*, Hobbes describes an original "premoral" state that he calls the "state of nature." It is premoral because there are no moral (or legal) rules yet in existence. In this state, each individual is free to act in ways that satisfy his or her own natural desires. According to Hobbes, our natural (or physical) constitution is such that in the state of nature, we act in ways that will enable us to satisfy our desires (or appetites) and to avoid what Hobbes calls our "aversions." While there is a sense of freedom in this natural state, the condition of our day-to-day existence is hardly ideal. In this state, each person must continually fend for herself, and, as a result, each must also avoid the constant threats of others, who are inclined to pursue their own interests and desires.

Hobbes describes this state of nature as one in which life is "solitary, poor, nasty, brutish, and short." Because we are rational creatures and because we see that it would be in our best interests to band together, Hobbes notes that we eventually establish a formal legal code. In doing this, Hobbes believes that we are willing to surrender some of our "absolute" freedoms to a sovereign. In return, we receive many benefits, including a system of rules and laws that are designed and enforced to protect individuals from being harmed by other members of the system.

One virtue of the social contract model of ethics is that it gives us a motivation for being moral. We see that it is in our individual self-interest to develop a moral system with rules. This type of motivation for establishing a moral system is conspicuously absent in both the utilitarian and deontological theories.[11] So a contract-based ethical theory might seem to have one advantage over them.

2.6.1 Some Criticisms of Contract-Based Theories

Some critics, such as Pojman (2006), point out that contract-based theories provide the foundation for only a minimalist morality. They are minimalist in the sense that we are obligated to behave morally only where an explicit or formal contract exists. So if I have no express contract with you or if a country such as the United States has no explicit contract with a developing nation, there is no moral obligation for me to help you or for the United States to come to the aid of that developing nation. Of course, we can think of many situations involving morality where there are no express contracts or explicit laws describing our obligations to each other. Yet we also tend to believe that in at least some of these cases, we are morally obligated to help others when it is in our power to do so.

Consider the case of Kitty Genovese who was murdered outside her apartment building in Queens, New York, in 1964, as 38 neighbors in her apartment building watched. During the incident, none of Genovese's neighbors came to her rescue or called the police. When interviewed after the fact, some of her neighbors responded that they did nothing wrong.[12] In one sense, they were correct, since there was no explicit law requiring that they do anything at all. So technically, these neighbors were correct, at least from a legal perspective. But we can certainly ask whether her neighbors had a moral obligation to do something rather than simply be indifferent. It is in this sense, then, that social contract theory can be seen as being minimalist and legalistic and not a robust theory of morality.

Another way to think about minimalist morality is to think of the difference between two principles: (i) doing no harm and (ii) doing good. A minimalist morality would insist merely that we do not harm others. As such, it does not require that we come to the aid of others. But is that an adequate view of morality? Should we accept such a moral system as complete? If you happen to see a child drowning in water that is four feet deep and it is in your power to rescue the child, are you not morally obligated to do so? Are you under no moral obligation to assist simply because you may have no explicit legal contract requiring you to rescue that particular child?

According to a minimalist account of morality, you are not *required* to make any effort to save the child. All that is required is that you not actively harm the child (or anyone else). But some argue that a moral system demands much more of us than simply doing no harm. That is, it may also obligate us to do good when it is in our power to do so. According to the latter view of morality, then, if we could rescue the child without any significant inconvenience to ourselves, we would be morally obligated to do so (even if we have no explicit contract).

2.6.2 Rights-Based Contract Theories

Closely associated with social contract ethical theories are rights-based theories of morality. Some philosophers have argued that independent of whether individuals happen to have any legal rights, all humans have certain moral rights or natural rights. Philosophers such as Thomas Aquinas (1225–1274), as well as several of the Founders of the United States, believed that humans possess some natural rights. In the Declaration of Independence, for example, Thomas Jefferson asserted that all humans are entitled to life, liberty, and the pursuit of happiness because these rights are "inalienable" and "self-evident."

Of course, it is one thing for philosophers and legal scholars to assert that humans are endowed with natural or moral rights; and it is something altogether different to ensure that such rights are guaranteed and protected by the state—hence, the need for explicit legal rights identified in a governing charter or constitution. Legal rights are grounded in "positive law," or civil law, whereas moral rights or natural rights are not. However, some argue that moral rights are derived from natural law; and because of this, they further argue that these rights exist independently of any legal rights that might happen to be granted to citizens of a certain nation via that nation's system of positive laws.[13]

Philosophers and legal scholars often differentiate between two kinds of legal rights: *positive rights* and *negative rights*. Having a negative right to something simply means that one has the right not to be interfered with in carrying out the privileges associated with that right. For example, your right to vote and your right to own a computer are both negative rights. They are negative rights in the sense that as a holder of those rights, you have the right (and the expectation) not to be interfered with in exercising your right to go to polls to cast your vote in a particular election or your right to purchase a computer. However, as the holder of a negative right, you cannot demand (or even expect) that others must either physically transport you to the voting polls if you are unable to travel there on your own or provide you with a computer if you cannot afford to purchase one.

Positive rights, it turns out, are very rare. And since those rights tend to be far more controversial than negative rights, philosophers and legal scholars have had a much more difficult time justifying them. In the United States, one's right to receive an education (through the twelfth grade of high school) is a positive right. All American citizens are entitled to such an education; thus, they must be provided with a free public education through the 12th grade. An interesting question, for our purposes, is, what would happen in the event that our formal education process requires that each student own a computer and that he or she has access at home to the Internet? In that case, would students also have to be provided with a home computer and free Internet access? (We take up the question of universal access issues and the "digital divide" in Chapter 10.)

Some would argue that access to adequate healthcare should also be a positive right as well, because they believe healthcare is something that citizens have a right to be provided (even if they cannot afford to pay for it). In Canada as well as in many European countries, universal healthcare is viewed as a positive right. In the United States, however, this view is still being debated. Although the Patient Protection and Affordable Care Act, also informally known as "Obamacare," was enacted into law in March 2010, it has since come under severe criticism and serious challenges from opponents. Depending on the outcome of the fall 2016 presidential elections, this law could be repealed, in which case healthcare in the United States would not be a positive right.

Discussion about the nature of rights can be both confusing and controversial. In the United States, many conservative political and religious leaders believe that in recent years, far too much emphasis has been placed on individual rights. As a result, they believe that we have not paid enough attention to corresponding responsibilities that individuals also have by virtue of possessing those rights. However, we will not pursue that line of controversy here.

▶ 2.7 CHARACTER-BASED ETHICAL THEORIES

A fourth type of ethical theory that must be considered, especially in light of the recent attention it has received, is *virtue ethics* (also sometimes described as "character ethics"). This ethical theory ignores the special roles that consequences, duties, and social contracts play in moral systems, especially with respect to determining the appropriate standard for evaluating moral behavior. Rather, it focuses on criteria having to do with the character development of individuals and their acquisition of good character traits from the kinds of habits they develop. The fundamental principles of virtue ethics were introduced in the writings of Plato and Aristotle nearly 2,500 years ago. In more recent times, virtue ethics has gained respect among ethicists as a viable contemporary ethical theory, in part, through the influential work of Philippa Foot, Alasdair MacIntyre, and others.[14]

2.7.1 Being a Moral Person vs. Following Moral Rules

Aristotle believed that ethics was something not merely to be studied, but rather to be lived or practiced. In fact, Aristotle (384-322 BC) thought of ethics as a "practical science," like politics. To become an ethical person, in Aristotle's view, one is required to do more than simply memorize and deliberate on certain kinds of rules. What is also needed, Aristotle argued, is that people develop certain *virtues*. The Greek word for virtue is *arete*, which means excellence. Aristotle believed that to be a moral person, one had to acquire the right virtues (strengths or excellences). Through the proper training and acquisition of good habits and character traits, Aristotle believed that one could achieve moral virtues such as temperance and courage that are needed to "live well."

Because virtue ethics focuses primarily on character development and moral education, it does not need to rely on a system of formal rules. Consider that both utilitarians and deontologists depend on having a system of rules when they ask a question such as, What should we do in such and such a case or situation? For utilitarians, the answer could be found by measuring the anticipated outcomes of following a general rule or principle. And for deontologists, the answer can be determined by using a formal rule such as the categorical imperative as a principle for determining which duties you have. For contract theorists, questions involving moral obligation ultimately rest on the principle or rule: What is the nature of my contract, if any, in this particular situation? Virtue ethicists take a very different tack. Instead of asking, "What should I *do* in such and such a situation?" a virtue ethicist asks, *What kind of person should I be?*—hence, the emphasis on *being a moral person* and not simply on understanding what moral rules are and how they apply in certain situations. Whereas deontological and utilitarian theories are action oriented and rule oriented, virtue ethics is "agent-oriented" because it is centered on the moral development and character of the agent himself/herself.

Virtue ethicists believe that a moral person is one who is necessarily disposed to do the right thing. They correctly point out that when we engage in routine acts in our daily lives, including many of our nonnormative actions, we do not deliberate by asking ourselves, What ought I to do in such and such a case? In our earlier criticism of act utilitarianism, we considered a situation in which an individual would be required to deliberate over whether or not to steal an item each time he or she entered a store. A virtue ethicist would point out that if that person had developed the right kind of moral character (through the acquisition of the "correct" moral habits), he or she would not be in a position that required such deliberation. That is, the moral person is already disposed not to steal items from stores (or from fellow human beings) because of the kinds of character traits that he or she has previously developed. And in the example involving the drowning child, considered in our criticism of contract-based ethical theory, a virtue ethicist would also likely point out that a moral person would not have to deliberate. Regardless of whether someone had an explicit legal contract to help rescue the child, the virtue ethicist would point out that a moral person is predisposed to attempt to rescue the child if it were in his or her power to do so.

2.7.2 Acquiring the "Correct" Habits

Consider the following illustration of a disposition to behave in a certain way. When you woke up this morning and began to prepare for your day's events, did you ask yourself the question, Should I brush my teeth today? Most likely, this question never crossed your mind. Why not? The answer, of course, is that you have already developed certain habits such that you are disposed to brush your teeth in the morning without having to question it or even think about it. Of course, the act of brushing one's teeth is not an act that has any moral significance. But it is the process of character formation, especially the development of moral habits, that is crucial to becoming a fully moral person, from the perspective of virtue ethics.

As noted earlier, Aristotle believed that ethics was something to be lived and practiced, not simply studied. Thus, some philosophers and ethicists believe that to teach ethics, one must first be an ethical person. The teacher who instructs students on the virtues but who himself lacks them would be a poor model for aspiring students. Moor (2002) suggests that virtue ethics instruction is the "first level" in teaching (computer) ethics. He believes that building habits of character such as kindness, truthfulness, honesty, trustworthiness, helpfulness, generosity, and justice is an important prerequisite in preparing for the second level of instruction. Once students have mastered the virtues, they can then move to the second level where they learn the established rules of a moral system.

Some instructors have argued that their students are better able to relate to classroom examples that involve virtue ethics than to those illustrating other traditional theories. For this reason, Grodzinsky (2001) has suggested that aspects of virtue ethics should be incorporated into the ethics training for computing professionals. Grodzinsky believes that aspiring computer professionals who wish to develop an appropriate level of sensitivity to ethical aspects of their profession often find the principles of virtue ethics far more useful than the kinds of rigid rules required in ethical theories such as utilitarianism and deontology. She notes that action-guiding rules associated with utilitarian and deontological theories often tend to be perceived by students as too abstract and formal. On the contrary, however, many of those students are able to grasp what it means to develop certain character traits and thus become (or be) a certain kind of person.

It would seem that the reemergence of virtue ethics, despite the fact that its origins can be traced back to classical Greece, has provided ethicists with some fresh insights. However, we should also note that virtue ethics is not without its critics. One of the chief drawbacks of taking virtue ethics as a complete theory of ethics is that it neither helps resolve conflicts that can arise among the competing virtues nor encourages examination of consequences. Some critics point out that a virtue- or character-based ethics would seem to have a better chance of taking hold in a society that is homogeneous rather than in one that is heterogeneous or pluralistic. The ancient Greek society could be considered fairly homogeneous in the sense that the world that Plato and Aristotle inhabited included a consensus as to what the ideal values, including the moral education of the young, were. In contemporary America, which is much more heterogeneous than classical Greek society, we have a diversity of views about which ideals and values are most important.

It is also worth pointing out that character-based ethical systems would most likely flourish in cultures where the emphasis placed on community life is stronger than that accorded to the role of individuals themselves. Beginning with the Enlightenment period in the West in the seventeenth and eighteenth centuries, considerable emphasis has been placed on the importance of individual autonomy and individual rights. As you might already have suspected, aspects of utilitarianism, deontological ethics, and contractualist ethics are strongly tied to the notions of individual rights and responsibilities. In the ancient Greek world of Aristotle's time, the notion of community was paramount. Thus, virtue ethics faces certain challenges in contemporary Western society that it would not have had to endure in the classical Greek *polis*, or city-state.

▶ 2.8 INTEGRATING ASPECTS OF CLASSICAL ETHICAL THEORIES INTO A SINGLE COMPREHENSIVE THEORY

We have completed our examination of the four main types of ethical theories, and we have noted some of the strengths and weaknesses of each theory. Consequentialist theories such as utilitarianism are useful because they aim at promoting happiness and the social good. Yet, we also saw that utilitarians tend to ignore the importance of justice and fairness in their preoccupation with promoting social utility for the majority. Deontologists, on the contrary, stress the importance of obligation and respect for all persons and thus emphasize the principles of fairness and justice. However, we saw that deontologists fail to pay sufficient attention to the promotion of happiness and the social good.

Contract theory seems useful in that it provides a motivation for being moral and it enables us to articulate which explicit moral obligations we have and do not have, both as individuals and as a society. However, the weakness of the social contract view is that it provides us with only a minimalist theory of morality. Virtue ethics stresses character development and the acquisition of good habits on the part of individuals, but its disadvantage is that it depends on homogeneous community standards for determining the correct virtues. Thus, each theory has its weakness, despite its strengths. Table 2-3 summarizes the advantages and disadvantages of each of the four ethical theories we examined.

Because of problems with the four types of traditional ethical theories that we considered, some have advocated for alternative ethical theories including feminist ethics. Adam (2008) has drawn from some of the insights of Carol Gilligan,[15] as well as from other authors who have contributed to the literature on feminist ethics, in making her case for why at least some computer ethics issues would be better understood if they were analyzed from the perspective of feminist ethical theory. We briefly examine Adam's arguments for a "gender-informed" computer ethics in Chapter 10, where we consider gender issues affecting cybertechnology.

Others have proposed ways in which elements of two or more traditional theories can be integrated into a single, more comprehensive framework. For example, Gert (2005, 2007) has integrated aspects of two theories by incorporating Kant's insights on the importance of impartiality with the claims of utilitarians about consequences, but he thinks that each theory, in itself, is inadequate. Gert has also shown how his moral system, which he calls "common morality," can be directly applied to issues involving computer ethics such as copying proprietary

TABLE 2-3 Four Types of Ethical Theory

Type of Theory	Advantages	Disadvantages
Consequence based (utilitarian)	Stresses promotion of happiness and utility	Ignores concerns of justice for the minority population
Duty based (deontology)	Stresses the role of duty and respect for persons	Underestimates the importance of happiness and social utility
Contract based (rights)	Provides a motivation for morality	Offers only a minimal morality
Character based (virtue)	Stresses character development and moral education	Depends on homogeneous community standards for morality

software.[16] Recall our discussion of Gert's notion of the moral system and its corresponding "moral rules" in Section 2.1.1.

Influenced by the work of Gert and others, Moor (2004) has proposed a scheme that integrates aspects of utilitarian and deontological theories into a framework he calls "just consequentialism." We next examine some key aspects of this theory.

2.8.1 Moor's Just-Consequentialist Theory and Its Application to Cybertechnology

Moor believes that only an ethical approach that combines considerations of *consequences* of action with more traditional deontological considerations of duties, rights, and *justice* can provide us with a defensible ethical theory—namely, *just consequentialism*—that yields a useful framework for applied ethics. Moor begins by considering what kind of conduct we want ethics to regulate. He believes first and foremost everyone wants to be protected against suffering unnecessary harms. We don't want to be killed or suffer great pain or have our freedom taken away. Human nature is such that people value the same kind of basic goods (life, happiness, abilities, security, knowledge, freedom, opportunities, and resources). The specifics of these may manifest somewhat differently in different cultures (e.g., some kinds of freedom may be more important in some cultures than others), but the general set of goods, which Moor calls "core values" (see Section 2.1.2), is shared by all. Losing any of these goods counts as harm, and all of us want ethics to protect us from others causing us harm. This point is captured by the familiar ethical maxim "Do no harm," described earlier. Stealing someone's computer causes a loss of resources to that person, and lying about software bugs undermines the purchaser's knowledge. Thus, it is not surprising that we regard stealing and lying as unethical activities in light of their harmful consequences.

Another desirable objective of ethics, according to Moor, is to support justice, rights, and duties. We want others to keep their promises and agreements, to obey the law, and to fulfill their duties in whatever roles they play. These specific obligations are generated within societies, and to the extent that they spring from just agreements, laws, and social situations, we justifiably expect others to fulfill their duties toward us. For example, we want a software engineer to produce reliable software. We believe it is her duty as a professional to develop effective and safe software and that we have a right to expect good quality when we buy it. Another familiar maxim of ethics is "Do your duty," where "duty" here designates specific duties people acquire by their roles in society such as a signer of contract, a citizen, a parent, an employer, or an employee. Violating one's just duty, such as knowingly designing defective software for later production and sales, in the absence of contravening considerations, is clearly unethical.

Moor believes that if all we had to do to be ethical were to do no harm and perform our duties, ethics would be challenging but at least easy to understand. But, as Moor argues, the ethical life is not nearly so simple. Often, actions involve a mixture of goods and evils as well as conflicts among duties. Sometimes, we need to make exceptions to our general policies for action. How do we decide what to do? His answer involves two steps: the deliberation stage and the selection stage. First, at the *deliberation stage*, we should consider the various possible policies for action from an impartial point of view. Impartial does not mean that everyone is treated the same but that the policy is regarded as a rule governing the situation without consideration of the particular individuals who happen to be involved. This is what Gert has in mind by his "blindfold of justice" (see Section 2.1.1) or what Rawls suggests with his "veil of ignorance." This is a technique to establish the justice of a policy—it will not be just if one will not accept the policy as a general rule of conduct, not knowing who plays which roles in the situation.

For example, consider the scenario involving the hacking of nude photos of celebrities from their mobile phones, discussed in Chapter 1. Let us assume that the hacker was obsessed with his victims and got significant gratification out of his deeds. If we consider a policy for justifying such an action impartially, we will clearly reject it. We will not endorse a policy of allowing people to hack into someone's electronic device to make controversial photos available online to the public even if people get significant pleasure from it. It is easy to reject such a policy as unjust and unethical when considered from an impartial point of view.

However, many policies will pass the impartiality test, and we will still need to consider whether we should adopt them. We need to move to the second step in the decision-making process, the *selection stage*, and carefully weigh the good consequences and the bad consequences of the remaining policies. In this second step, it may be less of a choice between ethical and unethical policies than between better and worse policies. Although we may be able to at least partially rank policies, legitimate disagreements about the rankings often exist.

For instance, consider the controversial issues as to whether we should adjust or even have a policy of intellectual property protection. For many years in many places, there were no laws protecting intellectual property. It is far from clear that this situation was unjust or even bad. A culture might maintain that sharing information and invention is more valuable to the society's members' welfare and the society's cohesiveness than trying to protect intellectual property. Witness the rationale given for the "open source movement" in software development. Critics of this movement, however, might maintain that having intellectual property protection laws is important to protect creators and to produce innovative products for everyone's benefit.

According to Moor, it is important to keep in mind that although we may disagree about the merits of various policies and how to rank them, rational discussion of the relevant policies is very possible and highly desirable. People may overlook values embedded in a situation and may change their rankings once informed. People may not be fully aware of the consequences of various policies. Moor does not believe that complete agreement on controversial policies can or necessarily should be reached, as people may ultimately rank benefits and harms differently. Nevertheless, considerable consensus about some policies being better than others can often be generated. Moor points out that frequently much of the disagreement hinges on differences about the facts of the case than on value differences. (Recall our early analysis of differences involving "disagreements about principles" and "disagreements about facts" in Section 2.2.1, in our discussion of discussion stoppers in ethics.) It would radically change much of the debate about the need for protecting MP3 files, for example, if it could be demonstrated that, *as a matter of fact*, downloading MP3 files to preview them dramatically increases sales or if it could be demonstrated that, *as a matter of fact*, downloading MP3 files to preview them dramatically decreased the quality of music that was produced.

2.8.2 Key Elements in Moor's Just-Consequentialist Framework

Moor's ethical framework of just consequentialism can be summarized in terms of a strategy that includes the following steps:

1. *Deliberate* over various policies from an impartial point of view to determine whether they meet the criteria for being ethical policies. A policy is ethical, if it:
    - **a.** Does not cause any unnecessary harms to individuals and groups and
    - **b.** Supports individual rights, the fulfilling of duties, etc.
2. *Select* the best policy from the set of just policies arrived at in the deliberation stage by ranking ethical policies in terms of benefits and (justifiable) harms. In doing this, be sure to:
    - **a.** Weigh carefully between the good consequences and bad consequences in the ethical policies and
    - **b.** Distinguish between disagreements about facts and disagreements about principles and values, when deciding which particular ethical policy should be adopted. (Knowledge about the facts surrounding a particular case should inform the decision-making process.)

As we noted in our discussion of virtue ethics in Section 2.7.2, Moor points out that developing the appropriate habits of character such as kindness, truthfulness, honesty, trustworthiness, helpfulness, generosity, and justice is an important prerequisite in moral behavior. So if one has not already developed the "correct" habits required for moral behavior, it may be difficult for an individual to successfully carry out the steps in Moor's just-consequentialist model. In this sense, elements of virtue ethics or character-based ethics are also presupposed in Moor's framework.

We apply the just-consequentialist framework, wherever appropriate, in suggesting policies in response to moral issues that arise from specific cyberethics issues examined in Chapters 4–12 of this textbook.

▶ 2.9 CHAPTER SUMMARY

In this chapter, we defined ethics as the study of morality. In elaborating on that definition, we drew some useful distinctions between morality (as a system of rules and principles) and ethics (as the study of that system). Acknowledging the distinction between normative and descriptive studies of morality, we saw that normative investigations into morality can be conducted from the perspectives of religion and law as well as from philosophy. We also noted that only philosophical ethics offers a method to analyze moral issues based exclusively on the application of ethical theory and logical argumentation. We briefly identified and analyzed some common "discussion stoppers" that are frequently invoked in ways that prematurely close down, even if unintentionally, the possibility of constructive ethical dialogue.

We also examined the roles that ethical theories ideally play in guiding us in our moral deliberations about cyberethics issues. We saw that consequence-based, duty-based, contract-based, and character-based theories each had certain strengths and weaknesses. Finally, we examined James Moor's proposal for a framework that incorporates aspects of consequence-based and duty-based theories (and to some extent character-based theories) into one unified, comprehensive theory, called "just consequentialism." We summarized Moor's framework into a two-step process that we will use, wherever possible, in our analysis of the cyberethics issues examined in this textbook.

▶ REVIEW QUESTIONS

1. What is *ethics*, and how can it be distinguished from *morality*?
2. What is meant by a *moral system*?
3. What are the "rules of conduct" that comprise a moral system? Give some examples of these (moral) rules.
4. Describe the key differences between rules of conduct that are individual "directives" and those that are "social policies." Provide an example of each.
5. What does Bernard Gert mean when he describes morality in terms of a system that is both "public" and "informal"?
6. Describe how the ideals of "rationality" and "impartiality" function in Gert's moral system.
7. What are *values*, and what criteria differentiate *intrinsic* values from *instrumental* values?
8. What does James Moor mean by "core values," and how are they both similar to and different from intrinsic values and instrumental values?
9. What factors differentiate *moral values* from *non-moral values*? Provide examples of each.
10. How do religion, law, and philosophy each provide different grounds for justifying a moral principle? How can each perspective be applied in analyzing the moral principle "Stealing is wrong?"
11. What are the basic differences separating *ethicists* from *moralists*?
12. Summarize each of the four different kinds of "discussion stoppers" that often arise in ethical discourse.
13. Why are these "discussion stoppers" problematic for the advancement of dialogue and debate about ethical issues?
14. What is *moral relativism*? How is it different from *cultural relativism*?
15. What is *moral objectivism*, and how is it different from *moral absolutism*?
16. What is ethical theory, and what important functions do ethical theories play in the analysis of moral issues?

17. What are the distinguishing features of consequence-based ethical theories?
18. Describe some of the key differences between act utilitarianism and rule utilitarianism.
19. Which features distinguish duty-based ethical theories from alternative types of theories?
20. Describe some of the main differences between act deontology and rule deontology.
21. What is meant by the expression "contract-based" ethical theories?
22. What features distinguish "character-based" (or "virtue-based") ethical theories from alternative schemes of morality?

▶ DISCUSSION QUESTIONS

23. Why does Gert believe that the notion of "personal morality" is an oxymoron? For Gert, how is a moral system both similar to and different from a game? Apply Gert's notion of a moral system to the analysis of a contemporary ethical issue affecting cybertechnology. Analyze that issue in terms of the four features that comprise a moral system for Gert.
24. How does James Moor's "just-consequentialist" theory incorporate aspects of utilitarian and deontological theories into one comprehensive ethical framework? Describe the strategies used in the two different stages of Moor's theory: the deliberation and the selection stage. Identify a contemporary moral issue affecting cybertechnology, and apply Moor's just-consequentialist theory to it.
25. Recall the four types of "discussion stoppers" that we examined in this chapter. Is that collection of "stoppers" complete? Can you think of any additional discussion stoppers that might also block or shut down moral discourse? Why is it so easy to fall victim to one or more of those stoppers when discussing moral issues in general, as well as moral issues involving the use of cybertechnology in particular?
26. Are any of the four traditional ethical theories we examined—that is, consequence based, duty based, contract based, and character based—adequate to handle moral issues that arise as a result of cybertechnology? If not, is an alternative kind of ethical theory needed, as some have argued (e.g., Adam 2008)? Or, can a comprehensive, integrated theory, such as the one proposed by James Moor (i.e., his theory of "just consequentialism") be used successfully to resolve moral issues involving cybertechnology?

Scenarios for Analysis

1. In analyzing the following scenario, describe how an *act utilitarian*, a *rule utilitarian*, a *rule deontologist*, and an *act deontologist* would each reach a solution to this dilemma. Which solution seems most plausible? Finally, apply Moor's just-consequentialism framework in your analysis of this scenario.

   You have just been appointed to the board of directors of XYZ.com. Unfortunately, the dot-com company has been experiencing some difficult financial times, resulting in revenue losses in three of the last four quarters. As you assume your new position, you discover that two proposals are on the table. Each proposal has been put forth as a means for dealing with XYZ's immediate financial problems. Proposal #1 recommends that all employees be retained but that an immediate freeze on salary increases (raises) for all employees be imposed for the next six months. (Employees may even be asked to take a 5% cut in pay if things do not improve by the end of that period.) Proposal #2 recommends that wages not be frozen but that 5% of the XYZ's workforce be laid off. (One piece of reasoning behind this proposal is that taking more drastic measures will "protect" 95% of XYZ's workers and will send a message to Wall Street and local investors that XYZ is serious about improving its financial position and that it will soon be a stable company once again.) The board is evenly split, seven members favoring proposal #1 and seven favoring proposal #2. Yours will be the tiebreaking vote.
2. Analyze the dilemma in the following scenario from the vantage point of both utilitarian and deontological ethical theories. In particular, how might Ross's theory of act deontology apply?

   The U.S. government, with the approval of the majority of Americans, has decided to round up all Arab-Americans and relocate them into internment camps. You have a friend who is an American citizen of Arab descent. She asks you to protect her from the authorities. You have known this person all of your life, and you are convinced that she is a loyal American. So you agree to hide her in the third floor of your house. Next, imagine that a U.S. federal agent knocks on your door and asks if you know the whereabouts of the person you are hiding. How would you respond to that agent?

You realize that you cannot both keep your promise to your friend and tell the truth to the federal agent. Initially, your gut reaction might suggest that the solution to your dilemma is really quite simple: A far greater good will be served by lying to the federal agent than by breaking your promise to your friend. However, to embrace the moral principle underlying that line of reasoning is to embrace a form of utilitarianism. And we have already seen some of the difficulties that can result from trying to be a consistent and thoroughgoing utilitarian. Furthermore, could you consistently universalize a moral principle that states: Whenever you must choose between telling the truth to authorities and breaking a promise to a friend, you should always keep your promise? Will that principle always work?

▶ ENDNOTES

1. Analyses of moral dilemmas based on examples using the (now classic) "trolley problem" have proliferated since this "thought experiment" was introduced by philosopher Philippa Foot in 1967. For an interesting variation of this dilemma (in the context of an autonomous computer-driven trolley), see Wallach and Allen (2009).
2. This classic definition of ethics has been used by many philosophers. See, for example, Paul W. Taylor's *Principles of Ethics: An Introduction* (Belmont, CA: Wadsworth, 1980).
3. Bernard Gert's "blindfold of justice" is similar in some ways to John Rawls' well-known "veil of ignorance," articulated in Rawls' class work *A Theory of Justice* (rev. ed. 1999). However, the two notions also differ in key respects.
4. See, for example, Pojman (2006).
5. For example, some critics point out that even though there appear to be significant differences in the moral beliefs held by various groups and cultures, when examined at the surface level, a closer analysis will suggest that there are also some ("deep") universal or core moral beliefs that lie under the surface.
6. Gert suggests that his ten "moral rules" are objective in nature. However, he does not use the label "objectivism" to describe his moral system.
7. Although Gert does not call himself a moral objectivist, I interpret his position to be compatible with the view I describe as moral objectivism.
8. Wallach and Allen (2009) also consider a variation of the "trolley case" in which the trolley's driver has been replaced by a computerized system.
9. The variations of Kant's Categorical Imperative expressed here closely follow the original formulation in Kant's writings.
10. For more detail on this strategy, see Ross (1930).
11. Pojman (2006) explains in more detail how this theory provides a "motivation" for someone or some group to behave morally.
12. For a classic account of this incident, see "Queens Woman Is Stabbed to Death in Front of Home," *New York Times*, March 14, 1964.
13. This is a basic distinction in Natural Law, a theory that we are not able to examine in detail in this chapter.
14. See, for example, Foot's *Theories of Ethics* (Oxford University Press, 1967) and MacIntyre's *After Virtue* (Notre Dame, IN: University of Notre Dame Press, 1981).
15. Gilligan's classic book *In a Different Voice* (Cambridge, MA: Harvard University Press, 1982) has influenced many authors writing on topics in feminist ethics.
16. See Gert (2004).

▶ REFERENCES

Adam, Alison. 2008. "The Gender Agenda in Computer Ethics." In K. E. Himma and H. T. Tavani, eds. *The Handbook of Information and Computer Ethics*. Hoboken, NJ: John Wiley and Sons, pp. 589–619.

Aristotle. 1962. *Nicomachean Ethics*. Trans. M. Oswald. New York: Bobbs-Merrill.

Bentham, Jeremy. 1948. In W. Harrison, ed. *Introduction to the Principles of Morals and Legislation*. London: Oxford University Press.

De George, Richard T. 2010. *Business Ethics*. 7th ed. Upper Saddle River NJ: Prentice Hall.

Ess, Charles. 2006. "Ethical Pluralism and Global Information Ethics." *Ethics and Information Technology* 8, no. 4: 215–66. p. 63–82.

Ess, Charles. 2014. *Digital Media Ethics*. 2nd ed. London, UK: Polity Press.

Gert, Bernard. 2004. "Common Morality and Computing." In R. A. Spinello and H. T. Tavani, eds. *Readings in CyberEthics*. 2nd ed. Sudbury, MA: Jones and Bartlett, pp. 96–106. Reprinted from *Ethics and Information Technology* 1, no. 1 (1999): 37–56.

Gert, Bernard. 2005. *Morality: Its Nature and Justification*. Rev. ed. New York: Oxford University Press.

Gert, Bernard. 2007. *Common Morality: Deciding What to Do*. New York: Oxford University Press.

Grodzinsky, Frances S. 2001. "The Practitioner from Within: Revisiting the Virtues." In R. A. Spinello and H. T. Tavani, eds. *Readings in CyberEthics*. Sudbury, MA: Jones and Bartlett, pp. 580–91. Reprinted from *Computers and Society* 29, no. 1 (1999): 9–15.

Hobbes, Thomas. 1962. *Leviathan*. New York: Collier Books.

Kant, Immanuel. 1965. *Fundamental Principles of the Metaphysics of Morals*. Trans. T. K. Abbott. London: Longman's.

Mill, John Stuart. 1965. *Utilitarianism*. New York: Bobbs-Merrill.

Moor, James H. 2002. "The Importance of Virtue in Teaching Computer Ethics." In M. Ochi, et al., eds. *Proceedings of the Foundations of Information Ethics*. Hiroshima, Japan: Hiroshima University Press, pp. 29–38.

Moor, James H. 2004. "Just Consequentialism and Computing." In R. A. Spinello and H. T. Tavani, eds. *Readings in CyberEthics*. 2nd ed. Sudbury, MA: Jones and Bartlett, pp. 107–13.

Pojman, Louis P. 2006. *Ethics: Discovering Right and Wrong*. 5th ed. Belmont, CA: Wadsworth.

Rawls, John. 1999. *A Theory of Justice*. Rev. ed. New York: Oxford University Press.

Ross, W. D. 1930. *The Right and the Good*. London: Oxford University Press.

Wallach, Wendell and Colin Allen. 2009. *Moral Machines: Teaching Robots Right from Wrong*. New York: Oxford University Press.

▶ FURTHER READINGS

Anderson, Michael and Susan Leigh Anderson. eds. 2011. *Machine Ethics*. Cambridge: Cambridge University Press.

Cahn, Steven and Peter Markie, eds. 2012. *Ethics: History, Theory, and Contemporary Issues*. 5th ed. New York: Oxford University Press.

Hinman, Lawrence M. 2013. *Ethics—A Pluralistic Approach to Moral Theory*. 5th ed. Belmont, CA: Wadsworth Publishing.

Rachels, James and Stuart Rachels. 2012. *The Elements of Moral Philosophy*. 7th ed. New York: McGraw-Hill.

Scalet, Steven and John Arthur, eds. 2013. *Morality and Moral Controversies: Readings in Moral, Social, and Political philosophy*. 9th ed. Upper Saddle River, NJ: Prentice Hall.

Sterba, James and Peter Bornschein. 2013. *Morality in Practice*. 8th ed. New York: Cengage.

Triplett, Timm. 2002. "Bernard Gert's *Morality* and Its Application to Computer Ethics." *Ethics and Information Technology* 4, no. 1: 79–92.

CHAPTER

3

Critical Reasoning Skills for Evaluating Disputes in Cyberethics

LEARNING OBJECTIVES

Upon completing this chapter, you will successfully be able to:

- Identify and construct alogical *argument*, and differentiate arguments from the various *claims*, or *statements*, that comprise them,
- Determine when an argument satisfies the conditions for being *valid,*
- Determine whether a valid argument is also *sound* (or *unsound*),
- Determine whether an argument is invalid,
- Determine when an invalid argument satisfies the conditions for being *inductive,*
- Determine when an invalid argument is *fallacious,*
- Apply a seven-step strategy for determining the *overall strength* of an argument,
- Identify a cluster of common "informal logical fallacies" that occur in everyday discourse and apply them in your analysis of cyberethics issues.

In this chapter, we examine some basic *reasoning* skills and concepts that aid us in our overall analysis of specific cyberethics issues examined in Chapters 4–12. We begin by briefly reflecting on a scenario that illustrates a particular kind of (conventional) reasoning process one might use in trying to determine whether it would be morally permissible to download content from a Web site.

▶ **SCENARIO 3–1:** Reasoning About Whether to Download Software from "Sharester"

You are contemplating downloading a software application that is available on a Web site called *Sharester*, a file-sharing P2P (peer-to-peer) site. Sharester is not officially designated as a "pirate site" because it mainly provides users with access to (freely available) open-source software applications. However, this site also contains a few proprietary (or copyrighted) software applications that users can download. It turns out that the particular application you are interested in downloading is proprietary; furthermore, there is no indication that the copyright holder has authorized the free downloading of that application. Although you wish to download this application for personal use (only), you are conflicted about what to do; so you discuss your concerns with a close friend, Charlie.

Charlie tries to convince you not to download a proprietary software program using the following rationale: *Downloading proprietary software (without permission from the copyright holder) is identical to stealing physical property. Stealing physical property is morally wrong. Therefore, downloading proprietary software (without permission) is morally wrong.* ■

How good is the reasoning process used by Charlie (in this scenario), and how do we determine our answer to that question? If we rely solely on our intuitions, we might be inclined to believe that Charlie's reasoning process is very solid (and in this case, the conclusion reached may indeed be true). But what about the reasoning process itself, that is, the "form of reasoning," used? Is the (assumed truth of the) evidence provided in Charlie' argument sufficient to guarantee the truth of the conclusion? While Charlie's reasoning process might seem to concur with our initial intuitions, can we always trust our intuitions (solely) when reasoning about what to do in situations similar to this one? Fortunately, there are some objective criteria that we can use to distinguish between good and bad reasoning (i.e., to determine whether Charlie's argument is valid, or whether it contains invalid/fallacious reasoning).

Later in this chapter (at the end of Section 3.8), we apply a seven-step strategy to evaluate the reasoning process used in the argument expressed in Scenario 3–1. First, however, we need to understand some basic terms and concepts that are typically used in critical reasoning.

▶ 3.1 WHAT IS CRITICAL REASONING?

Critical reasoning is a subfield of *informal logic*.[1] So, you may wonder why a chapter dedicated to this topic is included in a book on cyberethics.[2] To appreciate the important role that critical reasoning skills play in our analysis of cyberethics issues,[3] recall the methodological framework that we developed in Chapter 1. There, we saw that the final step of that methodology requires that we defend or justify our position by evaluating it vis-à-vis the rules of (logical) argumentation. Also, recall that in Chapter 2 we saw how a typical cyberethics issue could be analyzed from the vantage point of one or more ethical theories, such as utilitarianism, deontology, etc. But then we must ask: How do we defend—give a (logical) reason for—our selection of one particular ethical theory over another in our analysis? And how would we convince others about which theory should be applied, for example, in a situation where we might be in a dispute with someone about how best to analyze one or more pressing cyberethics issues?[4]

Consider also that there may be occasions where someone might try to influence your thinking about which kinds of behavior are, and are not, appropriate online. As we saw in Scenario 3–1, for example, it is possible that you may be conflicted about what to do in cases where online policies and laws might seem unclear, or might not seem to be unethical (even if they are illegal). In this chapter, we will see how critical reasoning skills can help us both to clarify our own thinking/reasoning and analyze the arguments others might use to try to persuade us with respect to some claim. We will also see how the various techniques for constructing and analyzing arguments will help us to frame our positions more precisely and defend them more rigorously.

3.1.1 Some Basic Concepts: (Logical) Arguments and Claims

Critical reasoning skills provide the tools necessary for evaluating the strength of (logical) *arguments*, which comprise various *claims*. For our purposes, an argument, which contains at least two claims, can be defined as a reasoning form, or structure, that attempts to establish the truth of one claim (called a *conclusion*) based on the assumed truth of the evidence in other claims (called *premises*) provided to support the conclusion. Thus, an argument is a *form of reasoning* that has two important characteristics or features in that it:

i. Includes at least two claims (but can include an indefinite number of claims)

ii. Aims at establishing a conclusion (i.e., the truth of one claim) based on evidence provided by one or more other claims called premises

We will see that whereas arguments are either *valid* or *invalid*, the claims that comprise them are either *true* or *false*. First, however, we examine an important role that arguments can play when someone is trying to support or defend a position that is being questioned or disputed.

3.1.2 The Role of *Arguments*

Consider a hypothetical scenario involving a claim about the development of a controversial and powerful new computer chip—code-named Chip X—in Japan. This new chip is purported to be so powerful in speed and performance that it will eclipse any computer chips that manufacturers in the United States will be capable of producing during the next several years. Chip X will also enable the manufacturer to monitor certain activities of those users whose devices contain the chip in ways that, potentially at least, pose serious threats to personal privacy.

Suppose that you are skeptical about my claim that Chip X is currently under development by Mishito Corporation and that it is planned for release sometime within the next year. There are a number of ways I could attempt to convince you that my claim is true; for example, I could try to persuade you to accompany me on a trip to Japan to see firsthand that Chip X is indeed being developed there. In this case, we could obtain direct evidence regarding the truth of my claim. But if you are unable or unwilling to accompany me to Japan, I will have to use some other, less direct, mode of verification to convince you. For example, I could show you a copy of the design specifications for Chip X extracted from a confidential Mishito Corporation document that I happened to acquire. Or perhaps I could ask a mutual colleague of ours who recently studied as an exchange student at the University of Hiroshima, where the field-testing for this new chip is being carried out, to corroborate my claim regarding Chip X. That is, I can put together various pieces of evidence to construct a logical argument that supports my claim.

Now we are in a position to debate the merits of my overall argument regarding Chip X, based on the form reasoning employed in it, without our having to travel to Japan to verify the truth of my claim. Before we debate the strength of my argument, however, we must first understand some essential features of an argument's *structure*.

3.1.3 The Basic Structure of an Argument

We noted in Section 3.1 that an argument consists of two or more claims, one of which is called the conclusion; the others are called the premises. The standard form for representing an argument is to list the premises first and then state the conclusion. The following structure represents an argument's standard form:

PREMISE 1

PREMISE 2 (optional)

PREMISE 3 (optional)

.

.

.

PREMISE *n* (optional)

CONCLUSION

To support my claim that Chip X is currently being developed in Japan, in the conclusion of my argument, I would need to list the evidence in the form of one or more premises. For example, I could use the following argument form:

> **PREMISE 1.** When I recently visited the computer science department at the University of Hiroshima in Japan, I noticed that graduate students and professors there were field-testing a new computer chip whose code name is Chip X.
>
> **PREMISE 2.** I have a copy of the design specifications for Chip X, which shows that it will be several times faster than any chip currently available in the United States.
>
> **PREMISE 3.** Lee Smith, a mutual colleague of ours who was recently an exchange student in the computer science program at the University of Hiroshima and who participated in the field-testing of Chip X, will corroborate my claim.
>
> ---
>
> **CONCLUSION.** Chip X is currently being developed in Japan.

This particular argument includes three premises and a conclusion; additional premises could be added. However, an argument requires at least one premise along with a conclusion. In this section, we are concerned only with an argument's structure and not with how strong the argument might be. An argument, however weak it may ultimately be, still qualifies as an argument if its structure (or reasoning form) includes one or more premises and a conclusion.

You might have observed that the claim expressed in the conclusion to our argument about Chip X could also be verified (i.e., determined to be either true or false) independent of the evidence provided in the argument's premises. Since the conclusion contains a statement that is descriptive, or empirical (i.e., capable of being observed through sensory experience), the truth or falsity of the conclusion could be resolved in this case simply by going to Japan to see whether such a chip was actually being developed there.

However, not all arguments have empirical or descriptive statements as their conclusions. Suppose that a friend wants to convince you that Internet users should be allowed to write a blog on how to build a bomb. (Note that this is a normative claim because it includes the word "should"; you may want to consult the distinction we drew in Chapter 1 between normative and descriptive claims.) Further, suppose that his reason for holding this view is based on the principle that people are allowed to write books on how to build bombs, and authors of blogs should have the same rights and freedoms as authors of books. And suppose your friend bases his reasoning for this claim on the right of authors to express themselves as guaranteed in the First Amendment of the U.S. Constitution. His argument could be constructed as follows:

> **PREMISE 1.** A person's right to author a book on how to build a bomb is protected by the First Amendment (of the U.S. Constitution).
>
> **PREMISE 2.** Authoring a book is similar to authoring a blog on the Internet.
>
> ---
>
> **CONCLUSION.** A person's right to author a blog on how to build a bomb ought to be protected by the First Amendment.

Notice how this argument differs from the preceding one. For one thing, we can't simply go to Japan to determine whether this conclusion is true or false. For another, the conclusion contains a normative statement (one that includes "ought"). Unlike the previous argument, which contained a descriptive statement in its conclusion that could be verified independent of the argument, we now depend on the *form of reasoning* alone to help us determine whether the conclusion is true. In doing this, we will *assume* that the premises in this argument are true and then ask whether the conclusion would logically follow from them.

Initially, the reasoning in this argument might seem plausible: The person constructing the argument cleverly uses an analogy based on a legal right that applies in physical space. So, we might assume that any legal rights that citizens enjoy in physical space should automatically be extended to cyberspace.

In this argument, we are also asked to consider certain features or characteristics that are common to both (printed) books and blogs. Clearly, we can draw a number of analogies here. For example, both books and blogs can communicate and disseminate information to readers, each is authored by one or more persons, and so forth. However, there is a danger in pushing some of these analogies too far: Whereas traditional books are tangible items existing in physical space, blogs are not. And the scope of a blog allows it to be accessed by members of the international community, some of whom may have no access to physical books or may lack sufficient funds to purchase such books. We now begin to see dissimilarities between books and blogs, so we must be cautious about drawing conclusions when reasoning by analogy. Later in this chapter, we will see why arguments of this kind are not valid. First, however, we consider some strategies for constructing arguments.

▶ 3.2 CONSTRUCTING AN ARGUMENT

Think of some situations in which arguments are used by those in powerful positions, as well as by ordinary persons. Lawyers, for example, use arguments to try to persuade juries, and politicians often use arguments to convey their positions to their constituencies. All of us use arguments when we try to convince a friend, a spouse, or a boss about some point or other. If you try to convince your parents that they should buy you a new iPad, for example, you will most likely be making an argument of some sort. Ultimately, arguments will succeed or not succeed depending on (i) how well they are constructed and (ii) how strong their reasoning forms are. We refer to (ii) as *argument strength*, and we examine that concept in Section 3.3 in our discussion of valid vs. invalid arguments. In this section, we focus on how arguments are constructed.

Arguments often appear as editorials in newspapers and periodicals where they are sometimes expressed in prose forms that can obscure the argument, making it difficult to isolate and analyze. When this happens, we must locate the arguments concealed in the text before we can analyze them. Consider the political debate over the need for a new national missile defense (NMD) system, which has been controversial from both a domestic and an international perspective. A fairly straightforward argument in favor of NMD in the editorial section of a newspaper might look something like the following:

> We must build a national missile defense system because without such a system we are vulnerable to nuclear attacks from rogue nations that might arise in the future. Engineers and computer scientists have testified that they can design a computer-guided missile defense system that is effective, safe, and reliable. It is our obligation as Americans to take whatever measures we can to protect the safety of our citizens.

Before we analyze this argument, however, it is perhaps worth making a few parenthetical remarks about certain events leading up to NMD. The debate in the U.S. Congress over NMD that occurred during the George W. Bush administration, and which has been resurrected in recent years, can be viewed as an updated version of the earlier "Star Wars" debate, officially known as the (or Strategic Defense Initiative (SDI)). That debate, which took place during the Reagan administration in the 1980s, was significant for cyberethics because it was one of the first ethical controversies to catch the attention of a group of computer ethics pioneers.[5] We will examine some specific ethical issues pertaining to Star Wars and NMD of interest to computer professionals in Chapter 4; our primary purpose in this chapter, however, is to consider the NMD controversy only insofar as it illustrates how logical arguments can be constructed and analyzed.

There has been strong support for NMD among many conservative politicians in the United States. As suggested above, a proponent of the NMD system could construct an argument for his or her case by first asserting that without such a new missile system, the United States is vulnerable to future attacks from potential "rogue" nations that might acquire nuclear weapons. The proponent might next want to assure us that there is sufficient and compelling evidence that such a missile defense system would be safe and reliable. Finally, the NMD supporter might assume the following principle: "We must do whatever is necessary to preserve the safety of America and its people." The structure of the proponent's argument can be represented as follows:

PREMISE 1. Without the NMD, the United States is vulnerable to nuclear attacks in the future from rogue nations.

PREMISE 2. Computer scientists and engineers have testified before Congress that they can design a computer-guided missile defense system that is both safe and reliable.

PREMISE 3. The United States must do whatever is necessary to preserve the military defense of the nation and the safety of its citizens.

CONCLUSION. The United States should build the NMD.

So far, we have considered only the structure of this argument. That is, we have described its two basic components—its premises and conclusion—and we have represented it in standard logical form. Now we ask: Is the reasoning used in the argument strong? Are there rules that will enable us to determine this? To answer these questions, we first need to understand the difference between valid and invalid arguments.

▶ 3.3 VALID ARGUMENTS

The first question we could ask about the sample argument described in the preceding section is whether its reasoning is strong or weak—that is, is the argument's reasoning *valid* or is it *invalid*? "Valid" and "invalid" are technical terms in logic. Whereas claims (the individual statements that make up an argument) are either true or false, arguments will be either valid or invalid; it is incorrect to refer to an argument as either true or false, and it is incorrect to refer to a claim as either valid or invalid.

How can we determine whether a particular argument is valid or invalid? In formal systems of logic, elaborate schemes that consist of symbols, rules, and tables have been constructed for determining when arguments are valid or invalid. Alternatively, however, some "informal" systems of logic, such as the system developed by Nolt (2002), also enable us to accomplish this task. Nolt's system does not require that we know anything about the *actual* truth or falsity of the claims in an argument's premise(s) in order to determine whether an argument is valid or invalid. Instead, we need only to determine whether the argument's conclusion would necessarily follow from its premises, when those premises are all *assumed* to be true.[6] In other words, we ask:

> Is the relationship between the premises and the conclusion such that if all of the premises in the argument are assumed true, it would be impossible for the conclusion to be false?

The concern here is with the relationship of truth conditions vis-à-vis the premises and the conclusion. The premises and the conclusion could be true or false (in the actual world), independent of each other, but that is not relevant for testing the argument's validity. We ask only whether the assumed truth of the premises is sufficient to guarantee the truth of the conclusion. If the answer is yes, then the argument is valid. If, however, it is logically possible for the argument's conclusion to be false at the same time that its premises are (assumed) true, then the argument is invalid.

You can apply this test for validity to the argument for the new NMD system that we considered above. Imagine that all of the argument's premises are true statements. Is it possible—that is, could you conceive of a possible instance such that—when those premises are true, the conclusion could still be false? Of course, the premises could be imagined to be false, and the conclusion could be imagined to be false as well. But the relevant questions here are: What happens when all of the premises are imagined to be true? Could the claim in the argument's conclusion (i.e., "The United States should build the new NMD.") be false even when Premises 1–3 are assumed true? The answer is yes. Hence, the argument is invalid.

The Counterexample Strategy

To show that an argument is invalid, all we need to do is to produce one *counterexample* to the argument. A counterexample is:

> A logically possible case in which the argument's conclusion could be imagined to be false while (at the same time) the argument's premises are assumed true.[7]

In the NMD argument, we can coherently imagine a logically possible situation (i.e., a situation that does not involve a logical contradiction) where the conclusion "The United States should build the new NMD" is false when the claims stated in Premises 1–3 are assumed true. For example, we can imagine a situation or case in which all three premises are true but some alternative strategy not involving the development of a new missile defense system could provide for the safety of America. So a counterexample is possible; thus, the argument is invalid.

Note, however, although this particular argument has been shown to be invalid, it does not follow that the argument's conclusion is, in fact, false. All that has been shown is that the argument is invalid because the form of reasoning it uses does not succeed in guaranteeing that the conclusion must be true. It is still possible, of course, that the conclusion could be true. But a different argument would need to be constructed to show that the inference is valid.

Suppose we added a fourth premise, "The new NMD system is necessary to preserve the defense and safety of the United States and its citizens," to the argument. The amended argument would be as follows:

PREMISE 1. Without the NMD, the United States is vulnerable to nuclear attacks in the future from rogue nations.

PREMISE 2. Computer scientists and engineers have testified before Congress that they can design a computer-guided missile defense system that is both safe and reliable.

PREMISE 3. The United States must do whatever is necessary to preserve the military defense of the nation and the safety of its citizens.

PREMISE 4. The new NMD system is necessary to preserve the defense and safety of the United States and its citizens.

CONCLUSION. The United States should build the NMD.

This argument would now be valid. If all of its premises are assumed true, then the conclusion cannot be false. Of course, we could next ask whether all of the premises in this argument are in fact true. Premises 1 and 2 are fairly uncontroversial claims, though Premise 2 might be challenged by programmers who believe that building a completely reliable computer system is not possible. However, both Premises 3 and 4 are controversial: Premise 4 can be shown to be false if it can be demonstrated that the United States could be adequately protected without the newly proposed missile defense system; Premise 3, which is a normative statement, can also be shown to be false if, for instance, we can provide an exception to the principle included in it. For one thing, we could ask both whether indeed the United States *must* do whatever is necessary to make the United States safe and what exactly we mean by the phrase "whatever is necessary"? For example, what if making the United States safe entailed closing down all systems of transportation, all government offices, and all schools for an indefinite period of time that could go on for years? It might protect U.S. citizens but would it be an acceptable alternative? And U.S. citizens might be willing to make trade-offs rather than shut down major institutions essential to their day-to-day lives. So Premise 3, as stated, is also false. However, even if all of the premises are eventually shown to be false, the argument itself is still valid because its conclusion follows from the premises if they are assumed true.

Figure 3-1 illustrates the basic distinction between valid and invalid arguments.

Next, consider the following argument:

PREMISE 1. People who own iPhones are smarter than those who own Droids (Android phones).

PREMISE 2. My roommate owns an iPhone.

PREMISE 3. I own a Droid.

CONCLUSION. My roommate is smarter than me.

This argument meets all of the criteria for validity: *If* all three of the premises in this argument are assumed true, then the conclusion ("My roommate is smarter than me.") must be true. In other words, no counterexample to this argument's reasoning form is possible. However, the argument's validity alone is not sufficient to establish that the argument

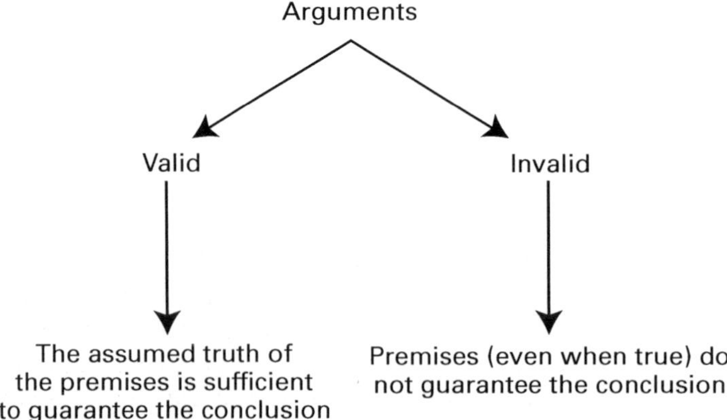

Figure 3-1 Valid and invalid arguments.

succeeds in the final analysis (as we will see in the following sections). It only shows that when all of the premises are assumed true, the conclusion would also be true.

This argument, like all valid arguments, is valid by virtue of its *logical form*; An argument's logical form, not its content, determines its validity and invalidity. An example of a valid logical form is as follows:

PREMISE 1. Every A is a B.

PREMISE 2. C is an A.

CONCLUSION. C is a B.

Any argument that has this form is valid, regardless of the content represented by A, B, or C. As long as the premises "Every A is a B" and "C is an A" are both assumed true, there is no way that the conclusion "C is a B" could be coherently conceived to be false. Even if the two premises in this particular argument turn out to be false in the actual world, the argument continues to be valid by virtue of its logical form.

We can now see that it is important to separate two distinct questions:

a. What is the *strength of reasoning* of the argument (i.e., is it valid or invalid)?

b. Are the argument's premises true in the actual world?

To say that an argument is valid does not necessarily mean that its premises are true in the actual world. An argument can be valid in terms of its logical form and yet still be unsound. One more step is required for an argument to qualify as a *sound argument*. To be sound, all of the premises (included in the valid argument) must be true in the real world and not merely assumed true as in the case of the test for validity. For information on how to determine whether a statement is true or false, see Appendix G (available at www.wiley.com/college/tavani).

▶ 3.4 SOUND ARGUMENTS

To assume that the premises of an argument are true is an important first step in the process of evaluating arguments, because doing so enables us to determine the logical relationship between the argument's premise(s) and conclusion and thus determine the argument's strength of reasoning. The reasoning strength will be either valid or invalid. If we can produce one counterexample by showing a possible case where the argument's conclusion can be false even when all of its premises are assumed true, we have shown the argument to be invalid. If the argument is shown to be invalid, we can stop here for the time being. To show that the argument was valid, all that we have to do is to show that no counterexample is possible. And to do that, we consider merely the hypothetical or assumed truth of the argument's premises vis-à-vis the argument's conclusion. If the argument is valid, then we must determine if it is also sound by going on to the next step, where we test the premises to see whether they are actually true or false in the empirical world.

Consider again the two arguments in the preceding section: one involving an NMD system and the other involving the intelligence of iMac users. Both arguments were shown to be valid. (The argument defending the need for an NMD system had to be modified, but once we modified it, it met the criteria for validity.) We can now further examine each argument to see if it is also sound. An argument will be sound if (i) it is valid, and (ii) all of the premises are actually true in the empirical world (and not merely assumed to be true).

First, consider the NMD system. If one or more of Premises 1–4 are false, then the argument will be unsound. Premise 3, "The United States must do whatever is necessary to preserve the military defense of the nation and the safety of its citizens," is clearly questionable. Surely, the goal of national defense is one of the highest priorities of a political administration. But we have already seen that the phrase "whatever is necessary" is problematic. For example, would such a principle give the U.S. government the right to use *any* means that it happened to deem necessary to bring about some desired end?

Suppose some government officials believed that it was necessary to put all non-U.S. citizens under house arrest? Or suppose that some of those officials believed that all U.S. citizens should be subject to constant search and seizure, both within and outside their homes? Would these measures be acceptable? Perhaps under the most severe and dire circumstances, some proposals of this type might seem plausible. But it is still not exactly clear that such drastic measures would be necessary. So Premise 3 in the missile defense argument cannot be confirmed to be true, even if Premises 1, 2, and 4 can. Thus, this argument is not sound even though it is valid. Because it is unsound, the argument does not succeed. However, once again, we should be careful to note that even when an argument is unsound, or even when it is invalid, it does not necessarily follow that the argument's conclusion is false. Rather, we can only infer that the evidence given, that is, the particular premises used to support the argument's conclusion, is not adequate because (when used alone) the premises fail to meet certain logical requirements.

Returning to the argument involving claims about the intelligence of iMac users, we saw that when we assume the truth of all three premises of that argument, the conclusion cannot be imagined to be false; hence, the argument is valid. But is it also sound? We need to examine each premise in more detail. Premises 2 and 3—"My roommate owns an iPhone" and "I own a Droid," respectively—are relatively easy to verify because both are descriptive claims. To see if they are true or false, we simply go to the dormitory room or to the apartment where my roommate and I live and observe whether my roommate indeed owns an iMac computer and whether I own a Droid.

Premise 1—"People who own iMac computers are smarter than those who own Droids"—however, is more controversial and hence more difficult to verify than the other premises. Clearly, more evidence would be needed to show that Premise 1 is true; in fact, it certainly seems suspect. So despite the fact that the argument is valid by virtue of its logical form, we cannot yet say that it is sound. Thus, the argument would appear, at best, to be not sound but inconclusive.

As you might suspect, sound arguments are not very common, and often they are about matters that are either trivial or uncontroversial. Consider the following argument:

PREMISE 1. CEOs of major computer corporations are high school graduates.

PREMISE 2. Bill Gates was the CEO of a major computer corporation.

CONCLUSION. Bill Gates is a high school graduate.

This argument is clearly valid because no counterexample can be constructed, that is, there is no possible case where Premises 1 and 2 could both be (assumed) true and the conclusion could be false at the same time. As it turns out, the premises are also true in the actual world, so this argument is sound; however, it is also not terribly informative. Perhaps you can now see why there are so few sound arguments that are also informative: relatively few valid arguments are sound, and relatively few sound arguments are informative or nontrivial.

Figure 3-2 illustrates the basic differences between valid arguments that are sound and those that are unsound.

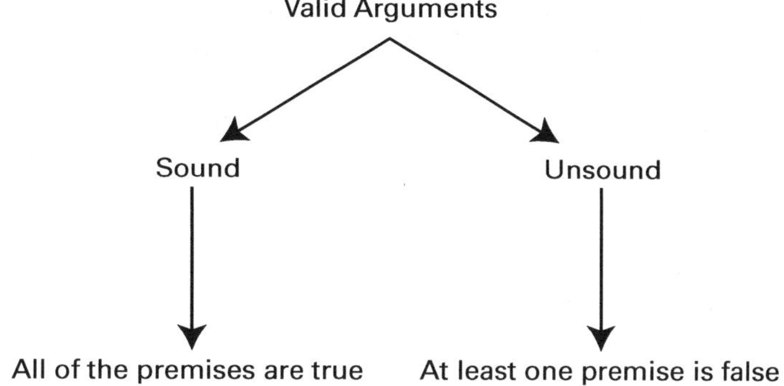

Figure 3-2 Sound and unsound (valid) arguments.

At this point, you might ask, what good is a valid argument if it contains false premises? You might also wonder whether certain types of invalid arguments whose premises are true in the actual world are stronger than valid arguments that contain one or more false premises.

▶ 3.5 INVALID ARGUMENTS

Consider the following argument:

PREMISE 1. All CEOs of major U.S. computer corporations have been U.S. citizens.
PREMISE 2. Steve Jobs was a U.S. citizen.

CONCLUSION. Steve Jobs was a CEO of a major computer corporation in the United States.

Even though all three of the claims included in this argument (i.e., the two premises and the conclusion) are true in the actual world, we can show that this argument is invalid by producing at least one counterexample. We can imagine a possible case where the premises in this argument are both true, but the conclusion—(the late) Steve Jobs was the CEO of a major computer corporation—is false. For example, we can imagine that he had been a consultant or a programmer, or he could have been employed outside the computer field. However, there is an even more serious flaw in this argument: If we substitute for "Steve Jobs" the names Hilary Clinton, LeBron James, Jessica Lawrence, or Brad Pitt, we see that although each of these persons is a U.S. citizen, none has been a CEO of a major computer corporation. Yet by the logic used in the above argument, it would follow that if any one of them is a U.S. citizen, then he or she must also be or have been a CEO. We have shown that this argument is invalid. If you had noticed that the reasoning in this argument was weak, now you know exactly why.

We next determine whether the following argument is valid or invalid:

PREMISE 1. Most CEOs of major computer corporations are college graduates.
PREMISE 2. Satya Nadella is the CEO of a major computer corporation.

CONCLUSION. Satya Nadella is a college graduate.

Notice that all of the statements included in this argument happen to be true in the empirical world. But is the reasoning valid? Clearly not! All we need is one counterexample to show why. If we substitute the name "Bill Gates" for "Satya Nadella," the present CEO of Microsoft (as of 2015), the premises of the argument remain true but the conclusion is false. The argument is invalid, but because the premises are true, this particular invalid argument is stronger overall than either of the two arguments we considered that were valid but unsound. Overall "argument strength," as opposed to an argument's "strength of reasoning," takes into account the actual truth condition of the argument's premises. We saw that an argument's strength of reasoning is concerned only with the hypothetical or assumed truth of those premises.

▶ 3.6 INDUCTIVE ARGUMENTS

Not all invalid arguments are necessarily weak arguments; in fact, some are quite strong. Hence, we should not automatically discard every invalid argument simply because it is not valid. Some invalid arguments are *inductive*. Although inductive arguments do not necessarily guarantee the truth of their conclusions in the way that valid arguments do, inductive arguments nonetheless provide a high degree of probability for their conclusions. Those invalid arguments that are not inductive are fallacious arguments; we will discuss them in the next section. In this section, we describe the criteria that must be satisfied for an argument to be inductive.

Let's determine the strength of reasoning of the following argument:

PREMISE 1. Seventy-five percent of people who own iPods also own iMacs.
PREMISE 2. My roommate owns an iPod.

CONCLUSION. My roommate owns an iMac.

Based on the technique discussed earlier in this chapter, we can see that this argument is not valid: A counterexample to the argument is possible. For instance, we can assume that both premises are true while the conclusion ("My roommate owns an iMac computer") is false. There is no contradiction in doing this since my roommate could be among the 25% of people who currently own iPods but who never owned iMacs. So the argument is clearly invalid.

This argument and the argument in the preceding section designed to show that Steve Jobs was the CEO of a major computer corporation are both invalid, but they are different in their strength of reasoning. The argument that tried to show that Jobs must have been a CEO because "Jobs is a U.S. citizen" and "all CEOs of major computer corporations have been U.S. citizens" has weak reasoning. On the other hand, the form of reasoning used in the argument to show that my roommate owns an iMac computer is much stronger. In fact, the conclusion ("My roommate owns an iMac computer") is *very likely* to be true when we assume the truth of both premises. Hence, this (invalid) argument is inductive.

As suggested above, some inductive arguments, although invalid, can be stronger overall than some valid arguments. But how is that possible? We have seen examples of valid arguments that contained premises that were false in the actual world. Inductive arguments consisting of premises that are all true in the actual world are generally stronger than arguments that are valid but unsound. As you consider the various arguments involving privacy, free speech, security, etc., in Chapters 4–9, determine which ones meet the criteria of being inductive with all true premises. Such arguments will be much more successful in establishing their

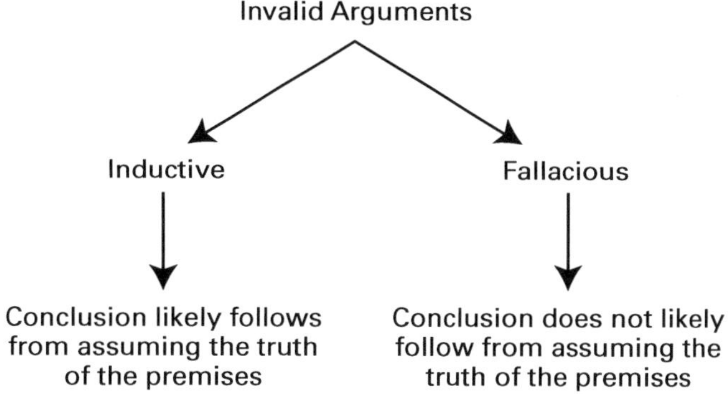

Figure 3-3 Inductive and fallacious (invalid) arguments.

positions (i.e., they will be much stronger overall) than will valid arguments that contain one or more false premises.[8]

Figure 3-3 illustrates the basic differences between invalid arguments that are inductive and invalid arguments that are fallacious.

▶ 3.7 FALLACIOUS ARGUMENTS

Recall the argument that we examined in Section 3.5 to show that Steve Jobs was the CEO of a major corporation. All of the statements or claims in that particular argument were true in the actual world, so the argument might have seemed fairly strong. Yet, because we could produce a counterexample (and, in fact, we saw that we could easily produce several counterexamples), clearly the argument was invalid.

We next ask whether the argument is inductive or fallacious. That is, how likely is it that the argument's conclusion, "Jobs was the CEO of a major computer corporation," would be true based simply on the assumed truth of the argument's premises? Even though the conclusion could be true—and even though it is, in fact, true—the truth or falsity would have to be established on grounds other than those given in the premises used to support the conclusion that Jobs had been a CEO. Hence, this argument is *fallacious*.

Note that an argument's being fallacious has nothing to do with the actual truth or falsity of its premises, so you have probably noticed a certain irony with respect to an argument's strength of reasoning. We have seen that an argument can be valid and yet contain one or more false premises and a false conclusion, and conversely, an argument can be fallacious despite the fact that all of its premises as well as its conclusion could be true.

Next, consider an argument in which someone tries to convince you that Internet users should not expect to retain their privacy when they engage in online activities, because the Internet is essentially a public forum or public space. Expressed in standard form, the argument reads:

PREMISE. The Internet is in public space.

CONCLUSION. Those who use the Internet should not expect to retain any personal privacy.

When we evaluate this argument's strength of reasoning, that is, whether it is valid or invalid, we first ask if a counterexample can be produced. Let us assume that the premise—The Internet is in public space—is true. We next ask: Is it possible for that statement to be true, and for the conclusion (Internet users should not expect to retain their privacy) to be false, at the same time? The answer is "yes." For example, a person's backpack can be in public space, yet its owner enjoys some expectation of privacy regarding the contents enclosed in the backpack. So a counterexample can be produced, and the argument is invalid. We can next ask whether the argument is inductive or fallacious. In the argument's current form, the conclusion does not likely follow from the premise, even when that premise is assumed true. So the argument is fallacious.

Also recall an argument that we examined in Chapter 1 for the view that at least some ethical issues involving cybertechnology must be unique. The argument had the following form:

PREMISE 1. Cybertechnology has some unique technological features.

PREMISE 2. Cybertechnology has generated some ethical concerns.

CONCLUSION. Some ethical concerns generated by cybertechnology must be unique ethical concerns.

You can no doubt see why this argument is fallacious. First, we construct a counterexample to show the argument is invalid, that is, we can imagine a case where both premises are true, but the conclusion is false. For example, we can imagine some ethical concern generated by the use of cybertechnology to be simply a variation of a traditional ethical problem that is neither new nor unique. Furthermore, we can construct a range of possible cases where both premises are assumed true, but the conclusion could be false. (In fact, in the majority of such cases, the conclusion would not likely be true merely because of what is assumed to be true in the premises.) As we noted in Chapter 1, this argument wrongly assumes that a characteristic that applies to

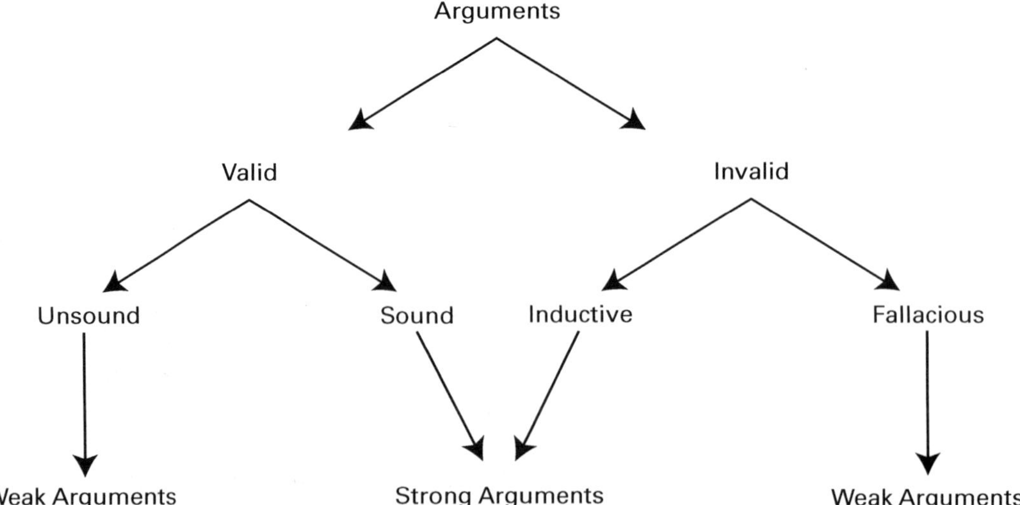

Figure 3-4 Comprehensive view of argument types.

the technology—namely, uniqueness—must also apply to the ethical issues generated by this technology. Of course, it is possible that some cyberethics issues may turn out to be unique ethical issues. But if that happens, it is not because of the evidence supplied in the premises of the above argument.

In Section 3.9, we will examine some "informal logical fallacies" that tend to recur in everyday reasoning. There, we will also examine techniques for spotting some of the more common fallacies, or "fallacy types," that occur in ordinary discourse. (These techniques do not require the counterexample strategy that we used to distinguish invalid from valid arguments.) First, however, we include a scheme that summarizes the techniques we have used so far to differentiate among valid and invalid, sound and unsound, and inductive and fallacious arguments.

Figure 3-4 presents an overview of the different kinds of argument forms that we have examined in this chapter.

▶ 3.8 A SEVEN-STEP STRATEGY FOR EVALUATING ARGUMENTS

The following strategy, which consists of seven steps, summarizes the techniques we used in Sections 3.3–3.7 to evaluate an argument's overall strength of reasoning:

Step 1. Convert the argument into standard form. (List the premises followed by the conclusion.)

Step 2. Test the argument for its strength of reasoning to see whether it is valid or invalid.

Strategy: Assume the premises to be true and ask yourself whether the conclusion must also be true when those premises are assumed true. Is a counterexample to the argument possible?

Step 3. Is the argument valid?

If yes, go to Step 4.

If no, go to Step 5.

Step 4. Is the (valid) argument also sound? That is, are the premises true in the actual world?

Strategy: To determine whether a claim is true or false in the actual world, see the guidelines in Appendix G (Available at www.wiley.com/college/tavani).

a. If the argument is valid and if all of the premises are true in the actual world, then the argument is also sound.

b. If the argument is valid, but one or more premises can be shown to be false, then the argument is unsound. (Note that if one or more premises are unable to be verified, i.e., determined to be either true or false, then the overall argument is inconclusive.)

Step 5. Is the (invalid) argument inductive or fallacious?

Strategy: To determine this, ask how likely the conclusion would be true when the premises are assumed true.

If the conclusion would likely be true because the premises are assumed true (i.e., the evidence for the conclusion is strong), the argument is inductive.

If the conclusion would not likely be true even when the premises are assumed true, the argument is fallacious.

Note: Keep in mind that a fallacious argument can be made up of individual claims or statements that are themselves true in the actual world.

Step 6. Determine whether the premises in your argument are either true or false in the actual world.

Strategy: Consult the guidelines for determining the truth or falsity of statements in Appendix G (available at www.wiley.com/college/tavani).

Step 7. Make an overall assessment of the argument by determining both (i) the argument's strength of reasoning (valid, inductive, or fallacious) *and* (ii) the truth conditions of each of the argument's premises.

Strategy: Determine, for example, whether the argument's overall strength is:

- Sound
- Valid but unsound
- Inductive with all true premises
- Inductive with some false premises
- Fallacious with a mixture of true and false premises
- Some other combination

Remember that an inductive argument with premises that are all true can be stronger overall than a valid argument with one or more false premises, which will be (valid but) unsound.

We next apply the seven-step strategy to the argument included in Scenario 3–1 at the beginning of this chapter. Applying Step 1, we convert the argument into standard form (which, in this case, it already happens to be presented):

PREMISE 1. Downloading proprietary software (without permission from the copyright holder) is identical to stealing physical property.

PREMISE 2. Stealing physical property is morally wrong.

CONCLUSION. Downloading proprietary software (without permission) is morally wrong.

At Step 2, we examine the argument's strength of reasoning and determine that the argument is valid because if we assume the truth of both its premises (Premises 1 and 2), the conclusion cannot be false (i.e., the combination of true premises and false conclusion in this example would be a logical contradiction). Having determined that the argument is valid (Step 3), we next go to Step 4 and ask whether it is sound or unsound. Whereas Premise 2 is a true statement (and is easily verifiable), the truth or falsity of Premise 1 is less clear cut. Although there would certainly seem to be a strong analogy between stealing physical property and downloading unauthorized software, there are also some disanalogies. Thus, the two behaviors are not, strictly speaking at least, "identical." (We examine this and some other disanalogies in Chapter 8 in our discussion of intellectual property.) So, Premise 1 may be either false or indeterminate (i.e., it is not literally true, as stated), and we now see that this argument is *unsound*.

However, the argument is still valid; so we can skip Step 5, which applies only to invalid arguments. At Step 6, we note that both Premise 2 and the conclusion are true, while Premise 1 may be either false or indeterminate (since it is not literally true). So our overall evaluation of this argument, at Step 7, is *valid but unsound*. Here, we note that the conclusion happens to be true even though its truth is not logically supported by the argument's premises.

The seven-step strategy is a useful tool for evaluating a wide range of arguments. However, we should note that some less formal techniques are also available for spotting fallacious arguments that commonly occur in ordinary, everyday reasoning. In the next section, we will see that there is an informal, and arguably simpler, way of identifying and cataloging many logical fallacies that frequently appear in everyday discourse.

▶ 3.9 IDENTIFYING SOME COMMON FALLACIES

Contrary to what many people assume, "fallacy" does not mean false statement; rather, it means *faulty reasoning*. As we saw in Section 3.6, it is possible for an argument to contain all true statements and still be fallacious. (We also saw that an argument can contain all false statements and still be valid, solely by virtue of its logical form.)

At this point, you might be unsure about your ability to recognize a fallacious argument without using the counterexample strategy described in this chapter or without applying some of the more sophisticated rules that comprise formal systems of logic. Because so many fallacies appear in everyday reasoning, logicians have categorized them in ways that are convenient for us to recognize. We refer to these kinds of fallacious arguments as *informal logical fallacies*.

The following 8 informal fallacies, or "fallacy types," each illustrated with one or more examples involving computers and cybertechnology, are typical of fallacious arguments that surface time and again in ordinary everyday discourse.

3.9.1 *Ad Hominem* Argument

In the *ad hominem* argument, an attack is directed at the person rather than the substance of what is being disputed. Consider an instance of this kind of attack that occurred in the Edward Snowden case of whistle-blowing, which involved the leaking of sensitive documents from the National Security Agency (NSA) in 2013 (a case that we examine in detail in Chapter 4):

> Edward Snowden was not a whistle-blower, but rather a self-serving narcissist who was more interested in promoting himself than in exposing any wrong doing. Also, he is reported to have lied both to his employer and his girlfriend. So, how could anyone possibly believe that Snowden's leaking of the sensitive NSA documents was morally justified?[9]

Why is the reasoning process used in this argument fallacious? For one thing, we could conjure up numerous counterexamples (and we include one below). But the nature of the fallacy in this particular argument is apparent in its sole focus on attacking Snowden's character rather than providing any relevant evidence to show that Snowden's whistle-blowing act was not morally justifiable. Consider, however, that even if Snowden is a narcissist (as asserted in the above attack), and even if Snowden had acted from purely selfish motives, it does not follow that "he is not a whistle-blower"—that is, did not engage in a genuine act of whistle-blowing. The reasoning process used in the above scenario reduces simply to an attack of Snowden's personal attributes (i.e., his character, alleged past behavior, etc.) and says nothing about why his act of leaking the NSA documents was not morally justified.

As already noted, one can easily imagine a counterexample to the kind of *ad hominem* attack directed against Snowden in the above argument. Consider, for instance, a situation where a member of Islamic State in Iraq and Syria (ISIS) (sometimes also referred to as ISIL) betrays his organization by intentional leaking information to an American journalist about a plan to blow up a government building in the United States. Further imagine that we later find out that this individual is narcissistic and that his or her motives for leaking the information were based solely on self-promotional grounds. Would we condemn this person's actions merely because they were the result of narcissistic/self-promotional motives? We may dislike this person for whatever reasons but that factor would be completely irrelevant in our evaluation of whether his or her actions constituted a genuine act of whistle blowing (as well as whether the whistle-blowing act was morally justified).

3.9.2 Slippery Slope Argument

The slippery slope argument has the form, "X could possibly be abused; therefore, we should not allow X." For example, one might argue:

> We should not continue to allow computer manufacturers to build computer systems that include CD burners. If we allow them to do so, young people will burn copies of copyrighted music illegally. If the rate of unauthorized copying of music continues, recording artists will lose more money. If they lose more money, the entire music industry could be in jeopardy. If the music industry in America declines, the entire U.S. economy will suffer. So, we must prohibit computer manufacturers from providing CD burners as part of the computer systems they build.

It should be fairly easy to spot the fallacy here. The author assumes that allowing computer manufacturers to continue to include CD burners as part of their computer systems will inevitably lead to an abusive slippery slope that logically implies a downturn in the overall U.S. economy. It is certainly possible that in the future, the U.S. economy does experience a downturn while computer manufacturers continue to produce computers with CD burners. And it may well be that some users abuse CD burners to make unauthorized copies of music. However, any claim that the bad economy was an inevitable result of the use of CD burners in computers cannot be substantiated merely in terms of the evidence provided in the above argument.

3.9.3 Fallacy of Appeal to Authority

Arguments that conform to the fallacy of authority (*argumentum ad verecundiam*) have the following form:

PREMISE 1. X is an authority in field Y.

PREMISE 2. X said Z.

CONCLUSION. Z.

As an example, imagine that Tim Berners-Lee, who designed the HTTP protocol that became the standard for the World Wide Web, has agreed to do an advertisement for Twitter, a social networking service (SNS). Further imagine that someone draws the following inference from the ad:

> Tim Berners-Lee believes that Twitter is superior to SNSs such as Facebook and Linked-In. And Berners-Lee is clearly an expert on matters involving the Web and the Internet. So, Twitter must be superior to alternative SNSs such as Facebook and Linked-In.

Can you spot the fallacy here? It is true that Berners-Lee is an expert on Web design; it may also be true that Twitter is superior to alternative SNSs (e.g., in certain respects). However, is the argument's conclusion that Twitter is superior to Facebook, Linked-In, and other SNSs (such as Pinterest), even if true, warranted by the premises? Simply because

Berners-Lee wrote the code that became the standard protocol for the World Wide Web, and thus is an expert on some matters involving the Web, does that make him an authority on SNSs?

3.9.4 False Cause Fallacy

The false cause argument (*post hoc ergo propter hoc*—after this, therefore because of this) reasons from the fact that event X preceded event Y to the conclusion that event X is necessarily the cause of event Y. Consider the following argument about Microsoft's Windows 10 operating system:

> Shortly after the release of the Microsoft Windows 10 operating system in 2015, Microsoft's stock plummeted severely. Hence, there is no doubt that the release of Windows 8 is responsible for the decline in Microsoft's loss in the stock market.

Can you identify the fallacy in the above argument? Even though it might be tempting to attribute Microsoft's decline in the price of its stock to the release of the Windows 10 operating system, the person making this argument has overlooked the possibility of other factors that might have caused this decline. For example, maybe there were factors in the economy in 2015 that affected all high tech stock prices, or maybe there were overall declines in the market during that year.

3.9.5 Fallacy of Composition/Fallacy of Division

The fallacy of composition confuses the characteristics that apply to the parts of a whole, or to the individual members of a group, with the characteristics of the whole itself. For example, consider the following form of reasoning:

> The new XYZ laptop computer is the best system on the market. XYZ has the fastest processor currently available on any laptop, it comes with twice the amount of RAM than any of its competitors, and it comes equipped with a suite of office applications that are superior to those on any currently available system. Also, its monitor has the best resolution and graphic display currently available on any commercial laptop.

Here, the fallacy should be obvious. Each of the components of this laptop computer is the best that is currently available. However, it clearly does not follow that the system will necessarily be the best one available. The connections between the various parts of this system might not be well designed; we are not told how reliable the computer system is vis-à-vis its competitors. These kinds of flaws are apparent in all argument forms that commit the fallacy of composition. A film that has the best cast (Tom Hanks, Julia Roberts), one of the best directors (Steven Spielberg), and one of the best soundtrack composers (John Williams) might still be a flop. The quality of the individual parts does not necessarily guarantee the same quality in the overall product.

Next, consider the flip side of this fallacy: the fallacy of division. The fallacy of division mistakenly infers that the same attributes or characteristics that apply to the whole or to the group must also apply to every part of the whole or to every member of the group. See if you can spot the fallacy in the following argument:

> Harvard University is the highest-ranked university in the United States. Thus, Harvard must have the nation's best computer science department.

Does the conclusion to the above argument follow from its premise? Clearly not! Harvard might be ranked first overall among universities in the United States, but the possibility remains that MIT, Stanford University, or some other institution has the nation's highest-ranked computer science department.

3.9.6 Fallacy of Ambiguity/Equivocation

Fallacious reasoning can occur whenever one or more terms are used either ambiguously or equivocally; ambiguous terms have more than one interpretation, and it is not always clear which interpretation the author intends. A term is used equivocally, on the contrary, when it has two (or more) different senses or meanings. Consider the following argument:

> Humans can think and highly sophisticated AI (artificial intelligence) computer systems can think; therefore, highly sophisticated AI computer systems are human.

In this case, it is possible that both premises are true in the actual world. However, the sense in which AI computer systems are said to think is not necessarily the same sense in which humans, in fact, think. Here, the term "think" is used equivocally. So even if it is true that computers can think in one sense of that term, it doesn't necessarily follow that computers can think in the same sense that humans do. Even if computers and humans could both think in the same sense, it doesn't follow that computers must be human. Consider that some animals, such as orangutans, do many things in ways that are similar to humans, yet we do not infer that orangutans are humans. (One might object to the above argument being called a fallacy by noting that if thinking is defined as something that only humans could do, then, by definition, computers (that "think") would have to be human. While this kind of move might avoid the fallacy of ambiguity/equivocation, it introduces other problems since the premise "computers can think" would now be more controversial and require further analysis.)

Another example of the fallacy of ambiguity/equivocation can be found in the following argument:

> Computers have memory. Humans have memory. Having memory enables humans to recall some of their childhood experiences. Therefore, computers can recall experiences from their childhood.

Notice that "memory" is used in two different senses in the above argument.

Although both examples of the fallacy of ambiguity/equivocation illustrate exaggerated cases, which might seem implausible, we should note that many arguments used in everyday discourse commit variations of this fallacy.

3.9.7 The *False Dichotomy/Either–Or Fallacy/All-or-Nothing* Fallacy

One fallacy type—frequently referred to by labels such as the False Dichotomy, the Either/Or Fallacy, or the All-or-Nothing Fallacy—typically presents us with two options that might initially seem to be mutually exclusive. For example, some political leaders assert, if you are not with us, you are against us. In this case, there would seem to be no possible neutral ground. Or, you might hear a politician in the United States claim, either you endorse the Patriot Act or you hate America. But often times, assertions of this kind can be very misleading. Of course, there are genuine situations where only two (mutually exclusive) options are possible, for example, a light switch is either in the on *or* off position. However, many claims, especially one's involving controversial political issues, appeal to a strict either/or rhetorical strategy in cases where additional options are available.

Solove (2011) notes that a variation of the All-or-Nothing Fallacy can be found in the reasoning process frequently used to defend what he calls the "false trade-off between privacy and security." Some people who use this line of fallacious reasoning assert, "we must give up our privacy if we want to be secure from terrorist attacks." This and similar kinds of refrains have been used by government leaders, national defense agencies, and conservative politicians to influence the enactment of controversial laws such as the USA Patriot Act. But are the choices that one must make in these kinds of situations always reducible to "all-or-nothing" (or to an "either/or") option? Or have we instead been presented with false dichotomies by those who use such fallacious reasoning?

Solove correctly points out that our surrendering privacy would not necessarily make us more secure; similarly, he notes that not every gain in privacy necessarily entails a loss in security. Consider that there are ways of increasing security that do not intrude on privacy. For example, Solove notes that making cockpits in airplanes more secure enhances the security of airline passengers, but it does not reduce their personal privacy.[10] So we can see that the concepts of privacy and security are not mutually exclusive and thus do not necessarily present us with either/or scenarios or false dichotomies, despite what many of those who use variations of the all-or-nothing fallacy in the privacy vs. security debate would have us believe. We revisit Solove's insight in more detail in our analysis of privacy in Chapter 5.

3.9.8 The Virtuality Fallacy

The *virtuality fallacy*, coined by James Moor, has the following form:

PREMISE 1. X exists in cyberspace.
PREMISE 2. Cyberspace is virtual.

CONCLUSION. X (or the effect of X) is not real.[11]

Those who defend questionable forms of online behavior, such as launching viruses and engaging in unauthorized entries into computer systems, sometimes suggest that these activities cause no real harm to people. Some reason that because these activities are carried out in the virtual world, their effects are only virtual and thus not real. You should be able to spot the fallacy in this line of reasoning. Imagine that someone has posted an insulting remark about you on Facebook or some other online forum. Arguably, the locus of offense is in cyberspace, or virtual space, as opposed to real (physical) space. Does it follow that the particular harm caused to you is any less real than it would have been had it occurred in a physical setting? In Chapter 11, we examine some arguments used by members of virtual communities who reason that no real harm can result in these forums because they are only in virtual space.[12] There, we will see how the virtuality fallacy applies.

We have considered some techniques for identifying fallacy types in ordinary language. The common fallacy types identified in this section represent only a small sample of those identified and labeled by logicians and philosophers. Yet, all have one feature in common: Their reasoning is so weak that even when the premises are assumed true, the conclusion would not likely be true because of the weak or insufficient evidence supporting it.

You can devise your own labels for some of the fallacious arguments we have encountered that have not yet been given names. For example, consider the fallacious argument we examined in Section 3.7 that tried to show that computer ethics issues must be unique because (i) computers have some unique technological features and (ii) computers raise ethical issues. We could call this the "Computer Ethics is Unique Fallacy." Also consider the fallacy we examined earlier in this chapter, which reasoned that Internet users should have no expectation of personal privacy while they are online because the Internet is in public space. We could label this the "Privacy in Public Fallacy." You can no doubt come up with additional labels for fallacious arguments that you encounter in your analysis of cyberethics issues. (For the names of some standard logical fallacies not covered in this chapter, see http://yourlogicalfallacyis.com/.)

These techniques for spotting logical fallacies in ordinary, everyday discourse are useful in helping us to evaluate some of the arguments we will examine in the remaining chapters in this textbook. We should also note that some authors, including Artz (2000), have suggested that "narrative reasoning" in the form of stories, as opposed to strict logical reasoning (even in the informal sense described in this chapter), can be very useful in helping us to understand and evaluate some cyberethics issues. However, we will not pursue this claim here, because the aim of this chapter has been to show how conventional critical reasoning skills for analyzing informal logical arguments can be applied in the context of cyberethics.

▶ 3.10 CHAPTER SUMMARY

In this chapter, we considered some basic critical reasoning skills, and we examined both the structure and the strength of logical arguments. We considered key criteria for differentiating among arguments that were valid and invalid, sound and unsound, and inductive and fallacious. We then considered a seven-step strategy for determining an argument's overall strength. We also identified eight common fallacies, or "fallacy types," that illustrated flaws in reasoning in the context of cybertechnology and cyberethics, and we considered some techniques that will help us to spot additional informal logical fallacies that occur in everyday reasoning. (Note that some additional material on critical reasoning skills is included in Appendix G, Available at www.wiley.com/college/tavani.) In the remaining chapters of this textbook, we will see how the critical reasoning skills introduced in this chapter can be used to evaluate arguments affecting many cyberethics disputes.

▶ REVIEW QUESTIONS

1. What is critical reasoning, and how can it be applied to ethical issues involving cybertechnology?
2. What is a logical argument, and how is it different from a claim or a statement?
3. Identify and briefly describe the two important characteristics or features of an *argument*.
4. What role or purpose do arguments play in helping us to resolve issues in cyberethics?
5. Describe the basic structure of an argument.
6. What is the essential difference between an argument that is valid and one that is invalid? Construct an example of each.
7. What is a counterexample, and how can it be used to show that an argument is invalid?
8. How is it possible for an argument to be valid but not successful?
9. What is required for an argument to be sound? Construct an example of a sound argument.
10. When is a valid argument unsound? Construct an example of an unsound argument.
11. What differentiates invalid arguments that are inductive from invalid arguments that are fallacious? Construct an example of each.
12. What is an "informal logical fallacy"?
13. What is the *Ad Hominem Fallacy*? Provide an example of this fallacy in the context of cyberethics.
14. What is the *Slippery Slope Fallacy*? Provide an example of this fallacy in the context of cyberethics.
15. What is the *Fallacy of Appeal to Authority* (*Ad Verecundiam*)? Provide an example of this fallacy in the context of cyberethics.
16. What is the *False Cause Fallacy*? Provide an example of this fallacy in the context of cyberethics.
17. What is the difference between the *Fallacy of Composition* and the *Fallacy of Division*? Provide an example of each fallacy in the context of cyberethics.
18. What is the *Fallacy of Ambiguity/Equivocation*? Provide an example of this fallacy involving either an issue in cyberethics or an aspect of cybertechnology.
19. What is the *False Dichotomy/Either–Or Fallacy/All-or-Nothing Fallacy*? Provide an example of this fallacy in the context of cyberethics.
20. What is the *Virtuality Fallacy*? Provide an example of this fallacy in the context of cyberethics.

▶ DISCUSSION QUESTIONS

21. Construct an argument for the view that your university should/should not have the right to monitor student e-mail. Next, analyze your argument to see if it is either valid or invalid. If it is valid, determine whether it is also sound. If it is invalid, determine whether it is inductive or fallacious.

22. Identify some of the arguments that have been made on both sides in the debate about sharing copyrighted MP3 files on the Internet. Evaluate the arguments in terms of their strength of reasoning. Can you find any valid arguments? Can you find any inductive arguments?

23. Based on what you have learned in this chapter, construct an argument to support or to refute the view that all undergraduate students should be required to take a course in cyberethics. Next, apply the seven-step strategy (in Section 3.8) to your argument.

24. Construct an argument for the view that privacy protection should be improved for ordinary users who conduct searches on Google. Next, evaluate your argument via the rules for validity versus invalidity. If your argument is invalid, check to see if it also includes any of the informal fallacies we examined in Section 3.9.

Scenarios for Analysis

1. Apply the seven-step strategy (in Section 3.8) to your evaluation of the argument in the following scenario:

A major association representing the music industry in the United States has determined that 4,000 copies of a new album featuring a popular rock group, called DUO, had been illegally downloaded last month. The cost of this album for those who elect to download it legally from online music stores is $10 per copy. So the association concludes that the music company that holds the copyright to this album lost $40,000 dollars in revenue last month (on that album alone).

2. Determine whether the strength of reasoning used in the argument in the following scenario is valid or invalid. If it is invalid, does it commit any of the fallacies we examined in Section 3.9?

You are engaged in an intense discussion with your friend, Bill, who works in the IT department at your university. Bill complains that many students are using P2P (peer-to-peer) file-sharing applications on the university's network to download excessive amounts of unauthorized copyrighted material. He also claims that the most effective solution to this problem would be to disable student access to all (existing) P2P sites and to prevent students at your institution from setting up their own P2P sites for any reason whatsoever (even to include noncopyrighted material). You convey to Bill your belief that this measure is too drastic. However, Bill argues that the only way to eliminate unauthorized file sharing among students at your institution is to disable access to all P2P software on the university's network.

▶ ENDNOTES

1. Philosophers and logicians often contrast "informal logic," comprising the fields of critical reasoning and critical thinking, with "formal logic." The latter is a much more rigorous system based on a framework of elaborate rules and symbols. Informal logic, on the contrary, focuses on the kind of reasoning that occurs in ordinary language, that is, in everyday discourse. As such, the critical reasoning skills described in this chapter can help us to analyze cyberethics-related arguments without having to master the rules in a formal system of (symbolic) logic.
2. Following Boyd (2003), Cederblom and Paulsen (2012), Thomson (2009), and others, I use the expression "critical reasoning" instead of "critical thinking" to describe the reasoning skills examined in this chapter. In my view, "critical thinking" has become far too broad a term, and it can now be interpreted to mean very different things in different academic disciplines. For our purposes, "critical reasoning" better captures the kind of precision and rigor required in the strategies and techniques used in this textbook to evaluate informal logical arguments.
3. See Søraker (2006) for an interesting account of the role that critical reasoning skills, especially in the context of "pragmatic arguments," can play in our analysis of cyberethics issues.
4. Many ethics instructors now recognize the importance of rigorous critical reasoning skills for analyzing issues examined in ethics courses, and an increasing number of introductory ethics and applied ethics textbooks include a separate chapter on logical arguments and critical reasoning. See, for example, Bowyer (2001), Vaughn (2010), and Waller (2010). See also Ruggiero (2012) who devotes an entire book to critical thinking in the context of ethics.

5. An analysis of key issues and arguments surrounding the classic SDI controversy, as well as NMD, is included in Bowyer (2001, 2002) and Yurcik and Doss (2002).
6. Both the methodology and the terminology that I use for argument evaluation in Sections 3.3–3.7 follow and build upon standard models of informal logic, such as those used by Nolt (2002) and others. In those sections, I also include several examples from my (Wiley custom) textbook on reasoning (Tavani 2010).
7. The notion of "counterexample" used here follows a classic definition of the term used in informal logic; see, for example, the description in Nolt (2002). Whereas I use the term "valid" to label the argument form for which no counterexample is possible, other authors (including Nolt) use "deductive" to refer to this argument form.
8. Whereas I use the term "strong" to describe the "overall reasoning strength" of arguments that are either sound or inductive with all true premises, and the term "weak" to refer to the overall reasoning strength of arguments that are either fallacious or valid with one or more false premises, Nolt uses "rational" and "irrational" to distinguish between the two kinds of "overall reasoning strengths."
9. See Tavani and Grodzinsky (2014) for an expanded discussion of how *ad hominem* attacks have been used in arguments involving the Edward Snowden controversy.
10. Solove (2011, p. 34). An example of the Either/Or Fallacy that applies in the controversial whistle-blowing controversy involving Edward Snowden is included in Tavani and Grodzinsky (2014).
11. Moor described this fallacy in a talk entitled "Just Consequentialism and Computing" at the *2000–2001 Humanities Lecture Series*, Rivier University: Nashua, NH, February 2001.
12. For an interesting discussion of "rationalist" vs. "emotivist" accounts of reasoning about issues involving virtual environments, see Søraker (2010).

▶ REFERENCES

Artz, John M. 2000. "Narrative vs. Logical Reasoning in Computer Ethics." In R. Baird, R. Ramsower, and S. Rosenbaum, eds. *Cyberethics: Social and Moral Issues in the Computer Age*. Amherst, NY: Prometheus, pp. 73–79.

Boyd, Robert. 2003. *Critical Reasoning and Logic*. Upper Saddle River, NJ: Prentice Hall.

Bowyer, Kevin W. 2001. *Ethics and Computing: Living in a Computerized World*. 2nd ed. New York: IEEE Press.

Bowyer, Kevin W. 2002. "Star Wars Revisited: Ethics and Safety Critical Software." IEEE Technology and Society 21, no. 1: 13–26.

Cederblom, Jerry and David W. Paulsen. 2012. *Critical Reasoning: Understanding and Criticizing Arguments and Theories*. 7th ed. Boston, MA: Wadsworth.

Nolt, John E. 2002. *Informal Logic: Possible Worlds and Imagination*. New York: McGraw Hill.

Ruggiero, Vincent R. 2012. *Thinking Critically About Ethical Issues*. 9th ed. New York: McGraw-Hill.

Solove, Daniel J. 2011. *Nothing to Hide: The False Tradeoff between Privacy and Security*. New Haven, CT: Yale University Press.

Søraker, Johnny Hartz. 2006. "The Role of Pragmatic Arguments in Computer Ethics." *Ethics and Information Technology* 8, no. 3: 121–30.

Søraker, Johnny Hartz. 2010. "The Neglect of Reason: A Plea for Rationalist Accounts of the Effects of Virtual Violence." In C. Wankel and S. Malleck, eds. *Emerging Ethical Issues of Life in Virtual Worlds*. Charlotte, NC: Information Age Publishing, pp. 15–32.

Tavani, Herman T. 2010. *The Elements of Reasoning: A Short Introduction to Informal Logic*. Hoboken, NJ: John Wiley and Sons (Custom Learning Solutions).

Tavani, Herman T. and Frances Grodzinsky. 2014. "Trust, Betrayal, and Whistle-Blowing: Reflections on the Edward Snowden Case." *Computers and Society* 44, no. 3: 8–13.

Thomson, Anne. 2009. *Critical Reasoning: A Practical Introduction*. 3rd ed. New York: Routledge.

Vaughn, Lewis. 2010. *Doing Ethics: Moral Reasoning and Contemporary Issues*. 2nd ed. New York: W. W. Norton.

Waller, Bruce N. 2010. *Consider Ethics*. 3rd ed. New York: Pearson.

Yurcik, William and David Doss. 2002. "Software Technology Issues for a U.S. National Missile Defense System." *IEEE Technology and Society Magazine* 21, no. 2: 36–46.

▶ FURTHER READINGS

Bergmann, Marie, James H. Moor, and Jack Nelson. 2013. *The Logic Book*. 6th ed. New York: McGraw Hill.

Copi, Irving M. and Carl Cohen. 2011. *Introduction to Logic*. 14th ed. Upper Saddle River, NJ: Prentice Hall.

Hurley, Patrick. 2015. *A Concise Introduction to Logic*. 12th ed. Belmont, CA: Wadsworth Publishing.

Kahane, Howard and Nancy Cavender. 2010. *Logic and Contemporary Rhetoric: The Use of Reason in Everyday Life*. 11th ed. Belmont, CA: Wadsworth Publishing.

Moore, Brooke Noel and Richard Parker. 2015. *Critical Thinking*. 11th ed. New York: McGraw-Hill.

Munson, Ronald and Andrew Black. 2012. *The Elements of Reasoning*. 6th ed. Boston, MA: Wadsworth.

Ruggiero, Vincent R. 2012. *Beyond Feelings: A Guide to Critical Thinking*. 9th ed. New York: McGraw-Hill.

CHAPTER

4

Professional Ethics, Codes of Conduct, and Moral Responsibility

LEARNING OBJECTIVES

Upon completing this chapter, you will successfully be able to:

- Define *professional ethics* and differentiate professional ethics issues from other kinds of applied ethics issues affecting cybertechnology,
- Determine whether computing/IT professionals have any special moral responsibilities (by virtue of their specific professional roles),
- Articulate the roles/purposes of *professional codes of ethics* and identify their strengths and weaknesses,
- Understand the kinds of conflicts of professional responsibility that can arise where an employee may be permitted, or possibly even required, to blow the whistle,
- Articulate the key distinctions that differentiate *moral responsibility*, *legal liability*, and *accountability* (in the context of the computing/IT profession),
- Determine whether some computer companies might have special moral responsibilities (because of the nature of the products they develop or the services they provide).

In this chapter, we examine a range of issues often categorized under the general heading "professional ethics." We begin by briefly reflecting on a scenario that raises questions about professional responsibility in the context of a serious malfunction in a semiautonomous, computerized weapon system.

▶ SCENARIO 4–1: Fatalities Involving the Oerlikon GDF-005 Robotic Cannon

In 2007, the South African army conducted a series of training exercises (in the Republic of South Africa) using the Oerlikon GDF-005, a semiautonomous, robotic cannon. The weapon was designed to use radar and laser technology to "lock on" to its targets, which include unmanned aerial vehicles (UAVs), cruise missiles, and helicopters. The robotic cannon was also designed to reload automatically when the magazines in its pair of 35 mm guns become empty. During a routine shooting exercise in October 2007, the cannon malfunctioned, resulting in 9 deaths and 14 injuries. Following an official investigation into the fatal incident, the South African National Defense Ministry issued a report that critics found vague and inconclusive. While some analysts suspected that a software glitch was responsible for the malfunction, others believed that the cannon's malfunctioning could have been caused by a hardware failure.[1] So, it was not clear whether the deaths and injuries resulting from the Oerlikon GDF-005's malfunctioning were due to a software flaw, a hardware problem, or possibly both. ■

To what extent can/should the professionals, especially the software and hardware engineers, involved in developing this robotic cannon be held accountable for its malfunctions? Determining the locus of responsibility for malfunctions of this kind is not only important; it is urgent. Consider that many of the advanced and sophisticated technologies developed by computing/information technology (IT) professionals, which include more and more robotic and autonomous components, are increasingly used in military defense systems and warfare; these technological systems could also malfunction in ways similar to the Oerlikon GDF-005. Furthermore, malfunctions in these kinds of systems increasingly threaten the lives of ordinary civilians, in addition to those of the military personnel who use them (and their intended enemy combatants). In 2010, for example, the U.S. military lost control of a helicopter drone for more than 30 minutes during a test flight; the drone veered toward Washington, D.C., violating air space intended to protect the White House and other official government buildings (Lin, 2012). Although no one was injured during this mishap, the outcome could easily have been quite different. So, we can see why there is good reason to be concerned with some of the broader societal implications of malfunctions involving these kinds of computerized/robotic systems.

We should note that malfunctions in computerized systems with "safety-critical" and "life-critical" applications (defined in Section 4.2) are by no means new. Consider an incident, now viewed by many as a classic case of a computer malfunction in the medical field, which occurred in the 1980s. Between 1985 and 1987, a series of malfunctions involving the Therac-25, a computerized radiation therapy machine, resulted in six serious accidents and three deaths. The problem was eventually traced to a bug in a software program that, in certain instances, caused massive overdoses of radiation to be administered to patients.[2] The Therac-25 case is examined in Section 4.5.2, in our analysis of moral accountability and the problem of "many hands." Before examining specific cases involving unreliable computer systems in the context of responsibility issues for computing/IT professionals, we first address some foundational questions in professional ethics.

▶ 4.1 WHAT IS *PROFESSIONAL ETHICS?*

Recall that in Chapter 1 we described professional ethics as one of the three main perspectives through which cyberethics issues can be identified and analyzed. We saw that, when applied to computing, professional ethics is a field of applied ethics concerned with moral issues that affect computer professionals. You may also recall from our discussion of professional ethics in Chapter 1 that Don Gotterbarn suggested that professional ethics is the principal, perhaps even exclusive, perspective through which ethical issues involving the computing field should be examined.[3] Although this claim is controversial and will not be further considered here, we have devoted this chapter to an analysis of cyberethics issues from the vantage point of professional ethics.

Why have a category called "professional ethics?" After all, one could reasonably argue that independent of whether a particular moral issue happens to arise in either a professional or a nonprofessional context, ethics is ethics; the same basic ethical rules apply to professionals as to ordinary individuals. In response, many ethicists argue that some moral issues affecting professionals are sufficiently distinct and specialized to warrant a separate field of study. Some ethicists also argue that, at least in certain cases, professionals have special moral obligations, which exceed those of ordinary individuals. To grasp the essential points in the arguments advanced by these ethicists, it is useful first to understand what is meant by "profession" and "professional."

4.1.1 What Is a Profession?

The meaning of "profession" has evolved significantly over time. Harris, Pritchard, and Rabins (2009) point out that while a profession was once associated with people "professing a religious or monastic life," that concept took on a more secular meaning in the late seventeenth century when it was first used to refer to one who "professed to be duly qualified." According to Davis (2015a), the term "profession" has at least four senses in its everyday usage; that is, it can mean:

1. a vocation (or calling),
2. an occupation,
3. an "honest occupation" (that one may "openly admit to profess"),
4. a "special kind of honest occupation."[4]

Davis claims that (4), which rules out dishonest occupations (e.g., such as in organized crime) and also emphasizes special skills/abilities/knowledge, is the primary sense in which we think of a profession today.

Some believe that one way of distinguishing a profession from many "ordinary occupations" has to do with certain kinds of characteristics that apply to the former, but not the latter. Having a code of ethics would be one such distinguishing factor. Consider that the field of computing/IT has a number of professional societies with ethical codes (see Section 4.3), as do professions such as medicine and law. However, the computing/IT profession also differs from some of the better-known traditional professions such as medicine and law in at least one key respect. While many doctors and lawyers work in private practice, most computer/IT professionals are not self-employed; even though some work as independent consultants, most are employed by corporations.

Based on criteria used to demarcate traditional professions, one might question whether the computer/IT field is a "true profession." Barger (2008) argues that it is; in his view, the field qualifies as a genuine profession because it satisfies two key criteria that have traditionally characterized a profession: (i) expert knowledge, which he describes as a "special technical knowledge that is certified by some authority and is not possessed by the layperson" and (ii) autonomy with respect to "independence in conducting one's professional practice."[5]

4.1.2 Who Is a Professional?

As in the case of "profession," the meaning of the term "professional" has also evolved. Traditionally, professionals included lawyers, medical doctors, and professors. In our current and expanded use of that term, we refer to a broader range of professional categories, such as real estate professionals, marketing professionals, and so forth. A defining attribute of traditional professions, such as medicine and law, is that members often find themselves in situations in which their decisions and actions can have significant social effects; for example, medical doctors can prescribe the use of certain drugs for their patients, who otherwise would have no legal access to them, and lawyers are bound by special obligations such as client confidentiality that would not apply if they were acting as ordinary citizens. In these cases, a professional's roles and responsibilities can exceed those of ordinary individuals. Sometimes, these roles and responsibilities are said to *differentiate* professionals from nonprofessionals.

Buchanan (2004) believes that the roles and responsibilities of professionals are differentiated from ordinary individuals because:

> . . . professionals are experts in a field, which provides them an advantage over the lay person and that professional's work has the potential to impact—either positively or negatively—the general public at large.[6]

Buchanan goes on to note that "information professionals" have the potential to adversely affect an "increasingly large and diverse clientele by failing to act responsibly, fairly, timely, and appropriately." So it would seem that these roles and responsibilities differentiate professionals working in the fields of computing and IT from ordinary individuals. The extent to which a computer/IT professional's roles and responsibilities are "highly differentiated," however, is a matter of some dispute. To understand why this is so, it would first help to understand what, exactly, is meant by the expression "computer/IT professional."

4.1.3 Who Is a Computer/IT Professional?

Broadly speaking, a computer/IT professional is anyone employed in the computing and IT fields—from software and hardware engineers to specialists such as support personnel, network administrators, and computer repair technicians. Computer professionals can also include faculty and instructors who teach in computer science and information management departments at universities, as well as in industry settings. We could possibly even extend "computer/IT professional" to include professionals who are responsible for providing access to electronic information in libraries, although they may prefer to describe themselves as "information professionals" or "information science professionals."[7]

A computer/IT professional might also be thought of in more narrow terms, in which case only software engineers would be included. Of course, there are various gradients in between the two ends of this spectrum. A computer/IT professional could be defined in a way that would exclude professionals in the fields of communications and library science yet still include professionals whose computer-specific job descriptions extend beyond software engineering per se, such as software technical writers, software quality analysts, and managers and supervisors who play key roles in the software development process and make up a software engineering team.[8]

For purposes of this chapter, we will consider *computer/IT professionals* to include software/hardware engineers and software/hardware engineering teams, as well as computer science instructors in colleges, universities, and industry settings who are responsible for educating and training the members of software engineering teams. We will also include IT professionals in end-user support roles (e.g., network administrators and computer support personnel) in our definition of computer/IT professionals. However, we will not include lawyers, accountants, nurses, or other professionals who are employed by computer companies or who work closely with computers as part of their regular employment.

▶ 4.2 DO COMPUTER/IT PROFESSIONALS HAVE ANY SPECIAL MORAL RESPONSIBILITIES?

Some ethicists believe that all professionals, regardless of their practice, have special moral obligations *as professionals*. But are there also specific moral obligations that apply to computer/IT professionals in the sense in which we have defined the term? As noted earlier, many computer/IT professionals include software engineers and members of software engineering teams. An important question for us to consider is whether this subgroup of professionals have any special moral obligations that differentiate them from other professionals who work in the computing/IT fields. Gotterbarn (2001) believes that because software engineers and their teams are responsible for developing safety-critical systems, they have significant opportunities to (i) do good or cause harm, (ii) enable others to do good or cause harm, and (iii) influence others to do good or cause harm. Thus, Gotterbarn suggests that the roles and responsibilities involved in the development of safety-critical systems constitute a differentiating factor.

Safety-Critical Software

What, exactly, is safety-critical software? Bowyer (2001) points out that the phrase "safety-critical system" is often used to refer to computer systems that can have a "direct life-threatening impact." He notes that, under this definition, examples of safety-critical software applications typically include:

- Aircraft and air traffic control systems
- Mass transportation systems
- Nuclear reactors
- Missile systems
- Medical treatment systems

However, Bowyer believes that an understanding of safety-critical systems that includes only these examples is too narrow. He suggests that a broader definition be adopted in which safety-critical systems are also understood as software applications used in the design of physical systems and structures whose failures can also have an impact that is life threatening. Here, the range of safety-critical applications can be expanded to include software used in the:

- Design of bridges and buildings
- Selection of water disposal sites
- Development of analytical models for medical treatment[9]

We use the expanded sense of "safety-critical software" in this chapter. And we examine two important cases of computer malfunctions involving safety-critical software in our discussion of moral accountability in Section 4.5. A related question is whether the computing/IT profession itself (as opposed to the individuals comprising that profession) has any special moral obligations. Also, we could ask whether certain kinds of computer corporations might have these kinds of moral obligations because of the significant social impact of their products and services. In Section 4.6, we briefly consider whether corporations that develop *autonomous systems*, that is, "machines" capable of making life-critical decisions independent of human oversight, might have some special moral obligations.

▶ 4.3 PROFESSIONAL CODES OF ETHICS AND CODES OF CONDUCT

We have already seen that many professions have established professional societies, which in turn have adopted codes of conduct. For example, the medical profession established the American Medical Association (AMA), and the legal profession established the American Bar Association (ABA). Both associations have formal codes of ethics/conduct for their members. How do the ethical guidelines/requirements included in professional codes differ from "ordinary morality?" Davis (2015b) argues that these codes, which are "morally binding" on those professionals to whom they apply, can "impose new moral obligations and requirements" on the members of a profession; to illustrate this point, he notes that an employee can be required to sign a contract to uphold an employer's code of ethics as a condition of employment. So, Davis believes that codes of ethics should not be understood as simply a restatement of "ordinary" or conventional morality.[10]

As in the case of the medical, legal, and other well-known professions, the computing profession has also established a number of professional societies, the largest of which are the Association for Computing Machinery (ACM) and the Institute of Electrical and Electronics Engineers Computer Society (IEEE-CS). Both organizations have adopted professional codes of ethics; the full texts of these two codes are included in Appendices A–E (www.wiley.com/college/tavani), as well as at the ACM and IEEE sites.

Both the ACM and IEEE codes contain general statements about what is expected, and in some cases what is required, to be a member in good standing. The IEEE Code of Ethics contains 10 general directives; the first four instruct members to:

1. accept responsibility in making engineering decisions consistent with the safety, health, and welfare of the public . . . ;

2. avoid real or perceived conflicts of interest wherever possible . . . ;

3. be honest . . . ;

4. reject bribery in all its forms . . .[11]

The ACM Code of Ethics and Professional Conduct, on the other hand, is more complex. It contains 24 imperatives, formulated as statements of personal responsibility. Like the IEEE Code, the ACM Code also lists general moral imperatives:

1.1 Contribute to society and human well-being.

1.2 Avoid harm to others.

1.3 Be honest and trustworthy.

1.4 Be fair and take action not to discriminate.

1.5 Honor property copyrights and patents.

1.6 Give proper credit for intellectual property.

1.7 Respect the privacy of others.

1.8 Honor confidentiality.

From these general imperatives, a list of more specific professional responsibilities follows. These include the directives:

2.1 Strive to achieve the highest quality . . . in . . . work.

2.2 Acquire and maintain professional competence.

These directives are then followed by six "organizational leadership imperatives," which include:

3.1 Articulate social responsibilities of members . . .

3.2 Manage personnel and resources to design and build information that enhance the quality of working life.

The fourth component of the ACM Code stresses "compliance with the code," and consists of two imperatives:

4.1 Uphold and promote the principles of this code.

4.2 Treat violations of this code as inconsistent with membership of the ACM.[12]

4.3.1 The Purpose of Professional Codes

Professional codes of ethics serve a variety of functions. For example, these codes can "regulate" the members of a profession, as Gotterbarn and Miller (2009) point out. Bynum and Rogerson (2004) identify five important functions that professional codes serve: inspiration, education, guidance, accountability, and enforcement. The authors point out that codes *inspire* members of the profession by "identifying values and ideals" to which members can aspire. Bynum and Rogerson also note that codes *educate* by informing members about the profession's values and standards and can *guide* members by specifying "standards of good practice." Additionally, codes describe the level of *accountability* and responsibility that is expected and demanded by a professional society. Finally, codes have an *enforcement* function with regard to behavior deemed to be "ethically unacceptable" in a society.[13] Martin and Schinzinger (2004) describe this feature as a "disciplinary or penal function" that codes can serve when members violate one or more policies stipulated by the professional code.

To be effective, a professional code must be broad, yet specific. Perlman and Varma (2002) point out that a code must be broad enough to cover the ethical conflicts and concerns likely to arise in its professional field (such as computing/IT), but, at the same time, a code cannot be so broad that it covers extraneous incidents. It must also be sufficiently specific to serve as a guide to making sound decisions for practical action in actual circumstances that are likely to arise in the computing field. To accomplish the first objective, Perlman and Varma believe that a code needs to encompass the principles that guide professions in general and ethics in particular. And to satisfy the second objective, a code is measured by the degree to which its rules serve as "effective guides" for computer/IT professionals and practitioners. Perlman and Varma also note that in engineering contexts, professional codes face a special challenge because the practice of engineering often dictates secrecy, whereas the ethics of engineering requires transparency, or openness.

4.3.2 Some Criticisms of Professional Codes

One might be surprised to learn that professional codes in general, as well as specific codes developed for computer/IT professionals, have been criticized. But we should note that some critics have pointed out that the ethical codes adopted by professional computer societies have no "teeth." For example, violations of the ACM or IEEE codes, unlike violations of professional codes in the fields of medicine and law, do not necessarily threaten the employment of those who violate them. Also, computer/IT professionals are not usually required to be members of the ACM, IEEE, or any other professional society to be employed in the computing field or to practice as computer/IT professionals.

Critics have pointed out numerous ways in which professional codes in general can be dismissed. For example, Davis (1995) notes that these codes are often perceived as "self-serving, unrealistic, inconsistent, mere guides for novices, too vague, or unnecessary."[14] To Davis' list, we could add yet another criticism—professional codes tend to be "incomplete." Fairweather (2004) believes that codes of conduct for computing professionals have been influenced by a conception of computer/information ethics that is limited to four traditional areas of concern: privacy, accuracy, property, and accessibility. He argues that a professional code built on a foundation that includes such a narrow range of ethical concerns can provide certain loopholes for unethical behavior in an organization.

Ladd (1995) has criticized ethical codes on slightly different grounds, arguing that these codes rest on a series of confusions that are both "intellectual and moral." His complex arguments can, for our purposes, be summarized in three main points. First, Ladd notes that ethics is basically an "open ended, reflective, and critical intellectual activity." Because ethics is a field of study that consists of issues to be examined, explored, discussed, deliberated, and argued, it requires a process of deliberation and argumentation. (Recall our definition of ethics in Chapter 2.) Directives listed in a professional code may give an employee the mistaken notion that all he or she needs to do is to locate a directive and then blindly follow it. More importantly, however, Ladd notes that individuals are not told what to do in a situation where two or more principles or directives (in a code) conflict with one another. Here, the individual needs to deliberate; yet professional codes do not typically provide any hierarchy of principles or any mechanism for choosing one directive over another.

Second, Ladd is critical of codes because of the confusions they introduce with respect to responsibilities involving microethics vs. macroethics issues (i.e., confusions about which responsibilities apply to individual professionals and which responsibilities apply to the profession itself). Recall that we briefly discussed the microethical/macroethical distinction in Chapter 2. In the context of professional ethics, microethical issues apply to personal relationships between individual professionals and other individuals, such as clients. Macroethical issues, on the contrary, apply to social problems that confront members of a profession collectively or as a group. As such, most microethical issues involve the application of ordinary moral notions (such as honesty and civility) that would also hold when dealing with other individuals in nonprofessional contexts. Macroethical issues, however, are more complex, since they involve the formulation of policies at the level of social organizations. Ladd believes that we need to distinguish between questions such as "Which responsibilities do I, as a computer professional, have in such and such a situation?" and "Which responsibilities does the computing profession, as a profession, have in such and such a situation?" He concludes that professional codes of ethics cannot help us to make this important distinction.

Third, Ladd believes that attaching disciplinary procedures and sanctions to codes effectively turns them into legal rules or "authoritative rules of conduct" rather than ethical rules. The role of ethics in general, he argues, is to appraise, criticize, and even defend the principles, rules, and regulations, but it is not to dictate or to punish. Also, when individuals are compelled to obey directives, they are deprived of their autonomy, that is, their ability to choose, which is crucial in moral deliberation. So Ladd argues that professional codes rest on some mistaken notions about both the nature and the purpose of morality, which ultimately result in a series of intellectual and moral confusions.

4.3.3 Defending Professional Codes

It is very important to point out at this stage of our discussion of professional codes that not everyone has been critical of them. In fact, even some critics who have identified specific limitations or weaknesses in professional codes have also defended and praised them. For example, Barger (2003), who concedes that the hope of finding a single professional code that everyone would accept might seem "dim," also notes that we should not infer that an effort to do so is futile. And Davis, whose criticisms of professional codes were described in the previous section, has argued that codes are extremely important for engineering professionals because they are central to guiding individual engineers in how to behave morally as professionals. Since an engineer cannot always rely on his or her own private conscience when making moral decisions, Davis believes that codes play an essential role in "advising individual engineers in how to conduct themselves."[15] He also believes that codes of conduct can help individual engineers to better understand "engineering as a profession." Bynum and Rogerson (2004), who also describe some positive functions that codes serve, point out that we should acknowledge the "limitations of codes." For example, they note that professional codes should not be viewed simply as laws or algorithms or as "exhaustive checklists."

Gotterbarn (2000) has suggested that some of the criticism leveled against professional codes might be eliminated if we think of them as serving three important, but distinct, functions, that is,

- Codes of ethics
- Codes of conduct
- Codes of practice

Gotterbarn describes codes of ethics as "aspirational," because they often serve as mission statements for the profession and can thus provide vision and objectives. Codes of conduct, on the other hand, address the professional and the professional's attitude and behavior. Finally, codes of practice relate to operational activities within a profession. Gotterbarn points out that the degree of enforcement possible with respect to specific violations of a professional code is dependent on the type of code violated. For example, he notes that violations involving codes of ethics, which are primarily aspirational, are often considered no more than "light concerns." Consequently, violations of these codes may not have any serious consequences for individuals. Violations involving codes of conduct, on the other hand, can range from warnings given to an individual to the possibility of exclusion from practicing in a profession. Violations of codes of practice go one step further, however, in that they may also lead to legal action.[16]

Gotterbarn notes that the hierarchy in the three types of codes parallels the three levels of obligation owed by professionals. The first level includes a set of ethical values, such as integrity and justice, which professionals share with other humans by virtue of a shared humanity. The second level of responsibility is shared by all professionals, regardless of their fields of specialization. The third (and deeper) level comprises several obligations that derive directly from elements unique to a particular professional practice, such as software engineering. This threefold distinction is incorporated in a professional code developed by a joint task force of the IEEE-CS/ACM, which we examine in the next section.

Table 4-1 lists some of the strengths and weaknesses of professional codes.

4.3.4 The IEEE-CS/ACM Software Engineering Code of Ethics and Professional Practice

In the 1990s, the ACM and IEEE approved a joint code of ethics for software engineers: the IEEE-CS/ACM (SECEPP). Gotterbarn (2001) believes that SECEPP, as a professional code for software engineers, is unique for two reasons: First, it is intended as the code for the software engineering profession, unlike the individual codes (such as those of the ACM and IEEE) designed for particular professional societies within the computing profession. Second, Gotterbarn believes that SECEPP is distinctive in that it has been adopted by two international computing societies: ACM and IEEE-CS.

TABLE 4-1 Some Strengths and Weaknesses of Professional Codes

Strengths	Weaknesses
Codes inspire the members of a profession to behave ethically	Codes include directives that tend to be too general and too vague
Codes guide the members of a profession in ethical choices	Codes are not always helpful when two or more directives conflict
Codes educate the members about their professional obligations	Codes comprise directives that are neither complete nor exhaustive
Codes discipline members when they violate one or more directives	Codes are ineffective (have no "teeth") in disciplinary matters
Codes inform the public about the nature and roles of the profession	Codes sometimes include directives that are inconsistent with one another
Codes "sensitize" members of a profession to ethical issues and alert them to ethical aspects they otherwise might overlook	Codes do not always distinguish between microethics issues and macroethics issues
Codes enhance the profession in the eyes of the public	Codes can be self-serving for the profession

SECEPP is organized into two main parts: a short version and a longer, or full, version. Each version has its own preamble, and the full text for each version is included in Appendix E (www.wiley.com/college/tavani). SECEPP comprises eight core principles:

1. PUBLIC: Software engineers shall act consistently with the public interest.
2. CLIENT AND EMPLOYER: Software engineers shall act in a manner that is in the best interests of their client and employer, consistent with the public interest.
3. PRODUCT: Software engineers shall ensure that their products and related modifications meet the highest professional standards possible.
4. JUDGMENT: Software engineers shall maintain integrity and independence in their professional judgment.
5. MANAGEMENT: Software engineering managers and leaders shall subscribe to and promote an ethical approach to the management of software development and maintenance.
6. PROFESSION: Software engineers shall advance the integrity and reputation of the profession consistent with the public interest.
7. COLLEAGUES: Software engineers shall be fair to and supportive of their colleagues.
8. SELF: Software engineers shall participate in lifelong learning regarding the practice of their profession and shall promote an ethical approach to the practice of the profession.[17]

Does SECEPP Provide an Appropriate Balance between Generality and Specificity?

We noted earlier that professional codes are often criticized for being too vague and too general to be useful, yet there is also a danger in being too specific. If a professional code is too specific, it might fail to instruct members about general principles regarding ethical behavior and ethical decision making. SECEPP does include some very specific language, but it also has general prescriptions found in most professional codes. And, at the general level, SECEPP emphasizes the profession's obligation to the public at large, including concern for the public's health, safety, and welfare. For example, in the preamble to the full version of the code, software engineers are encouraged to:

- Consider broadly who is affected by their work
- Examine if they and their colleagues are treating other human beings with due respect
- Consider how the public, if reasonably well informed, would view their decisions
- Analyze how the least empowered will be affected by their decisions

The preamble to the short version of SECEPP summarizes aspirations at a high level of abstraction. The specific clauses included in the full version, on the other hand, give examples of how these aspirations change the way that software engineering professionals act as professionals. The code's principal authors note that "without the aspirations, the details can become legalistic and tedious; without the details, the aspirations can become high sounding but empty; together, the aspirations and the details form a cohesive code."[18] SECEPP's supporters believe that this code achieves an ideal balance between the general and the specific.

Can SECEPP Avoid Criticisms of Earlier Professional Codes?

One criticism often directed at professional codes is that they are incomplete; recall Ben Fairweather's argument in Section 4.3.2. Another criticism notes that most codes provide no mechanism for choosing between principles when two or more of them conflict; recall

John Ladd's critique, included in Section 4.3.2. Gotterbarn (2000) believes that SECEPP has overcome both difficulties.

Regarding the charge of incompleteness, Gotterbarn is willing to concede that the principles included in SECEPP are not intended to be exhaustive. He also acknowledges that no code could reasonably anticipate every possible moral controversy that can arise. However, he believes that SECEPP addresses the problem of completeness by providing "general guidance for ethical decision making." Gotterbarn argues that ethical tensions that arise can best be addressed by "thoughtful consideration of fundamental principles, rather than blind reliance on detailed regulations." He also points out that SECEPP should not be viewed as a simple algorithm that generates ethical decisions. And Gotterbarn notes that the individual principles that comprise SECEPP are not intended to be used in isolation from one another.

With respect to the second major criticism of professional codes, Gotterbarn points out that SECEPP has a "hierarchy of principles." This hierarchy enables engineers to prioritize their roles and responsibilities and to determine which ones are overriding when two or more conflict. Recall the list of eight principles that make up SECEPP: The ordering of these principles is intended to offer some guidance in cases where two or more rules conflict. SECEPP's hierarchy of principles states that concern for the health, safety, and welfare of the public is primary in all ethical judgments.

In concluding Section 4.3, we acknowledge that professional codes clearly have some limitations. However, we should be careful not to underestimate the important contributions that well-developed professional codes, such as SECEPP, have made to the computing profession so far. Critics may be correct in pointing out that merely following the directives of a professional code can never be a substitute for the kind of careful moral deliberation that is needed in certain controversial cases. Nevertheless, well-developed codes of conduct provide professionals with an important first step in the overall ethical deliberation process.

▶ 4.4 CONFLICTS OF PROFESSIONAL RESPONSIBILITY: EMPLOYEE LOYALTY AND WHISTLE-BLOWING

What, exactly, is employee loyalty? Do employees and employers have a special obligation of loyalty to each other? Should loyalty to one's employer ever preclude an employee's "blowing the whistle" in critical situations? In which cases can whistle-blowing be justified? Each of these questions is examined in this section.

4.4.1 Do Employees Have an Obligation of Loyalty to Employers?

Many ethicists believe that while loyalty may not be an obligation that is absolute, we nonetheless have a *prima facie* obligation of loyalty in employment contexts. In other words, all things being equal, an employee should be loyal to his or her employer and vice versa. For our purposes, however, we ask, What is the origin of the concept of employee loyalty in an engineering context? Carl Mitcham points out that, historically, engineers believed that they had a basic obligation to be loyal to "institutional authority."[19] He also notes that, originally, an engineer was a "soldier who designed military fortifications or operated engines of war, such as catapults." Mitcham further notes that early civil engineering could be viewed as peacetime military engineering in which engineers were "duty bound to obey their employer," which was often some branch of the government.[20] So it may be the case that this historical precedent has indeed contributed to the sense of loyalty that many engineers currently have for their institutions and employers.

Does employee loyalty still make sense in the context of employment in a large computer corporation in the twenty-first century? Skeptics might argue that loyalty makes sense only in employment contexts where there is a mutual commitment on the part of both parties involved—employer and employee. In good economic times, many employees seem to assume that their employers are very loyal to them. And in the past, it was not uncommon for employees in many professional fields to expect to be able to spend their entire career working for one employer, provided he or she was a loyal employee. But downturns in the U.S. economy, especially during the past three decades, have caused many employers to reassess their obligations to employees. As a result of significant downsizing in many corporations, beginning in the 1980s and continuing into the second decade of this century, employees can reasonably question the degree of loyalty that their employers offer them. In fairness to corporations, however, CEOs also have an obligation of loyalty to stockholders to ensure that the company remains viable and profitable. This obligation can sometimes conflict with a corporation's obligations to its employees.

In one sense, the skeptic's arguments seem plausible. Consider, for instance, how many corporations have gone through downsizing and restructuring phases in which loyal employees who have served a company faithfully for several years have been laid off or dismissed as part of restructuring plans. Also consider that many computer programming jobs in the United States are now being "outsourced" by major corporations to countries where programmers are willing to write the software code for much lower wages.

On the contrary, however, some employers have shown what would certainly appear to be a strong sense of loyalty to employees. For example, there have been instances where an employer will keep an employee on the payroll even though that employee has a chronic illness that causes him/her to miss several months of work. There have also been cases in which several employees have been kept on by a company despite the fact that their medical conditions have caused the corporation's health insurance costs to increase significantly, thereby reducing the company's overall profits. Also, you may have heard of a case involving the owner of Malden Mills whose physical plant in Massachusetts was destroyed by fire. The mill's proprietor, Aaron Feuerstein, could have been excused from any future obligations to his employees, and he could have chosen to rebuild his facility in either a different state (within the U.S) or a different country where employees would work for lower wages. Instead, Feuerstein continued to pay and provide benefits for his employees while a new facility was being built in Massachusetts. So there have been instances where employers have been very loyal to their employees.

How should the notion of employee loyalty apply in computing/IT contexts? Do computer/IT professionals necessarily have an obligation to be loyal to their employers? Let us assume for the sake of argument that, all things being equal, computer/IT professionals should be loyal to their employers. However, sometimes, an employee's obligation of loyalty can conflict with other obligations, such as those to society in general, especially where health and safety considerations are at stake.

How are computer/IT professionals supposed to balance their obligation of loyalty to an employer against their obligations of loyalty that lie elsewhere? Even if a computer/IT professional has a prima facie obligation (i.e., all things being equal) of loyalty to his or her employer, it does not follow that he or she has an absolute obligation of loyalty! Consider that computer/IT professionals, because of the nature of the critical-safety projects they work on, can also have an obligation to society as a whole, especially since safety and health issues can arise. Divided loyalties of this type, of course, can result in serious conflicts for employees, and in certain cases, the moral dilemmas they generate are so profound that an employee must determine whether to blow the whistle.

4.4.2 Whistle-Blowing

What, exactly, is whistle-blowing? We first note that there is no "standard" or universally agreed-upon definition of this controversial activity. However, a plausible definition has been put forth by John Boatright, who describes whistle-blowing as

> the voluntary release of nonpublic information, as a moral protest, by a member or former member of an organization outside the channels of communication to an appropriate audience about illegal and/or immoral conduct in the organization that is opposed in some significant way to the public interest.[21]

Boatright's description identifies three key requirements regarding the nature of the *information* revealed in a whistle-blowing act, noting that this information must be:

1. Nonpublic
2. Voluntarily disclosed by a member, or former member, of an organization
3. Presented to an "appropriate" audience

Additionally, Boatright's description requires that the information revealed to the appropriate source is about conduct deemed to be (i) illegal and/or immoral in nature and (ii) harmful to the general public (if not revealed). Each point deserves further development and elaboration; to do that, however, would take us beyond the scope of this section and chapter. For our purposes, we will accept Boatright's description as our working definition of whistle-blowing. We should also note, however, that this definition does not specifically mention any of the kinds, or distinct categories, of whistle-blowing that can be articulated. To that end, Luegenbiehl (2015) and De George (2010) both draw helpful distinctions for differentiating some relevant categories of whistle-blowing. For example, Luegenbiehl distinguishes between what he calls "open" and "anonymous" whistle-blowing, noting that the identity of the whistle-blower is known in the former type but not in the latter. And De George articulates some helpful distinctions that he bases on three contrasting sets of concepts:

- Internal vs. external
- Personal vs. impersonal
- Governmental vs. nongovernmental[22]

We briefly consider examples of each. De George's category of "internal whistle-blowing" includes the typical kinds of disclosures made by employees to their supervisors, or by students to their teachers or administrators, that is, *within* their respective organizations. Situations where an employee or a student reports an incident of harassment affecting oneself would fall under De George's category of "personal whistle-blowing," as opposed to what we think of as more typical instances of "impersonal whistle-blowing" that are directed to broader kinds of concerns (i.e., beyond merely the interests of oneself). His category of "governmental whistle-blowing" includes examples in which government employees (as well as employees of firms that have government contracts) divulge abuse (e.g., involving the misuse of power, money, etc.) in one or more government agencies. Instances in which one or more employees—either governmental or nongovernmental employees—go outside the organization to make their revelations fall under De George's category of external whistle-blowing.[23] Note that our focus in this chapter will be mainly on instances of ("open") whistle-blowing that qualify both as impersonal and external, but which also span governmental and nongovernmental contexts.

Having articulated some distinct categories of whistle-blowing, we next ask, Who, exactly, is—i.e., who qualifies as—a legitimate *whistle-blower*? Bok (2003) defines a whistle-blower as an individual who makes "revelations meant to call attention to negligence, abuses, or dangers that threaten the public interest."[24] Bok also points out that because whistle-blowers make public their disagreement with their employers or with some authority, their activities can be viewed as a form of "dissent." As Brenkert (2010) notes, however, the whistle-blower's act of (voluntary) disclosure or revelation must also be *deliberate*; in other words, it cannot be accidental.

Are whistle-blowers heroes or are they villains, or perhaps something in between? Although they are sometimes perceived as traitors and snitches, whistle-blowers have also been viewed by others as brave and heroic individuals. In 2002, for example, three whistle-blowers—Cynthia Cooper (a WorldCom employee), Coleen Rowley (an FBI employee), and Sherron Watkins (an Enron employee)—were named "Persons of the Year" by *Time* magazine. But many whistle-blowers have been maligned by their supervisors and coworkers, and they have sometimes been described as "enemies" of business or of the public good (even in cases where the disclosures they made would seem morally justified in light of the harm that otherwise could have resulted). In the past, many whistle-blowers have put their professional careers on the line, and in some cases, they have even put their lives in danger. So, it would seem prudent for prospective whistle-blowers to be well aware of the risks involved before following through with their actions.

Determining When to Blow the Whistle

When should an employee blow the whistle? Consider an incident in which Colleen Rowley came forth to describe how critical messages had failed to be sent up the Federal Bureau's chain of command in the days immediately preceding the tragic events of September 11, 2001. Was it appropriate for her to blow the whistle on her supervisor, or was she being disloyal to her supervisor and her fellow employees in doing so? Also, consider employees in positions of authority in corporations and major financial institutions who were in positions to blow the whistle about their companies' illegal accounting practices, as Cynthia Cooper (at WorldCom) and Sherron Watkins (at Enron) had both done. One could argue that failure to blow the whistle on key individuals and corporations involved in deceptive practices leading up to the 2008–2009 downturn in the U.S. economy resulted in thousands of people losing their retirement savings, and in some cases, their entire lifesavings. For example, if someone had blown the whistle on Bernie Madoff (and other notorious financiers who used "Ponzi," or Ponzi-like, schemes to deceive investors), the financial losses suffered by many investors, as well as the damage to the U.S. economy (in general) during that period, might have far less severe.

In other cases, an employee's blowing could result in saving human lives. Consider, for example, the Space Shuttle Challenger disaster (in 1986), which resulted in the deaths of the seven crew members. Subsequent reports of this incident in the press revealed that the engineers who designed the space shuttle were well aware of the safety risks in launching the shuttle in cooler temperatures. In fact, some engineers, when learning that the Challenger was scheduled for launch on a cool January morning, went to their supervisors to express their concerns. Despite the worries of these engineers, however, NASA officials elected to stick with the original launch date. Given that the engineers received no support from their supervisors, should they have gone directly to the press? Many believe that the engineers involved had a professional responsibility to blow the whistle on their management team.

We have not yet considered a case of whistle-blowing in a computing/IT context per se. One that occurred in the early 1980s, which some now view as a classic whistle-blowing case in cyberethics, involved a U.S. military proposal called the Strategic Defense Initiative (SDI). SDI, which was more informally referred to in the media during that time as "Star Wars," was a national missile defense (NMD) system whose purpose was to provide a "defense shield" in the United States against incoming ballistic missiles. While supporters argued that SDI was essential for America's national security and defense, some critics countered that the system's software was unreliable and thus could not be counted on to perform adequately. One critic, David Parnas, went public with his concerns about SDI, one of which was based on his conclusion that there would not be sufficient time during an attack to repair and reinstall software that failed.[25]

Some SDI supporters accused Parnas of being disloyal, as well as acting out of his own self-interest. With respect to the latter charge, however, Parnas' defenders pointed out that he had walked away from a very lucrative consulting contract. (As a consultant on the SDI project in the early 1980s, he was paid $1,000 per day for his expertise.) Yurcik and Doss (2002) believe some of the concerns expressed by Parnas also apply in the controversy surrounding the most recent proposal for an SDI-like initiative—namely, the NMD proposed by the George W. Bush administration in 2001. (Recall that in Chapter 3, we briefly described that version of NMD in connection with our sample arguments illustrating both valid and invalid logical forms.) We next consider a more recent case of whistle-blowing that also involves a national security-related concern.

▶ SCENARIO 4–2: NSA Surveillance and the Case of Edward Snowden

In May 2013, Edward Snowden, a former employee of the National Security Agency (NSA) contractor Booz Allen Hamilton, leaked sensitive national security-related material both to *Washington Post* and *The Guardian*. The leaked reports revealed that the NSA used at least three Internet surveillance programs, known internally as Tempora, PRISM, and XKeyscore. The reports also revealed that the NSA collected "metadata" from telephone communications that it had intercepted both in the United States and Europe. Many of Snowden's critics have since claimed that the sheer scale of the material involved in this incident makes it the "most significant leak" in U.S. history. Whereas some of Snowden's critics have described him as a dissident and a "traitor" (who has also caused grave damage to U.S. intelligence capabilities), at least some of his defenders view him as a "hero" and a "patriot" (in part, at least, because they believe that Snowden's disclosure showed how the U.S. government had gone too far in its surveillance practices on its own citizens as well as on many of the leaders of closely allied nations).[26] ■

Does Snowden's voluntary and deliberate act of leaking this information to the press qualify as a genuine instance of whistle-blowing? As we saw in Chapter 3, some of Snowden's critics claimed that he was "not a whistle-blower" but instead a traitor, a liar, and a narcissist. But as we also noted in Chapter 3, some of these attacks commit logical fallacies (such as the *Ad Hominem* fallacy and the False Dichotomy). We saw, for example, that even if Snowden were a narcissist (an *ad hominem* attack on Snowden as a person), that would not necessarily preclude his having been a (genuine) whistle-blower as well. And one's being both a traitor and a whistle-blower is not a contradiction, since all whistle-blowers (by definition) betray the trust of an organization on which they blow the whistle. So, criticisms to the effect that someone is *either* a whistle-blower *or* an organizational betrayer commit the False Dichotomy Fallacy.

Although the kinds of arguments described in preceding paragraph may fail to establish the conclusions drawn by Snowden's critics, we can still ask whether Snowden's actions meet the conditions for being a (genuine) whistle-blower. Following the criteria put forth by Bok (described previously), it would appear that Snowden had indeed made "revelations" that were meant to call attention to abuses that "threaten the public interest," and that his act could also be viewed as a form of "dissent." And in compliance with Brenkert's insight, Snowden's act was "deliberate" (and not accidental). So, Snowden's actions seem to meet the relevant criteria. As to questions about which kind or category of whistle-blowing Snowden engaged in, we can see that it complies with Luegenbiehl's criterion for "open" (as opposed to anonymous). And, finally, Snowden's actions would seem to satisfy De George's criteria for *external, impersonal, and governmental* whistle-blowing. However, whether Snowden was also morally justified in blowing the whistle is a question that has been and continues to be hotly disputed.

We should note that Snowden, in defending his actions (as an American citizen), pointed out that he took an oath to support and defend the U.S. Constitution, whose fourth and fifth Amendments forbid "systems of massive, pervasive surveillance."[27] Snowden also claimed that his "sole motive" for leaking the documents was "to inform the public as to that which is done in their name and that which is done against them."[28] Nevertheless, in June 2013, the U.S. government officially charged Snowden with "theft of government property, unauthorized communication of national defense information" and "willful communication of classified communications intelligence information to an unauthorized person."[29]

Can Snowden's actions be defended on moral grounds, even if they violated one or more U.S. laws? Unfortunately, much of the highly charged rhetoric on both sides of this debate has failed to address the key question of whether Snowden's behavior was morally justifiable. (In fact, we have already noted some of rhetoric in the *ad hominem* attacks against Snowden.) To analyze the moral aspects of this case, we need a viable framework or model of whistle-blowing. While numerous frameworks have been advanced, Brenkert (2010) notes the most popular have been variations of what he calls the "harm theory" of whistle-blowing. He also points out that the most well-known version of this theory is the model articulated by De George (1999, 2010). We next examine that model, which draws an important distinction between whistle-blowing actions that are morally permissible and those that are morally obligated.[30]

De George's Model for Evaluating Whistle-Blowing

De George proposes a series of conditions for determining when an employee is (i) morally permitted to blow the whistle and (ii) morally obligated to do so. He believes that employees are morally permitted to go public with information about the safety of a product, or a policy, when three key conditions are satisfied. For our purposes, we can summarize De George's three conditions as follows:

1. The "policy" will do "serious and considerable harm" to the public.
2. The employee(s) have reported the "serious threat" to their immediate supervisor and have made "their moral concern known."
3. The employee(s) have exhausted the "internal procedures and possibilities" within the organization, including going to the board of directors, if necessary.[31]

While De George argues that one is morally permitted to blow the whistle when conditions 1–3 are satisfied, he does not believe that a person is yet morally required to do so. To have a strict moral obligation to blow the whistle, De George believes that two additional conditions must be satisfied:

4. The employee(s) have "accessible, documented evidence that would convince a reasonable, impartial, observer that one's view of the situation is correct."
5. The employee(s) have "good reasons to believe that by going public the necessary changes will be brought about."[32]

Applying De George's Model in the Snowden Case

We should note that De George includes a caveat with Condition 5, pointing out that the whistle-blower's chance of "being successful must be worth the risk one takes and the danger to which one is exposed."[33] We should also note that De George intends his model to be applied in *nongovernmental* cases of whistle-blowing, which would seem to rule out the Snowden case (since Snowden was an employee of a company that had contracts with the U.S. government). But De George also suggests that his model might work in some instances of external whistle-blowing involving governmental organizations/agencies as well.[34] So, it would be interesting to see whether his model could apply in the Snowden controversy (which on De George's criteria would be an instance of "governmental, external, impersonal" whistle-blowing).

In extending his model to this case, we begin by asking whether Snowden's actions satisfy De George's first three criteria, which pertain to "moral permissibility." Arguably, Snowden had satisfied De George's first criterion, or condition, insofar as Snowden showed how the NSA's massive surveillance techniques targeting the phone uses and Internet practices of U.S. citizens caused "serious and considerable harm" to the public. Even if one objects that no American citizens were "physically harmed" because of the NSA's surveillance techniques, the psychological harm caused to U.S. citizens as well as the international fallout resulting from the disclosure that "friendly" heads of states were among those being monitored (in the NSA surveillance scheme) would clearly seemed to have caused "considerable harm" to American citizens as well as to the U.S.'s reputation abroad.

It is more difficult to show that Snowden had also satisfied De George's second and third conditions. But we should note that Snowden has claimed (in various interviews, including a televised *NBC News* interview with Brian Williams) that he had indeed gone to his immediate supervisors first.[35] So, he may have satisfied Condition 2. However, it is less clear that Snowden satisfied De George's third condition, that is, by going up the appropriate chain of command. And if Snowden had failed to do that, it would seem to follow (on De George's criteria) that Snowden's act of whistle-blowing was not morally permissible. Yet, some of Snowden's supporters believe that he had good reasons for not pursuing the chain of command.[36]

If, however, Snowden failed to satisfy the third condition in De George's model, we could infer that Snowden was not morally permitted to blow the whistle. Yet, we also noted that if some of Snowden's supporters are correct, there may have been very good reasons for why Snowden did not (and could not successfully) comply with Condition 3. So, given these mitigating circumstances, it still might be useful for us to go ahead and ask whether Snowden's actions satisfied De George's fourth and fifth conditions. Consider that Snowden's actions seem to comply with Condition 4, in that Snowden arguably had "documented evidence that would convince a reasonable, impartial, observer that [his] view of the situation is correct." Also, consistent with Condition 5 in De George's framework, Snowden had "good reasons to believe that by going public the necessary changes w[ould] be brought about." So, it is possible that Snowden may well have satisfied De George's criteria for being "morally required" to go public, even if he failed to satisfy one (or more) of De George's first three conditions for being "morally permitted" to blow the whistle.

Of course, we can question whether De George's criteria are too stringent, as some critics have suggested, or too lenient, as others have argued. We could also question whether De George's model puts too much emphasis on the criterion of "serious harm," at the expense of other important criteria that also apply in evaluating whistle-blowing cases; this critique has also been made by some of De George's critics.[37] However, we will not pursue those criticisms here. And, in fairness to De George, we should also note that he intends to limit the application of his model to nongovernmental cases whistle-blowing. Nevertheless, we chose to apply it in the Snowden case because his model is both well known and well respected and because De George himself has also suggested that it might be extended to some governmental cases as well.[38] We should also note that a virtue of De George's model is that it has been very helpful in analyzing instances of whistle-blowing in engineering contexts (including the classic Ford Pinto case). His model also provides engineers with a fairly clear and straightforward set of guidelines to consider in morally complex cases, without also requiring them to be what some call "moral saints" and what De George calls "moral heroes."[39]

We conclude this section by noting that much more could be said about whistle-blowing and about the Snowden case. We also note that other prominent controversial cases associated with whistle-blowing were not examined here. For example, one might ask why the WikiLeaks controversy was not considered. That controversy is examined instead in Chapter 7, in Section 7.9.

▶ 4.5 MORAL RESPONSIBILITY, LEGAL LIABILITY, AND ACCOUNTABILITY

So far, our examination of issues involving the moral responsibility of computing/IT professionals has focused mainly on questions concerning employee loyalty and whistle-blowing. We have seen that some of these questions have centered on the responsibilities of computing/IT professionals as individuals, whereas others have dealt with responsibilities facing the computing/IT profession. We have also noted that these questions illustrate essential differences between issues of responsibility involving microethics and macroethics. However, we have not yet fully considered the concept of moral responsibility itself.

Philosophers often describe the concept of moral responsibility in terms of two conditions that must be satisfied: causality and intent. In other words, some agent, X, is held morally responsible for an act, Y, if X caused Y. Here, a person could be held responsible even if he or she did not intend the outcome. Consider a scenario in which a camper, whose careless behavior in failing to put out a camp fire properly resulted in a major forest fire that caused millions of dollars in damage, claims that he did not intend the damage that resulted. Nonetheless, the camper can be held responsible as a moral "agent" for the outcome caused by his careless behavior. Agents can also be held morally responsible when they intend for something to happen, even if they ultimately fail to cause (or to bring about) the intended outcome. For example, consider a scenario in which a disgruntled student intends to blow up a college's computer lab, but at the last minute is discovered and prevented from doing so. Even though the student failed to carry out his objective—cause the bomb to detonate in the computer lab—we hold the student morally culpable because of his intentions.

4.5.1 Distinguishing Responsibility from Liability and Accountability

It would be helpful at this point to distinguish responsibility from the related notions of liability and accountability. Responsibility differs from liability in that the latter is a legal concept, sometimes used in the narrow sense of "strict liability." To be strictly liable for harm is to be liable to compensate for it even though one did not necessarily bring it about through faulty action. Here, the moral notion of blame may be left out. A property owner may be legally liable for an injury to a guest who falls in the property owner's house, but it does not necessarily follow that the property owner was also morally responsible for any resulting injury. (We elaborate on the notion of liability in Section 4.5.3, where we examine some legal liability issues affecting producers of defective computer software.)

Nissenbaum (2007) distinguishes between responsibility and accountability by suggesting that responsibility is only part of what is covered by the "robust and intuitive notion of accountability." In Nissenbaum's scheme, accountability is a broader concept than responsibility, and means that someone, or some group of individuals, or perhaps even an entire organization, is "answerable." In a computing context, she notes that accountability means:

> there will be someone, or several people to *answer* . . . for malfunctions in life-critical systems that cause or risk grave injuries and cause infrastructure and large monetary losses . . .[40]

Table 4-2 summarizes the elements we have used to differentiate moral responsibility, legal liability, and accountability.

TABLE 4-2 Responsibility, Legal Liability, and Accountability

Moral Responsibility	Legal Liability	Accountability
Attributes blame (or praise) to individuals	Does not attribute blame or fault to those held liable	Does not necessarily attribute blame (in a moral sense)
Usually attributed to individuals rather than collectivities or groups	Typically applies to corporations and property owners	Can apply to individuals, groups of individuals, and corporations
Notions of guilt and shame apply, but no legal punishment or compensation need result	Compensation can be required even when responsibility in a formal sense is not admitted	Someone or some group is answerable (i.e., it goes beyond mere liability)

Nissenbaum believes that the notion of accountability has been "systematically undermined" in the computer era, despite the fact that we are increasingly dependent on safety-critical and life-critical systems controlled by computers. In Section 4.2, we saw that safety-critical applications included software used in aircraft and air traffic control systems, in nuclear reactors, in missile systems, and in medical treatment systems, as well as in the selection of water disposal sites and in the design of bridges and buildings. Nissenbaum argues that a major barrier to attributing accountability to the developers of safety-critical software is the problem of "many hands."

4.5.2 Accountability and the Problem of "Many Hands"

Computer systems are typically developed in large organizational settings. Because these systems are the products of engineering teams or of corporations, as opposed to the products of a single programmer working in isolation, Nissenbaum notes that "many hands" are involved in their development. Thus, it is very likely that no single individual grasps all of the code used in developing a particular safety-critical system.[41] As a result, it is difficult to determine who exactly is accountable whenever one of these safety-critical systems results in personal injury or harm to individuals; it is not always clear whether the manufacturer of the system hardware (the machine itself) or the engineering teams that developed the system's software, or both, should be held accountable.

When thinking about the problem of many hands from the perspective of strict moral responsibility, as opposed to accountability, two difficulties arise: First, we tend to attribute moral responsibility for an accident to an individual, but not to groups or "collectivities." Thus, we sometimes encounter difficulties when we try to attribute blame to an organization. Nissenbaum suggests that by using "accountability", we can avoid the tendency to think only at the level of individuals in matters typically associated with assigning moral responsibility.

The second difficulty arises because the concept of moral responsibility is often thought of as exclusionary, as Ladd (1995) points out. In other words, if we can show that A is responsible for C, then we might infer that B cannot be held responsible for C. Ladd believes that moral responsibility should be viewed as nonexclusionary because both A and B (and possibly others) can be responsible for C. Nissenbaum suggests that we can avoid this confusion if we use "accountability" instead of "responsibility"; in her scheme, holding Sally accountable for making unauthorized copies of proprietary software does not necessarily preclude holding Harry accountable as well (e.g., if Harry pays Sally for making copies of the pirated software).

So Nissenbaum believes that holding one individual accountable for some harm need not necessarily let others off the hook, because several individuals may be accountable. Nor does it mean letting organizations off the hook, because they too may be accountable. As Nissenbaum puts the matter, "We should hold each fully accountable because many hands ought not necessarily lighten the burden of accountability." The following scenario (involving the Therac-25 machine, which we described briefly in the opening section of this chapter) illustrates how the involvement of "many hands" can obscure the process in determining accountability for accidents affecting some safety-critical systems.

▶ **SCENARIO 4–3:** The Case of the *Therac-25 Machine*

The Therac-25 was a computer-controlled radiation treatment machine built by Atomic Energy of Canada Limited (AECL). Between 1985 and 1987, six reported incidents occurred in which patients were severely overdosed by the Therac-25. As a result of the severe burns caused by the excessive radiation dosages, three individuals died, and three others had irreversible injuries.[42] ■

Eventually, the Therac-25 malfunction was traced not to a single source but to numerous faults, including two significant software coding errors ("bugs") and a faulty microswitch. One bug involved radiation dosage errors: If a subsequent request to change a previously entered radiation dosage was entered in a certain sequence through the user interface, a software bug caused the new entry to be ignored, and the entry instructing the original dosage was used. Instead of receiving 200 RADs, one radiation patient received 20,000 RADs; this patient died shortly afterward from excessive radiation (Leveson and Turner 2001).

Several interesting questions regarding the locus of responsibility were raised in the wake of the Therac-25 accidents. Who, exactly, should be held accountable for the deaths and injuries that resulted from the computer malfunction? Is the hospital, which may be found legally liable, also accountable in a larger sense? Should the company that manufactured and sold the Therac system to the hospital be held accountable? Were the engineers and programmers who worked on the design and development of this system ultimately responsible for the injuries and deaths caused to the radiation patients? Should they be held legally liable?

Nissenbaum argues that guidelines for producing safer and more reliable computers should include a standard of care that incorporates (i) a formal analysis of system modules (as well as of the entire system), (ii) meaningful quality assurance and independent auditing, and (iii) built-in redundancy.[43] She believes that a standard comprising these criteria would provide a nonarbitrary means for determining accountability; it would offer a tool for distinguishing between malfunctions due to inadequate practices and those that occur in spite of a programmer or designer's best efforts. Nissenbaum also suggests that if such standard had existed at the time Therac-25 was produced, the software developers of the system could have been held accountable for the deaths and injuries that resulted.

4.5.3 Legal Liability and Moral Accountability

In Section 4.5.1, we saw that legal liability can be distinguished from both moral responsibility and accountability. Nissenbaum believes that in computer/IT contexts, it is important to keep "accountability" distinct from "liability to compensate." She concedes that liability offers a partial solution to problems resulting from computer malfunctions, because at least it addresses the needs of the victims; however, she also notes that accepting liability as a substitute for accountability can further obscure the process of determining who is accountable for computer malfunctions.

Is it reasonable to hold computer corporations legally liable for products they sell that are either unreliable or defective? Supporters of liability law believe that holding owners legally liable makes sense because owners are typically in the best position to directly control their property. Nissenbaum believes that because ownership implies a "bundle of rights," it should also imply responsibilities such as being liable. Software owners (who are also usually the software's producers) are in the best position to directly affect the quality of the software they release to the public. Yet, ironically, the trend in the software industry, Nissenbaum points out, is to "demand maximal property protection while denying, to the extent possible, accountability." Software manufacturers frequently include disclaimers of liability on their products such as "This software is sold as is."

Nissenbaum also suggests that strict liability would shift the accountability to the producers of defective software, thereby addressing an anomaly (perhaps even a paradox) with respect to our current understanding of overall accountability: While liability laws protect the public against potential harm, most producers of software deny accountability for software errors. Producers sometimes base their argument on the notion that software is prone to error in ways that other technologies are not. Nissenbaum concludes that strict liability laws can send a message cautioning software producers to take extraordinary care to produce safe and reliable systems.

▶ 4.6 DO SOME COMPUTER CORPORATIONS HAVE SPECIAL MORAL OBLIGATIONS?

Before concluding our chapter on professional responsibility, we return to a question raised in Section 4.2 concerning whether computer/IT professionals in particular or the computing profession in general has any special moral responsibilities. There, we focused on (microlevel) professional responsibility-related issues for those individuals (e.g., software engineers) responsible for developing life-critical and safety-critical applications. However, we postponed our consideration of whether any computer corporations themselves, by virtue of the social impact of their products and services, might also have some special moral obligations to society (a macrolevel, professional responsibility concern). In Section 4.5, we saw that it indeed made sense to attribute moral accountability to computer corporations (as well as to the individuals who comprise them). So, we are now in a much better position (than we were in Section 4.2) to ask whether any of those corporations might also have some special moral obligations that differentiate them from other kinds of corporations.

Among the kinds of computer companies that might have special moral obligations, at least two would seem to be plausible candidates: (i) major search engine companies and (ii) companies that develop autonomous systems. Regarding (i), many have pointed out the critical roles that search engines play in our current information society, including the dissemination of knowledge. Hinman (2005), for example, has argued that because of their privileged place in our society as "gatekeepers of the Web," major search engine companies should shoulder significant social responsibility. However, we will not analyze his argument here.[44] Instead, we will focus on (ii) in the remainder of this section.

Why should companies that develop autonomous systems have special responsibilities to society? We begin by noting that an influential report published in the United Kingdom by The Royal Academy of Engineering (2009) pointed out that *autonomous systems*—from "unmanned vehicles and robots on the battlefield, to autonomous robotic surgery devices, applications for technologies that can operate without human control, learn as they function and ostensibly make decisions"—will soon be available and that these systems raise a number of ethical, legal, and social issues. To this list, we could also add professional responsibility issues for the companies that develop these systems.

In Scenario 4–1, we examined an actual case that closely mirrors one kind of concern described in the Royal Academy's report—that is, the malfunction of a semiautonomous cannon designed to make some decisions "independent of human oversight." Recall that this incident, involving a routine test of a military weapon system in the Republic of South Africa, resulted in in human casualties. We can easily imagine similar kinds of incidents occurring in the near future where other autonomous systems are involved.

However, it is not only with life-critical applications that we need to worry about autonomous systems malfunctioning. For example, Wallach and Allen (2009) present a hypothetical scenario (set in the near future) in which autonomous software agents have been designed to make financial recommendations for their human clients about when to buy and sell stock. A cluster of financial transactions initiated by these autonomous agents then triggers a series of cascading events in which other agents make decisions that ultimately result in an international catastrophe where (i) hundreds of people lose their lives and (ii) billions of dollars are lost in the financial sector. Wallach and Allen ask whether disasters of this kind could be avoided if autonomous systems are embedded with the appropriate kinds of ethical decision-making procedures (software code) that will enable them to make "good moral decisions."

Should the companies that develop these systems be held responsible for "moral-decision-making software code" that they build into them? Wallach, Allen, and others suggest that they should.[45] But to whom, exactly, should these companies be responsible in the event that the autonomous machines they develop result in accidental human deaths or in severe economic loss? The lack of a clear answer to this question would seem to suggest that explicit policies and laws are needed to anticipate, rather than have to react to, this and related concerns in light of the profound societal impact that autonomous systems will likely have.

In Chapter 12, we examine some broader ethical issues involving the development and use of autonomous machines. There, for example, we consider some implications that the future development of these machines will likely have for our notions of autonomy and trust. In this chapter, however, we simply pose the question of whether the companies that develop autonomous machines may have some special moral responsibilities to society. It would seem that a plausible case can be made for the view that they do.

We conclude this section by noting that there may indeed be other kinds of computer corporations that also have special responsibilities to society in light of the significant social impacts of their products and services. In some ways, concerns of this type are more appropriately analyzed under the category "business ethics." To the extent that these concerns particularly affect computer/IT professionals, however, they also warrant discussion within the context of cyberethics (and professional responsibility) as well.

▶ 4.7 CHAPTER SUMMARY

In this chapter, we examined some ethical problems that confront computer/IT professionals, and we focused on some specific issues and challenges that software engineers and their team members sometimes face in the development of safety-critical software. We saw that professional codes of ethics/conduct are useful insofar as they inspire and educate professionals entering and working in the fields of computing and IT. We also saw, however, that many professional codes have serious limitations. We noted that the IEEE-CS/ACM SECEPP was designed to avoid many of the shortcomings of earlier professional codes of ethics.

We also considered questions having to do with employee loyalty, especially in cases where computer/IT professionals have conflicting obligations involving their employers and the public good. We then considered criteria for determining when these professionals would be morally justified in blowing the whistle; in particular, we examined conditions for distinguishing between when professionals may be "permitted" to blow the whistle vs. situations in which they might also be "required" to blow the whistle. Next we saw that because the notion of accountability in the context of computing has become diffused by the "problem of many hands," it is not always easy to determine where accountability and responsibility for computer malfunctions and errors in safety-critical software systems ultimately lie. We also saw why it was important to differentiate among the concepts of accountability, responsibility, and liability. Finally, we asked whether some computer corporations may have special moral responsibilities due to the significant societal impact of the technologies they develop.

Among the relevant professional ethics-related concerns not considered in this chapter are issues involving the notions of risk and risk analysis in the context of computing/IT systems; these are examined in Chapter 6. Also not examined in this chapter are professional ethics issues surrounding "open" vs. "closed" software development methodologies. Some ethical aspects of methodologies used in software development are examined in Chapter 8 in our discussion of open-source software (OSS) and free software foundation (FSF) development. An ethical issue that also has implications for computer professionals but not examined in this chapter involves the global outsourcing of programming jobs. This controversy is briefly considered in Chapter 10 in connection with our discussion of globalization and the transformation of work. Another professional-ethics-related question not considered in this chapter is whether computer/IT professionals should participate in nanocomputing research and development, given certain kinds of controversies surrounding nanotechnology. This question is briefly examined in Chapter 12.

▶ REVIEW QUESTIONS

1. What is professional ethics?
2. What is a profession, and who is a professional?
3. Who is a computer/IT professional?
4. Do computer/IT professionals have special moral responsibilities that ordinary computer users do not have?
5. How do Don Gotterbarn, Keith Miller, and Simon Rogerson propose that we define the profession of software engineering?
6. According to Gotterbarn, what responsibilities do software engineers and their teams have that differentiate them from other professionals working in the computer field?
7. How is "safety-critical software" defined by Kevin Bowyer?
8. What are professional codes of ethics, and what functions do they serve?
9. Briefly describe John Ladd's criticisms of professional codes.
10. Explain Gotterbarn's threefold distinction: codes of ethics, codes of conduct, and codes of practice.
11. Do Gotterbarn's distinctions help to eliminate any of the criticisms that have been raised against professional codes?
12. How does the IEEE-CS/ACM SECEPP improve on earlier professional codes affecting software engineers?
13. What, exactly, is whistle-blowing? What are the key elements in John Boatright's definition of whistle-blowing?
14. How does Richard De George differentiate the following whistle-blowing categories: internal vs. external, personal vs. impersonal, and governmental vs. nongovernmental?
15. According to Sissela Bok, what conditions must an employee satisfy to qualify a legitimate whistle-blower?
16. Can professional codes of conduct adequately guide engineers in determining when it would be appropriate to blow the whistle and when it would not?
17. What does Helen Nissenbaum mean by "accountability" in a computing context?
18. How is Nissenbaum's notion of accountability different from the concepts of liability and responsibility?
19. What does Nissenbaum mean by "the problem of many hands" in a computing/IT context?
20. Why do some computer corporations, including companies that develop autonomous systems, have special societal obligations?

▶ DISCUSSION QUESTIONS

21. Evaluate Richard De George's criteria for when it is morally permissible, as opposed to when it is morally required, for an engineer to blow the whistle (described in Section 4.4.2). Apply these criteria to a recent controversy where you believe that blowing the whistle would have been morally permissible or perhaps even morally required.
22. Describe some virtues of the ethical codes of conduct adopted by professional societies such as the ACM and IEEE-CS, and list some shortcomings of these professional codes as well. In the final analysis, do the advantages of having a code outweigh the prospects of not having one? Use either an actual or a hypothetical case to establish the main points in your answer. Do you believe that a coherent and comprehensive code of conduct for the computing/IT profession is possible? Does SECEEP satisfy those conditions?
23. Recall the various arguments that we examined as to when it is appropriate, and sometimes mandatory, for software engineers and IT professionals to blow the whistle. The criteria for when whistle-blowing is permissible, at least for those working in some federal government agencies, changed following the September 11, 2001, terrorist attacks. In November 2002, the Homeland Security Act was passed in both houses of Congress and was signed into law by former President George W. Bush. On one interpretation of the revised law, whistle-blowing acts similar to that of Colleen Rowley—who blew the whistle on her FBI superiors who failed to act on information they received in the days preceding September 11—would be illegal and thus a punishable offense. What implications could this have for software engineers and other computer professionals whose employment comes under the auspices of the Homeland Security Department? In this case, what set of rules should computer/IT professionals follow?

Scenarios for Analysis

1. Describe the process of ethical deliberation that you would use in trying to resolve the following dilemma.

   You have been working for the XYZ Computer Corporation as an entry-level software engineer since you graduated from college last May. You have done very well so far; you are respected by the management team, are well liked by your fellow engineers, and have been assigned to a team of engineers that has consistently worked on the most critical and valued projects and contracts that XYZ Corp. has secured. XYZ's most recent contract is for a U.S. defense project involving the missile defense system, and again you have been assigned to the engineering team that will develop the software for this project. However, you are staunchly opposed to the project's objectives, so you ask to be reassigned. Your supervisor and coworkers, as well as upper management, are disappointed to learn of your strong feelings about this project. You are asked to reconsider your views, and you are promised a bonus and a substantial pay increase if you agree to work on this project during the next year. You also discover from a colleague that refusing to work on this project would greatly diminish your career advancement at XYZ and may even make you vulnerable in the event of future layoffs. To compound matters, you and your spouse are expecting your first child in about three months, and you recently purchased a home. What would you do in this case?

2. In analyzing the following scenario, what course of action would you take? Would you be willing to blow the whistle? Explain your position.

   For the past six months, you have worked on a project to develop a transportation-related software program for the city of Agropolis, a project designed to make some much needed improvements to Agropolis's system of public transportation. You and your team of programmers have worked very hard on this project, but you have encountered difficulties that could not possibly have been anticipated in the original design plan; these difficulties have put your project significantly behind schedule. The city transportation planners are nervous, because they depend on the software from your company to get the new transportation system up and running. And the management at your company is very uncomfortable because it signed a contract to deliver the required software on time. Although the software is not yet foolproof, testing so far reveals that it works about 99% of the time. The few glitches that remain apply only to the transportation system's backup code, which arguably would be needed in only the most severe emergencies. Residents of the city are also eager to have the new transportation system in place.

   A decision is made by the management of your company and by the managers of the city transportation system to go ahead and implement the software as it is. They base their decision on the probability that a backup system would not be needed for several months (at which time the remaining bugs should be fixed). A decision was also made by the management groups on both sides not to announce publicly that the software still has a few bugs. You and a few of your coworkers believe that the bugs are more dangerous than the managers are willing to admit. What would you do in this case?

▶ ENDNOTES

1. See Shachtman (2007) for an interesting account of this incident, which is also briefly described in Wallach and Allen (2009).
2. See Leveson and Turner (2001).
3. See, for example, Gotterbarn (1995).
4. See Davis (2015a, pp. 489–90) for more details on these distinctions.
5. Barger (2008, p. 85).
6. Buchanan (2004, p. 620).
7. Buchanan suggests that an "information professional" can be conceived of along these lines.
8. Gotterbarn, Miller, and Rogerson (1999) suggest that a "software engineering team" can be thought of in terms of as those who contribute by direct participation to "the analysis, specification, design, development, certification, maintenance and testing of software systems."
9. See Bowyer (2001, p. 165).
10. See Davis (2015b, pp. 283–9).
11. The full text of IEEE Code of Ethics is available at http://www.ieee.org/web/membership/ethics/code_ethics.html.
12. The full text of the ACM Code of Ethics is available at http://web.mit.edu/afs/athena.mit.edu/course/2/2.95j/Codes-of-Ethics/ACM-Code-of-Ethics.html.
13. For a full description of these five features, see Bynum and Rogerson (2004, pp. 135–36).
14. Davis (1995, p. 586).
15. *Ibid.*
16. See Gotterbarn (2000, pp. 209–10) for more detail on these three distinctions.
17. The text of both versions of the SECEPP Code (short and full) is available at http://seeri.etsu.edu/Codes/TheSECode.htm.

18. See Gotterbarn, Miller, and Rogerson (1999).
19. Mitcham (1997, p. 262).
20. *Ibid.*
21. Boatright (2000, p. 109).
22. De George (2010, p. 300).
23. *Ibid.*
24. Bok (2003, p. 53). We should note that one virtue of Bok's definition is that it explicitly acknowledges the role that negligence can play independently of any specific and overt abuses.
25. See Parnas (1990).
26. Much has been written about the Edward Snowden controversy in the context of whistle-blowing. For an analysis of this (whistle-blowing) case from the perspectives of trust and betrayal, see Tavani and Grodzinsky (2014).
27. See Snowden (2013) for more detail. See also Griggs and Gross (2014).
28. Rieder (2013).
29. See Finn and Horwitz (2013).
30. In this section, we focus on the whistle-blowing model articulated in De George (2010). An earlier version of that model, which focuses on the classic "Pinto Case" in the context of an engineering environment, is included in De George (1999).
31. The full text for these three conditions is included in De George (2010, pp. 306–8). In Condition 1, De George also includes the notion of a "product," as well as a policy, that can cause serious harm. And he uses the expression "the firm," where we use "organization."
32. De George's fourth and fifth conditions are also presented in summarized form here. See De George (pp. 310–11) for the full text of his two conditions for being "morally required" to blow the whistle.
33. De George, p. 311.
34. *Ibid*, p. 312.
35. See Esposito, Cole, and Schone (2014).
36. For example, Daniel Ellsberg (a former whistle-blower who leaked the notorious "Pentagon Papers" in the early 1970s) believes that the reason Snowden did not pursue the appropriate chain of superiors in his organization was because he saw what had happened to those employees who had done so in previous incidents (Democracynow.org, 2014). So Ellsberg suggests that Snowden had reasonable grounds for not complying with the kind of requirement stated in De George's third condition.
37. For example, Brenkert (2010, pp. 567–70) has criticized De George's whistle-blowing model for placing too much emphasis on the criterion of "harm."
38. See, for example, De George (2010, p. 312).
39. See De George (1999, p. 184).
40. Nissenbaum (2007, p. 274). [Italics Added]
41. *Ibid*, p. 275.
42. For more detail, see Leveson and Turner (2001).
43. See Nissenbaum, p. 279. Note that she also includes some additional guidelines, such as "independent auditing" and "excellent documentation."
44. For a more detailed discussion of Hinman's argument in this context, see Tavani (2012).
45. See, for example, the views expressed on this topic by various contributors in Anderson and Anderson (2011).

▶ REFERENCES

Anderson, Michael, and Susan Leigh Anderson, eds. 2011. *Machine Ethics*. Cambridge: Cambridge University Press.

Barger, Robert N. 2003. "Can We Find a Single Ethical Code?" In M. David Ermann and Michele S. Shauf, eds. *Computers, Ethics, and Society*. New York: Oxford University Press, pp. 42–7.

Barger, Robert N. 2008. *Computer Ethics: A Case-Based Approach*. New York: Cambridge University Press.

Boatright, John R. 2000. *Ethics and the Conduct of Business*. 3rd ed. Upper Saddle River, NJ: Prentice Hall.

Bok, Sisela. 2003. "The Morality of Whistle Blowing." In M. David Ermann and Michele S. Shauf, eds. *Computers, Ethics, and Society*. 3rd ed. New York: Oxford University Press, pp. 47–54.

Bowyer, Kevin, ed. 2001. *Ethics and Computing: Living Responsibly in a Computerized World*. 2nd ed. New York: IEEE Press.

Brenkert, George G. 2010. "Whistle-Blowing, Moral Integrity, and Organizational Ethics." In George G. Brenkert and Tom L. Beauchamp, eds. *The Oxford Handbook of Business Ethics*. New York: Oxford University Press, pp. 563–601.

Buchanan, Elizabeth A. 2004. "Ethical Considerations for the Information Professions." In R. A. Spinello and H. T. Tavani, eds. *Readings in CyberEthics*. 2nd ed. Sudbury, MA: Jones and Bartlett Publishers, pp. 613–24.

Bynum, Terrell Ward, and Simon Rogerson, eds. 2004. *Computer Ethics and Professional Responsibility*. Malden, MA: Blackwell.

Davis, Michael. 1995. "Thinking Like an Engineer." In D. G. Johnson and H. Nissenbaum, eds. *Computing Ethics and Social Values*. Englewood Cliffs, NJ: Prentice Hall, pp. 586–97.

Davis, Michael. 2015a. "Profession and Professionalism." In J. Britt Holbrook and Carl Mitcham, eds. *Ethics, Science, Technology, and Engineering: A Global Resource*. Vol. 3, 2nd ed. Farmington Hills, MI: Macmillan Reference, pp. 489–93.

Davis, Michael. 2015b. "Codes of Ethics." In J. Britt Holbrook and Carl Mitcham, eds. *Ethics, Science, Technology, and Engineering: A Global Resource*. Vol. 1, 2nd ed. Farmington Hills, MI: Macmillan Reference, pp. 283–9.

De George, Richard T. 1999. "Ethical Responsibilities of Engineers in Large Corporations: The Pinto Case." In D. G. Johnson, ed. *Ethical Issues in Engineering*. Englewood Cliffs, NJ: Prentice Hall, pp. 175–86.

De George, Richard T. 2010. *Business Ethics*. 7th ed. Upper Saddle River, NJ: Pearson Prentice-Hall.

Democracynow.org. 2014. "Debate: Was Snowden Justified? Former NSA Counsel Stewart Baker vs. Whistleblower Daniel Ellsberg." Available at http://www.democracynow.org/2014/2/14/debate_was_snowden_justified_former_nsa#. Accessed 3/19/14.

Esposito, Richard, Matthew Cole, and Mark Schone. 2014. "Exclusive, Edward Snowden Gives Wide-Ranging Interview to Brian Williams." http://www.nbcnews.com/storyline/nsa-snooping/exclusive-edward-snowden-gives-wide-ranging-interview-brian-williams-n110351. Retrieved July 6.

Fairweather, N. Ben. 2004. "No PAPA: Why Incomplete Codes of Ethics are Worse than None at All." In T. W. Bynum and S. Rogerson, eds. *Computer Ethics and Professional Responsibility*. Malden, MA: Blackwell, pp. 142–56.

Finn, Peter and Sari Horwitz. 2013. "U.S. Charges Snowden with Espionage." *The Washington Post,* June 21. Available at http://www.washingtonpost.com/world/national-security/us-charges-snowden-with-espionage/2013/06/21/507497d8-dab1-11e2-a016-92547bf094cc_story.html. Accessed 1/19/15.

Gotterbarn, Don. 1995. "Computer Ethics: Responsibility Regained." In D. G. Johnson and H. Nissenbaum, eds. *Computers, Ethics and Social Values*. Englewood Cliffs, NJ: Prentice Hall, pp. 18–24.

Gotterbarn, Don. 2000. "Computer Professionals and YOUR Responsibilities." In D. Langford, ed. *Internet Ethics*. New York: St. Martin's Press, pp. 200–19.

Gotterbarn, Don. 2001. "The Ethical Software Engineer." In K. W. Bowyer, ed. *Ethics and Computing: Living Responsibly in a Computerized World*. 2nd ed. New York: IEEE Press, p. 67.

Gotterbarn, Don and Keith Miller. 2009. "The Public is Priority: Making Decisions Using the Software Code of Ethics," *IEEE Computer* 42, no. 6: 66–73.

Gotterbarn, Don, Keith Miller, and Simon Rogerson. 1999. "Software Engineering Code of Ethics Approved." *Communications of the ACM* 42, no. 10: 102–7.

Griggs, Brandon and Doug Gross. 2014. "Edward Snowden Speaks at SXSW, Calls for Public Oversight of U.S. Spy Programs". Available at http://www.cnn.com/2014/03/10/tech/web/edward-snowden-sxsw/. Accessed 1/19/15.

Harris, Charles E., Michael S. Pritchard, and Michael J. Rabins. 2009. *Engineering Ethics: Concepts and Cases*. 4th ed. Belmont, CA: Wadsworth.

Hinman, Lawrence M. 2005. "Esse Est Indicato in Google: Ethical and Political Issues in Search Engines." *International Review of Information Ethics* 3: 19–25.

Ladd, John. 1995. "The Quest for a Code of Professional Ethics: An Intellectual and Moral Confusion." In D. G. Johnson and H. Nissenbaum, eds. *Computers, Ethics and Social Values*. Englewood Cliffs, NJ: Prentice Hall, pp. 580–5.

Leveson, Nancy G. and Clark S. Turner. 2001. "An Investigation of the Therac-25 Accidents." In K. W. Bowyer, ed. *Ethics and Computing: Living Responsibly in a Computerized World*. 2nd ed. New York: IEEE Press, pp. 200–24. Reprinted from *IEEE Computer* 26, no. 7 (1993): 18–41.

Lin, Patrick. 2012. "Introduction to Robot Ethics." In P. Lin, K. Abney, and G. Bekey, eds. *Robot Ethics: The Ethical and Social Implications of Robotics*. Cambridge, MA: MIT Press, pp. 3–16.

Luegenbiehl, Heinz. 2015. "Whistleblowing." In J. Britt Holbrook and Carl Mitcham, eds. *Ethics, Science, Technology, and Engineering: A Global Resource*. Vol. 4, 2nd ed. Farmington Hills, MI: Macmillan Reference, pp. 529–31.

Martin, Michael W. and Roland Schinzinger. 2004. *Ethics in Engineering*. 4th ed. New York: McGraw-Hill.

Mitcham, Carl. 1997. "Engineering Design Research and Social Responsibility." In K. Schrader-Frechette and L. Westra, eds. *Technology and Values*. Lanham, MD: Rowman and Littlefield, pp. 261–78.

Nissenbaum, Helen. 2007. "Computing and Accountability." In J. Weckert, ed. *Computer Ethics*. Aldershot, UK: Ashgate, pp. 273–80. Reprinted from *Communications of the ACM* 37 (1994): 37–40.

Parnas, David Lorge. 1990. "Professional Responsibility to Blow the Whistle on SDI." In M. D. Ermann, M. B. Williams, and C. Guiterrez, eds. *Computers, Ethics, and Society*. New York: Oxford University Press, pp. 359–72.

Perlman, Bruce and Roli Varma. 2002. "Improving Engineering Practice," *IEEE Technology and Society* 21, no. 1: 40–7.

Rieder, Rem. 2013. "Snowden's NSA Bombshell Sparks Debate." *USA Today*, June 13. Available at http://www.usatoday.com/story/money/columnist/rieder/2013/06/12/rem-rieder-surveillance/2415753/. Accessed 1/19/15.

Shachtman, Noah. 2007. "Robotic Cannon Kills 9, Wounds 14." Wired, 10.18.07. Available at http://www.wired.com/2007/10/robot-cannon-ki/.

Snowden, Edward. 2013. "Statement to Human Rights Group (in Full)." *The Daily Telegraph*, July 12. Available at http://www.telegraph.co.uk/news/worldnews/europe/russia/10176529/Edward-Snowdens-statement-to-human-rights-groups-in-full.html. Accessed 11/30/13.

Tavani, Herman T. 2012. "Search Engines and Ethics." *Stanford Encyclopedia of Philosophy*. Available at http://plato.stanford.edu/entries/ethics-search/.

Tavani, Herman T. and Frances Grodzinsky. 2014. "Trust, Betrayal, and Whistle-Blowing: Reflections on the Edward Snowden Case." *Computers and Society* 44, no. 3: 8–13.

The Royal Academy of Engineering. 2009. *Autonomous Systems: Social, Legal and Ethical Issues*. London, UK. Available at www.raeng.org.uk/autonomoussystems.

Wallach, Wendell and Colin Allen. 2009. *Moral Machines: Teaching Robots Right from Wrong*. New York: Oxford University Press.

Yurcik, William and David Doss. 2002. "Software Technology Issues for a U.S. National Missile Defense System." *IEEE Technology and Society* 21, no. 2: 36–46.

▶ FURTHER READINGS

Allen, Colleen, and Wendell Wallach. 2012. "Moral Machines: Contradiction in Terms or Abdication of Human Responsibility." In P. Lin, K. Abney, and G. Bekey, eds. *Robot Ethics: The Ethical and Social Implications of Robotics*. Cambridge, MA: MIT Press, pp. 55–68.

Birsch, Douglas. 2004. "Moral Responsibility for Harm Caused by Computer System Failures." *Ethics and Information Technology* 6, no. 4: 233–45.

Buchanan, Elizabeth A. and Kathrine A. Henderson. 2009. *Case Studies in Library and Information Science Ethics*. Jefferson, NC: McFarland.

Friedman, Batya, Peter H. Kahn, Jr., and Alan Borning. 2008. "Value Sensitive Design and Information Systems." In K. E. Himma and H. T. Tavani, eds. *The Handbook of Information and Computer Ethics*. Hoboken, NJ: John Wiley and Sons, pp. 69–101.

Moor, James H. 2000. "If Aristotle Were a Computing Professional." In R. Baird, R. Ramsower, and S. E. Rosenbaum, eds. *Cyberethics: Social and Moral Issues in the Computer Age*. Amherst, NY: Prometheus, pp. 34–40.

Rashid, Awais, John Weckert, and Richard Lucas. 2009. "Software Engineering Ethics in a Digital World." *IEEE Computer* 42, no. 6: 34–41.

CHAPTER

5

Privacy and Cyberspace

LEARNING OBJECTIVES

Upon completing this chapter, you will successfully be able to:

- Describe the ways in which personal privacy is threatened in the digital era and determine whether cybertechnology has introduced any new or unique privacy issues,
- Explain why *privacy* is a difficult concept to define and describe the key elements of a comprehensive privacy theory that helps us to distinguish between a *loss* of privacy and a *violation* of privacy,
- Explain why privacy is valued and why it is an important social value as well as an individual good,
- Describe how one's privacy is impacted by *data-gathering* techniques such as RFID technologies and (Internet) cookies,
- Assess privacy-related concerns generated by *data-analysis* techniques involving Big Data, such as data mining and Web mining,
- Explain what is meant by the problem of protecting "privacy in public," especially in light of challenges posed by routine uses of online search facilities such as Google and social networking sites such as Facebook,
- Evaluate the debate between proponents of stronger privacy legislation and those who advocate for industry self-regulation practices as an alternative,
- Describe and assess the arguments for whether people should, in certain cases, have a right to have online personal information about them "erased," or at least "delinked" from search engine indexes.

In this chapter, we examine a wide range of privacy issues, including concerns that affect the day-to-day activities of ordinary individuals carried out in both online and offline contexts. We begin by reflecting on a scenario that illustrates some privacy concerns surrounding the opening of a controversial data center by the National Security Agency (NSA) in 2014.

▶ **SCENARIO 5–1:** A New NSA Data Center

The NSA, officially formed in 1952 and headquartered at Ft. Meade, Maryland, is one of the largest intelligence organizations in the United States (and in the world). Although the NSA's original charter was to conduct surveillance on "foreign" sources—that is, non-U.S. governments, organizations, and individuals—many critics, including reputable journalists, claim that the agency's mission has since been significantly expanded to include surveillance on American citizens as well. Sensitive documents that Edward

Snowden leaked to the press in May 2013 allegedly revealed some of the controversial surveillance techniques the NSA uses to collect data on U.S. citizens. These revelations have resulted in increased public awareness of the NSA, as well as closer media scrutiny of that organization's activities, especially in light of some embarrassing details about foreign government officials that were included in the leaked documents. (See Scenario 4–2 in Chapter 4 for more detail about controversies resulting from the documents leaked by Snowden.)

In the aftermath of the Snowden leaks, the NSA not only continued to defend its activities but has also recently opened a controversial data center, or "data farm" as some refer to it, in Utah. The new data center, which is able to gather significantly more information than was previously possible, reportedly collects phone records, text messages, e-mails, and other forms of electronic data. Privacy advocates in the United States are concerned that the new center also provides NSA with enhanced tools to analyze much of the electronic data generated by ordinary American citizens. Many NSA critics believe that the organization would have collected more data in the past but that it was hampered from doing so by limitations affecting both (i) storage capacity and (ii) the technology-related resources needed to conduct more extensive searches. But the new NSA data center (whose contents are officially classified) is reported to have 100,000 square feet of computers (to harvest data) and five zettabytes of storage capacity to house it.[1] So, critics worry that the NSA's activities now pose an even greater threat than before to the privacy of ordinary American citizens. ■

Are privacy advocates justified in their concerns about the NSA's increased ability to "spy" on American citizens and to collect vast amounts of data about them? The NSA has argued that its surveillance and data-collection techniques simply follow the organization's charter, which is to keep Americans safe. That organization's defenders suggest that in an era of global terrorism, U.S. citizens should be less concerned about their privacy and more worried about their safety. Arguably, this tension underlies one of the crucial dilemmas facing American citizens, as well as citizens in many countries around the world—namely, how much individual privacy should be we willing to trade off for increased security? But is the dichotomy between privacy and security, as articulated here, a "genuine dilemma"?[2] (Recall our analysis of the False Dichotomy/Either–Or fallacy in Chapter 3.) We examine key issues at the heart of the privacy-versus-security debate in detail in Chapter 6, and we briefly describe some concerns affecting governmental surveillance and data-collection techniques in Section 5.4.4.

The main purpose of Scenario 5–1 has been to get us to begin thinking about the value of privacy in general, especially in light of the serious challenges it faces in the second decade of the twenty-first century. For example, we will see that our privacy is threatened not only by governmental surveillance but by many of the data-collection and data-analysis techniques currently used in the commercial sector as well. This is especially apparent in the case of major search engine companies like Google, which collect vast amounts of personal information on ordinary users. So, our privacy is currently threatened on many different levels and in many different sectors.

▶ 5.1 PRIVACY IN THE DIGITAL AGE: *WHO* IS AFFECTED AND WHY SHOULD WE WORRY?

Of all the ethical and social issues associated with the digital era, perhaps none has received more media attention than concern about the loss of personal privacy. As we shall see, however, cybertechnology is not the first technology to threaten personal privacy. Nevertheless, that technology now threatens privacy in ways that were not previously possible.

5.1.1 Whose Privacy Is Threatened by Cybertechnology?

Virtually no one living today in a developed nation is exempt or immune from some kind of cybertechnology-related privacy threat. In fact, people who have never owned or never even used a networked computer are still affected. Consider that in carrying out many of our day-to-day activities, we supply information to organizations that use computers and electronic devices to record, store, and exchange those data. These activities can include information we provide in filling out various forms, or they can include information acquired from our commercial transactions in a bank or a store.

Some might assume that using the Internet only for noncommercial activities will help them to avoid many of the typical privacy threats associated with the online world, such as privacy risks associated with shopping at e-commerce sites. However, even users who navigate the Web solely for recreational purposes are at risk with respect to their privacy. For example, if you use a major search engine (such as Google) or interact in a social media site (such as Facebook), personal data about your interests and preferences can be acquired by those organizations, whose methods for collecting this information are not always obvious to ordinary users. Furthermore, personal data about us collected via our online activities can be sold to third parties.

Also consider that applications such as Google Street View (a feature of Google Earth and Google Maps) make use of satellite cameras and GPS software that enable Internet users to zoom in on your house or place of employment and potentially record information about you. Additionally, closed-circuit televisions (CCTVs) located in public places and in shopping malls record many of your daily movements as you casually stroll through those environments. So even if you have never owned or used a computer, cell phone, (Internet-enabled) electronic device, and so forth, your privacy is threatened in ways that were not possible in the past.

Concerns about privacy now affect many aspects of one's life—from commerce to healthcare to work to recreation. So, some analysts organize these concerns into categories such as consumer privacy, medical/healthcare privacy, employee/workplace privacy, etc. Although some cyber-related privacy concerns are specific to one or more spheres or sectors—that is, employment, healthcare, and so forth—others cut across multiple dimensions of our lives and thus affect each of us regardless of our employment or health status.

Unfortunately, we cannot examine all of the current privacy concerns in a single chapter. So, we will have to postpone our analysis of certain kinds of privacy issues until the later chapters in the book. For example, we will examine some cyber-related privacy concerns that conflict with cybersecurity issues and national security interests in Chapter 6, where privacy-related concerns affecting "cloud computing" are also considered. Some specific employee/workplace privacy-related issues are examined in our discussion of workplace surveillance and employee monitoring in Chapter 10. And in our analysis of emerging and converging technologies (such as nanotechnology and ambient intelligence) in Chapter 12, we examine some controversies surrounding a relatively new category of privacy called "location privacy."

Despite the significant impact that cybertechnology has had and continues to have for our privacy, one still might ask: Do any of the current privacy concerns differ in kind from privacy issues that arose in the predigital era? In other words, is there anything new, or even special, about cyber-related privacy issues? We next propose a strategy for addressing that question.

5.1.2 Are Any Privacy Concerns Generated by Cybertechnology Unique or Special?

We begin by noting that concerns about personal privacy existed long before the advent of computers and cybertechnology. Prior to the digital era, for example, technologies such as the camera and the telephone presented challenges for privacy. So we can ask: What, if anything, is special about the privacy concerns that are associated with cybertechnology? Consider the impact that changes involving this technology have had on privacy with respect to the:

- Amount of personal information that can be collected
- Speed at which personal information can be transmitted
- Duration of time that the information can be retained
- Kind of information that can be acquired and exchanged

Cybertechnology makes it possible to collect and store much more information about individuals than was possible in the predigital era. The *amount* of personal information that could be collected in that era was determined by practical considerations, such as the physical space required to store the data and the time and difficulty involved in collecting the data. Today, of course, digitized information that can be stored electronically in computer databases takes up very little storage space and can be collected with relative ease. As we will see in Section 5.5, many people are now worried about the sheer volume of personal data that can be collected and analyzed by various techniques associated with "big data" and data mining.

Next, consider the *speed* at which information is exchanged and transferred between databases. At one time, records had to be physically transported between filing destinations; the time it took to move them depended upon the transportation systems—for example, motor vehicles, trains, airplanes, and so forth—that carried the records. Now, of course, records can be transferred between electronic databases in milliseconds through wireless technologies, high-speed cable lines, or even ordinary telephone lines.

With so much information being collected and transferred so rapidly, many have expressed concerns about its accuracy as well as the difficulties in tracking down and correcting any inaccuracies that might have been transferred. In an interview conducted for the BBC TV series *The Machine that Changed the World*, Harvard law professor Arthur Miller points out that trying to correct such information is like "chasing a greased pig"—you may get your hands on the pig, but it is very difficult to keep the pig firmly in your grip.[3] Although issues concerning the accuracy of personal information are clearly distinguishable from those concerning privacy per se, accuracy issues are frequently associated with privacy issues, and both are impacted by cybertechnology.

Also, consider the *duration* of information—that is, how long information can be kept. Before the digital era, information was manually recorded and stored in file cabinets and then in large physical repositories; it is unlikely that report cards my parents received as high school students still exist somewhere as physical records in file cabinets, for at that time report cards were not computerized but instead existed, literally, as ink marks on paper. But the report cards my daughter received when she was a high school student were both generated and stored using computer technology. As an electronic record, her report card can be kept indefinitely, and the grades she received as a high school student (as well as the grades she received in elementary school and in college) can follow her throughout her life.

In the past, practices involving the retention of personal data were perhaps more "forgiving." Because of practical limitations, such as physical storage space, that affected how long personal data could be kept on file, much of the personal information collected and stored had to be destroyed after a certain number of years. Since information could not be archived indefinitely, people with blemished records sometimes had the opportunity to start over again by physically relocating. Today, however, one's electronic dossier would likely follow, making it very difficult, if not impossible, for that person to start over with a clean slate. We can argue whether the current means of data retention is a good thing, but it is difficult to dispute the claim that now, because of cybertechnology, most of us have what Arthur Miller calls a "womb-to-tomb dossier." It is also worth noting, however, that a 2014 court ruling by the European Court of Justice (ECJ) gave citizens in European nations the right, in certain cases, to have some kinds of online personal information about them deleted or "erased." We examine this principle, commonly referred to as the right to "be forgotten" or "to erasure," in detail in Section 5.8.

Cybertechnology has also generated privacy concerns because of the *kind* of personal information that can now be collected. For example, every time you engage in an electronic transaction, such as making a purchase with a credit card or withdrawing money from an ATM, transactional information is collected and stored in several computer databases; this information can then be transferred electronically across commercial networks to agencies that request it. Personal information, retrieved from transactional information that is stored in computer databases, has been used to construct electronic dossiers containing detailed information about an individual's commercial transactions, including purchases made and places traveled—information that can reveal patterns in a person's preferences and habits.

Additionally, we should note that cybertechnology raises privacy concerns because of the myriad ways in which it enables our personal information to be manipulated once it has been collected. For example, unrelated pieces of information about us that reside in separate databases can be combined to construct electronic personal dossiers or profiles. Also, information about us included in one database can be matched against records in other databases that contain information about us. Furthermore, our personal information can be mined (from databases, as well as from our activities on the Web) to reveal patterns in our behavior that would have been very difficult to discern in the predigital era. Of course, our personal data could have been, and in some instances was, manipulated in the predigital era as well. But there were practical limitations to the amount of data collection and analysis that could be done manually by humans.

Although the privacy concerns that we now associate with cybertechnology may not be totally new, or even altogether different in kind, from those we associate with earlier technologies, few would dispute the claim that cybertechnology has exacerbated them. In Sections 5.4–5.5, we examine some controversial uses of cybertechnology that raise specific concerns for personal privacy. First, however, we examine the concept of personal privacy to better understand what privacy is and why we value it.

▶ 5.2 WHAT IS PERSONAL PRIVACY?

Although many definitions have been put forth, there is no universally agreed upon definition. To understand why this concept has been so difficult to define, consider the diverse range of metaphors typically associated with privacy. Sometimes, we speak of privacy as something that can be lost or diminished, suggesting that privacy can be understood in terms of a repository of personal information that can be either diminished altogether or gradually eroded. Contrast this view with descriptions of privacy as something that can be intruded upon or invaded, where privacy can be understood in terms of a spatial metaphor, such as a zone, that deserves protection. Alternatively, privacy is sometimes described as something that can be violated or breached, when we think of it in terms of either a right or an interest that deserves legal protection. Because of these different conceptions of privacy, we will see that it is useful to distinguish between the notions of one's having privacy (in a descriptive sense) and one's having a (normative) right to privacy. We will say more about this distinction in Section 5.2.4.

Privacy analysts have pointed out that in the United States, the meaning of privacy has evolved since the eighteenth century. Initially, privacy was understood in terms of freedom from (physical) intrusion. Later, it became associated with freedom from interference into one's personal affairs, including one's ability to make decisions freely. Most recently, privacy has come to be closely identified with concerns affecting access to and control of personal information—a view that is also referred to as "informational privacy." Although the main emphasis in this chapter is on informational privacy, we also briefly describe the other two views.

5.2.1 Accessibility Privacy: Freedom from Unwarranted Intrusion

In a seminal paper on privacy, Samuel Warren and Louis Brandeis suggested that privacy could be understood as "being let alone" or "being free from intrusion." Appearing in the *Harvard Law Review* in 1890, the Warren and Brandeis article made the first explicit reference to privacy as a legal right in the United States. Many Americans are astonished to find out that there is no explicit mention of privacy in either the Constitution or its first ten amendments, the Bill of Rights. However, some legal scholars believe that a right to privacy can be inferred from the Fourth Amendment, which protects citizens against unreasonable searches and seizures of personal affects (i.e., papers, artifacts, etc.) by the government. Some legal scholars suggest that the Fourth Amendment may also provide legal grounds for a right to privacy protection from nongovernmental intrusion as well.

Warren and Brandeis also suggested that our legal right to privacy is grounded in our "right to inviolate personality." In part, they were responding to a certain use of a new technology—not the computer, of course, but rather the camera—which had begun to threaten individual privacy in new ways.[4] Photographs of people began to appear in newspapers, for example, in gossip columns, along with stories that were defamatory and sometimes even false. Warren and Brandeis believed that individuals have a (legal) right not be intruded upon in this manner. Because this definition of privacy as freedom from unwarranted intrusion focuses on the harm that can be caused through physical access to a person or to a person's possessions, DeCew (1997, 2006) and others have described this view as *accessibility privacy*.

5.2.2 Decisional Privacy: Freedom from Interference in One's Personal Affairs

Privacy is also sometimes conceived of as freedom from interference in one's personal choices, plans, and decisions; some refer to this view as decisional privacy. This kind of privacy has also been associated with reproductive technologies having to do with contraception. In *Griswold v. Connecticut* (1965), the court ruled that a person's right to get counseling about contraceptive techniques could not be denied by state laws. The view of privacy as freedom from external interference into one's personal affairs has since been appealed to in legal arguments in a series of controversial court cases, such as those involving abortion and euthanasia. For example, this view of privacy was appealed to in the landmark Supreme Court decision on abortion (*Roe v. Wade* 1973), as well as in a state court's decision involving Karen Ann Quinlan's right to be removed from life-support systems and thus her "right to die."[5] Because it focuses on one's right not to be interfered with, decisional privacy can be distinguished from both accessibility privacy and informational privacy.

5.2.3 Informational Privacy: Control over the Flow of Personal Information

Because of the increasing use of technology to gather and exchange personal information, many contemporary analysts view privacy in connection with one's ability to restrict access to and control the flow of one's personal information. Privacy concerns are now often framed in terms of questions such as: Who should have access to one's personal information? To what extent can individuals control the ways in which information about them can be gathered,

TABLE 5-1 Three Views of Privacy

Accessibility privacy	Privacy is defined as one's (physically) being let alone, or being free from intrusion into one's physical space
Decisional privacy	Privacy is defined as freedom from interference in one's choices and decisions
Informational privacy	Privacy is defined as control over the flow of one's personal information, including the ways in which that information is collected and exchanged

stored, mined, combined, recombined, exchanged, and sold? These are our primary concerns in this chapter, where we focus on informational privacy.

Table 5-1 summarizes the three views of privacy.

5.2.4 A Comprehensive Account of Privacy

James Moor has put forth a privacy framework that incorporates important elements of the nonintrusion, noninterference, and informational views of privacy. According to Moor,

> An individual [has] privacy in a *situation* with regard to others if and only if in that situation the individual [is] protected from intrusion, interference, and information access by others.[6]

An important element in this definition is Moor's notion of "situation," which he deliberately leaves broad so that it can apply to a range of contexts, or zones, that can be "declared private." For example, a situation can be an "activity" or a "relationship," or it can be the "storage and access of information" in a computer (Moor 2000).

Central to Moor's theory is a distinction between naturally private and normatively private situations, enabling us to differentiate between the conditions required for (i) having privacy and (ii) having a right to privacy. This distinction, in turn, enables us to differentiate between a loss of privacy and a violation of privacy. In a naturally private situation, individuals are protected from access and interference from others by natural means, for example, physical boundaries such as those one enjoys while hiking alone in the woods. In this case, privacy can be lost but not violated, because there are no norms—conventional, legal, or ethical—according to which one has a right, or even an expectation, to be protected. In a normatively private situation, on the other hand, individuals are protected by conventional norms (e.g., formal laws and informal policies) because they involve certain kinds of zones or contexts that we have determined to need normative protection. The following two scenarios will help us to differentiate between normative and natural (or descriptive) privacy.

▶ SCENARIO 5–2: Descriptive Privacy

Mary enters her university's computer lab at 11:00 P.M. to work on a research paper that is due the next day. No one else is in the lab at the time that Mary arrives there, and no one enters the lab until 11:45 P.M., when Tom—the computer lab coordinator—returns to close the lab for the evening. As Tom enters, he sees Mary typing on one of the desktop computers in the lab. Mary seems startled as she looks up from her computer and discovers that Tom is gazing at her. ■

Did Mary lose her privacy when Tom entered the lab and saw her? Was her privacy violated? Before Tom noticed her in the lab, we could say that Mary had privacy in the descriptive, or natural, sense of the term because no one was physically observing her while she was in the lab. When Tom entered and noticed that Mary was typing on a computer, Mary lost her natural (or descriptive) privacy in that situation. However, we should not infer that her privacy was violated in this incident, because a university's computer lab is not the kind of situation or zone that is declared normatively private and thus protected.

▶ **SCENARIO 5–3:** Normative Privacy

Tom decides to follow Mary, from a distance, as she leaves the computer lab to return to her (off-campus) apartment. He carefully follows her to the apartment building, and then stealthily follows Mary up the stairway to the corridor leading to her apartment. Once Mary is safely inside her apartment, Tom peeps through a keyhole in the door. He observes Mary as she interacts with her laptop computer in her apartment. ■

Has Mary's privacy been violated in this scenario? In both scenarios, Tom observes Mary interacting with a computer. In the first scenario, the observation occurred in a public place. There, Mary may have lost some privacy in a descriptive or natural sense, but she had no expectation of preserving her privacy in that particular situation. In the second scenario, Mary not only lost her privacy but her privacy was violated as well, because apartments are examples of zones or "situations" that we, as a society, have declared normatively private.

We have explicit rules governing these situations with respect to privacy protection. Note that it was not merely the fact that Tom had observed Mary's interactions with a computer that resulted in her privacy being violated in the second scenario. Rather, it was because Tom had observed her doing this in a normatively protected situation. So, there was nothing in the information per se that Tom acquired about Mary that threatened her privacy; it was the situation or context in which information about Mary was acquired that caused her privacy to be violated in the second scenario.

5.2.5 Privacy as "Contextual Integrity"

We have seen the important role that a situation, or context, plays in Moor's privacy theory.[7] But some critics argue that the meaning of a situation or context is either too broad or too vague. Helen Nissenbaum elaborates on the notion of a context in her model of privacy as "contextual integrity," where she links adequate privacy protection to "norms of specific contexts." She notes that the things we do, including the transactions and events that occur in our daily lives, all take place in some context or other. In her scheme, contexts include "spheres of life" such as education, politics, the marketplace, and so forth (Nissenbaum 2004a, 2010).

Nissenbaum's privacy framework requires that the processes used in gathering and disseminating information (i) are "appropriate to a particular context" and (ii) comply with norms that govern the flow of personal information in a given context.[8] She refers to these two types of informational norms as follows:

1. Norms of appropriateness
2. Norms of distribution

Whereas norms of appropriateness determine whether a given type of personal information is either appropriate or inappropriate to divulge within a particular context, norms of distribution restrict or limit the flow of information within and across contexts. When either norm has been "breached," a violation of privacy occurs; conversely, the contextual integrity of the flow of personal information is maintained when both kinds of norms are "respected."[9]

As in the case of Moor's privacy model, Nissenbaum's theory demonstrates why we must always attend to the context in which information flows, and not to the nature of the information itself, in determining whether normative protection is needed. To illustrate some of the nuances in her framework of privacy as contextual integrity, consider the following scenario in which a professor collects information about students in his seminar.

▶ **SCENARIO 5–4:** Preserving Contextual Integrity in a University Seminar

Professor Roberts teaches a seminar on social issues in computing to upper-division, undergraduate students at his university. Approximately half of the students who enroll in his seminar each semester are computer science (CS) students, whereas the other half are students majoring in humanities, education, business, etc. At the first class meeting for each seminar, Professor Roberts asks students to fill out an index card on which they include information about their major, their year of study (junior, senior, etc.), the names of any previous CS courses they may have taken (if they are non-CS majors), their preferred e-mail address, and what they hope to acquire from the seminar. Professor Roberts then records this information in his electronic grade book. ■

Has Professor Roberts done anything wrong in requesting and collecting this information? For the most part, it is information that he could have gathered from the registrar's office at his university—for example, information about which CS courses and which general education courses the students have previously taken, and so forth. But Roberts finds it much more convenient to collect information in the classroom, and he informs the students that he uses that information in determining which kinds of assignments he will decide to give to the class in general and which kinds of criteria he will use to assign students to various group projects.

Because Professor Roberts has informed the students about how the information they provided to him will be used in the context of the classroom, and because the students have consented to give him the information, no privacy violation seems to have occurred. In fact, the process used by Professor Roberts satisfies the conditions for Nissenbaum's norm of appropriateness with respect to contextual integrity.

Next, suppose that Professor Roberts has lunch a few weeks later with a former student of his, Phil, who recently graduated and now has a job as a software engineer for a publishing company. Phil's company plans to release its first issue of a new magazine aimed at recent CS graduates, and it has launched an advertising campaign designed to attract undergraduate CS majors who will soon graduate. Phil asks Professor Roberts for the names of the CS majors in the seminar he is teaching. Professor Roberts is initially inclined to identify some students that Phil would likely know from classes that he had taken the previous year at the university. But should Professor Roberts reveal those names to Phil?

If he did, Professor Roberts would violate the privacy norm of distribution within the context of the seminar he is teaching. Consider that the students gave information about themselves to Professor Roberts for use in the context of that seminar. While his use of that information for purposes of the seminar is context appropriate, passing on (i.e., distributing) any of that information to Phil is not, because it would violate the integrity of that context. Even though the information about the students that Professor Roberts has collected is neither sensitive nor confidential in nature, it was given to him for use only in the context of the seminar he is teaching. Insofar as Professor Roberts uses the information in that context, he preserves its integrity. But if he elects to distribute the information outside that context, he violates its integrity and breaches the privacy of his students.

▶ 5.3 WHY IS PRIVACY IMPORTANT?

Of what value is privacy? Why does privacy matter and why should we care about it? In 1999, Scott McNealy, then CEO of Sun Microsystems, uttered his now famous remark to a group of reporters: "You have zero privacy anyway. Get over it." And in 2013, Facebook CEO Mark Zuckerberg proclaimed that privacy "is no longer a social norm." So, should we infer from these remarks that the idea of personal privacy is merely a relic of the past? Although Froomkin (2000), Garfinkel (2000), and others speak of the "death of privacy," not everyone has been willing to concede defeat in the battle over privacy. Some privacy advocates staunchly believe that we should be vigilant about retaining what little privacy we may still have. Others note that we do not appreciate the value of privacy until we lose it, and by then, it is usually too late. They point out that once privacy has been lost, it is difficult, if not impossible, to get back. So perhaps, we should heed their warnings and try to protect privacy to the degree that we can.

We might also question whether the current privacy debate needs to be better understood in terms of differences that reflect generational attitudes. For many so-called Millennials, who are now college aged, privacy does not always seem to be of paramount importance. Most Millennials, as well as many members of Generations X and Y, seem all too eager to share their personal information widely on social networking services such as Facebook, and many also seem willing to post "away messages" on AIM or Skype that disclose their whereabouts at a given moment to a wide range of people. But for many older Americans, including Baby Boomers, privacy is something that is generally still valued. So the relative importance of privacy may vary considerably among the generations; however, we will proceed on the assumption that privacy has value and thus is important.

Is privacy universally valued? Or is it valued mainly in Western, industrialized societies where greater importance is placed on the individual? Solove (2008) notes that privacy is a "global concern," which suggests that it is valued universally. However, it has also been argued that some non-Western nations and cultures do not value individual privacy as much as we do in the West. Alan Westin believes that countries with strong democratic political institutions consider privacy more important than do less democratic ones.[10] Nations such as Singapore and the People's Republic of China seem to place less importance on individual privacy and greater significance on broader social values, which are perceived to benefit the state's community objectives. Even in countries such as Israel, with strong democratic systems but an even stronger priority for national security, individual privacy may not be as important a value as it is in most democratic nations. So, even though privacy has at least some universal appeal, it is not valued to the same degree in all nations and cultures. As a result, it may be difficult to get universal agreement on privacy laws and policies in cyberspace.

5.3.1 Is Privacy an Intrinsic Value?

Is privacy something that is valued for its own sake—that is, does it have intrinsic value? Or is it valued as a means to an end, in which case it has only instrumental worth? Recall our discussion of intrinsic and instrumental values in Chapter 2. There, we saw that happiness has intrinsic value because it is desired for its own sake. Money, on the other hand, has instrumental value since it is desired as a means to some further end or ends.

While few would argue that privacy is an intrinsic value, desired for its own sake, others, including Fried (1990), argue that privacy is not merely an instrumental value or instrumental good. Fried suggests that unlike most instrumental values that are simply one means among others for achieving a desired end, privacy is also essential, that is, necessary to achieve some important human ends, such as trust and friendship. We tend to associate intrinsic values with necessary conditions and instrumental values with contingent, or non-necessary conditions; so while privacy is instrumental in that it is a means to certain human ends, Fried argues that it is also a necessary condition for achieving those ends. Solove also believes that privacy has aspects that cut across the intrinsic–instrumental divide, and he argues "intrinsic and instrumental value need not be mutually exclusive."[11]

Although agreeing with Fried's claim that privacy is more than merely an instrumental value, and with Solove's insight that privacy is a value that spans the intrinsic–instrumental divide, Moor (2004) takes a different approach to illustrate this point. Like Fried, Moor argues that privacy itself is not an intrinsic value. But Moor also believes that privacy is an articulation, or "expression" of the "core value" security, which in turn is essential across cultures, for human flourishing. (We examine the concept of security as it relates to privacy in Chapter 6.) And like Fried, Moor shows why privacy is necessary to achieve certain ends. Moor further suggests that as information technology insinuates itself more and more into our everyday lives, privacy becomes increasingly important for expressing (the core value) security.

Does privacy play a key role in "promoting human well-being," as Spinello (2010) claims? Perhaps, one way it does is by serving as a "shield" that protects us from interference. DeCew (2006), who believes that the value of privacy lies in the "freedom and independence" it provides for us, argues that privacy shields us from "pressures that preclude self-expression and the development of relationships."[12] She claims that privacy also acts as a shield by protecting us from coercion and the "pressure to conform." In her view, the loss of privacy leaves us vulnerable and threatened because we are likely to become more conformist and less individualistic.

5.3.2 Privacy as a Social Value

Based on the insights of DeCew and others, one might infer that privacy is a value that simply benefits individuals. However, some authors have pointed out the social value that privacy also provides, noting that privacy is essential for democracy. Regan (1995) points out that we often frame the privacy debate simply in terms of how to balance privacy interests as individual goods against interests involving the larger social good; in such debates, Regan notes that interests benefiting the social good will generally override concerns regarding individual privacy. If, however, privacy is understood as not solely concerned with individual good but as contributing to the broader social good, then in debates involving the balancing of competing values, individual privacy might have a greater chance of receiving equal consideration.

Solove (2008) also believes that privacy has an important social dimension, when he notes that the value of privacy is both communal *and* individual. Employing an argument similar to Regan's, Solove points out that privacy becomes "undervalued," when it is viewed as an overly individualistic concept. Arguing instead for what he calls a "pragmatic approach," Solove believes that it is important to assess the value of privacy in terms of its "contribution to society."[13]

Since privacy can be of value for greater social goods, such as democracy, as well as for individual autonomy and choice, it would seem that it is important and worth protecting. But privacy is increasingly threatened by new cyber- and cyber-related technologies. In Sections 5.4 and 5.5, we examine how privacy is threatened by two different kinds of practices and techniques that use cybertechnology:

a. *Data-gathering* techniques used to collect and record personal information, often without the knowledge and consent of users

b. *Data-analysis* techniques, including data mining, used to manipulate large data sets of personal information to discover patterns and generate consumer profiles (also typically without the knowledge and consent of users)

▶ 5.4 GATHERING PERSONAL DATA: SURVEILLANCE, RECORDING, AND TRACKING TECHNIQUES

Collecting and recording data about people is hardly new. Since the Roman era, and possibly before then, governments have collected and recorded census information. Not all data-gathering and data recording practices have caused controversy about privacy. However, cybertechnology makes it possible to collect data about individuals without their knowledge and consent. In this section, we examine some controversial ways in which cybertechnology is used to gather and record personal data, as well as to monitor and track the activities and locations of individuals.

5.4.1 "Dataveillance" Techniques

Some believe that the greatest threat posed to personal privacy by cybertechnology lies in its capacity for surveillance and monitoring. Others worry less about the monitoring per se and more about the vast amounts of transactional data recorded via cybertechnology. Roger Clarke uses the term *dataveillance* to capture both the surveillance (data monitoring) and data recording techniques made possible by computer technology.[14] There are, then, two distinct controversies about dataveillance: one having to do with surveillance as a form of data monitoring and one having to do with the recording and processing of data once the data are collected. We examine both controversies, beginning with a look at data monitoring aspects of surveillance.

First, we should note the obvious, but relevant, point that privacy threats associated with surveillance are by no means peculiar to cybertechnology. Long before the advent of cybertechnology, individuals (e.g., private investigators and stalkers) as well as organizations, including governmental agencies all over the world, have used the latest technologies and techniques available to them to monitor individuals and groups.

Telephone conversations have been subject to government surveillance by wiretapping, but phone conversations have also been monitored in the private sector as well; for example, telephone conversations between consumers and businesses are frequently monitored, sometimes without the knowledge and consent of the consumers who are party to them. So surveillance is neither a recent concern nor one that should be associated exclusively with the use of cybertechnology to monitor and record an individual's online activities. However, surveillance has clearly been exacerbated by cybertechnology. Consider that video cameras now monitor consumers' movements while they shop at retail stores, and scanning devices used by "intelligent highway vehicle systems," such as E-ZPass, subject motorists to a type of surveillance while they drive through tollbooths. Sue Halpern notes that, as of 2011, approximately 500 companies monitor and track all of our movements online.[15]

In the past, it was not uncommon for companies to hire individuals to monitor the performance of employees in the workplace. Now, however, there are "invisible supervisors," that is, computers, that can continuously monitor the activities of employees around the clock without failing to record a single activity of the employee. We will examine workplace monitoring in detail, including some arguments that have been used to defend and to denounce computerized monitoring, in Chapter 10, where we consider some impacts that cybertechnology has for the contemporary workplace. In the remainder of this section, we consider surveillance techniques that involve nonworkplace-related monitoring and recording of personal data in both off- and online activities.

Although users may not always realize that they are under surveillance, their online activities are tracked by Web site owners and operators to determine how frequently users visit their sites and to draw conclusions about the preferences users show while accessing their sites. We next consider some controversies associated with a type of online surveillance technology known as cookies.

5.4.2 Internet Cookies

Cookies are text files that Web sites send to and retrieve from the computer systems of Web users, enabling Web site owners to collect information about a user's online browsing preferences whenever that user visits a Web site. The use of cookies by Web site owners and operators has generated considerable controversy, in large part because of the novel way that information about Web users is collected and stored. Data recorded about the user are stored on a file placed on the hard drive of the user's computer system; this information can then be retrieved from the user's system and resubmitted to a Web site the next time the user accesses that site.

Those who defend the use of cookies tend to be owners and operators of Web sites. Proprietors of these sites maintain that they are performing a service for repeat users of a Web site by customizing the user's means of information retrieval. They also point out that, because of cookies, they are able to provide a user with a list of preferences for future visits to that Web site. Privacy advocates, on the other hand, see the matter quite differently. They argue that information gathered about a user via cookies can eventually be acquired by online advertising agencies, which can then target that user for online ads. For example, information about a user's activities on different Web sites can, under certain circumstances, be compiled and aggregated by online advertising agencies. The information can then be combined and cross-referenced in ways that enable a marketing profile of that user's online activities to be constructed and used in more direct advertisements. Also consider that Google now integrates information gathered from cookies with its wide array of applications and services, which include Gmail, Google+, Google Chrome, and others. As Zimmer (2008) notes, Google's ability to integrate this information provides the search engine company with a "powerful infrastructure of dataveillance" in which it can monitor and record users' online activities.

Some critics have also argued that because cookie technology both (a) monitors and records a user's activities while visiting Web sites (often without the user's knowledge and consent) and (b) stores that information on a user's computer or device, it violates the user's privacy. To assist Internet users who may be concerned about cookies, a number of privacy-enhancing tools (PETs), which are briefly described in Section 5.7, are available. Also, most current Web browsers provide users with an option to disable cookies. So with these browsers, users can either opt-in or opt-out of (accepting) cookies, assuming that they (i) are aware of cookie technology and (ii) know how to enable/disable that technology on their Web browsers. However, some Web sites will not grant users access unless they accept cookies.

Many privacy advocates also object to the fact that the default status for most Web browsers is such that cookies will automatically be accepted unless explicitly disabled by the user. So, cookie technology has raised a number of privacy-related concerns because of the controversial methods it uses to collect data about users who visit Web sites.

5.4.3 RFID Technology

Another mode of surveillance made possible by cybertechnology involves the use of radio frequency identification (RFID) technology. In its simplest form, RFID technology consists of a tag (microchip) and a reader. The tag has an electronic circuit, which stores data, and an antenna that broadcasts data by radio waves in response to a signal from a reader. The reader also contains an antenna that receives the radio signal, and it has a demodulator that transforms the analog radio information into suitable data for any computer processing that will be done (Lockton and Rosenberg 2005).

Although the commercial use of RFIDs was intended mainly for the unique identification of real-world objects (e.g., items sold in supermarkets), the tags can also be used to monitor those objects after they are sold. This relatively new mode of (continuous or "downstream") tracking of consumers' purchases has caused concern among some privacy advocates; for example, Nissenbaum (2004a) worries that consumers may not realize how RFID tags now make it possible for store managers to record, track, and share information about their purchases well beyond the initial point of sale.[16]

In one sense, the use of these tags in inventory control in retail contexts would seem uncontroversial. For example, Garfinkel (2002) notes that a company such as Playtex could place an RFID tag in each bra it manufactures to make sure that shipments of bras headed for Asia are not diverted to New York. He also points out, however, that a man with a handheld (RFID) reader in his pocket who is standing next to a woman wearing such a bra can learn the make and size of her bra. Additionally, and perhaps more controversially, RFID technology can be used for tracking the owners of the items that have these tags. So, on the one hand, RFID transponders in the form of "smart labels" make it much easier to track inventory and protect goods from theft or imitation. On the other hand, these tags pose a significant threat to individual privacy. Critics of this technology, which include organizations such as the Electronic Privacy Information Center (EPIC) and the American Civil Liberties Union (ACLU), worry about the accumulation of RFID transaction data by RFID owners and how those data will be used in the future.

RFID technology is already widely used—as Garfinkel notes, it has been incorporated into everything from automobile keys to inventory control systems to passports. If you have an E-ZPass (or some other intelligent highway systems) transponder in your car, for example, you already possess a wireless tag; E-ZPass uses the serial number on it to debit your account when your car passes through a tollbooth. Garfinkel notes that these tags now also appear in some of our clothing.

Many ranchers in the United States now track their cattle by implanting RFID tags in the animals' ears. In the future, major cities and municipalities might require RFID tags for domestic animals and pets; in Taiwan, for example, owners of domesticated dogs are required to have a microchip containing an RFID tag inserted in their pet dog's ear. In this case, the tag identifies the animal's owner and residence. Policies requiring RFID tags for some humans, especially for the elderly, may also be established in the near future. In the United States, some nursing homes now provide their patients with RFID bracelets. And chips (containing RFID technology) can now be implanted in children so that they can be tracked if abducted. On the one hand, this use of RFID technology may seem to empower parents of young children; on the other hand, however, Adam (2005) fears that we may come to rely too heavily on these technologies to care for children.

Like Internet cookies and other online data-gathering and surveillance techniques, RFID clearly threatens individual privacy. But unlike surveillance concerns associated with cookies, which track a user's habits while visiting Web sites, RFID technology can be used to track an individual's location in the offline world. We examine some specific privacy-and-surveillance concerns affecting RFID in connection with "location privacy" and "pervasive surveillance" issues in Chapter 12 in our discussion of ambient intelligence.

5.4.4 Cybertechnology and Government Surveillance

So far, we have examined surveillance techniques involving cybertechnology that are used mainly in the business and commercial sectors to monitor the activities of consumers and to record data about them. Another mode of surveillance that is also associated with cybertechnology involves governments and government agencies that monitor the activities of citizens, a practice that is sometimes referred to as "domestic spying."

Some cybertechnologies, despite their initial objectives and intent, can facilitate government surveillance. Consider, for example, that cell phone companies in the United States are required by law to include a GPS locator chip in all cell phones (manufactured after December 2005). This technology, which assists "911 operators" in emergency situations, also enables any cell phone user to be tracked within 100 meters of his or her location; so some privacy advocates worry that this information can also be used by the government to spy on individuals.

Government agencies currently use a variety of technologies that enable them to intercept and read private e-mail messages. In Chapter 6, we will see that this practice, initiated by the George W. Bush administration to monitor e-mail between U.S. residents and people living outside the United States, has been controversial. And in Section 5.6.1, we will see why the U.S. government's decision to subpoena the records of online search requests made by users of search engines such as Google, which are recorded and archived in computer databases, has also been controversial. In Chapter 7, we describe in detail some of the specific technologies (such as keystroke monitoring and biometric technologies) that have been used by government agencies in the United States to conduct surveillance on individuals. There, we will also see why these technologies, which have been used to combat terrorism and crime in cyberspace, have been controversial from the point of view of privacy and civil liberties.

While few would object to the desirable ends that increased security provides, we will see that many oppose the means—that is, the specific technologies and programs supporting surveillance operations, as well as legislation such as the USA Patriot Act—that the U.S. government has used to achieve its objectives. Our main purpose in this section has been to briefly describe how government surveillance of citizens illustrates one more way that cybertechnology both contributes to and enhances the ability of organizations to gather and record data about individuals.

In concluding this section, you may wish to revisit Scenario 5–1, where we noted that NSA's original charter was to conduct surveillance on entities (countries, organizations, and individuals) outside the United States. We also noted, however, that there is now compelling evidence to suggest that the NSA's mission has been broadened to include as surveillance on U.S. citizens as well. For more details on NSA-related surveillance in connection with the Edward Snowden controversy, see Scenario 4–2 in Chapter 4.

▶ 5.5 ANALYZING PERSONAL DATA: BIG DATA, DATA MINING, AND WEB MINING

In the previous section, we examined some ways in which personal data could be gathered using surveillance techniques. Other tools, however, have been devised to manipulate and analyze that (collected) data before it is transferred across, and exchanged between, electronic databases. Our focus in this section is on data analysis, as opposed to data collection. Simply collecting and recording personal data, per se, might not seem terribly controversial if, for example, the data were never manipulated (e.g., combined, recombined, matched, transferred, and exchanged) in preparation for further analysis. Some would argue, however, that the mere collection of personal data without someone's knowledge and consent is in itself problematic from a privacy perspective. Others assume that if data are being collected, there must be some motive or purpose for its collection. Of course, the reason, as many now realize, is that transactions involving the sale and exchange of personal data are a growing business.

Much of the personal data gathered or collected electronically by one organization is later exchanged with other organizations; indeed, the very existence of certain institutions depends on the exchange and sale of personal information. Some privacy advocates believe that professional information-gathering organizations, such as Equifax, Experian (formerly TRW), and TransUnion (credit reporting bureaus), as well as the Medical Information Bureau (MIB), violate the privacy of individuals because of the techniques they use to transfer and exchange personal information across and between databases. Many also believe that this process has been exacerbated by the phenomenon of *big data*.

5.5.1 Big Data: What, Exactly, Is It, and Why Does It Threaten Privacy?

Ward and Barker (2013) note that while the term "big data" has become "ubiquitous," it has no precise or "unified single" meaning. They also point out that the definitions of big data put forth thus far are not only "diverse," but are often "contradictory" as well.[17] However, Ward and Barker also propose a working definition based on an "extrapolation" of key factors that cut across various definitions of big data, which they describe as an "analysis of large and/or complex data sets using a series of techniques."[18] So, in their view, big data can be understood in terms of one or more of three key factors: size, complexity, and technologies/tools (used to analyze the data).

Initially, one might assume that the concept of big data simply refers to the size or scale of the data being analyzed. For example, Boyd and Crawford (2012) suggest that big data can be understood mainly in terms of its "capacity to search, aggregate and cross-reference *large data sets*."[19] Definitions that focus on capturing the large size of the data sets involved often view big data primarily in terms of its *volume*. Other definitions, however, include factors sometimes referred to as the "three Vs": *variety*, *velocity*, and *veracity*.[20] The "variety" component or element describes the wide range of sources involved in the data analysis, which include social media, scientific applications, business transactions, Internet search indexing, medical records, and Web logs. Whereas "velocity" captures the speed ("fast data in/out") involved in the process, "veracity," refers to the notion of trust in the (big) data analysis that needs to be established for business decision making. So the concept of big data is a far more complex phenomenon than merely the size, or volume, of the data involved. As Poskanzer (2015) points out, in the case of big data, "more isn't just more—more is different." She further suggests that big data can be better understood as a "new mode of knowledge production."[21]

Others believe that the concept of big data can be understood in terms of certain "insights" it purportedly provides into new and emerging types of data and content. Some also suggest that big data can be viewed as an "emerging paradigm," or perhaps even as providing a "paradigm shift" for analyzing data. But has a genuinely new or an emerging paradigm been provided or has the expression "big data" simply become a "new buzzword"—one that is now so ambiguous, as well as ubiquitous, that it is no longer effective? Perhaps the real "shift" (paradigm or otherwise) in data analysis was ushered in when the technique commonly known today as *data mining* (defined in the following section) first became available—that is, when certain kinds of pattern-matching algorithms made possible by AI research were first used to analyze terabytes of data to "discover" information that otherwise would not have been obvious. For example, some data mining techniques led to the "discovery" of new (and mostly nonobvious) groups and of "new facts" about people. This technique or process has also been referred to as "knowledge discovery in databases" (KDD).

Regardless of which expression we use to describe this phenomenon—big data, data mining, or KDD—serious privacy concerns have been generated by it. Some believe that these kinds of concerns justify the need for a new legal category of privacy, which some call "group privacy."[22] However, we will see that many, if not most, of the kinds of privacy concerns currently associated with big data had already been introduced by the use of various data mining techniques, beginning in the 1990s. We next examine the concept of data mining in detail to understand how these specific privacy issues arose and why they are problematic.

5.5.2 Data Mining and Personal Privacy

Data mining can be defined as a technique that involves the manipulation of information, including personal information, through an analysis of implicit patterns discoverable in large data sets. (In this respect, it is very similar to many definitions of big data.) Also, data mining can generate new and sometimes nonobvious classifications or categories of persons (which is again similar to some definitions of big data); as a result, individuals whose data are mined can become identified with or linked to certain newly created groups that they might never have imagined to exist. This is further complicated by the fact that current privacy laws offer individuals relatively little protection with respect to how information about people acquired through data mining activities is subsequently used, even though important decisions can be made about those individuals based on the patterns found in the mined personal data. So, data mining technology can be used in ways that raise special concerns for personal privacy.[23]

But what is so special about the privacy concerns raised by data mining? For example, how do they differ from privacy issues introduced by more traditional data retrieval and exchange techniques? For one thing, privacy laws as well as informal data protection guidelines have been established for protecting personal data that are:

- Explicit in databases (in the form of specific electronic records)
- Confidential in nature (e.g., data involving medical, financial, or academic records)
- Exchanged between databases

However, relatively few legal or normative protections apply to personal data manipulated in the data mining process, where personal information is typically:

- Implicit in the data
- Nonconfidential in nature
- Not necessarily exchanged between databases

Unlike personal data that reside in explicit records in databases, information acquired about persons via data mining is often derived or inferred from implicit patterns in the data. The patterns can suggest "new" facts, relationships, or associations about a person, placing that person in a "newly discovered" category or group. Also, because most personal data collected and used in data mining applications is considered neither confidential nor intimate in nature, there is a tendency to presume that such data must, by default, be public data. And unlike the personal data that are often exchanged between or across two or more databases in traditional database retrieval processes, in the data mining process, personal data are often manipulated within a single database or within a large "data warehouse."

Next, consider a scenario involving data mining practices at a lending institution in determining whether or not to grant mortgages to its customers. As you consider the privacy issues raised in the following scenario, keep in mind Nissenbaum's distinction between "norms of appropriateness" and "norms of distribution" for determining contextual integrity (described in Section 5.2.5).

▶ **SCENARIO 5–5:** Data Mining at the XYZ Credit Union

Jane, a senior real estate professional at CBA Real Estate, wishes to purchase a condominium, and she has recently applied for a mortgage at the XYZ Credit Union. To be considered for this loan, Jane is required to fill out a number of mortgage-related forms, which she willingly completes. For example, on one form, she discloses that she has been employed by CBA for more than seven years and that her current annual salary is $95,000. On another form, Jane discloses that she has $50,000 in her savings account at a local bank (much of which she plans to use for the down payment on the house she hopes to purchase). Additionally, she discloses that she has $1,000 of credit card debt and still owes $3,000 on an existing car loan. The amount of the loan for the mortgage she hopes to secure is for $100,000 over a 30-year period.

After Jane has completed the forms, the credit union's computing center runs a routine data mining program on information in its customer databases and discovers a number of patterns. One reveals that real estate professionals earning more than $80,000 but less than $120,000 annually are also likely to leave their current employers and start their own businesses after 10 years of employment. A second data mining algorithm reveals that the majority of female real estate professionals declare bankruptcy within two years of starting their own businesses. The data mining algorithms can be interpreted to suggest that Jane is a member of a group that neither she nor possibly even the mortgage officers at the credit union had ever known to exist—namely, the group of female real estate professionals likely to start a business and then declare bankruptcy within two years. With this newly inferred information about Jane, the credit union determines that Jane, because of the newly created category into which she fits, is a long-term credit risk. So, Jane is denied the mortgage. ■

Does the credit union's mining of data about Jane raise any significant privacy concerns? At one level, the transaction between Jane and the credit union seems appropriate. To secure the mortgage from XYZ Credit Union, Jane has authorized the credit union to have the information about her, that is, her current employment, salary, savings, outstanding loans, and so forth, that it needs to make an informed decision as to whether or not to grant her the mortgage. So, if we appeal to Nissenbaum's framework of privacy as contextual integrity, it would seem that there is no breach of privacy in terms of norms of appropriateness.

However, Jane gave the credit union information about herself for use in one context, namely, to make a decision about whether or not she should be granted a mortgage for her condominium. She was also assured that the information given to the credit union would not be exchanged with a third party, without first getting Jane's explicit consent. So, no information about Jane was either exchanged or cross-referenced between external databases—that is, there is no breach of the norms of distribution (in Nissenbaum's model, described in Section 5.2.5). However, it is unclear whether the credit union had agreed not to use the information it now has in its databases about Jane for certain in-house analyses.

Although Jane voluntarily gave the credit union information about her annual salary, previous loans, and so forth, she gave each piece of information for a specific purpose and use, in order that the credit union could make a meaningful determination about Jane's request for a mortgage. However, it is by no means clear that Jane authorized the credit union to use disparate pieces of that information for more general data mining analyses that would reveal patterns involving Jane that neither she nor the credit could have anticipated at the outset. Using Jane's information for this purpose would now raise questions about "appropriateness" in the context involving Jane and the XYZ Credit Union.

The mining of personal data in Jane's case is controversial from a privacy perspective for several reasons. For one thing, the information generated by the data mining algorithms suggesting that Jane is someone likely to start her own business, which would also likely lead to her declaring bankruptcy, was not information that was "explicit" in any of the data (records) about Jane per se; rather, it was "implicit" in patterns of data about people similar to Jane in certain respects but also vastly different from her in other respects. For another thing, Jane's case illustrates how data mining can generate new categories and groups such that the people whom the data mining analysis identifies with those groups would very likely have no idea that they would be included as members. And we have seen that, in the case of Jane, certain decisions can be made about members of these newly generated groups simply by virtue of those individuals being identified as members. For example, it is doubtful that Jane would have known that she was a member of a group of professional individuals likely to start a business and that she was a member of a group whose businesses were likely to end in bankruptcy. The "discovery" of such groups is, of course, a result of the use of data mining tools.

Even though no information about Jane was exchanged with databases outside XYZ, the credit union did use information about Jane internally in a way that she had not explicitly authorized. And it is in this sense—unauthorized internal use by data users—that many believe data mining raises serious concerns for personal privacy. Note also that even if Jane had been granted the mortgage she requested, the credit union's data mining practices would still have raised privacy concerns with respect to the *contextual integrity* of her personal information.

Jane was merely one of many credit union customers who had voluntarily given certain personal information about themselves to the XYZ for use in one context—in this example, a mortgage request—and subsequently had that information used in ways that they did not specifically authorize.

Controversial Consumer Profiles Generated by Data Mining Techniques

The scenario involving Jane is, of course, hypothetical. But there is now empirical evidence to suggest that banks and consumer credit organizations are using data mining techniques to determine an individual's "credit worthiness" in ways that are not so different from the process described in Scenario 5–5. So, in some cases, a consumer's credit rating is actually determined via profiling schemes that can suggest "guilt by association." For example, a consumer could be denied a credit card, or have one revoked, merely because of where she shops or where she lives. Also, consider that people living in neighborhoods where there have been high rates of home foreclosures, or people holding mortgages with certain banks or lending institutions that have experienced high rates of home foreclosures, may now be considered credit risks by virtue of their association with either a certain neighborhood or bank, even though they have been responsible in paying their mortgages and other loans on time.

Similarly, if individuals shop at a certain kind of retail store, say, Walmart, information about their purchases at such a store can associate them with other individuals who shop there, and who may have a higher-than-average default rate on their credit cards. For example, Stuckey (2008) describes an incident where a 37-year-old computer consultant had two of his American Express cards canceled and the limit on a third card reduced based on criteria having to do with (i) where he shopped and (ii) the financial institution with whom he held his mortgage. When this person questioned American Express's decision, he was informed that the criteria it uses to decide to reduce the spending limit on someone's credit card include:

> credit experience with customers who have made purchases at establishments where you have recently used your card.
>
> analysis of the credit risk associated with customers who have residential loans from the creditor(s) indicated in your credit report.

While there had been suspicion for many years that credit card companies did indeed engage in the kind of profiling scheme used by American Express, consumer advocates and credit analysts believe that this may have been the first time that a major credit company admitted to using such criteria. In its defense, however, American Express claimed that it needed to analyze its exposure to risk as it reviews its cardholder's credit profiles in light of the economic turndown in the United States (in 2008–2009) that severely affected the credit industry at that time (Stuckey 2008).

Can Data Mining Techniques also Be Used in Ways that Protect Consumer Privacy?

We have seen how data mining can be used to threaten consumer privacy. But can it also be used to protect consumers against fraudulent activities? Perhaps not surprisingly, data mining, like other technologies, can be viewed as a "double-edged sword" with respect to consumers' interests, as the following story suggests. One day, to my surprise, I received a telephone call from my credit card company informing me that a purchase, which the company apparently viewed as suspicious, had been charged earlier that day to my credit card account. When asked about the purchase, I informed the company's representative that it had not been made by me, and I also thanked the person for notifying me so promptly about this transaction. The company representative then immediately canceled my existing credit card and issued me a new card with a new account number.

Why did the company suspect that the purchase made that day with my credit card was questionable? It would seem that the data mining algorithms used by the credit card company to determine the patterns of my purchases—which kinds of purchases and credit card transactions I typically make, with whom and where I make them, and when—generated suspicion about the questionable purchase made that day with my credit card. So in this instance, data mining appeared to have been used in a way that protected the interests of a consumer.

5.5.3 Web Mining: Analyzing Personal Data Acquired from Our Interactions Online

Initially, the mining of personal data depended on large (offline) commercial databases called *data warehouses*, which stored the data, consisting primarily of transactional information. Data mining techniques are now also commonly used by commercial Web sites to analyze data about Internet users. This process is sometimes referred to as *Web mining*, which has been defined as the application of data mining techniques to discover patterns from the Web.[24] The various kinds of patterns discovered via Web mining are often used by marketers, especially in their online advertisements and promotional campaigns.

A now classic case of Web mining involved Facebook's Beacon initiative in 2007, which enabled Facebook friends to share information about their online activities, including online purchases they made. This initiative was controversial from the outset, however, because it also allowed targeted advertisements by the Web sites sending the data to Facebook. In response to the outpouring of criticism Facebook received for collecting more user information for advertisers than it had originally admitted, the popular social networking service decided to cancel Beacon in December 2007.[25] However, critics worry that Facebook and other social networking services still engage in various forms of Web mining.

Because the amount (or volume) of data currently available on the Web is so vast, one might assume that it is impossible to mine those data in ways that could be useful. However, current data mining tools employ sophisticated techniques that can "comb" through the massive amounts of data on the Web; collecting and analyzing this volume of data would not have been possible using earlier kinds of information gathering/analysis techniques. (Recall our brief examination of "big data" in Section 5.5.1, where we saw how easy it is now to analyze extremely large data sets.) Also, sophisticated search engines have programs (called "spiders") that "crawl" through the Web in order to uncover general patterns in information across multiple Web sites. Halpern (2011) points out that approximately 500 companies now mine the "raw material of the Web" and then sell it to data mining companies. And Pariser (2011) notes that one of these companies, Acxiom, has managed to accumulate 1,500 pieces of data, on average, for each person in its database; this personal data ranges from people's credit scores to the kinds of medications they use.

Pariser also notes that Google and other major search engine companies use "prediction engines" to construct and refine theories about us and the kinds of results we desire from our search queries. In Section 5.7.1, we examine some specific ways in which the use of Internet search engines raise privacy concerns, even though the kind of personal information about us that is acquired by search engine companies might not initially seem to warrant explicit privacy protection. To see why such protection might indeed be needed in these cases, however, we first examine some questions underlying a concern that Nissenbaum (2004b) calls the "problem of privacy in public."

▶ 5.6 PROTECTING PERSONAL PRIVACY IN PUBLIC SPACE

So far, we have examined how cybertechnology can be used to gather, exchange, and mine personal information. With the exception of data mining, which manipulates personal, but nonconfidential information, the kind of personal information gathered and exchanged was often confidential and sensitive in nature. For example, financial and medical records could be exchanged between two or more databases using computerized merging and matching techniques. This confidential/sensitive personal information is sometimes referred to as non-public personal information (NPI). Privacy analysts are now concerned about a different kind of personal information—public personal information (PPI), which is neither confidential nor sensitive and which is also being gathered, exchanged, and mined via cybertechnology.

5.6.1 PPI vs. NPI

PPI includes information about you, such as where you work or attend school or what kind of car you drive. Even though it is information about you as a particular person, PPI has not enjoyed the privacy protection that has been granted to NPI. Until recently, most concerns about personal information that was gathered and exchanged electronically were limited to NPI, and because of the attention it has received, privacy laws and policies were established to protect NPI. But now, privacy advocates are extending their concern to PPI; they argue that PPI deserves greater legal and normative protection than it currently has. As noted previously, Nissenbaum refers to this challenge as the problem of protecting privacy in public.

Why should the collection and exchange of PPI raise privacy concerns? Suppose that I discover some of the following information about you: you are a junior at Technical University, you frequently attend your university's football games, and you are actively involved in your university's computer science club. In one sense, the information that I have discovered about you is personal, because it is about you (as a person), but it is also public, because it pertains to things that you do in the public sphere. Should you be worried that this information about you is so easily available?

In the past, the public availability of such seemingly harmless and uncontroversial information about you was no cause for concern. Imagine that 80 years ago a citizen petitioned his or her congressperson to draft legislation protecting the privacy of each citizen's movements in public places. It would have been difficult then to make a strong case for such legislation; no one would have seen any need to protect that kind of personal information. But today, many argue that we need to protect privacy in public, pointing out that our earlier assumptions are no longer tenable. Nissenbaum (2004b) believes that many in the commercial sector proceed from an assumption that she believes is "erroneous"—namely, "There is a realm of public information about persons to which no privacy norms apply."[26] Keep this assumption in mind as you consider the following two scenarios.

▶ **SCENARIO 5–6:** Shopping at SuperMart

On your way home from class, you decide to stop at SuperMart to shop for groceries. If I also happen to shop there and see you enter or leave SuperMart, or if we are both shopping in this store at the same time, I now have information that you shop (or, at least, have once shopped) at SuperMart. (This information could be considered "public" because it was acquired in a public forum and because it is neither intimate nor confidential in nature.) If I also happen to pass by you in one of the aisles at SuperMart, I can observe the contents of your shopping basket; I may notice, for example, that your cart contains several bottles of wine but relatively little food. Again, I have acquired this information about you by observing your activity in a public forum. ■

Because the information I have acquired about you in the above scenario can be considered public information, it would not warrant any legal privacy protection. And even though this information is about you as a person, it is not the kind of personal information to which we, as a society, would typically grant normative privacy protection. What, exactly, is the privacy problem regarding the kind of personal information about your public activities in shopping at SuperMart? Why should you be concerned about information that is gathered about what you do at SuperMart or, for that matter, in any public place? Let us continue the shopping metaphor, but this time, we consider shopping that takes place in an online forum.

▶ **SCENARIO 5–7:** Shopping at Nile.com

Imagine that you visit an online bookstore called Nile.com to view a particular book that you are considering purchasing. Because you are visiting this bookstore via a computer or electronic device, you cannot be physically observed by other users who also happen to be visiting Nile's Web site at that time. However, from the moment you enter that site, information about you is being intentionally gathered and carefully recorded—that is, information about the exact time that you entered Nile, as well as the exact time that you leave. As you make your initial contact with the Nile Web site, Nile requests a cookie file from your device to determine whether you have previously visited this site. If you have visited this site before and have clicked on items that interested you, Nile can find a record of these items. The information stored in that cookie file can also be used by Nile to alert you to newly released books that it believes might interest you, based on an analysis of the data Nile collected from your previous visits to its site. ■

The information that Nile now has about you does not seem categorically different from the information that SuperMart might also have about you (assuming, for example, that you used that store's "courtesy card" or discount card in making your purchases). However, there are significant differences in the ways that information about you can be gathered, recorded, and then used as a result of your shopping at each store.

When you shopped in physical space at SuperMart, only a list of your actual purchases could be recorded and stored in SuperMart's databases. Items that might have only caught your attention and items that you might also have picked up or even placed in your cart at one point while shopping but did not eventually purchase at the checkout register are not recorded by SuperMart's data-collection system. However, as you shop, or even browse, at Nile, there is a record of virtually every move you make—every book that you search, review, etc., as well as the one(s) you purchase. Yet, just like the information gathered about your shopping habits in physical space at SuperMart, this personal information that Nile has gathered about your browsing and shopping habits online is considered and treated as public information (i.e., not treated as NPI).

Now, we can see why some people worry about having their movements online tracked and recorded. The information Nile gathered about you is, in effect, Nile's information, even though it pertains to you as a person; Nile now owns that information about you, as well as the information it has about its other customers, and is, in principle at least, free to do with that information whatever it chooses (so long as it is consistent with any consumer privacy policies it may happen to have). On the one hand, the information seems fairly innocuous—after all, who really cares which books you happen to browse or purchase? On the other hand, however, this information can be combined with other information about your online transactions at additional Web sites to create a consumer profile of you, which can then be sold to a third party.

One argument that online entrepreneurs might advance to defend these business practices is that if a user puts information about him- or herself into the public domain of the Internet, then that information is no longer private. Of course, one response to this line of reasoning could be to question whether users clearly understand the ways that data they submit might subsequently be used.

In Scenario 5–7, Nile used information about you in ways that you neither explicitly authorized nor likely intended—an example of the kind of practice that Nissenbaum (2004a, 2010) describes as violating "contextual integrity" (see Section 5.2.5). Also, we can question whether businesses, such as Nile.com, should be able to "own" the information about us that they collect and then do with that information whatever they please and for as long as they want?

Fulda (2004) questions whether the old legal rule that states, "Anything put by a person in the public domain can be viewed as public information," should still apply. He admits that such a rule may have served us well, but only before data were "mined" to produce profiles and other kinds of patterns about individuals.[27]

5.6.2 Search Engines and the Disclosure of Personal Information

Internet search engines are valuable for directing us to available online resources for academic research, commerce, recreation, and so forth; so it might be surprising to find that search engine technology, too, can be controversial from the perspective of personal privacy. How can search engine technology conflict with personal privacy? At least two different kinds of concerns affecting privacy arise because of practices involving search engines: (i) search engine companies such as Google record and archive each search request made by users and (ii) search engines enable users to acquire a wealth of personal information about individuals, with relative ease. We begin with a brief examination of (i).

Google and Its Practice of Collecting Records of Users' Searches

Google creates a record of every search made on its site, which it then archives. The topic searched for, as well as the date and time the specific search request is made by a user, are included in the record. These data can be linked to the IP address and the ISP of the user requesting the search. So individual searches made by a particular user could theoretically be analyzed in ways that suggest patterns of that individual's online behavior, and, perhaps more controversially, these records could later be subpoenaed in court cases. Yet, until relatively recently, many (if not most) Google users were unaware of the company's policy regarding the recording and archiving of users' search requests.

On the one hand, this information might seem relatively innocuous—after all, who would be interested in knowing about the kinds of searches we conduct on the Internet, and who would want to use this information against us? On the other hand, however, consider the case of a student, Mary, who is writing a research paper on Internet pornography. Records of Mary's search requests could reveal several queries that she made about pornographic Web sites, which in turn might suggest that Mary was interested in viewing pornography. Following a controversial decision by the George W. Bush administration in 2005, Google users discovered that any worries they may have had about the lack of privacy protection concerning their Internet searches were justified. That year, the Bush administration informed Google that it would be required to turn over a list of all users' queries entered into its search engine during a one-week period. Initially, Google refused to comply with the subpoena on the grounds that the privacy rights of its users would be violated. Yahoo, however, which also had its search records subpoenaed, complied with the government's initial request.[28]

The Bush administration's decision to seek information about the search requests of ordinary users has since drawn significant criticism from many privacy advocates. Critics argued that although the Bush administration claimed that it had the authority to seek electronic information in order to fight the "war on terror" and to prevent another September 11-like attack, the records at issue in this particular case had to do with the number of users requesting information about, or inadvertently being sent to, pornographic Web sites. Some critics further argued that the Bush administration was interested in gathering data to support its stance on the Children's Internet Protection Act (CIPA), which had been challenged in a U.S. District Court (see Chapter 9). So, many critics were quick to point out that the Bush administration's rationale for obtaining records of search requests made by ordinary citizens seemed politically and ideologically motivated and may have had nothing to do with protecting national security.

Using Search Engines to Acquire Information about People

It is not only the fact that an individual's search requests are recorded and archived by major companies such as Google that make Internet search engines controversial from the perspective of personal privacy. Search engine-related privacy issues also arise because that technology can be used for questionable purposes such as stalking. In fact, one search facility—Gawker-Stalker (www.gawker.com/stalker)—has been designed specifically for the purpose of stalking famous people, including celebrities. For example, suppose that Matt Damon is spotted ordering a drink at an upscale café in Boston. The individual who spots Damon can send a "tip" via e-mail to Gawker-Stalker, informing the site's users of Damon's whereabouts. The Gawker site then provides its users, via precise GPS software, with information about exactly where, and at what time, Damon was sighted. Users interested in stalking Damon can then follow his movements electronically, via the Gawker site, or they can locate and follow him in physical space, if they are in the same geographical vicinity as Damon.

But it is not just celebrities who are vulnerable to information about them being acquired by others via search engines. Consider the amount and kind of personal information about ordinary individuals that is now available to search engines. In some cases, that information may have been placed on the Internet inadvertently, without the knowledge and consent of those affected. Yet information about those persons can be located by an Internet user who simply enters their names in a search engine program's entry box. The fact that one can search the Internet for information about someone might not seem terribly controversial. After all, people regularly place information about themselves on Web sites (or perhaps they authorize someone else to do it for them) and on social networking services such as Facebook. And it might seem reasonable to assume that any online personal information that is currently available to the public should be viewed simply as public information. But should such information about persons be unprotected by privacy norms merely because it is now more easily accessible for viewing by the public? (In Section 5.8, we consider whether users should have a "right" to have some kinds of online personal information about them either deleted or "de-linked" from search engine indexes.)

We have seen how the use of search engines can threaten the privacy of individuals in two distinct ways: (i) by recording and archiving records of a user's search queries that reveal the topic of the search and the time the request was made by the user and (ii) by providing users of search engines with personal information about individuals who may have no idea of the wealth of personal information about them that is available online (and have no control over how it is accessed and by whom it is accessed). The latter concern is further complicated by the fact that individuals who are the subject of online searches, including celebrities who can be stalked (as we saw in the case of Gawker), enjoy no legal protection because of the presumed "public" nature of the personal information about them that is available via online searches.

So far, we have seen how our personal information can be collected and then manipulated by search engines in ways that are controversial.[29] A variation of this privacy-related controversy involves access to personal information that resides in public records made available online via online searches. In Section 5.1.2, we saw that once information is converted to digital form, it can live on indefinitely; so there is no time limit or expiration date for most public records. As we will see in our analysis of a recent European privacy principle called "the right to be forgotten" in Section 5.8, links to documents about an unfortunate incident in one's distant past, which may no longer be "relevant," can continue to be available online and thus haunt that person indefinitely. So one might ask: Do we need stricter privacy laws, especially in the United States, to protect us in the digital era?

▶ 5.7 PRIVACY LEGISLATION AND INDUSTRY SELF-REGULATION

Many privacy advocates believe that stronger privacy laws are needed to protect the interests of online consumers, as well as ordinary users. Others, however, especially those in the commercial sector, argue that additional privacy legislation is neither necessary nor desirable. Instead, they suggest the use of voluntary controls regulated by industry standards. Generally, privacy advocates have been skeptical of voluntary controls, including most industry standards affecting "self-regulation," arguing instead for stricter privacy/data protection frameworks backed by explicit legislation. We begin this section with an examination of some industry-initiated, self-regulatory schemes designed to protect consumer privacy.

5.7.1 Industry Self-Regulation and Privacy-Enhancing Tools

Some who advocate for the use of (voluntary) self-regulatory controls point out that various privacy enhancing tools (PETs), designed to protect a user's privacy while navigating the Internet, are already available. For example, some PETs enable users to navigate the Web anonymously; perhaps, one of the best-known tools of this type is the *Anonymizer* (available from Anonymizer.com).[30] Another useful tool is TrackMeNot (http://cs.nyu.edu/trackmenot/), which was designed to work with the Firefox Web browser to protect users against surveillance and data profiling by search engine companies. Rather than using encryption or concealment tools to accomplish its objectives, TrackMeNot instead uses "noise and obfuscation." In this way, a user's Web searches become "lost in a cloud of false leads." By issuing randomized search queries to popular search engines such as Google and Bing, TrackMeNot "hides users' actual search trails in a cloud of 'ghost' queries." This technique makes it difficult for search engine companies to aggregate the data it collects into accurate user profiles.

Although some users have found anonymity tools (and other kinds of PETs) helpful, many question their overall effectiveness in protecting the privacy of online consumers, as well as ordinary Internet users. In fact, even many industry self-regulation proponents would likely concede that PETs alone are not sufficient. But they still oppose the idea of any additional privacy legislation, arguing instead for better enforcement of industry standards that have already been accepted and implemented. Some of these standards are similar to PETs in their intended objective, that is, to protect an online consumer's privacy, but are also unlike PETs in that they cannot be classified as "tools" in the strict (or technological) sense of the term.

One industry-backed (self-regulatory) framework, designed to help ensure that commercial Web sites adhere to the privacy policies they advertise, is TRUSTe. This framework uses a branded system of "trustmarks" (i.e., graphic symbols) to represent a Web site's privacy policy regarding personal information. Trustmarks provide consumers with the assurance that a Web site's privacy practices accurately reflect its stated policies. If a Web site bearing its trust seal does not abide by the stated policies, users can file a complaint to TRUSTe. Any Web site that bears the TRUSTe mark and wishes to retain that seal must satisfy several conditions: The Web site must clearly explain in advance its general information-collecting practices, including which personally identifiable data will be collected, what the information will be used for, and with whom the information will be shared. Web sites that bear a trust seal but do not conform to these conditions can have their seal revoked. And Web sites displaying trust seals, such as TRUSTe, are subject to periodic and unannounced audits of their sites.

Critics have pointed out some of the difficulties that users encounter interacting with frameworks like TRUSTe. For example, the amount of information users are required to provide can easily discourage them from carefully reading and understanding the agreement. Also, the various warnings displayed may appear unfriendly and thus might discourage users; "friendlier" trustmarks, on the contrary, might result in users being supplied with less direct information that is important for protecting their privacy. But advocates of self-regulatory frameworks such as TRUSTe argue that, with them, users will be better able to make informed choices regarding online commercial transactions.

Some critics also worry that schemes like TRUSTe do not go far enough in protecting consumers. Consider, for example, a now classic incident involving Toysmart.com, an e-commerce site that once operated in the state of Massachusetts. Consumers who purchased items from Toysmart were assured, via an online trust seal, that their personal data would be protected. The vendor's policy stated that personal information disclosed to Toysmart would be used internally but would not be sold to or exchanged with external vendors. So, users who dealt with Toysmart expected that their personal data would remain in that company's databases and not be further disclosed or sold to a third party. In the spring of 2000, however, Toysmart was forced to file for bankruptcy.

In the bankruptcy process, Toysmart solicited bids for its assets, which included its databases containing the names of customers.[31] One question that arose was whether the parties interested in purchasing that information were under any obligation to adhere to the privacy policy that Toysmart had established with its clients? If they were not, then whoever took over Toysmart's site or purchased its databases, would, in principle, be free to do whatever they wished with the personal information in the databases. They would conceivably be able to do this, despite the fact that such information was given to Toysmart by clients in accordance with an explicit privacy policy that guaranteed that personal information about them would be protected indefinitely.

A slightly different, but related, kind of privacy policy concern arises in the context of search engine companies. Unlike e-commerce sites, which users can easily avoid if they wish, virtually every Internet user depends on search engines to navigate the Web. In Section 5.6.1, we saw how major search engine companies such as Google record and keep a log of users' searches. This practice, as we also saw, has generated privacy-related concerns for ordinary users and was further complicated by the fact that Google offers many other kinds of services in addition to its well-known search engine. These include Gmail, Google Maps, Google+, Google Calendar, Google Chrome, Picasa, AdSense/AdWords, YouTube (which was acquired by Google), and so forth. So, Google had developed separate privacy policies for its services, and these policies varied from service to service.

In 2012, Google announced a new comprehensive privacy policy, which replaced its individual privacy policies for each of its services. The new policy, however, also allowed the sharing of user account data across all its services, subsidiary services, and Web-based applications. When Google implemented its new privacy policy, critics noted that a user's search engine history could now be shared with YouTube, or vice versa, and that a user's Google+ account data might be shared with AdWords to generate more targeted advertising.[32]

Google's 2012 privacy policy, while explicit and transparent, has nonetheless been controversial for several reasons. For one thing, it is not clear how Google will use all of the personal information that it can now access so easily. For another, no one outside Google fully understands how the search engine company uses that information to manipulate (i.e., tailor or personalize) the search results a user receives for his or her search queries. Additionally, it is not clear whether one's personal information collected from the various Google services will be used only internally or will also be available to advertisers and information merchants outside the company (e.g., those Web sites that include embedded Google ads to generate revenue).

Other critics worry whether users can trust Google—a company that officially embraces the motto: "do not be evil"—to abide by its new privacy policy. Some note, for example, that many people who used Apple's Safari Web browser on their computers and iPhones were under the impression that Google was not able to track their browsing activities. In 2012, however, it was discovered Google had used software code that tricked the Safari browser, thus enabling Google to track the activities of those using that browser. Google disabled the controversial software code shortly after the incident was reported in *The Wall Street Journal*, and Safari users were informed by Google that they could rely on Safari's privacy settings to prevent tracking by Google in the future (Anguin and Valentino-DeVries 2012). But some critics remain skeptical.

Because of concerns involving distrust of major search engine companies like Google, as well as commercial Web sites in general, to regulate themselves, many privacy advocates believe that the only plausible alternative for protecting users is to enact better, and more explicit, privacy laws. We next briefly examine some existing privacy legislations in the North America (mainly the United States) and Europe.

5.7.2 Privacy Laws and Data Protection Principles

Many nations, especially in the West, have enacted strong privacy legislation. The United States, however, has not taken the lead on legislation initiatives in this area; in fact, some would argue that the United States is woefully behind Canada and the European nations when it comes to protecting its citizens' privacy. For example, in the United States, there is currently very little privacy protection provided in legal statutes. In 1974, Congress passed the Privacy Act, which has been criticized both for containing far too many loopholes and for lacking adequate provisions for enforcement. Also, it applies only to records in federal agencies and thus is not applicable in the private sector.

Critics also point out that there is virtually no explicit legal protection for private e-mail communications in the United States. Julian Sanchez notes that the Electronic Communications Privacy Act (ECPA) of 1986, which was "tweaked in the early 1990s," was written before most people had even heard of the Internet. Some U.S. citizens might assume that the Fourth Amendment (prohibiting government search and seizure) also applies to the protection of e-mail communications. However, Sanchez points out that it was not until 2010 that a court in the United States finally ruled in favor of privacy protection for an e-mail communication—and he notes that this ruling was handed down only at the circuit court level of one federal court.[33]

In 2003, the Health Insurance Portability and Accountability Act (HIPAA), which provides protection for "individually identifiable" medical records from "inappropriate use and disclosure," was enacted into law in the United States. But the kind of privacy protection provided by HIPAA does not apply to an individual's nonmedical/health records such as consumer data, or even to one's genetic data. Enactment of the Genetic Information Nondiscrimination Act (GINA), in 2008, explicitly extended privacy protection to personal genetic information. So, some federal privacy laws have successfully targeted specific contexts such as healthcare and genetic information. However, critics argue that privacy legislation in the United States has resulted mostly in a "patchwork" of individual state and federal laws that are neither systematic nor coherent.

Generally, U.S. lawmakers have resisted requests from privacy advocates and consumer groups for stronger consumer privacy laws. Instead, they have sided with business interests in the private sector, who believe that such legislation would undermine economic efficiency and thus adversely impact the overall economy. Critics point out, however, that many American businesses that have subsidiary companies or separate business operations in countries with strong privacy laws and regulations, such as nations in Western Europe, have found little difficulty in complying with the privacy laws of the host countries; furthermore, profits for those American-owned companies have not suffered because of their compliance. In any event, there has been increased pressure on the U.S. government, especially from Canada and countries in the European Union (EU), to enact stricter privacy laws (as well as pressure on American businesses to adopt stricter privacy policies and practices to compete in e-commerce at the global level).

EU nations, through the implementation of strict "data protection" principles, have been far more aggressive than the United States in both anticipating and addressing privacy concerns raised by cybertechnology. In the early 1990s, the European community began to synthesize the "data protection" laws of the individual European nations.[34] The European community has since instituted a series of "directives," including the EU Directive 95/46/EC of the European Parliament and of the Council of Europe of 24 October 1995.[35] The latter, also sometimes referred to simply as the EU Directive on Data Protection, was designed to protect the individual rights of citizens who reside within the EU, while also facilitating the flow of data beyond the EU nations. As such, the EU Directive on Data Protection prohibits the "transborder flow" of personal data to countries that do not provide adequate protection of personal data. Elgesem (2004) has pointed out that a central focus of this directive, unlike earlier privacy legislation in Europe that focused simply on the recording and the storage of personal data, is on the "processing and flow" of that data.

Several principles make up the European Directive on Data Protection; among them are the principles of Data Quality and Transparency. Whereas the Data Quality Principle is concerned with protecting the data subject's reasonable expectations concerning the processing of data about that subject (ensuring that the personal data being processed is true, updated, and properly kept), the Transparency Principle grants the data subject the rights to be informed, to contest, to correct, and "to seek judicial redress."[36] What helps to ensure that each of these principles is enforced on behalf of individuals, or "data subjects," is the presence of privacy protection commissions and boards in the various European nations. As in the case of Canada, which has also set up privacy oversight agencies with a Privacy Commissioner in each of its provinces, every member state of the EU is required to institute a Data Protection Authority (DPA). (This "authority" can consist of a board, a commission, or an individual commissioner.) DPAs are empowered to check to see that all of the laws are being followed in the processing of personal data, and they can impose very severe sanctions when personal data is processed illegally. In Europe, willful data protection breaches may also be criminal offenses, and can even rise to the level of felonies in certain circumstances.

A recent challenge for the EU Directive on Data Protection—and one that has international implications because of the flow of personal information across the porous boundaries of cyberspace—has involved the question of whether users should have a right to have certain kinds of personal information about them deleted, or at least "delinked" from search engine indexes. This right would apply mainly to personal information in digital form that is shown to be either inaccurate or no longer "relevant."

▶ 5.8 A RIGHT TO "BE FORGOTTEN" (OR TO "ERASURE") IN THE DIGITAL AGE

In our discussion of privacy issues affecting online public records in Section 5.6.3, we saw that a record about an unfortunate incident in one's past can now live on indefinitely—that is, once it has been converted into digital form and identified with a digital link or universal resource locator (URL). Is this necessarily a bad thing? One might argue that our being able to access information about a person's past convictions for crimes such as child molestation or pedophilia is very important; for example, a community's residents would be able to view information concerning past criminal records of prospective home buyers wishing to move into their neighborhood. But do we always need access to an online public record about someone's past to accomplish this specific objective? In the United States, and possibly in other countries well, some explicit laws are already in place requiring that the names of past offenders of various kinds of child- and sex-related crimes be included on a "list" or index, and also requiring these people register with police departments in communities where they wish to live. So, in these instances, individuals who have been convicted of certain kinds of crimes are required to self-report, even though information about their past may also be readily available via online public records as well. A more interesting challenge, however, can arise in the case of access to online records about a person's past arrest for a less serious offense, such as underage drinking. This kind of situation is illustrated in the following scenario.

▶ **SCENARIO 5–8:** An Arrest for an Underage Drinking Incident 20 Years Ago

Philip Clark is a 39-year-old resident of Amityville, where he lives with his wife and two school-age children. He is a respectable member of his community, active in his local church as well as in several civic organizations. Philip is employed by the DEF Corporation in Amityville, where he has worked for several years and is a highly valued employee. However, when Philip attempted to change jobs a few years ago, he was unsuccessful. He strongly suspects that this may be due to an online document about an incident in Philip's past that shows up whenever someone searches his name: a newspaper story describing Philip Clark's arrest (along with the arrests of two of his friends) in an underage drinking incident that occurred 20 years ago, when Philip was a sophomore in college. Philip had pleaded guilty to the charge and received a reduced sentence of 30 hours of work-related service in his community; the judge presiding over Philip's case informed Philip that because it was his first offense, the conviction would not be included in his permanent record. So, Philip believed that the incident was behind him and that he would not have to worry about any official public record affecting his future.

Since the time of his arrest as a teenager, Philip has not violated any laws; in fact, he is viewed by many in his community as a "model citizen" because of his volunteer work with youth groups and his various contributions to neighborhood initiatives. Yet Philip continues to be haunted by the unfortunate incident in his past because of the online link to the (20-year-old) newspaper story about his arrest, which cannot be expunged in the same way that a public record can. And since a prospective employer who searches for "Philip Clark" will almost certainly discover the link to the newspaper article describing Philip's arrest, which is featured prominently in the list of search returns, Philip believes that his future employment prospects are not very promising. In fact, during the past few years, Philip has been turned down by a number of prospective employers who initially seemed very interested in hiring him. Unable to change jobs, and feeling locked out of potential career opportunities, Philip concludes that he will be stuck in his current employment position as long as the information about his past underage-drinking arrest continues to be available online. So Philip decides to contact Google, Bing, and other major search engine companies with requests to have their links to that 20-year-old newspaper story removed from their indexes. ■

Does, or should, Philip have a right to make this request? If not, what alternative recourse, if any, does/should Philip have to get the link to this old, and arguably now "irrelevant," information removed? While some might be sympathetic to Philip's request, others oppose any legislation that would give people a right to have any online personal information about them deleted, or even "de-linked" or deindexed, from search engines. The questions raised in Scenario 5–8 reflect some of the key issues at stake in the current debate in Europe about the Right to Be Forgotten (RTBF), sometimes also referred to as the "right to erasure." Whereas the scenario depicting Philip Clark is hypothetical, an actual case in Spain, involving Mario Costeja González, triggered a controversial debate in Europe (and elsewhere), the ramifications of which are still being sorted out.

In 2010, González, a Spanish citizen, sought to have some unflattering (and arguably no longer "relevant") information about him removed from Google's list of returns for searches of his name. Specifically, he wanted Google to delete a link to an article in a Spanish newspaper about his home foreclosure that occurred 16 years earlier. So González appealed to Spain's National Data Protection Agency to have the link to the report about his foreclosure removed, arguing that because the information was no longer relevant, it should not be prominently featured in Google's list of returns on searches of his name. The Spanish court ruled in González's favor. While this court's decision arguably set a precedent that is favorable to Spanish citizens with respect to RTBF requests, it was not clear whether this ruling should apply in other EU countries as well.

Google Inc. challenged the Spanish court's ruling, and the European Court of Justice (ECJ), which presides over all of the EU countries, agreed to consider the case. Initially, it seemed that the European court might side with Google. However, when the ECJ formally considered the case in May 2014, it upheld the Spanish court's ruling.[37] Two important qualifications affecting the ECJ's ruling on RTBF are worth mentioning: (i) the right is not absolute (but instead needs to be balanced against other rights, including freedom of expression) and (ii) the right does not apply in the same way to "public figures" in Europe, including politicians and celebrities. Google (in Europe) agreed to comply with the ECJ's decision, which affected only its European users (e.g., those using a service like Google.co.uk in England, but not to the Google.com users outside Europe). However, many of those outside (as well as inside) Europe have been critical of the ECJ's ruling. We briefly examine some of their arguments.

5.8.1 Arguments Opposing RTBF

Major search engine companies and journalists/publishers have been among RTBF's staunchest opponents. Search engine companies generally make two different kinds of claims, arguing that they:

a. Do not control *content* on the Internet (and thus cannot be held responsible for the relevance, or even the accuracy, of the content on sites to which they provide links)

b. Cannot be expected to respond to all of the links requested by users (even if the information being linked to is either inaccurate or no longer relevant, because doing so would be too *impractical*, if not impossible)

Regarding (a), search engine companies tend to view themselves as "services" that provide links to online content, and not as "content providers." In the United States, search engine companies are not held legally liable for the content to which they link, as long as they comply with official legal requests to remove links to sites whose content explicitly violates the law—for example, sites that willingly and intentionally violate U.S. laws involving copyright, child pornography, and so forth. So if search engine companies make a good faith effort to remove those links, they are immune from legal liability (in accordance with Section 512 of the Digital Millennium Copyright Act). In Europe, however, search engine companies are viewed as "controllers of personal data" that are responsible/liable for the content that is accessible through their services. So, American search engine companies, as well as all non-European companies, operating in Europe are required to comply with RTBF.

According to (b), Google and other major search engine companies have argued that it would be extremely difficult, as well as very time consuming, for them to have to respond to every RTBF-like request made by users. For example, some critics have noted that in the time period between the ECJ's ruling on RTBF, in May 2014 and April 2015, Google received more than 244,000 requests for delinking.[38] So, these critics might also argue that Google's obligation to sort through these requests would not only be a daunting task but that being required to respond meaningfully to all of those requests in a timely manner would seem virtually impossible. However, we can ask whether these factors in themselves would be sufficient for someone or some company not to comply with a law. As Bottis (2014) points out, we do not cease to enact and comply with laws simply because their enforcement could not possibly eliminate certain crimes. She notes, for example, that even though it has not been possible to eliminate crimes like prostitution, drug dealing, and so forth, we do not "de-legislate" those crimes. Bottis further points out that in the digital world, protecting privacy and copyright has sometimes seemed impossible to achieve, but we still propose, enact, and enforce laws to protect both as best we can.[39]

Those who defend (b) might seem to have stronger case when Google's situation is examined from the vantage point of RTBF requests it receives to remove personal information solely on grounds that the information is embarrassing (e.g., one of the arguments made in the Mario González case). However, one could respond to this objection by noting that there is a critical difference between a company being required to comply with requests to delete or delink to personal information that is merely "unflattering" or "embarrassing" versus requests to delink to personal information that is either inaccurate or no longer relevant. So, perhaps a different set of standards could apply in the case of requests to delete/delink from personal information of the latter type, as opposed to the former.

We next examine two kinds of arguments typically used by journalists and publishers against RTBF. Essentially, these groups believe that being required to comply with RTBF is:

c. Tantamount to "Internet censorship" (because it violates "freedom of expression")

d. Harmful to the general public (because it interferes with a citizen's "right to know")

Regarding (c), many critics believe that requiring publishers to delete some kinds of online personal information (but not other kinds), or requiring search engine companies to remove links to that information, is a step toward censoring the Internet. Some American journalists and publishers also worry that RTBF, and principles like it, violate the First Amendment of the U.S. Constitution. For example, they argue that the RTBF principle interferes with the free flow of information (as well as freedom of expression), which is essential to their news reporting and journalistic investigations. But RFTB's supporters counter by claiming that "the spirit" of this privacy principle is "to empower individuals to manage their personal data" while also "explicitly protecting the freedom of expression and of the media."[40]

With respect to (d), many journalists and publishers also argue that RTBF threatens the public's right to access information and thus their right to know. So, these critics believe that the general public is harmed by RTBF and principles like it. Some of these critics also suggest that since RTBF would contribute to making the Internet less robust and would "degrade" its (overall) quality, because of the deleted online information and/or the removal of links to it.

5.8.2 Arguments Defending RTBF

In making their case for RTBF, many European supporters begin by pointing out that personal privacy is a human right (as stated in the United Nation's Declaration of Human Rights). Some of these supporters also see RTBF as a subset of a (principle in the) EU Data Protection Directive that already exists—namely, Article 12, which enables a user to request the deletion of personal data that is "no longer necessary."[41] But some also believe that Article 12 needs to be "updated and clarified for the digital age," and that this would include an explicit right to delete online personal information that is no longer *relevant*, as well as online personal information that is "inadequate" or "excessive."[42] Arguments supporting RTBF generally fall into two broad categories, claiming that this privacy principle is needed to:

i. Prevent innocent people from being harmed

ii. Protect people whose personal identity evolves over time

Regarding (i), supporters argue that without a principle like RTBF, many people are at "risk" and thus vulnerable to "harm" in a variety of ways. For example, Bottis (2014) notes that people can easily be "defamed, humiliated, and degraded" by the kinds of inappropriate personal information about them that is readily accessible on the Internet. Consider some relatively recent incidents involving "revenge porn" sites, where victims have unfairly suffered significant psychological harm.[43] Arguably, these victims should have the right to have this kind of inappropriate information about them deleted, or at least delinked.

In addition to the kinds of psychological harm caused to these victims, however, Bottis notes that without RTBF, some people may even be at risk of being put in serious physical danger. To illustrate this claim, she points to an actual case involving a rape victim from the past whose name was later revealed to the public via a newspaper article in the *Florida Star*. (While this newspaper had legally acquired the name of the victim via a court record, its decision to print the name violated a Florida state statute.) In this incident, the past victim, whose real identity had been exposed, was "*threatened again* with rape, forced to move and change jobs [and suffered] from deep distress and public humiliation."[44] This particular incident involved personal information that had been published in a physical newspaper. But many newspaper articles have since been converted to digital form and made available online, which means that these articles are now discoverable by, and accessible to, a much wider audience. So, the rape victim whose name was disclosed by the *Florida Star* (several years ago) could now potentially be at an even greater risk regarding her physical safety. However, with an RFTB-like privacy principle in place, that victim would have some legal recourse in being able to request the removal of any links to the online version of that newspaper article (and possibly to having the online version of the article deleted altogether).

With respect to (ii), some RTBF supporters worry about a person's ability to protect his or her *personal identity* and *autonomy*—for example, to develop one's identity in an autonomous way in a digital world. Earlier (in Section 5.3), we noted some connections between autonomy and privacy and showed how the latter can be essential for the former. Some also believe that privacy is essential for one's personal identity. For example, Floridi (2014) has argued that a society in which "no informational privacy is possible . . . is one in which no personal identity can be maintained."[45] So, some RTBF advocates argue that people who are continually "stigmatized" by the presence of online personal information about their distant past would not have the level of privacy that is essential to protect their personal identities. These advocates believe that because the Internet "never forgets," a principle like RTBF is needed to protect those whose personal identities may evolve over time.

RTBF supporters further argue that since one's personal identity can evolve significantly over one's lifetime, certain kinds of information about a person's characteristics in the distant past may no longer be relevant or appropriate. For example, Bottis notes that some kinds of information revealed about one's past religious beliefs, sexual orientation, and so forth, may no longer reflect that person's present identity. Consider the case of a person who had a sex change 40 years ago. Does information about that incident need to be available online? Unless the person who had the sex change is a public figure, in which case he or she would not be protected by RTBF anyway, information about that person's past sexual identity could be viewed as neither relevant nor something that the general public has a need to know.

We have briefly examined some arguments for and against RTBF. While this privacy principle may never extend beyond the EU countries, RTBF is nevertheless the law in Europe; so, any search engine company, or any other kind of company, doing business in Europe must comply with it. But a difficult challenge facing those companies is determining the appropriate criteria for whether or not the digital links to a specific incident in one's past warrant removal.

5.8.3 Establishing "Appropriate" Criteria

Although the ECJ ruled in favor of RTBF in May 2014, it did not provide precise criteria for search engine companies to comply with the new privacy principle. Google has since established an advisory council to come up with appropriate criteria. It would seem that at least two important factors need to be taken into consideration: (i) the nature of the *personal information* itself and (ii) the *context(s)* in which this information flows. With regard to (i), Floridi raises an interesting point by asking: "Is the information this person would like to see de-linked, or even perhaps removed, *constitutive* of that person . . . [o]r is it something completely irrelevant?"[46] Initially, at least, Floridi's distinction would seem to provide a very helpful criterion for search engine companies and online content providers to consider. Recall, for example, the hypothetical incident involving "Philip Clark" (in Scenario 5–8). Is the information about Philip's arrest 20 years ago for underage drinking "constitutive" of Philip's identity? How relevant is that information about Philip? Based simply on what has been disclosed about him in Scenario 5–8, the information would not seem very relevant at all. So, Floridi's (constitutive) criterion would seem to work well in this scenario.

Suppose, however, we were to alter that scenario slightly, that is, in such a way that Philip is considering running for a political office in Amityville (e.g., as a city alderman). Arguably, that information about Philip's past would now seem more *relevant*, even if it is nor more *constitutive* of Philip's identity than it was before. It is one thing if Philip, as a private citizen of Amityville, wishes to have a link to a story about a 20-year-old underage drinking arrest removed because it causes problems for him in trying to change jobs. But if Philip decides to run for public office, even at a very low level, it is reasonable to argue that this information about his past arrest may indeed be relevant. So, it would seem that in this case, the question of whether such-and-such personal information is constitutive of Philip's identity does not play a key role in our decision. (Of course, once someone becomes a "public figure," the RTBF principle no longer applies to that person in the same way that it does to an ordinary citizen.)

While there may indeed be many clear-cut cases where Floridi's "constitutive" criterion can be applied fairly easily, borderline cases will also likely arise where its application might be less effective. Consider again the case of Philip Clark, but this time suppose Philip's arrest had been made when he was 21 years of age (i.e., when he was legally an adult in the U.S.) and that it involved driving while intoxicated (DWI) instead of underage drinking in a home or dorm room. Information about Philip in the DWI incident may be no more constitutive of Philip's identity than the information about his underage drinking. Yet, there may be compelling reasons not to delete the former information about Philip, even if there is agreement that information about his underage drinking arrest does warrant removal.

We now turn to (ii)—namely, criteria affecting the *context* in which ones online personal information flows. Recall Helen Nissenbaum's framework of "privacy as contextual integrity," which we examined in Section 5.4. There we saw that Nissenbaum's privacy framework requires that the processes used in disseminating personal information must not only be "appropriate" to a particular context but must also comply with "norms that govern the flow of personal information" within that context. We saw that in Nissenbaum's framework, "norms of distribution" can restrict or limit the flow of information both within and across various contexts. We also saw that when that norm is "breached," a violation of privacy occurs. So, in Nissenbaum's scheme, it is not necessarily the information itself—for example, whether it happens to be constitutive of one's identity—that is germane; rather it is the context and the "norms" that govern the flow of the personal information in that context.

We can now see why attempts at resolving the question about which *kinds* of personal information should be eligible for deletion, and which should not, may be more difficult than anticipated. But even if clear-cut criteria could, in principle, be established, questions still remain about the process involved for removing and deindexing the personal information. For example, should users contact the search engine companies that provide the links to the information (or content) or should they instead contact the publishers who make the online content available? Floridi (2014) notes that while a search engine company has "no creative power with respect to the personal information it indexes," a publisher "has both creative and controlling power over the personal information in question." So, he argues that a publisher, unlike a search engine, can "block access to personal information quite easily." In light of this distinction, Floridi argues for a procedure whereby a user would first make a request to a publisher to remove the information in question. If that fails, then the user could next request the search engine company to delink it. If that still does not work, the user could then appeal to the national Data Protection Authority (DPA) in his or her country (in Europe). And, finally, if that does not work, the user could appeal to the ECJ.[47]

An additional RTB-related question to consider has to do with the principle's scope: how widely should it apply? As already noted, the ECJ's ruling affects only those search engines operating in Europe. (We should also note that the Google search engine in Europe displays the "removal notification" at the bottom of the search page in the case of "name searches" it has delinked.) So, people living outside Europe can still access information that has been removed (e.g., information about Mario Gonzalez) via Google.com, but not through Google.co.es (in Spain). Finally, it is worth noting that the ECJ allows Google, as well as other search engine companies operating in Europe, to assess RTBF requests on a case-by-case basis in determining which requests must be honored and which can be rejected.

▶ 5.9 CHAPTER SUMMARY

We began this chapter by examining some ways that cybertechnology has exacerbated privacy concerns introduced by earlier technologies. We then briefly examined the concept of privacy and some theories that have attempted to explain and defend the need for privacy protection. We saw that "informational privacy" could be distinguished from "accessibility privacy" and "decisional privacy," and that Moor's privacy theory was able to integrate key components of three traditional theories into one comprehensive theory of privacy. We also saw that privacy is an important value, essential for human ends such as friendship and autonomy.

Next, we saw how personal privacy is threatened by data-gathering techniques such as RFID technologies and Internet cookies and by data-analysis techniques such as those associated with Big Data. We then saw the impact that data mining technologies have for privacy, especially for many forms of "public personal information" that have no explicit normative protection. In our analysis of the problem of "protecting privacy in public," we examined ways in which contemporary search engines pose some significant challenges. We then examined the debate between those who advocate for stricter privacy laws and those who champion (industry) self-regulation standards as an alternative to additional privacy legislation. Finally, we examined the current dispute involving an individual's alleged "right to be forgotten" (or "right to erasure") in a digital world.

We also noted at the outset that not all computer-related privacy concerns could be examined in this chapter. For example, specific kinds of privacy issues pertaining to employee monitoring in the workplace are examined in Chapter 10, while surveillance concerns affecting "location privacy" made possible by pervasive computing and ambient intelligence are examined in Chapter 12. Although some privacy concerns affecting personal information collected by governmental organizations were briefly identified and considered in this chapter, additional privacy issues in this area are examined in Chapter 6 in the context of our discussion of computer/cyber security.

▶ REVIEW QUESTIONS

1. Describe four ways in which the privacy threats posed by cybertechnology differ from those posed by earlier technologies.
2. What is personal privacy and why is it difficult to define?
3. Describe some important characteristics that differentiate "accessibility privacy," "decisional privacy," and "informational privacy."
4. How does James Moor's theory of privacy combine key elements of these three views of privacy? What

does Moor mean by a "situation," and how does he distinguish between "natural privacy" and "normative privacy"?

5. Why is privacy valued? Is privacy an intrinsic value or is it an instrumental value? Explain.
6. Is privacy a social value or is it simply an individual good?
7. What does Roger Clarke mean by "dataveillance"? Why do dataveillance techniques threaten personal privacy?
8. What are Internet cookies and why are they considered controversial from the perspective of personal privacy?
9. What is RFID technology and why is it a threat to privacy?
10. Describe some surveillance techniques that the U.S. government has used to collect data on its citizens. Why are they considered controversial?
11. What is meant by "Big Data"? Why is this notion difficult to define?
12. What is data mining and why is it considered controversial?
13. What is Web mining and how is it similar to and different from traditional data mining?
14. What is the difference between public personal information (PPI) and nonpublic personal information (NPI)?
15. What is meant by "privacy in public"? Describe the problem of protecting personal privacy in public space.
16. Why are certain uses of Internet search engines problematic from a privacy perspective?
17. Describe some of the voluntary controls and self-regulation initiatives that have been proposed by representatives from industry and e-commerce.
18. Why do many privacy advocates in the U.S. believe that industry self-regulation and voluntary controls are not adequate and that stronger privacy legislation is needed?
19. What are some of the criticisms of U.S. privacy laws such as HIPAA and the Privacy Act of 1974?
20. Describe some principles included in the EU Directive on Data Protection. What do you believe to be some of the strengths and weaknesses of those principles when compared to privacy laws in the United States?
21. What is the meant by the "Right to Be Forgotten"? Why is this "right" so controversial?

▶ DISCUSSION QUESTIONS

22. Review Helen Nissenbaum's framework of privacy in terms of "contextual integrity." What are the differences between what she calls "norms of appropriateness" and "norms of distribution"? Give an example of how either or both norms can be breached in a specific context.
23. Through the use of currently available online tools and search facilities, ordinary users can easily acquire personal information about others. In fact, anyone who has Internet access can, via a search engine such as Google, find information about us that we ourselves might have had no idea is publicly available there. Does this use of search engines threaten the privacy of ordinary people? Explain.
24. In debates regarding access and control of personal information, it is sometimes argued that an appropriate balance needs to be struck between individuals and organizations: individuals claim that they should be able to control who has access to their information and organizations, including government and business groups, claim to need that information in order to make appropriate decisions. How can a reasonable resolution be reached that would satisfy both parties?
25. Reexamine the arguments made by the U.S. government and by Google regarding the government's requests for information about users' search requests made during the summer of 2005. Are the government's reasons for why it should have access to that information reasonable? Does Google have an obligation to protect the personal information of its users, with respect to disclosing information about their searches? Could this obligation be overridden by certain kinds of national defense interests? If, for example, the government claimed to need the information to prevent a potential terrorist attack, would that have changed your analysis of the situation? Or does the government have the right, and possibly an obligation to the majority of its citizens, to monitor the searches if doing so could positively affect the outcome of child pornography legislation?
26. Initially, privacy concerns involving computer technology arose because citizens feared that a strong centralized government could easily collect and store data about them. In the 1960s, for example, there was talk of constructing a national computerized database in the United States, and many were concerned that George Orwell's prediction of Big Brother in his classic book 1984 had finally arrived. The centralized database, however, never materialized. Prior to September 11, 2001, some privacy advocates suggested that we have fewer reasons to be concerned about the federal government's role in privacy intrusions (Big Brother) than we do about privacy threats from the commercial sector (Big Bucks and Big Browser). Is that assessment still accurate? Defend your answer.

Scenarios for Analysis

1. In the days and weeks immediately following the tragic events of September 11, 2001, some political leaders in the United States argued that extraordinary times call for extraordinary measures; in times of war, basic civil liberties and freedoms, such as privacy, need to be severely restricted for the sake of national security and safety. Initially, the majority of American citizens strongly supported the Patriot Act, which passed by an overwhelming margin in both houses of Congress and was enacted into law on October 21, 2001. However, between 2001 and 2005, support for this act diminished considerably. Many privacy advocates believe that it goes too far and thus erodes basic civil liberties. Some critics also fear that certain provisions included in the act could easily be abused. Examine some of the details of the Patriot Act (which can be viewed on the Web at www.govtrack.us/congress/bills/107/hr3162/text) and determine whether its measures are as extreme as its critics suggest. Are those measures also consistent with the value of privacy, which many Americans claim to embrace? Do privacy interests need to be reassessed, and possibly recalibrated, in light of ongoing threats from terrorists? To what extent does the following expression, attributed to Benjamin Franklin, affect your answer to this question: "They who can give up essential liberty to obtain a little temporary safety, deserve neither liberty nor safety."
2. At the beginning of this chapter, we suggested that concerns about the loss of privacy may have a generational dimension or element—that is, younger people may be less concerned about privacy loss involving cybertechnology than older people. To further explore this possibility, conduct a series of informal interviews with individuals that represent three generations: Millennials, Gen X/Y, and Baby Boomers. Ask members of each group how much they value their privacy and how much of it they are willing to trade off for the convenience of cybertechnology. Compare the results of the answers you get from the three groups. Are their respective views about the importance of privacy as far apart as some might expect? Explain.

▶ ENDNOTES

1. See, for example, Berkes (2014). Berkes notes that a zettabyte of data is roughly equivalent to the amount of data that would "fill 250 billion DVDs" and that it is estimated that five zettabytes of data could store approximately "100 years worth of [all] worldwide communications." For additional information about the controversy surrounding the opening of this new NSA data facility, see http://www.npr.org/2013/06/10/190160772/amid-data-controversy-nsa-builds-its-biggest-data-farm. See also the description of the new NSA facility in Bamford (2012).
2. See, for example, Solove (2011).
3. See the interview with Arthur Miller in the video, "The World at Your Fingertips," in the BBC/PBS Series, *The Machine that Changed the World*, 1990.
4. See Warren and Brandeis (1890) for more detail.
5. For a discussion of the right to privacy in the Quinlan case, see "Court at the End of Life—The Right to Privacy: Karen Ann Quinlan" at http://www.libraryindex.com/pages/582/Court-End-Life-RIGHT-PRIVACY-KAREN-ANN-QUINLAN.html.
6. Moor (2000, p. 207). [Italics added]
7. Key aspects of Moor's privacy framework are more fully developed in Tavani and Moor (2001).
8. Nissenbaum (2004a, p. 137).
9. *Ibid*, p. 135. For examples of ways in which Nissenbaum's contextual integrity model of privacy can be applied to the blogosphere and to "the Cloud," see Grodzinsky and Tavani (2010, 2011), respectively.
10. See Westin (1967) for more detail on this point.
11. Solove (2008, p. 84).
12. DeCew (2006, p. 121). Moor (2006, p. 114) also describes privacy as a kind of "shield" that protects us.
13. Solove, p. 91.
14. See Clarke's account of dataveillance, available at http://www.rogerclarke.com/DV/.
15. See Halpern (2011) for more detail.
16. Nissenbaum, p. 135.
17. Ward and Barker (2013, p. 1). Available at Ar Xiv:1309.5821lvl [cs.DB]. In their view, this lack of consistency both "introduces ambiguity" and "hampers discourse" about issues affecting big data.
18. *Ibid*, p. 2. [Italics Ward and Barker] Although their definition also includes the "collection," as well the analysis of data, we focus solely on the analysis aspect of big data in this section.
19. Boyd and Crawford (2012, p. 663). [Italics added]
20. Two of these categories—variety and velocity (along with "volume")—were first articulated in the now classic Gartner Report (2001).
21. Poskanzer (2015, p. 210).
22. Vedder (2004) refers to the kind of privacy protection needed for groups as "Categorial Privacy."
23. In composing this section on data mining, I have drawn from and expanded upon some concepts and distinctions introduced in Tavani (1999, 2007).
24. See "Web Mining." In *Wikipedia*. Available at http://en.wikipedia.org/wiki/Web_mining.
25. See, for example, the account of Facebook Beacon in http://en.wikipedia.org/wiki/Facebook.
26. Nissenbaum (2004b, p. 455).

27. Fulda (2004, p. 472).
28. See, for example, Nissenbaum (2010).
29. For an extended discussion of privacy issues generated by search engine technology, see Tavani (2012).
30. Critics point out that tools like *Anonymizer* are not effective in e-commerce contexts; they also note that even in non-e-commerce contexts, users' online activities can still be tracked via their IP addresses.
31. For more information about the Toysmart case, see Morehead (2000), who notes that Toysmart made the mistake of separating its customer list as a "separate asset" instead of grouping it together with other aspects of its "corporate package."
32. See Werner (2012) for a more detailed analysis of this controversy.
33. See Julian Sanchez (2013) interviewed in *Online Privacy: How Did We Get Here?* PBS/Digital Studios. Available at http://www.theatlantic.com/video/archive/2013/07/what-we-talk-about-when-we-talk-about-privacy/278134/.
34. See http://www.oecd.org/document/18/0,3343,en_2649_34255_1815186_1_1_1_1,00.html.
35. See http://www.cdt.org/privacy/eudirective/EU_Directive_.html.
36. For more detail about the various principles and how each works, see http://eur-lex.europa.eu/LexUriServ/LexUriServ.do?uri=CELEX:31995L0046:en:HTML.
37. According to the revisions included in Article 17 of the EU Directive, individuals have the right—under certain conditions—to ask search engines to remove links with personal information about them.
38. See "A New Ethics Case Study." Available at http://www.scu.edu/ethics-center/ethicsblog/internet-ethics.cfm?c=22135&utm_source=feedburner&utm_medium=email&utm_campaign=Feed%3A+EthicalIssuesInTheOnlineWorld+%28Ethical+Issues+in+the+Online+World%29. See also Herritt (2014).
39. See Bottis (2014). I am grateful to Professor Bottis for some additional points she raised in a series of e-mail exchanges with me on the topic of RTBF, which are included here.
40. See the *Factsheet on the "Right to Be Forgotten" Ruling C131/12*. Available at http://ec.europa.eu/justice/data-protection/files/factsheets/factsheet_data_protection_en.pdf.
41. Article 12 (Right of Access) states "the rectification, erasure, or blocking of data the processing of which does not comply with the provisions of the Directive because the information is incomplete or inaccurate and a notification to whom the data has been disclosed of any rectification, erasure, or blocking . . . unless this proves impossible or involves disproportionate effort."
42. These criteria are in included in Article 17 ("Right to be forgotten and to erasure") of the EU Directive.
43. Of course, the topic of "revenge porn" is one that warrants separate discussion because of the cluster of ethical issues it raises. But it is mentioned here because it makes available one kind of online personal information that an injured party should clearly be able to have deleted.
44. Bottis (2014, p. 3). [Italics Bottis]
45. See the interview with Floridi in Herritt (2014, p. 2).
46. *Ibid*, p. 4. [Italics added]
47. *Ibid*. This procedure would follow one that is already in place for requesting the deletion of "unnecessary personal information," in accordance with Article 12 of the EU Privacy Directive.

▶ REFERENCES

Adam, Alison. 2005. "Chips in Our Children: Can We Inscribe Privacy in a Machine?" *Ethics and Information Technology* 7, no. 4: 233–42.

Anguin, Julia and Jennifer Valentino-DeVries. 2012. "Google's iPhone Tracking: Web Giant, Others Bypassed Apple Browser Settings for Guarding Privacy." *Wall Street Journal*, February 17. Available at http://online.wsj.com/article_email/SB1000142405297020488040457722538045659917 6-lMyQjAxMTAyMDEwNjExNDYyWj.html

Bamford, James. 2012. "The NSA Is Building the Country's Biggest Spy Center (Watch What You Say)." *Wired*, March 15. Available at http://m.wired.com/threatlevel/2012/03/ff_nsadatacenter/all/1.

Berkes, Howard. 2014. "Amid Data Controversy NSA Builds Its Biggest Data Farm." Available at http://www.npr.org/2013/06/10/190160772/amid-data-controversy-nsa-builds-its-biggest-data-farm.

Bottis, Maria. 2014. "Allow Me to Live the Good Life, Let me Forget: Legal and Psychological Foundations of the Right to Be Forgotten and the New Developments in the European Union Laws." In *Well-Being, Flourishing, and ICTs: Proceedings of the Eleventh International Conference on Computer Ethics–Philosophical Enquiry*. Menomonie, WI: INSEIT, Article 10.

Boyd, Danah and Kate Crawford. 2012. "Critical Questions for Big Data: Provocations for a Cultural, Scholarly, and Technological Phenomenon." *Information, Communication, and Society* 15, no. 5: 62–79.

DeCew, Judith W. 1997. *In Pursuit of Privacy: Law, Ethics, and the Rise of Technology*. Ithaca, NY: Cornell University Press.

DeCew, Judith W. 2006. "Privacy and Policy for Genetic Research." In H. T. Tavani, ed. *Ethics, Computing, and Genomics*. Sudbury, MA: Jones and Bartlett, pp. 121–35.

Elgesem, Dag. 2004. "The Structure of Rights in Directive 95/46/EC on the Protection of Individuals with Regard to the Processing of Personal Data and the Free Movement of Such Data." In R. A. Spinello and H. T. Tavani, eds. *Readings in CyberEthics*. 2nd ed. Sudbury, MA: Jones and Bartlett Publishers, pp. 418–35.

Floridi, Luciano. 2014. "The Right to Be Forgotten – The Road Ahead." *The Guardian*, October 8. Available at http://www.theguardian.com/technology/2014/oct/08/the-right-to-be-forgotten-the-road-ahead.

Fried, Charles. 1990. "Privacy: A Rational Context." In M. D. Ermann, M. B. Williams, and C. Gutierrez, eds. *Computers, Ethics, and Society*. New York: Oxford University Press, pp. 51–67.

Froomkin, Michael. 2000. "The Death of Privacy?" *Stanford Law Review* 52. Available at www.law.miami.edu/~froomkin/articles/privacy-deathof.pdf.

Fulda, Joseph S. 2004. "Data Mining and Privacy." In R. A. Spinello and H. Tavani, eds. *Readings in CyberEthics*. 2nd ed. Sudbury, MA: Jones and Bartlett Publishers, pp. 471–5.

Garfinkel, Simson. 2000. *Database Nation: The Death of Privacy in the 21st Century*. Cambridge, MA: O'Reilly and Associates.

Garfinkel, Simson. 2002. "RFID Bill of Rights." *Technology Review*, October. Available at http://www.technologyreview.com/article/401660/an-rfid-bill-of-rights/.

Grodzinsky, Frances S. and Herman T. Tavani. 2010. "Applying the 'Contextual Integrity' Model of Privacy to Personal Blogs in the Blogosphere," *International Journal of Internet Research Ethics* 3, no. 1, pp. 38–47.

Grodzinsky, Francis, S. and Herman T. Tavani. 2011. "Privacy in 'the Cloud': Applying Nissenbaum's Theory of Contextual Integrity." *Computers and Society* 41, no. 1: 38–47.

Halpern, Sue. 2011. "Mind Control and the Internet." *New York Review of Books*, June 23. Available at http://www.nybooks.com/articles/archives/2011/jun/23/mind-control-and-internet/.

Herritt, Robert. 2014. "Google's Philosopher." *Nature and Technology*, December 30. Available at http://www.psmag.com/navigation/nature-and-technology/googles-philosopher-technology-nature-identity-court-legal-policy-95456/.

Lockton, Vance and Richard S. Rosenberg. 2005. "RFID: The Next Serious Threat to Privacy." *Ethics and Information Technology* 7, no. 4: 221–31.

Moor, James H. 2000. "Towards a Theory of Privacy for the Information Age." In R. M. Baird, R. Ramsower, and S. E. Rosenbaum, eds. *Cyberethics: Moral, Social, and Legal Issues in the Computer Age*. Amherst, NY: Prometheus Books, pp. 200–12.

Moor, James H. 2004. "Reason, Relativity, and Responsibility in Computer Ethics." In R. A. Spinello and H. T. Tavani, eds. *Readings in CyberEthics*. 2nd ed. Sudbury, MA: Jones and Bartlett Publishers, pp. 40–54.

Moor, James H. 2006. "Using Genetic Information While Protecting the Privacy of the Soul." In H. T. Tavani, ed. *Ethics, Computing, and Genomics*. Sudbury, MA: Jones and Bartlett, pp. 109–19.

Morehead, Nicholas. 2000. "Toysmart: Bankruptcy Litmus Test." *Wired* 7, no. 12. Available at http://archive.wired.com/techbiz/media/news/2000/07/37517.

Nissenbaum, Helen. 2004a. "Privacy as Contextual Integrity." *Washington Law Review* 79, no. 1: 119–57.

Nissenbaum, Helen. 2004b. "Toward an Approach to Privacy in Public: Challenges of Information Technology." In R. A. Spinello and H. T. Tavani, eds. *Readings in CyberEthics*. 2nd ed. Sudbury, MA: Jones and Bartlett, pp. 450–61. Reprinted from *Ethics and Behavior* 7, no. 3 (1997): 207–19.

Nissenbaum, Helen. 2010. *Privacy in Context: Technology, Policy, and the Integrity of Social Life*. Palo Alto, CA: Stanford University Press.

Pariser, Eli. 2011. *The Filter Bubble: What the Internet Is Hiding from You*. New York: Penguin.

Poskanzer, Deborah. 2015. "Big Data." In J. Britt Holbrook and Carl Mitcham, eds. *Ethics, Science, Technology, and Engineering: A Global Resource*. Vol. 1, 2nd ed. Farmington Hills, MI: Macmillan Reference, pp. 210–12.

Regan, Priscilla M. 1995. *Legislating Privacy: Technology, Social Values, and Public Policy*. Chapel Hill, NC: The University of North Carolina Press.

Solove, Daniel J. 2008. *Understanding Privacy*. Cambridge, MA: Harvard University Press.

Solove, Daniel J. 2011. *Nothing to Hide: The False Tradeoff between Privacy and Security*. New Haven, CT: Yale University Press.

Spinello, Richard A. 2010. "Informational Privacy." In G. Brenkert and T. Beauchamp, eds. *The Oxford Handbook of Business Ethics*. Oxford, UK: Oxford University Press, pp. 366–87.

Stuckey, Mike. 2008. "Amex Rates Credit Risk by Where You Live, Shop." *MSNBC.Com*. Available at http://www.msnbc.msn.com/id/27055285/.

Tavani, Herman T. 1999. "Informational Privacy, Data Mining and the Internet." *Ethics and Information Technology* 1, no. 2: 137–45.

Tavani, Herman T. 2007. "Philosophical Theories of Privacy: Implications for an Adequate Online Privacy Policy." *Metaphilosophy* 38, no. 1, pp. 1–22.

Tavani, Herman T. 2012. "Search Engines and Ethics." *Stanford Encyclopedia of Philosophy*. Available at http://plato.stanford.edu/entries/ethics-search/.

Tavani, Herman T. and James H. Moor. 2001. "Privacy Protection, Control over Information, and Privacy-Enhancing Technologies." *Computers and Society* 31, no. 1: 6–11.

Vedder, Anton. 2004. "KDD, Privacy, Individuality, and Fairness." In R. A. Spinello and H. T. Tavani, eds. *Readings in CyberEthics*. 2nd ed. Sudbury, MA: Jones and Bartlett, pp. 462–70.

Ward, Jonathan Stuart and Adam Barker. 2013. "Undefined by Data: A Survey of Big Data Definitions." Cornell University Library. Available at http://arxiv.org/abs/1309.5821.

Warren, Samuel and Louis Brandeis. 1890. "The Right to Privacy." *Harvard Law Review* 4, no. 5: 193–220.

Werner, Jeff. 2012. "Should You Be Worried about Google's New Privacy Policy?" *NWFDailyNews.com*, March 25. Available at http://www.nwfdailynews.com/articles/google-48355-new-policy.html.

Westin, Alan. 1967. *Privacy and Freedom*. New York: Atheneum Press.

Zimmer, Michael 2008. "The Gaze of the Perfect Search Engine: Google as an Institution of Dataveillance." In A. Spink and M. Zimmer, eds. *Web Search: Multidisciplinary Perspectives*. Berlin: Springer-Verlag, pp. 77–99.

▶ FURTHER READINGS

Alfino, Mark. 2001. "Misplacing Privacy." *Journal of Information Ethics* 10, no. 1: 5–8.

Floridi, Luciano. 2014. "Right to Be Forgotten: Who May Exercise Power, over which kind of Information." *The Guardian*. Available at http://www.theguardian.com/technology/2014/oct/21/right-to-be-forgotten-who-may-exercise-power-information?CMP=twt_gu. October 22.

Lyon, David. 2014. "Surveillance, Snowden, and Big Data: Capacities, Consequences, Critique." Big Data and Society 1:1–13.

Schneier, Bruce. 2015. *Data and Goliath: The Hidden Battles to Collect your Data and Control Your World*. New York: W. W. Norton.

Shoemaker, David W. 2010. "Self Exposure and Exposure of the Self: Informational Privacy and the Presentation of Identity." *Ethics and Information Technology* 12, no. 1: 3–15.

Spinello, Richard A. 2011. "Privacy and Social Networking." *International Review of Information Ethics* 16: 42–6.

Zimmer, Michael. 2005. "Surveillance, Privacy, and the Ethics of Vehicle Safety Communication Technologies." *Ethics and Information Technology* 7, no. 4: 201–10.

CHAPTER

6

Security in Cyberspace

LEARNING OBJECTIVES

Upon completing this chapter, you will successfully be able to:

- Articulate what is meant by *security* in the context of cybertechnology and differentiate issues in cybersecurity from both *cyberprivacy*-related issues and *cybercrime*-related issues,
- Distinguish among three distinct categories of security affecting cybertechnology: *data* security, *system* security, and *network* security,
- Describe key challenges that *cloud computing* poses for cybersecurity,
- Explain what is meant by the terms *hacking*, *Hacker Ethic*, and *hacktivism*,
- Describe the parameters of *cyberterrorism* and show how it can be distinguished both from hacktivism and information warfare,
- Explain what is meant by *information warfare* and show how it is both similar to and different from cyberterrorism.

In this chapter, we examine a wide range of issues affecting cybersecurity. Among them is the question whether cyber intrusions can ever be justified on ethical grounds? For example, would it ever be morally permissible for governmental organizations in (sovereign) nation states to engage in cyberattacks and computer break-ins? The following scenario, illustrating an alleged intrusion involving three nations, briefly addresses that question.

▶ **SCENARIO 6–1:** The "Olympic Games" Operation and the Stuxnet Worm

In June 2012, the *New York Times* reported that the United States and Israeli governments had been cooperating on an initiative code-named *Olympic Games*. Originally conceived and developed during the George W. Bush administration, the Olympic Games operation aimed at disrupting Iran's uranium enrichment program and thus damaging that nation's nuclear capability. At the core of this joint operation was a computer worm known as Stuxnet, a "cyberweapon" that targeted "electronic program controllers" developed by Siemens Corporation (in Germany) for industrial controlled computers (ICCs) that were installed in Iran. The Stuxnet worm was allegedly responsible for (i) sending misleading data to computer monitors in Iran and (ii) causing several of that nation's centrifuges—that is, fast-spinning machines that enrich uranium—to spin out of control. The Stuxnet attack was estimated to have destroyed approximately 1,000 of Iran's (then) 6,000 centrifuges.[1] ■

Was the Olympic Games operation a justified breach of cybersecurity? If it is wrong for ordinary individuals and nongovernmental actors/organizations to break into and disrupt someone's computer system, is it also wrong for sovereign nation states to do this as well? Or, can exceptions be made in the case of cyberwarfare that would justify such actions? We should point, however, that during the Olympic Games incident, no formal declaration of war existed among the three nations allegedly involved (Iran, Israel, and the United States). So, we might modify our original question slightly by asking instead whether imminent threats regarding the development of nuclear weapons by "rogue" nations could be used to justify cyber intrusions on the part of any "legitimate" sovereign nation(s) affected. For example, one might be inclined to argue that such actions against rogue nations could be justified on consequentialist or utilitarian grounds (i.e., based on the principle of "the greatest good for the greatest number"), examined in Chapter 2.

But if it is permissible for sovereign nations states such as the United States and Israel to engage in cyber intrusions against so-called rogue nations like Iran, simply on consequentialist grounds, we can ask the following question: Why would it not also be permissible for some nonstate actors—for example, members of the computer hacking community—to launch cyberattacks against those nations, if an overall greater good could result from their actions? After all, if our concern is merely with the kinds of desirable consequences that would likely be achieved, couldn't the same utilitarian principles justify cyberattacks from hacker groups or from other kinds of nonstate actors/organizations as well? Furthermore, we could ask whether those same actors/organizations might also be justified in attacking "unofficial states" such as Al Qaeda and Islamic State in Iraq and Syria (ISIS), which are not officially recognized by the international community as legitimate and sovereign states.

In February 2015, a well-known international hacker group, called *Anonymous*, announced its plans to take down ISIS by attacking that organization's social media sites used to spread ISIS propaganda and recruit new members.[2] (We describe the Anonymous hacker group in more detail in Scenario 6–3, where we examine that group's activities and practices in the context of our discussions involving some distinctions between hacktivism and cyberterrorism.) On the one hand, some might be inclined to applaud Anonymous' objectives in the case of ISIS. On the other hand, however, we can ask what the unintended consequences might be if we legitimize such activities by international hacker groups like Anonymous, who do not act officially on the part of any legitimate or recognized nation state(s).

We examine controversies affecting cyberterrorism and information warfare (IW) in detail in Sections 6.5 and 6.6, respectively. The purpose of Scenario 6–1, and our brief discussion here of the controversies it raises, is simply to get us to begin thinking about the kinds of state-sponsored hacking/cyber-intrusion incidents that have become commonplace and how these activities pose some significant challenges for implementing coherent cybersecurity polices at the international level. We begin our analysis of cybersecurity issues by defining some basic concepts and drawing some key distinctions.

▶ 6.1 SECURITY IN THE CONTEXT OF CYBERTECHNOLOGY

What, exactly, do we mean by "computer security" and "cybersecurity"? Like privacy, security—especially in the context of computing and cybertechnology—has no universally agreed-upon definition. The expressions computer security and cybersecurity are often associated with issues having to do with the reliability, availability, and safety of computer systems, as well as with the integrity, confidentiality, and protection of data. Epstein (2007) suggests that security concerns affecting computers and cybertechnology can be viewed in terms of three key elements:

- Confidentiality
- Integrity
- Accessibility

In Epstein's scheme, confidentiality has to do with "preventing unauthorized persons from gaining access to unauthorized information," while integrity is about "preventing an attacker from modifying data." And accessibility has to do with "making sure that resources are available for authorized users."[3]

Are any additional elements or criteria useful for understanding cybersecurity? Neumann (2004) notes that, in addition to providing desired confidentiality, integrity, and accessibility, cybersecurity aims at preventing "misuse, accidents, and malfunctions" with respect to computer systems. Neumann also notes, however, that cybersecurity can be a "double-edged sword"; for example, it can be used to protect privacy, but it can also be used to undermine "freedom of access" to information for users.[4]

In defining cybersecurity, it is important to point out that sometimes issues involving security in cyberspace overlap with concerns pertaining to cybercrime; other times, however, they intersect with issues involving privacy. We briefly examine some ways in which security issues intersect and overlap with both kinds of concerns, also noting how security concerns can be distinguished from those of privacy and crime.

6.1.1 Cybersecurity as Related to Cybercrime

How are cybersecurity violations both similar to and different from cybercrime? First, we should note that some cyberethics textbooks link together issues involving cybersecurity and cybercrime by covering them in the same chapter. Consequently, these issues could easily be viewed as subcategories of a single cyberethics category. But while most intentional cybersecurity violations are illegal and often criminal, not every crime in cyberspace involves a breach, or violation, of cybersecurity.

Consider three cyber-related crimes that have no direct implications for cybersecurity: A pedophile can use a computer to solicit sex with young children, a drug dealer can use the Internet to traffic in drugs, and a student can use an electronic device to pirate copyrighted music. Although each of these activities is clearly illegal, it is not clear that any of them necessarily result from insecure computers. Perhaps greater security mechanisms on computer networks could deter crimes and detect criminals in cyberspace, but cyber-assisted crimes involving pedophilia, drug trafficking, and pirating music do not typically result from security flaws in computer system design. There are, then, important distinctions between issues of security and crime involving cybertechnology. We will examine issues pertaining specifically to cybercrime in Chapter 7, while focusing our attention in this chapter on concerns affecting security in cyberspace. Just as cybersecurity issues are sometimes lumped together with cybercrime, security concerns involving cybertechnology can also overlap with worries about personal privacy. We briefly considered some of these security-related privacy concerns in Chapter 5. Now we ask: How are issues pertaining to security in cyberspace different from those involving privacy?

6.1.2 Security and Privacy: Some Similarities and Some Differences

The concepts of privacy and security are not always easy to separate, especially when civil liberties and basic human rights are discussed. In the United States, arguments for a right to privacy that appeal to the Fourth Amendment have often been made on the basis of securing the person (and the person's papers and so forth) from the physical intrusion of searches and seizures. Thompson (2001) believes that many of our claims for a right to privacy can be better understood as claims about a "right to being secure." And Moor (2000) argues that privacy can be understood as an expression of (the value) *security*, which he claims is a "core value."

Although cyber-related issues involving privacy and security can overlap, some important distinctions are nonetheless worth drawing. Privacy concerns affecting cybertechnology often arise because people fear losing control over personal information that can be accessed by organizations (especially businesses and government agencies), many of whom claim to have some legitimate need for that information in order to make important decisions. Security concerns, on the contrary, can arise because people worry that personal data or proprietary information, or both, could be retrieved and possibly altered by unauthorized individuals and organizations.

Privacy and security concerns can be thought of as two sides of a single coin: People need personal privacy, and they wish to have some control over their personal information, especially with respect to how that information is accessed by others. Making sure that personal information stored in computer databases is secure is important in helping them achieve and maintain their privacy. In this sense, then, the objectives for protecting privacy would seem compatible with, and even complementary to, those of maintaining security. In another sense, however, there appears to be a tension between privacy and security. From the perspective of security, protecting (computer) system resources and proprietary data (residing in those systems) is critical, whereas from the vantage point of privacy, protecting personal information and personal autonomy will have a higher priority.

In analyzing the tension involving privacy vs. security interests, Himma (2007a) has argued that threats to security outweigh comparable threats to the right to privacy. On the contrary, Nissenbaum (2010) and Solove (2011) both offer a more sympathetic appeal to the value of privacy in their analyses of the "trade-offs" between the two competing interests. The following quotation, attributed to Ben Franklin (1706–1790), is sometimes cited by privacy advocates to express their interpretation of what is at stake in the dispute involving security vs. privacy interests: "They who can give up essential liberty to obtain a little temporary safety, deserve neither liberty nor safety." However, in an era where concerns about cyberterrorism now influence our public policy debate, many people may be more willing to give up aspects of their liberty and privacy for greater security. (We examine some impacts that cyberterrorism has for this debate in Section 6.5.)

In the context of cybersecurity, privacy-related concerns include protecting personal data from unauthorized access, abuse, and alteration and thus reflect values that preserve individual autonomy and individual respect for persons. And while anonymity tools (briefly described in Chapter 5) help protect the privacy of individuals navigating in cyberspace, those tools can also cause serious concerns for security because anonymous behavior makes it difficult to identify security violators. So, in some cases, there is a natural tension between security and privacy, as we have seen; at other times, however, the objectives and goals of privacy and security—for example, with respect to confidentiality and data integrity—are the same.[5]

▶ 6.2 THREE CATEGORIES OF CYBERSECURITY

Security issues involving cybertechnology span a range of concerns having to do with three distinct kinds of vulnerabilities:

- **I.** Unauthorized access to data, which are either resident in or exchanged between computer systems
- **II.** Attacks on system resources (such as computer hardware, operating system software, and application software) by malicious computer programs
- **III.** Attacks on computer networks, including the infrastructure of privately owned networks and the Internet itself[6]

We refer to the first of these three categories of security concerns as "data security." The second category of concerns can be described under the heading "system security," and the third can be understood as "network security."

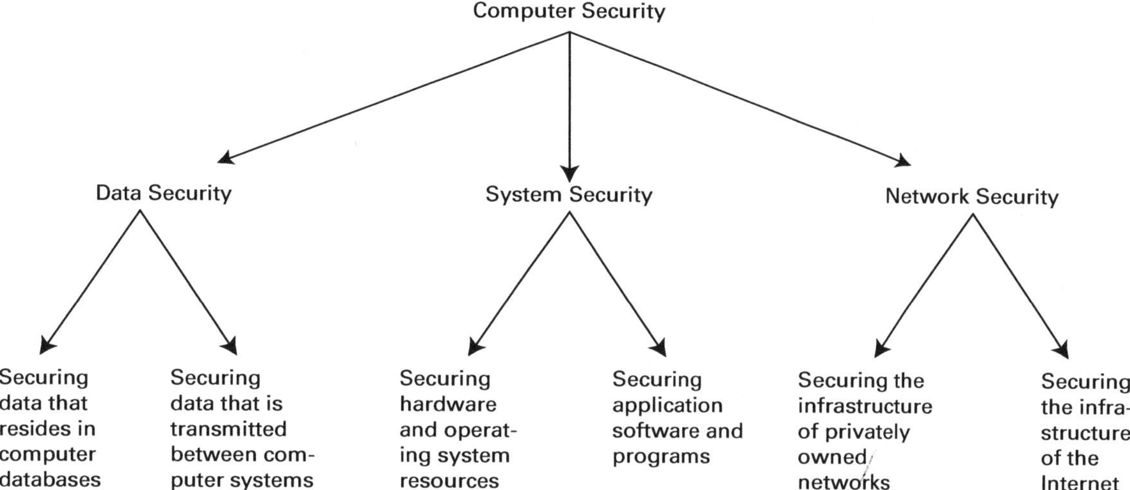

Figure 6-1 Three kinds of computer security.

We briefly describe some key aspects of each category of security, as summarized in Figure 6-1.

6.2.1 Data Security: Confidentiality, Integrity, and Availability of Information

Data security is concerned with vulnerabilities pertaining to unauthorized access to data. Those data can either (i) reside in one or more computer storage devices or (ii) be exchanged between two or more computer systems, or both. In particular, data security issues affect the confidentiality, integrity, and availability of information. Spinello (2000) aptly describes what is required for data security when he points out that

> . . . proprietary or sensitive information under one's custodial care is kept confidential and secure, that information being transmitted is not altered in form or content and cannot be read by unauthorized parties, and that all information being disseminated or otherwise made accessible through Web sites and online data repositories is as accurate and reliable as possible.[7]

Three points in this description are worth highlighting. First, the information to be protected can be either personal or proprietary, or both. (Proprietary information, as we will see in Chapter 8, is legally protected by schemes such as copyrights and patents and thus can be "owned" by corporations or by individuals, while sensitive information is generally considered to be intimate or confidential because it includes personal, medical, and financial records.)

Second, the information must be secured not only from tampering and alteration by unauthorized parties but also from merely being accessed (and read) by those parties. Third, and finally, the stored information must be accurate, readily available, and accessible to authorized parties. So, not only must the information residing in a computer database or in a password-protected Web site be available at optimal times; it must be able to be accessed by authorized users at any time—that is, accessible "on demand."

Data security is now also threatened by "cloud-computing" services (described in Section 6.3), as more and more corporations and ordinary users elect to store their data in "the cloud." Cloud storage devices provide users with one means to secure their data by ensuring that their data could survive (i) "crashes" on the hard drives of their personal computers and (ii) physical damages involving their electronic "tablets" and electronic devices. However, cloud storage also poses a threat to data security because unauthorized users could gain access to, and potentially manipulate, personal and proprietary data that is stored there.

6.2.2 System Security: Viruses, Worms, and Malware

System security is concerned with vulnerabilities to system resources such as computer hardware, operating system software, and application software. As such, it is concerned with various kinds of viruses, worms, and related "malicious programs" that can disrupt and sometimes destroy computer systems. What are the key differences between computer viruses and worms? Dale and Lewis (2016) define a virus as a "malicious, self-replicating program that embeds itself into other code" and a worm as a "malicious stand-alone program that often targets network resources."[8] Worms also differ from viruses because the former do not require human interaction in order to "propagate" in spreading via computer networks (Skoudis 2004). Also, worms can replicate and propagate without needing a host or program (Simpson 2006).

Some security analysts differentiate further between the two types of disruptive programs by pointing out that a worm is less virulent than a virus. However, worms can spread more quickly than viruses, because worms, as noted earlier, do not need any human action to trigger them. Also, worms can move from machine to machine across networks and thus can have parts of themselves "running" on different machines. Viruses, on the contrary, are not capable of running on their own, and they are often activated when an unsuspecting user opens an e-mail attachment.

Some worms and viruses have become well known by their infamous names—not only in the computer community but in the popular media as well. In recent years, prominent viruses and worms have had names such as "Blaster," "Slammer," "Code Red,"[9] "Conficker,"[10] and "Heartbleed."[11] If the distinction between viruses and worms were not confusing enough, some analysts suggest that we further differentiate disruptive programs to include Trojan horses and logic bombs. A Trojan horse often appears to be a benign program, but it can do significant system damage behind the scenes. Logic bombs, on the contrary, check for certain conditions or states in a computer system and then execute when one of those conditions arises. However, many now refer collectively to these various kinds of "malicious programs," including viruses and worms, via the single heading "malware."

Miller (2015) defines malware as "software designed to produce, damage, or provide unauthorized access to computers or computer systems."[12] Employing this broad definition, some forms of "spyware" would also come under the category of malware (i.e., in addition to viruses, worms, Trojan horses, logic bombs, etc.). So, the effects of malware can range from minor annoyances with individual computer systems to preventing an entire organization from operating, to shutting down computer networks, and to disrupting major segments of the Internet.

6.2.3 Network Security: Protecting our Infrastructure

A third category of computer security, which we call network security, is concerned with securing computer networks—that is, from privately owned computer networks such as local area networks (LANs) and wide area networks (WANs)) to the Internet itself—against various kinds of attacks. The Internet's infrastructure has been the victim of several attacks. These attacks have ranged from programs launched by individuals with malicious intentions to individuals who claimed their intentions were benign. In many cases, these attacks have severely disrupted activities on segments of the Internet. In a few cases, they have also rendered the Internet virtually inoperable.

We should note that it is not always easy to determine whether a major computer network disruption is the result of the work of malicious individuals who launch various kinds of malware or is due to the failure of some aspect of the network infrastructure itself. For example, a significant power outage experienced by the AT&T long-distance telephone service in 1990 was attributed to a software glitch in the system's programming code that caused the network to crash. However, some have questioned the official explanation given by AT&T, suggesting instead that the crash may have resulted from an attack involving malware.

Because many nations now depend on a secure cyberspace for their physical infrastructures, including power grids, there has been increased concern over threats from international hacking groups, including governments and state-sponsored organizations. The following scenario illustrates how vulnerable our national infrastructure may be to attacks by foreign governments.

▶ SCENARIO 6–2: The "GhostNet" Controversy

In 2009, the Information Warfare Monitor (IWM), a Canadian organization that monitors cyberespionage, discovered a network of at least 1,295 compromised computers in 103 countries. Approximately 30% of these were considered "high-value" targets, which (according to the IWM Report) included ministries of foreign affairs, embassies, international organizations, news media, and nongovernmental organizations (NGOs). The computer systems were compromised in ways that suggested China was responsible, but the IWM report refused to identify any one nation. The circumstantial evidence implicating China was tied to the fact that IWM's investigation was launched in response to a request by the Dalai Lama, the exiled leader of Tibet (and longtime enemy of the Chinese government), who reported that his computer network had been hacked. (The IWM report referred to the cyberespionage system as "GhostNet" because it resembled the Ghost RAT (sometimes referred to as Gh0st RAT) Trojan horse malware that was traced back to Hainan, China.) The IWM report concluded that regardless of which country or countries were responsible for the cyberespionage, the discovery of these activities should serve as a warning to policy makers that network security requires serious attention.[13] ■

In one sense, this scenario might initially seem to be more concerned with information warfare (IW), which we examine in Section 6.6, than with network security. However, the GhostNet controversy has also raised concerns about the vulnerability of a nation's network-based infrastructure, including its power grids. We will return to the GhostNet controversy later in this chapter in our discussion of IW, where we also examine the impact of the Flame virus in 2012.

In this section, we have differentiated three categories of cybersecurity, and we have briefly described some typical kinds of threats associated with each category. Table 6-1 summarizes key concerns identified with each cybersecurity category.

For the most part, the specific cybersecurity issues we identified in this chapter tend to fall into one (or at most two) of these categories. However, in the next section, we will see why some relatively recent security issues associated with "cloud computing" can potentially span all three of the categories comprising our security framework.

TABLE 6-1 Data, System, and Network Security

Cybersecurity Category	Corresponding Area(s) of Concern
Data security	Concerned with vulnerabilities pertaining to unauthorized access to data, as well as with threats to the confidentiality, integrity, and availability of data that resides in computer storage devices or is exchanged between computer systems
System security	Concerned with attacks on system resources (such as computer hardware, operating system software, and application software) by malicious programs
Network security	Concerned with attacks on computer networks, including the infrastructure of privately owned networks as well as the Internet itself

▶ 6.3 CLOUD COMPUTING AND SECURITY

What is meant by *cloud computing*? Knorr and Gruman (2008) note that in the past, "the cloud" has often been used as a "metaphor for the Internet." In fact, the graphical interfaces on the screens of older desktop computers typically included an icon or visual of a cloud, which a user could click on to connect to the Internet. But Knorr and Gruman point out that in the current context of "cloud computing," the cloud (in its broad sense) can now refer to any computer resources that are used "outside the firewall."

According to the National Institute of Standards and Technology (NIST; 2011), cloud computing is officially defined as

> a model for enabling ubiquitous, convenient, on-demand network access to a shared pool of configurable computing resources (e.g., networks, servers, storage, applications and services).[14]

Among the "essential characteristics" included in the NIST definition of cloud computing are three key elements: "on-demand self-service," "broad network access," and "resource pooling" (Mell and Grance 2011).

Zeng and Cavoukian (2010) note that while cloud computing is still at an early stage of development, it currently provides a wide range of services—that is, from "full-blown applications to storage services to spam filtering." The authors also believe that cloud computing is changing the way we now think about computing by "decoupling data" and "in effect, divorcing components from location." Consider, for example, that this technology affects not only where users can store their data but also where many of the applications they use can ultimately reside. Four popular examples of cloud-computing applications include photo storing services, such as Google's Picasa; Web-based e-mail services, such as Yahoo; file transfer services, such as YouSendIt; and online computer backup services, such as Mozy.[15]

6.3.1 Deployment and Service/Delivery Models for the Cloud

The NIST definition of cloud computing identifies four distinct "deployment models" and three kinds of "service models," which are also sometimes also referred to as "delivery models" (Zeng and Cavoukian). Deployment models include the following:

1. Private cloud
2. Community cloud
3. Public cloud
4. Hybrid cloud

Whereas (1) is used mainly by "a single organization" that can comprise "multiple consumers (e.g., business units)" and while (2) is used mainly by a "specific community" of organizations and users that have "shared concerns," (3) can be used by the general public. The infrastructure of (4), however, is typically some combination of 1–3 (NIST 2011; Mell and Grance 2011).

As mentioned earlier, cloud computing also provides three important service (or delivery) models:

- Software as a service (SaaS)
- Platform as a service (PaaS)
- Infrastructure as a service (IaaS)

Zeng and Cavoukian note that while SaaS models deliver various kinds of applications to consumers (i.e., either enterprises or individuals) via a "multitenant architecture," PaaS models deliver "development environments" to consumers. The authors also note that IaaS models

TABLE 6-2 Possible Configurations of Cloud Computing

SaaS—Private cloud	PaaS—Private cloud	IaaS—Private cloud
SaaS—Community cloud	PaaS—Community cloud	IaaS—Community cloud
SaaS—Public cloud	PaaS—Public cloud	IaaS--Public cloud
SaaS—Hybrid cloud	SaaS—Hybrid cloud	SaaS—Hybrid cloud

deliver various "resources," which include servers, connections, and "related tools" needed for building "an application from scratch." So if we consider the possible configurations of the cloud-computing services generated by the combination of deployment and service/delivery models, 12 distinct permutations of cloud computing are possible (i.e., based on private/community/public/hybrid modes of deployment and SaaS/PaaS/IaaS modes of service/delivery). Table 6-2 illustrates the permutations.

So it would appear that there is no monolithic scheme for describing and understanding cloud computing in general, given the multifaceted nature of the cloud services currently available. And perhaps more importantly for our purposes, there is no single "context" from which security concerns involving the cloud can be analyzed.[16] Thus, it would seem that any attempt to frame a comprehensive cloud-security policy would need to take into account all 12 elements in Table 6-2. Additionally, it is worth noting that the kinds of challenges involved in securing these elements can impact all three categories of cybersecurity (described in Section 6.2): data security, system security, and network security. In the following section, we focus our analysis on cloud-security concerns that pertain to data/information security, in particular.

6.3.2 Securing User Data Residing in the Cloud

Cavoukian (2008) argues that for cloud computing to be fully realized, users will have to be confident that their personal information is protected and that their data (in general) is both secure and accessible. At present, however, users have at least four kinds of worries along these lines. One concern has to do with how users can control their data stored in the cloud—currently, users have very little "control over or direct knowledge about how their information is transmitted, processed, or stored."[17] Another concern involves the integrity of the data—for example, if the host company goes out of business, what happens to the users' data? A third concern affects access to the data; that is, can the host deny a user access to his/her own data? And a fourth concern has to do with who actually "owns" the data that is stored in the cloud.[18]

Despite these concerns, Cavoukian notes that the cloud offers flexibility and security to users, because they no longer have to worry about how to protect their data. She also notes that the cloud enables users to work on local, less expensive platforms, which could appeal to business owners who would be relieved of the burden of having to secure their data. However, Cavoukian argues that cloud computing can only be effective if users and businesses trust their cloud service providers. But do users have good reasons to place their trust in the businesses that currently provide cloud-computing services? Consider that in 2009, for example, Google reported that a bug in Google Docs (a cloud storage system) had allowed unintended access to some private documents and it was estimated that "0.05% of documents stored via the service were affected by the bug." However, Google claimed that the bug had been fixed within a few days.[19]

According to Talbot (2011), many businesses—especially those in the healthcare and finance sectors—remain leery about turning over their data to third parties. In particular, Talbot identifies three main kinds of concerns that these businesses have: (i) accidental loss of data, (ii) fear of hacking attacks, and (iii) theft by "rogue employees of cloud providers." So it would seem that until these kinds of concerns are resolved, users have good reasons to be skeptical about placing their trust in cloud-computing services to protect their data. In addition to questions concerning confidence and trust on the part of businesses and ordinary users who subscribe or are considering subscribing to cloud-computing services, some related concerns affecting risk analysis also arise.

6.3.3 Assessing *Risk* in the Cloud and in the Context of Cybersecurity

What is meant by *risk analysis*, and how does it apply in the context of cybersecurity and cloud computing? Schneier (2004), who argues that security is an "ongoing process," believes that a key element in that process involves an understanding of the concept of risk. But who exactly is responsible for understanding risk, as well as for assessing and managing it in computing/information technology (IT) security contexts? Unfortunately, it is not altogether clear where the moral responsibility lies for carrying out these functions. One reason why it is becoming even more difficult to determine who is responsible for doing this may have to do with a factor that Pieters and van Cleeff (2009) call the "deperimeterization" of the security landscape.

Arguing that the information security landscape has become increasingly "de-perimeterized," Pieters and van Cleeff point out that IT systems now "span the boundaries of multiple parties" and they "cross the security perimeters." The authors also note that deperimeterization-related concerns lead to "uncertain risk" for IT security, because of the lack of clear boundaries defining the security landscape. To the extent that there is no secure "digital fence" or perimeter safeguarding the users' data, however, it would seem that ordinary users and businesses alike will be required to assume some level of *uncertain risk* with regard to their data and system resources that reside in the cloud.[20]

So far in Chapter 6, we have examined some key elements in cybersecurity, but we have not yet elaborated on their ethical implications. Next, we examine ethical aspects of cybersecurity that pertain to hacking-related activities.

▶ 6.4 HACKING AND "THE HACKER ETHIC"

Individuals who have launched malicious programs of various kinds, which we collectively refer to as malware, have commonly been described in the media as computer hackers. Who are hackers, and what is hacking in the context of computers and cybertechnology? According to Simpson (2006), a hacker is anyone who "accesses a computer system or network without authorization from the owner." (He defines "crackers," on the contrary, as hackers who break into a computer system with "the intention of doing harm or destroying data.") Note that we also examine the concept of hacking in our analysis of cybercrime in Chapter 7, where we focus on hacking as it relates to crime and criminal behavior. In this chapter, we examine hacking and the notion of a "hacker ethic" as it relates to primarily to cybersecurity.

Many in the computer science community are unhappy with how the word "hacker," which now has a negative connotation, is used in the conventional media. Kaufman, Perlman, and Speciner (2002) describe "true computer hackers" in a very different way—that is, as individuals who play with computers for the "pure intellectual challenge" and as "master programmers, incorruptibly honest, unmotivated by money, and careful not to harm anyone." They go on to note that people identified in the media as hackers tend to be malicious individuals who are neither brilliant nor accomplished. The authors also note that "early hackers" have been described as individuals who aimed at accessing computer systems to see how they worked, not to cause any harm to those systems.

In this chapter, we use "hacker" in the sense of the term often attributed to early computer enthusiasts. In documenting early computer hackers, many of whom were associated with the "MIT culture," some authors have used the expressions "hacker ethic" and "hacker code of ethics."

6.4.1 What Is "The Hacker Ethic"?

Levy (2001) suggests that a strong and distinctive code of ethics could be found in the original hacker community. He describes the hacker code as "a philosophy, an ethic, and a dream," based on the following principles:

- **I.** Access to computers should be unlimited and total.
- **II.** All information should be free.
- **III.** Mistrust authority–promote decentralization.
- **IV.** Hackers should be judged by their hacking (not by bogus criteria such as degrees, age, race, or position).
- **V.** You can create art and beauty on a computer.
- **VI.** Computers can change your life for the better.[21]

Perhaps what Levy really describes is not so much a code of ethics but rather a code for the way that hackers approach their craft, that is, in terms of a certain ethic, as in "work ethic." Himanen (2001) has described the hacker ethic as a "new work ethic," which he contrasts with the classic "Protestant work ethic" (coined originally by Max Weber in his classic work *The Protestant Ethic and the Spirit of Capitalism*). In addition to an ethic, hackers also seem to have a distinct "ethos"—that is, they have a distinct way of looking at the world, especially the world of computers.

Many of the early hackers believed that computer systems were inherently flawed and thus needed to be improved. As a result, some hackers believed that they needed total access to all computer systems in order to take them apart, see how they work, and make the needed improvements. Not surprisingly, then, these hackers wanted to remove any barriers to free access to computers. Many hackers have embraced and some continue to embrace, either explicitly or implicitly, the following three principles:

1. Information should be free.
2. Hackers provide society with a useful and important service.
3. Activities in cyberspace are virtual in nature and thus do not harm real people in the real (physical) world.

We briefly examine each principle.

Information Should Be Free

Should information be totally free? If so, on what grounds can this claim be justified? The expression "Information wants to be free" has become a mantra for many hackers who see proprietary software and systems as obstacles to realizing the freedom of the Internet, where users would otherwise have total access to information. The debate over whether information should be free, or even to what extent information should be freely accessible to Internet users, is a complicated one. As we shall see in Chapter 8, this debate is rooted in complex property laws and policies that have been disputed in the courts, often times resulting in Supreme Court decisions. So we will postpone our fuller discussion of this particular point raised by hackers until our analysis of intellectual property in cyberspace. However, a few brief comments need to be made at this point.

Some critics regard the view that (all) information should be free as overly idealistic. According to Spafford (2007), it is also a very naïve view. He points out that if all information were free, privacy would not be possible because individuals could not control how information about them was collected and used. Also, it would not be possible to ensure integrity and accuracy of that information, since information that was freely available could always be modified and changed by anyone who happened to access it. So from the points of view of privacy and confidentiality, a world in which all information was literally and completely free would not be desirable. Thus, there would seem to be good reasons not to embrace the principle that information should be free.

Hackers might object, however, by pointing out that they do not claim that all information should be free because they recognize that some information should be kept private. Hence, they would argue for a position along the following lines: keep private any information that should be private and keep free any information that should be free. They recognize that there is much information that should be kept private but is not, and there is much information that should be publicly available but is not.[22]

Hackers Provide Society with an Important Service

Does the second hacker principle fare any better? Many are suspicious of claims that hackers perform a useful service for society by searching for and exposing security holes in cyberspace. According to this rationale, hackers are doing us a favor, because pointing out these security holes will force those responsible for the holes to fix them.

Spafford has produced a series of counterexamples to this version of the hacker argument, and he uses an analogy to counter the hacker's position that exposing security vulnerabilities is doing the computer user community a favor. Spafford asks whether we would permit someone to start a fire in a crowded shopping mall in order to expose the fact that the mall's sprinkler system was not adequate. Similarly, we could also ask whether you would be willing to thank a burglar who, in the process of burglarizing your house, was able to show that your home security system was inadequate. If you would not, then why, Spafford would ask, should we thank hackers for showing us that our computers are insecure? We return to Spafford's argument in Section 6.4.2.

However, we will see how some nonmalicious hackers have discovered holes in security systems that have also revealed questionable, and possibly illegal, behavior on the part of content providers in cyberspace (as in the case of Sony BMG, which we describe in the next section). So, one might make a utilitarian argument that users are better served if these kinds of abuses are discovered by nonmalicious hackers.

Hacking Causes Only Virtual Harm, Not Real Harm

According to the third principle we identified, unauthorized access in cyberspace causes no real harm because those activities occur only in the virtual world. This argument commits a logical fallacy in that it confuses the relationship between the notions of "harm" and "space" by reasoning that

> the virtual world is not the real (physical) world; so any harms that occur in the virtual world are not real harms.

Consider how this reasoning is flawed. If someone sends you an e-mail message in which they unfairly accuse you of being a malicious person, they have communicated with you in cyberspace, which is "virtual," as opposed to physical, space. But does it follow that the content of the e-mail is any less real than if it had been printed in a hardcopy letter that had been sent to you in the physical mail? Would any harm you experience because of the e-mail's content be any less real than the harm you would experience from identical information in a letter written on physical paper? James Moor has described a variation of this type of reasoning involving incidents in virtual contexts as the "virtuality fallacy,"[23] which we briefly examined in Chapter 3. In Chapters 9 and 11, we will see how harms involving virtual child pornography can arguably cause real harms to real people, even if they involve only virtual (or computer-generated) images or virtual characters.

Of course, nonmalicious hackers could argue that they are not causing any harm, virtual or real. In fact, some might argue that they are helping to reduce the amount of harm that can occur because of their discoveries of abuses of power by content providers on the Internet, including corporations that provide digital media for electronic devices. For example, it was because of hackers that we discovered that Sony BMG was able to monitor the activities of some unsuspecting customers who purchased digital music products.[24] This questionable, and arguably illegal, activity on Sony's part would likely not have been discovered had it not been for hackers. In this sense, the argument that hackers can prevent harm is similar to, and perhaps builds on, the rationale that hackers provide society with an important service, which we examined in the preceding section.

We have now considered some counterexamples for each of the three principles that we identified as key elements in the "hacker code of ethics." And we have considered some ways in which nonmalicious hackers can respond to those counterexamples. In the following section, we consider the question of whether unauthorized access to a computer in the form of an explicit break-in could ever be ethically justified.

6.4.2 Are Computer Break-Ins Ever Ethically Justifiable?

Eugene Spafford believes that in certain extreme cases, breaking into a computer could be the "right thing to do."[25] He also argues, however, that computer break-ins always cause harm, which suggests that they are not ethically justified. How can Spafford defend what some might interpret as a contradictory claim: Sometimes, it could be right to do something that is ethically unjustifiable? Spafford asks us to consider a scenario in which vital medical data that resided in a computer are needed in an emergency to save someone's life. Further, imagine that the authorized users of the computer system cannot be located. In this case, Spafford believes that breaking into that computer system would be the right thing to do. We might assume that Spafford's rationale is based on utilitarian grounds because, arguably, a greater good (or at least a lesser harm) would result from the computer break-in in this situation.

However, Spafford does not appeal to utilitarian or consequentialist principles to defend his position. Instead, he bases his argument on deontological grounds (see the discussion of deontological and nonconsequentialist ethical theories in Chapter 2) because he believes that morality is determined by actions, not results. He correctly notes that we cannot evaluate morality based on consequences or results because we would not "know the full scope of those results," which are based on the "sum total of all future effect." Thus, Spafford believes that we must base our moral decisions primarily on the actions themselves and not on possible results. In this sense, his view is compatible with the ethical theory of Act Deontology, which we analyzed in Chapter 2.

Critics might point out that Spafford has not provided us with a general principle for determining which kinds of break-ins are ethically justifiable. But using the criteria underlying the act-deontology framework, Spafford could respond by noting that each situation where our two or more (*prima facie*) duties conflict would have to be analyzed on a case-by-case basis in order to determine which duty would take precedence in that particular situation. In deliberating over and weighing between the conflicting duties in those situations, Spafford shows why we cannot simply base our decision on absolute duties (as in Kant's version of rule deontology). (You may want to review David Ross's account of act deontology, examined in Chapter 2, to see how it applies to Spafford's argument for justifying a computer break-in a situation such as the one he presents.)

Independent of whether some computer break-ins can be justified on moral grounds is the question whether certain forms of hacking, especially for nonmalicious purposes, ought to be legally permissible (a question we examine in detail in Chapter 7). Another interesting question is whether the expression "ethical hacker" is an oxymoron. We should note that at least one organization believes that there can be "ethical hackers" and they offer a program that certifies individuals to engage in authorized hacking activities for companies who employ them. According to the Certified Ethical Hacker (CEH) Web site, an "ethical hacker" is an employee within an organization who has been authorized by the organization to "probe" and "penetrate" a targeted computer system or network. Interestingly, but perhaps not at all surprisingly, a "certified ethical hacker" often uses the same tools and knowledge as a "malicious hacker."[26]

Of course, few would disapprove of training people—whether or not we choose to call them "ethical hackers"—to thwart the malicious actions carried by individuals that, for better or worse, we have traditionally called hackers. And the official process of certifying such individuals would seem to give them a sense of legitimacy. But these are not the kind of hackers—if we still wish to use that term to describe these individuals—whose activities would seem to raise moral concerns. However, insofar as these certified hackers' activities also allow "preemptive" hacking attacks, we can question the moral and legal status of some of their actions. We take up this particular question in detail in Chapter 7.

Additional questions regarding hacking could include whether we should distinguish between "white hat" and "black hat" hackers and whether we need to distinguish between hacking and "cracking," as some computer security analysts do. We also address these and similar questions in Chapter 7, where we examine legal issues involving hacking in connection with our discussion of cybercrime.

We have not yet considered the various implications that break-ins involving malicious hacker attacks have had for our financial infrastructure, which increasingly depends on available networked computers. Nor have we yet considered some of the threats that certain forms of malicious hacking pose to our national security. In the next two sections, we examine both security-related concerns.

▶ 6.5 CYBERTERRORISM

Concerns about the threats posed by cyberterrorism have been on the rise in the United States and around the world. In 2002 the U.S. Congress passed legislation that specifically responded to this new kind of terrorism, and in 2009 U.S. President Barack Obama established a "cybersecurity czar" to address concerns about cyberterrorism. Obama also announced his plans to create and implement a top-level post called "Cybersecurity Coordinator" to oversee "a new comprehensive approach to securing America's digital infrastructure" and to respond to the threat of cyberattacks from Al Qaeda and other terrorist groups.[27]

What, exactly, is cyberterrorism? Dorothy Denning defines it as the "convergence of terrorism and cyberspace."[28] As such, cyberterrorism covers politically motivated hacking operations intended to cause grave harm—that is, resulting in either loss of life or severe economic loss, or both. Denning (2007) also notes that acts of cyberterrorism are typically performed by "nonstate actors" in their goal of intimidating or coercing governments and societies. In some cases, however, it is difficult to separate acts of malicious hacking (e.g., computer break-ins and cybervandalism) from cyberterrorism. As noted in our discussion of network security in Section 6.2.3, it is sometimes even difficult to determine whether a major computer network disruption is due to a system failure (in either the hardware or the software of a networked computer system) or is the result of the work of either malicious hackers or cyberterrorists.[16] Additionally, it is possible that some of these disruptions are caused a third group: *hacktivists*.

6.5.1 Cyberterrorism vs. Hacktivism

In the past, several coordinated cyberattacks directed at major e-commerce Web sites, such as Yahoo and eBay, prevented tens of thousands of people from accessing them. These cyber intrusions, called distributed denial-of-service (DDoS) attacks, resulted in severe economic loss for major corporations. Should these DDoS attacks be classified as cyberterrorism? Or are they better understood as a form of hacking by individuals with some particular political agenda or ideology—a kind of behavior that Manion and Goodrum (2004) describe as hacktivism or "electronic political activism"?

Noting that some hackers and political activists expressed their outrage over the ways in which the Internet had become "commodified" by the early twenty-first century, Manion and Goodrum question whether the actions taken by those individuals could be viewed as a new form of "civil disobedience" that integrates the talent of traditional computer hackers with the interests and social consciousness of political activists. The authors also point out that while many hackers continue to be portrayed in the media as vandals, terrorists, and saboteurs, only a few have considered the possibility that at least some of these individuals might be hacktivists. But they also point out that a key factor in making this distinction is to show that political activists are engaging in acts of electronic civil disobedience (ECD).

Is the distinction drawn by Manion and Goodrum plausible? Can acts of hacktivism be justified on grounds of civil disobedience? Himma (2007b) describes the line of reasoning that hacktivists and their supporters use to justify their acts of civil disobedience, via the following kind of argument:

PREMISE 1. Because civil disobedience is justifiable as a protest against injustice, it is permissible to commit digital intrusions as a means of protesting injustice.

PREMISE 2. Insofar as it is permissible to stage a sit-in in a commercial or governmental building to protest, say, laws that violate human rights, it is permissible to intrude on commercial or government networks to protest such laws.

CONCLUSION. Digital intrusions that would otherwise be morally objectionable are morally permissible if they are politically motivated acts of electronic civil disobedience, or hacktivism.[29]

Based on our analysis of arguments in Chapter 3, we see that the form of this argument is valid. But in order to be a sound argument, the premises must also be true (statements or claims); otherwise, the argument will be valid and unsound. Both of the argument's premises are controversial, and they assume that an appropriate analogy can be drawn between civilly disobedient acts in the physical and the electronic realms. But how are we to understand the notion of "electronic civil disobedience"? Manion and Goodrum claim that for an act to qualify as "civilly disobedient," it must satisfy the following conditions:

- No damage done to persons or property
- Nonviolent
- Not for personal profit
- Ethical motivation—the strong conviction that a law is unjust, or unfair, to the extreme detriment of the common good
- Willingness to accept personal responsibility for the outcome of actions[30]

Based on these criteria, Manion and Goodrum believe that a number of nonviolent, politically motivated cyberattacks could qualify as ECD. Denning (2008), however, argues that Manion and Goodrum's analysis of hacktivism suggests that some acts of Web defacement may also be morally justified as ECD insofar as they are "ethically motivated." But she points out that defacing a Web site seems to be incompatible with Manion and Goodrum's first condition for ECD—that is, "no damage." As Denning notes, defacements can "cause information property damage that is analogous to physical property damage," and both forms of damage can "require resources to repair."[31] So she suggests that at least some of the cases that Manion and Goodman count as hacktivism are questionable, given their own criteria.

Based on Denning's analysis of criteria involving ECD and hacktivism, we ask whether the incident described in the following scenario can be justified on hacktivist grounds.

▶ SCENARIO 6–3: *Anonymous* and the "Operation Payback" Attack

In 2012, a self-described hacktivist group called *Anonymous* launched a series of DDoS attacks against commercial and government Web sites in response to two different incidents. For one thing, the group stated that its attack, called "Operation Payback," was in retaliation against the (U.S.) Department of Justice for taking down Megaupload, a massive file-sharing site. For another, Anonymous stated that it was supporting the coordinated January 18 (2012) online protest against two controversial legislative proposals in the U.S. Congress: Protect Intellectual Property Act (PIPA) and Stop Online Piracy Act (SOPA).

While most of the participants in this online protest, including Wikipedia and Google, used tactics that were nondisruptive, Anonymous launched DDoS attacks against the Web sites of organizations that supported the two congressional bills. The sites attacked included not only those of the Recording Industry Association of America (RIAA) and Motion Picture Association of America (MPAA) but also the sites for the U.S. Copyright Office and Broadcast Music, Inc. (BMI), which collects fees from businesses that use music. (The online protest involving SOPA and PIPA, as well as controversial aspects of these two legislative proposals that sparked this protest, is described in detail in Chapter 8.) ■

Can these attacks by Anonymous qualify as hacktivism, or are they yet another instance of cyberterrorism? One could argue that because of the *scale* of these attacks, they border on cyberterrorism; but this, in turn, may cause us to question of whether a meaningful distinction can be drawn between acts of hacktivism and cyberterrorism. Is the sheer scale of the attack paramount, or do we need to take into account other aspects affecting the act—for example, the *motive* behind it or possibly its *consequences*? Recall our brief discussion of Anonymous in the opening section of this chapter, where we described this group's intention to take down ISIS Web sites. Could that incident be justified as hacktivism because of the desirable consequences it would likely have for Western nations (as well as other countries currently targeted and victimized by ISIS)? But if that kind of attack qualifies as hacktivism, why wouldn't Anonymous' "Operation Payback" attack in 2012 (on commercial interests on the Web) also qualify as a kind of hacktivism. Consider that Anonymous' motives for taking down both entities were the same.

Denning (2001) has drawn some interesting distinctions between hacktivism and cyberterrorism. She notes that hacktivism, the convergence of activism and computer hacking, uses hacking techniques against a target Internet site in a way that (i) intends to disrupt normal operations, but (ii) does not intend to cause serious damage. Denning also notes that these disruptions could be caused by "e-mail bombs" and by "low-grade viruses" that can cause minimal disruption but would not result in severe economic damage or loss of life.

Cyberterrorism, as we saw earlier, consists of activities intended to cause great harm, such as loss of life or severe economic damage, or both. For example, a cyberterrorist might attempt to bring down the U.S. stock market or take control of a transportation unit in order to cause trains to crash. Denning believes while these conceptual distinctions can be used to differentiate hacktivism and cyberterrorism, the boundaries can become fuzzy as we progress from the former to the latter. For example, should an e-mail bomb sent by a hacker who is also a political activist be classified as a form of hacktivism or as an act of cyberterrorism? Many in law enforcement would no doubt argue that rather than trying to understand the ideological beliefs, goals, and objectives of those who engage in malicious forms of hacking, much more effort should be devoted to finding ways to deter and catch these individuals. However, the category distinctions that Denning has drawn can help determine the degree of punishment that these individuals should receive.

6.5.2 Cybertechnology and Terrorist Organizations

A major security concern, especially since September 11, 2001, has been how and when terrorist organizations, such as Al Qaeda and ISIS might use cybertechnology to carry out their objectives. We discovered that the terrorists who carried out the highly coordinated attacks on the Twin Towers of the World Trade Center communicated by e-mail in the days preceding the attack. We also have discovered that many members of Al Qaeda, despite the fact that some operated out of caves in Afghanistan and Pakistan, had fairly sophisticated computer devices. Yet it does not seem that these terrorists have yet taken full advantage of currently available forms of cybertechnology in executing their campaigns. For example, some fear a scenario which terrorists use cybertechnology to gain control of an airplane's onboard computer systems and even block the ability of a pilot to override those controls.

Denning (2007) notes that there is evidence that terrorist groups and "jihadists" are interested in conducting cyberattacks. She also notes that there is evidence to suggest they have at least some capability to carry out such attacks and that they are undergoing online training on how to develop the necessary skills. However, Denning also points out that (as of 2007, at least) there is no evidence to suggest either that the threat of cyberattacks from these terrorist groups is imminent or that they have acquired the knowledge or the skills to conduct "highly damaging attacks against critical infrastructure."[32] However, we do know that some of these groups now have the skills necessary to set up and successfully operate social media sites to spread jihadist propaganda and to recruit internationally. We also know that they have adeptly used the latest digital devices and mobile technologies to coordinate high-profile terrorist attacks, such as the "Charlie Hebdo"-related attacks in Paris in January 2015.

▶ 6.6 INFORMATION WARFARE (IW)

In the preceding section, we saw that it is not always easy to differentiate acts of cyberterrorism from those of hacktivism. It can also be difficult to distinguish between acts of cyberterrorism and acts of IW. Denning (1999) defines IW as "operations that target or exploit information media in order to win some objective over an adversary." But certain aspects of cyberterrorism also conform to Denning's definition of IW, so what distinguishes the latter from the former? For our purposes, IW is distinguishable from cyberterrorism in three ways. First, IW can include cyberattacks that send misleading information to an enemy. Second, while IW is disruptive and sometimes destructive, it need not involve loss of life or severe economic loss, even though such results can occur. Third, IW typically involves cyberattacks launched by sovereign nations, or nation states, as opposed to "rogue" political organizations and terrorist groups.

6.6.1 Information Warfare vs. Conventional Warfare

Moor (2004) notes that while information has always played a vital role in warfare, now its importance is overwhelming, because the battlefield is becoming increasingly computerized. In the past, warfare was conducted by physical means: human beings engaged in combat, using weapons such as guns, tanks, and aircraft. Moor notes that during the first Gulf War, in the early 1990s, we saw for the first time the importance of IT in contemporary warfare strategies. Arguably, the war was won quickly by the multinational coalition because it had advantages in cybertechnology. Destroying the Iraqi communications technologies at the outset put the Iraqi army at a severe disadvantage. Moor points out that in the future, warfare may have more to do with information and cybertechnology than with human beings going into combat.

Some analysts point out that IW, unlike conventional or physical warfare, often tends to be more disruptive than destructive. The "weapons" of IW, consisting of logic bombs, viruses, worms, and DDoS attacks deployable from cyberspace, typically strike at a nation's infrastructure. Although these are not the traditional weapons of warfare, the disruption can be more damaging than physical damage from conventional weapons.

Consider once again the GhostNet controversy (described in Scenario 6-2) and its implications for IW. Recall that a report issued by the IWM (2009) included circumstantial evidence that linked various cyberattacks (associated with GhostNet) to China but also suggested that other countries might be involved as well. For example, in 2009, the government of South Korea accused North Korea of running a cyberwarfare unit that attempted to hack into both United States and South Korean military networks to gather confidential information and to disrupt service. North Korea was also suspected of launching the DDoS attacks that disrupted the Web sites of 27 American and South Korean government agencies as well as commercial Web sites such as the New York Stock Exchange, Nasdaq, and Yahoo's finance section (Sang-Hun and Markoff 2009). Next, we consider an IW incident that allegedly involves two Western nations: the United States and Israel.

Recall our brief discussion of *Operation Olympic Games* and the Stuxnet worm in Scenario 6–1. Does this "operation" qualify as an example of IW (or "cyberwarfare")? Insofar as the Stuxnet worm sent misleading information to the Iranian government and its scientists, it complies with the first aspect of IW we described. And because this worm was disruptive (regarding Iran's nuclear program), as well as destructive (i.e., with respect to its effect on Iran's centrifuges), it complies with the second aspect of IW. Third, the Stuxnet attacks were launched (allegedly, at least) by two nation states. So, Stuxnet complies with all three conditions for IW (described earlier). But as we noted in our early discussion of the Olympic Games incident, no formal declaration of war had been made by any of the three nations allegedly involved.

6.6.2 Potential Consequences for Nations That Engage in IW

Why has the Stuxnet/Operation Olympic Games incident caused so much controversy at the international level? To see why, consider once again some of the concerns that arose in the international community in response to the 2009 IW incidents allegedly involving China (in GhostNet) and South Korea. One question that arose in the aftermath of the Stuxnet attacks was whether the United States and Israeli governments were now guilty of the same kind of questionable behavior attributed to China and North Korea three years earlier. If so, should the U.S. government worry about the possible repercussions that its involvement in "Olympic Games" could have for its standing in the international community, as well as for its credibility involving any future complaints that it might make against other nations, especially China? Sanger (2012) suggests that the United States did not think through the international implications of its use of cyberwarfare in the Olympic Games operations (just as he believes that it also did not think through some of the major political and legal consequences of its policy regarding the use of armed drones).

Another question is whether the U.S. government, and the nation's infrastructure and commerce, will also become focal points of retaliation for its IW activities involving Olympic Games. Vijayan (2012) notes that the United States, as a result of the Stuxnet attacks, may have "painted a huge target on [its] back." And the Obama administration seemed to recognize this vulnerability when it warned American businesses—immediately following the media's announcement of the effects that Stuxnet had in Iran—to prepare for similar attacks by bolstering the security apparatus on their computers.

We should note that the Stuxnet worm, discovered in 2010, is sometimes confused with the Flame virus (also known as "Flamer" and "Skywiper"). Like Stuxnet, this virus also has significant implications for IW. Ladner (2012) points out that the Flame virus, discovered in 2012, is "an espionage tool" that can "eavesdrop on data traffic, take screenshots and record audio and keystrokes." Kamlyuk (2012), a security (malware) expert at the Kaspersky Lab in Russia, describes Flame as the "most powerful computer virus in history." Pointing to some differences between Stuxnet and Flame, Kamlyuk notes that while the former was a "small application developed for a particular target with the specific objective to interact with industrial control systems," the latter is a "universal attacking tool kit used mostly for cyberespionage."

Some security experts, including Kamlyuk, also point to a few things that Flame and Stuxnet have in common, in addition to the widely held view that both pieces of malware were developed by nation states. Lee (2012) points out that there is growing evidence to suggest that the development teams responsible for Stuxnet and Flame worked together, in the early stages, on the code for both malware applications. One way in which the two applications are similar is that both take advantage of a "zero day" type of "vulnerability" in the systems they attack. In most cases, software developers are the first to become aware of vulnerabilities (such as bugs or "holes") in their systems that need to be fixed. But in some cases, these vulnerabilities are initially discovered and exploited by malicious hackers. In this sense, the vulnerability is discovered on the "zeroth day," or a(ny) day preceding the discovery of that software's vulnerability by its developer(s).

We should note that IW-related concerns affecting both the Flame virus and Stuxnet worm are further complicated by the recent development of a new kind of search engine, called Shodan. Not only can Shodan locate and return the URLs for relevant Web sites (as traditional search engines do), but it is also able "to map and capture the specifications of everything from desktop computers to network printers to Web servers" that are connected to the internet (Charette 2012). O'Harrow (2012) points out that between 2010 and 2012, Shodan gathered data on approximately 100 million devices, "recording their exact locations and the software systems that run them." He also notes that during that period, Shodan users had discovered numerous ("uncounted") industrial control computers—that is, the systems that automate power grids and water plants—and that these computers were "linked in, and in some cases they were wide open to exploitation by even moderately talented hackers." As Robert Charette observes, it is not difficult to imagine what "a government intent on doing harm to U.S. infrastructural and business systems could do with that information." So, it would seem that the United States (and other countries as well) may indeed have something to worry about in the aftermath of the IW activities involving Stuxnet and the Olympic Games operation.

In concluding our discussion of IW, we acknowledge that some controversial issues surrounding this topic were not able to be examined. One interesting question concerns whether IW could, in principle, satisfy the conditions traditionally required for a "just war." For example, one requirement is that a distinction between combatants and noncombatants be drawn and respected. Another condition is that attacks typically cannot be preemptive. However, it may not be possible for these and other conventional just-war requirements to be satisfied in the context of IW. So, some conclude that IW can never be justified solely on moral grounds. Unfortunately, however, an examination of the necessary conditions articulated for just-war theory in the context of IW is beyond the scope of this chapter.[33]

In this and the preceding section, we have discussed various security threats, from malicious hacking to hacktivism and from cyberterrorism to information warfare. Table 6-3 summarizes these distinctions.

TABLE 6-3 Hacktivism, Cyberterrorism, and Information Warfare

Hacktivism	The convergence of political activism and computer hacking techniques to engage in a new form of civil disobedience
Cyberterrorism	The convergence of cybertechnology and terrorism for carrying out acts of terror in (or via) cyberspace
Information warfare	Using malware in cyberattacks designed to mislead the enemy and disrupt/damage an opponent's military defense system and its critical infrastructure

▶ 6.7 CHAPTER SUMMARY

In this chapter, we examined some ethical implications of a wide range of cybersecurity issues, including the question whether unauthorized computer break-ins can ever be ethically justified. We also described some ways in which some cybersecurity issues overlap with cybercrime, while others overlap with privacy. Additionally, we briefly identified some of the tensions that exist between security and privacy in the context of cybertechnology. We then argued that it is useful to draw distinctions involving data, system, and network security, and we briefly considered some of the challenges that cloud computing provides for cybersecurity. Finally, we drew some distinctions between concepts such as hacking and hacktivism and IW and cyberterrorism.

We also drew some distinctions between the traditional and current meanings of "hacker," in our discussion of the "hacker ethic." In Chapter 7, we will examine some criminal aspects of (malicious) hacking from a legal perspective.

▶ REVIEW QUESTIONS

1. What do we mean by "computer security" or "cybersecurity"?
2. Which three key elements does Richard Epstein include in his description of computer security/cybersecurity?
3. Why does Peter Neumann believe that computer security/cybersecurity can be a "double-edged sword?"
4. How can cybersecurity concerns be differentiated from issues in cybercrime?
5. How are cybersecurity issues similar to and different from privacy issues affecting cybertechnology?
6. What is meant by *data security*?
7. What is *system security*, and how is it similar to and different from *network security*?
8. What is *cloud computing*, and what challenges does it pose for securing one's personal information in cyberspace?
9. Identify the four kinds of *deployment* models and the three types of *service/delivery* models comprising cloud computing.
10. Who are computer hackers, and how has the term "hacker" evolved?
11. What is meant by the expression "hacker code of ethics"?
12. According to Steve Levy, what are the six "principles" of this code?
13. Describe and briefly evaluate the argument used by some hackers who assert that "information wants to be free."
14. Assess the argument that (nonmalicious) hackers can provide society with a valuable service. Is it a plausible argument?
15. Describe the kind of argument that some hackers use to support their claim that hacking causes only virtual harm, not real harm.
16. What exactly is cyberterrorism?
17. What is meant by "hacktivism"? How is it distinguished from traditional computer hacking?
18. Can "hacktivist activities" be justified on the grounds of civil disobedience toward unjust laws?
19. What is meant by "information warfare"?
20. How can information warfare be distinguished from cyberterrorism?

DISCUSSION QUESTIONS

21. Is the expression "ethical hacker" an oxymoron? Do you agree that some individuals should be allowed to be "certified" as hackers to work on behalf of industry or for the interests of other organizations? Do the kinds of activities permitted by certified hackers in the CEH program raise any moral issues? Explain.

22. Revisit the GhostNet controversy described in Scenario 6-2 and the "Olympic Games" incident discussed in Scenario 6-1. What kinds of actions should sovereign nations take against countries that engage in cyberespionage and that launch cyberattacks in the form of various worms, viruses, and DDoS requests? Would such attacks be acceptable between nations that have formally declared war with one another?

23. In Section 6.4.1, we examined some issues surrounding a "hacker code of ethics." We also saw why this code, containing the six principles described by Steven Levy, has been controversial. Is it possible to establish an appropriate set of guidelines for a hacker code of ethics, that is, for nonmalicious hackers, without becoming a moral relativist? You may want to revisit our discussion of moral relativism in Chapter 2 in deciding your answer to this question.

24. Revisit the Olympic Games operation (described in Scenario 6–1). Is it morally, or even legally, permissible for "legitimate" (or sovereign) nation states to conduct cyberwarfare against one another? Would it ever be morally permissible for a nation to solicit the help of an international hacking organization, such as Anonymous, in launching cyberattacks against other sovereign nation states or even against radical organizations such as Al Qaeda or ISIS?

Scenarios for Analysis

1. In our discussion of hacking-related security concerns, we saw how some forms of anonymous behavior in cyberspace can cause harm to others. What course of action would you recommend be taken in the following scenario?

A very close political race is underway in your state, where two candidates are running for a seat in the U.S. Senate. The weekend before citizens will cast their votes, one candidate decides to defame his/her opponent by using an anonymous remailer service (which strips away the original address of the sender of the e-mail) to send a message of questionable truth to an electronic distribution list of his opponent's supporters. The information included in this e-mail is so defamatory that it may threaten the outcome of the election by influencing many undecided voters, as well as the libeled candidate's regular supporters, to vote against him/her. Does the "injured" candidate in this instance have the right to demand that the identity of the person using the anonymous remailer (whom she suspects is her opponent in this election) be revealed?[34]

2. Recall Eugene Spafford's argument as to why computer break-ins can be justified under extraordinary circumstances. Apply his rationale in the following scenario.

You determine that you will need to break into a neighbor's car in order to drive a friend, who will otherwise die, to the hospital. You realize that you are morally obligated to save a person's life when it is in your power to do so. But you are also obligated to obey the law, which forbids breaking into someone's motor vehicle. How is the reasoning process that you use to evaluate this scenario similar to or different from the one Spafford used in determining whether it is morally permissible to break into a computer database containing the medical information needed to save someone's life?

ENDNOTES

1. Scenario 6–1 draws from information in the accounts of the Olympic Games operation in Charette (2012) and Nakashima and Warrick (2012). See both works for more details regarding the controversies surrounding the Olympic Games controversy and the Stuxnet worm.
2. See Viebeck (2015). Also see the interview with Anonymous in *France 24*, available at http://www.bing.com/videos/search?q=anonymous+isis+interview+in+france+24&FORM=VIRE7#view=detail&mid=8460F5CF64BDD4CCAD428460F5CF64BDD4CCAD42.
3. Epstein (2007), p. 176. Note that Kizza (2008), who has a similar threefold distinction regarding the key elements of cybersecurity, describes the third element as *availability* rather than *accessibility*.

4. Neumann (2004), pp. 208–09. Here, Neumann also provides more examples of how security can be viewed as a double-edged sword that "cuts both ways."
5. Some of the distinctions I make between privacy and security in Section 6.1.2 draw from and expand upon concepts and frameworks introduced in Tavani (2000).
6. We should note that some authors suggest that two categories—data security and system security—are sufficient to cover the issues that fall under the heading "Cybersecurity." The framework I use in Section 6.2, with three separate categories, draws from some distinctions introduced in Spinello and Tavani (2004) and expanded upon in Tavani (2007).
7. Spinello (2000), p. 158.
8. Dale and Lewis (2016), pp. 655–656.
9. Bottis (2007) points out that Code Red infected approximately 395,000 servers during a 14-hour period in 2000.
10. Lawton (2009) notes that the Conficker worm turned the computers it infected into "a botnet capable of launching mass attacks" and that in a four-day period in January 2009, the number of "individual infections grew from 2.4 to 8.9 million."
11. See, for example, the descriptions of this virus included in Aamoth (2014) and Arrouas (2014).
12. Miller (2015), p. 48.
13. Scenario 6–2 draws from information included in Maidment (2009) and the *Information Warfare Monitor Report* (2009). See also "Tracking GhostNet: Investigating a Cyber Espionage Network" (2009). Available at http://www.scribd.com/doc/13731776/Tracking-GhostNet-Investigating-a-Cyber-Espionage-Network.
14. See the fuller description available at http://csrc.nist.gov/publications/nistpubs/800-145/SP800-145.pdf.
15. Privacy Rights Clearinghouse (2008). My analysis of cloud computing in Sections 6.3–6.3.2 draws from and expands upon some concepts and distinctions introduced in Grodzinsky and Tavani (2011).
16. See Grodzinsky and Tavani (2011) for a more detailed discussion of this point.
17. Privacy Rights Clearinghouse (2008).
18. *Ibid.*
19. See the account of this incident in Breitbart (2010).
20. For an excellent discussion of "risk assessment" in the context of cybersecurity, see the extended analysis in Schneier (2004); a detailed study of risk methodologies affecting cloud computing is included in Pauley (2012).
21. See Levy (2001) for a full explanation of the six principles identified in this list.
22. I am grateful to Mason Cash for pointing out this distinction to me.
23. Moor described this fallacy in a talk titled "Just Consequentialism and Computing," presented at the 2000–2001 Humanities Lecture Series, Rivier University, Nashua, NH, February 2001.
24. See, for example, the analysis of the "Sony Rootkit" controversy in Russinovich (2005). See also the account of this incident in *Wikipedia*. Available at http://en.wikipedia.org/wiki/2005_Sony_BMG_CD_copy_protection_scandal.
25. Spafford (2007), p. 57.
26. See www.eccouncil.org/ceh.htm. I am grateful to Hien Nguyen for pointing out this Web site to me.
27. See http://edition.cnn.com/2009/POLITICS/05/29/cyber.czar.obama/index.html.
28. Denning (2004), p. 536.
29. Himma (2007b), pp. 73–74. Note that Himma's original text has been transposed into the form of a logical argument (with the author's permission). See also Himma (2008).
30. Manion and Goodrum (2004), p. 528.
31. Denning (2008), p. 421.
32. Denning (2007), p. 136.
33. See, for example, Arquilla (2002), De George (2003), Denning (2008), and Lin, Allhoff, and Rowe (2012) for some excellent discussions of the possibility of "just warfare" in the cyber era.
34. I am grateful to an anonymous reviewer who suggested this hypothetical scenario, illustrating an ethical dilemma involving Internet anonymity.

▶ REFERENCES

Aamoth, Doug. 2014. "How to Protect Yourself Against the Heartbleed Bug." *Time*, April 9. Available at: http://time.com/55337/how-to-protect-yourself-against-the-heartbleed-bug/.

Arquilla, John. 2002. "Can Information Warfare Ever Be Just?" In J. Rudinow and A. Graybosch, eds. *Ethics and Values in the Information Age*. Belmont CA: Wadsworth, pp. 403–14.

Arrouas, Michelle. 2014. "Change Your Passwords: A Massive Bug Has Put your Details at Risk." *Time*, April 9. Available at: http://time.com/55037/heartbleed-internet-security-encryption-risk/.

Bottis, Maria C. 2007. "Disclosing Software Vulnerabilities." In K. E. Himma, ed. *Internet Security: Hacking, Counterhacking, and Society*. Sudbury MA: Jones and Bartlett, pp. 255–68.

Breitbart, Andrew. 2010. "Google Software Bug Shared Private Online Documents." Available at http://www.breitbart.com/article.php?id=CNG.54c3200980573ae4c.

Cavoukian, Ann. 2008. "Privacy in the Clouds: A White Paper on Privacy and Digital Identity: Implications for the Internet." Available at: http://www.ipc.on.ca/images/resources/privacyintheclouds.pdf.

Charette, Robert N. 2012. "Gone Missing: The Public Policy Debate on Unleashing the Dogs of Cyberwar." *IEEE Spectrum*, June 4. Available at http://spectrum.ieee.org/riskfactor/telecom/security/gone-missing-the-public-policy-debate-on-unleashing-the-dogs-of-cyberwar/?utm_source=techalert&utm_medium=email&utm_campaign=060712.

Dale, Nell, and John Lewis. 2016. *Computer Science Illuminated*. 6th ed. Burlington, MA: Jones and Bartlett.

De George, Richard T. 2003. "Post-September 11: Computers, Ethics, and War." *Ethics and Information Technology* 5, no. 4: 183–90.

Denning, Dorothy E. 1999. *Information Warfare and Security*. New York: ACM Press, and Reading MA: Addison Wesley.

Denning, Dorothy E. 2001. "Activism, Hacktivism, and Cyberterrorism: The Internet as a Tool for Influencing Foreign Policy." In J. Arquilla and D. Ronfelt, eds. *Networks and Netwars*. Santa Monica CA: Rand Corp., pp. 229–88.

Denning, Dorothy E. 2004. "Cyberterrorism." In R. A. Spinello and H. T. Tavani, eds. *Readings in CyberEthics*. 2nd ed. Sudbury MA: Jones and Bartlett, pp. 536–41.

Denning, Dorothy E. 2007. "A View of Cyberterrorism Five Years Later." In K. E. Himma, ed. *Internet Security: Hacking, Counter-Hacking, and Society*. Sudbury MA: Jones and Bartlett, pp. 123–29.

Denning, Dorothy E. 2008. "The Ethics of Cyber Conflict." In K. E. Himma and H. T. Tavani, eds. *The Handbook of Information and Computer Ethics*. Hoboken NJ: John Wiley & Sons, pp. 407–28.

Epstein, Richard G. 2007. "The Impact of Computer Security Concerns on Software Development." In K. E. Himma, ed. *Internet Security: Hacking, Counter-Hacking, and Society*. Sudbury MA: Jones and Bartlett, pp. 171–202.

Grodzinsky, Francis, S., and Herman T. Tavani. 2011. "Privacy in 'the Cloud': Applying Nissenbaum's Theory of Contextual Integrity." *Computers and Society* 41, no. 1: 38–47.

Himanen, Pekka. 2001. *The Hacker Ethic: A Radical Approach to the Philosophy of Business*. New York: Random House.

Himma, Kenneth Einar. 2007a. "Privacy vs. Security: Why Privacy is Not an Absolute Value or Right," *University of San Diego Law Review* 45: 857–921.

Himma, Kenneth Einar. 2007b. "Hacking as Politically Motivated Digital Civil Disobedience: Is Hacktivism Morally Justified?" In K. E. Himma, ed. *Internet Security: Hacking, Counter-Hacking, and Society*. Sudbury MA: Jones and Bartlett, pp. 61–71.

Himma, Kenneth Einar. 2008. "Ethical Issues Involving Computer Security: Hacking, Hacktivism, and Counterhacking." In K. E. Himma and H. T. Tavani, eds. *The Handbook of Information and Computer Ethics*. Hoboken NJ: John Wiley and Sons, pp. 191–217.

Information Warfare Monitor Report. 2009. Available at http://www.nartv.org/mirror/ghostnet.pdf.

Kamlyuk, Vitaly. 2012. "'Flame' Virus Explained: How it Works and Who's Behind it." Interview in *RT*, May 29. Available at http://www.rt.com/news/flame-virus-cyber-war-536/.

Kaufman, Charlie, Radia Perlman, and Mike Speciner. 2002. *Network Security: Private Communication in a Public World*. 2nd ed. Upper Saddle River NJ: Prentice Hall.

Kizza, Joseph M. 2008. *Ethical and Social Issues in the Information Age*. 3rd ed. New York: Springer-Verlag.

Knorr, Eric and Galen Gruman. 2008. "What Cloud Computing Really Means." *InfoWorld*. Available at http://www.infoworld.com/d/cloud-computing/what-cloud-computing-really-means-031?page=0,0.

Ladner, Richard. 2012. "Sophisticated Cyber-battles Raise Fears of Cyber-blowback." *MSNBC News*, June 2. Available at http://www.msnbc.msn.com/id/47658329/ns/technology_and_science-security/.

Lawton, George. 2009. "On the Trail of the Conficker Worm." *IEEE Computer* 42, no. 6: 19–22.

Lee, David. 2012. "Flame and Stuxnet Makers 'Co-operated' on Code." *BBC News*, June 11. Available at http://www.bbc.co.uk/news/technology-18393985.

Levy, Steve. 2001. *Hackers: Heroes of the Computer Revolution*. Rev. ed. New York: Penguin.

Lin, Patrick, Fritz Allhoff, and Neill Rowe. 2012. "Is It Possible to Wage a Just Cyberwar?" *The Atlantic*, June 5. Available at http://www.theatlantic.com/technology/archive/2012/06/is-it-possible-to-wage-a-just-cyberwar/258106/.

Maidment, Paul. 2009. "GhostNet in the Machine." *Forbes.com*. Available at http://www.forbes.com/2009/03/29/ghostnet-computer-security-internet-technology-ghostnet.html.

Manion, Mark and Abby Goodrum. 2004. "Terrorism or Civil Disobedience: Toward a Hacktivist Ethic." In R. A. Spinello and H. T. Tavani, eds. *Readings in CyberEthics*. 2nd ed. Sudbury MA: Jones and Bartlett, pp. 525–35. Reprinted from *Computers and Society* 30, no. 2 (2000): 14–19.

Mell, Peter and Timothy Grance. 2011. "The NIST Definition of Cloud Computing." National Institute of Standards and Technology. U.S. Department of Commerce. Available at http://csrc.nist.gov/publications/nistpubs/800-145/SP800-145.pdf.

Miller, Keith W. 2015. "Malware." In J. Britt Holbrook and C. Mitcham, eds. *Ethics, Science, Technology, and Engineering: A Global Resource*. Vol. 3, 2nd ed. Farmington Hills, MI: Macmillan Reference, pp. 48–52.

Moor, James H. 2001. "Towards a Theory of Privacy for the Information Age." In R. M. Baird, R. Ramsower, and S. E. Rosenbaum, eds. *Cyberethics: Social and Moral Issues in the Computer Age*. Amherst NY: Prometheus Books, pp. 200–12.

Moor, James H. 2004. "Reason, Relativity, and Responsibility in Computer Ethics." In R. A. Spinello and H. T. Tavani, eds. *Readings in CyberEthics*. 2nd ed. Sudbury MA: Jones and Bartlett, pp. 40–54.

Nakashima, Ellen, and Joby Warrick. 2010. "Stuxnet Was Work of U.S. and Israeli Experts." *The Washington Post*, June 1. Available at http://www.washingtonpost.com/world/national-security/stuxnet-was-work-of-us-and-israeli-experts-officials-say/2012/06/01/gJQAlnEy6U_story.html.

National Institute of Standards and Technology. 2011. "The NIST Definition of Cloud Computing." U.S. Department of Commerce. Special Publication 800-145. Available at http://csrc.nist.gov/publications/nistpubs/800-145/SP800-145.pdf.

Neumann, Peter G. 2004. "Computer Security and Human Values." In T. W. Bynum and S. Rogerson, eds. *Computer Ethics and Professional Responsibility*. Malden MA: Blackwell, pp. 208–26.

Nissenbaum, Helen. 2010. *Privacy in Context: Technology, Policy, and the Integrity of Social Life*. Palo Alto, CA: Stanford University Press.

O'Harrow, Robert. 2012. "Cyber Search Engine Shodan Exposes Industrial Control Systems to New Risks." *The Washington Post*, June 3. Available at http://www.washingtonpost.com/investigations/cyber-search-engine-exposes-vulnerabilities/2012/06/03/gJQAIK9KCV_story.html.

Pauley, Wayne. 2012. *An Empirical Study of Privacy Risk Methodologies in Cloud Computing Environments*. Dissertation. Nova Southeastern University.

Pieters, Wolter, and Andre van Cleeff. 2009. "The Precautionary Principle in a World of Digital Dependencies." *IEEE Computer Society* 42, no. 8: 50–56.

Privacy Rights Clearing House. 2008. "The Privacy Implications of Cloud Computing." Available at http://www.privacy rights.org/ar/cloud-computing.htm.

Russinovich, Mark. 2005. "Sony, Rootkits, and Digital Rights Management Gone Too Far." Available at http://www.sysinternals.com/blog/2005/10sony-rootkits-and-digital-rights.html.

Sang-Hun, Choe, and John Markoff. 2009. "Cyberattacks Jam Government and Commercial Web Sites in U.S. and South Korea." *New York Times*, July 9. Available at http://www.nytimes.com/2009/07/09/technology/09cyber.html.

Sanger, David. 2012. "Mutually Assured Cyberdestruction." *New York Times*, June 2. Available at http://www.nytimes.com/2012/06/03/sunday-review/mutually-assured-cyberdestruction.html?.

Schneier, Bruce. 2004. *Secrets and Lies: Digital Security in a Networked World*. Rev. ed. New York: John Wiley and Sons.

Simpson, Michael T. 2006. *Hands-On Ethical Hacking and Network Defense*. Boston, MA: Thomson.

Skoudis, Ed. 2004. *Malware: Fighting Malicious Code*. Upper Saddle River, NJ: Prentice Hall.

Solove, Daniel J. 2011. *Nothing to Hide: The False Tradeoff between Privacy and Security*. New Haven, CT: Yale University Press.

Spafford, Eugene H. 2007. "Are Computer Hacker Break-Ins Ethical?" In K. Himma, ed. *Internet Security: Hacking, Counter-Hacking, and Society*. Sudbury, MA: Jones and Bartlett, pp. 49–59. Reprinted from *Journal of Systems Software*, 17: 41–47.

Spinello, Richard A. 2000. "Information Integrity." In D. Langford, ed. *Internet Ethics*. London, UK: Macmillan Publishers, pp. 158–80.

Spinello, Richard A., and Herman T. Tavani. 2004. "Introduction to Chapter 5: Security and Crime in Cyberspace." In R. A. Spinello and H. T. Tavani, eds. *Readings in Cyberethics*. 2nd ed. Sudbury, MA: Jones and Bartlett Publishers, pp. 501–12.

Talbot, David. 2011. "Improving the Security of Cloud Computing," *Technology Review*, June 15. Available at http://www.technologyreview.com/business/37683/.

Tavani, Herman T. 2000. "Privacy and Security." In D. Langford, ed. *Internet Ethics*. London, UK: Macmillan, and New York: St. Martin's Press, pp. 65–95.

Tavani, Herman T. 2007. "The Conceptual and Moral Landscape of Computer Security." In K. E. Himma, ed. *Internet Security: Hacking, Counter-Hacking, and Society*. Sudbury, MA: Jones and Bartlett, pp. 29–45.

Thompson, Paul B. 2001. "Privacy, Secrecy, and Security." *Ethics and Information Technology* 3, no. 1: 13–19.

Viebeck, Elise 2015. "Anarchist Hackers Go to Cyber War with ISIS." *The Hill*, February 12. Available at http://www.msn.com/en-us/news/it-insider/anarchist-hackers-go-to-cyber-war-with-isis/ar-AA9iukK.

Vijayan, Jaikumar. 2012. "Government Role in Stuxnet Could Increase Attacks Against U.S. Firms." *Computer World*, June 2. Available at http://www.computerworld.com/s/article/9227696/Government_role_in_Stuxnet_could_increase_attacks_against_U.S._firms.

Zeng, Ke, and Ann Cavoukian. 2010. *Modeling Cloud Computing Architecture without Compromising Privacy: A Privacy by Design Approach*. Available at: www.privacybydesign.ca.

▶ FURTHER READINGS

Bidgoli, Hossein, ed. 2005. *The Handbook of Information Security*. Hoboken NJ: John Wiley and Sons.

Jordan, Tim. 2008. *Hacking*. Cambridge, UK: Polity Press.

Schneir, Bruce. 2012. *Liars and Outliers: Enabling the Trust that Society Needs to Thrive*. Hoboken, NJ: John Wiley and Sons.

Tetmeyer, Annette, and Hossein Saiedian. 2010. "Security Threats and Mitigating Risk for USB Devices." *IEEE Technology and Society Magazine* 29, no. 4: 44–49.

Wallace, Kathleen A. 2008. "Online Anonymity." In K. E. Himma and H. T. Tavani, eds. *The Handbook of Information and Computer Ethics*. Hoboken NJ: John Wiley and Sons, pp. 165–89.

Wright, Marie, and John Kakalik. 2007. *Information Security: Contemporary Cases*.

CHAPTER

7

Cybercrime and Cyber-Related Crimes

LEARNING OBJECTIVES

Upon completing this chapter, you will successfully be able to:

- Identify numerous examples of *cybercrimes* and *cyber-related* crimes and determine whether it makes sense to speak of a *typical computer criminal*,
- Differentiate among the notions of *hacking*, *cracking*, and *counter hacking*,
- Describe three key categories of "genuine" cybercrime: *cyberpiracy*, *cybertrespass*, and *cybervandalism*,
- Differentiate (genuine) cybercrimes from cyber-related crimes and show how the latter category can be further divided into crimes that are either cyber-assisted or cyber-exacerbated,
- Describe the various kinds of tools and technologies that law enforcement agencies have used to combat cybercrimes and cyber-related crimes,
- Explain some key governmental programs and techniques that have been used in the ongoing battle involving cybercrimes,
- Identify some national and international laws currently in place to prosecute cybercrimes and explain the challenges involved in prosecuting those crimes,
- Describe the current tension between free speech (when used by individuals to justify leaking sensitive information on the Internet) and international governmental efforts to prosecute individuals and organizations that leak such information (as in the case of the WikiLeaks).

In Chapter 6, we examined cybersecurity issues independent of their implications for crime, even though issues involving crime and security in cyberspace sometimes overlap. In this chapter, we focus specifically on criminal activities involving cybertechnology. We begin by briefly reflecting on a scenario illustrating a law enforcement agent's controversial use of a social media site to catch suspected criminals.

▶ **SCENARIO 7–1:** Creating a Fake Facebook Account to Catch Criminals

In October 2014, the *Washington Post* reported a story about a Drug Enforcement Agency (DEA) officer who created a fake Facebook account using the identity of a real person. The DEA official, Timothy Sinnigen, set up the fake account using a profile of woman named Sondra Prince, who had been arrested in 2010 (and sentenced to probation). The Facebook profile, which Sinnigen believed would help him to locate suspected criminals in a drug ring, also included posts of some photos of Prince retrieved from her cell phone when it was confiscated at the time of her arrest. Two of the photos were controversial and deemed to be "racy": One was a picture of Prince wearing a scantily clad bikini (hardly distinguishable from a bra and underpants), and the other showed her in a suggestive pose while sitting on the hood of a BMW. Prince, who now goes by the name Sandra Arquiett, became aware of the fake Facebook profile only after a friend had asked why she posted the photos in question. She decided to sue the DEA for having fraudulently represented her on Facebook.[1] ■

Can the DEA officer's actions be defended on legal grounds? Sinnigen believed that using the fake account would help him to catch a wanted fugitive who had been romantically involved with Prince at the time of her arrest. He also believed that it might lead to the arrest and prosecution of suspected members of a drug ring. We should note that Sinnigen's actions have since been defended by the U.S. Justice Department, which claimed that the DEA agent had the right to impersonate the young woman and to create a Facebook account using her name without explicitly getting her permission. But we can ask whether there is either a legal precedent or a specific statute to support the DEA's claim.

First, we should note that police officers and law enforcement agents have often gone undercover, using fictitious names for the sole purpose of luring and catching criminals. For example, we will examine a case of Internet entrapment in Scenario 7–2, where an undercover police officer used a false name and profile to lure and eventually arrest a pedophile. But does it also follow that it is legal for a police officer to impersonate a real person in an online forum and then post controversial photos of her on the forum, without first getting that person's explicit consent? We can also reasonably ask: If it is a criminal act for an ordinary citizen to create a fraudulent Facebook account using the identity of a real person, why should it be permissible for a law enforcement agent to do so?

We should note that in recent years, some law enforcement agencies have used social media sites such as Facebook and Twitter to catch criminals. Consider, for example, that it is well known that police officers have monitored the (authentic) Facebook accounts of people they happen to be investigating for crimes. However, that practice is very different from creating a fake social media account that uses the name (and photos) of a real person. We can further ask what it would mean for the integrity of Facebook and similar social media sites, and what the implications for our civil liberties would likely be, if law enforcement agencies like the DEA could routinely set up fake social media accounts using the profiles of real people. While Facebook officially declined to comment on specific aspects of the DEA controversy involving the Sondra Prince incident, Facebook's chief security officer (CSO) expressed his concern that allowing the use of false accounts would undermine the social media site's integrity (McCoy 2014). We should note that in January 2015, the Justice Department reached a $134,000 settlement with Sondra Prince (Arquiett); however, the government did not admit to any wrongdoing in this incident.[2]

The purpose of Scenario 7–1 was not to arrive at any conclusive answers to the cluster of questions posed in this controversial incident; rather, its aim is to get us to begin thinking about cybercrime, especially with regard to some of the new ways that crimes can now be combated, as well as committed, in the digital age. When discussing cybercrimes, we typically think about rouge individuals and organizations using the latest technologies to commit (what might at least initially appear to be) novel kinds of crimes. We do not tend to think about those technologies and tools also being used by some law enforcement agencies to combat crime in ways that may potentially, even if unintentionally, violate our civil liberties. In a later section of this chapter, we examine some specific ways in which civil liberties issues can arise in the context of using the latest cyber-related tools to catch cybercriminals. First, however, we examine some basic concepts and background issues in cybercrime, and we begin with a brief look at some classic cybercrimes that have received worldwide media attention.

7.1 CYBERCRIMES AND CYBERCRIMINALS

Reports of criminal activities involving cybertechnology have appeared as cover stories in periodicals, as headlines in major newspapers, and as lead stories on television news programs in the United States and around the globe. In the 1970s and 1980s, we heard about numerous crimes that involved the use of computers to launch viruses and to break into financial and government institutions. In the 1990s, as the Internet insinuated itself into mainstream society, we heard stories about crimes involving digital piracy, cyberstalking, cyberpornography, and Internet pedophilia. In the first and second decades of this century, high-profile cyber-related crimes have expanded to include cyberbullying, sexting, identity theft, phishing, and so forth. In light of the evolutionary aspects of crimes involving cybertechnology, Wall (2007) differentiates "three generations" of computer crimes.

In recent years, there have been reports of "hacks" into people's pacemakers and even into a person's genome.[3] It seems as if novel cyber-related crimes continue to arise as new cyber-related technologies are developed and implemented. But we will see that despite the increase in the number and kinds of cyber-related crimes in recent years, the use of computers and cybertechnology to carry out criminal activities is hardly new.

7.1.1 Background Events: A Brief Sketch

In our analysis of cybercrime, it is useful to trace the developments of some key criminal activities involving computers and cyberspace. As noted earlier, some of the earliest incidents occurred in the 1970s. During that period, stories began to surface about disgruntled employees who altered files in computer databases or who sabotaged computer systems to seek revenge against employers. Other highly publicized news stories described computer-savvy teenagers, sometimes described in the media as "hackers," breaking into computer systems, either as a prank or for malicious purposes. There were also reports, frequently sensationalized and occasionally glamorized by some members of the press, involving "hackers" who used computers to transfer money from wealthy individuals and corporations to poorer individuals and organizations.

In Chapter 6, we saw that malicious hackers have engaged in a wide range of illicit, or at least questionable, activities. As a society, our attitude toward activities associated with hacking, as that concept has been used in the media, has changed. In the past, young computer enthusiasts who figured out ways of gaining unauthorized access to computer systems were sometimes portrayed as countercultural heroes who single-handedly took on the establishment, like David taking down Goliath (i.e., big government or big business) or Robin Hood robbing the rich to give to the poor. By the turn of the twenty-first century, however, there was a growing concern in both the private and the public sectors about whether any types of activities leading to unauthorized access should be tolerated. The media which itself had become a victim of cyberattacks (e.g., distributed denial-of-service [DDoS] attacks directed at *The New York Times*, CNN, and other well-known media Web sites) as well as ordinary computer users shifted their attitude considerably. Perhaps this change in sentiment is due to our society's increased dependence on networked computers and the Internet, as we noted in Chapter 6.

Of course, unauthorized break-ins are only one of the many kinds of crimes made possible by computers and cybertechnology. Power (2000), who believes that most computer crimes involve either fraud or abuse, or both, distinguishes between the two notions in the following way: He identifies *computer fraud* as computer-related crimes involving "deliberate misrepresentation or alteration of data in order to get something of value"; he defines *computer abuse*, on the contrary, as "willful or negligent unauthorized activity that affects the availability, confidentiality, or integrity of computer resources." Power notes that these abuses can include "embezzlement, theft, malicious damage, unauthorized use, denial of service, and misappropriation."[4]

Analysts believe that many cybercrimes go unreported. Wall (2007) notes that in at least some cases, organizations are reluctant to report cybercrimes because of the embarrassment it might cause them. Other analysts believe that many of these crimes go unreported because the victims fear the negative repercussions: Reporting the crimes would be tantamount to admitting that their computer security practices are inadequate. Consider, for example, what might happen if a customer discovered that the bank where he/she deposits and saves money had been broken into—he/she might decide to transfer her funds to a bank that he/she perceives to be more secure. And if cyber-related crimes committed by employees working inside a financial institution were reported and publicized, the institution could also suffer a loss of customer confidence.

7.1.2 A Typical Cybercriminal

Can we construct a profile for a typical cybercriminal? Some people associate cybercriminals with "hackers," or what we described in Chapter 6 as "malicious hackers." Many people think of a typical computer hacker in terms of the very bright, technically sophisticated, young white male in the popular 1983 movie *War Games*. Is such a portrayal accurate? Donn Parker, one of the first authors to write on the topic of computer crime, points out that a traditional hacker tended to perceive himself "as a problem solver rather than as a criminal."[5] Parker's classic study also suggested that we should carefully distinguish between hackers who commit crimes, that is, as people who are primarily nonprofessional or amateur criminals, and "professional criminals." He believes that stereotypical computer hackers, unlike most professional criminals, are not generally motivated by greed; some seem to thrive on a kind of "joyriding" (the thrill experienced in figuring out how to break into unauthorized systems). Along somewhat similar lines, Sagiroglu and Canbek (2009) point out that in the early days of computing, "idealistic hackers" were inclined to attack computers merely to prove that they could or to "show off" to one another. Characteristics such as these would seem to differentiate many traditional hackers from professional criminals.

Although many malicious hackers are considered amateur criminals, some possess an expertise with computers comparable to that of the best technical experts in computer science. However, it is also worth noting that many malicious hackers do not possess outstanding technical skills but are savvy enough to locate sophisticated "hacking tools" that can be downloaded from the Internet for free, and many of these individuals are sufficiently astute to take advantage of "holes" in computer systems and programs. Simpson (2006) notes that these individuals, who tend to be young and inexperienced, are sometimes referred to by sophisticated computer programmers as "script kiddies" or "packet monkeys," because they copy code from knowledgeable programmers as opposed to creating the code themselves.

▶ 7.2 HACKING, CRACKING, AND COUNTER HACKING

We have already noted that computer criminals are often referred to in the media as hackers and that, as a result, "hacker" now has a negative connotation. In Chapter 6, we saw why this definition of "hacker" is controversial and why many believe it to be both an inaccurate and unfortunate use of the term. Himanen (2001) notes that "hacker" originally meant anyone who "programmed enthusiastically" and who believed that "information sharing is a powerful positive good." The hacker Jargon File (maintained on the Web by Eric Raymond at www.catb.org/jargon/html/H/hacker.html) defines a hacker as "an expert or enthusiast of any kind." Note that, according to this definition, a hacker need not be a computer enthusiast; for example, someone could be an astronomy hacker. In fact, a hacker, in the generic sense of the term, might have no interest in computers or cybertechnology at all.

7.2.1 Hacking vs. Cracking

Himanen points out that the meaning of "hacker" began to change in the 1980s when the media started applying the term to criminals using computers. In order to avoid confusion with virus writers and intruders into information systems, traditional hackers began calling these destructive computer users *crackers*. According to the hacker Jargon File, a cracker is one "who breaks security on a system." Crackers often engage in theft and vandalism once they have gained access to computer systems.

Some authors, including Wall (2007), also use the expressions *white hat* and *black hat* to distinguish between the two types of hacking behavior. The phrase "white hat hackers" is used to refer to those "innocent," or nonmalicious, forms of hacking, while "black hat hackers" refers roughly to what we described earlier as "cracking." However, distinctions between hacking and cracking, and between white hat and black hat hackers, are generally not recognized and observed in the world beyond the computer community. So the media often refers to crackers, or "black hat hackers," simply as hackers. This, in turn, has perpetuated the negative image of hackers and hacking in society at large.

In this chapter, our uses of "hacker" sometimes reflect the broader societal (i.e., negative) meaning of the term. Because of the way "hacker" has been used in the media, it is difficult, if not impossible, to refer to some classic cases of cybercrime without invoking it. So it is important to keep in mind that many activities and crimes described in this chapter in terms of hacking would be better understood as instances of cracking.

7.2.2 Active Defense Hacking: Can Acts of "Hacking Back" or Counter Hacking Ever Be Morally Justified?

A more recent controversy associated with hacking activities has to do with *active defense hacking*, sometimes also referred to as "counter hacking" or "hacking back against hackers." Counter hacking activities have been carried out both by individuals and corporations; they are directed against those who are suspected of originating the hacker attacks. In some cases, counter hacking has been preemptive; in other cases, it has been reactive. Both forms are controversial, but preemptive counter hacking is arguably more difficult to defend. Is counter hacking an act of "self-defense," as some argue? Or is it simply another case of "two wrongs making a right?" Should counter hacking be legalized? Can it ever be ethically justified?

In Chapter 6, we saw that at least one organization offers a certification program to train "ethical hackers." Individuals who successfully complete this program—that is, Certified Ethical Hackers (CEH)—are trained and certified not only in the use of defensive measures to ensure the security of their employers but also appear to be authorized to engage in security-related activities that involve preemptive strikes as well. CEH draws an analogy between preemptive hacking on the part of its "certified" programmers and the kind of typical "penetration testing" done by programmers in corporations who are employed to "attack" their own systems to check for vulnerabilities (www.eccouncil.org/ceh.htm). But we can ask whether the "ethical hackers" certified by CEH are, in fact, similar to penetration testers and whether their cyberattacks should be perfectly legal even if they are performed under a "contract" that an organization has with CEH.

Some who defend preemptive acts of counter hacking on the part of organizations such as CEH believe that the attacks can be justified on utilitarian, or consequentialist, grounds. For example, they argue that less overall harm will likely result if preemptive strikes are allowed. However, it would seem that many of the same difficulties that arose in applying a utilitarian justification for computer break-ins in extraordinary cases (examined in Chapter 6) also arise in the case of extending a utilitarian argument to defend counter hacking in its preemptive form.

Because counter hacking can cause harm to innocent individuals, we can question whether this practice can be defended on moral grounds. Himma (2004, 2008) points out that in the case of hacking back against those who launch DDoS attacks, many innocent persons are adversely affected because the attacks are routed through their computer systems. As we noted in Chapter 6, perpetrators of DDoS attacks use "host computers," which often include the computers of innocent persons, to initiate their attacks (a technique sometimes referred to as "IP spoofing"). This would suggest to the victims of these attacks that they originated from the host computer, as opposed to the computer of the initiator of the attack. So when victims hack back, they can unintentionally cause the intermediate computer to be assaulted.

So, even if utilitarian arguments showed that counter hacking resulted in more desirable outcomes for the majority of society, deontologists (and other nonconsequentialists) would argue that such practices are morally unacceptable if they do not respect the rights of innocent individuals. In this case, those individuals would be unfairly used as a means to an end, which, as we saw in Chapter 2, is not permissible in deontological ethical theories.

It is difficult to provide a moral justification for counter hacking; and from a legal perspective, it is not clear whether "hacking back" can be viewed in a way that is not criminal. For example, if hacking is illegal, then it would seem that hacking back would be no less illegal. However, until a case of counter hacking—especially one that involves a preemptive attack in the form of a DDoS—is officially tried in court, it is difficult to say how our legal system will respond.

In Chapter 6, we considered whether at least some computer break-ins, under extraordinary conditions, might be ethically justifiable. In this chapter, we analyze computer break-ins and hacking-related issues mainly from a legal perspective. For example, we ask: Should all forms of computer hacking be declared illegal? Should every hacker be prosecuted as a criminal?[6] Before answering these questions, however, we examine some reasons why it is important to define what we mean by "cybercrime."

▶ 7.3 DEFINING CYBERCRIME

We have seen that crimes affecting cybertechnology, especially those associated with hacking, have received considerable attention in the popular media. The criteria used for determining which kinds of crimes should be labeled "computer crimes" or "cybercrimes" have been neither clear nor consistent. Initially, some news reporters and journalists seemed to suggest that any crime involving the use, or even the presence, of a computer is a computer crime; others, however, have argued that there was nothing special about crimes that happen to involve computers. Don Gotterbarn was an early skeptic regarding much of the media hype surrounding computer-related crimes, which he criticized as "a new species of yellow journalism."[7] As we saw in Chapter 1, Gotterbarn argues that a crime in which an individual uses a surgeon's scalpel to commit a murder would not be considered an issue in medical ethics, even though a medical instrument was used in the criminal act; so, by analogy, Gotterbarn concludes that crimes involving computers are not necessarily issues in computer ethics.

Gotterbarn's position can be interpreted in a way to suggest that no distinct category of computer crime or cybercrime is needed. Leman-Langlois (2008) makes a similar suggestion in stating that cybercrime, or what she calls "technocrime," "does not exist." In Leman-Langlois' view, cybercrime "is simply a convenient way to refer to a set of concepts . . . shaping the ways we understand matters having to do with the impact of technology on crime, criminals and our reactions to crime—and vice versa."[8]

If Gotterbarn and Leman-Langlois are correct, we can reasonably ask whether a separate category, cybercrime, is necessary or even useful. Consider the crimes that have involved technologies other than computers. Do we have separate categories for them? People steal televisions, but we don't have a category, television crime. People also steal automobiles, and some people have used automobiles to assist criminals in "getaway" operations, but we don't have a category, automobile crime. So why do we need a separate category, cybercrime, for criminal acts involving cybertechnology? Yet lawmakers have determined it necessary, or at least useful, to enact specific laws for crimes involving computers and cybertechnology.

In this chapter, we use "computer crime" and "cybercrime" interchangeably, even though some authors draw a distinction between the two. For example, Moore (2011) notes that a computer crime can be viewed as a "subdivision" of cybercrime and thus warrants its own definition. Moore prefers the expression "high-technology crime," which he uses to refer to any crime "involving the use of a high-technology device in its commission." However, in following the conventional nomenclature in the cyberethics literature, we use "cybercrime" and "computer crime" to refer to the full range of crimes covered in Moore's category of high-technology crime.

We next take up the question of criteria for distinguishing computer crimes/cybercrimes from other kinds of crimes. In particular, we ask whether the criteria used by lawmakers to frame various categories of computer crime or cybercrime has been coherent.[9]

7.3.1 Determining the Criteria

Do any of the following three incidents, each of which illustrates criminal activity involving a computer lab, convincingly demonstrate the need for a distinct category of computer crime?

- **a.** Sandra steals a computer device (e.g., a laser printer) from a computer lab.
- **b.** Bill breaks into a computer lab and then snoops around.
- **c.** Ed enters a computer lab that he is authorized to use and then places an explosive device, set to detonate a short time later, on a computer system in the lab.

Clearly, (a)–(c) are criminal acts, but should any of these acts necessarily be viewed as a computer crime or cybercrime? One could point out that it would not have been possible to commit any of them if computer technology had never existed, and this might initially influence some to believe that the three criminal acts are somehow unique to computer technology. Even though each act involves the presence of computer technology, each of them can easily be understood and prosecuted as a specific example of ordinary crime involving theft, breaking and entering, and vandalism, respectively. So we might infer that there are no legitimate grounds for having a separate category of computer crime. Can we justify such an inference?

7.3.2 A Preliminary Definition of Cybercrime

Moore (2011) suggests that a computer crime can include any criminal activity involving a computer, while a cybercrime would include any criminal activity involving a computer and a network. He also claims that a computer "may or may not have played an instrumental part in the commission of the crime." But some authors would find these definitions far too broad. Perhaps a computer crime could, as Forester and Morrison suggest, be defined as "a criminal act in which a computer is used as the *principal tool*" [italics added].[10] According to this definition, the theft of a computer hardware device (or, for that matter, the theft of an automobile or a television which also happened to contain a computer component) would not qualify as a computer crime. If we apply Forester and Morrison's definition to incidents (b) and (c) above—that is, breaking and entering into the computer lab and vandalizing a computer system in the lab, respectively—we see that these criminal acts are also ruled out as computer crimes. So their definition of computer crime might seem plausible. But is it adequate?

Consider a scenario in which a young woman named Sheila uses a computer or electronic device to enter the data for her annual income tax forms, which she will submit electronically. In the process of completing her income tax forms, she decides to enter false information and thus files a fraudulent tax return. Since income tax fraud is a crime and since Sheila uses a computer in committing this crime, is this criminal act a computer crime? Arguably, Sheila has used a computer as the "principal tool" to commit a crime of fraud. So according to Forester and Morrison's definition, it would seem that Sheila has committed a computer crime. But has she? Sheila could commit the same crime by manually filling out a hardcopy version of the income tax forms using a pencil or pen. So it would seem that Sheila's using a computer is coincident with, but by no means essential to, this particular criminal act. Thus, Forester and Morrison's definition of computer crime, which fails to rule out Sheila's criminal act of income tax fraud as a computer crime, is not adequate.

Girasa (2002) defines cybercrime as a crime that involves a "computer as a central component." Is this definition any more helpful than Forester and Morrison's? What does it mean for a crime to have a computer as its "central component"? Was a computer a central component in our example of Sheila's filing a fraudulent income tax return? It is difficult to distinguish which crimes have and which do not have a computer as their central component; so Girasa's definition of computer crime is not much of an improvement over the one advanced by Forester and Morrison.

7.3.3 Framing a Coherent and Comprehensive Definition of Cybercrime

Strickwerda (2013) defines a cybercrime as

> any new or different human act that is carried out through the use of computers or computer networks and is prohibited by the enactment of . . . law.[11]

On the one hand, defining a cybercrime simply as an act that is carried out through the use of computers and computer networks would not seem to be much of an improvement over earlier definitions that we considered. For example, we saw that many kinds of crimes carried out through those means would not clearly qualify as genuine cybercrimes. However, one component in Strikweda's definition merits further analysis—namely, her insight that a cybercrime involves *a new or different human act*. Recall our discussion in Chapter 1 of James Moor's insight that computer technology creates "new possibilities for human action" (because that technology is "logically malleable"). There, we also saw that these new possibilities, in turn, sometimes generate both "policy vacuums" and "conceptual muddles" (Moor 2007). By extension, these new possibilities for human action also include new possibilities for crime. Many of these possibilities have resulted in criminal actions that have forced us to stretch traditional concepts and laws dealing with crime. Applying Moor's insight, we can further ask whether any new forms of crime have been made possible by cybertechnology. If we answer "yes," then some crimes may be unique to computers and cybertechnology.

By thinking about cybercrimes in terms of their unique or special features—that is, conditions that separate them from ordinary crimes—we could distinguish authentic, or "genuine," cybercrimes from other crimes that merely involve the use or the presence of cybertechnology. We propose a definition of a genuine cybercrime as a crime in which

> the criminal act can be carried out *only* through the use of cybertechnology and can take place *only* in the cyberrealm.

Note that this definition would rule out the scenario where Sheila used a computer to file a fraudulent income tax return as an example of a genuine cybercrime. Of course, it also rules out the three examples of crimes involving a computer lab that we considered.

▶ 7.4 THREE CATEGORIES OF CYBERCRIME: PIRACY, TRESPASS, AND VANDALISM IN CYBERSPACE

Using our definition of cybercrime, we can further categorize genuine cybercrimes as follows:

1. Cyberpiracy—using cybertechnology in unauthorized ways to:
   a. Reproduce copies of proprietary information
   b. Distribute proprietary information (in digital form) across a computer network
2. Cybertrespass—using cybertechnology to gain unauthorized access to:
   a. An individual's or an organization's computer system
   b. A password-protected Web site
3. Cybervandalism—using cybertechnology to unleash one or more programs that:
   a. Disrupt the transmission of electronic information across one or more computer networks, including the Internet
   b. Destroy data resident in a computer or damage a computer system's resources, or both

Consider three incidents that can each illustrate one of the three categories: (i) the unauthorized exchanging of copyrighted music files over the Internet (beginning with the original Napster site); (ii) the launching of cyberattacks on major (commercial and government) Web sites in 2012, in response to PIPA and SOPA legislation (described in Chapter 8), that resulted in "denial of service" to thousands of users wishing to access those sites; and (iii) the unleashing of the Heartbleed computer virus in 2014 (mentioned in Chapter 6), which infected computers around the world.

Using our model of cybercrime, activities involving the unauthorized exchange of copyrighted music on the Internet via Napster and later versions of P2P-related file-sharing sites are examples of cyberpiracy (Category 1); the launching of the Heartbleed virus is an instance of cybervandalism (Category 3); and the DDoS attacks on government and commercial Web sites illustrate an example of cybertrespass (Category 2), because they involved the breaking into, as well as the unauthorized use of, third-party computer systems to send spurious requests to commercial Web sites (as opposed to the kind of "genuine" requests sent by users who wish to access those sites for legitimate purposes). Since DDoS attacks also cause serious disruption of services for the targeted Web sites, they can also be classified as cybervandalism (Category 3); so, some (genuine) cybercrimes can span more than one category.

If our model is correct, then many crimes that use cybertechnology are not genuine cybercrimes. For example, crimes involving pedophilia, stalking, and pornography can each be carried out with or without computers and cybertechnology; there is nothing about them that is unique to cybertechnology, so crimes such as Internet pedophilia, cyberstalking, and Internet pornography would not qualify as genuine cybercrimes. (We will see in Section 7.5 that they are examples of *cyber-related* crimes that have been exacerbated by cybertechnology.)

In Chapter 6, we saw that it was difficult to draw a coherent distinction between cyberterrorism and hacktivism. We now see that both can be understood as instances of cybertrespass, regardless of whether they were perpetrated by "electronic political activists" (called hacktivists) or by cyberterrorists. If, however, hacktivists and cyberterrorists also break into computer systems in order to disrupt or vandalize computer systems and networks, then they have committed cybervandalism as well. Using our definition of cybercrime, there is no need to consider motive, political cause, ideology, etc., when determining how the criminal acts best fit into one of our three categories. (However, motive or intention could influence the ways that cybercrimes are prosecuted and that convicted cybercriminals are sentenced.)

▶ 7.5 CYBER-RELATED CRIMES

So far, we have differentiated genuine cybercrimes, that is, crimes that are specific to cybertechnology, from crimes that are cyber-related. We next see that *cyber-related* crimes can, in turn, be divided into two subcategories: *cyber-exacerbated* crimes and *cyber-assisted* crimes. This distinction enables us to differentiate between a crime in which someone merely uses cybertechnology (e.g., a personal computer or electronic device to file a fraudulent income tax return) and crimes such as Internet pedophilia and cyberstalking, which are significantly exacerbated by computers and cybertechnology. The role that cybertechnology plays in the first example seems at best trivial and possibly altogether irrelevant, but in the latter two examples, cybertechnology does much more than merely *assist* someone in carrying out a crime—cybertechnology *exacerbates* the crimes.

7.5.1 Some Examples of Cyber-Exacerbated vs. Cyber-Assisted Crimes

Certain kinds of crimes aided by cybertechnology can increase significantly because of that technology. For example, in the case of cyber-exacerbated crimes, the scale on which crimes of a certain type can be carried out is significantly affected. Consider the potential increase in the number of stalking-, pornography-, and pedophilia-related crimes that can now occur because of cybertechnology vs. the likely increase in the number of income tax crimes, which are also assisted by computer technology.

Along lines that are somewhat similar to the distinctions we have drawn in separating three categories of cybercrime—cyber-assisted, cyber-exacerbated, and cyber-specific (or genuine cyber) crimes—Wall (2007) proposes the following scheme based on three "generations" of cybercrime. What we call cyber-assisted crimes, he describes as "first-generation" cybercrimes that are, in effect, "traditional" or "ordinary" crimes that happen to involve the use of a computer. Corresponding to our category of cyber-exacerbated crimes is Wall's notion of second-generation or "hybrid crimes." For this set of cyber-related crimes, Wall points out that network technology has "created entirely new global opportunities." His third generation of cybercrimes comprises a category that Wall calls "true cybercrimes," which corresponds to our category of genuine cybercrimes in that they are "solely the product of the Internet" (or, in our case, the product of cybertechnology).

Wall notes that in the case of cybercrimes involving the first two generations, individuals and organizations could still find ways of carrying out the criminal activities in the event that either the computer or the Internet was eliminated. In the case of true cybercrimes, however, Wall points out that if you eliminate the Internet, those crimes "vanish." He uses the examples of spamming and phishing to illustrate this point. These examples complement the set of crimes we identified earlier as genuine cybercrimes.

Figure 7-1 illustrates some ways in which crimes involving the use of cybertechnology can be catalogued according to this threefold scheme.

We should not underestimate the significance of many cyber-related crimes, even if they fail to qualify as genuine or true cybercrimes. Consider that many professional or career criminals, including those involved in organized crime, are using cybertechnology to conduct illicit gambling, drug trafficking, and racketeering scams. When cybertechnology is used, these crimes can be viewed as cyber-related crimes. Yet these kinds of crimes, which some describe as "old-style" crimes, receive far less attention in the popular media than those perpetrated by malicious hackers, many of whom are young and could be viewed as "amateur criminals." Because stories about these amateur criminals tend to grab the headlines, our attention is diverted from crimes committed in cyberspace by professionals. Power (2000) believes that youthful hacker stereotypes provide a "convenient foil" for both professional criminals and foreign intelligence agents. In Section 7.1.2, we saw that unlike many individuals who are

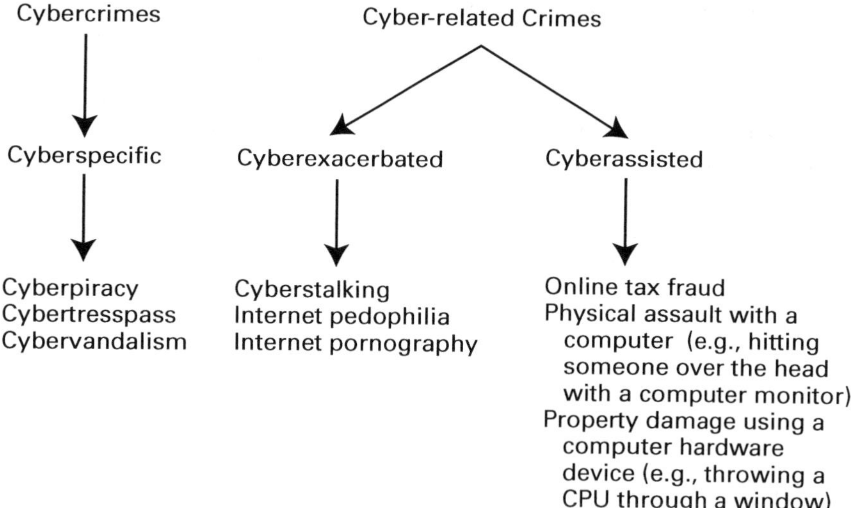

Figure 7-1 Cybercrimes and cyber-related crimes.

described in the media as "hackers" and who are amateurs, professionals do not seek technological adventure; rather, they hope to gain a financial advantage. But Power points out that since professional criminals have superior skills, they are less likely than amateurs to get caught in carrying out their criminal acts.

Also consider that some cyber-related crimes, including cyberstalking and cyberbullying, have resulted in deaths.[12] Bocij (2004) describes the wide range of criminal activities made possible by cyberstalking in a book dedicated to that topic.[13] And Kowalski, Limber, and Agatston (2008), in their book on cyberbullying, identify many of the ways by which cybertechnology has provided new opportunities for traditional bullying.[14] Although the authors of both books suggest that there may be some aspects of cyberstalking (vs. offline stalking) crimes and cyberbullying (vs. traditional bullying) crimes, respectively, that challenge our conventional laws, neither succeeds in making a convincing case for why those criminal acts should qualify as examples of what we call genuine cybercrimes. But, in describing the many ways that stalking and bullying crimes have increased significantly because of cybertechnology, the authors make a very strong case for why those cyber-related crimes would qualify as what we call cyber-exacerbated crimes (as opposed to merely cyber-assisted crimes).[15]

Next, we examine, in more detail, a cyber-related crime that also has been significantly exacerbated by cybertechnology: identity theft.

7.5.2 Identity Theft

What is identity theft, and how is it exacerbated by cybertechnology? Lininger and Vines (2005) define identity theft as

> a crime in which an imposter obtains key pieces of personal information, such as social security or driver's license numbers, in order to impersonate someone else. The information can be used to obtain credit, merchandise, and services in the name of the victim, or to provide the thief with false credentials.[16]

Identity theft crimes can also include the taking of another person's identity through the fraudulent acquisition of personal information in credit card numbers. However, Wall (2007) notes that identity theft is often mistakenly used to describe crimes involving credit card theft. So, not all instances of the latter kind of theft qualify as identity theft.

Of course, identity theft, like other cyber-related crimes, does not require cybertechnology. In the past, identity thieves have combed through dumpsters (and some still do) looking for copies of bank statements and for papers containing account information on credit card bills that people dispose of in their trash. (This behavior is sometimes referred to as "dumpster diving.") But identity thieves have been very successful in scams involving cybertechnology in general (e.g., in recording credit card "swipes"), independent of the Internet per se.

Factors such as lax security and carelessness involving customer information contained in computer databases and in company-owned laptop computers have made it easy for some identity thieves to acquire personal information about their victims. Simon (2005) describes two examples that occurred in 2005: (i) The Bank of America lost computer tapes containing data on 1.2 million federal employees, and (ii) ChoicePoint Inc. and LexisNexis disclosed that the dossiers of more than 170,000 Americans on the companies' databases had been illegally accessed by criminals and that at least 750 of them had their identities stolen. The information in these databases contained the addresses and Social Security numbers of individuals—all of the information that identity thieves needed to open up a credit card account. Simon points out that another incident linked to lax security and carelessness involved an MCI laptop computer containing the names of 165,000 MCI employees. (MCI was acquired by Verizon Communications in 2005.) The computer was stolen from the car of an MCI employee, which was parked in front of his home garage.[17]

As we saw in Chapter 5, information merchants purchase and sell personal information, including Social Security numbers and credit card information. And many are willing to pay for this information. So information brokering has become a lucrative business, and this has not gone unnoticed by professional criminals as well as by some employees in organizations that have access to sensitive information about people's financial records. Simon describes an incident where a former bank employee of Wachovia Corporation allegedly sold information about account numbers and account balances to a person who then sold them to data collection agencies. Some data brokers, such as ChoicePoint, have tried to screen customers to avoid selling information to criminals. But critics, especially privacy advocates, remain skeptical; many believe that for information brokers, concerns about privacy and security are more of an "afterthought" than a priority.[18]

Many kinds of identity theft scams have also been carried out on the Internet. One common example is a scheme involving an e-mail that appears to have been sent by a reputable business. For example, you may receive an e-mail that looks as if it were sent by eBay, Amazon, or PayPal. Often, these e-mail messages include the official logos of the companies they purport to represent; the message informs you that your account is about to expire and that you need to update it by verifying your credit card number. Although the e-mail might look legitimate, it could have been sent to you by identity thieves or other individuals whose objective is to get your credit card number as well as other kinds of personal information. How can a potential victim differentiate legitimate e-mail sent from businesses such as eBay or PayPal from that sent by identity thieves? Typically, e-mail from identity thieves will not address the potential victim by name; so this can be an indication that the e-mail is not from a legitimate source. Users wishing to verify the authenticity of the e-mail can contact the company by phone, or through the company's legitimate e-mail address, if they are in doubt.

Many e-mail messages sent from identity thieves are generated through spam (examined in Chapter 9). Using spam to gather personal information is sometimes referred to as *phishing*, which Lininger and Vines (2005) describe as "automated identity theft." They point out that phishing "combines the power of the Internet with human nature to defraud millions of people out of billions of dollars."[19] They also believe that phishing may soon overtake spam as "the main Internet headache." Lininger and Vines cite a study by the Anti-Phishing Working Group (APWG), which reports that the number of phishing incidents is increasing at a rate of about 56% per month.[20]

An automated version of phishing, sometimes called "pharming," automatically "redirects the victim to the offending site" (Wall 2007). Activities involving pharming and phishing, along with conventional e-mail spam, increase the amount of identity theft that can be accomplished over the Internet. And we have seen how other nonnetworked uses of cybertechnology also exacerbate identity theft crimes.

In our analysis of cybercrime and cyber-related crimes so far, we have examined some ways in which individuals and organizations have used cybertechnology to carry out criminal activities. Some of these crimes were "genuine" cybercrimes because they could not have been committed without the use of cybertechnology; others, however, were crimes that were either assisted or exacerbated by the use of cybertechnology. Not only has this technology enabled criminals to carry out their crimes, but it has also provided law enforcement agencies with new tools to track down criminals, including cybercriminals. We have already examined some ethical issues that arise because of the ways individuals can use cybertechnology to carry out criminal acts. Next, we consider some ways in which the use of cybertechnology by law enforcement agencies to combat crime can also raise ethical concerns.

▶ 7.6 TECHNOLOGIES AND TOOLS FOR COMBATING CYBERCRIME

Since the 1970s (and possibly earlier), the U.S. government has used cybertechnology to track down criminals via a technique called computerized record matching. For example, this technique has been used to match records in databases containing the names of federal government employees against the records in databases with the names of welfare recipients in order to identify "welfare cheats." Many privacy advocates, as well as civil liberties groups, have objected to the use of this technique in combating crime. However, one popular line of reasoning frequently used to defend computerized techniques (including record matching) in tracking down individuals suspected of committing crimes is: If you have done nothing wrong, you have nothing to worry about.[21]

From a utilitarian perspective, it could be argued that the end (e.g., catching welfare cheats or "deadbeat" parents) justifies the means used (matching the records of many innocent citizens in the process). But we can also see why techniques involving the computerized record matching of ordinary citizens (who are presumed to be innocent) can raise concerns about basic civil liberties. Civil liberties issues often lie at the heart of the controversies surrounding the use of cybertechnology by law enforcement agencies in tracking down criminals. Not surprisingly, law enforcement organizations desire to use the latest available technologies in pursuing criminals, including cybercriminals. We next consider some controversies surrounding the use of biometric technologies to fight crime.

7.6.1 Biometric Technologies

Power defines biometrics as "the biological identification of a person, which includes eyes, voice, hand prints, finger prints, retina patterns, and hand-written signatures."[22] van der Ploeg (1999, 2004) points out that through biometric technologies, one's iris can be read in the same way that one's voice can be printed. She also notes that one's fingerprints can be read by a computer that, in turn, has become touch sensitive and endowed with hearing and seeing capacities. The digital representation of these biometric data is usually transformed via some algorithm to produce a template, which is stored in a central computer database.

Possibly you have heard the expression, "Eyes are the window to the soul." In an age of biometrics, however, one's eyes may become the window to one's identity in a much more tangible sense than the classic metaphor ever intended. While biometric devices are a highly accurate means for validating an individual's identity, they are also controversial. In an incident involving Super Bowl XXXV (in January 2001), a biometric identification tool using face recognition technology scanned the faces of people entering the football stadium. The scanned images were then instantly matched against the facial templates of suspected criminals and terrorists, which were contained in a central computer database.[23]

Initially, the use of this technology at Super Bowl XXXV drew scathing criticism from civil liberties groups and privacy advocates. In the post-September 11 world, however, practices that employ biometric technologies such as face recognition devices have received overwhelming support from the American public; a poll conducted in October 2001, for example, indicated that more than 86% of Americans approved of using biometric technologies in public places, including sports stadiums and airports.[24]

Does the use of biometric technologies violate human rights? Do arguments against the government's traditional uses of computerized record matching apply equally in the case of biometric techniques? In nonbiometric-based computerized matching, including record-matching techniques used by the U.S. government in the 1970s, the databases involved contained records of individuals who were, or should have been, presumed to be innocent; for example, records of government workers were matched against records of welfare recipients to generate "hits." In matching practices involving biometric technology, such as the one used at Super Bowl XXXV, images of people who are presumed innocent were recorded and matched against a database of known or suspected criminals and terrorists. So, there is at least one key difference involving the two kinds of computerized matching.

But critics still raise questions regarding the use of biometric technologies by law enforcement agencies. Brey (2004) notes that critics of face recognition technologies in particular and biometrics in general point to at least three problems: error, abuse, and privacy. First, errors can occur in matches resulting from biometric technology, and the rate of error increases when the criteria used to determine what qualifies as an acceptable match is expanded. Second, the uses for which biometric technologies are originally authorized can expand significantly and can lead to possible abuses. And finally, the net security gained in the use of biometrics is not, in the view of many privacy advocates, commensurate with the loss of privacy and civil liberties for individuals. But those who favor using biometric technology argue that it provides increased security, even if using this technology undercuts some civil liberties for ordinary citizens.

7.6.2 Keystroke-Monitoring Software and Packet-Sniffing Programs

In addition to biometric technologies, law enforcement agencies have used other forms of cybertechnology to track the activities of criminals who themselves use cybertechnology. One such technique is *keystroke monitoring*, which Power describes as "a specialized form of audit-trail software . . . that records every key struck by a user and every character of the response that the system returns to the user."[25] This software can trace the text included in electronic messages back to the original sequence of keys and characters entered at a user's computer keyboard. So it is especially useful in tracking the activities of criminals who use encryption tools to encode their messages. Wall (2007) notes that "keystroke loggers" were originally designed to "identify errors in systems." The later use of this technology by law enforcement groups, however, has been controversial.

Government agencies such as the Federal Bureau of Investigation (FBI) have also tracked criminals and their activities via *Carnivore*, a "packet-sniffing" program that monitors the data traveling between networked computers; a packet sniffer or "sniffer" is a program that captures data across a computer network. However, these kinds of software programs have also been used by malicious hackers to capture user IDs and passwords. So Carnivore became somewhat controversial, and because of the negative publicity it received in the media, the FBI officially changed the name from Carnivore to DCS1000. However, DCS (Digital Collection System) has functioned in much the same way as Carnivore.[26]

▶ 7.7 PROGRAMS AND TECHNIQUES DESIGNED TO COMBAT CYBERCRIME IN THE UNITED STATES

In the preceding section, we saw that the government and law enforcement groups, in their efforts to track suspected criminals, have used a variety of technologies and tools—including biometrics, keystroke monitoring software, and packet-sniffing programs—all of which are controversial from the perspective of civil liberties groups. Next, we examine some programs and practices, as well as some interpretations of controversial laws, that government and law enforcement agencies have also used to apprehend and catch individuals, including professional criminals who use cybertechnology to carry out their criminal activities. We begin with a look at the practice of entrapment on the Internet.

7.7.1 Entrapment and "Sting" Operations to Catch Internet Pedophiles

Police and federal agents have used "sting" operations and entrapment techniques to catch members of organized crime involved in drug dealing, gambling, pornography, and so forth. Consider a controversial case of entrapment involving cybertechnology that was intended to lure and catch a pedophile who used the Internet to solicit sex with an under-aged person.

▶ **SCENARIO 7–2:** Entrapment on the Internet

Using an alias or pseudonym, detective James McLaughlin of Keene, New Hampshire, posed as a young boy in "boy-love chat rooms" on the Internet. There, he searched for adults attempting to solicit sex with underage boys and gathered evidence from conversations recorded in the chat rooms. Philip Rankin, a British marine insurance expert living in Norway, communicated with McLaughlin under the assumption that the police officer was a young boy. Rankin then agreed to travel to Keene to meet his online contact in person at a Dunkin' Donuts restaurant. Upon his arrival at the restaurant, Rankin was arrested by McLaughlin on the charge of using the Internet to solicit sex with an underage person.[27] ■

Critics of Internet entrapment have questioned whether such practices for catching child molesters are ethically justifiable, even if they are legal. In the United States, numerous cases of child molestation have been investigated by the FBI where pedophiles have crossed over a state line to meet and molest children they met via an Internet forum such as a chat room. Sometimes, police officers have entered chat rooms, posing as young girls to lure unsuspecting pedophiles. In 2003, a three-week sting operation was conducted in Spokane, Washington, where a policeman posing as a 13-year-old girl in an Internet chat room arrested a 22-year-old man on charges of attempted (second-degree) rape of a child.[28]

Supporters of online entrapment operations argue that they can save many innocent lives and can significantly lessen the harm that might otherwise occur to some individuals. Of course, a critical question from the point of view of many civil libertarians is whether the ends achieved by entrapment operations justify the means. Are such means morally acceptable? At the root of this question are some of the same issues involving civil liberties and computerized record matching, where we saw that the end achieved, catching criminals, was desirable, but the means used to accomplish this end were questionable.

7.7.2 Enhanced Government Surveillance Techniques and the Patriot Act

Another controversial practice involving government surveillance of criminal activities is supported by provisions in the Uniting and Strengthening America by Providing Appropriate Tools Required to Intercept and Obstruct Terrorism (USA PATRIOT) Act. This act, which was passed by the U.S. Congress in October 2001 and renewed (in a slightly modified form) in

2006 and 2015, provides law enforcement agencies with increased powers to track down suspected terrorists and criminals by allowing those agencies to closely monitor e-mail communications and cell phone conversations.

The Patriot Act works in conjunction with, and in some cases expands on, two related acts: the Foreign Intelligence Surveillance Act (FISA) of 1978 and the Electronic Communications Privacy Act (ECPA) of 1986. The original FISA, which was amended in 2008, established legal guidelines for federal investigations of foreign intelligence targets.[29] The Patriot Act amended FISA: Whereas the original FISA applied only to "snooping" in foreign intelligence investigations, the Patriot Act permits "domestic surveillance" as well.

In late 2005, reports began to surface that the George W. Bush administration had been monitoring the e-mails and phone calls of U.S. citizens who were communicating with individuals outside the United States. Opponents of this practice, including many members of the U.S. Congress, argued that the administration's practices violated the law because no court order was requested in conducting the surveillance on U.S. citizens. Others, however, supported the Bush administration's decision because of the positive effect it could have on national security. Some supporters also noted that it is legal for the National Security Agency (NSA) to conduct wiretaps on non-U.S. citizens, because of the authority given to it by FISA. However, critics objected that NSA is not authorized to intercept the communications of American citizens without first getting a court order. But, in its defense, the Bush administration argued that it was acting within the law because its primary obligation was to protect the American public against terrorist attacks.[30]

While many conservative organizations have supported the enhanced domestic surveillance provisions made possible by the Patriot Act, critics argue that this increased surveillance has eroded basic civil liberties. Some critics also worry that certain provisions in this act could be abused by those in power, under the convenient excuse of crime prevention and national defense, to achieve certain political ends. So, controversial aspects of the Patriot Act once again illustrate the classic tension between interests involving civil liberties and national security (as it affects terrorism and crime).[31] (In Chapters 4 and 5, we also saw how Edward Snowden's leaks to the media concerning the NSA's snooping on U.S. citizens have further exacerbated the tensions between civil liberties groups and governmental organizations.)

▶ 7.8 NATIONAL AND INTERNATIONAL LAWS TO COMBAT CYBERCRIME

Laws are typically limited in jurisdiction to nations where they are enacted. For example, the (U.S.) Economic Espionage Act is enforceable only in the United States. Some laws involving cybercrime are intended to have international reach, but issues involving legal jurisdiction have often impeded their prosecution in many instances.

7.8.1 The Problem of Jurisdiction in Cyberspace

Traditionally, crimes are prosecuted in the legal jurisdictions in which they were committed. In certain cases, suspected criminals have been extradited from one legal jurisdiction to another (and sometimes from one country to another) to stand trial for an accused crime. Girasa (2002) points out that jurisdiction is based on the concept of boundaries and laws are based on "territorial sovereignty." Because cyberspace has no physical boundaries, it can be difficult to prosecute cybercrimes involving multiple nations, as well as multiple states within nations. So, some have questioned whether the concept of legal jurisdiction makes any sense in cyberspace.

Enforcing Cybercrime Laws across States/Provinces within Nations

States and provinces within nations have often been challenged in determining how to enforce local laws when crimes are committed within their jurisdictional boundaries by criminals residing outside those boundaries. In the United States, for example, different states have different laws regarding gambling. How can those laws be prosecuted in the case of online gambling, which can span multiple states? Individual state laws affecting online gambling are evolving and thus seem to be in flux. In the following (hypothetical) scenario, we will assume that online gambling is legal in the state of Nevada but not in Texas.

▶ **SCENARIO 7–3:** A Virtual Casino

Sarah and Phil are U.S. citizens who live in different states. Phil, a resident of Nevada, has decided to set up an online gambling site called "Virtual Casino." His casino, which complies with all of Nevada's gambling regulations, is fully licensed by the state. Sarah, a resident of Texas, decides to visit Phil's Virtual Casino, which is physically located on a server in Nevada. She then places a bet at one of the virtual tables in Phil's casino.[32]

When Sarah engages in gambling activities on Phil's site (located on a server in Nevada) from her home computer, she has technically broken the law in Texas; but where, exactly, has the violation of the law taken place—in Texas, where the illegal gambling activities are carried out from Sarah's home, or in Nevada, where the server for the Virtual Casino resides? And where should this "crime" be prosecuted? Can the state of Texas demand the extradition of the Nevada resident who owns and operates the online gambling site, on grounds that the Web site owner has assisted (or has made possible) the "crime" that was committed by the resident of Texas? Note that in Scenario 7–3, no interstate transmission of illegal material, in the strict legal sense of that definition, has occurred. (Interstate statutes have been established to prosecute that type of crime.)

Although the "virtual casino" scenario is merely hypothetical, there have been some actual jurisdictional quagmires involving cybertechnology. A now classic incident involved an online forum, whose California-based server contained pornographic material that was legal in that state. But this content was illegal in Tennessee, where it had been viewed online by a resident of that state. We examine this incident in detail in our discussion of pornography laws in Chapter 9.

Enforcing Cybercrime Laws Involving Multiple Nations

Not only have there been problems in prosecuting Internet crimes that span state borders within nations, but criminal enforcement has been hampered as well by a lack of international legal agreements and treaties. This was quite apparent in 2001 when the notorious the ILOVEYOU virus, launched by Onel de Guzman from the Philippines, wreaked havoc worldwide. Where, exactly, did the crime take place? In the Philippines? In the United States? In Europe? Or in all of the above? Even though the virus originated in the Philippines, its effect was global. Suppose that in 2001, the Philippines had no explicit criminal law against launching computer viruses. In that case, did an actual crime even occur? Furthermore, if no crime had been committed by de Guzman in the Philippines, should he, as a citizen of that nation, still have been able to be extradited to nations that do have strict cybercrime laws, and should he be required to stand trial in those nations?

On the one hand, it might be argued that de Guzman should stand trial in any country that was affected by the virus he launched; after all, individuals and institutions in those countries were harmed by de Guzman's act. On the other hand, we might also wish to consider the flip side of that argument: Would we want all cases of crimes or of controversial Internet practices that have a global reach prosecuted by multiple nations? Consider the following scenario.

▶ **SCENARIO 7–4:** Prosecuting a Computer Corporation in Multiple Countries

XYZ Corporation, a major computer company in the United States, has developed and released a new software product that has been distributed globally. However, this product has a serious defect that causes computer systems using it to crash under certain conditions. These system crashes, in turn, result in both severe disruption and damage to system resources. QTRON, a company headquartered in eastern Asia that purchased this product from XYZ, has experienced multiple system crashes since installing it, which has also resulted in a severe loss of revenue for that company. What legal recourse does/should QTRON have in its complaint against XYZ Corp., given that its complaint involves companies in two sovereign nations? ■

In the United States, there are strict liability laws, but there are also disclaimers and caveats issued by manufacturers to protect themselves against litigation. Suppose that several countries where XYZ Corporation has sold its new software product also have strict liability laws but do not recognize disclaimers. Should XYZ Corporation be held legally liable in each of these countries? Would the fact that some of those countries did not recognize XYZ's disclaimer clause for computer products it sells in those countries have any bearing on deciding this question? It would seem that we need to think through some of the ramifications that broadening the sphere of legal jurisdiction at the international level could have for corporations that produce software products, which are susceptible to system failures in ways that other kinds of products are not.

For information about specific cybercrime laws in the United States, see http://www.cybercrime.gov. We next examine some international laws and treaties.

7.8.2 Some International Laws and Conventions Affecting Cybercrime

The Council of Europe (COE) has considered some ways to implement an international legal code that would apply to members of the European Union. Because cybercrimes can involve multiple law enforcement agencies and multiple ISPs in diverse countries under diverse rules of law, the G8 countries met in 2000 to discuss an international treaty involving cybercrime. (The G8 was, at that time, an informal group of eight countries: Canada, France, Germany, Italy, Japan, Russia, the United Kingdom, and the United States of America.) In conjunction with the G8 conference, the COE released its first draft of the COE Convention on Cybercrime in April 2000 (http://conventions.coe.in/treaty/en/projects/cybercrime.htm).[33] It addresses four types of criminal activity in cyberspace:

- Offenses against the confidentiality, availability, and integrity of data and computer systems
- Computer-related offenses (such as fraud)
- Content-related offenses (such as child pornography)
- Copyright-related offenses

Crimes involving economic espionage are not considered in the COE draft. However, international crimes involving copyright offenses are included, and this may prove to be important because of the sheer volume of unauthorized file sharing at the global level.

Many crimes affecting digital intellectual property are international in scope. Beginning in the late 1990s, Internet users around the world downloaded proprietary music from the original Napster Web site, whose central servers resided in the United States. In subsequent years, many illicit file-sharing sites that built upon the Napster system have operated outside the United States. For example, the servers for KaZaA, a well-known P2P file-sharing site, resided in the Netherlands before it ceased operations in 2005. But other sites, including Limewire, have taken the place of earlier sites such as Napster and KaZaA and have enabled the illicit sharing of proprietary music internationally. Perhaps one of the most "successful" sites dedicated to the unauthorized sharing of proprietary music, videos, games, and other copyrighted materials was The Pirate Bay, which operated out of Sweden. In 2009, an international trial took place, which determined the fate of that site.

▶ **SCENARIO 7–5:** The Pirate Bay Web Site

Established in 2003 by a Swedish anticopyright organization, ThePirateBay (hereafter referred to as Pirate Bay) is a well-known Web site that tracks and indexes files known as BitTorrent or "torrent" files. (Torrents are small files that contain "metadata," which are required to download the data files from other users.) In 2008, Pirate Bay announced that it had more than 25 million "unique peers" (unregistered users) and about 3,600,000 registered users. (Only users who wanted to download pornography from that site were required to register.) In 2006, Pirate Bay's servers were raided by Swedish police. Since then, Pirate Bay has faced a series of legal battles. In 2009, the four cofounders of Pirate Bay were found guilty by a Swedish court of "assisting the distribution of illegal content online." The verdict has since been appealed.[34] ■

The prosecution of Pirate Bay received international attention, and the verdict in this case no doubt pleased those who favor the strict international enforcement of intellectual property laws. In this case, there was no need to dispute jurisdictional boundaries; nor was there any need to extradite individuals across nationally sovereign borders to prosecute a cybercrime that was international in scope.

▶ 7.9 CYBERCRIME AND THE FREE PRESS: THE WIKILEAKS CONTROVERSY

In the previous section, we examined some challenges for law enforcement groups in their efforts to prosecute cybercrimes in the international arena. A relatively recent challenge for law enforcement in cyberspace, especially at the international level, has emerged in response to controversial "journalistic" practices involving some new online media outlets and organizations. Do these practices explicitly violate existing laws, in which case they would clearly qualify as criminal? Or should they be viewed as journalistic activities that are protected by a free press? This question lies at the heart of the WikiLeaks controversy.

WikiLeaks was founded in 2006 by the Sunshine Press organization (allegedly under the direction of Julian Assange, who has since become the "face of WikiLeaks"). Describing itself as a "not-for-profit media organization," WikiLeaks claims that its main objective is "to bring important news and information to the public" by publishing original source material so that readers "can see evidence of the truth" (http:wikileaks.org). Comparing itself to other "media outlets" that conduct "investigative journalism," WikiLeaks states that it accepts (but does not solicit) sources of information that are anonymous. However, WikiLeaks also states that unlike the other outlets, it provides a "high security anonymous drop box" and that when it receives new information, the organization's journalists analyze and verify the material before writing a "news piece about it describing its significance to society." The organization then publishes "both the news story and the original material" so that readers can analyze the story "in the context of the original source material themselves" (http:wikileaks.org/About.html).

By 2010, WikiLeaks had released thousands of controversial documents, in redacted form, to five traditional media organizations: *The Guardian*, *Le Monde*, *Der Spiegel*, *El Pais*, and *The New York Times* (Benkler 2011). The released documents included:

- A video of a U.S. helicopter attack in which the crew members allegedly fired on and killed innocent civilians, in addition to enemy soldiers

- Two large-scale documents involving the Iraq and Afghanistan wars
- Several U.S. state department diplomatic cables

We analyze the WikiLeaks controversy in terms of three key questions: (i) Can WikiLeaks' practices be justified on ethical grounds (even if they may be criminal)? (ii) Do WikiLeaks' practices clearly violate existing laws (and thus rise to the level of a crime)? (iii) Should WikiLeaks' practices be interpreted as a new form of journalism (and thus be protected under the provisions of a free press)?

7.9.1 Are WikiLeaks' Practices Ethical?

WikiLeaks claims that it "combines high-end security technologies with journalism and *ethical principles*" [Italics Added] (*http:wikileaks.org/About.html*). However, many critics have challenged WikiLeaks' claim regarding its adherence to ethical principles. For example, Wieneke (2011), who describes the organization's objectives and practices as naïve, reckless, and dangerous, believes that WikiLeaks' activities are unethical for at least two reasons: (i) The leaks involved have been "vast and indiscriminate," and (ii) the leaks were intended more to "embarrass" rather than to "fix." So, Wieneke exposes two kinds of concerns that would make it difficult for WikiLeaks to defend its claim regarding the organization's compliance with ethical principles.

Floridi (2013) also examines some ethics-related aspects of WikiLeaks' activities, which he analyzes from the vantage point of whistle-blowing. (Recall our discussion of whistle-blowing in the context of computing/IT professionals in Chapter 4.) He identifies two key problems with trying to support the organization's (whistle-blowing) activities on ethical grounds:

1. WikiLeaks' motivation was based on resentment (and the intent to cause harm to its target).
2. WikiLeaks' activities put some innocent people at risk.

Floridi also points out that some of WikiLeaks' supporters have tried to justify the organization's practices by appealing either to consequentialist (e.g., utilitarian) or deontological theories (see Chapter 2), or both. But Floridi believes that neither kind of ethical theory can be used successfully to justify WikiLeaks' practices.

Floridi also questions WikiLeaks' so-called "information liberation" argument, which holds that its practice of publishing leaked documents "improves transparency, and this transparency creates a better society for all people" (http://www.wikileaks.ch/about.html). He believes that this argument is "naïve," at best. Additionally, Floridi is concerned that the kind of threat/retaliation tactics used by WikiLeaks constitute a form of "whitemail"—that is, because it blackmails organizations by threatening to disclose even more damaging information about them via the organization's "insurance file,"—in the event anything should happen to WikiLeaks or to Julian Assange. Following Floridi, we question whether an organization that threatens its adversaries with these kinds of retaliatory measures can be viewed as acting ethically? We conclude this section by noting that both Floridi and Wieneke provide some compelling examples to show why it is difficult to justify WikiLeaks' practices on ethical grounds.

7.9.2 Are WikiLeaks' Practices Criminal?

Many see WikiLeaks' activities as not only unethical but also crossing the threshold of criminal behavior. But do these activities rise to the level of a cybercrime? And if they do, what specific criminal statutes do they violate? Former U.S. Attorney General Eric Holder and U.S. Senator Dianne Feinstein (D-CA) have argued that Julian Assange, as the spokesman for (and generally recognized leader of) WikiLeaks, should be prosecuted under the U.S. Espionage Act. But others, including U.S. Congressman Peter King (R-NY), have taken a different tack by arguing that WikiLeaks should be placed on the list of terrorist organizations that include Al Qaeda and ISIS. And some analysts have interpreted former U.S. Vice Presidential candidate Sara Palin's remarks as (effectively) calling for the assassination of Assange, when Palin suggested that Assange be treated the same as a high-ranking member of Al Qaeda.

Should Assange be assassinated, as Palin and a few other conservative politicians in the United States seem to imply? Would that be ethically justifiable? And is Assange really a "high-tech terrorist," as U.S. Vice President Joseph Biden asserts? It would certainly be helpful if we could separate the rhetoric used by some political leaders from the "facts" (or descriptive accounts) of the WikiLeaks criminal case. Much of the controversial material released by WikiLeaks was given to the organization by Pfc. Bradley Manning (U.S. Army), who was charged in 2010 with leaking the sensitive military information to WikiLeaks. [Bradley Manning currently goes by the name "Chelsea Manning."] Specific charges against Manning included downloading and sending vast amounts of diplomatic cables and sensitive documents to WikiLeaks. Manning was also charged with indirectly aiding Al Qaeda. At Manning's court martial, the U.S. military's prosecutors claimed that the documents sent by Manning to WikiLeaks included "nearly half a million sensitive battlefield reports from Iraq and Afghanistan" as well as "hundreds of thousands of diplomatic cables" that WikiLeaks, in effect, shared with the world.[35] In July 2013, Manning was convicted of several charges, including violating the U.S. Espionage Act, and was sentenced to 35 years' imprisonment in August of that year.

Of course, the criminal charges brought against Manning (for leaking sensitive military/national security information to WikiLeaks), which resulted in Manning's conviction and prison sentence, are very different from the kinds of criminal charges that have been levied against the WikiLeaks organization itself for disseminating that information. In the remainder of this section, we limit our discussion to assessing the grounds (or lack thereof) for the criminal charges directed against WikiLeaks in general and Julian Assange in particular.

Despite what might have appeared to be widespread international support for prosecuting Assange, some countries have seen the matter differently. For example, law enforcement authorities in Australia, where Assange is a citizen (but not currently residing), are not convinced that he has violated any Australian laws. Also, some U.S. legal scholars and analysts do not believe that WikiLeaks' activities qualify as "criminal" under American law. Yochai Benkler, an eminent Harvard law professor, argues that "there is no sound Constitutional basis for a criminal prosecution of Assange" and that neither WikiLeaks nor Assange should be treated any differently than *The New York Times* (and its reporters). Benkler also believes that the reports issued by both the American news media and the U.S. government have dramatically overstated the extent of the "actual threat of WikiLeaks." He further argues that the vast overreaction by both groups has helped to frame and reinforce an image of WikiLeaks as some kind of terrorist organization, as opposed to presenting an accurate picture of what the organization, in his view, is: a "journalistic enterprise."[36]

7.9.3 WikiLeaks and the Free Press

We next briefly consider the interests of the "free press" tradition in the dispute about whether it was legal to shut down WikiLeaks and to prosecute Assange. Benkler believes that WikiLeaks' activities were "fundamentally a moment of journalistic exposure," despite the fact that public and political response was, in his view, overstated, overheated, and irresponsible. If Benkler is correct, then it would seem plausible to argue that the journalistic protections consonant with a free press should also apply to WikiLeaks. But some disagree that this organization's activities can be defended under the guise of "journalistic exposure," at least not in the traditional sense of that phrase. For example, Wieneke (2010) argues that if WikiLeaks' motivation had been simply "to disseminate factual information," there would have been little distinction between an attempt to prosecute Assange or other WikiLeaks organizers and "more established media outlets" such as *The New York Times* and its journalists. Of course, a critic might point out that it was precisely the status of so-called factual information previously reported in the media that was being challenged in some of the leaked documents and reports. That critic might further point out that exposing (and correcting) false information previously reported in the press is an important part of "responsible journalism."

Can the WikiLeaks organization qualify as a traditional journalistic organization, in which case it would also qualify for the legal protections that apply to traditional journalists and their organizations? Benkler argues that WikiLeaks can best be understood as participating in a "joint venture" with "other traditional news organizations." In this role, Benkler believes that WikiLeaks has (whether intentionally or not) helped to form a new mode of journalism—that is, one that cannot be adequately understood simply as a "traditional media organization." But we can still ask whether this "new" kind of media organization deserves the same legal protections that have been accorded to traditional media outlets and their journalists.

Benkler believes that there is a "difficult but important relationship" between the traditional media and the "new, networked media" that have now come together to characterize what he calls the "new media environment." This environment, Benkler points out, is much more global and diverse, and it also includes a wider "range of actors." And in response to the kinds of journalistic practices made possible by this new media environment, Benkler believes that we need a "reformed legal regime." He also believes that these laws are needed to protect forms of "unpopular speech" that otherwise would not be able to be expressed in this new environment.

We conclude this section by noting that the WikiLeaks controversy is still not fully settled; for one thing, Julian Assange currently resides in Ecuador, where he has been granted political asylum. We also note that there are aspects of this controversy that could not be examined in this chapter. For example, we did not consider WikiLeaks vis-à-vis concerns affecting national security, as issues affecting that topic were examined in Chapter 6. While it may be difficult to defend the view that WikiLeaks should be rewarded for "exposing corruption around the world," as some proponents seem to suggest, it also not clear that "vigilante groups" that support the U.S. government's concerns—for example, some private commercial organizations—should have been encouraged in their efforts to shut down WikiLeaks by launching DDoS attacks on that organization's Web site. And even if international law enforcement agencies succeed in permanently shutting down WikiLeaks, other like-minded Web sites will probably emerge sooner or later. In the meantime, however, it would seem prudent to follow Benkler's advice as far as gaining a better understanding of what constitutes the new media environment for journalism, so that we can enact the appropriate legislation that may be needed.

▶ 7.10 CHAPTER SUMMARY

In this chapter, we examined crimes involving cybertechnology. We considered arguments as to whether a profile for a typical cybercriminal could be constructed and whether a reasonable distinction could be drawn between hacking and cracking. We also questioned whether "hacking back" or counter hacking is ever morally permissible. We then drew a distinction between "genuine" cybercrimes and cyber-related crimes and considered some examples of each type. We also considered some roles that biometric technologies have played in assisting law enforcement to combat crime in cyberspace. Next, we identified and briefly described some international laws that have been enacted in response to criminal activities involving cybertechnology. Finally, we described some problems that the WikiLeaks controversy poses for both understanding and prosecuting international cybercrimes where journalistic interests affecting a free press are also at stake.

It is important to note that many cyber-related crimes were either not examined or not discussed in the detail they would seem to deserve. A principal objective of this chapter, however, was to clear up some conceptual confusions about the way that many of the crimes involving cybertechnology are analyzed; no attempt was made to provide an exhaustive analysis of cyber-related crimes. As a result, very little was said about crimes affecting software piracy, spam, sexting, online child pornography, etc.—all of which use cybertechnology at some level. These topics are discussed in detail in appropriate sections of later chapters. For example, criminal aspects of software piracy are examined in our discussion of intellectual property in Chapter 8. Issues affecting spam, child pornography, and sexting are discussed in our examination of regulatory challenges affecting cyberspace in Chapter 9.

▶ REVIEW QUESTIONS

1. How did the popular media's portrayal of computer-related crimes carried out in the 1970s and 1980s romanticize the behavior of some individuals who engaged in these criminal activities?
2. Can we construct a profile of a "typical cybercriminal"?
3. Why have many members of the professional computer community opposed the use of "hacker" to describe cybercriminals?
4. Can a meaningful distinction be drawn between hacking and "cracking"?
5. What is meant by "active defense hacking" or "counter hacking"?
6. Can this kind of hacking be justified on either legal or ethical grounds?
7. What are the objectives of the Certified Ethical Hacker (CEH) organization?
8. Can CEH's practices be justified on ethical grounds, even if they happen to be legal?
9. What, exactly, is cybercrime?
10. How can a coherent definition of cybercrime be framed?
11. Identify and briefly describe the three categories of "genuine cybercrime" that we examined.
12. How can we distinguish between genuine cybercrimes and "cyber-related" crimes?
13. How might we distinguish between cyber-related crimes that are "cyber-exacerbated" and those that are "cyber-assisted"?
14. What is identity theft, and how has it been exacerbated by cybertechnology?
15. What are biometric technologies, and how are they used in fighting cybercrime?
16. How have packet-sniffing programs and keystroke-monitoring technologies assisted law enforcement authorities in fighting cybercrime?
17. What is "entrapment on the Internet," and why has it been controversial?
18. What is the Patriot Act, and why is it controversial?
19. What problems do issues of jurisdiction pose for understanding and prosecuting crimes committed in cyberspace?
20. What is WikiLeaks, and why is it controversial?

▶ DISCUSSION QUESTIONS

21. Recall our brief discussion of a case involving Internet entrapment to lure and arrest a pedophile in Section 7.7.1. Which arguments can be made in favor of entrapment and "sting operations" on the Internet? From a utilitarian perspective, entrapment might seem like a good thing because it may achieve desirable consequences. Should sting operations be used to lure pedophiles? Justify your position by appealing to one or more of the ethical theories described in Chapter 2.
22. Recall the distinctions that we drew between cyber-specific and cyber-related crimes. Why would cyberstalking be classified as a cyber-related crime, according to this distinction? When analyzing cyber-related crimes, why is it useful to distinguish further between cyber-exacerbated and cyber-assisted crimes? Why would cyberstalking also be categorized as a "cyberexacerbated" rather than a cyber-assisted crime? Why not simply call every crime in which cybertechnology is either used or present a cybercrime?
23. Assess arguments for and against the use of biometric technologies for security purposes, especially in airports and large stadiums. Should biometric technologies such as face recognition programs and iris scanners be used in these and other kinds of public places? In the post-September 11 world, there is much more support for these technologies than there was

when biometrics technologies were used at Super Bowl XXXV in January 2001. Granted that such technologies can help the government to catch criminals and suspected terrorists, what kinds of issues does the use of these technologies raise from a civil liberties perspective?

24. What implications does the conviction of the four cofounders of The Pirate Bay Web site (in 2009) have for international attempts to prosecute intellectual property crimes globally? Should the four men also have been required to stand trial in all of the countries in which copyrighted material had been downloaded from their Web site? Will the outcome of The Pirate Bay trial likely deter individuals and organizations, worldwide, from setting up future P2P sites that allow the illicit file sharing of copyrighted material?

Scenarios for Analysis

1. Your brother, Phil, is a sergeant in the U.S. Army. He has just returned home (on military leave) from his second tour of duty in Iraq, where he was part of a multination security coalition (peacekeeping force) during the transition period for a new government regime in that country. Phil's first tour in Iraq went relatively smoothly, but during his second tour, he witnessed a tragic event involving "friendly fire" in his unit, which has since troubled him deeply. He tells you that three members of his platoon were killed by coalition forces as a result of mistaken identity, although the official report issued by the U.S. Army was that the three soldiers were killed by enemy combatants. Phil also tells you that he was advised by his close friends in the military not to report the truth about this incident to the press, for fear of possible retaliation by some of Phil's (Army) superiors. It turns out that you are aware of a controversial journalistic/media outlet (similar to WikiLeaks) that accepts anonymous tips about incidents falsely reported by governments and military organizations around the world.

Phil has made it clear to you that he will not report the incident to the media outlet in question. However, you believe that the truth about the cover-up should be reported (while you also believe that your anonymity, as well as Phil's, should be protected). So, you seriously consider giving the information to this media outlet; but you also have some concerns about how the release of this information might adversely affect the families of the three victims, once the truth about the incident is revealed. After much deliberation, you decide to send the information to the media organization through an "anonymous drop box." Later, you learn that this organization has been under criminal investigation for leaks of sensitive diplomatic and military information in the past. Even after learning this, you still believe that providing the information about the cover-up of the "friendly fire" incident to this organization was the right thing to do. Next, assume that that media organization releases the information about this incident and that it is subsequently charged with criminal behavior for doing so. Would it be appropriate for you to be considered an accessory to that crime? Explain.

2. In France and Germany, it is illegal to sell Nazi memorabilia (from the World War II era), as well as neo-Nazi items, on Web auction sites. In fact, France had a dispute with Yahoo, Inc. about this point in 2000, and Yahoo agreed to install filtering technology that would block access to information about these items on the Yahoo site in France (even though advertising and selling the same kinds of items on U.S. Web auction sites is legal). Your sister, Jane, has recently founded a new Web auction site in the United States, which, of course, will have to compete with well-known sites such as eBay to succeed. Jane's newly launched auction site is eager to attract as much business as it can, as long as the items being traded on it are in compliance with U.S. law. Two potential clients, both of whom are U.S. citizens living in America, wish to auction some Nazi memorabilia and neo-Nazi items on this new site.

Initially, Jane is conflicted about what to do, but she is then informed by a few of her business associates that auctioning these items on Web sites in the United States is perfectly legal. Jane also realizes that if she turns down the prospective clients, they will only go elsewhere to a site that will list the items in question. What would you advise Jane to do in this case? Suppose her Web auction company decides to accept these items, and further suppose that they eventually end up for sale in Germany or France where they would have been acquired illegally. Would Jane and her online auction site bear any responsibility in aiding and abetting a crime in a country outside the United States? Explain.

ENDNOTES

1. See, for example, McCoy (2014). McCoy also points out that when the police seized Sondra Prince's cell phone at the time of her arrest (in 2010), they found several photos on it. However, Prince did not give her express consent for the police to use her photos to set up an account on Facebook.
2. See the account of this settlement in Eric Tucker (Associated Press), available at http://www.msn.com/en-us/news/us/apnewsbreak-us-settles-case-over-fake-facebook-page/ar-AA8oURN.
3. See Ragan (2009), Feder (2008), and Aldhous and Reilly (2009).
4. Power (2000), p. 329.
5. Parker (1988), p. 142.
6. Some critics suggest that many of today's "computer heroes" including some successful entrepreneurs in the computer industry, could also be accused of having been hackers in the past. See, for example, Jordan (2008) for an interesting discussion of this topic.
7. Gotterbarn (1995), p. 19.
8. Leman-Langlois (2008), p. 1.
9. My discussion and analysis of categories of cybercrime, in Sections 7.3 and 7.4, draws from and expands upon some concepts and distinctions introduced in Tavani (2000).
10. Forester and Morrison (1994), p. 29.
11. Strickwerda (2013), p. 502.
12. For example, Amy Boyer was murdered in 1999 by a someone who had stalked her on the Internet, and Megan Meier committed suicide in 2006 following a cyberbullying incident.
13. Bocij (2004, p. 14) defines cyberstalking as a "group of behaviors in which an individual, group of individuals, or an organization uses information and communications technology to harass another individual, group of individuals, or organization."
14. Kowalski, Limber, and Agatston (2008, p. 1) define cyberbullying as "bullying through e-mail, (IM), in a Chat Room, on a Web site, or through digital messages or images sent to a cellular phone."
15. See the arguments in Grodzinsky and Tavani (2001) for why cyberstalking crimes do not qualify as "genuine cybercrimes."
16. Lininger and Vines (2005), p. 268.
17. For more details, see the account of these incidents in Simon (2005).
18. *Ibid*.
19. Lininger and Vines (2005), p. 5.
20. *Ibid*, p. xxi.
21. See Solove (2011) for an interesting critique of this view.
22. Power (2000), p. 328.
23. See the account in Brey (2004).
24. For example, see the Harris Interactive Poll taken in late September 2001.
25. Power, p. 332.
26. See, for example, http://en.wikipedia.org/wiki/Carnivore_(FBI).
27. See Sinnott-Armstrong (1999) for an excellent analysis of key issues described in this scenario.
28. See the account of this incident in Martinez (2009).
29. See http://www.fas.org/irp/agency/doj/fisa/.
30. In some ways, this dispute lies at the heart of the NSA controversy generated by the Edward Snowden leaks in 2013, which we examined in Chapter 4 in our discussion of whistle-blowing. Interested readers may want to revisit our discussion there in connection with our analysis of related issues examined in this section of Chapter 7.
31. Critics note that many, possibly even most, crimes involving cybertechnology have involved neither terrorists nor members of organized crime syndicates. So, they ask whether the government should be permitted to use the same aggressive tactics that it claims are needed to counter terrorism and organized crime in catching lesser criminals who commit crimes that do not impact our security and safety as a nation.
32. For more information about online gambling, see the description in *Wikipedia*. Available at http://en.wikipedia.org/wiki/Online_gambling.
33. The former G8 countries have since expanded to include Australia, Belgium, Spain, Switzerland, and others; this group is currently referred to as the G20.
34. See Jemima Kiss. "The Pirate Bay Trial: Guilty Verdict." *The Guardian*, April 17, 2009. Available at http://www.guardian.co.uk/technology/2009/apr/17/the-pirate-bay-trial-guilty-verdict.
35. See "Bradley Manning Hearing: Attorney Asks For Dismissal In WikiLeaks Case." *Huffington Post*, March 16, 2012. Available at http://www.huffingtonpost.com/2012/03/15/bradley-manning-trial-attorney-dismiss-case_n_1349309.html.
36. References to Benkler's views in the remaining sections of this chapter are from the transcript of his interview with June Wu in *Harvard Law Today* (Wu 2011).

REFERENCES

Aldhous, Peter, and Michael Reilly. 2009. "Special Investigation: How my Genome was Hacked."*New Scientist*. Available at http://www.newscientist.com/article/mg20127013.800-special-investigation-how-my-genome-was-hacked.html.

Benkler, Yochai. 2011. "A Free Irresponsible Press: Wikileaks and the Battle over the Soul of the Networked Fourth Estate." *Harvard Civil Rights – Civil Liberties Journal* 46, 311–97.

Bocij, Paul. 2004. *Cyberstalking: Harassment in the Internet Age and How to Protect Your Family*. Westport CT: Praeger.

Brey, Philip. 2004. "Ethical Aspects of Facial Recognition Systems in Public Places." In R. A. Spinello and H. T. Tavani, eds. *Readings in CyberEthics*. 2nd ed. Sudbury MA: Jones and Bartlett, pp. 585–600.

Feder, Barnaby J. 2008. "A Heart Device Is Found Vulnerable to Hacker Attacks."*New York Times*, March 12. Available at http://www.nytimes.com/2008/03/12/business/12heart-web.html?_r=1.

Floridi, Luciano. 2013. "The Ethical Evaluation of WikiLeaks." In L. Hinman, ed. *Contemporary Moral Issues: Diversity and Consensus*. Upper Saddle River, NJ: Pearson, pp. 475–477.

Forester, Tom, and Perry Morrison. 1994. *Computer Ethics: Cautionary Tales and Ethical Dilemmas in Computing*. 2nd ed. Cambridge MA: MIT Press.

Girasa, Roy J. 2002. *Cyberlaw: National and International Perspectives*. Upper Saddle River, NJ: Prentice Hall.

Gotterbarn, Don. 1995. "Computer Ethics: Responsibility Regained." In D. G. Johnson and H. Nissenbaum, eds. *Computers, Ethics, and Social Values*. Englewood Cliffs, NJ: Prentice Hall, pp. 18–24.

Grodzinsky, Frances S., and Herman T. Tavani. 2001. "Is Cyberstalking a Special Type of Computer Crime?" In T. W. Bynum, et al., eds. *Proceedings of the Fifth International Conference on the Social and Ethical Impacts of Information and Communications Technologies: Ethicomp 2001*. Vol. 2. Gdansk, Poland: Mikom Publishers, pp. 73–85.

Himanen, Pekka. 2001. *The Hacker Ethic: A Radical Approach to the Philosophy of Business*. New York: Random House.

Himma, Kenneth. 2004. "Targeting the Innocent: Active Defense and the Moral Immunity of Innocent Persons from Aggression." *Journal of Information, Communication, and Ethics in Society* 2, no. 1: 31–40.

Himma, Kenneth Einar. 2008. "Ethical Issues Involving Computer Security: Hacking, Hacktivism, and Counterhacking." In K. E. Himma and H. T. Tavani, eds. *The Handbook of Information and Computer Ethics*. Hoboken, NJ: John Wiley & Sons, pp. 191–217.

Jordan, Tim. 2008. *Hacking. Digital Media, and Technological Determinism*. Malden, MA: Polity.

Kiss, Jemima. 2009. "The Pirate Bay Trial: Guilty Verdict." *The Guardian*, April 17. Available at http://www.guardian.co.uk/technology/2009/apr/17/the-pirate-bay-trial-guilty-verdict.

Kowalski, Robin M., Susan P. Limber, and Patricia W. Agatston. 2008. *Cyber Bullying*. Malden, MA: Blackwell.

Leman-Langlois, Stephane, ed. 2008. *Technocrime: Technology, Crime, and Social Control*. Portland, OR: Willan Publishing.

Lininger, Rachael, and Russell Dean Vines. 2005. *Phishing: Cutting the Identity Theft Line*. Indianapolis, IN: John Wiley and Sons.

Martinez, Michael. 2009. "To Catch a Predator: An Ethical Analysis of Sting Journalism." Available at http://michaeltmartinez.org/documents/predator.pdf.

McCoy, Terrence. 2014. "DEA Created a Fake Facebook Profile in this Woman's Name using Seized Pics – then Impersonated Her." *The Washington Post*, October 7. Available at: http://www.washingtonpost.com/news/morning-mix/wp/2014/10/07/dea-created-a-fake-facebook-profile-in-this-womans-name-using-seized-pics-then-impersonated-her/.

Moor, James H. 2007. "What Is Computer Ethics?" In J. Weckert, ed. *Computer Ethics*. Aldershot, UK: Ashgate, pp. 31–40. Reprinted from *Metaphilosophy* 16, no. 4 (1985): 266–75.

Moore, Robert. 2011. *Cybercrime: Investigating High-Technology Cybercrime*. 2nd ed. Burlington, MA: Anderson Publishing.

Parker, Donn B. 1998. *Fighting Computer Crime: A Framework for Protecting Information*. New York: John Wiley and Sons.

Power, Richard. 2000. *Tangled Web: Tales of Digital Crime from the Shadows of Cyberspace*. Indianapolis, IN: Que Corp.

Ragan, Steve. 2009. "Facebook Accounts Hacked for $100." *The Tech Herald*. Sep. 18. Available at http://www.thetechherald.com/article.php/200938/4468/Facebook-accounts-hacked-for-100.

Sagiroglu, Seref, and Gurol Canbek. 2009. "Keyloggers: Increasing Threats to Computer Security and Privacy." *IEEE Technology and Society Magazine* 28, no. 3: 11–17.

Simon, Ellen. 2005. "Identities Get Harder to Keep." *The Nashua Telegraph*, May 24, pp. 14–15.

Simpson, Michael. 2006. *Hands-On Ethical Hacking and Network Defense*. Boston, MA: Thompson.

Sinnott-Armstrong, Walter. 1999. "Entrapment in the Net?" *Ethics and Information Technology* 1, no. 2: 95–104.

Solove, Daniel J. 2011. *Nothing to Hide: The False Tradeoff between Privacy and Security*. New Haven, CT: Yale University Press.

Strickwerda, Litska. 2013. "Should Virtual Cybercrime Be Brought Under the Scope of Criminal Law?" In M. Bottis, ed. *Honorary Volume for Evi Laskari*. Athens, Greece: Nomiki Bibliothiki, pp. 495–545.

Tavani, Herman T. 2000. "Defining the Boundaries of Computer Crime: Piracy, Trespass, and Vandalism in Cyberspace." *Computers and Society* 30, no. 3: 3-9. A revised version of this article is reprinted in R. A. Spinello and H. T. Tavani, eds. (2004). *Readings in CyberEthics*. 2nd ed. Sudbury, MA: Jones and Bartlett, pp. 513–24.

van der Ploeg, Irma. 1999. "The Illegal Body: Eurodac and the Politics of Biometric Identification." *Ethics and Information Technology* 1, no. 2, 295–302.

van der Ploeg, Irma. 2004. "Written on the Body: Biometrics and Identity." In R. A. Spinello and H. T. Tavani, eds. *Readings in CyberEthics*. 2nd ed. Sudbury MA: Jones and Bartlett, pp. 571–84.

Wall, David S. 2007. *Cybercrime: The Transformation of Crime in the Information Age*. Malden MA: Polity.

Wieneke, David. 2010. "Is WikiLeaks Ethical, Criminal, or an Immune Nuisance?" *Useful Arts*. Dec 3. Available at http://usefularts.us/2010/12/03/is-wikileaks-ethical-criminal-or-an-immune-nuisance/.

Wu, June. 2011. Interview (with Yochai Benkler): "Benchler Argues Against the Prosecution of WikiLeaks." *Harvard Law Today*. Available at http://www.law.harvard.edu/news/2011/03/14_benkler-argues-against-prosecution-of-wikileaks.html.

▶ FURTHER READINGS

Brin, David. 2008. "Crime and Lawfulness in an Age of All-Seeing Techno-Humanity." In S. Leman-Langlois, ed. *Technocrime: Technology, Crime, and Social Control*. Portland, OR: Willan Publishing, pp. 14–26.

Easttom, Chuck, and Jeffrey Taylor, eds. 2011. *Computer Crime, Investigation, and the Law*. Boston, MA: Course Technology/Cengage.

Fairweather, N. Ben, and S. Rogerson. 2004. "Biometric Identification." *Journal of Information, Communication and Ethics in Society* 2, no. 1: 3–8.

Gagnon, Benoit. 2008. "Cyberwars and Cybercrimes." In S. Leman-Langlois, ed. *Technocrime: Technology, Crime, and Social Control*. Portland, OR: Willan Publishing, pp. 46–65.

Singel, Ryan. 2008. "National ID: Biometrics Pinned to Social Security Cards." In P. De Palma, ed. *Computers in Society 08/09*. New York: McGraw Hill, pp. 48–49.

Schneir, Bruce. 2012. *Liars and Outliers: Enabling the Trust that Society Needs to Thrive*. Hoboken, NJ: John Wiley and Sons.

Willard, Nancy. 2006. *Cyber Bullying and Cyberthreats: Responding to the Challenge of Online Social Threats*. Eugene, OR: Center for Safe and Responsible Internet Use.

CHAPTER

8

Intellectual Property Disputes in Cyberspace

LEARNING OBJECTIVES

Upon completing this chapter, you will successfully be able to:

- Define what is meant by *intellectual property* (IP) and explain the relevant ways in which IP is both similar to and different from tangible property,
- Explain what copyright laws entail and describe the evolution of copyright law as it applies to digital media,
- Explain the key features that differentiate three distinct forms of protection for IP: patents, trademarks, and trade secrets,
- Understand the challenges that jurisdictional issues pose for enforcing IP laws at the international level,
- Describe the philosophical foundations for three kinds of theories used to justify IP rights,
- Articulate the key differences between the Free Software Foundation and Open Source Initiative,
- Explain what is meant by the "common good" approach to IP and describe how it offers an alternative framework for analyzing the current IP debate,
- Assess key issues underlying three controversial IP-related legislative proposals: Protect Intellectual Property Act (PIPA), Stop Online Piracy Act (SOPA), and Research Works Act (RWA).

Perhaps no single issue in the digital era has been more contentious than intellectual property rights affecting cybertechnology. The following scenario briefly illustrates how contentious, as well as how confusing, that issue has become in the context of digital music.

▶ **SCENARIO 8–1:** Streaming Music Online

Online music streaming services have become popular with many Internet users. Spotify, one of the fastest growing streaming services, has (as of January 2015) approximately 60 million users with 15 million paid subscribers or "premium members." While many recording artists have entered into contractual agreements with one or more streaming services, some well-known artists (including Beyoncé) have not. In November 2014, Taylor Swift publicly announced that she would not allow her newly released album *1989* to be streamed on Spotify and that she also planned to remove all of her earlier music from that online service. Swift's announcement generated considerable debate about current policies affecting online music streaming services in general and Spotify in particular. At the heart of the controversy is the question of whether the royalty structure used by Spotify and similar streaming services is fair to recording artists.

Swift defended her decision to break with Spotify by claiming that "music should not be free." She argued that "music is art, and art is important and rare," and since "important, rare things are valuable," those things "should be paid for."[1] However, some critics have responded by pointing out that (i) the music on streaming services is not completely free and (ii) recording artists receive payment for their streamed music in the form of royalties which are typically based on the number of times their music is streamed. But some recording artists, including Swift, have complained that the income they receive from Spotify and similar services pales in comparison to the amount of money they collect when their music is purchased either as an MP3 download, from a service like iTunes or Amazon, or as a CD. In response to these complaints, Spotify pointed out that its streaming service has paid out approximately 70% of its total revenue (estimated to reach $1 billion by early 2015) to rights holders, which is income that these recording artists and record labels otherwise would not enjoy.[2] ■

Arguably, intellectual-property-rights battles involving digital music have evolved considerably since the media coverage of the original Napster controversy in the late 1990s. Many illicit music-sharing Web sites have since been shut down, due in large part to the aggressive stance taken by the Recording Industry Association of America (RIAA). As a result, it has become less easy for users to "pirate," or illegally download, copyrighted music. Online music stores have also made it possible for users to purchase (i.e., legally download) individual songs without having to purchase an entire CD—a requirement that had annoyed many music fans in the days of pre-MP3-formatted music. Overall, stricter enforcement of copyright laws has also seemed to favor musicians and their recording labels; so, arguably, consumer trends with respect to purchasing habits in the music industry have tilted in favor of the interests of the RIAA.

As Scenario 8–1 also illustrates, however, online streaming services have recently opened up a new challenge for the music industry. While some recording artists claim that their income from music sales has diminished significantly because of streaming, Spotify has responded by arguing that its service provides users with an alternative to piracy. The claims made on both sides of this debate are controversial and they need to be examined in more detail. We do this in Section 8.2.4, where we examine a wide range of issues affecting copyright laws in the context of digital music. The purpose of Scenario 8–1 was simply to get us to begin thinking about some of the controversies surrounding copyright-and-access issues with respect to one form of digital intellectual property (IP).

In this chapter, we will see that disputes about IP rights involving cybertechnology range from claims pertaining to ownership of software programs to arguments about who has the right to distribute (or even make available for use) other forms of proprietary information on the Internet, including movies and books. We will also see that decisions affecting who should have ownership rights to, and thus control over, digitized information will ultimately determine who can and cannot access that form of information. Before examining specific issues, however, we first need to understand the concept of IP.[3]

▶ 8.1 WHAT IS INTELLECTUAL PROPERTY?

An adequate analysis of *intellectual property* issues requires that we first have an understanding of the concept of property in general. Like privacy, property is a complex notion that is not easy to define. Yet, as legal scholars and philosophers have pointed out, property laws and norms play a fundamental role in shaping a society and in preserving its legal order; that is, laws and norms involving property rights establish relationships between individuals, different sorts of things or objects, and the state. When discussing issues involving property, we tend to think of tangible items. Originally, property referred to land; however, it now also includes various kinds of objects that an individual can own, such as an automobile, a wardrobe of clothing, or a DVD collection.

However, many legal theorists and philosophers suggest that property should not be understood simply in terms of objects or things that can be owned but rather as a *relationship between individuals in reference to things*.[4] Hence, in this relational view of property, three elements need to be considered: (i) some individual (*X*), (ii) some thing or object (*Y*), and (iii) *X*'s relation to other individuals (*A*, *B*, *C*, etc.) in reference to *Y*. In this sense, *X* (as the owner of property *Y*) can control *Y* relative to persons *A*, *B*, *C*, etc. So if Tom owns a Dell laptop computer, then he can control who has access to his computer and how it is used; for example, Tom has the right to exclude Mary from using the laptop computer, or, as its owner, he can grant her unlimited access to it. Ownership claims involving "intellectual objects" are similar in certain respects but are also less straightforward, in other respects, to claims involving the ownership of tangible objects.

8.1.1 Intellectual Objects

Some philosophers use the expression *intellectual objects* when referring to forms of IP.[5] Unlike physical property, IP consists of objects that are not tangible. These nontangible, or intellectual, objects represent literary/creative works and inventions, which are the manifestations or expressions of ideas. Unlike tangible objects, which are exclusionary in nature, intellectual objects (e.g., software programs) are *nonexclusionary*: Consider once again Tom's laptop computer, which is a physical object. If Tom is its sole owner, then Mary cannot own it, and vice versa. Tom's laptop is an example of an exclusionary object. Next, consider a word processing program that resides in Tom's computer. If Tom makes a copy of that program for Mary, then both Mary and Tom have copies of it. Thus, the word processing program is nonexclusionary.

Note that scarcity (which often causes competition and rivalry when applied to physical objects) need not exist in the case of intellectual objects, which can be easily reproduced. Note also that there are practical limitations to the number of physical objects one can own, and there are natural and political limitations to the amount of land that can be owned; however, countless digital copies of a software program can be produced and each at a relatively low cost.

Another feature that distinguishes intellectual objects from physical objects has to do with exactly what it is that one can lay legal claim to. One cannot own an idea in the same sense that one can own a physical object; ideas themselves are not the kinds of things for which governments are willing to grant ownership rights to individuals. As Moore (2008) points out, ownership rights do not apply to an intellectual object as an "abstract physical entity" but rather to "physical manifestations or expressions" of that object. In other words, legal protection is given only to the tangible *expression* of an idea that is creative or original. And as Moore and Himma (2014) note, IP laws grant the owner of the creative work the right to control and to produce physical manifestations of that work.

For a literary or artistic idea to be protected, it must be expressed (or "fixed") in some tangible medium such as a physical book or a sheet of paper containing a musical score. If the idea is functional in nature, such as an invention, it must be expressed as a machine or a process. Whereas authors are granted copyright protections for expressions of their literary ideas, inventors are given an incentive, in the form of a patent protection, for expressions of their functional ideas. Copyright law and patent law, along with other legal schemes for protecting IP, are discussed in detail in Sections 8.2 and 8.3.

8.1.2 Why Protect Intellectual Objects?

What is our basis for saying that IP, or for that matter any kind of property, ought to be protected? One answer lies in our current system of laws. Of course, we could then further ask: On what philosophical grounds are our laws themselves based? In Section 8.5, we will see that in

Anglo-American law, the philosophical justification for granting property rights for intellectual objects is generally grounded in either (one or both) of two very different kinds of theories about property. One theory is based on the rationale that a property right is a type of "natural right" that one has to the ownership of an intellectual object because of the *labor* he or she has expended in producing a creative work or a practical invention. The other theory is based on the notion that property rights themselves are not natural rights but rather social constructs designed to encourage creators and inventors to better serve society in general by bringing forth their creative works and practical inventions into the marketplace. To encourage authors and inventors, *utilitarians* believe that it is necessary to grant them property rights in the form of limited monopolies that can result in financial advantages for them.

In many continental European countries, neither individual labor nor social utility is used as a justification for granting IP rights and corresponding protections. Instead, creative works and inventions are viewed as expressions of the *personalities* of their creators and inventors, who should, it is argued, have the right to determine how their works are displayed and distributed. This view is sometimes referred to as the personality theory of IP. In Section 8.5, where we examine the labor, utilitarian, and personality theories of property in detail, we will also see that some critics reject the notion that IP property rights should be extended to computer software.

Philosophers and legal theorists point out that the introduction of computer software has created questions regarding IP laws for which there are no easy answers. Innovations in computer hardware, on the contrary, have clearly qualified for patent protection, and in this sense, computer hardware inventions are no different than other kinds of inventions involving physical objects. But questions about whether and how software, as a kind of intellectual object, should be protected have been vehemently debated in the courts.

8.1.3 Software as Intellectual Property

Is computer software a special kind of intellectual object that deserves both copyright and patent protection? Software, which consists of lines of programming code (or codified thought), is not exactly expressed, or "fixed," in a tangible medium as literary works are. To complicate matters, a program's code takes many forms: source code, object code, and the final executable code. Because of conceptual muddles and confusions surrounding the nature of programming code, computer programs were not, initially, eligible for either copyright or patent protection. Eventually, however, they were granted both forms of legal protection. Although software programs seem to be like inventions that could be patented, they also resemble algorithms, which, like mathematical ideas or "mental steps," are not typically eligible for patent protection.

Initially, software was not conceived of as a distinct commodity, since computer corporations tended to bundle together their software and hardware offerings as part of a single package. But Grodzinsky, Miller, and Wolf (2004) note that in the late 1960s, IBM adopted a new marketing policy that separated software (and services) from hardware, which also suggested the need for "closed-source software" so that its programming division could be profitable. Grodzinsky et al. also note that the practice of separating these components became further entrenched when IBM contracted with Intel and Microsoft to develop the personal computer in 1981. However, in the early 1970s, AT&T Bell Laboratories in New Jersey decided to make the source code for one of its software products "open" or freely accessible. AT&T gave away the source code and licenses for its Unix operating system to universities.[6] So two very different strategies emerged in the 1970s with respect to whether software code should be protected as proprietary information.

As late as the 1970s and early 1980s, software programs and software code were often freely exchanged among computer enthusiasts without concern for copyright law. I worked in the software industry in the early 1980s, and I recall incidents where software developers freely exchanged with each other copies of programs on which they were working: A software developer might lend a fellow developer a copy of a database program in return for a copy of a word processing program. (As we will see in our discussion of the Free Software Movement and the Open Source Initiative in Section 8.6, some programmers believe that these kinds of exchanges actually improved the quality of the software products that eventually went to market.) By the mid-1980s, the cavalier attitude that once surrounded the exchange of software programs had changed considerably, and by the 1990s, software companies carefully guarded their proprietary software, sometimes to the point of encouraging law enforcement officials to raid private homes where they suspected that unauthorized software was being used.

Some people believe that a distinction should be drawn between an individual's unauthorized copying of a friend's software program for personal use and the pirating of software in a systematic way for profit by corporations and criminals. The economic impact of systematic software piracy by organizations is far more significant than the impact of a few individuals copying their friends' programs. From a moral point of view, however, if unauthorized copying of proprietary software is wrong, then it is just as wrong for individuals as it is for organizations interested in profiting from it.

8.1.4 Evaluating a Popular Argument Used by the Software Industry to Show Why It Is Morally Wrong to Copy Proprietary Software

Why, exactly, is the unauthorized copying of proprietary software morally wrong? Many in the software industry have made the following kind of argument:

PREMISE 1. Stealing a tangible object is morally wrong.

PREMISE 2. Making an unauthorized copy of a proprietary software program is identical to stealing a tangible object.

CONCLUSION. Making an unauthorized copy of a proprietary software program is morally wrong.

If we apply the rules for logical validity that we examined in Chapter 3, we see that this argument is valid because of its logical form—in other words, if Premises 1 and 2 are both assumed to be true, the conclusion cannot be false. Even though the argument's form is valid, however, we could still show the argument to be unsound if either or both of the premises are false. (You may want to review the rules for valid and sound arguments in Chapter 3.)

Premise 1 is fairly straightforward, and few would question its truth. But Premise 2 is more controversial and thus we can question whether it is empirically true. For example, is duplicating a software program *identical* to stealing a physical item? We noted that intellectual objects, such as software programs, are nonexclusionary, which means that my having a copy of Program X does not exclude you from also having a copy of that program, and vice versa. The computer hardware on which that software program runs—for example, my laptop computer—is exclusionary in the sense that if I own it, you do not, and vice versa. So, the act of your making an unauthorized copy of the proprietary software program that resides on my laptop computer is *not* identical to your stealing my (physical) computer, in at least one important sense. Because the truth of Premise 2 is questionable, we cannot infer that the above argument (in its present form) is sound.

Even if the original argument turns out to be unsound, however, it does not follow that its conclusion is false. Note that the conclusion—"making unauthorized copies of a proprietary software program is morally wrong"—could be true for reasons other than those stated in the original argument's premises. In fact, there could be several reasons why the conclusion can be true, despite the fact that the second premise may be false. For example, even if duplicating software is not identical to stealing physical property, we can show that it may cause harm. Consider that copying the proprietary software program, like the theft of someone's physical property, deprives the property owner of the legitimate use of his or her property. If someone steals my laptop, he or she deprives me of my right to use a device that I own; similarly, when someone makes an unauthorized copy of a proprietary program that I own (as the copyright holder), he or she deprives me of income to which I am entitled. Spinello (2008) argues that unauthorized copying is harmful because it is a misuse, misappropriation, or "unfair taking" of another person's property against the property owner's will.

But some still might object by claiming that while an individual programmer, who is self-employed, may be harmed by the unauthorized copying of his program, most proprietary software programs are owned by wealthy corporations; for instance, they might argue that Microsoft is so well-off that it will not suffer if it loses the revenue from a few sales of its Word program. However, you can probably see the danger that might result if everyone used this line of reasoning. (Recall our discussion of the Slippery Slope Fallacy in Chapter 3.) Thus, the unauthorized copying of software can be shown to be morally wrong, independent of whether it has a negative financial impact for the company that has ownership rights to the program.

Many nations have enacted specific laws and statutes to protect the rights and interests of the "owners" of computer software programs and applications (as forms of IP). We examine four different types of schemes for protecting IP rights: copyright law, patents, trademarks, and trade secrets. We begin, however, with a detailed analysis of copyright law.

▶ 8.2 COPYRIGHT LAW AND DIGITAL MEDIA

Arguably, elements of contemporary IP frameworks in general, and copyright law in particular, can be traced back to ancient Greece and the Roman era (Moore and Himma 2014). However, legal scholars and philosophers in the Anglo-American sphere now tend to focus more specifically on historical developments in copyright law that arose in response to the widespread publishing of pamphlets made possible by the printing press. Two elements undergird this phenomenon. On the one hand, the British monarchy wanted to control the spread of "subversive" and "heretical" works that were being printed. On the other hand, authors had a vested interest in protecting their works from unauthorized reproduction. The Statute of Anne, enacted in England in 1710, was the first law to give protection to authors for works attributed to them. The American colonies followed British law regarding copyright; the Framers later included these ideas in Article 1, Section 8, of the U.S. Constitution:

> The congress shall have the power . . . to promote the Progress of Science and the useful Arts, by securing for limited Times to authors and inventors the exclusive Rights to their respective Writings and Discoveries.

8.2.1 The Evolution of Copyright Law in the United States

The first copyright law in the United States, enacted in 1790, applied primarily to books, maps, and charts. As newer forms of media were developed, it was extended to include photography, movies, and audio recordings. In 1909, the copyright law was amended to include any form that could be seen and read visually by humans; this modification was motivated by a new technology (viz., the player piano) in which a song could be copied onto a perforated roll. Since the musical copy could not be read from the piano roll visually (by humans), the copy was not considered a violation of the song's copyright. The "machine readable" vs. "human readable" distinction has implications for decisions as to whether software programs qualify for copyright protection: Although a program's source code can be read by humans, its executable code, which runs on a computer, cannot. Beginning in the 1960s, however, the computer industry argued that software programs, or at least parts of those programs, should be eligible for copyright protection.

The Copyright Act was amended in 1980 to address the status of software programs, and the concept of a literary work was extended to include programs, computers, and "databases that exhibit authorship." The amendment defined a computer program as "a set of statements or instructions to be used directly in a computer in order to bring about certain results." To obtain copyright protection for a computer program, however, its author had to show that the program contained an original expression (or arrangement) of ideas and not simply the ideas themselves.[7]

In 1998, two important amendments were made to the Copyright Act: the Sonny Bono Copyright Term Extension Act (SBCTEA) and the Digital Millennium Copyright Act (DMCA). The SBCTEA extended the length of copyright protection from the life of the author plus 50 years to the life of the author plus 70 years. Protection for works of hire produced before 1978 were extended from 75 to 95 years. (When an author receives payment from someone—e.g., an individual, corporation, or organization—to produce a creative or artistic work, it can be considered a work of hire.) Critics of the SBCTEA noted that the law was passed just in time to keep Mickey Mouse from entering the public domain, and they also pointed out that the Disney Corporation lobbied very hard for the passage of this act.

The DMCA has also been severely criticized—not because it extends the amount of time that a copyrighted work is protected but because of the manner in which copyrights are extended. For example, Henderson, Spinello, and Lipinski (2007) point out that DMCA's critics identify three areas of controversy that need to be addressed: its "chilling effect" on *fair use* (defined in Section 8.2.2), its suppression of *innovation*, and its *overreach*. (We examine each of these points in later sections of this chapter.) Many critics also believe that these controversies are, in turn, closely linked to DMCA's highly controversial anticircumvention clause, which prohibits the development of any software or hardware technology that *circumvents* (or devises a technological work-around) to copyrighted digital media.

DMCA laws have also been passed at the individual state level in the U.S. These laws, sometimes called "Super-DMCA" or "S-DMCA," have been very controversial because some are interpreted as exceeding the conditions specified in the federal DMCA. Critics, including the Electronic Frontier Foundation (EFF), argue that the Motion Picture Association of America (MPAA) has been pressing states to pass S-DMCA-type legislation that is aimed at criminalizing the possession of what the MPAA calls "unlawful communication and access devices." EFF also argues that this legislation would constitute "an unprecedented attack on the rights of technologists, hobbyists, tinkerers and the public at large."[8]

8.2.2 The Fair-Use and First-Sale Provisions of Copyright Law

Two important provisions have been developed to balance the exclusive controls given to copyright holders against the broader interests of society: *fair use* and *first sale*. The fair-use principle enables authors and publishers to make limited use of another person's copyrighted work for the following purposes: comment, criticism, news, reporting, research, scholarship, and teaching. This principle is important to the computer industry in particular and to engineering in general because it also supports the practice of "reverse engineering," which allows someone to buy a product for the purpose of taking it apart to see how it works.

Another important scheme for balancing the otherwise exclusive controls of copyright law is the first-sale provision, which applies once the original work has been sold for the first time. At this point, the original copyright holder loses his or her rights to the previously protected work. For example, once you purchase a copy of a (physical) book, you are free to give away, resell, or even destroy your copy. However, we will see why it is not clear that one can easily give away media in digital format that is licensed for use but not, strictly speaking, owned by a user.

Critics believe that the fair-use provision of copyright law has been significantly threatened by both SBCTEA and DMCA. Some believe that SBCTEA threatens fair use because it has delayed many proprietary works from entering the public domain and thus being freely available for general use. Critics argue that the DMCA has also had serious implications for the fair-use principle, mainly because its anticircumvention clause makes it illegal to reverse engineer a competitor's (digital) product. Innovators and competitors have depended on the use of reverse engineering, which has traditionally been protected by the Copyright Act's fair-use principle.

The DMCA also has implications for the first-sale provision because works formatted in digital media are often licensed by a user rather than purchased and owned by a consumer. For example, contrast an e-book with a physical (i.e., "paper and glue") book, where one can do whatever one wishes after purchasing it. Consider that after purchasing a physical book, one can resell that book, in compliance with the first-sale provision of copyright law. One can also give the book to a friend, or one can even destroy the copy of the book if so inclined. The same is not true, however, of e-books, because the digitized information contained in those books cannot be subsequently exchanged without permission of the copyright holder. Note, for example, that if you own a Kindle (or some competitor to this e-book reader) and you purchase an e-book, you have the legal right to read that book on your device but not necessarily to share the book with a friend in the same way that you could a physical book.

8.2.3 Software Piracy as Copyright Infringement

With the proliferation of personal computers in the 1980s, many users discovered how easy it was to duplicate software; but as we saw in Chapter 1, there was some legitimate confusion during that period as to whether it was legal to make a copy of someone else's software program. So, a "policy vacuum" (to use James Moor's terminology) existed with respect to copying proprietary software for personal use. This "vacuum" arose, in large part, because of certain confusions or (what Moor calls) "conceptual muddles" in our understanding of software.[9] Earlier in this chapter, we noted that in the 1970s and early 1980s, software developers sometimes shared and exchanged programs with one another, and that by the late 1980s, many software companies had become extremely zealous when it came to protecting their proprietary software.

Software manufacturers, who claim to have lost millions of dollars of potential revenue because of software piracy, seem justified in their concerns regarding the pirating of proprietary software by individuals and organizations, both nationally and globally. However, some critics have argued that claims made by American software manufacturers about their loss of revenue due to the use of pirated software in developing countries are either greatly exaggerated or altogether bogus. They point out that many people and organizations in those countries could not afford to pay the prices set by American software companies for their products; so, the companies have not necessarily lost any (real) revenues, because their (expensive, by international standards) software would not have sold on the open market in most developing countries.

Software companies also worry about revenues lost in developed nations, including the United States, due to the illegal copying of software. Corporations such as Microsoft have been far more concerned with piracy as a form of organized crime, both domestically and internationally, than they have been about individuals making occasional unauthorized copies of their proprietary software. From a financial point of view, it would seem to make perfectly good sense for Microsoft to allow some illicit copying of its software by individuals rather than spend money to pursue their arrest and prosecution. However, many corporations have been quite willing to pursue those who engage in software piracy for commercial gain. And corporations have been especially concerned about the ways that their proprietary information can be pirated over a computer network. As we saw in Chapter 7, cyberpiracy applies to more than the mere unauthorized copying of software; it also covers the unauthorized distribution (or facilitation of the distribution) of digital information on a computer network. The software industry confronted this phenomenon for the first time in 1994 in an incident involving Robert LaMacchia, then a student at MIT.

LaMacchia operated an online forum at MIT called *Cynosure*, which resided on an anonymous server in Finland. He invited users to upload and download (for free) copyrighted software to and from Cynosure. LaMacchia was arrested on charges that he had pirated software, but since he did not make unauthorized copies of the proprietary software, and since he did not receive a fee for his services, law enforcement authorities had a difficult time bringing piracy charges against him. In fact, they had a difficult time finding any clear criminal grounds for prosecuting LaMacchia at that time. For example, there were no explicit provisions in the 1986 Computer Fraud and Abuse Act (see Chapter 7) under which he could be prosecuted. Eventually, federal authorities decided to bring charges against him by appealing to the Wire Fraud Act, a federal statute. Charges against LaMacchia were eventually dropped, however, and the indictment was officially struck down by a district judge who ruled that any criminal copyright charge must be brought under copyright laws and not under general federal criminal laws.[10]

The software industry followed the case closely and, not surprisingly, was disappointed with the outcome. It had hoped that a conviction in the LaMacchia case would set a clear precedent. In the aftermath of this incident, however, the 1986 Computer Fraud and Abuse Act was amended to broaden the scope of criminal behavior that could be prosecuted under it, and the No Electronic Theft (NET) Act was passed in 1997, criminalizing the "dissemination" of copyrighted information by electronic means. While many agree with the spirit of the NET Act, some also believe that it went too far. Prior to the NET Act, a person had to "infringe a copyright willfully" and for "purposes of commercial or financial gain" in order to be punished under the criminal provisions of the Copyright Act. The NET Act, however, has made criminal the reproduction or distribution, including by electronic means, of one or more copyrighted works, which have a total retail value of more than $1,000.[11]

Grosso (2000) has argued that the meaning of copyright infringement was "expanded" under the Net Act. He points out that a copyright infringement can now occur either in fixation (in print or paper) or in virtual space, that is, by means of a mere electronic distribution, regardless of whether the copyrighted work is ever printed on paper or downloaded on to a disk, etc. According to the NET Act, merely viewing a copyrighted work posted on the Internet can be interpreted as a criminal violation of copyright. One possible interpretation is that "fixation" occurs in online viewing, because a temporary copy is "fixed" in the memory (i.e., in RAM) of the host computer, no matter how briefly the information is stored there.

8.2.4 Napster and the Ongoing Battles over Sharing Digital Music

Many of the controversial issues underlying the LaMacchia incident foreshadowed those in the highly publicized Napster case. Although Napster did not traffic in proprietary software, it did facilitate the distribution of another kind of proprietary digital information: music in the form of MP3 files. Through its online service, Napster's users exchanged copyrighted music files with one another. In December 1999, the RIAA sued the Napster Web site for illegally distributing copyrighted music on the Internet. Napster responded by arguing that its activities were perfectly legal under the fair-use provision of copyright law. However, the courts ultimately ruled against Napster.[12] Although the original Napster site ceased operations, it later reopened as a pay-per-song Web site, similar to iTunes, in cooperation with the RIAA.

The Napster controversy was just the beginning of an ongoing battle involving the recording industry and file-sharing sites over the unauthorized exchange of proprietary music online. Internet music providers such as Morpheus, KaZaA, and LimeWire have also supported the online exchange of MP3 files containing copyrighted music. Initially, they were able to avoid the plight of Napster, which used a centralized distribution point consisting of a centralized server, index, and registry of names in the file-exchange process. The later file-sharing services used either decentralized or "supernode" systems, based on peer-to-peer (P2P) technologies developed by Gnutella. As P2P file-sharing sites have evolved, they have become increasingly decentralized.

Spinello (2008) notes that the methods for indexing the files that are exchanged in P2P systems comprise three categories: a centralized indexing system (such as in the original Napster site), a decentralized indexing system, and a supernode system (where a group of computers can act as indexing servers). Another P2P protocol is Bit Torrent, which enables large files, such as entire music CDs, to be exchanged more efficiently through a system of networked computers designated as "peers" and "seeds." Whereas KaZaA used the supernode system, the Pirate Bay service used the Bit Torrent protocol. (We briefly examined the outcome of the trial involving the Pirate Bay site in Chapter 7.)

The recording industry, in its effort to crack down on illicit file sharing, has not been deterred by the fact that later P2P systems were able to avoid the legal pitfalls surrounding the centralized indexing method used by Napster. Alternatively, the RIAA employed some new strategies and techniques in the ongoing battle with file-sharing sites. For example, it began to track down individuals that it suspected of exchanging proprietary music online. In 2003, the RIAA issued court subpoenas to Internet service providers (ISPs) such as Comcast and Verizon, as well as to major universities, for the names of users who it suspected of downloading and exchanging large volumes of copyrighted music via those online services. While many ISPs and universities complied with the recording industry's request, Verizon challenged the RIAA in court on the grounds that complying with such requests violated the privacy rights of their subscribers (*Verizon v. RIAA*, 2003). Since that time, most universities have developed strict policies that prohibit the use of their networks to exchange copyrighted music; some have even disabled their P2P file-sharing systems altogether.[13]

The recording industry has also taken other tacks in its efforts to deter the unauthorized sharing of copyrighted music files online. For example, one way it fought back was by uploading "corrupted" music files onto the popular P2P sites, so that users downloading these files would be discouraged from using those sites again. And in what could be viewed as an even more aggressive attempt to prevent students from freely downloading copyrighted music on university campuses, the RIAA tried to influence legislation in 2007 that would tie the unauthorized downloading of files by college students to a loss of financial aid.[14]

Music Streaming Services

The ongoing controversies involving digital music have recently expanded to include the current dispute between some prominent recording artists and online services that *stream* copyrighted music to users. (Recall our brief description of this controversy in Scenario 8–1, which you may wish to revisit at this point.) Some critics of streaming services believe that these online services both (i) contribute to piracy and (ii) are responsible for the decline of CD sales. One very popular streaming service—Spotify—has rejected both claims. With respect to (i), Spotify has argued that its service provides members with an alternative to piracy (while, at the same time, providing revenue to recording artists that they otherwise would not receive). Regarding (ii), Spotify points out that its members reported (in a survey conducted by Spotify) that they had paid either very little or nothing for music before joining that streaming service.

So, Spotify claims that if the sale of CDs had fallen, it is not because of its service; thus, it cannot be held responsible for any decline in sales.[15]

Is Spotify's argument in this dispute plausible? In its defense, the streaming service cites some 2014 statistics showing that the average American spends approximately $17 per year on music. So, Spotify believes that its service has not significantly affected the overall amount of money that its average listener would otherwise spend on music. Spotify also points out that it offers a two-tier level of membership: a premium level for users willing to pay $9.99 per month and one that is completely free for users who are willing to listen to advertisements (both of which generate the income used to pay royalties to recording artists). As we saw in Scenario 8–1, Spotify claims that it has paid approximately 70% of its revenue (estimated to reach $1 billion by early 2015) to rights holders. However, Doctorow (2014) points out that it is the record labels, not the recording artists, who have benefited from the royalties paid by streaming services, the bulk of which "stay in the pockets of the labels."[16]

Perhaps a more important point that Spotify could use in its defense, at least from a legal perspective, is that the streaming service has explicit contractual agreements with the recording artists and record labels featured on its service. In this sense, Spotify and similar streaming services (like Pandora) are very different from the various P2P music-sharing sites in the past, which enabled users to download unauthorized copies of proprietary recordings in violation of copyright law.

While many recording artists have agreed to Spotify's terms, others have refused to grant Spotify the right to have their songs played or have subsequently changed their mind and had their music removed. As we saw in Scenario 8–1, for example, Taylor Swift did not allow her (2014) album *1989* to be aired on Spotify and she has since removed all of her earlier music from that streaming service as well. Swift believes that Spotify's policies are "unfair" to recording artists because they significantly decrease the amount of income those artists would receive if Spotify's users instead purchased music in the form of CDs and MP3s.

Are Spotify's practices unfair, as Swift claims, and for the reasons she suggests? First, we should note that Spotify is a service whose practices are in strict compliance with copyright law. So unlike "pirate" music sites, beginning with Napster and evolving to the present day, Spotify has legal contracts with recording artists and record labels; these contracts also include a royalty structure to which both parties agree. However, Swift is correct in claiming that recording artists—at least some of them—stand to gain far more royalty income by "going the song-for-purchase route" than from the royalties offered by Spotify. For example, recording artists who are currently in their prime, such as Swift and Beyoncé, may be significantly affected by the amount of royalty income they can potentially lose.

Nevertheless, we can ask whether all, or even most, recording artists are negatively affected in the same way as Swift apparently is by Spotify's policies, as well as those of other major streaming services. As defenders of these services point out, some solo artists and bands who may be starting out in their careers can gain more exposure through services like Spotify than they otherwise would. Also, recording artists who are past the primes of their careers can benefit from still having their songs aired to Spotify users. So, Swift's claim that Spotify is "unfair" to (all) recording artists does not seem to be completely accurate, since many artists do indeed stand to gain from exposure to their music via this online service.

It would also seem that the debate over access to digital music has moved well beyond the earlier Napster-era questions pertaining to illegal downloading. For example, that debate now includes questions about legitimate modes of freely accessing/listening to copyrighted music via a process that financially rewards musicians and the recording industry. This ongoing battle over digital music also illustrates the complex nature of copyright law with its (traditional) exclusive-rights provisions vis-à-vis the interests of "fair use" and greater online access to digital music (and other forms of creative content) by the public.

The Movie Industry's Response to Unauthorized Access/Distribution

The debate over sharing copyrighted material in digital form has not been limited to proprietary software and copyrighted music. The motion picture industry has also been significantly affected because of the ease with which copyrighted movies can be illegally downloaded and freely exchanged in (P2P) file-sharing systems. In 2003, Metro-Goldwyn-Mayer (MGM) Studies Inc. (along with several music and motion picture studios) sued Grokster (and Morpheus, which was owned by Streamcast) for "contributory copyright infringement" through its file-sharing service (*MGM v. Grokster*).

MGM claimed that over 90% of the material exchanged on Grokster was copyrighted material and that the P2P service was legally liable for the copyright infringement. However, a district court disagreed with MGM, ruling that Grokster could not be held liable for the distribution of copyrighted material. The court reasoned that Grokster both (i) lacked sufficient knowledge of the infringement and (ii) did not "materially contribute" to it.[17] MGM then appealed to the U.S. Supreme Court, which disagreed with the lower court's ruling.

The Supreme Court justices deliberated over two key principles that seemed to be in conflict in the Grokster case—namely, the need to (i) "protect new technologies" (such as P2P networks) and (ii) provide "remedies against copyright infringement." The justices unanimously agreed that using Grokster's service for exchanging copyrighted material was illegal.[18] Although the Court found Grokster liable for "inducing" copyright infringement through its practices, such as advertising, it did not rule that P2P technology itself violated copyright law. So, some legal analysts such as Samuelson (2005) believe that MGM did not get the victory in court that it sought, even though Grokster was forced to pay $50 million to the music and recording industries.

We conclude our discussion of digital copyright controversies—or the "copyfight," as Doctorow (2014) describes this "multifaceted political struggle" involving copyright and the Internet—by once again noting how rapidly the issues have evolved from concerns about pirating proprietary software to worries about the unauthorized downloading and sharing of music and movies in digital format. Many believe that the next phase in the ongoing battle involving digital copyright will significantly impact the publishing industry—that is, in light of the financial impact resulting from the unauthorized downloading and sharing of e-books and e-journals. However, we will not examine specific copyright issues affecting digital publications, since many of the piracy-related challenges currently facing the publishing industry are similar in kind to those already experienced by the software, music, and movie industries, which we have examined in this section.

▶ 8.3 PATENTS, TRADEMARKS, AND TRADE SECRETS

We noted earlier that in addition to copyright law, three alternative legal frameworks have been devised to protect IP: patents, trademarks, and trade secrets. We examine examples of each form of protection with respect to how each can be applied to cybertechnology.

8.3.1 Patent Protections

A patent is a form of legal protection given to individuals who create an invention or process. Unlike copyright protection, patents offer a 20-year exclusive monopoly over an expression or implementation of a protected work. Patent protection can be applied to inventions and discoveries that include "utilitarian or functional" devices such as machines and "articles of manufacture." Patent law requires that inventions satisfy three conditions: usefulness, novelty, and nonobviousness.

First, an invention must have a certain *usefulness*, or utility, in order to be awarded a patent; inventing a machine or process that does nothing "useful" would not merit its inventor a patent. Also, the invention must be *novel*, or new, in order to qualify for a patent. One cannot simply modify an existing invention and expect to be granted a patent for it; the modification would have to be significant enough to make a qualified difference. Finally, the invention or process must be *nonobvious*.[19] For example, it is possible that no one has yet recorded directions for how to travel from Buffalo, New York, to Cleveland, Ohio, through Pittsburgh, Pennsylvania, but describing the route would not satisfy the condition of nonobviousness.

Although computer hardware inventions clearly satisfied the requirements of patent law, this was not initially the case with computer software. Snapper (1995) points out that in the 1960s, most of the discussion involving the protection of software focused on patents. He also notes that in a series of decisions beginning with *Gottschalk v. Benson* (1972), the U.S. Patent Office and the courts established a strong opposition to patenting software. Benson had applied for a patent for an algorithm that translated the representation of numbers from base 10 to base 2; this algorithm was an important feature of all software programs. So, some critics worried that if Benson were granted a patent for his algorithm, he would be able to control almost every computer in use for a number of years.[20]

However, Benson was denied the patent because his algorithm was viewed as an abstract process or mathematical formula that could be performed by a series of mental steps with the aid of pencil and paper (Snapper 1995). But the goal of obtaining patents for computer programs did not end with Benson. And in 1981, the U.S. Supreme Court ruled in what many now consider a landmark case for patents affecting computer software: *Diamond v. Diehr* (1981).

In that pivotal case, the Supreme Court decided 5–4 that a patent could be awarded for a computer program under certain conditions; in this instance, the program assisted in converting rubber into tires. Critics note that on the one hand, Diehr had developed a new process that physically transformed raw rubber into rubber tires; on the other hand, however, Diehr had only a new computer program, since every other part of the machinery used in the conversion process consisted of traditional technology. Initially, Diehr's request for a patent was denied by Diamond, the director of the Patent Office. But Diehr appealed, and his case was eventually heard and upheld by the Supreme Court. However, in their ruling, the justices also continued to affirm the view that computer algorithms themselves are not patentable. They pointed out that the patent awarded to Diehr was not for the computer program per se but for the "rubber tire transformation process" as a whole.[21]

Since the Diehr case, numerous patents have been granted to computer programs and software applications. Some fear that patent protection has now gone too far. Aharonian (2001) points out that between 1990 and 1999, the number of patents increased from 1,300 to 22,500; and between 1993 and 1999, the number of patents issued increased 10-fold. He also points out that between 1979 and 1999, more than 700,000 patents were issued for electronics inventions, including software products. And it is estimated that since 1994, more than 100,000 additional patents for "computer-implemented inventions" have been granted by the U.S. Patent Office.[22]

8.3.2 Trademarks

A trademark is a word, name, phrase, or symbol that identifies a product or service. In 1946, the Lanham Act, also referred to as the Trademark Act, was passed to provide protection for registered trademarks.[23] To qualify for a trademark, the "mark" is supposed to be distinctive. Consider, for example, the distinctive apple that has come to symbolize Apple computers and devices. But not all trademarks have necessarily been distinctive in ways that one might assume to be relevant. As Halbert (1999) notes, for example, the trademark "uh-huh," which is not very "distinctive," was granted to Pepsi-Cola. Because of decisions such as this, critics have argued that trademark protections are being expanded in ways that are inappropriate.

Consider the following example, which may support the view that some entrepreneurs have tried to expand the scope of trademark protection inappropriately. In the 1990s, America Online (AOL) applied for trademarks for its expressions "You've Got Mail," "Buddy List," and "IM" (Instant Messenger). If AOL had been allowed to own these trademarks, other ISPs that used these or very similar expressions could have been sued for infringing on AOL's registered trademarks. So, in 2000, AT&T decided to challenge AOL. In this case, the court ruled that the expressions were not unique to AOL.[24]

8.3.3 Trade Secrets

A *trade secret* consists of information that is highly valuable and considered crucial in the operation of a business or other enterprise. The "secret" is accessible to only a few select individuals within the organization. Trade secrets can be used to protect formulas (such as the one used by Coca-Cola) and blueprints for future projects. They can also protect chemical compounds and processes used in manufacturing. Owners of a trade secret have exclusive rights to make use of it, but they have this right only as long as the secret is maintained.[25]

One problem with protecting trade secrets is that trade secret law is difficult to enforce at the international level. Not only have corporate spies in the United States tried to steal secrets from their corporate rivals, but there is evidence to suggest that international industrial espionage has become a growing industry. The Trade Relationship Aspects of Intellectual Property Standards (TRIPS) agreement, which was part of the World Intellectual Property Organization (WIPO) agreements, includes a provision for protecting trade secrets at the international level; specifically, Article 39 of the TRIPS agreement protects trade secrets by stating explicitly that disclosure of trade secrets comes within the meaning of unfair competition in the global community.[26] (Both WIPO and TRIPS are described in detail in Section 8.4.)

Of course, protecting trade secrets is not something that is peculiar to the high-tech industry. However, because of the considerable amount of research and development conducted in that industry and the fortunes that can be made from computer-based products, it is highly vulnerable to trade secret violations.

▶ 8.4 JURISDICTIONAL ISSUES INVOLVING INTELLECTUAL PROPERTY LAWS

The specific IP laws described in this chapter apply mostly to the United States even though their implications are global. Some international treaties pertaining to IP have also been signed; for example, the TRIPS agreement has implemented requirements from the Berne Convention for the Protection of Literary and Artistic Works.[27] This agreement is recognized by signatories to WIPO.[28]

International IP laws have been very difficult to enforce globally, in large part because of jurisdictional issues. In recent years, however, there has been considerable international cooperation in prosecuting digital piracy cases across jurisdictional lines. For example, in 2009, the owners and operators of the internationally controversial (Sweden-based) Pirate Bay site, who were found guilty of "unlawful transfer" of copyrighted material, received both fines and jail sentences.[29]

In some countries, including the United States, copyright laws affecting IP have also been enacted at the state level. These laws, which often vary from state to state, can apply to the sale of goods, as well as to contracts involved in those sales. With regard to sales and contracts involving computers and electronic devices, two pieces of legislation have aimed at establishing uniformity across states: the Uniform Computer and Information Transactions

TABLE 8-1 Acronyms Corresponding to Intellectual Property Laws and Agreements

DMCA	Digital Millennium Copyright Act
NET Act	No Electronic Theft Act
SBCTEA	Sonny Bono Copyright Term Extension Act
S-DMCA	Super-DMCA (DMCA legislation passed at the state level in the United States)
TRIPS	Trade Relationship Aspects of Intellectual Property Standards
UCITA	Uniform Computer and Information Transactions Act
UETA	Uniform Electronic Transactions Act
WIPO	World Intellectual Property Organization

Act (UCITA) and the Uniform Electronic Transactions Act (UETA).[30] Whereas UETA applies to electronic contracts in general, UCITA is designed to govern transactions, including contracts, involving the development, sale, licensing, maintenance, and support of computer software. It would also extend to all shrink-wrap licenses and "click-wrap" agreements (Girasa 2002). So far, UCITA has been enacted into law in the states of Virginia and Maryland.

In our discussion of various schemes for protecting IP, we used several acronyms and abbreviations to describe and refer to national and international policies, treaties, and statutes. Table 8-1 contains a list of those acronyms.

▶ 8.5 PHILOSOPHICAL FOUNDATIONS FOR INTELLECTUAL PROPERTY RIGHTS

Even though some philosophers and political theorists have opposed the notion of private property rights, we will assume that property ownership is justifiable. We should note that some believe that property ownership rights make sense in the physical realm but are skeptical that property rights can be extended to intellectual objects in cyberspace. We will examine arguments for this position in Section 8.6. Earlier, in Section 8.1.2, we alluded to three philosophical theories—labor, utilitarian, and personality theories—that have been used to justify property rights. We next examine each of those theories in greater detail.[31]

8.5.1 The Labor Theory of Property

The labor theory of property traces its origins to seventeenth-century philosopher John Locke. In his *Second Treatise on Civil Government*, Locke argues that when a person "mixes" his or her labor with the land, that person is entitled to the fruit of his or her labor. So if a person tills and plants crops on a section of land that is not already owned by another—an act which, Locke notes, requires considerable toil—that person has a right to claim ownership of the crops. Analogously, if a person cuts down a tree in the woods and saws it into several pieces, then the person is entitled to the pieces of wood that result from his or her labor. Hence, for Locke, a person's right to property is closely tied to that person's labor.

Locke also includes an important qualification with respect to the appropriation of property, which has come to be known as the "Lockean proviso." The proviso states that when someone either encloses a section of land from the commons or appropriates objects from it, "enough and as good" must be left for others. So, in Locke's account of property, a person has neither the right to cut down all of the trees in a "commons" nor the right to take the last tree. Even with this qualification, however, some argue that Locke's theory fails to provide an adequate account of property rights.

Locke's property theory has been attacked on several fronts. For example, some critics argue that even if Locke's labor theory makes sense for physical property, it does not follow that it can be extended to IP. Noting that Locke associates labor with arduous physical work, these critics point out that the production of intellectual objects does not necessarily require the same kind of onerous toil (or "sweat of the brow") that goes into producing tangible goods. But we can see how an author might claim a right to the ownership of intellectual objects generated by his or her labor, because writing a book, a poem, or a software program can often require a fair amount of mental toil.

Other critics of Locke's property theory point out that intellectual objects are nonexclusionary in nature (as we saw in Section 8.1.2) and thus are not scarce. From this, they go on to infer that there is no need to grant property rights for those objects in a way that would be strictly analogous to rights involving physical property.

Others dispute Locke's claim that a property right is a *natural right*. They ask, What evidence is there for Locke's assertion that an individual's right to own property is a natural right, as opposed to an artificial (or man-made) right? Also, Locke's theory of property presupposes that persons making property claims "own their own bodies." If the right to own property is indeed a natural right, then it should apply to all persons, but consider the example of slavery, a relevant issue in Locke's time. Slaves do not legally own their bodies and it would seem to follow, on Locke's reasoning, that they have no claim to the fruits of their labor—that is, they do not have property rights. So property rights, according to Locke's labor theory, do not apply equally to all people; if they did, Native Americans who mixed their labor with the soil should have been granted property rights to their land in North and South America. It is not clear how Locke can claim that property ownership is a natural right and yet at the same time imply that such a right could possibly be denied to some individuals who happen to be slaves or Native Americans.

Despite these objections, however, some believe that Locke's property theory can be used to justify the protection of intellectual objects.[32] We next consider a scenario in which an appeal for copyright protection is made on the basis of the labor theory of property.

▶ **SCENARIO 8–2:** DEF Corporation vs. XYZ Inc.

DEF Corporation, a software company with 80 employees, has spent the last year developing a sophisticated database program that it is about to release. Thirty software developers have been employed full time on this project, and each software developer worked an average of 60 hours per week. The company expects that it will take more than one year to recoup the investment of labor and time put into this project. DEF applies for a copyright for its product.

XYZ Inc., which also produces database software, files a suit against DEF Corporation for allegedly infringing on its copyright: XYZ claims that DEF has copied a feature used in the interface in one of XYZ's software products. DEF objects by arguing that the feature is, in fact, not original and thus XYZ Inc. should not be eligible for copyright protection. More importantly, DEF further argues that it has invested considerable labor and "sweat" in its database program, so it should be rewarded for its hard work. ■

Does DEF's claim make sense in light of the labor theory of property? Is the labor expended on a particular project, in itself, sufficient to make the case for copyright protection? According to Locke's labor theory, DEF would seem to have a reasonable case, but XYZ sees the matter very differently. Do you agree with DEF's position or with the case made by XYZ?

8.5.2 The Utilitarian Theory of Property

Critics of the labor theory argue that a rationale for granting property rights should not be confused with an individual's labor or with a natural right; rather, property rights are better understood as artificial rights or conventions devised by the state to achieve certain practical ends. According to the utilitarian theory, granting property rights will maximize the good for the greatest number of people in a given society. (Recall our Chapter 2 discussion of utilitarianism and Jeremy Bentham's and John Stuart Mill's arguments for it.) Arguably, utilitarian theory was used by the framers of the U.S. Constitution to justify the granting of property rights for intellectual objects (creative works and inventions) to individuals. The Founders seemed to assume that incentives in the form of copyrights and patents would motivate individuals to bring out their creative products and that, as a result, American society in general would benefit.

An advantage of the utilitarian theory is that it does not need to appeal to the abstract principle of a natural right to justify the granting of property rights to creators and inventors of intellectual objects. However, utilitarians have their critics as well. In Chapter 2, we saw some shortcomings of utilitarian theory with respect to protecting the interests of individuals who fall outside the scope of the greatest number (or majority) in a given society. Also, utilitarians tend to appeal to an economic/financial incentive as a necessary motivation for bringing creative works into the marketplace. For these reasons, many critics find the utilitarian rationale for granting property rights to be inadequate. The following scenario considers some incentives one might have for bringing forth a creative work based on the utilitarian argument for property rights.

▶ **SCENARIO 8–3:** Sam's e-Book Reader Add-on Device

Sam is a very talented and creative person, but he is not terribly industrious when it comes to following through with his ideas. He has an idea for an add-on device that would enable a popular e-book reader to store and play music (MP3 files) on the e-reader. Many of Sam's friends are interested in his idea, and some have strongly encouraged him to develop this device so that they can use it on their e-book readers. But Sam remains unconvinced and unmotivated. Then Sam's friend, Pat, tells him that an acquaintance of hers patented an analogous invention and has since earned several thousand dollars. Pat tries to persuade Sam that not only would his invention benefit his friends but also that he would stand to gain financially if he patents the product and it is successful. After considering Pat's advice, Sam decides to work on his invention and apply for a patent for it. ▩

Was a utilitarian incentive (i.e., in the form of a financial benefit) necessary to get Sam to follow through on his invention? Would he have brought his invention into the marketplace if there were not a financial enticement? Do people only produce creative works because of financial rewards they might receive? On the one hand, it would seem that financial incentives could motivate some individuals, such as Sam, to produce a creative work that benefits society in general. However, it is not clear that all great authors or composers have written literary works (such as novels or poems) or have composed musical works (such as symphonies or songs) solely because of the prospects of becoming wealthy. It is possible, for example, that some gifted composers wrote music for the sheer enjoyment it brought them as creators of one or more artistic works. So there may be factors other than financial incentives that influence creators to bring forth their works.

8.5.3 The Personality Theory of Property

Critics of the labor and utilitarian theories believe that any theory that links the granting of property rights to either (i) an individual's onerous labor or (ii) the notion of social utility misses an important point about the nature of the creative work involved in the production of intellectual objects. Both the labor and utilitarian theories appeal to criteria external to the individual himself/herself as the rationale for granting a property right. Note that in each case, the criterion is a reward that is directly monetary in the case of utilitarian theory and indirectly monetary in the case of labor theory. Both theories assume an extrinsic criterion—that is, either one's labor or some economic incentive—for justifying property rights; neither considers the possibility that an internal criterion could justify these rights. In this sense, both theories underestimate the role of the persona or *personality* of the creator of the intellectual work. According to the personality theory of property, the intellectual object is an extension of the creator's personality (i.e., the person's being or soul). And it is because of this relationship between the intellectual object and the creator's personality that advocates of the personality theory believe that creative works deserve legal protection. As Moore and Himma (2014) also note, the personality theory of property distinguishes the "personal rights of creators" from "their economic rights."

The personality theory traces its origins to the writings of G. W. F. Hegel, a nineteenth-century philosopher, and it has served as a foundational element in IP laws enacted by nations in continental Europe. In France, the personality account of property is sometimes referred to as the "moral rights" (*droits morals*) theory of property. The personality theory provides an interesting interpretation of *why* an author should have control over the ways in which his or her work can be displayed and distributed. To ensure this control, personality theorists suggest that authors should be given protection for their artistic work even if they have no legal claim to any monetary reward associated with it.

Consider a case in which the personality theory of property might apply—namely, the use of a Beatles' song in commercial advertisement. In mid-1987, the Nike Corporation aired a television commercial for its sneakers that featured the song "Revolution," composed by John Lennon in the late 1960s (when he was a member of the Beatles). Lennon was murdered in 1980, so when the Nike ad aired on commercial television, he could neither approve nor disapprove of how his song was being used. Many of Lennon's fans, however, were outraged that a song penned by Lennon to address the serious political and social concerns of the turbulent 1960s could be used so frivolously in a TV commercial. Critics argued that Lennon would not have approved of his song being used in this manner. However, even if Lennon had been alive, he may not have had any legal recourse when the TV commercial aired, because the entire Lennon–McCartney corpus of songs was purchased by Michael Jackson prior to 1987; Michael Jackson owned the copyright to "Revolution."[33]

By appealing to the personality theory, however, the case could be made that Lennon—or in this instance, his widow—should have some say in how his song was represented in a commercial forum. Next, consider a hypothetical scenario in which we can also apply the personality theory of property.

▶ **SCENARIO 8–4:** Angela's B++ Programming Tool

Angela, a CS graduate student who has been struggling to make ends meet, has developed a new programming tool, called B++. This software application, which employs the notion of a "reduced instruction set" technique, can be used in conjunction with the standard C++ programming language to execute certain tasks more quickly than the C++ instruction set. Angela has recently published an article that describes, in detail, the reduced set of instructions, how they work, and why she was motivated to develop B++. She was delighted to have her article published in the prestigious journal *CyberTechnology*. As part of the conditions for publication, however, Angela had to agree to sign over the copyright for her article to CyberPress (the publisher of *CyberTechnology*). ■

Angela is then informed that a textbook publisher, CyberTextbooks Inc., wishes to include a portion of her article in a textbook. As the copyright holder for Angela's article, CyberPress is legally authorized to allow CyberTextbooks to reprint all or selected portions of her article. Suppose, however, that Angela protests that mere excerpts from her article neither truly convey the important features of her programming tool nor explain how it works. She further argues that the article is an extension of her persona and that only in total does the article reveal her creative talents as a programmer.

TABLE 8-2 Three Philosophical Theories of Property

Labor theory	Argues that a property right is a natural right and that property rights can be justified by the labor, or toil, that one invests in cultivating land or in creating a work of art
Utilitarian theory	Argues that property rights are not natural rights but rather artificial rights created by the state. Property rights are granted to individuals and to corporations because they result in greater overall social utility
Personality theory	Argues that a property right is a moral right and that property rights are justified not because of labor or social utility but because creative works express the personalities of the authors who create them

Does Angela have a legitimate objection in this case? Should she, the original author of the article and the creator of the new programming tool, have the right to prevent her article from being published in abridged form? Can her argument, based on the notion of IP as an expression of one's personality, be defended on moral grounds? Because she signed over the copyright for her article to CyberPress, she has no legal grounds for objecting to how that article is subsequently used. However, on moral grounds, she could claim that the publication of her abridged article does not fairly present her creative work.

Table 8-2 summarizes the three philosophical theories of property.

▶ 8.6 THE "FREE SOFTWARE" AND "OPEN SOURCE" MOVEMENTS

We have examined three traditional theories that have been used to justify the protection of IP from a philosophical perspective. In the introduction to Section 8.5, however, we also noted that some have argued for the view that no formal legal protection should be given to IP even if we do grant such protection to physical property. One of the best known, and perhaps most controversial, arguments for why conventional IP rights should not be granted to computer software has been made by Stallman (2004), who views software ownership as a form of "hoarding" that disregards the general welfare of society. As an alternative scheme, Stallman proposes that programmers work together to make software freely available for humankind rather than supporting efforts to restrict its use.

Although Stallman has been a staunch advocate for the view that software should be free, we should note that he intends "free" to refer to liberty, not to price (or "free" as in free speech vs. free beer). Grodzinsky, Miller, and Wolf (2004) suggest that Stallman's position on why software should be free may have been influenced by the culture of the 1970s at the Massachusetts Institute of Technology, where a program's source code could be freely exchanged. As we saw in Section 8.3, however, that practice began to change in the late 1970s and early 1980s. Also during that period, the burgeoning computer industry hired many of the best software developers and programmers from academic computing labs, and some of those individuals took the software they developed with them. As a result, some of that software eventually became proprietary. In response to these trends, Stallman began his Gnu's Not Unix (GNU) project in 1984. GNU's goal was to develop an entire Unix-like operating system, complete with system utilities, that was "open" and freely accessible.

8.6.1 *GNU* and the Free Software Foundation

As stronger IP rights began to be granted to software "owners" in the early 1980s and as more and more software became proprietary, some programmers were concerned about whether they would be able to exchange software programs with each other in the future. They also worried that someone other than themselves would "own" their creative works. In 1985, the Free Software Foundation (FSF) was formed in response to these concerns, as well as to support Stallman's GNU project.

According to FSF, four "freedoms" are essential for free software. These include *freedom to*:

1. Run the program, for any purpose
2. Study how the program works and adapt it for your needs
3. Redistribute copies so you can help your neighbor
4. Improve the program and release your improvements to the public so that the whole community benefits[34]

The software that is produced by programmers adhering to "free software" requirements (freely downloadable from www.fsf.org/) is typically accompanied by a licensing agreement that is designed to keep it freely available to other users "downstream," who can continue to modify the source code. This agreement is spelled out in the GNU General Public License (GPL). The kind of protection granted by this license is also known as *copyleft*. ("Copyleft" refers to a group of licenses that currently apply to documents, music, and art, as well as software.) Whereas copyright law is seen by FSF's proponents as a way to restrict the right to make and redistribute copies of a particular work, a copyleft license included in GPL uses an alternative scheme that "subverts" the traditional copyright mechanism in order to ensure that every person who receives a copy, or derived version of a work, can use, modify, and also redistribute both the work and the derived version of the work. All derivative works of GPL software must also be licensed under GPL. In this way, the four freedoms of FSF are propagated in the future software developed under this agreement.[35]

By the early 1990s, the GNU project had produced many important software development tools in compliance with FSF guidelines and the specifications for Unix-like source code. Throughout the 1980s, however, there was some confusion as to just what "Unix" meant, since several versions of that operating system existed—some at universities such as Berkeley and others in the private sector such as AT&T Bell Laboratories where Unix was originally developed. This resulted in lawsuits and counter lawsuits regarding which sections of Unix software source code could be freely distributed and which sections were proprietary. The legal problems created some difficulties for Stallman and the GNU project because GNU still lacked the core of its (Unix-like) operating system—that is, the kernel. However, this issue was finally resolved in the early 1990s, when Linus Torvalds developed the kernel for a Unix-like operating system that he called Linux. At this point, GNU realized its goal of having a complete, functional operating system with all of the source code freely available for inspection, modification, and improvement.[36] The GNU project and FSF significantly influenced another related software development initiative known as the open source software (OSS) movement.

8.6.2 The "Open Source Software" Movement: OSS vs. FSF

OSS, which began in 1988, shares many of the same goals as FSF—most notably, the ability of a software user to look at, understand, modify, and redistribute the source code for that software. Like FSF, OSS requires that its source code be freely available. So, both movements are similar with respect to their requirements for the free use of their source code in the software development process. And some authors, including Chopra and Dexter (2009), use the expression "FOSS" to describe "free and open source software." However, as Raymond (2004) notes, there are significant differences in the "attitudes" or philosophies of these two groups. Whereas FSF continues to focus on promoting its philosophical position that software should be free, OSS has concentrated its efforts more on promoting the open-source model as an alternative methodology to "closed-source" development for software. OSS and FSF also differ with respect to requirements for how the software is used "downstream." For example, FSF requires that all derivative pieces of software be subject to the original requirements and thus remain "open" and nonproprietary. OSS, on the contrary, is more flexible with respect to its derivative software. Unlike FSF, which requires that users strictly adhere to its GPL license in all derivative uses of its software, OSS supports less restrictive licenses such as Berkeley's Software Distribution (BSD) and Netscape's Mozilla Public License (MPL). These licenses are considered more "lenient" than GPL because they permit programmers to alter the OSS and to release it as a proprietary product.[37]

Another difference between OSS and FSF can be found in their attitudes toward the business community. The former is less anticommercial than the latter. In fact, many in the open-source community interact comfortably with members of the business community. Because of its success in the software world, OSS now poses a significant threat to companies that produce proprietary software, such as Microsoft Corp. In addition to the Linux operating system, other well-known open-source products include the Apache Web server and the Perl programming language. Whereas Torvalds believes that OSS and commercial software can coexist, Stallman does not believe that this is possible in the long run because of the profit incentives that drive investors in the commercial sector. Stallman also condemns the business community's practice of producing proprietary or "closed" code as unethical, and he claims that signing a typical software licensing agreement is like "betraying your neighbor." Spinello (2003) notes that some of Stallman's followers have gone so far as to suggest that FSF is "morally superior" to proprietary software. However, we will not pursue that debate here. Instead, a more important question for our purposes is how the OSS and FSF movements can help us to think about at an issue at the heart of the contemporary IP debate: Is the free flow of information still possible in a digital world?

As we saw in Chapter 6, some of Stallman's followers subscribe to the mantra *information wants to be free*. We should not assume that Stallman himself holds this view with respect to all information, however, because he focuses his arguments specifically on why computer software should be free. One point that Stallman makes in his discussion of software is particularly useful in helping us think about issues involving the concept of information (in general) vis-à-vis IP from a radically different perspective—namely, information is something that humans desire to *share* with one another. Although this insight undergirds Stallman's view that software should be free, we do not need to embrace his position on software to appreciate the force of Stallman's insight with respect to the broader notion of information. In order to be shared, information must be communicated; so elaborate IP structures and mechanisms that prohibit, or even discourage, the communication of information would seem to undermine its very purpose as something to be shared.

▶ 8.7 THE "COMMON GOOD" APPROACH: AN ALTERNATIVE FRAMEWORK FOR ANALYZING THE INTELLECTUAL PROPERTY DEBATE

In the preceding section, we focused our discussion on the question of whether software should be unrestricted and thus freely available to distribute and modify in conformance with certain "open" or "free" licensing agreements, as opposed to being legally protected by strict copyright and patent laws. Although our discussion centered on computer software, in particular, we saw that a more general question that arises is whether the free flow of information itself, in digital form, should be restricted. While not everyone may agree with the claim that software should be free, we noted that some have found Stallman's insight about the nature and purpose of *information* (i.e., as something that humans naturally want to share and communicate) to be compelling.

Some authors writing on the topic of IP have noted that Stallman's insights are compatible with key elements in virtue ethics, which we discussed in Chapter 2. McFarland (2004, 2005), who suggests that we can draw from principles in virtue ethics in understanding and analyzing issues involving IP, appeals to Stallman's insight that the essential purpose of information is to be shared. McFarland also notes how this insight supports the "common good" view of IP.

McFarland's notion of a "common good" approach to computer ethics draws from insights in Aristotle's *Nicomachean Ethics*. In Chapter 2, we saw that some key elements of Aristotle's theory serve as the cornerstone for virtue ethics; but how can this view provide a framework for discussing IP issues? McFarland suggests the following strategy. First, he points out that Aristotle believed that every object had a nature, end, or purpose, which he called its *good*. Following Aristotle's method of inquiry, McFarland suggests that we begin any philosophical investigation by asking what the good, or purpose, of an object *is*. So, in our investigation of information as an intellectual object, we should aim at understanding its ultimate purpose.

Although information can certainly be understood as a form of self-expression (as the personality theory rightly suggests) and as a product that performs some useful functions (as utilitarians correctly suggest), it also has an even more fundamental purpose than personal expression and utility. Information, McFarland argues, is ultimately about communication; hence, the nature and purpose of IP in the form of information is communication, and thus an adequate account of the purpose of information (as something to be communicated) must take that into consideration.

McFarland believes that traditional concepts of property often overlook the ethically significant relationships that some kinds of property have with the rest of the society. The three traditional theories of property that we examined in Section 8.6 focus on criteria such as an individual's (or a corporation's) labor, social utility (cost benefit), or the author's personality. But they fail to consider that the purpose of information is something whose essential nature is to be shared and communicated. Hence, McFarland believes that a "common good" analysis of property, which examines the nature of information in terms of a broader social context, can provide us with an attractive alternative to the traditional property theories.

How is a common-good approach to IP issues, which takes into account the overall good of society, different from a utilitarian theory? We noted earlier that a utilitarian system's primary concern is with maximizing the good for the majority, but utilitarianism does not always take individual rights into consideration in producing the greatest good for the greatest number. McFarland points out that a utilitarian analysis based solely on cost-benefit criteria might suggest that it is desirable to publish a person's private diary because many people would enjoy reading it. Although the benefit to the overall majority would outweigh any embarrassment to the individual writer of the diary, such a practice is not morally correct, because it violates the basic right of humans to be respected.

McFarland also points out that if we begin our analysis of IP issues simply by analyzing the notion of property itself, then the central point of debate tends to be about ownership and control; this is indeed how property issues are typically conceived and debated. McFarland believes that if we are willing to step outside that conventional framework, we can get a more complete view of the important societal role that information plays in IP debate. In doing this, we gain the insight that an adequate theory of information must take into account its *social nature*, an important feature that we tend to overlook when we think of information only in terms of rights and property.

Before proceeding any further, it is important to ask, What do we mean by "information" in the context of our common-good approach to IP disputes? We should note that there are both technical and colloquial (or everyday) senses of "information." While many highly technical definitions of "information" have been proposed by scholars in the field of information science (especially since the 1950s), our concern in this chapter is with the term's colloquial use and meaning. Capurro and Hjørland (2003) point out that "the concept of information as we use it in everyday English, in the sense *knowledge communicated*, plays a central role in contemporary society" (Italics Capurro and Hjørland). We limit our analysis to this sense of "information" (i.e., in the broad context of "knowledge communicated"), which includes academic, literary, scientific, health, and general information that either already is or eventually should be in the "public domain." It is this sense of "information" that Capurro, Hjørland, McFarland, and others believe plays a very important social role.

8.7.1 Information Wants to be Shared vs. Information Wants to be Free

Arguably, a new (guiding) principle can be derived from the insights of Stallman and McFarland: *Information wants to be shared.*[38] Note, however, that this principle is very different from the claim "information wants to be free." We do not need to embrace the latter in order to defend the former. As we saw in Chapter 6, the view that all information should be free is not only naïve but is also conceptually flawed. For example, Spafford (2007) has described some of the undesirable consequences that such a principle would have for individual privacy if all personal information were freely accessible. Also, Himma (2005) has shown why the view that information should be free is problematic as a "normative principle" since it is not clear who, exactly, should be responsible for making it free. For example, is the government or the state obligated to make this information freely available to its citizens?

Doctorow (2014) argues that, strictly speaking, "information doesn't want to be free—people do." He further claims that because information is an "abstraction," it does not (and cannot) "want" anything. But even if information were capable of having "wants," or broader "desires," Doctorow notes that those desires would be completely "irrelevant to the destiny of the Internet." Arguably, Doctorow's insight is not so much in attacking the metaphor used in describing information in terms of various wants/desires (which, admittedly, is somewhat confusing, as others have pointed out as well) but rather noting that people "want to be free"—that is, free in terms of what *they want* "from computers and the internet."[39] However, Doctorow's insight is also compatible with our "presumptive principle in favor of sharing information"—in spite of the awkward metaphor suggesting the attribution of wants, or any other kinds of sentient desires, to information.

So it is primarily our "presumptive principle" about the nature and status of information as "something that *people freely wish to share and communicate*" that is at the heart of the "information-wants-to-be-shared" strategy that we defend in this chapter (and that we distinguish from the more controversial view that all information should be free). Perhaps it is also important to reiterate that our sense of "information" in this context has to do with "knowledge communicated" (and thus does not necessarily apply to all forms of information).

Not only is our presumptive principle regarding the sharing of information compatible with McFarland's "common-good" approach to IP, but it is also compatible with positions that others have expressed with regard to the social benefits of being able to share knowledge and information freely. For example, De George (2003) points out that because cybertechnology enables us to share information in ways that were not previously possible, it has also provided us with the opportunity of greater information access at the level of community. Yet he also notes that, paradoxically, by focusing on information as a commodity, the software industry has highlighted its commercial value, and, as a result, policies and schemes have been constructed to control information for commercial purposes rather than to share it freely.

To see the force of De George's claim, consider that copyright laws, originally intended to cover print media, were designed to encourage the distribution of information. We have seen that these laws have since been extended to cover digital media, inhibiting the distribution of electronic information. The distribution of digitized information is now being discouraged in some sectors. To illustrate this point, consider the traditional practice of borrowing books from public libraries. Physical books had always been available for an indefinite number of loans for library patrons; that is, there was no limit on how many times a book could circulate. However, the same practice does not hold in the case of all e-books. Consider that in 2011, HarperCollins had a policy that any e-book it published could be checked out of a library a maximum of 26 times before the e-book's license expired. (HarperCollins has since changed its policy in response to protests by librarians and library patrons.) But it is worth noting that some publishers do not even allow their e-books to circulate at all in public libraries. Such practices clearly tend to discourage the sharing of copyrighted information in digital format.

Copyright laws were originally designed to encourage the flow of information in print media, via their fair-use provisions. Yet, for digital media, they have been revised in a way that discourages the flow, and thus the sharing, of electronic information. What implications could this trend have for the future? Consider that the ability to share, not to hoard, information contributed to the development of the World Wide Web. Also consider what might have happened if the inventors of the Internet and the Web had been more entrepreneurial-minded and less concerned with sharing information. Tim Berners-Lee, who invented HTTP (the protocol used on the Web), never bothered to apply for a patent for his invention or for a copyright for his programming code. As a physicist working at CERN (a physics laboratory on the Franco–Swiss border), he desired to develop a common protocol for Internet communication so that scientists could share information more easily with each other.

Note that Berners-Lee's goal in developing the Web was to provide a forum where information could be *shared*. A person whose interests were more entrepreneurial could have sought IP protection for his or her contributions, thereby reducing the amount of information that could be shared. Also consider that Doug Engelbart, who invented the mouse, never applied for patent for his contribution. Yet, virtually every major computer manufacturer, as well as every computer user who has used a graphical interface, has benefited from his seminal contribution to what came to be called the "Windows interface" in computing. Like Berners-Lee, Engelbart was interested in developing a tool that would enable the sharing information, rather than its commodification.

Consider also how the sharing of information has benefited many of those entrepreneurs who now seek to control the flow of information in cyberspace. It has been argued that Microsoft benefited significantly from the work done by Apple Corporation on its graphical user interface (the system of icons that users can point to and click on to accomplish a task). And it is well known that when Steve Jobs was at Apple in the 1970s, he visited Xerox PARC (Palo Alto Research Center), where he discovered that a graphical interface had already been invented by researchers there. So it is reasonably accurate to say that current user interfaces have benefited from the sharing of information along the way. Would it be fair to credit any one company or person with exclusive rights to a graphical user interface? Would doing so not also eliminate, or certainly impede, the possibility of incremental development and innovation? And more importantly, would it not also prevent us from sharing that important information?

Warwick (2004) argues that the original copyright framework, which valued the interests of the people as a whole over the interests of creators of IP, is being "slowly dismantled" to give more weight to the interests of the latter group. And Burk (2003) notes that "overreaching" in copyright licensing has now begun to be recognized by some courts to "constitute a new form of misuse." In fact, many critics worry that digital information is now becoming less available and that we, as a society, are worse off because of it. Some also fear that if the public domain of ideas continues to shrink, our "information commons" may eventually disappear.

8.7.2 Preserving the Information Commons

What do we mean by *information commons*? One way of understanding this concept is by comparing it to a "physical commons," a common area that has been set aside and is open to the general public or to residents of a community. Garret Hardin, in his classic account of the "tragedy of the commons," describes the disappearance of the public space, or commons, that farmers living in a certain community had once enjoyed. In Hardin's tale, a public plot of land is shared by many farmers but owned by none of them; by sharing the land in a reasonable and mutually agreed manner, the commons benefits all of the farmers. Suppose that they agree collectively that each is allowed to have no more than 10 cows graze on the commons on a given day. Further suppose, however, one day a farmer decides to cheat a little by having 11 or 12 of his cattle graze on the commons, reasoning that having 1 or 2 additional cows graze will not deplete the land's resources and will also enable him to profit slightly.[40] If other farmers also use the same rationale, you can see that before long the entire commons would be depleted.

It is very easy to underestimate the importance of the commons, or the public domain. We often take for granted the public parks, public beaches, and public gathering places that have been set aside for general use. Imagine the quality of our lives without them and consider that without proper foresight, planning, and management, our parks could easily have been turned over to entrepreneurs for private development. Imagine, for example, if early city planners in New York City had not had the wisdom to set aside the area of Manhattan called Central Park; yet there was nothing inevitable about this. An entrepreneurial-minded city council might have sold the land to developers and businesses on the grounds that doing so would bring revenue to the city. In the short term, the city might have realized significant financial gain; but that kind of decision would have been very shortsighted, and it would have been economically disadvantageous in the long term. Although Central Park is a tourist attraction that draws many people to New York City, it is not valued simply as a tourist attraction. For example, it is also a gathering place for city residents as well as visitors—a place to hear a concert on a summer evening, have a picnic in the fall, or ice skate in the winter. Imagine if Central Park were to disappear from the New York City landscape.

We have briefly considered some ways in which the physical commons has been threatened, but how is this analogous to the current threat posed to the information commons? Buchanan and Campbell (2005) describe the information commons as

> a body of knowledge and information that is available to anyone to use without the need to ask for or receive permission from another, providing any conditions placed on its use are respected.[41]

Just as the physical commons in England began to vanish in the seventeenth and eighteenth centuries when property laws passed by Parliament prohibited peasants from fishing and hunting in newly enclosed territories that had previously been accessible to everyone, some now worry that the information commons is now undergoing a similar fate.[42] Boyle (2006), who describes this trend as the "second enclosure movement," draws some useful comparisons to the original enclosure movement that resulted in the "fencing off" of much of the "grassy commons of old England." In the current enclosure movement, of course, it is ideas and information that are being fenced off or enclosed. So, just as there is reason to be concerned about the tragedy of the physical commons, as described by Hardin, there would also seem to be good reasons to worry about what Onsrud (1998) calls "the tragedy of the information commons." Buchanan and Campbell note that what is especially tragic is that the information commons is now

> . . . being enclosed or even destroyed by a combination of law and technology that is privatizing what had been public and may become public, and locking up and restricting access to ideas and information that have heretofore been shared resources.[43]

A different way of expressing the concern about what is being lost in this second enclosure movement is offered by Heller (1998) in his description of the "tragedy of the anti-commons"—a phenomenon that occurs whenever resources are *underconsumed* or *underutilized*. As more and more of the information commons is fenced off because of strong IP laws, critics such as Heller fear that fewer and fewer intellectual resources will be available to ordinary individuals and that, as a result, our information resources will be underutilized.

8.7.3 The Fate of the Information Commons: Could the Public Domain of Ideas Eventually Disappear?

Now imagine what it would be like if the public domain of ideas, which we have all enjoyed and benefited from, disappeared. In a book subtitled *The Fate of the Commons in a Connected World*, Lessig (2002) raises some serious concerns about the future of ideas in a medium that is overly regulated and controlled by economic interests. In Section 8.2.2, we saw that the passage of SBCTEA extended copyright protection for rights holders by 20 years. Laws such as this seem to run counter to the notion in which the public domain of ideas has traditionally become populated—that is, intellectual objects are supposed to enter the public domain after a reasonable period of time. As Coy (2007) notes, this factor distinguishes intellectual objects from physical objects, since the latter can always remain proprietary.

Of course, governments could continue to pass laws extending the term limits of copyright law (as in the case of SBCTEA in the United States) to the point where precious few intellectual objects, if any, will enter the public domain in the future. We have already seen how the DMCA, with its controversial anticircumvention clause, also contributes to the erosion, and possible future elimination, of the information commons. We may wish to consider the short-term vs. long-term gains and losses that can result from current trends in information policy. In the near term, corporations and some individuals will profit handsomely from privatization of information policy. In the long term, however, our society may be worse off intellectually, spiritually, and even economically if the short-term goals of privatization are not balanced against the interests of the greater public good.

Imagine if more of the information that we have traditionally shared freely were to disappear from the public domain and enter the world of copyright protection. Suppose, for example, that beginning tomorrow every recipe will be copyrighted and thus not be able to be disseminated without the permission of the new rights holder (i.e., the legal owner of that recipe). We would not even be permitted to use, let alone improve on, a particular recipe without first getting permission from the copyright holder. In the past, chefs could use recipes freely and improve upon them. Would it be fair if those chefs who had previously benefited from the sharing of recipes were all of a sudden awarded exclusive rights to them? And would it be fair if they were awarded the exclusive rights simply because they just happened to be experimenting with food at a time when the legal system favored the privatizing of information for commercial interests? Does it matter that society would be deprived of communicating freely the kind of information it has always had the luxury to share? What would this mean for the public domain of ideas and for ordinary discourse and information exchange? Critics like Boyle (2004) worry that the public domain of information is "disappearing" under the IP system built around the interests of the current stakeholders.

In defending the view that the ultimate purpose of information is something to be shared and communicated, we have made the case that the public domain of ideas should be preserved. Of course, the rights and interests of both software manufacturers and individual creators of literary and artistic works also deserve serious consideration in any debate about IP rights in cyberspace. And we do not need to advocate for the controversial view that all information should be absolutely free to move the debate forward. Indeed, companies and individuals need fair compensation for both their costs and the risks they undertake in developing their creative products and bringing them to market. The key phrase here, of course, is "fair compensation"; a fair IP system is one that would enable us to achieve a proper balance. In reaching that state of equilibrium, however, we must not lose sight of the fact that information is more than merely a commodity that has commercial value.

If we defend the principle that information wants to be shared (but not totally free), then perhaps it will be possible to frame reasonable IP policies that would both encourage the flow of information in digital form *and* reward fairly the creators of intellectual objects, including software manufacturers. One promising scheme for accomplishing these objectives can be found in the kind of licensing agreements currently issued in the Creative Commons (CC) initiative.

8.7.4 The Creative Commons

The CC, launched in 2001, provides a set of licensing options that help artists and authors give others the freedom and creativity to build upon their creativity. Lessig (2004) points out that such a "creative" scheme for licensing is needed because many people now realize that the current IP rights regime does not make sense in the digital world. We should note that CC does not aim to undermine the principle of copyright. Lessig concedes that copyrights protect important values and are essential to creativity, even in a digital age. He also believes that if the essence of copyright law is to allow creators to have control, then there should be a way to maintain ownership of copyrighted works and still make it possible for the average person to license the use of those works. Lessig notes that, unfortunately, the current version of copyright, which was not written for a world of digital creativity, "restricts more than it inspires." Traditional copyright regimes tend to promote an "all or nothing" kind of protection scheme with their "exclusive rights" clauses.

Lessig believes that the Internet allows for an "innovation commons" and that the CC licensing schemes help to promote this vision. CC provides options with four levels of permission: attribution, noncommercial, derivative, and share alike. At the level of attribution, others would be permitted to copy, distribute, display, and perform your work (as well as derivative works based upon it), only if they give you credit. The noncommercial option would permit others to copy, distribute, display, and perform your work (as well as derivative works based upon it), only for noncommercial purposes. At the derivative level, you would permit others to copy, distribute, display, and perform only verbatim copies of the work (but not derivative works based upon it). And, finally, the share-alike option permits others to distribute derivative works, but only under a license identical to the license that governs your work (http://creativecommons.org). By specifying one or more of these options, you can retain the copyright for your creative work while also allowing others to use it under some circumstances.

Lessig believes that artists, authors, and other creators who use the CC license are, in effect, saying:

> We have built upon the work of others. Let others build upon ours.

Building on the notion that every author "stands on the shoulders of giants," CC's proponents believe that musicians and artists who use the CC license are, in effect, "standing on the shoulders of peers" and allowing peers to "stand on their shoulders."

We can see how CC, via its creative and flexible licensing schemes, both encourages the flow of information in digital form and protects the legal rights and interests of artists and authors. Artists and authors can be recognized and rewarded, financially and otherwise, for their creative contributions, yet still share their works (or portions of their works) with others. This, in turn, enables us to realize Lessig's notion of an "innovation commons" because it allows authors and artists to build upon the works of others. It also contributes to the future of the commons, and it promotes the kind of spirit of cooperation and sharing among creators that Stallman and the FSF movement advocate for software development (although FSF does not endorse CC's licensing scheme). In promoting these and related goals, CC provides an implementation scheme for the presumptive principle defended in this chapter—namely, "information wants to be shared." Implementing our presumptive principle through a mechanism such as CC enables us to frame IP policies that avoid the kinds of problems inherent in both:

a. The claim that information should be absolutely free

b. Overly strong copyright laws that discourage sharing and innovation and also diminish the information commons.

▶ 8.8 PIPA, SOPA, AND RWA LEGISLATION: CURRENT BATTLEGROUNDS IN THE INTELLECTUAL PROPERTY WAR

In the previous sections, we defended a principle that presumes in favor of sharing information, which would help to prevent the information commons from further erosion; however, we did not argue that copyright protection should be altogether eliminated. In Section 8.2, we saw that the intent of the original U.S. Copyright Act (1790) was to "promote the progress of the sciences and useful arts," thereby *encouraging creative production* for society's benefits, by giving authors exclusive rights over literary and artistic works for a *limited time.* Ng (2011) argues that while this was clearly a "desirable goal" on the part of the Founders, granting exclusive rights to authors can, unfortunately, also "unnecessarily limit society's ability to access works in the public domain" (as we saw in Section 8.7).

We have also seen that authors are not only persons but now include many large corporations; the latter, of course, can profoundly influence lawmakers. Some of these corporations have recently tried to convince the U.S. Congress to pass stronger copyright protection laws. Many critics believe that such laws, if passed, would significantly threaten the flow of information on the Internet. In this section, we briefly examine three relatively recent legislative proposals that could have such an effect: Protect Intellectual Property Act (PIPA), Stop Online Piracy Act (SOPA), and Research Works Act (RWA).

8.8.1 The PIPA and SOPA Battles

In 2011, two controversial pieces of legislation, PIPA and SOPA, were introduced in the U.S. House of Representatives and the U.S. Senate, respectively. Supporters of these legislative proposals included the RIAA, the MPAA, and the American Entertainment Software Association (AESA). PIPA's and SOPA's supporters argued that stronger laws were needed to enforce copyright protection online and to crack down on pirates, especially those operating from Web sites in countries outside the United States. However, many critics of the proposed legislation argued that the enactment of SOPA and PIPA into law would grant the U.S. government, as well as some major corporations, broad powers that allow them to shut down Web sites that they merely suspect are involved in copyright infringement. Moreover, they would be able to do this without first having to get a court order and go through the traditional process of having either a trial or court hearing.[44]

On January 18, 2012, the date that legislative hearings for these controversial bills were set to begin in the U.S. Congress, a series of coordinated online protests ensued. Many prominent Web sites, including Wikipedia and Google, participated in the protest. Wikipedia had considered temporarily closing its site that day, while Google and many other online supporters elected to remain open but displayed protest signs on their sites. (Many sites "went dark" for the entire day to show their support for the online protest.) It is estimated that as many as

115,000 Web sites joined the protest and that 4.5 million protestors (mostly ordinary users) signed the online petition to denounce PIPA and SOPA.

Following the January 2012 protests, leaders in both houses of Congress decided to postpone voting on the two controversial measures. Although the bills were eventually shelved, they have not been abandoned by their original sponsors in Congress. However, several prominent lawmakers who initially had come out in favor of the controversial legislation have withdrawn their support (at least temporarily). Yet the battle is far from over; in fact, key supporters of the original SOPA and PIPA bills have vowed to introduce alternate versions in the near future. And some critics worry that the Cyber Intelligence Sharing and Protection Act (CISPA), which has been subsequently introduced in Congress, is a "back door" effort to get PIPA- and SOPA-like legislation passed.

8.8.2 RWA and Public Access to Health-Related Information

As in the case of PIPA and SOPA, RWA was also introduced in the U.S. Congress in late 2011. This bill, which was concerned mainly with scientific and academic research that was accessible online, was designed to replace the National Institute of Health (NIH) Public Access Policy. That policy had mandated that any NIH research funded by U.S. tax payers would be freely available online. RWA's critics, who worried that future online access to important health information would be severely restricted, included the American Library Association, the Alliance for Taxpayer Access, the Confederation of Open Access Repositories, and the Scholarly Publishing and Academic Resources Association. However, supporters of the RWA legislation included powerful groups such as the Copyright Alliance and the Association of American Publishers.

Some RWA opponents worried that the proposed legislation, if enacted into law, would not only block the sharing of important health-related information (generated by NIH grants), including the public availability of biomedical research results, but could also significantly restrict the sharing of much scientific and academic information in general. Other critics pointed out that taxpayers had already paid once for this research, via their taxes that funded NIH grants; so people who wish to access this information in the future would effectively be required to pay twice because of the proposed new fees. Opponents have also noted that many large (privately owned) publishing companies, who stood to gain financially, were staunch supporters of RWA. It turned out that one of these companies, Elsevier Press, had contributed money to the political campaign for U.S. Congressman Darrell Issa (a cosponsor of the original RWA legislation). This publishing company became the target of an international boycott, described in the following scenario.

▶ **Scenario 8–5:** Elsevier Press and "The Cost of Knowledge" Boycott

Elsevier Press is a prestigious academic publisher, headquartered in the Netherlands. Noted for its quality publications in science and mathematics, Elsevier publishes approximately 2,000 journals and roughly 20,000 books. Some of its journals, such as *The Lancet* and *Cell*, are highly regarded. However, many scientists and mathematicians have been displeased with Elsevier's pricing and policy practices, which they believe restrict access to important information. In 2011, distinguished mathematician Timothy Gowers (of the University of Cambridge) organized a formal boycott of Elsevier Press. As of August 2015, the boycott has collected close to 16,000 signatures from scholars around the world; they have signed a petition pledging not to publish in or review manuscripts for Elsevier. The boycott has come to be called "The Cost of Knowledge."[45] ■

The boycotters have two major complaints against Elsevier, claiming that it (1) charges excessive prices for its journals and (2) bundles subscriptions for their publications in a way that lesser journals are included together with valuable ones. Because of (1), some academic libraries cannot afford to purchase important journals. And because of (2), libraries are required to spend a considerable amount of money to pay for many journals they don't want in order to get a few journals they consider essential. So, those college and university libraries that cannot afford the cost of individual Elsevier journals, or the price of the bundled subscription service established by the publisher, are unable to provide their students and professors with access to some important academic publications.[46]

What many of the signatories of this petition also find troublesome is the business scheme used by Elsevier and other leading academic publishers (such as Springer, Wiley, and Informa, who were also later included in the boycott). These publishers depend on scholars to submit their manuscripts for publication and to serve as (peer) reviewers for submitted manuscripts in determining which ones are eventually accepted for publication. Additionally, scholars also organize and guest-edit special issues (on topical themes) for many of these journals. Yet, these contributing scholars typically receive no payment for either their (authored) publications or their reviewing and guest-editing services. While this is generally not a problem for many professors seeking promotion or tenure at their universities—as their professional service can enhance their academic careers—many scientists argue that their published research (which was both freely submitted by them and funded by taxpayer money) should be more generally available to the public.

However, most scholars have virtually no control over how their published work is either disseminated or restricted, because they are typically required to transfer copyright of their work (as we saw in Chapter 8) to publishers such as Elsevier. This means that the publisher and not the author(s), or the taxpayers who helped fund the research, have total control over the publications. As a result, access to these published works can be limited only to large or well-off universities that can pay the high prices charged by Elsevier and other major publishers.

RWA's critics also worried about the profit incentives that drive major publishers. Whereas scholars enjoy having their published work widely accessible, publishing companies are motivated by the corporate profit model. So, restricting access to scholarly papers can work in the publisher's favor by driving up the cost to ensure greater revenue and profit margins. In 2011, Elsevier's revenues were in excess of 3.2 billion dollars (U.S.) and its profit rate was 36%, which is well above the average of many industries.[47] Elsevier has defended its profits by pointing to its efficient business model. But critics have responded by noting that those profits were significantly subsidized by "free labor" from scholars and by taxpayers who funded the research. In light of the Elsevier boycott and other protests, RWA's cosponsors—Darrell Issa (R-CA) and Carolyn Maloney (D-NY)—announced that they would not proceed with pushing the bill through the formal legislative process. In early 2012, Elsevier also formally withdrew its support for RWA. The publishing company has since claimed, however, that its decision had nothing to do with the boycott.

The Cost of Knowledge boycott is still in effect (as of August 2015, and, as noted earlier, has acquired nearly 16,000 signatories of prominent scholars in multiple academic disciplines). Despite Elsevier's decision to withdraw its support for RWA, however, one thing seems fairly clear: the dispute about whether academic information should be greatly restricted or freely accessible remains hotly contested. One factor that may also influence the future direction of academic publishing is the recent proliferation of "open-access" journals. Just as OSS is freely available to the computer community (as we saw in Section 8.6), open-access journals are freely available to the academic community, as well as to ordinary users. These journals are still relatively new and have not yet earned the reputation of many of the prestigious journals published by Elsevier and other leading academic publishers. So, some skeptics of open-access publishing fear that the quality of the articles published in these journals may not be as high as those in journals using the traditional model. However, the current trend seems to be favoring a movement toward open access, especially as many of these journals are gaining respect in the academic community. And if this trend continues, it may help to preserve the information commons and thus make scientific- and health-related information more accessible to the general public.

8.8.3 Intellectual Property Battles in the Near Future

We conclude this section and chapter by noting that current IP disputes over digital information seem to be as contentious as ever. Both sides stand prepared to muster their resources for the future battles that inevitably lie ahead. Copyright owners and corporations will no doubt continue to lobby the U.S. Congress for stronger copyright protections. On the other side, academic and library organizations will likely continue to press hard with their objective of keeping online scientific and academic information freely accessible to students and the general public.

One thing that is clearly at stake in the ongoing IP dispute is the future status of the information commons, which as we saw in Section 8.7 appears to be shrinking. We have seen how difficult it can be to strike a balance that is acceptable to both sides in the dispute about digital IP. However, we have argued that if we employ the presumptive principle defended in this chapter—information wants to be shared—in our future policy debates about IP rights vs. the free flow of information, it may be possible to prevent the information commons from further erosion.

▶ 8.9 CHAPTER SUMMARY

In this chapter, we have examined disputes involving intellectual-property-right claims affecting digital information. In particular, we considered how current IP laws, especially those involving copyright and patents, can be applied to software and other forms of digital media. We saw that three distinct philosophical theories of property have been used to defend our current schemes of legal protection, and we examined some arguments used in the FSF and OSSS movements. We also saw that an alternative framework for analyzing property disputes affecting digital media, based on the "common good" approach, suggests that we need to take into account the fact that information's essential purpose or nature is to be shared and communicated. Ironically, however, we noted that the latest copyright laws, including the SBCTEA and DMCA, restrict the distribution, and thus the sharing, of information. We defended the view that "information is something that needs to be shared and communicated" as a (presumptive) guiding principle that can inform the contemporary debate about IP rights affecting digitized information. We also saw how the Creative Commons initiative provides a scheme that enables us to implement our presumptive principle in the digital world. Finally, we examined three recent legislative proposals that threaten the future of the information commons.

▶ REVIEW QUESTIONS

1. What is intellectual property?
2. How is intellectual property different from tangible property?
3. What is meant by the expression "intellectual object"?
4. Describe the difficulties that arose in determining whether computer software (as a kind of intellectual object) should be eligible for the kinds of legal protection (i.e., copyrights and patents) that are typically granted to authors and inventors of creative works.
5. Describe some of the key differences in the four legal schemes designed to protect intellectual property: copyrights, patents, trademarks, and trade secrets.
6. What is the SBCTEA, and why is it controversial?
7. What is the DMCA, and why is it controversial?
8. What is the principle of fair use?

9. What is the principle of "first sale" with respect to copyright law?
10. How were some controversies in the Napster dispute anticipated in the LaMacchia incident (involving Cynosure) at MIT in the mid-1990s?
11. What are the arguments for and against protecting software with patents?
12. Describe some of the jurisdictional issues/challenges involving intellectual property laws. What roles do TRIPS and WIPO play in addressing these issues?
13. Describe the rationale behind the labor theory of property. Is it a plausible philosophical theory when used to justify intellectual property rights?
14. What is the utilitarian theory of property? Can it justify the protection of software?
15. How does the personality theory of property differ from both the labor and the utilitarian property theories?
16. What is the Free Software Foundation (FSF), and what does it advocate?
17. What is GNU?
18. What is the Open Source Software (OSS) initiative, and how is it different from FSF?
19. What is meant by the expression "information commons"?
20. What is the Creative Commons (CC) initiative?
21. What are PIPA and SOPA, and why are they controversial?
22. What is RWA, and how did it influence "The Cost of Knowledge" boycott?

▶ DISCUSSION QUESTIONS

23. Why does Richard Stallman believe that software should be free? How is Stallman's view about the ownership of computer programs both similar to and different from that advocated by the Open Source Software initiative? What do we mean by the expression "information wants to be shared"? How is it different from the position "information wants to be free"?
24. Why does Lawrence Lessig believe that the information commons, or what he calls the "innovations commons," is disappearing? How can Lessig's position be compared to Boyle's analysis of the "fencing off" of digital information in what he calls the "second enclosure" movement? Can the Creative Commons (CC) initiative help to preserve the information commons? Explain.
25. Critics argue that more and more information in digital form is being "fenced off" because of recent copyright legislation. Yet owners of proprietary information fear that they could lose control of their property without those laws. How can we achieve an appropriate balance between those who hold legal rights to proprietary information and ordinary users who wish to access, share, and communicate that information?
26. In Chapter 5, we saw that privacy advocates argue for greater control of personal information by individuals, while many in the commercial sector argue for increased access to that information. In this chapter, we saw that those positions have become reversed—entrepreneurs argue for increased control over the flow of information on the Internet, while ordinary users argue for greater access to that information. Is there an irony, perhaps even an inconsistency, here? Can this inconsistency be resolved in a logically coherent manner? How? Explain.

Scenarios for Analysis

1. You are taking a course on the history of computing at your university. One of the requirements for the course is a 25-page research paper. Your professor for that course is concerned that some students may be purchasing research papers from Internet sites, while others may be submitting papers that are highly plagiarized. So, your professor decides to use an online plagiarism-detecting system to have all of the papers submitted in this class verified (by being matched against a large repository or database of student papers) for their originality and authenticity. The company that owns the plagiarism-detecting system, however, has a controversial policy with regard to ownership of student papers. Specifically, they claim to own—that is, hold the copyright to—every paper your professor submits to them, so that those papers can be included in the company's proprietary database. Thus, all of the students in your class are required to sign a transfer of copyright form when they submit their research papers. You are very annoyed by this, however, because you want to maintain ownership of your paper. In fact, you plan to use some material in your paper in a section of your senior thesis project. Next, you approach your professor about your concern. Although she is sympathetic

to your position, she also points out that she is not able to make any exceptions because of the agreement the university has with the company contracted to verify the authenticity of student papers.

What would you do in this scenario? Based on the theories of property that we examined in Chapter 8, what kind of argument would you make to your professor (and to your university's administration, if necessary) that you, and you alone, should be able to retain ownership (i.e., hold the copyright) for your paper?

2. Professor Bill Smith, who teaches computer science courses at Technical University in the United States, recently received an email from a graduate student in India, named Raj, who is working on a master's degree in computer science. Raj notes in the email that he came across an abstract of a paper by Smith, which appears to be very important for a final project that is required for Raj to complete his master's degree. Unfortunately, the library at the university where Raj is studying does not subscribe to the journal in which Smith's paper is published. When Raj contacted the journal about purchasing the article, he was informed that the cost was $50 (U.S.). Unfortunately, Raj does not have the money to pay for this article; so he asks Professor Smith if he would be willing to email him a copy for personal use (i.e., to read and reference in his project). Smith is eager to help Raj, but is also concerned about copyright issues in distributing the article electronically. Although Smith has a copy of the article (in PDF format) on his desktop computer, he is reluctant to send Raj an electronic copy because of his interpretation of the DMCA (described in Section 8.2). But Smith is conflicted because he is eager to help Raj. Smith also wishes to have his article available as widely as possible for scholars to use; furthermore, he believes that the publisher is charging Raj (and others) an excessive price for the article. What should Professor Smith do in this situation?

▶ ENDNOTES

1. Swift remarks are quoted in Linshi (2014).
2. In composing Scenario 8–1, I have cited some statistical data included in two sources: Becker (2012) and "Can You Use Spotify and Still Be an Ethical Music Buyer?" (2013). *Every Record Tells a Story*, July 28. Available at: http://everyrecord-tellsastory.com/2013/07/28/can-you-use-spotify-and-still-be-an-ethical-music-buyer/.
3. In composing Sections 8.1 and 8.2, I have drawn from and expanded upon some concepts and distinctions introduced in Tavani (2002).
4. For example, see Averill (2015).
5. See, for example, Hettinger (1997) and Spinello and Tavani (2005).
6. For more details, see Grodzinsky, Miller, and Wolf (2004).
7. See http://www.austlii.edu.au/au/legis/cth/num_act/caa1980213/.
8. See https://w2.eff.org/IP/DMCA/states/.
9. See Moor's definitions of "policy vacuum" and "conceptual muddle" included in Chapter 1.
10. For more details affecting this ruling, see *United States v. LaMacchia*. (1994). 871 F Supp 535.
11. See http://www.copyright.gov/docs/2265_stat.html.
12. For more details affecting this ruling, see *A&M Records Inc. v. Napster Inc.* (2001). 239 F 3d 1004.
13. See Grodzinsky and Tavani (2005) for more details about some of the controversies affecting the RIAA vs. Verizon case.
14. For more detail, see S. Kalara (2007). "Now the RIAA wants Universities to get campus-wide Napster subscription or 'lose all federal aid.'" Available at http://ngemu.com/threads/riaa-tells-universities-to-stop-p2p-downloading-or-lose-all-federal-funding.95933/. Also see Grodzinsky and Tavani (2008) for an analysis of some of the privacy-vs.-property issues at stake in this controversy.
15. My analysis of streaming controversies in this section draws from information included in three sources: Linshi (2014), Becker (2012), and "Can You Use Spotify and Still Be an Ethical Music Buyer?" (2013). Available at http://everyrecord-tellsastory.com/2013/07/28/can-you-use-spotify-and-still-be-an-ethical-music-buyer/.
16. Doctorow (2014), p. 471.
17. Samuelson (2004). Also see Samuelson (2005) for an excellent analysis of key legal issues involving this controversial case, including the accounts of the lower court's ruling leading up to the Supreme Court's decision.
18. *Ibid.* For more details affecting this ruling, see *MGM Studios Inc. v. Grokster Ltd.* (2005). 545 US 913.
19. See http://www.uspto.gov/.
20. For more details affecting this ruling, see *Gottschalk v. Benson* (1972). 409 U.S. 63. A description of key issues in this case is included in Snapper (1995).
21. See *Diamond v. Diehr* (1981). 450 U.S. 175. Also, see Snapper (1995) for an excellent analysis of this case.
22. See, for example, http://en.wikipedia.org/wiki/Software_patent.
23. See http://www.uspto.gov/sites/default/files/trademarks/law/Trademark_Statutes.pdf.
24. For more details affecting this ruling, see *America Online Inc. v. AT&T Corp.* (2001). 243 F. 3d 812.
25. See http://www.wipo.int/sme/en/ip_business/trade_secrets/trade_secrets.htm.
26. See http://www.wto.org/english/tratop_E/trips_e/trips_e.htm.
27. See http://www.wipo.int/treaties/en/ip/berne/trtdocs_wo001.html.
28. See http://www.wipo.int/portal/index.html.en.
29. See https://torrentfreak.com/the-pirate-bay-trial-the-verdict-090417/

30. See http://www.law.cornell.edu/ucc/; http://www.satisfice.com/articles/kanersweng.pdf; and http://www.law.upenn.edu/bll/archives/ulc/ecom/ueta_final.pdf.
31. In composing Section 8.5, I have drawn from and expanded upon some concepts and distinctions introduced in Tavani (2002).
32. For a more detailed discussion of the ways in which Locke's labor theory applies to the contemporary IP debate, see Tavani (2005).
33. See http://www.pophistorydig.com/?tag=the-beatles-revolution.
34. See http://www.gnu.org/philosophy/free-sw.html.
35. See http://www.gnu.org/copyleft/gpl.html.
36. See Grodzinsky, Miller, and Wolf (2004).
37. See http://www.opensource.org/.
38. In composing Sections 8.7.1–8.7.3, I have drawn from and expanded upon some concepts and distinctions introduced in Tavani (2002).
39. Doctorow (2014), p. 93.
40. See Hardin (1968) for more detail.
41. Buchanan and Campbell (2005), p. 229.
42. See the account of the original "fencing off" of the physical commons in Rose, Mark. 1993. *Authors and Owners: The Invention of Copyright*. Cambridge, MA: Harvard University Press.
43. Buchanan and Campbell, p. 226.
44. See "PIPA Vote: Sen. Harry Reid Postpones Vote, Seeking Compromise On Anti-Piracy Bill." *Huffington Post*, January 20. Available at http://www.huffingtonpost.com/2012/01/20/pipa-vote-harry-reid-piracy_n_1218702.html?ir=Technology.
45. See, for example, Fischman (2012) and The Cost of Knowledge (2015), available at http://thecostofknowledge.com/.
46. For more detail, see http://thecostofknowledge.com/.
47. See http://en.wikipedia.org/wiki/Elsevier.

▶ REFERENCES

Aharonian, Gregory. 2001. "Does the Patent Office Respect the Software Community?" In K. W. Bowyer, ed. *Ethics and Computing: Living Responsibly in a Computerized World*. 2nd ed. New York: IEEE Press, pp. 296–98.

Averill, Marylin. 2015. "Intellectual Property." In J. Britt Holbrook and Carl Mitcham, eds. *Ethics, Science, Technology, and Engineering: A Global Resource*. Vol. 1, 2nd ed. Farmington Hills, MI: Macmillan Reference, pp. 569–75.

Becker, Jeff. 2012. "Spotify vs. iTunes vs. File-Sharing vs. Streaming and the Ethical Battle over Music Ownership," July 15. Available at http://twths.org/opinion-spotify-vs-itunes-vs-file-sharing-vs-streaming-and-the-ethical-battle-over-music-ownership/.

Boyle, James. 2004. "A Politics of Intellectual Property: Environmentalism for the Net." In R. A. Spinello and H. T. Tavani, eds. *Readings in CyberEthics*. 2nd ed. Sudbury, MA: Jones and Bartlett Publishers, pp. 273–93.

Boyle, James. 2006. "Enclosing the Human Genome: What Squabbles Over Genetic Patents Can Teach Us." In H. T. Tavani, ed. *Ethics, Computing, and Genomics*. Sudbury, MA: Jones and Bartlett, pp. 255–77.

Burk, Dan L. 2003. "Anti-Circumvention Misuse: How I Stopped Worrying and Love the DMCA." *IEEE Technology and Society Magazine* 22, no. 3: 40–47.

Buchanan, Elizabeth A., and James Campbell. 2005. "New Threats to Intellectual Freedom: The Loss of the Information Commons Through Law and Technology in the U.S." In R. A. Spinello and H. T. Tavani, eds. *Intellectual Property Rights in a Networked World: Theory and Practice*. Hershey, PA: Idea Group/Information Science Publishing, pp. 225–42.

Capurro, Ralphael, and Birger Hjørland. 2003. "The Concept of Information." In B. Cronin, ed. *Annual Review of Science and Technology*. Vol. 37, Chapter 8, 343–411. Available at http://www.capurro.de/infoconcept.html.

Chopra, Samir, and Scott D. Dexter. 2009. "Free Software, Economic 'Realities' and Information Justice." *Computers and Society* 39, no. 3: 12–26.

Coy, Wolfgang. 2007. "On Sharing Intellectual Properties in Global Communities." In J. Fruhbauer, R. Capurro, and T. Hassmanninger, eds. *Localizing the Internet: Ethical Issues in Intercultural Perspective*. Munich: Fink Verlag, pp. 279–88.

De George, Richard T. 2003. *The Ethics of Information Technology and Business*. Malden, MA: Blackwell.

Doctorow, Cory. 2014. *Information Doesn't Want to Be Free: Laws for the Internet Age*. San Francisco, CA: McSweeney's.

Fischman, Josh. 2012. "Elsevier Publishing Boycott Gathers Steam Among Academics." *Chronicle of Higher Education*, January 30. Available at http://chronicle.com/blogs/wiredcampus/elsevier-publishing-boycott-gathers-steam-among-academics/35216.

Girasa, Roy J. 2002. *Cyberlaw: National and International Perspectives*. Upper Saddle River, NJ: Prentice Hall.

Grodzinsky, Frances S., Keith Miller, and Marty J. Wolf. 2004. "Ethical Issues in Open Source Software." In R. A. Spinello and H. T. Tavani, eds. *Readings in CyberEthics*. 2nd ed. Sudbury, MA: Jones and Bartlett, pp. 305–21.

Grodzinsky, Frances S., and Herman T. Tavani. 2005. "P2P Networks and the *Verizon v. RIAA* Case: Implications for Personal Privacy and Intellectual Property." *Ethics and Information Technology* 7, no. 4: 243–50.

Grodzinsky, Frances S., and Herman T. Tavani. 2008. "Online File Sharing: Resolving the Tensions between Privacy and Property Interests." *Computers and Society* 38, no. 4: 28–39.

Grosso, Andrew. 2000. "The Promise and the Problems of the No Electronic Theft Act." *Communications of the ACM* 43, no. 2 (February): 23–26.

Halbert, Debora J. 1999. *Intellectual Property in the Information Age: The Politics of Expanding Ownership Rights*. Westport, CT: Quorum Books.

Hardin, Garret. 1968. "The Tragedy of the Commons." *Science* 162: 1243–48.

Heller, Michael. 1998. "The Tragedy of the Anticommons: From Marx to Markets." *Harvard Law Review* 111: 611–28.

Henderson, Katherine A, Richard A. Spinello, and Tomas A. Lipinski. 2007. "Prudent Policy? Reassessing the Digital Millennium Copyright Act." *Computers and Society* 37, no. 4: 25–40.

Hettinger, Edwin. 1997. "Justifying Intellectual Property." In A. D. Moore, ed. *Intellectual Property: Moral, Legal, and International Dilemmas*. Lanham, MD: Rowman and Littlefield, pp. 57–80.

Himma, Kenneth Einar. 2005. "Information and Intellectual Property Protection: Evaluating the Claim That Information

Should Be Free." *APA (American Philosophical Newsletter) on Philosophy and Law* 4, no. 2: 3–8.

Lessig, Lawrence. 2002. *The Future of Ideas: The Fate of the Commons in a Connected World*. New York: Random House.

Lessig, Lawrence. 2004. "Creative Freedom for All: Done Right, Copyrights Can Inspire the Next Digital Revolution." *Wired* (November): 188–89.

Linshi, Jack. 2014. "Here's Why Taylor Swift Pulled Her Music from Spotify." *TIME Magazine*, Nov. 3. Available at http://time.com/3554468/why-taylor-swift-spotify/.

Moore, Adam. 2008. "Personality-Based, Rule-Utilitarian, and Lockean Justifications of Intellectual Property." In K. E. Himma and H. T. Tavani, eds. *The Handbook of Information and Computer Ethics*. Hoboken, NJ: John Wiley and Sons, pp. 105–30.

Moore, Adam, and Kenneth E. Himma. 2014. "Intellectual Property." *Stanford Encyclopedia of Philosophy*. Available at http://plato.stanford.edu/entries/intellectual-property/.

McFarland, Michael C. 2004. "Intellectual Property, Information, and the Common Good." In R. A. Spinello and H. T. Tavani, eds. *Readings in CyberEthics*. 2nd ed. Sudbury MA: Jones and Bartlett Publishers, pp. 294–304.

McFarland, Michael C. 2005. "Whose Bytes? A Common Good View of Computer Ethics." Paper presented at the 2005–2006" *Humanities Lecture Series*, Rivier University, Nashua NH, November 10.

Ng, Alina. 2011. *Copyright Law and the Progress of Science and the Useful Arts*. Cheltenham, UK. Edward Elgar.

Onsrud, Harlan. 1998. "The Tragedy of the Information Commons." In D. Taylor, ed. *Policy Issues in Modern Cartography*. Oxford, UK: Pergamon, pp. 141–58.

Raymond, Eric. 2004. "The Cathedral and the Bazaar." In R. A. Spinello and H. T. Tavani, eds. *Readings in CyberEthics*. 2nd ed. Sudbury, MA: Jones and Bartlett Publishers, pp. 367–96.

Samuelson, Pamela. 2004. "What's at Stake in *MGM v. Grokster*? Seeking to Balance the Needs of Copyright Holders and Technology Developers." *Communication of the ACM* 47, no. 2: 15–20.

Samuelson, Pamela. 2005. "Legally Speaking: Did MGM Really Win the Grokster Case?" *Communication of the ACM* 48, no. 10: 19–24.

Snapper, John W. 1995. "Intellectual Property Protections for Computer Software." In D. G. Johnson and H. Nissenbaum, eds. *Computing, Ethics, and Social Values*. Englewood Cliffs, NJ: Prentice Hall, pp. 181–89.

Spinello, Richard A. 2003. "The Future of Open Source Software: Let the Market Decide." *Journal of Information, Communication, and Ethics in Society* 1, no. 4: 217–34.

Spinello, Richard. 2008. "Intellectual Property: Intellectual and Moral Challenges of Online File Sharing." In K. E. Himma and H. T. Tavani, eds. *The Handbook of Information and Computer Ethics*. Hoboken, NJ: John Wiley and Sons, pp. 553–69.

Spinello, Richard A., and Herman T. Tavani. 2005. "Intellectual Property Rights: From Theory to Practical Implementation." In R. A. Spinello and H. T. Tavani, eds. *Intellectual Property Rights in a Networked World: Theory and Practice*. Hershey, PA: Idea Group, pp. 1–65.

Stallman, Richard. 2004. "Why Software Should Be Free." In T. W. Bynum and S. Rogerson, eds. *Computer Ethics and Professional Responsibility*. Malden, MA: Blackwell, pp. 294–310.

Tavani, Herman T. 2002. "'Information Wants to Be Shared': An Alternative Framework for Approaching Intellectual Property Disputes in an Information Age." *Catholic Library World* 73, no. 2: 94–104.

Tavani, Herman T. 2005. "Locke, Intellectual Property, and the Information Commons." *Ethics and Information Technology* 7, no. 2: 87–97.

Warwick, Shelly. 2004. "Is Copyright Ethical? An Examination of the Theories, Laws, and Practices Regarding the Private Ownership of Intellectual Work in the United States." In R. A. Spinello and H. T. Tavani, eds. *Readings in CyberEthics*. 2nd ed. Sudbury, MA: Jones and Bartlett Publishers, pp. 305–21.

▶ FURTHER READINGS

Barrett, William, Christopher Price, and Thomas Hunt. 2008. *iProperty: Profiting from Ideas in an Age of Global Information*. Hoboken, NJ: John Wiley and Sons.

Boyle, James. 2008. *The Public Domain: Enclosing the Commons of the Mind*. New Haven, CT: Yale University Press.

Chopra, Samir, and Scott D. Dexter. 2008. *Decoding Liberation: The Promise of Free and Open Source Software*. New York: Routledge.

De George, Richard T. 2010. "Intellectual Property Rights." In G. G. Brenkert and Tom L. Beauchamp, eds. *The Oxford Handbook of Business Ethics*. New York: Oxford University Press, pp. 408–38.

Grodzinsky, Frances S., and Marty J. Wolf. 2008. "Ethical Interest in Free and Open Source Software." In K. E. Himma and H. T. Tavani, eds. *The Handbook of Information and Computer Ethics*. Hoboken, NJ: John Wiley and Sons, pp. 245–72.

Merges, Robert. 2011. *Justifying Intellectual Property*. Cambridge, MA: Harvard University Press.

Spinello, Richard A., and Maria Bottis. 2009. *A Defense of Intellectual Property Rights*. Cheltenham, UK: Edward Elgar.

CHAPTER

9

Regulating Commerce and Speech in Cyberspace

LEARNING OBJECTIVES

Upon completing this chapter, you will successfully be able to:

- Differentiate and explain the relevance of key questions, concepts, and categories at the core of *Internet regulation*,
- Understand digital rights management (DRM) technology and explain why it is controversial from the perspective of regulating cyberspace,
- Describe the different kinds of regulation-related challenges posed by e-mail spam and assess the different kinds of arguments that have been advanced to show why spam is morally objectionable,
- Explain the difficulties involved in balancing free speech and censorship in online contexts and forums,
- Describe the difficulties involved in framing online pornography laws that will adequately protect children and evaluate the arguments that have been advanced to restrict and to abolish online pornography,
- Differentiate between online hate speech and online speech that can cause physical harm to others,
- Understand what is meant by "network neutrality," and explain how the outcome of the network neutrality debate will likely affect the future of the Internet.

In this chapter, we examine a wide range of issues and controversies that have led to a call for strong regulatory proposals in cyberspace. We begin our analysis with a scenario that briefly describes a recent incident involving two highly controversial organizations.

▶ SCENARIO 9–1: *Anonymous* and the Ku Klux Klan

The "Anonymous" group is an international network of hackers and hacktivists who have gained notoriety by disrupting governmental and commercial Web sites to make political statements and/or advance political causes. (Recall our earlier discussions of controversial aspects of Anonymous in Chapters 6 and 8.) In November 2014, Anonymous targeted the Ku Klux Klan (KKK) when that controversial group threatened protestors in Ferguson, Missouri (following an incident in which Michael Brown, a young black man, was shot dead by a white police officer). Some members of Anonymous hacked into two KKK Twitter accounts, and others launched cyberattacks against the Web sites of white supremacist groups that Anonymous believed to be either sympathetic to or affiliated with the KKK. Following these attacks, Anonymous also made public the names of specific individuals it believed to be KKK members.[1] ■

Was Anonymous justified in carrying out these cyber-related attacks against the KKK? Should some form of Internet regulation that bans groups like the KKK from conducting racist online activities have been in place beforehand? On the one hand, many of the KKK's activities, as well as those of other white supremacist groups, are protected by free speech, whether their activities are carried out in physical space or in cyberspace. On the other hand, these kinds of groups also engage in a form of speech that "can cause physical harm to others." The latter kind of speech, as we shall see, is not clearly protected. But who, if anyone, is responsible for regulating the Internet with regard to both kinds of speech?

In the case involving the KKK and Ferguson protestors, Anonymous decided to intervene in a way that was not officially sanctioned by any existing laws. Furthermore, Anonymous' tactics in this incident clearly violated the law, since (as we saw in Chapters 6 and 7) acts of hacking and hacktivism are illegal. (And, in this case at least, it is not clear that "two wrongs make a right"!) The Anonymous–KKK scenario not only illustrates why Internet regulation is so controversial but also suggests how one's political ideology can influence his or her beliefs about which forms of online speech should be regulated and which should not.

The purpose of Scenario 9–1 was not to offer a resolution to the thorny issues underlying the Anonymous–KKK controversy, but to get us to begin thinking about some reasons why clearer and more explicit Internet regulation might be needed. Other cases and scenarios also could have been used to illustrate some of the reasons why many believe that stronger regulatory frameworks could help make the Internet a safer place. Consider, for example, the case of Tyler Clementi, an 18-year-old student at Rutgers University who committed suicide in 2010, following a cyber-related incident that received international attention. Clementi's roommate, Dharun Ravi, had secretly set up a Web cam(era) in their dorm room that exposed Clementi in a romantic encounter with a male student. Ravi was never formally charged in Clementi's suicide/death, but the incident raised questions about whether explicit regulatory schemes were needed to prevent a user's making a video of someone's activities publicly available on the Web without first getting that person's consent. So, we can begin to see why arguments for stronger regulation on the Internet have been advanced.

Disputes about whether and how to regulate cyberspace are hardly new; in fact, they have been going on at some level since the inception of the Internet itself. In this chapter, we will see that many conservative organizations have argued for regulatory schemes in the form of censorship of certain kinds of speech in cyberspace. Some liberal groups, on the contrary, who oppose any restrictions on free speech in cyberspace, argue that e-commerce, not speech, needs to be regulated.

For our purposes, regulatory concerns affecting "speech" will include issues involving pornography and hate speech, while e-commerce regulation issues include concerns affecting e-mail spam and digital rights management (DRM). With respect to the latter, we will also see why many are now concerned about a kind of cyberspace regulation that can be enforced via technology itself, that is, by means of "regulation by code" (which is exacerbated by DRM technologies). Some critics worry that regulation by code is becoming the default regulatory scheme in cyberspace. Before examining specific topics, however, we first consider some conceptual distinctions and clarifications that can better inform both our understanding and analysis of Internet regulation.

▶ 9.1 INTRODUCTION AND BACKGROUND ISSUES: SOME KEY QUESTIONS AND CRITICAL DISTINCTIONS AFFECTING INTERNET REGULATION

Weckert (2007) suggests that when discussing cyberspace regulation, we need to ask two separate questions:

1. *Can* it be regulated?
2. *Should* it be regulated?

Asking question (1) implies that it is not clear whether cyberspace can be effectively regulated. In this chapter, we will operate on the assumption that it can, in fact, be regulated. However, we acknowledge that regulation schemes can be difficult to implement and enforce, and we concede that regulation can have undesirable side effects in terms of both cost and efficiency.

Our main focus is on question (2), that is, the normative question as to whether cyberspace *ought* to be regulated. This question, as Weckert points out, can also be broken down into two separate questions. For example, we can ask whether the Internet should be "regulated in general" or whether it should be "regulated in any one country in the absence of cooperation by others."[2] In a later section of this chapter, we examine some controversies affecting consensus at the international level with regard to regulatory schemes and practices.

Despite some of the challenges that arise in the various schemes proposed for regulating cyberspace, Weckert and Al-Saggaf (2008) note that we should not presume against Internet regulation. In fact, they believe that a "strong moral case" can be made for regulating the Internet's content.[3] Others have suggested that a similar case can be made for regulating commerce in cyberspace. Before examining specific issues affecting the regulation of cyberspace, however, it is useful to consider two additional questions:

a. What do we mean by *cyberspace*?
b. What do we mean by *regulation*, particularly as it applies to cyberspace?

We postpone our analysis of (b) until Section 9.1.2. In answering (a), we first consider whether cyberspace is an actual "place" or whether it is best understood as a medium of some sort.

9.1.1 Is Cyberspace a Medium or a Place?

In Chapter 1, we loosely defined the Internet as the network of interconnected computers and devices, and we suggested that the terms "Internet" and "cyberspace" were roughly equivalent. In this chapter, we use the two terms interchangeably. But we have not yet described the ontology of cyberspace, that is, we have not said what, exactly, cyberspace *is*. For example, is it a *place*, that is, a virtual space that consists of all the data and information that resides in the connected servers and databases that make up the Internet? Or is cyberspace a (relatively new) *medium*?

Some believe that the Internet is best understood as a new kind of medium, significantly different from earlier media, such as the telephone or television. Whereas the telephone is a "one-to-one medium" and television is a "one-to-many medium," Goodwin (1995, 2003) describes the Internet as a "many-to-many medium." He also notes that one does not need to be wealthy to have access to this medium; nor does one need to win the approval of an editor or a publisher to speak his or her mind there. But should the Internet be viewed as a medium, or can it be better understood as a public space? Camp and Chien (2000) argue for the latter view.

Camp and Chien differentiate four types of media: *publisher*, *broadcast*, *distributor*, and *common carrier*. An example of a publisher is a newspaper or a magazine, and broadcast media include television and radio. Telephone companies and cable companies are instances of common carriers, conduits for the distribution of information. Camp and Chien argue that none of the media models are appropriate for understanding the Internet. Instead, they believe that a spatial model—one in which cyberspace is viewed as a public space with certain digital characteristics—is more plausible.

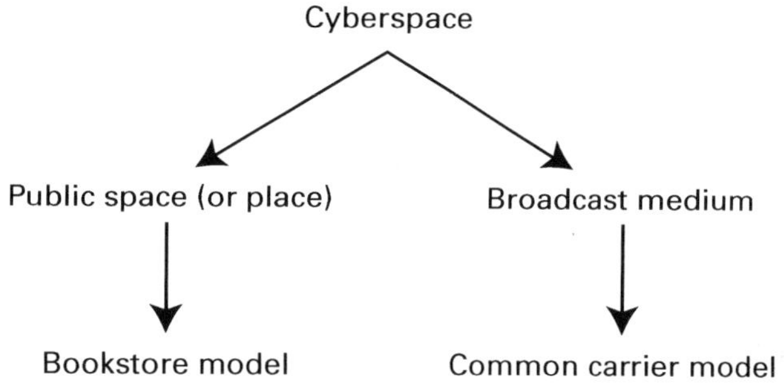

Cyberspace → Public space (or place) → Bookstore model
Cyberspace → Broadcast medium → Common carrier model

Figure 9-1 The ontology of cyberspace.

But can we model the Internet accurately as a public space, as Camp and Chien suggest? Or is it better understood as a new kind of *medium*, as Goodwin and others have argued? We are making more than a mere semantic distinction, because, as Camp and Chien point out, the model we use can influence our decisions about public policies on the Internet. If the Internet is viewed as a public space, for example, then there are good legal and moral reasons for ensuring that everyone has access to it. The ontology of cyberspace will ultimately determine whether and how we should (or perhaps should not) regulate it.

Consider the rules used to regulate the distribution and sale of "adult" magazines and videos in physical space. Bookstores and video rental stores are permitted to carry and sell such merchandise, and because a store is a physical place, certain sections can be partitioned so that adults can visit them but individuals under a certain age cannot. The rules are drastically different, however, for broadcast media such as television, where the Federal Communications Commission (FCC) regulates which kinds of content can be broadcast over the airwaves. Movies that can be rented and sold only to adults in stores can also be deemed inappropriate (by the FCC) for general television viewers. So before we can successfully resolve questions about Internet regulation, we need to keep in mind that the model we use to understand cyberspace will also strongly influence which regulatory schemes are appropriate.

Figure 9-1 illustrates our two models of cyberspace.

9.1.2 Two Categories of Cyberspace Regulation: Regulating Content and Regulating Process

To "regulate" means to monitor or control a product, process, or set of behaviors according to certain requirements, standards, or protocols. Sometimes regulatory discussions about cyberspace have centered on its *content*, for example, whether online pornography and hate speech should be censored. And sometimes the regulatory discussions have focused on which kinds of processes, that is, rules and policies, should be implemented and enforced in commercial transactions in cyberspace. Physical space is regulated in both ways.

Some regulatory agencies monitor the content, and others the process, of items in physical space. The Food and Drug Administration (FDA) monitors food products on the shelves of supermarkets to ensure that they meet health and nutrition standards; FDA regulations ensure that the contents of each food item both match and are accurately described by its label. Unlike the FDA, state public health boards do not regulate content; their regulations apply to conditions for compliance with community health standards. For example, public health officials inspect restaurants and grocery stores to ensure that they meet sanitation standards in their preparation and sale of food. So, an agency can regulate for content or process, or both.

In the commerce sector, federal and state agencies, such as the Federal Trade Commission (FTC) and the Security and Exchange Commission (SEC), enforce laws and policies that

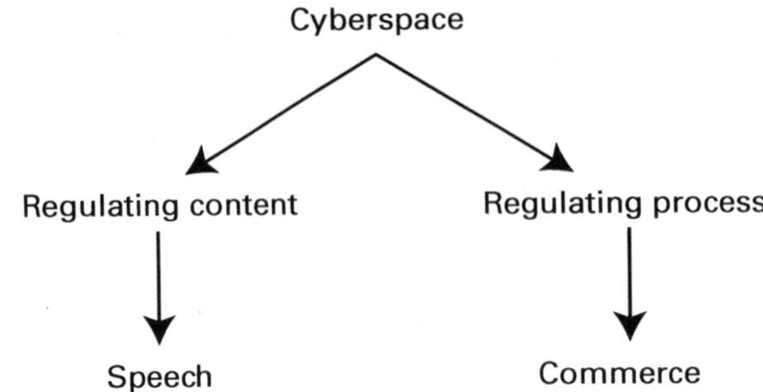

Figure 9-2 Two categories of cyberspace regulation.

apply to commercial activities and transactions; for example, they regulate against monopolies and other unfair business practices, such as those alleged in the Microsoft antitrust case in the late 1990s. Regulatory principles in the commerce sector also determine whether to permit mergers, such as the one between America Online (AOL) and Time Warner.

Figure 9-2 illustrates the ways in which cyberspace can be regulated.

It is not difficult to point out the positive effects that regulatory practices in physical space have for health and safety. Consider, for example, the role that state liquor boards (in the U.S.) play in regulating the distribution and sale of liquor: They determine who is and is not eligible for a license to distribute liquor in their state, and if a board determines that a licensed distributor has violated its licensing agreement with the state, its license can be revoked. And boards that regulate liquor can help to keep liquor out of the hands of minors and help to discourage an underground, or black, market for the sale of "bootleg liquor," which is not tested and certified as meeting standards of quality and authenticity. State liquor boards also help determine fair pricing to prevent unscrupulous merchants from price gouging. So, there are many good reasons for regulating the distribution and sale of liquor. But how can we extend this analogy to the Internet?

First, we can ask how we can possibly regulate cyberspace, which is inherently decentralized. Cyberspace is not compartmentalized neatly into state jurisdictions that can set up their own control boards. Does this mean that effective regulation of any type is impossible in cyberspace? Not according to Lessig (2000) and Agre (2005), who suggest that a decentralized cyberspace does not preclude Internet regulation from being carried out quite effectively. In describing the architecture of P2P (peer-to-peer) networks in cyberspace, Agre notes that decentralized institutions do not imply decentralized architectures, and vice versa. Lessig believes that in cyberspace, understanding architecture, or what he calls *code*, is the key to understanding how regulation works.

9.1.3 Four Modes of Regulation: The Lessig Model

Lessig describes four distinct but interdependent constraints, which he calls "modalities," for regulating behavior: *laws*, social *norms*, *market* pressures, and *architecture*. Before we apply each modality to cyberspace, consider how each can be applied in regulating behaviors in the physical world.

Cigarette smoking can be regulated through the passage and enforcement of explicit laws that make it illegal to smoke in public buildings. And we have specific laws that prohibit cigarette manufacturers from advertising on television or in magazines targeted at teenage audiences. Independent of explicit laws, however, social norms can also discourage cigarette smoking in public; for example, it is socially acceptable for homeowners to place "Thank you for not smoking in our house" signs on their front doors. And hotel owners and operators can, under social pressure from prospective guests, partition smoking and nonsmoking rooms and sections of their establishments even if there is no explicit law requiring them to do so.

Market pressures can also affect smoking behavior. Cigarettes can be priced so that only the wealthiest people can afford to buy them. Finally, merchants can impose an "architecture of control" on cigarettes by using physical constraints. All cigarettes sold in grocery stores could be located behind locked doors, causing interruptions in checkout transactions. A cashier might have to temporarily suspend the transaction, locate the store's manager, and get the proper authorization and the key to open the locked doors to remove the cigarettes. Contrast this architecture with one in which cigarettes are available in vending machines easily accessible to everyone, including minors.

To apply Lessig's fourfold distinction to cyberspace, we replace architecture, which is in physical or geographic space, with *code*. Code, for Lessig, consists of programs, devices, and protocols—that is, the sum total of the software and hardware—that constitute cyberspace. Like physical architecture in geographic space, code sets the terms upon which one can enter or exit cyberspace. Also like architecture, code is not optional. Lessig notes that we do not choose to obey the structures that architecture establishes. Just as we are subject to architectures of physical space, so we are subject to code in cyberspace; a physical door can block you from entering a physical building, and a password requirement can prevent your entering a Web site. And code can be used to limit access to Web sites by requiring that users accept cookies (see Chapter 5) if they wish to visit those sites. Lessig believes that code can either facilitate or deter access to, or transfer of, information in cyberspace.

In Chapter 1, we saw that Moor (2007) described computer technology as "logically malleable" because, unlike most other technologies that are dedicated to performing specific tasks, computers can be instructed through software to perform an indefinite number of diverse functions. Lessig (2004) also illustrates an aspect of this technology's malleability, describing how different computer architectures create very different kinds of environments. He draws an interesting comparison between early and present-day computer networks, noting that whereas the Internet of 1995 (or what he calls "NET 95") had a "libertarian architecture," current networks do not.

To illustrate differences between these two architectures, Lessig compares the computer network systems at the University of Chicago and Harvard University in the late 1990s. During that period, the University of Chicago's network was still like NET 95, because anyone could connect his or her machine directly to (phone) jacks on the campus. As such, the code at Chicago favored freedom, or free speech. At Harvard, on the other hand, one first had to register his or her machine before getting on to the Harvard's network. Once registered, all interactions with the network could be monitored and identified by Harvard's network administrators. Lessig points out that at the University of Chicago, "facilitating access" had been the ideal (at that time); at Harvard, on the contrary, "controlling access" was (and still is) the ideal.

Note that the underlying network protocols (i.e., TCP/IP) were the same for the computer systems at both Harvard University and the University of Chicago. But layered on top of Harvard's TCP/IP protocol was an additional set of protocols, or *code*, which, Lessig argues, "facilitates control." Why should we care about the differences between the two kinds of architectures? Lessig points out that in the NET 95 environment, one could roam the Internet freely and anonymously. Today, one cannot. Lessig concludes from this that we have moved from what was once an "architecture of freedom" to an "architecture of control." He also concludes that in cyberspace, code is a more effective regulator than law. In fact, Lessig claims that in cyberspace, *code is the law*.[4]

▶ 9.2 DIGITAL RIGHTS MANAGEMENT (DRM)

To understand the force of Lessig's claim that (software) code is law, consider the role that "code" in the form of DRM tools plays in regulating digital media. DRM technologies allow content owners to regulate the flow of digital information by blocking access to it via "digital locks" supported by encryption mechanisms. The combination of DRM technology and copyright protection laws, such as the Digital Millennium Copyright Act (DMCA), makes it possible for the regulation and enforcement of policies and laws in cyberspace to a degree that never existed in the physical realm. DRM also makes it possible for corporations to make up new copyright-related rules and to enforce those rules via their own technologies and tools.

How is it possible for corporations to do this? First consider that, as Doctorow (2014) points out, there is no copyright law stating that it is illegal to skip through "piracy warnings" when viewing a movie on a DVD player. But suppose a viewer wishes to bypass or fast-forward through those warnings, as well as through a series of advertisements, displayed prior to the start of the movie. In this case, the viewer would likely have to break a "digital lock" (on the DVD player) to skip these segments of the DVD. But breaking that lock would violate DMCA's anticircumvention clause. (As we saw in Chapter 8, any program or device that circumvents DRM controls is in violation of Section 1201 of the DMCA.) Because the DMCA makes it illegal for someone to "descramble" a movie without permission, the (code that makes possible the) digital lock on the DVD player serves the same regulatory function as law (even where no explicit law exists). And because DMCA prohibits the development and use of technologies that could circumvent copyright management systems, it works hand in hand with DRM technology to control access to significant amounts of information now in digitized form.

9.2.1 Some Implications of DRM for Public Policy Debates Affecting Copyright Law

Critics worry about the many ways in which DRM technology can be used to enforce copyright law. Because software code in DRM systems is being developed and used with the express purpose of precluding the possibility of copyright infringement, Elkin-Koren (2000) fears that the traditional mechanism for debating public policy may now be closed to us. She notes that if the manufacturers of digital devices can decide what the copyright rules should be and if they are permitted to embed code in their products that enforces those rules, then there is no longer a need for, or even the possibility of, public policy debate about copyright issues.

Elkin-Koren notes that in the past, when individuals duplicated proprietary information by using the latest available technologies, we were often forced to question the viability of existing copyright laws in light of those new technologies vis-à-vis principles such as fair use (described in Chapter 8). She also notes that we could then engage in meaningful public policy debates about whether traditional copyright laws should apply or whether some new laws are needed. Thus we were able to challenge the viability and constitutionality of such laws through the judicial process.

However, Elkin-Koren worries that a framework for *balancing* the interests of individuals and the public, which in the past had been supported by "spirited policy debates" and judicial review, will no longer be possible in a world in which copyright policies are predetermined by code. As Spinello (2003) notes, restrictions embedded into computer code end up having the force of law without the checks and balances provided by the legal system. And Elkin-Koren argues that because of the technological controls embedded in software code (such as in DRM systems), our policies affecting information and digital media are becoming increasingly *privatized*. She also suggests that this trend toward privatization has enabled software companies to design code that reflects their own interests and values, without having to worry about any adverse effects that code can have for the public's interests.

Samuelson (2003), who also has been critical of technologies that regulate through embedded code, believes that DRM systems may violate the fair-use provision of copyright law. For example, she notes that DRM technology allows content owners to exercise far more control over uses of copyrighted works in digital media than what is provided by conventional copyright law. The claim that DRM threatens fair use has also been echoed by Grodzinsky and Bottis (2007) who argue that this technology has not only become an obstacle to fair use but has also changed our conventional understanding of "private use as fair use." Like Elkin-Koren, Samuelson, and other critics, Grodzinsky and Bottis worry that DRM is designed to protect digital content in a way that enables private interests to define the parameters of copyright law. In this sense, DRM schemes have clearly tipped the balance in favor of copyright owners who can now determine how and by whom their content may be used.

9.2.2 DRM and the Music Industry

One controversial use of DRM in the music industry, which has alarmed many critics, gained public attention because of an incident involving Sony BMG Music Entertainment and its "rootkit" technology. What, exactly, are *rootkits*, and what purpose(s) do they serve? Doctorow (2014) defines rootkits as "programs that covertly modify a computer's operating system to blind it to certain files and processes."[5] The DRM-related rootkit controversy involving Sony is illustrated in the following scenario.

▶ SCENARIO 9–2: The Sony Rootkit Controversy

Sony BMG used a DRM system called Extended Copy Protection (XCP) to protect its music CDs. In 2005, a blogger named Mark Russinovich posted an article that described the characteristics of the software protection scheme used by Sony. In that article, Russinovich (2005) disclosed certain flaws in the design of Sony's software that manifested themselves as security holes that could be exploited by malicious software such as viruses or worms. He also noted that Sony provided no "uninstall" program to remove XCP. Sony responded to this criticism by releasing a "software removal utility."

But Russinovich, in a follow-up blog article, noted that Sony's removal utility had only exacerbated privacy and security concerns about the software. For example, he pointed out that the program merely "unmasked" the hidden files in the "rootkit" component of XCP, but did not actually remove the rootkit itself. In November 2005, Sony offered a "new and improved" removal tool to uninstall the rootkit from affected Microsoft Windows computers.

Some of Sony's critics accused Sony of violating the privacy of its customers by using code that created a "backdoor" into their customers' machines. Other critics also claimed that Sony's DRM program, which gave the company control over its customers' machines in the name of copyright protection, itself infringed copyright law. And some critics argued that Sony violated the open source license agreement (see Chapter 8) because of the way in which it used some open source software code to build its protection system. In late 2005, Sony decided to back out of its copy protection software, recalling unsold CDs from all stores and allowing customers to exchange their CDs for versions that did not include the controversial software.[6] ■

One DRM-related question that arises in connection with Sony's use of its controversial rootkit software is: Can users trust content owners (such as Sony BMG) who, via DRM-related tools, are easily able to (i) spy on them and (ii) control aspects of their computers and electronic devices? Another question that arises in this case is whether Sony's actions can be justified solely on the grounds that music (and entertainment) companies require DRM systems (like the one used by Sony BMG) to protect their intellectual property. But even if the answer to the latter question is "yes," we can still ask if that justifies a company's use of rootkits to surreptitiously track and spy on its customers.

Another area of tension involving the use of DRM by the music industry has to do with "interoperability" across the devices on which digital music can be played. Interoperability enables users to download and play music on a variety of digital devices. However, it also challenges the notion that downloadable content can and should be restricted to proprietary devices controlled by the company that owns an "online store," such as iPods in the iTunes store. Internationally, there have been some efforts to promote interoperability. For example, in 2006, France's National Assembly passed a law that would force distributors of online music in France to remove DRM so that music could be played on any device (Hesseldahl 2006). However, many owners and distributors of music content feared that removing DRM to support interoperability would also result in opening the door to file sharing of copyrighted material without compensation for the content owners and distributors.

In 2007, EMI announced that it would sell its music without DRM on Apple Inc.'s iTunes music store. One trade-off, however, was that non-DRM-formatted music would cost slightly more than DRM versions. Proponents of this change, including the late Steve Jobs, have suggested that if DRM restrictions were lifted on music, there might be an influx of new stores and players (Jobs 2007). The ongoing debate about which kinds of roles DRM will play in the contexts of online music and interoperability will likely continue.[7]

Our discussion of Internet regulation thus far has focused mainly on controversies associated with regulating *process* (i.e., in the commercial sector), as opposed to regulating content. As we will see, the latter type of regulation often becomes embroiled in thorny issues affecting free speech. We examine some of those concerns in Section 9.4. First, however, we consider a particular kind of challenge for Internet regulation that straddles the divide between process and content: e-mail spam.

▶ 9.3 E-MAIL SPAM

What is *spam*, and why is it problematic from a social and moral perspective? It is interesting to note that some defenders of spam see it as an activity protected by free speech. However, most Internet users see spam as something that is at best a nuisance and at worst a serious threat to the efficient and safe functioning of their computers and devices. Miller and Moor (2008) point out that according to some estimates, as much as 80% of e-mails sent could qualify as spam. But they also note that there are "dramatically different definitions" of what can count as spam.

9.3.1 Defining Spam

While there is no universally agreed-upon definition of spam, it is typically viewed as e-mail that is *unsolicited*, *commercial*, and sent in *bulk* to multiple users. Is this definition adequate? Because spam is *unsolicited*, it is also nonconsensual. However, not all nonconsensual e-mails are spam. If you have an e-mail account, you have probably received unsolicited e-mail messages requesting information from you or informing you about an upcoming event; they may have been sent to you because you are a member of a particular social networking service (SNS) or because you have an e-mail address associated with an academic institution, government organization, and so forth. You may have considered some of these messages annoying, but are they necessarily spam?

Another feature of our working definition of spam is that it is *commercial*. However, some commercial e-mail you receive can be in the form of advertisements that you have authorized a commercial Web site to e-mail you. For example, you could have registered on an e-mail distribution list for a department store at which you frequently shop, requesting to be informed about upcoming sales and discount items. The e-mails you receive from this site, while commercial or promotional in nature, would not qualify as spam.

Spam is distributed in *bulk*, but not all e-mails distributed in that form necessarily qualify as spam. For example, some messages sent in bulk form (i.e., to an e-mail list) might have been directed at people in the group who are known by the sender; there could be some personal or professional connection between the sender and receiver of the e-mail message. So, our initial working definition of spam as e-mail that is "unsolicited, promotional, and sent in bulk" to multiple users would not seem adequate.

Miller and Moor believe that much of the popular discussion about spam in terms of what they describe as unsolicited commercial bulk e-mail (UCBE) is both "confused and degraded" because it fails to distinguish between UCBE that is "deceptive" and "intended to harm" and UCBE that is not. They also believe that the problems affecting e-mail spam can be better analyzed by focusing on a series of distinct, but interrelated, criteria such as the following:

- Content of the e-mail
- Intent of the sender
- Consequences of the receiver
- Consent of the receiver
- Relationship between the sender and the receiver
- Accountability of the sender and the degree of deception
- Number of identical e-mails sent[8]

Miller and Moor disagree with many critics of spam who tend to assume that all e-mail advertisements are deceptive. Alternatively, they believe that it is possible to distinguish between UCBE advertisements that (i) "misrepresent and are fraudulent" and (ii) "present information in a favorable light." They refer to the former as fraudulent UCBE (*F-UCBE*) and distinguish it from the nonfraudulent version they call nonfraudulent UCBE (*NF-UCBE*). They also believe that NF-UCBE requires a more complex ethical analysis than F-UCBE.

9.3.2 Why Is Spam Morally Objectionable?

Spinello (2006) believes that spam is morally objectionable for two reasons: one based on utilitarian grounds and the other on deontological considerations. In his view, spam not only has harmful consequences, but it also violates the individual autonomy of Internet users. First, consider some of the harmful consequences of spam—that is, its financial impacts, such as cost shifting and the consumption of valuable network resources. For example, spam consumes and strains valuable computing resources and thus contributes to the degradation of what Spinello calls the "fragile ecology of the Internet." Miller and Moor describe these kinds of abuses of the Internet as one more instance of "spoiling of the commons." (Recall our discussion of the "tragedy of the commons" in Chapter 8.)

Spinello argues that even if Internet resources were infinite and there were no negative utilitarian consequences, spam would still be morally objectionable because it does not respect individual users as persons. He believes that deontological arguments, such as Kant's (see Chapter 2), can be used to show why this is so. Recall that Kant argues that a practice has moral worth only if it can be universalizable. And, in Kant's system, a practice is universalizable only if it can coherently apply to all persons without exception. So, we need to ask: Could we universalize a coherent practice in which each e-mail user would allow spam to be sent and received by every other user? Could such a practice, if instituted, be logically coherent? On Kantian grounds, if spammers did not accept the principle that everyone should be able to send and receive spam, then they would be inconsistent. If spammers believed that only they should be permitted to send spam, then they would be making an exception for themselves. And if they granted themselves this exception while relying on the good will of ordinary users not to engage in the practice of spamming others, then spammers would be treating ordinary users merely as a means to their ends. So, Spinello makes a plausible case for why spam can be considered morally objectionable on deontological as well as utilitarian grounds.

Miller and Moor believe that an adequate ethical analysis of spam also needs to take into consideration criteria such as accountability and deception—generally, the "more deceptive the content and the less accountable the sender, the more blameworthy the sender becomes." Employing their distinction between NF-UCBE and F-UCBE, they argue that F-UCBE should always be condemned, whereas some cases of NF-UCBE can be justifiable from a moral point of view. For example, they point out that a whistle-blower might send a message to a large commercial mailing list to alert recipients of an injustice or a danger. Here, the whistle-blower may have justifiable reasons for sending the e-mail broadly and for wishing to be anonymous. Miller and Moor believe that in this whistle-blowing scenario, the "intent" of the sender needs to be taken into consideration. So, there can be some cases where sending spam in the form of NF-UCBE would be justifiable.

It is one thing to say that spam, at least in its F-UCBE form, is morally objectionable, but it is another to ask what can be done about it from a legal and public policy perspective. Because spam is very similar to the "junk mail" that we receive via the postal delivery system, we might ask why the same laws that apply to physical junk mail do not also apply to electronic spam. Although there are similarities between the two forms of junk mail, there are also relevant differences; practical and financial constraints determine how much physical junk mail merchants can send, but the same kinds of constraints do not apply in the case of electronic spam.

Miller and Moor believe that e-mail spam is also analogous to unsolicited commercial phone calls. And they point out that the latter have been significantly reduced in the United States through legislation, even though they have not been altogether eliminated. But they also note that because of the "open" nature of Internet architectures and protocols, spam has been far more resistant to the kinds of legislative and technological solutions used to discourage unsolicited commercial phone calls.

Various state laws against spam have been enacted in the United States, and in 2003, the U.S. Congress passed the Controlling the Assault of Non-Solicited Pornography and Marketing (CAN-SPAM) Act. That law, which went into effect in 2004, specifies criminal penalties that include a fine of $250 for each spam e-mail. However, critics of the CAN-SPAM Act note that spammers who use ISPs outside the United States to send their spam e-mail cannot be prosecuted under this act, which cannot be enforced internationally. Some critics are also skeptical as to whether any kind of legislation, even international laws, can solve the problem of spam.

▶ 9.4 FREE SPEECH VS. CENSORSHIP AND CONTENT CONTROL IN CYBERSPACE

So far in this chapter, we have examined a set of regulatory issues that either involved, or had implications for, electronic commerce. We next turn our attention to regulatory issues involving the *content* of cyberspace. Such issues center on the question as to whether all forms of online speech should be tolerated. In some instances, regulatory concerns affecting online speech and online commerce overlap. For example, questions concerning spam, considered in the preceding section, straddle the divide; some purveyors of spam have defended their practice on the grounds of free speech. However, the issues we examine in the remainder of this chapter affect the regulation of Internet content and thus tend to fall mainly under the category of speech.

Note that in this and in the following sections, we do not address the censorship or suppression of "political speech" by nation-states—an issue that is hotly debated because of practices involving governmental regulation of the Internet in the People's Republic of China and other nondemocratic countries. That concern is however addressed in Chapter 10 in our examination of democracy and democratic ideals in cyberspace. In Section 9.6.1, we examine some tensions between free speech and censorship that arise mainly in the United States and in the European Union countries.

9.4.1 Protecting Free Speech

Do all forms of online speech in the United States deserve to be protected under the U.S. Constitution's guarantee of free speech? According to the First Amendment of the U.S. Constitution, "Congress shall make no law . . . abridging the freedom of speech, or of the press." This passage, consisting of merely 14 words, has often been quoted by libertarians who strongly believe that the government should not intrude in matters involving our constitutionally guaranteed right to free speech. We should note, however, that free speech is not an absolute right. As in the case of other rights contained in the Bill of Rights, which comprise the first ten amendments to the Constitution, the right to free speech is *conditional* in the sense that it is only a right if "all things are equal." While one's right to free speech protects his/her freedom to express controversial ideas concerning politics, religion, and so forth, it does not grant him/her the right to shout "Fire!" in a crowded shopping mall or a movie theater (an analogy frequently made by analysts describing the limits of free speech as a conditional right).

Also, during times of war, one's ability to speak freely is sometimes constrained. For example, in the period immediately following the attacks of September 11, 2001, some Americans labeled the news commentators, reporters, and talk show hosts who criticized the Bush White House as "unpatriotic." Ordinarily, such criticisms are considered normal and in accordance with the principle of free speech, which is presumed by political commentators and the press. But at other times, social norms and market forces rather than the law itself can regulate free speech. Television viewers who were offended by remarks they perceived as either anti-Bush or antigovernment pressured advertisers not to sponsor programs that expressed viewpoints that they believed were "unpatriotic." This, in turn, caused television networks either to cancel some programs or not to broadcast them in certain areas of the country. (Note that this is an example of Lessig's claim that, in certain cases, social norms and market forces can be more effective regulators than laws themselves.) Nonetheless, free speech is a broad right, cited time and again by publishers of unpopular tabloids and also appealed to by many who distribute pornography. Many believe, however, that some forms of speech on the Internet, including pornography, should be censored.

9.4.2 Defining Censorship

What, exactly, is censorship? Mathiesen (2008) characterizes censorship as limiting access to content by deterring either (i) the speaker from speaking or (ii) the hearer from receiving the speech. She also advances a more formal definition of censorship, claiming that to censor is to

> *restrict or limit access to an expression, portion of an expression, or category of expression, which has been made public by its author, based on the belief that it will be a bad thing if people access the content of that expression.*[9]

Catudal (2004) points out that an important distinction can be drawn between two types of censorship that he describes as "censorship by suppression" and "censorship by deterrence." Both forms presuppose that some "authorized person or group of persons" has judged some text or "type of text" objectionable on moral, political, or other grounds.

Censorship by suppression prohibits the objectionable text or material from being published, displayed, or circulated. Banning certain books from being published and prohibiting certain kinds of movies from being made are both examples of censorship by suppression. In this scheme, pornography and other objectionable forms of speech would not be allowed on the Internet.

Censorship by deterrence, on the contrary, is less drastic. It neither suppresses nor blocks out objectionable material, nor does it forbid such material from being published. Rather, it depends on threats of arrest, prosecution, conviction, and punishment of both those who make an objectionable text available and those who acquire it. Heavy fines and possible imprisonment can deter the publication and acquisition of objectionable content. Again, using Lessig's regulatory model, social norms, such as social disenfranchisement, personal disgrace, and public censure, can also work to deter individuals from engaging in the publication, display, and transmission of objectionable speech.

In the next two sections, we examine three key forms of "objectionable speech" in cyberspace: pornography, hate speech, and speech that can cause physical harm to others. In the following section, we focus on various forms of online pornography, including virtual child pornography, and we look at a series of laws that have been enacted to protect children and minors.

▶ 9.5 PORNOGRAPHY IN CYBERSPACE

Before examining the issue of pornography on the Internet, or what some call "cyberporn," it is instructive to understand what legally qualifies as pornography in general. It is often debated in terms of notions such as obscenity and indecent speech. In *Miller v. California* (1973), the court established a three-part guideline for determining whether something is obscene under the law and thus not protected by the First Amendment. According to these criteria, something is obscene if it

1. depicts sexual (or excretory) acts whose depiction is specifically prohibited by law;
2. depicts these acts in a patently offensive manner, appealing to prurient interest as judged by a reasonable person using community standards;
3. has no serious literary, artistic, social, political, or scientific value.[10]

These criteria have proved problematic in attempts to enforce pornography laws. For example, the second criterion includes three controversial notions: "prurient interest," "reasonable person," and "community standards." *Prurient* is usually defined as having to do with lust and lewd behavior, concepts that, in turn, have been challenged as being vague and arbitrary. Also, many ask who, exactly, counts as a "reasonable person." The notion of "community standard" would likely seem the most straightforward or least controversial of the three concepts—that is, until the advent of cybertechnology, when a community had been traditionally defined in terms of geographical space. But what, exactly, is a community in cyberspace? And when more than one community is involved in a dispute involving pornography, whose community standards should apply?

9.5.1 Interpreting "Community Standards" in Cyberspace

Interpretations of "community" and "community standards" were among the issues debated in a court case involving pornography and the Amateur Action (Electronic) Bulletin Board System. (Electronic bulletin board systems could be viewed as a type of online forum that functioned as a predecessor to contemporary Internet sites such as craigslist.) This bulletin board system (BBS), which made sexually explicit images available to its members, was operated by a married couple who lived in California. Because it was an online forum, its contents were available not only to residents of California but also to users who had Internet access in other states (in the U.S.) and in other countries as well. A resident of Memphis, Tennessee, became a member of the BBS and then downloaded sexually explicit pictures onto his computer in Tennessee. Although including sexually explicit images on a BBS may not have been illegal in California, viewing such images was illegal under Tennessee state law. So, criminal charges were eventually brought against the operators of the BBS, who (though California residents) were prosecuted in Tennessee.[11]

The operators of this BBS were found guilty under Tennessee law of distributing obscenity, as defined under the local community standards that applied in Memphis. Not surprisingly, this case raised issues concerning what, exactly, was meant by "community standards" on the Internet. Can a community still be viewed or defined simply in terms of geography? Or, in an era of Internet-based social networking services (SNSs), such as Facebook and Twitter, should "community" be defined by other criteria? For example, can an online community be better understood as a computer-mediated forum where individuals who share common interests, regardless of geographical distance or proximity, come together? (We examine online communities in detail in Chapter 11.)

The Amateur Action case also raised another important issue affecting BBSs and online forums: Were the pornographic files actually *distributed* over the Internet by the operators of the BBS in California, as alleged? Or, instead, did the resident in Tennessee who downloaded them via the interstate telephone lines that transmit information between the two states *retrieve* those controversial files from the Internet? Questions involving both distribution and community standards in cyberspace contribute to the difficulty of interpreting and enforcing pornography laws online.

Many people first became aware of the amount of pornographic material available on the Internet through a news story entitled "CyberPorn," which appeared in *TIME* magazine in the summer of 1995. *TIME* reported that there were then 900,000 sexually explicit pornographic materials (pictures, film clips, etc.) available on the Internet. Many people, including most lawmakers, were outraged when they learned about the amount of pornographic materials that were so easily accessible to Internet users, including minors. Later, however, the *TIME* magazine story, based on an Internet study that had been conducted by a researcher at Carnegie Mellon University, was shown to be seriously flawed.

Although the Carnegie Mellon University study accurately reported the number of pornographic images and pornographic Web sites that were available, it failed to put this information into proper perspective—it made no mention of the fact that the percentage of pornographic sites relative to other sites on the Web was very low. However, the report caught the attention of many influential politicians, some of whom drafted legislation in response to what they saw as the growth of the "pornography industry" on the Internet. The result was the passage of the Communications Decency Act (CDA) in 1996.

9.5.2 Internet Pornography Laws and Protecting Children Online

The CDA caused controversy from the outset, especially the section referred to as the Exon Amendment, which dealt specifically with online pornography. The American Civil Liberties Union (ACLU) and other organizations challenged the constitutionality of CDA. A court in Philadelphia struck down CDA on grounds that it violated the U.S. Constitution; this court's ruling was upheld by the Supreme Court in 1997.[12] However, one section of the CDA, known as the Child Pornography Protection Act (CPPA) of 1996, was determined to be constitutional. According to CPPA, it was a crime to "knowingly send, receive, distribute, reproduce, sell, or possess more than three child pornographic images."[13] So even though CDA itself had been struck down, supporters of that legislation were pleased that the section on child pornography still held.

In 1998, the U.S. Congress passed the Child Online Pornography Act (COPA). (We should note that COPA is sometimes confused with COPPA, the Children's Online Privacy Protection Act of 2000, which was designed to reduce the amount of information that could be collected from children under the age of 12 who use the Internet.) Many of COPA's proponents believed that this act would be upheld by the courts; but as in the case of CDA, COPA was ill-fated. In 1999, the U.S. Supreme Court ruled that COPA was unconstitutional.[14] The only remaining federal law in 1999 that was specifically directed at online pornography was the CPPA of 1996, a section of the original CDA. Although it appeared that CPPA would remain intact, many critics argued that provisions of this act also conflicted with the U.S. Constitution. In 2002, the Supreme Court, in a 6-3 ruling, struck down portions of CPPA as unconstitutional.[15]

In 2000, the U.S. Congress enacted into law the Children's Internet Protection Act (CIPA), designed to address concerns about children's access to "offensive content" over the Internet via school and library computers. CIPA was targeted specifically at schools and libraries, where federal and local governments have greater control. This law affects any schools or public libraries that receive federal funding in the form of "E-Rate" discounts (described in Chapter 10), which make certain technologies more affordable for eligible schools and libraries. According to CIPA requirements, schools and libraries would not receive the discounts offered by the E-Rate program unless they certified that they had an "Internet safety policy" in place. This policy also included technology-based protection measures to block or filter Internet access by minors to pictures that are considered (i) obscene, (ii) child pornographic, and (iii) harmful to minors.[16]

As in the case of CPPA and COPA, CIPA was eventually challenged in the courts. In 2001, several groups, including the American Library Association (ALA) and the ACLU, filed suit to prevent the enforcement of CIPA's filtering requirement in public libraries. In 2002, the U.S. District Court for the Eastern District of Pennsylvania ruled that the CIPA filtering mandate was unconstitutional. However, the District Court's decision was overturned by the U.S. Supreme Court, which upheld CIPA in a 6–3 decision in June 2003 (*United States v. American Library Assn. Inc.*, 2003).

Many legal analysts who closely followed the Supreme Court's ruling in CIPA suggested that no clear precedent had been established with respect to how online child pornography laws will be interpreted in the future. They believed that this was especially apparent in legal precedents for interpreting an appropriate scope of filtering in public libraries. (The Supreme Court's ruling in CIPA was a "plurality decision" because there was less than a clear majority in the justices' written opinions.[17]) Although CIPA provides protection for children in school and library settings, proponents of broad-based pornography legislation worried that CIPA fell short because it did not provide the kind of protection they believed children need outside those contexts. However, CIPA's critics argued that too much nonpornographic content was blocked in the process of protecting children.

Table 9-1 identifies the four online child pornography laws that have been enacted at the federal level (in the U.S.), and includes information about when the laws were passed and when three of them were eventually struck down.

9.5.3 Virtual Child Pornography

Critics have argued that online pornography laws, especially CPPA, broaden the definition of child pornography to include entire categories of images that many would not judge to be "child pornographic." Catudal (2004) notes that under CIPA, visual depictions of sexually explicit conduct that do not involve *actual* minors would still be included as child pornography. In fact, Catudal believes that the CPPA's definition of child pornography includes categories of images that some would judge "not pornographic at all."

TABLE 9-1 Internet-Specific Child Pornography Laws

CDA (Communications Decency Act)	Passed in January 1996 and declared unconstitutional in July 1996. The Supreme Court upheld the lower court's decision in 1997
CPPA (Child Pornography Protection Act)	Passed as part of the larger CDA, but not initially struck down in 1997 with the CDA. It was declared unconstitutional in April 2002
COPA (Child Online Pornography Act)	Passed in June 1998 and (portions) declared unconstitutional by the Supreme Court in February 1999
CIPA (Children's Internet Protection Act)	Passed in December 2000 and declared unconstitutional by a U.S. district court in 2002. The Supreme Court overturned the lower court's ruling in June 2003

Child pornography, according to CPPA, is "any depiction, including a photograph, film, video, picture, or computer or computer-generated image or picture, whether made or produced by electronic, mechanical, or other means, of sexually explicit conduct." The definition goes on to list four categories of such depictions:

A. the production of such visual depiction involves the use of a minor engaging in sexually explicit conduct;

B. such visual depiction is, or appears to be, of a minor engaging in sexually explicit conduct; or

C. such visual depiction has been created, adapted, or modified to appear that an identifiable minor is engaging in sexually explicit conduct; or

D. such visual depiction is advertised, promoted, presented, described, or distributed in such a manner that conveys the impression that the material is or contains a visual depiction of a minor engaging in sexually explicit conduct.[18]

Whereas category (A) images represent depictions of what has been traditionally regarded as child pornography, Catudal argues that the same is not true of category (B) images. For example, he considers the case of a 19-year-old girl who appears in a pornographic image in which she looks much younger. Sexual depictions of this sort are sometimes referred to as the "little girl" genre; they have been used in many artistic works. (The "little girl" type does not, by definition, actually involve little girls or minors of any age.) In the United States, the sexually explicit depiction of a "young-looking" 19-year-old would be considered child pornography under CPPA, but in some other countries, such as Norway, it would not. Catudal believes that CPPA fails to note that category (A) and category (B) depictions represent two different types of prurient images.

Note also that in categories (C) and (D), the pornographic image can consist of a depiction of someone who *appears* to be a minor engaging in sexual activity or a depiction that *conveys the impression* of a minor engaging in such an activity. So, a computer-generated image that does not refer to an actual human being would also qualify as a child pornography image under CPPA. In its decision to strike down portions of the CPPA, the Supreme Court reasoned that a distinction needed to be made between a pornographic image of an actual child and that of a "virtual," or computer-generated, image of a minor.

Some argue that because no real children are used in the production of virtual child pornography, no children are harmed in the process. However, Sandin (2004) argues that even if the production of virtual child pornography does not harm real children, it does not follow that the *use* of virtual child pornography causes no harm to real children. Sandin suggests that a utilitarian argument could be made against allowing virtual child pornography if it is shown to have harmful consequences for real children. But Andrews (2010), who also makes an interesting case against virtual child pornography, worries that utilitarian arguments in and of themselves may not be sufficient to show that such behavior is unethical. So, Adams concludes that this issue should be tied to a

> much broader debate about the access of children to information of a sexual nature, without ignoring the differences between passive viewing of sexual activity (whether 'real' or 'virtual') and active virtual engagement.[19]

In our discussion of virtual reality (VR) in Chapter 11, we will see that "objectionable behavior" performed in virtual environments such as VR games, which portray only virtual or computer-generated images, can nonetheless cause real harm to real people. However, we will not continue with the debate about real vs. virtual harm here. Our purpose in this section has been to examine Internet pornography legislation that has been enacted to protect children online and to show why that legislation has been controversial, especially when it is extended to include virtual child pornographic images. We next consider how those laws apply in the case of "sexting."

9.5.4 *Sexting* and Its Implications for Current Child Pornography Laws

What is sexting, and what challenges does it pose for existing child pornography laws? Sexting is typically defined as the use of cell phones (or similar handheld electronic devices) to send nude or seminude photos of oneself to others. In some cases, these photos become widely distributed and can eventually end up on the Internet.

▶ **SCENARIO 9–3:** A Sexting Incident Involving Greensburg Salem High School

In 2009, six teenagers—three girls and three boys—at the Greensburg Salem High School in Pennsylvania were charged under child pornography laws in a sexting incident. The three girls, aged 14 and 15, who took nude or seminude photos of themselves on their cell phones and sent them to male classmates, faced charges involving the "manufacturing and dissemination of child pornography." The boys, who were aged 16 and 17, faced charges of possession of child pornography. (The nude pictures were discovered by Greensburg Salem High School officials when they seized a cell phone from a male student who was using it in violation of school policy.) The charges were later reduced to misdemeanors.[20] ■

Should the six teenagers have been charged with either dissemination or possession of child pornography? Were the original felony charges brought against them too harsh? Alternatively, are misdemeanor charges too lenient in cases such as this one? There does not yet seem to be any clear consensus on the answer to this question. Yet, the number of reported sexting incidents involving teenagers has increased sharply in recent years.

Next, consider two sexting incidents that each had very unfortunate outcomes—one resulting in the suicide of an 18-year-old female and one resulting in a felony charge brought against a male who had just turned 18. An Ohio resident—we will call her "Jill"—sent nude photos of herself via her cell phone to a boy, who then forwarded the pictures to others. The nude pictures of Jill were seen by some of her classmates at school as well as by others who lived in her community. As the photos became more widely distributed, Jill was taunted by some of her classmates as well as by others in her community. In May 2008, Jill took her life by hanging herself in her bedroom.[21]

A Florida resident, whom we will call "Phil," sent a nude picture of his ex-girlfriend to his friends and family, via his cell phone, following the couple's breakup. His ex-girlfriend was 16, and Phil had recently turned 18 (the age at which one can be legally prosecuted as an adult in the U.S.). He was arrested by the police in Florida who charged Phil with sending child pornography, and he was later convicted of a felony offense. Consequently, Phil was required to register as a sex offender, which means that his name will appear on an Internet registry of sex offenders in Florida until he is 43. Phil was also expelled from college and was unable to find employment. Additionally, he is required to check with his probation officer if he plans to travel outside his home county (in the state of Florida).[22]

Can sexting crimes be understood and prosecuted in a manner that is consistent with our current legal framework? It would seem that sexting incidents have generated a "conceptual muddle" (Moor 2007), which needs to be resolved before we can frame coherent policies and laws to punish sexting offenses. Legal analysts point out that the current laws are inconsistent in their application from state to state. We have seen that states such as Pennsylvania and Florida have prosecuted, or have tried to prosecute, sexting cases as a felony offense. However, in other states, including Vermont, lawmakers have introduced legislation that would exclude teenagers who engage in sexting from being tried under child pornography laws and would instead make sexting a misdemeanor.[23] Advocates on both sides of this view, however, can agree on one thing: more consistent laws are needed.

Hilden (2013) believes that instead of applying older child pornography laws that were designed for "graver and much more exploitative contexts," we should "craft new laws designed specifically for sexting." She agrees with the critics of the Greensburg case, including the ACLU, who argue that the initial charges brought against the six Pennsylvania teenagers were "ill-grounded," because the child pornography laws under which the teenagers were first charged were intended to cover "lascivious displays of the genitals and/or sexual activity." Hilden believes that the teenagers involved in the Greensburg Salem High School incident were not guilty of this kind of behavior, especially since two of the girls were wearing bras and one was topless in the photos sent to the three boys. So, prosecuting the three girls under strict child pornography laws would be inappropriate.

Hilden also believes, however, that the prosecution of some teenagers under such laws would be appropriate in future cases of sexting that might involve "underage teens having sex, displaying their genitals in a lascivious way, or both." In these cases, she suggests that the behavior of the teenagers could validly "form the basis of child-pornography charges." Hilden also suggests that lawmakers should consider two kinds of exceptions to child pornography laws in sexting cases:

i. A "Romeo and Juliet" exception (which is sometimes used in statutory rape laws where consensus is involved)

ii. An "age-specific" exception

Hilden believes that the Romeo and Juliet exception could apply when the two parties to an act of sex are close in age (say, 18 and 16, or 15 and 17). She notes, for example, that a 16-year-old sexting a nude photo of herself or himself to someone roughly the same age is far less disturbing than a 16-year-old doing so at the invitation of a 40-year-old. Hilden asks us to imagine a 16-year-old, named Jane, who sends a nude photo of herself to her 18-year-old boyfriend, Bill. Here, Jane might be protected under the Romeo and Juliet exception (and thus be immune from prosecution).

But Hilden also points out that if Bill forwards the photo to one or more persons without Jane's consent, he should not be immune from prosecution. Hilden believes that while these exceptions do not provide a "bright line" in prosecuting sexting cases, they at least enable authorities to differentiate between a high school senior who takes and "sexts" a photo of a 13-year-old eighth grader, and is truly engaging in child pornography, and a sexting incident involving two teenagers in the same-age category. In this way, the exceptions would avoid the need to impose severe criminal penalties on more or less same-age kids for what Hilden describes as "ugly immaturity," not crime.

One question that Hilden does not consider, however, is what would happen in the case where a teenage girl sends an uninvited nude photo of herself to an older man. In this case, would the man receiving the unsolicited photo be liable for prosecution under child pornography laws merely for having (or having had at some point) the nude photo of the teenager on his cell phone or electronic device? An actual case involving sexting between a 52-year-old man and a 14-year-old female occurred in Georgia in 2009. In this incident, the older man was trying to set up a "sexual rendezvous" with the young female. The girl sent him nude photos that she had taken of herself on her cell phone. Here, of course, the controversies raised go well beyond sexting—for example, they also include questions of intended child molestation or pedophilia.[24]

It would be interesting to consider what would happen if this 52-year-old man had made no sexual advances toward the 14-year-old girl and still received the pictures? It is not clear whether he still could be criminally charged with possessing child pornography on his cell phone. So, it would seem that answers to questions of this type would also need to be spelled out more clearly and explicitly in any future legislation drafted for sexting that incorporates "age-specific exceptions."

What can we conclude about sexting as it relates to our examination of child pornography in this section? We can agree with critics that most teenagers who have been prosecuted so far for sexting have not engaged in behavior that meets the threshold of crimes intended for prosecution as felonies under child pornography laws. Yet, sexting is a serious offense and thus needs to be dealt with appropriately in the legal and judicial systems. In the meantime, it seems that enacting some kind of federal legislation with standards that could be applied to sexting cases occurring in all states would be the best short-term solution.

▶ 9.6 HATE SPEECH AND SPEECH THAT CAN CAUSE PHYSICAL HARM TO OTHERS

In addition to pornography, which is sometimes viewed as "obscene" speech, hate speech and forms of speech that can cause physical harm to individuals and communities have both caused controversy in online contexts. We briefly examine some controversies affecting each.

9.6.1 Hate Speech on the Web

Hate speech on the Internet often targets racial and ethnic groups. For example, white supremacist organizations such as the Ku Klux Klan (KKK) can include offensive remarks about African Americans and Jews on their Web pages. (Recall our brief discussion of the KKK in Scenario 9–1.) Because of the Internet, international hate groups, such as "skin heads" in America, Europe, and Russia, can spread their messages of hate in ways that were not previously possible. Whereas much of the focus in the United States has been on controversial Internet speech issues that involve online pornography, European countries such as France and Germany have been more concerned about online hate speech. For example, Germany's Information and Communications Act was designed to censor neo-Nazi propaganda. But the law applies only to people who live in Germany; it cannot regulate the speech transmitted by ISPs outside that country. Girasa (2002) believes that if the German government had tried to enforce this law, countries such as the United States would likely have refused to extradite individuals to Germany.

In France, it is illegal to sell anything that incites hate and racism. However, Nazi and KKK memorabilia are auctioned daily on Web sites such as Yahoo that have an international reach.

In 2000, a French judge ruled that Yahoo must "make it impossible" for people in France to access sites selling that kind of material. Yahoo complied, and as a result, Nazi-related items are no longer available on Yahoo's French site (www.yahoo.fr). But French citizens who use an ISP outside France could potentially access the sites that are banned in France.[25]

In the United States, some "hate-watch" Web sites, such as the Southern Poverty Law Center (SPLC) "Intelligence Project" (http://www.splcenter.org), monitor online hate speech aimed at racial minorities. In an effort to counter the effectiveness of "hate sites," these hate-watch Web sites have exposed the existence of various hate organizations to the public. The SPLC site also features a Hatewatch blog and it includes a detailed map with physical locations of various hate groups, which it identifies under categories such as KKK, neo-Nazi, racist skinhead, and so forth. Ironically, perhaps, the information available on these sites also provides an easy way for consumers of hate speech to locate and visit particular hate sites that serve their interests. (In Chapter 10, we examine some of these concerns from the vantage point of race and cybertechnology, as opposed to the perspective of online hate speech.)

Numerous Web sites have promoted white supremacist hate speech. One such site was operated by James von Brunn who fatally shot an African American museum guard at the Holocaust Museum in Washington, DC, in 2009. On his site (holywesternempire.com), von Brunn included hate speech aimed at Jews and African Americans. (In fact, his site was included on the SPLC's list of notorious hate sites.) A few days before von Brunn shot his victim, he transferred control of his Web site to Steve Reimink who described the 88-year-old von Brunn as a "sick individual." But Reimink's message also included "code," familiar to many white supremacists, suggesting that Reimink's remarks were not sincere.[26]

Some antiabortion groups in the United States have set up Web sites dedicated to distributing (hate-related) information about doctors who perform abortions. These sites have also included information about where these doctors live, what times they travel to and from abortion clinics, where they go in their free time, etc. As in the case of the white supremacist rhetoric used by radical groups in the United States, this type of speech can also result in physical harm to others. Some information made available on antiabortion Web sites has been linked to the murder of doctors who perform abortions. In 2009, for example, Dr. George Tiller, who performed late-term abortions in Kansas, was murdered by an antiabortionist. Information about Tiller was available to Tiller's murderer via a Web site set up by an antiabortionist group (http://www.dr-tiller.com/), which described Tiller as "America's most notorious abortionist" and as "Tiller the Killer." This site also included information about Tiller's employees and assistant abortionists.

9.6.2 Online "Speech" that Can Cause Physical Harm to Others

Some forms of hate speech on the Internet are such that they might also result in physical harm being caused to individuals (as in the case of the antiabortionist sites described earlier). Other forms of this speech, however, are by the very nature of their content, biased toward violence and physical harm to others. Consider two examples of how speech communicated on the Internet can result in serious physical harm: one involving information on how to construct bombs and another that provides information on how to abduct children for the purpose of molesting them. Should this information be censored in cyberspace? Information of this kind was available before the Internet era and it may even have been (and still may be) available in some libraries. If it is available elsewhere, should it be censored on the Internet?

Critics point out that Internet access now makes it much easier to acquire all kinds of information, including information about how to make and do things that cause physical harm. They also note that it is possible to access and read this information in the privacy and comfort of one's home. Even more disturbing is that it is now far easier for international and domestic terrorists to obtain information about how to construct bombs. So, some believe that these are good enough reasons for censoring this kind of speech on the Internet.

Recall our discussion in Section 9.1.1 about whether the Internet should be conceived as a broadcast medium, like television or radio, or as a place, like a bookstore. We saw that the rules that apply in each are significantly different. Viewing the Internet as a medium of some sort makes it far easier to control the dissemination (or broadcast) of certain kinds of information than viewing it as a public place, such as a bookstore or library. If the Internet is viewed in the latter sense, however, it is more difficult to ban controversial forms of speech such as hate speech and speech that can cause physical harm to others. So, the debate continues about which kinds of speech, if any, should be regulated on the Internet.

▶ 9.7 "NETWORK NEUTRALITY" AND THE FUTURE OF INTERNET REGULATION

So far in this chapter, we have analyzed a wide range of controversies affecting cyberspace regulation. While some concerns have focused on issues involving the regulation of commerce, others have centered mainly on issues that affect speech (or content) in cyberspace. All of these regulatory concerns, however, have been examined within the context of a "neutral" Internet. We conclude this chapter by examining the controversial debate involving *network neutrality*, and we consider what kinds of implications the outcome of this debate will likely have for regulating and accessing the Internet in the future.

9.7.1 Defining Network Neutrality

What, exactly, is network neutrality, or "net neutrality," as it has commonly come to be called? Tim Wu, an Internet policy expert at Columbia University, describes it as a principle in which "a maximally useful public information network aspires to treat all content, sites, and platforms equally."[27] In explaining the key elements underpinning the net neutrality principle, Wu draws an interesting analogy between a neutral Internet and other kinds of networks, which he claims are also implicitly built on a "neutrality theory." Using the example of the neutral nature of the electric grid, he notes that the same grid that "worked for the radios of the 1930s" also works for the "flat screen TVs of the 2000s." Wu also notes that the electric grid doesn't care whether you plug in a computer, an iron, or a toaster; thus, it is the grid's "general purpose and neutral nature" that make it extremely useful, as well as a "model of a neutral, innovation-driving network."[28]

Will the Internet, like the electric grid, remain a neutral network? The principle of net neutrality has been at the center of a contentious debate between two groups: *neutrality opponents*, which include major U.S. telecommunication companies as well as some conservative law makers, and *neutrality proponents*, consisting of a wide coalition comprising numerous organizations that are commercial and noncommercial, liberal and conservative, and public and private. Proponents also include many consumer groups and ordinary users, as well as the founders of the Internet (Lessig and McChesney 2006).

Proponents argue that the Internet had been conceived of and implemented as a neutral network from the outset, even if no regulatory laws or formal policies had been in place to enforce it. However, this basic principle has been questioned and challenged in recent years by neutrality opponents. The tension that had been brewing between the two groups came to the fore in the U.S. in 2005, when the FCC officially adopted four broad neutrality principles in an effort to (i) "deregulate the Internet services provided by telephone companies" and (ii) "give consumers the right to use the content, applications, services and devices of their choice when using the Internet."[29]

In 2008, one service provider, Comcast, was accused of deliberately slowing down access to (and effectively blocking users from) a popular P2P file-sharing site. That year, the FCC filed a formal complaint against Comcast for its actions; although it did not fine the service provider, the FCC did require that Comcast cease blocking the P2P site in question. Next, Comcast challenged the FCC's position in court, and in 2010 a federal appeals court ruled in Comcast's favor.

Following the appeals court's decision, the FCC approved a policy that some viewed as a "compromise" position, which effectively created two classes of Internet access: one for "fixedline providers" and one for the "wireless net." Some critics saw this compromise as a policy of "net semineutrality." While that FCC policy officially banned fixed line broadband providers' services from both "outright blocking" and "unreasonable discrimination" of Web sites or applications, it also arguably provided more "wiggle room" to wireless providers such as Verizon and AT&T.[30]

9.7.2 Some Arguments Advanced by Net Neutrality's Proponents and Opponents

Proponents of net neutrality tend to argue that America's largest telecommunications companies, including AT&T, Comcast, Time Warner, and Verizon, want to be "Internet gatekeepers" who can:

- guarantee speedy delivery of their data via "express lanes" for their own content and services, or for large corporations that can afford to pay steep fees;
- slow down services to some sites, or block content offered by their competitors;
- discriminate "in favor of their own search engines, Internet phone services and streaming video."[31]

Net neutrality's opponents tend to respond to these charges by claiming that the telecommunications companies have no plans to block content or services, slow down or "degrade" network performance for some sites, or discriminate against any users. Instead, they argue that these companies simply want to stimulate competition on the Internet and that doing this will result in increased:

- Internet speed, reach, and availability for users (in the United States)
- Economic growth, job creation, global competitiveness, and consumer welfare[32]

However, many critics remain skeptical about the neutrality opponents' real intentions, and some point to an incident in 2008 (mentioned earlier) in which Comcast intentionally degraded network performance by slowing down access to a popular file-sharing site.

9.7.3 Future Implications for the Net Neutrality Debate

Lessig and McChesney (2006) argue that one important benefit of net neutrality in the past has been that it has served to minimize control by the network owners. So, many neutrality proponents worry about the future of the Internet in the absence of a net neutrality principle. In general, proponents believe that the consequences of an Internet without a neutrality principle would be devastating for at least three reasons:

1. access to information would be restricted, and innovation would be stifled;
2. competition would be limited because consumer choice and the free market would be sacrificed to the interests of a few corporations;
3. the Internet will look more like cable TV, where network owners will decide which channels, content, and applications are available (and consumers will have to choose from their menus).[33]

However, the opponents of net neutrality—especially large telephone and cable companies in the United States—see the matter very differently. For one thing, broadband providers claim that since 2008 they have invested more than $250 billion dollars to expand Internet access to broadband technology to homes and businesses in the United States. For another, they claim that broadband industry is now responsible for supporting more than six million American jobs.[34]

Neutrality opponents have continued to press hard for policies that would grant the telecommunication companies more flexibility and control. In January 2014, the FCC proposed a regulatory policy that some neutrality proponents believed would protect key aspects of net neutrality. However, this policy was also challenged in the courts and was rejected by a federal court on the grounds that the FCC was trying to regulate Internet providers as if they were the same as public utilities. (The latter are typically more heavily regulated than "information services" providers.) However, net neutrality supporters were encouraged that the federal court, in its 2014 ruling, upheld and confirmed the FCC's authority to regulate broadband on the Internet.[35]

In early 2015, the FCC deliberated over a new policy that would reclassify broadband as "telecommunications services," similar to traditional telephone service; this move would also enable Internet broadband to be regulated more heavily. Additionally, it would give the FCC more authority in regulating business mergers and agreements between content companies like Netflix and (service) providers like Comcast. Under the FCC's enforcement, Comcast and other Internet providers would be also banned from entering into so-called "paid prioritization" agreements with content providers.[36]

On February 26, 2015, the FCC officially adopted its new policy. According to Fernholz (2015), this policy can be summarized as requiring ISPs to follow three principles: (i) no blocking of legal content; (ii) no "throttling," or deliberately slowing down the delivery of data; and (iii) no paid prioritization, where ISPs could set up "fast lanes" for some content providers but not for others. Baum (2015) believes that ordinary Internet users will benefit from the policy because they will not be "relegated to a second class information highway," while ISPs may be adversely affected because they may now feel pressure to "invest more resources on building additional bandwidth." And because building more bandwidth is very expensive and would likely result in less profit for ISPs, those companies may elect not to make that investment.[37]

Some believe that the net neutrality dispute is far from settled and that it is still not yet clear which direction the U.S. government will ultimately take on it in the long term. But if, as some fear, the Internet eventually becomes a multitiered entity with respect to access, that is, where some parties (e.g., those who either control content or can afford to pay for premium access) are privileged or favored at the expense of ordinary users, the future Internet may become a "discriminatory medium." Concerns about discriminatory online access may also raise some new, or at least exacerbate some existing, equity and access-related issues affecting the "digital divide"—a topic that we examine in detail in Chapter 10.

▶ 9.8 CHAPTER SUMMARY

In this chapter, we have considered some challenges to regulating cyberspace. Specifically, we considered Internet regulation issues from two different perspectives: the regulation of commercial activities on the Internet and the regulation of content in cyberspace. We saw that decisions to view cyberspace as a medium rather than as a public place or space, or vice versa, are significant, because they determine which kinds of rules apply to regulating speech on the Internet. We also saw that the enactment of formal or explicit laws is only one way to regulate cyberspace. As Lessig and others have noted, much regulation of the Internet is being accomplished through technology itself, especially (software) "code." Future regulatory decisions will determine whether the Internet remains "neutral," or open, or whether it evolves into a different kind of entity.

Unfortunately, not all Internet regulation controversies were able to be examined in the limited space of this chapter. For example, one concern not considered here has to do with online defamation and who should be legally liable for defamatory remarks made in a particular online forum. (To date, many online defamation-related questions are still not resolved.) Another controversy not examined in this chapter involves the question of who should be responsible for regulating online "classifieds services" such as craigslist.com and backpage.com, especially with regard to ads affecting "adult services." While craigslist.com has taken a self-regulatory kind of approach by eliminating these kinds of services from its site, backpage.com has since been accused of facilitating sex trafficking and child exploitation by listing various adult services on its site. Yet, as of August 2015, there does not seem to be any clear regulatory body in place to monitor the kinds of sites that engage in these services. So, it would seem that some significant policy vacuums still need to be filled regarding Internet regulation.

▶ REVIEW QUESTIONS

1. In discussing "cyberspace regulation," why is it useful to distinguish the question "Can cyberspace be regulated?" from the question "Should cyberspace be regulated?"
2. Describe the arguments for why cyberspace should be viewed as a medium, and why it should be viewed as a "place."
3. How does the way we interpret cyberspace—that is, as a "place" or as a medium—affect the kinds of policies that can be used to regulate it?
4. What are the two different senses of "regulation" we examined, and how can they be applied to the regulatory issues involving cyberspace?
5. Identify the four modalities that Lawrence Lessig believes can be used to regulate behavior, and give an example of how each can be applied to regulating behavior on the Internet.
6. What does Lessig mean by the following claim: "In cyberspace, code is the law"?
7. What is digital rights management (DRM) technology, and why is it controversial?
8. Why does Cory Doctorow believe that the DMCA (Digital Millennium Copyright Act) works hand in hand with DRM technology to control the flow of digital information?
9. What does Niva Elkin-Koren mean when she asserts that information policy is becoming increasingly "privatized"? Why does she believe this is a problem?
10. What is e-mail spam, and why is it controversial?
11. What is the CAN-SPAM Act? Is it effective in deterring spam? Explain.
12. How does Kay Mathiesen define censorship? Describe the criteria that Jacques Catadul uses to distinguish between "censorship by suppression" and "censorship by deterrence."
13. What is pornography? Why is interpreting what is meant by "community standards" especially difficult in establishing pornography laws for cyberspace?
14. Describe the three Internet-specific child pornography laws that were passed in the 1990s but later struck down by the U.S. Supreme Court.
15. How is the Child Internet Pornography Act (CIPA) of 2000 both similar to and different from earlier laws affecting child pornography online?
16. What is "virtual child pornography," and why is it controversial?
17. What do we mean by "hate speech"? Give some examples of hate speech in cyberspace.
18. What is meant by "speech that can cause physical harm to others"?
19. What is network neutrality (or "net neutrality"), and why is it controversial?
20. Describe some of the arguments advanced by "neutrality proponents" and by "neutrality opponents." Which position do you find more convincing?

▶ DISCUSSION QUESTIONS

1. Have DRM systems gone too far, as some critics claim? Recall the 2005 Sony BMG copy protection case involving the controversial "rootkit" problem (examined in Scenario 9-2). Should Sony have been allowed to use a DRM system that cannot easily be uninstalled when circumstances warrant it? Do companies like Sony need strong DRM systems to ensure the protection of their intellectual property rights? What kind of compromise position might be reached between users and content owners in the ongoing debate about DRM systems?
2. Assess the (consequence-based and duty-based) arguments that Richard Spinello uses to show that e-mail

spam is morally objectionable. Are his arguments convincing? How does the distinction that Keith Miller and James Moor draw between fraudulent and nonfraudulent UCBE (unsolicited commercial bulk e-mail) inform the debate about the moral implications of spam?

3. What is sexting, and what challenges does it pose for prosecuting current child pornography laws? Recall our examination of the sexting incident at Greensburg Salem High School, PA (in Scenario 9–3). Should the teens involved in that case have been subject to felony charges under existing child pornography laws? Explain.
4. Review Julie Hilden's arguments for why some "exceptions" should be made in cases of prosecuting sexting crimes under current child pornography laws. What does she mean by the "Romeo and Juliet" exception and by the "age-specific" exception? Are these exceptions plausible in the kinds of sexting cases that we examined? Describe some of the challenges posed by the age-specific exception. For example, what would happen if a middle-aged man received an unsolicited nude photo from a teenage girl on his cell phone? Should he be prosecuted for possessing a pornographic image of a minor? Should the teenage girl who sent this photo to him be prosecuted for transmitting the image? Defend your answers.

Scenarios for Analysis

1. Your friend, Jane, a senior at Suburban High School, was recently suspended for three days by her principal for violating her school's cell phone policy. In retaliation, Jane decides to post a picture of her principal, along with some disparaging remarks about him, on Facebook. However, Jane also cleverly uses a fake name (instead of the principal's real name) to identify the person in the Facebook photo, who she describes as a pedophile and drug dealer. (Only a few of Jane's close friends on Facebook will recognize that the person in the photo is her high school principal; other "friends" will not likely make the connection involving this photo with the real identity of the person in it.) Should Jane's remarks in her Facebook posting be protected under her constitutional right to free speech? If not, would it be appropriate for her principal to file a lawsuit against Jane, given that she is still legally considered a minor (at the age of 17) in the state where she resides? What kind of punishment, if any, should Jane receive for posting the disparaging and false remarks (implicating her high school principal) on Facebook?[38]
2. Bob, an acquaintance of yours, has been interested in fireworks technology from a very young age. He has read volumes on this topic, as well as on how to design devices that detonate, since he was in junior high school. He has also experimented with various kinds of explosive devices on his parent's property, all of which have been in compliance with the law. Bob recently came up with a novel recipe for building a homemade bomb, and he plans to post the instructions (for assembling the bomb) on his blog and then announce them to his Facebook friends. You, along with a few of Bob's close friends, are very concerned about his plans to do this. But Bob argues, in his defense, that writing and publishing a book on how to build a bomb is perfectly legal in the United States, because it is protected by the First Amendment. He analogizes that if it is legally permissible to publish a physical book or document on this topic, it should also be permissible to write a blog (or even an entire e-book) on it as well. But you are not convinced that posting such a document on the Internet should be protected under "free speech." (And even if it is protected under the most generous reading of the constitutional guidelines affecting free speech, you worry about the broader implications of what his publication could have for terrorists who might be eager to read his "recipe" for building a bomb.) What argument would you make to try to persuade Bob not to publish his bomb-building recipe online? If Bob refuses to take your advice, what would be your next step?

▶ ENDNOTES

1. See, for example, http://www.huffingtonpost.com/2014/11/17/anonymous-kkk_n_6173332.html.
2. Weckert (2007), p. 95.
3. Weckert and Al-Saggaf (2008), p. 491.
4. For an extended discussion of Lessig's four modalities in the context of cyberspace, see his highly influential book, *Code and Other Laws of Cyberspace* (Lessig 2000). Also see Spinello (2001) for an excellent review of Lessig's book.

5. Doctorow (2014), p. 23. Doctorow goes on to note that when a computer has been "compromised by a rootkit, it will not 'see' the files associated with the malicious software the rootkit was designed to conceal."
6. This scenario is based on the account of the Sony BMG rootkit controversy in *Wikipedia*, available at http://en.wikipedia.org/wiki/2005_Sony_BMG_CD_copy_protection_scandal. See also the description of this incident in Doctorow (2014).
7. See Grodzinsky and Tavani (2008) for an analysis of how this affects some of the property-versus-privacy interests at stake in the dispute involving DRM.
8. Miller and Moor (2008), pp. 518–20.
9. Mathiesen (2008), p. 576.
10. See http://www.oyez.org/cases/1970-1979/1971/1971_70_73.
11. See http://www.spectacle.org/795/amateur.html.
12. See http://www.cdt.org/speech/cda/.
13. See https://en.wikipedia.org/wiki/Child_Pornography_Prevention_Act_of_1996.
14. See http://74.125.47.132/search?q=cache:sltTkgMAUmMJ:www.lc.org/profamily/copa.pdf+COPA+History&cd=1&hl=en&ct=clnk&gl=us.
15. See http://www.ala.org/ala/aboutala/offices/oif/ifissues/issuesrelatedlinks/cppacopacipa.cfmhttp://www.repository.law.indiana.edu/fclj/vol55/iss1/4/.
16. See http://www.universalservice.org/sl/applicants/step10/cipa.aspx.
17. For example, Justices Kennedy and Breyer, who sided with the majority, did not concur with the rationales stated in Justice Reinquist's majority opinion. Although they agreed with Reinquist's conclusion, they wrote a separate opinion supporting the majority decision only to the extent that it provides filtering for children; Kennedy and Breyer also stated that filtering must be easily disabled for adults who request it in public libraries. See http://www.oyez.org/cases/2000-2009/2002/2002_02_361.
18. See the full text of CPPA for more detail. This section of CPPA (A–D) is cited in Catudal (2004, p. 201).
19. Adams (2010), p. 68.
20. See Bunker (2009) for a detailed account of this incident.
21. For more detail, see Stiles (2008).
22. See Szustek (2009).
23. *Ibid.*
24. See Bunker (2009) for more details about this incident.
25. See http://news.bbc.co.uk/2/hi/europe/760782.stm.
26. See http://www.dailykos.com/storyonly/2009/6/12/741537/-von-Brunns-website-attacks-von-Brunn!
27. Tim Wu. "Network Neutrality FAQ." Available at http://timwu.org/network_neutrality.html.
28. *Ibid.*
29. See "Net Neutrality." 2010. *New York Times* (Updated December 22). Available at http://topics.nytimes.com/topics/reference/timestopics/subjects/n/net_neutrality/index.html.
30. *Ibid.*
31. See http://www.freepress.net/policy/internet/net_neutrality.
32. See Broadband for America. "Hands off the Internet." Available at http://www.broadbandforamerica.com/handsofftheinternet?gclid=CLbFmZHRlq8CFQjd4AodbHxsxA.
33. See http://www.freepress.net/policy/internet/net_neutrality and http://en.wikipedia.org/wiki/Network_neutrality.
34. See Broadband for America. "Hands off the Internet." Available at http://www.broadbandforamerica.com/handsofftheinternet?gclid=CLbFmZHRlq8CFQjd4AodbHxsxA.
35. See, for example, the account in Selyukh (2015).
36. *Ibid.*
37. See the interview with Baum in Fowler (2015).
38. This hypothetical scenario mirrors, in some important respects, an actual incident where a high school principal in Pennsylvania was indirectly insulted (or "parodied") on MySpace by two teenagers. See, for example, Dale (2011).

▶ REFERENCES

Adams, Andrew. 2010. "Virtual Sex with Child Avatars." In C. Wankel and S. Malleck, eds. *Emerging Ethical Issues of Life in Virtual Worlds*. Charlotte, NC: Information Age Publishing, pp. 55–72.

Agre, Philip E. 2005. "P2P and the Promise of Internet Equality." In P. De Palma, ed. *Computers in Society 05/06*. Dubuque, IA: McGraw-Hill/Dushkin, pp. 12–15. Reprinted from *Communications of the ACM* 46, no. 2 (2003): 39–42.

Bunker, Mike. 2009. "Sexting Surprise: Teens Face Child Porn Charges." Available at http://www.msnbc.msn.com/1d/28679588/. http://www.nbcnews.com/id/28679588/print/1/displaymode/1098

Camp, L. Jean, and Y. T. Chien. 2000. "The Internet as Public Space: Concepts, Issues, and Implications in Public Policy." *Computers and Society* 30, no. 3: 13–19.

Catudal, Jacques. 2004. "Censorship, the Internet, and the Child Pornography Law of 1996: A Critique." In R. A. Spinello and H. T. Tavani, eds. *Readings in CyberEthics*. 2nd ed. Sudbury, MA: Jones and Bartlett Publishers, pp. 196–213.

Dale, MaryClaire. 2011. "Pa. Teens Can't Be Suspended for MySpace Parodies." *The Washington Times*, June 14. Available at http://www.washingtontimes.com/news/2011/jun/13/pa-teens-cant-be-suspended-for-myspace-parodies/?page=all.

Doctorow, Cory. 2014. *Information Doesn't Want to Be Free: Laws for the Internet Age*. San Francisco CA: McSweeney's.

Elkin-Koren, Niva. 2000. "The Privatization of Information Policy." *Ethics and Information Technology* 2, no. 4: 201–09.

Fernholz, Tim. 2015. "What America's Historic Net Neutrality Rules Mean in Plain English." *MSN.COM*, February 26. Available at: http://www.msn.com/en-us/news/it-insider/what-america%e2%80%99s-historic-net-neutrality-rules-mean-in-plain-english/ar-BBhZW8x.

Fowler, Jenny Li. 2015. "What Net Neutrality Means for You, the Internet User: Interview with Matt Baum." *Harvard Gazette*, February 27. Available at (Harvard Kennedy School of Government): http://www.hks.harvard.edu/news-events/news/articles/net-neutrality?utm_source=SilverpopMailing&utm_medium=email&utm_campaign=02.27.2015%20(1).

Girasa, Roy J. 2002. *Cyberlaw: National and International Perspectives*. Upper Saddle River, NJ: Prentice Hall.

Goodwin, Mike. 1995. "Alt.sex.academic.freedom." *Wired* 3, no. 2: 72. Available at http://www.wired.com/wired/archive/3.02/cyber_rights_pr.html.

Goodwin, Mike. 2003. *CyberRights: Defending Free Speech in the Digital Age*. Rev. ed. Cambridge, MA: MIT Press.

Grodzinsky, Frances S., and Maria Bottis. 2007. "Private Use as Fair Use: Is it Fair?" *Computers and Society* 37, no. 4: 11–24.

Grodzinsky, Frances S. and Herman T. Tavani. 2008. "Online File Sharing: Resolving the Tensions between Privacy and Property." *Computers and Society* 38, no. 4: 28–39.

Hesseldahl, Arik. 2006. "Apple vs. France." *Business Week*, March 21. Available at http://www.businessweek.com/technology/content/mar2006/tc20060321_144066.htm.

Hilden, Julie. 2013. "How Should Teens' 'Sexting'—the Sending of Revealing Photos—Be Regulated?" In D. Hall, ed. *Taking Sides: Clashing Views in Family and Personal Relationships*. 9th ed. New York: McGraw Hill. Reprinted from *Find Law*, April 28, 2009. Available at http//writ.news.findlaw.com/hilden/20090428.html.

Jobs, Steve. 2007. "Thoughts on Music." *Apple.com*, February 6. Available at http://www.apple.com/hotnews/thoughtsonmusic/.

Lessig, Lawrence. 2000. *Code and Other Laws of Cyberspace*. New York: Basic Books.

Lessig, Lawrence. 2004. The Laws of Cyberspace. In R. A. Spinello and H. T. Tavani, eds. *Readings in CyberEthics*. 2nd ed. Sudbury, MA: Jones and Bartlett, pp. 134–44.

Lessig, Lawrence, and Robert W. McChesney. 2006. "No Tolls on the Internet." *The Washington Post*, June 8. Available at http://www.washingtonpost.com/wp-dyn/content/article/2006/06/07/AR2006060702108.html.

Mathiesen, Kay. 2008. "Censorship and Access to Expression." In K. E. Himma and H. T. Tavani, eds. *The Handbook of Information and Computer Ethics*. Hoboken, NJ: John Wiley and Sons, pp. 573–87.

Miller, Keith, and James H. Moor. 2008. "Email Spam." In K. E. Himma and H. T. Tavani, eds. *The Handbook of Information and Computer Ethics*. Hoboken, NJ: John Wiley and Sons, pp. 517–31.

Moor, James H. 2007. "What Is Computer Ethics?" In J. Weckert, ed. *Computer Ethics*. Aldershot, UK: Ashgate, pp. 31 40. Reprinted from *Metaphilosophy* 16, no. 4 (1985): 266–75.

Russinovich, Mark. 2005. "Sony, Rootkits, and Digital Rights Management Gone Too Far." Available at http://www.sysinternals.com/blog/2005/10sony-rootkits-and-digital-rights.html.

Samuelson, Pamela. 2003. "DRM {and, or, vs.} the Law." *Communications of the ACM* 46, no. 4: 41–45.

Sandin, Per. 2004. "Virtual Child Pornography and Utilitarianism." *Journal of Information, Communication and Ethics in Society* 2, no. 4: 217–23.

Selyukh, Alina. 2015. "Tougher Internet Rules to Hit Cable, Telecoms Companies." *MSN.Com*, February 26. Available at http://www.msn.com/en-us/news/us/tougher-internet-rules-to-hit-cable-telecoms-companies/ar-BBhYTNz.

Spinello, Richard A. 2001. "Code and Moral Values in Cyberspace." *Ethics and Information Technology* 3, no. 2: 137–150.

Spinello, Richard A. 2003. *Cyberethics: Morality and Law in Cyberspace*. 2nd ed. Sudbury, MA: Jones and Bartlett.

Spinello, Richard A. 2006. "Ethical Reflections on the Problem of Spam." In L. Hinman, ed. *Contemporary Moral Issues: Diversity and Consensus*. 3rd ed. Upper Saddle River, NJ: Prentice Hall, pp. 502–10. Reprinted from *Ethics and Information Technology* 1, no. 3 (1999): 185–91.

Stiles, Bob. 2008. "Effort Begins to Standardize Sexting Penalty." *Tribune-Review*, April 2. Available at http://m.triblive.com/triblive/db_7240/contentdetail.htm;jsessionid=198F0CC68FFC5176D6581C1E539F8C62?contentguid=tScPcIMY&full=true.

Szustek, Anne. 2009. "Authorities Treat Those Accused of 'Sexting' as Sex Offenders." *Finding Dulcinea*. Available at http://www.findingdulcinea.com/news/Americas/2009/April/Authorities-Treat-Those-Accused-of-Sexting-as-Sex-Offenders.html.

Weckert, John. 2007. "What Is So Bad about Internet Content Regulation?" In J. Weckert, ed. *Computer Ethics*. Aldershot UK: Ashgate, pp. 95–102. Reprinted from *Ethics and Information Technology* 2, no. 2 (2000): 105–11.

Weckert, John, and Yeslam Al-Saggaf. 2008. "Regulation and Governance of the Internet." In K. E. Himma and H. T. Tavani, eds. *The Handbook of Information and Computer Ethics*. Hoboken, NJ: John Wiley and Sons, pp. 475–95.

▶ FURTHER READINGS

Armstrong, Timothy K. 2006. "Digital Rights Management and the Process of Fair Use." *Harvard Journal of Law & Technology* 20. Available at http://ssrn.com/abstract=885371.

Bohman, James. 2008. "The Transformation of the Public Sphere: Political Authority, Communicative Freedom, and Internet Publics." In J. van den Hoven and J. Weckert, eds. *Information Technology and Moral Philosophy*. New York: Cambridge University Press, pp. 66–92.

Grossman, Wendy M. 2005. "The Spam Wars." In. P. De Palma, ed. *Annual Editions: Computers in Society 05/06*. Dubuque, IA: McGraw-Hill/Dushkin, pp. 147–51.

Levy, David M. 2008. "Information Overload." In K. E. Himma and H. T. Tavani, eds. *The Handbook of Information and Computer Ethics*. Hoboken, NJ, pp. 497–515.

Spinello, Richard A. 2002. *Regulating Cyberspace: The Policies of Technology and Control*. Westport, CT: Quorum Books.

White, A. 2004. "The Obscenity of Internet Regulation in the United States." *Ethics and Information Technology* 6, no. 2: 111–19.

Zittrain, Jonathan. 2008. *The Future of the Internet—And How to Stop It*. New Haven, CT: Yale University Press.

CHAPTER

10

The Digital Divide, Democracy, and Work

LEARNING OBJECTIVES

Upon completing this chapter, you will successfully be able to:

- Explain what is meant by phrase *digital divide* and why this "divide" is morally significant at the global as well as local levels,
- Describe key strategies and policies proposed by the Web Accessibility Initiative (WAI) to make access to cybertechnology more accessible to disabled persons and groups,
- Articulate key issues affecting cybertechnology and race, as they apply both to technology–access affecting racial and minority groups (in the United States and globally) and the use of the Internet to reinforce racism,
- Assess the impact that cybertechnology has had for gender issues, particularly as they apply to concerns about access to high-tech jobs for women and to gender bias in software design,
- Describe the many ways in which cybertechnology can both enhance and threaten democracy, as well as democratic values and ideals,
- Understand the impacts that cybertechnology has had for employment and work in the twenty-first century, both in terms of the *transformation* of work and the *quality* of work life.

Unlike Chapters 5–9, which focused on the impacts that cybertechnology has for specific moral, legal, and social problems—namely, privacy, security, crime, intellectual property, and Internet regulation—This chapter considers the impacts that this technology has for a wide range of issues that cut across three broad (social) categories:

- *Sociodemographic groups* (affecting social/economic class, race, and gender)
- *Social and political institutions* (such as education and government)
- *Social sectors* (including the workplace)

A common characteristic unifies the otherwise disparate issues examined in this chapter: They are often approached from the perspective of *sociological/descriptive ethics*. Recall that in Chapter 1 we drew a distinction between descriptive and normative approaches to the study of moral issues, noting that while social scientists conduct research that is essentially designed to report (or describe) sociological aspects of cybertechnology, those aspects often have normative implications as well. In this chapter, we examine some issues primarily from the vantage point of descriptive ethics, especially as they require an analysis of statistical and empirical data. In other cases, we also examine normative aspects of those issues. The latter perspective is particularly apparent in our analysis of concerns involving social equity/access to digital technology. We begin with a scenario that briefly illustrates a cluster of issues examined in greater detail in later sections of this chapter.

▶ **SCENARIO 10–1:** Digital Devices, Social Media, Democracy, and the "Arab Spring"

In early 2011, large political protests erupted in many Arabic-speaking countries in North Africa and the Middle East—including Egypt, Tunisia, Libya, and Yemen—where protestors, many of them young persons, demanded governmental reforms. In Egypt, for example, protestors used social media sites, accessible via their mobile devices, to organize demonstrations in Cairo. Subsequently, the government led by then President Hosni Mubarak soon fell (as did the ruling governments in Tunisia, Libya, and Yemen). This political uprising, bordering on what some describe as a "revolution," has since been described by many journalists and media outlets in the West as the "Arab Spring." Many optimists, especially in the West, believed that a wave of democratic governments would soon emerge across the Arab world.[1] Even though that outcome has not been realized (at least not so far), organized protestors were nevertheless able to topple the regimes of powerful governments in the Arab world—something that would have seemed unthinkable just a few years before. ■

In the past, political regimes in the countries that were affected in this region of the world were able to squash political protests by preventing the mobilization of their citizens into large-scale demonstrations and rallies. So, one might naturally ask: What was so different in the Arab Spring movement, and why did it succeed (at one level, at least, even if no democratic governments have yet taken hold in these countries)? Although many of the political leaders, including the Mubarak administration in Cairo, had reacted immediately to the protestors by shutting down the country's Internet services and mobile phone resources, their actions were too late. The protestors in Egypt, anticipating the government's reaction in advance, had already unified and planned out their organized demonstrations via social media sites such as Facebook and Twitter before the online services in Egypt were able to be shut down. So it would seem that these protestors' success in bringing down a powerful government could be attributed, in large part, to their adept use of electronic devices and online social media to organize their large demonstrations.

Historically, many governments have taken advantage of the latest technologies in ways that have enabled them to remain in power by controlling their citizens; for example, some governments have used surveillance technologies to monitor the movements of their citizens, thereby making it very difficult for them to mobilize. Also, some governments have used these technologies to eavesdrop on citizens and to intercept communications among dissenters and protestors. So the myriad uses of technology in the political/governmental sphere had often seemed one sided—that is, favoring the interests of those political regimes already in power. During the Arab Spring, however, ordinary citizens, including the protestors and their sympathizers, were able to turn the tables and use the latest technologies available to them (e.g., mobile phones, digital devices, etc.) and social media services (such as Twitter and Facebook) to bring down some firmly entrenched (and what many would also describe as "repressive") political regimes.

The purpose of Scenario 10–1 was not to provide a detailed analysis of the Arab Spring. Rather its objective was to get us to begin thinking about the relationship between technology and government in general, and technology and democracy in particular. One question this scenario might also cause us to consider is: How different would the political outcome in Egypt (and the other affected governments in North Africa and the Middle East) likely have been if ordinary citizens, or even specific groups/classes of citizens, in those countries were not able to afford or to access the kinds of digital technologies they used? So it would seem that issues concerning democracy (and democratic forms of government) are now becoming increasingly intertwined with issues involving a government's policies affecting (affordable) access to digital technologies for all of its citizens.

We examine some access-related issues affecting specific demographic groups in Sections 10.1–10.4 in our analysis of the digital divide (socioeconomic class), disabled persons, racial minorities, and women, respectively. Concerns associated with the impact of cybertechnology on our political/social institutions are considered in our discussion of democracy and the Internet in Section 10.5, whereas cybertechnology-related issues impacting the contemporary workplace (as a social sector) are examined in Section 10.6.

▶ 10.1 THE DIGITAL DIVIDE

What, exactly, is the digital divide? Compaine (2001) suggests that the phrase *digital divide* is basically a new label for an earlier expression used to describe the "information haves and have-nots." He defines the digital divide as the gap, or "perceived gap," between those who have and do not have access to "information tools." According to Himma and Bottis (2014), however, this "divide" or gap can be more accurately understood as a "series of gaps" affecting the technological haves and have-nots. For example, there are gaps between those have and do not have digital devices and Internet access and also gaps (or divisions) between those who have and do not have the knowledge and ability to use digital tools (and thus enjoy their benefits). So, the digital divide refers not only to a division or gap affecting mere access to information technology; it also reflects, as Ryder (2015) points out, the significant gap between those who can and those who cannot "effectively benefit" from that technology.[2]

For our purposes, issues affecting the digital divide can be organized into two broad categories: the divide *between* nations and the divide *within* nations. The division between information-rich and information-poor nations is sometimes referred to as the "global digital divide"; the technological divides within nations, on the contrary, typically exist between rich and poor persons, racial majority and minority groups, men and women, and so forth. We begin with a look at the global digital divide.

10.1.1 The Global Digital Divide

Consider some statistics ranging from 2000 to 2014. In 2000, it was estimated that 361 million people, approximately 5.8% of the world's population, were online; the vast majority of those users lived in North America and Europe.[3] Since then, global Internet usage has expanded significantly. In June 2014, it was estimated that there were slightly more than three billion Internet users.[4] A significant shift had already occurred by 2005 when the list of countries or regions where more than 50% of the population used the Internet had grown to 30.[5] That year, seven nations—Australia, Canada, Japan, South Korea, Taiwan, the United Kingdom, and the United States—had an Internet penetration rate of higher than 60%.

As of 2014, the disparity between the percentage of Internet users in developed and developing countries continues to be significant. In India, for example, the penetration rate for Internet users is 15.8%, while in the United Kingdom, it is 89.8%.[6] The disparity is especially apparent when viewed from the perspective of continents or world regions. For example, in Africa (which includes approximately 15% of the world's population), the Internet penetration rate is 26.5%, whereas in North America, the Internet penetration rate is 87.7% (as of June 2014). On a positive note, however, the Internet usage growth in Africa was 2,527.4% between 2000 and 2011.[7] So, one might be encouraged by some reports describing the growth in Internet usage at the global level. Yet, despite the progress that has been made in the African continent, critics worry that much more work still needs to be done to narrow, and perhaps one day even bridge, the global divide.

One obstacle to eliminating the global digital divide altogether is that developing countries struggle with low literacy rates; many people in developing nations cannot read and write in their native language, let alone in English. And much of the material on the Internet is in English. This has influenced advocates for improved Internet service for global users to lobby for the development of Web applications that include more graphics and images that can serve as universal symbols. (We return to this point in our discussion of technology-related access issues affecting disabled persons, in Section 10.2.) However, O'Hara and Stevens (2006) note that regardless of whatever explanation we give for the perpetuation of a global digital divide, one thing is patently clear: Inequalities regarding access to cybertechnology are closely tied to "economic inequality."[8]

10.1.2 The Digital Divide within Nations

Many developed nations still have significant divides within them regarding access to cybertechnology. For example, O'Hara and Stevens point to one such discrepancy in the United Kingdom. They note that in 2004, approximately one-half of all households were online, while only 3% of the poorest households were included in this number. As one might expect, there are also significant disparities within some developing nations as well. And in rapidly developing countries like India, the divisions that currently exist may eventually deepen. Consider that a growing segment of India's population is fluent in English and has the technical literacy required to work on many of the highly skilled jobs outsourced there; those on the other side of the divide, comprising the majority of the population of India, tend to have a low level of literacy and little or no access to digital/cybertechnology.

Some countries, including the United States, have instituted specific strategies designed to bridge the divide within their national borders. In response to concerns about the gap that existed in America in the early 1990s between those with and without access to computers, the Clinton administration initiated the National Information Infrastructure (NII) to ensure that all Americans would have access to information technology. To accomplish this objective, the National Telecommunications and Information Administration (NTIA) conducted a series of studies that investigated computer use among various groups.

One question that arose from the NTIA reports was whether a *universal service* policy was needed to ensure that all Americans have an appropriate level of access to Internet technology. Universal service policies have been controversial because they require subsidies, which often result either in user fees or higher taxes. However, proponents of a universal service policy for the Internet have pointed to the model that was used to subsidize telephone technology when that became available in the early part of the twentieth century. Without some kind of government-supported subsidy, people living in less-populated rural areas would not have been able to afford this new technology. So the U.S. Congress passed the Communications Act of 1934, which distributed the cost for telephone service in a way to make it affordable to all Americans. Today, the question is whether Internet access should be subsidized in a similar manner. In the case of telephone technology, arguments were made that having a telephone was necessary for one's well-being. Can the same argument be made in the case of digital/cyber technology and Internet access?

As we saw in Chapter 9, subsidies in the form of "E-rates" (i.e., federal technology discounts) have helped to defray the cost of Internet access for public schools and libraries in the United States. Unlike universal service policies involving telephones, which are aimed at subsidizing residential telephone service, E-rates for Internet access apply only to "community points of access" such as public libraries. While E-rates may support universal Internet *access*, they do not provide universal Internet *service*. So, critics such as Chapman and Rotenberg (1995) have argued that merely providing community points of access to the Internet would be similar to a policy that simply placed telephones in public locations rather than making telephone service affordable for all Americans.

Some critics worry that the absence of a (universal) Internet service policy in the United States could adversely affect school-age children in low-income families. Consider the following scenario where someone tries to convince you that an Internet service policy is needed to level the playing field for economically disadvantaged students attending U.S. public schools.

▶ SCENARIO 10–2: Providing In-Home Internet Service for Public School Students

Sara, an advocate for disadvantaged youth in low-income families in America, asks you to review a short editorial she is preparing for a blog (dedicated to education-related issues). In that editorial, she argues: There are several reasons why the U.S. government should provide in-home Internet service for all students (Grades 1–12) whose families cannot afford to pay for it. First, the federal government mandates that all school-age children (of U.S. citizens) receive a free public school education. Second, the government is required to provide those children with the resources they need to complete their education (i.e., classrooms, labs, textbooks, etc.). Today, having in-home Internet service is a critical resource for students to be able to complete their homework assignments. School-aged students whose families cannot afford in-home Internet service are at a significant disadvantage in competing in the educational system. So, students whose families cannot afford the cost of in-home Internet service should have that service subsidized by government funding. ■

Is Sara's argument convincing? One might initially be inclined to object by noting that these students could go to public libraries to get the online resources needed to complete their homework assignments. However, Sara could reply that libraries are mere "points of access" (as noted above) and thus do not provide the kind of (universal) service needed by these economically disadvantaged students. Furthermore, Sarah might note that if we adopt the rationale used in her critics' objection, we should also require students to go to libraries to get the textbooks needed for their homework assignments as well, rather than having schools freely provide students with these resources. For example, she might invoke the following analogy: Because textbooks, like home Internet access, are essential resources for students completing their homework assignments, the same policies should apply for textbooks as for Internet access. But it is unlikely that Sarah's opponents would want to eliminate free textbooks for school-aged children.

Two points in Sara's argument are also worth reiterating. First, she is not advocating (government subsidized) universal Internet service at home for *all* school-aged children; rather, this subsidy would apply only for those students in families below a certain economic/income threshold. Second, this subsidized (Internet) service would apply for those eligible school-age children only while they are students and only during those periods of the year when they are actually in school; in other words, there would be appropriate constraints, especially in the form of time limitations, for this Internet service policy.

It would be interesting to evaluate Sara's argument via the seven-step strategy described in Chapter 3 to see whether it satisfies the requirements for being both valid and sound. Of course, even if the argument can be shown to be valid, that is, merely in virtue of its logical form, one could still ask whether the premises are all empirically true. Assuming that they are, we could also ask whether a key claim made in this argument—namely, that school-age children in families unable to afford in-home Internet service are at a significant disadvantage in competing in the educational system—describes an issue that is fundamentally *ethical* in nature.

10.1.3 Is the Digital Divide an Ethical Issue?

What does it mean to say that the digital divide is an ethical issue? Is every kind of divide regarding unequal access to goods and services necessarily an ethical problem? Some skeptics have pointed to the divide between those who have and do not have Mercedes-Benz automobiles, arguing that there is a "Mercedes-Benz divide" and that many of us fall on the "wrong side" of it; they also correctly note that this kind of divide is not an ethical issue. But we could respond to these skeptics by pointing to the divisions that exist between those who do and those who do not have access to vital resources such as food and healthcare—divisions that many ethicists believe raise questions affecting the just distribution of primary goods and resources. So, how should we view unequal access to cybertechnology? Is it closer to the Mercedes-Benz divide, or is it closer to divisions involving access to food and healthcare?

Distributive Justice and Access to Vital Human Resources

As suggested above, some question whether the digital divide raises concerns affecting distributive justice. But what do we mean by "distributive justice," especially in the context of cybertechnology? According to van den Hoven and Rooksby (2008):

> Distributive justice in contemporary information societies concerns, among other issues, the distribution of information, information services, and information infrastructures.[9]

The authors note that while there has been much enthusiasm about the emergence of new technologies, there is also concern over "the uneven distribution of the new information wealth, both within nations and internationally."[10] To argue that the unequal distribution of information wealth is a moral issue would require that we show that information is a kind of "primary good" that is vital for human flourishing. So, we need to consider whether information meets the criteria of a kind of good or resource that is *vital* for one's well-being. Additionally, if we can show that not having access to cybertechnology either denies or unfairly limits access to information or to certain kinds of basic goods—what Moor (2004) calls "core goods" (or "core values"), such as knowledge, ability, freedom, and so forth—then we can make a fairly strong case that unequal access to cybertechnology is a moral issue affecting distributive justice.

In his classic work, *A Theory of Justice*, philosopher John Rawls introduces the notion of *primary social goods*, which are resources that satisfy basic human needs and thus have a special value or "moral weight" in society. Rawls notes that with these goods, humans "can generally be assured of greater success in carrying out their intentions and in advancing their needs."[11] Van den Hoven and Rooksby argue that Rawls' theory of justice in general, and his notion of a primary social good in particular, can be extended to include "information goods." They further argue, however that a "fully fledged theory of justice that takes adequate account of the new information goods" still needs to be fleshed out.[12] In the meantime, however, we can examine some recent models that have been advanced to show why the digital divide is indeed a moral issue affecting distributive justice.

One model has been articulated by Moss (2002) who argues that persons lacking access to cybertechnology are deprived of resources that are *vital for their well-being*. He points out that without access to cybertechnology, people are unfairly disadvantaged because their:

1. Access to knowledge is significantly lessened or prevented.
2. Ability to participate fully in the political decision-making process and to receive important information is greatly diminished.
3. Economic prospects are severely hindered.[13]

First, Moss claims that people who are deprived of access to cybertechnology are not able to benefit from the increasing range of information available on the Internet and thus are falling further behind in the information era. Second, because of political barriers to participation in the decision-making processes in developing countries, people in remote areas without access to the Internet may have no means at all of participating in national debates or of receiving information about important developmental matters and policies that can significantly affect them. Third, Moss believes that because so much economic growth is driven by the information and communication sector, people living in countries that are not part of this sector are disadvantaged.

With regard to Moss's second and third points, Norris (2001) makes a similar observation by noting that "the underclass" of information poor may become "further marginalized" because they will lack the skills needed both for "civic engagement" and economic success. Norris also worries that because people in this group will not possess essential computer-related skills, they will not be able to enjoy the kinds of good careers made possible by "educational opportunities."[14]

In response to advocates like Moss and Norris, however, one could argue that some people (and some nations) have always been disadvantaged in accessing new technologies such as automobiles, household appliances, and so forth. But, once again, we can respond by pointing out that this kind of criticism misses a crucial point. As we have noted, disparities in access to certain technologies and goods, such as Mercedes-Benz automobiles, do not in themselves constitute an ethical issue. We should also point out that divisions of this type are generally accepted in capitalist societies. However, if Moss's thesis about why cybertechnology is important is correct, then having access to cybertechnology is essential for one's *well-being* in ways that having access to other kinds of technologies—for example, "discretionary technologies" that provide convenience and entertainment—is not. So, one question that arises is: Do we have a moral obligation to bridge the digital divide? And if we do, are affluent nations the ones responsible for bridging this divide?

Making the Case for a Moral Obligation to Bridge the Digital Divide

Bottis and Himma (2008), in presenting their argument for the view that "affluent nations" have a moral obligation to bridge the divide, begin by clarifying some important points. For example, they note that we first need to draw a critical distinction between saying that "X is a good thing to do" and saying that "we are obligated to do X." Bottis and Himma believe that most people would likely agree that eliminating the digital divide would be a good thing to do; they also suggest, however, that there would likely be far less consensus as to whether we (i.e., some affluent nations) have an obligation to do it.

Bottis and Himma point out that one's failing to do something morally good is not necessarily morally wrong; they use the example of someone's risking his or life to save a person caught in a fire in a building. Failure to risk one's life to save another here, they correctly note, is not something that necessarily merits either blame or punishment. Of course, the act of attempting to save someone's life in the fire would be a good thing, but (assuming that you and I are not firefighters) we are not morally obligated to do it. Doing an act such as that crosses over to a category that philosophers and ethicists call "supererogatory." That is, the act of risking one's life in a fire to save another is morally good but is also "beyond the call of moral obligation." Bottis and Himma also note that we "praise supererogatory acts, but not obligatory acts" and we "blame nonperformance of obligatory acts, but not supererogatory acts."[15] So in this scheme, should we view the act of bridging the digital divide as a supererogatory act, in which case we are not morally obligated to do anything?

Himma (2007) points out that because many people believe that we are morally obligated only to do no harm, they infer that we have no obligation to bridge the digital divide. But he also believes that such a view is "inconsistent with the ethics of every classically theistic religion as well as our ordinary intuitions, as well as classic theories of deontology and consequentialism." In the case of deontology, for example, Himma notes that virtually all deontological theories hold that we "have an obligation to help the poor."[16] For example, he points to the *prima facie* obligation of *beneficence* that we have to help those in need, as implied in Ross' deontological theory. (You may wish to review Ross' ethical theory of act deontology described in Chapter 2.)

In Chapter 2, we saw that contract-based ethical theory holds that while we are morally obligated to "do no harm," we have no explicit obligation to do good—in this case, no moral obligation to bridge the digital divide. According to this view, we are behaving morally as long as we do nothing to prevent others from acquiring cybertechnology and Internet access. But is this minimalist view of morality adequate? Recall that in our discussion of contract-based ethical theories in Chapter 2, we saw that individuals and nations have a moral obligation to do good (to others) only in cases where individuals or nations have an explicit contract in which they are required to come to the aid of others. However, we also saw that there are some compelling reasons to be skeptical about such a limited theory of moral obligation.

In our critique of contract-based ethical theories, we saw that a more robust theory of morality requires that we come to the aid of those who are in danger of being harmed, whenever it is in our power to do so. For one thing, we saw that doing this could help to make cyberspace a safer place, especially for those individuals and groups vulnerable to online harm. And we can construct an analogous argument to show why coming to the aid of other kinds of vulnerable (or at least disadvantaged) individuals and groups—that is, those without Internet access—would also be the right thing to do. If Moss is correct in claiming that access to cybertechnology is vital to one's well-being, then is it plausible to suggest that we have at least some obligation to provide access to those who are disadvantaged?

▶ 10.2 CYBERTECHNOLOGY AND THE DISABLED

Not only do equity-and-access issues involving cybertechnology affect poor people in developing nations and people in low-income groups within developed nations, they also affect many disabled people. So, some suggest that core equity-and-access issues underlying the digital divide apply to this group of people as well. There has been much discussion about implementing strategies and policies to make the Internet and digital technologies more accessible to disabled persons. Tim Berners-Lee, director of the World Wide Web Consortium (W3C) and the inventor of the HTTP protocol that underlies the Web, has stated, "The power of the Web is in its universality. Access by everyone regardless of disability is an essential aspect."

The W3C was formed, in large part, to promote standards that ensure universal Web access. It established a Web Accessibility Initiative (WAI), which has produced guidelines and protocols for developing software applications that improve access for disabled persons. These applications range from software used in speech synthesizers and screen magnifiers to proposed software applications that will benefit people with visual, hearing, physical, cognitive, and neurological disabilities.[17]

WAI representatives have worked with industry groups and governmental organizations to establish guidelines for the design of "user agents," which are intended to lower barriers to Web accessibility for people with disabilities. These user agents include Web browsers and other types of software that retrieve and render Web content; the agents are designed to conform and communicate with other technologies, especially "assistive technologies" such as screen readers (which perform a function similar to Braille applications in offline contexts). Grodzinsky (2000) argues that computers equipped with assistive technologies and "adaptive devices" can be "equalizers" in the era of information technology because they enable people with disabilities to participate in and compete for jobs in the contemporary workplace.

Some critics might ask why we should continue to fund initiatives such as WAI, especially because of the financial commitment involved and because disabled persons comprise a relatively small portion of the overall population. In response to those critics, WAI proponents such as Asakawa (2012) argue that access to technology is not simply a privilege but rather a "human right." Other WAI supporters, however, take a different tack in pressing their case for why initiatives for the disabled should continue to be supported. For example, they point out that some measures taken for the disabled have had positive outcomes for other groups, especially poor people who are often forced to deal with literacy problems and inadequate equipment. It may well turn out that voice-recognition technology designed to assist disabled persons who are unable to use keyboards will ultimately also benefit nondisabled persons with low literacy skills. So we see that larger groups of (nondisabled) people have benefited and could continue to benefit from some Web-based initiatives designed for disabled persons, even though the resulting positive effects in the past may have been unanticipated and unintended.

We can also point to an example of an accessibility-related initiative in the nondigital world that was intended to accommodate disabled persons yet has benefited the public in general. Ramps designed for wheelchair accessibility have not only benefited people in wheelchairs but have also been very useful to nondisabled persons as well, such as parents pushing baby carriages. Also, consider some of the advantages that sloped curbs on street corners have provided many nondisabled persons—bicyclists and skaters have benefited from these features, which were initially intended to serve disabled persons (Woodbury 2002). So, many of WAI's proponents argue, analogously, that ordinary users will likely continue to benefit from the computer design enhancements to user interfaces that are initially intended to assist disabled persons.

Because improving access to cybertechnology for the disabled has potential benefits for society as a whole, we can formulate a utilitarian argument to advance this cause. However, we should also be cautious about extending this argument too far. What would happen if, in the future, the broader population did not realize any benefits from improving access to cybertechnology for the disabled? Could this kind of outcome lend support to a utilitarian argument against investing in initiatives that improved access for the disabled? After considering this, you can better understand some of the possible dangers of relying too heavily on utilitarian principles when advancing a moral argument for improved access for the disabled.

We conclude this section by noting that there are additional concerns affecting cybertechnology and the disabled that are unable to be examined here. Our main objective in this section, however, was to identify and briefly describe some key issues and concerns involving the ongoing debate about which kinds of initiatives ought to be implemented to improve cybertechnology access for disabled persons. Next, we examine the impact of that technology for racial minorities.

▶ 10.3 CYBERTECHNOLOGY AND RACE

We have seen that even in developed countries like the United States, many lower-income individuals and families still do not have in-home Internet access; not surprisingly, many of these individuals also belong to racial and ethnic minority groups. In this section, we examine race-related issues affecting cybertechnology from two distinct perspectives:

1. Statistical data concerning Internet usage patterns of racial minority groups
2. The role(s) that the Internet can play in either exacerbating or reducing racism

We begin our analysis with a brief discussion of (1).

10.3.1 Internet Usage Patterns

Consider some statistics ranging from 2000 to 2011 that correlate income (social class) and race with the digital divide in the United States. In 2000, 51% of all homes had at least one computer, and 41.5% of all homes had Internet access. In terms of income, 86.3% of households earning more than $75,000 per year had Internet access, while of those households earning below $15,000 per year, only 12.7% had access. From the vantage point of race, 46.1% of white Americans and 56.8% of Asian Americans had access, contrasted with only 23.5% of African Americans and 23.1% of Hispanics who did.[18]

By 2008, 73% of adult men and women in the United States had Internet access at home, while 90% of young people between the ages of 18 and 29 used the Internet. However, the penetration rate for black Internet users in the United States then was 59%, which was still well below the penetration for the American population as a whole.[19] In 2011, however, statistics for African American vs. white users changed significantly. Whereas Internet usage among whites was estimated to be 88%, the rate of African Americans using the Internet had grown to 80%. Perhaps even more interesting was the rate at which the use of access to broadband Internet connection had grown for African Americans. Whereas 65% of African American Internet users had broadband access, only 53% of white American Internet users enjoyed this service; nearly half of these users had not migrated from earlier forms of Internet access such as dial-up technologies.[20]

Yet, despite the gains made by African Americans (vis-à-vis their white counterparts) regarding Internet use, some significant differences in usage patterns between the two groups continue to persist. For example, Burn (2011) notes that whereas 26% of white Americans used the Internet for entertainment purposes, 68% of African Americans used it for this purpose. African American Internet users also used the Web more frequently than white users for activities such as news, health, and sports.

Our analysis of technology and race thus far has focused primarily on statistical data pertaining to racial groups—mainly African Americans—with regard to levels of Internet access. We have not yet considered other kinds of technology- and race-related questions. For example, have Internet-based technologies exacerbated racism? Or, have they helped to reduce—or possibly even eliminate—racism? While one might initially be inclined to assume the latter to be true, we need to question that assumption.

10.3.2 Racism and the Internet

Kretchmer and Karveth (2001) note that the study of race in cyberspace has often lead to paradoxical inferences. For example, they point out that on the one hand, the Internet has provided both an opportunity to discover and a forum to confront racial issues; On the other hand, however, cyberspace could be viewed as providing forums that have perpetuated, or perhaps even enhanced, aspects of racism. In support of the latter point of view, the Internet has introduced new tools, techniques, and forums for harassing members of racial and ethnic groups. In this sense, Internet technology can be viewed as a vehicle that has magnified both the significance and rhetoric of some racially motivated hate groups.

Lynn Theismeyer has examined some of the "rhetorical roles" that the Internet plays with respect to race. Her analysis of the rhetoric of racism does not focus on specific racial and minority groups in the United States, such as African Americans and Hispanics, but rather on the rise of neo-Nazi propaganda internationally. Theismeyer describes two distinct kinds of racist speech that have proliferated on the Internet: (i) online communications (music, images, broadcasts, etc.) that "exhort users to act against target groups" and (ii) rhetoric that indirectly promotes or justifies violence.[21] We should note, however, that some instances of what Theismeyer describes as racially controversial "rhetoric" would likely be protected in the

United States under the First Amendment right to free speech. So, it has not been easy to control certain forms of online racist rhetoric in the United States.

As we saw in Chapter 9, some European countries, especially Germany and France, have made a greater effort than the United States to restrict online hate speech that has targeted racial groups; this has been especially apparent in the case of neo-Nazi organizations. We also saw (in Chapter 9) that the U.S. government has focused more on censoring pornography, which many also view as offensive speech, than it has on efforts to combat online hate speech affecting race. This has allowed for some White supremacist groups in the United States, including the Ku Klux Klan (KKK), to establish Web sites for organizing demonstrations and spreading their messages of racial prejudice.[22] The designers and operators of these Web sites have also sometimes used misleading and deceptive keywords to attract visitors. For example, racist Web sites have deceptively used keywords, such as "Martin Luther King Jr.," to lure unsuspecting persons to their sites. So, someone searching for information about Dr. King's life might be directed to a Web site where he or she is instead subjected to racist hate speech directed against African Americans.

To what extent have racist Web sites influenced and possibly exacerbated, racial prejudice in the United States, as well as at the international level? Theismeyer believes that, at this point, it is not yet possible to know whether online technologies have been the main cause of the rapid spread of racism, especially in the neo-Nazism movement in Europe. However, she is convinced that the Internet has been its principal tool.[23]

In Section 10.5.2, we examine some ways in which blogs and the blogosphere also can either directly or indirectly contribute to the promotion of racial prejudice online. For example, some extreme right-wing political blogs have portrayed U.S. President Barack Obama in ways that are generally considered to be offensive and demeaning to African Americans. On the one hand, these blogs include content that is protected by free speech; on the other hand, they can reinforce racial stereotypes and perpetuate racial prejudice.

▶ 10.4 CYBERTECHNOLOGY AND GENDER

Other equity-and-access concerns associated with cybertechnology in general, and with the digital divide in particular, can be analyzed with respect to gender. Feminist authors and others who advocate for women's issues proffer arguments similar to those advanced by or on behalf of African Americans (and other racial minorities), which we examined in the preceding section. Women, like the members of many racial and ethnic groups, have not always been included in important decisions about technology policies and, until very recently, have not participated to the same degree as men in the use of technology.

We can begin by noting that the gap that has traditionally existed between the percentage of female and male Internet users in the United States had narrowed significantly by the beginning of the twenty-first century. A report by the *Pew Internet & American Life Project* in 2005 noted that young women were slightly more likely to be online than young men and that the number of black women online surged between 2002 and 2005 (to the point where black women who used the Internet outnumbered black men by about 10%). Pew Internet Project surveys conducted in 2005 also reported that in the United States, 66% of women went online, as opposed to 68% of men. But some analysts noted that women slightly outnumbered men in the Internet-user population because women made up a greater share, that is, proportionally, of the overall U.S. population. By 2008, however, even the percentage of women who used the Internet was equal to that of men.[24]

Although the gap between female and male Internet users has narrowed considerably in many Western countries, this has not been the case globally. However, some specific global initiatives have been introduced to address problems underlying gender equity and access in non-Western nations.[25] But even if the global divide between men and women who enjoy access to digital technology has been narrowed, we can ask whether that fact in itself is sufficient to resolve the core gender-related controversies? Adam (2005) argues that gender issues involving cybertechnology are much more complex than concerns about levels of online access. For example, we will see that gender issues also arise because of bias in software design, as well as the portrayal of women in many video games.

We next examine gender-related cybertechnology issues in terms of two important categories:

i. Women's access to high-technology jobs/careers
ii. Gender bias in software design (especially in video games)

10.4.1 Access to High-Technology Jobs

Some authors believe that to better understand gender-related issues affecting cybertechnology, we need to examine the challenges facing women who consider jobs and careers in computer science and engineering. To that end, Camp (1997) has conducted research on what she and others call "pipeline issues" by analyzing statistics involving the number of women entering the computer science and engineering professions; the data collected during the past 25 or so years suggest that proportionately few women elect to pursue degrees in either field. Wessells (1990) pointed out that in 1989, fewer than 5% of those awarded PhD degrees in computer science were women. According to slightly later statistics provided by Camp, in 1997, that number had increased to 15.4% (during 1993–1994). However, Camp also noted that the percentage of women pursuing bachelors and masters degrees in computer science had declined slightly during those years.

Kirlidog, Aykol, and Gulsecen (2009) cite more recent evidence to support the ongoing concerns about the "pipeline," and they argue that computer science is still typically regarded as a "male profession," both in industry and academia. The authors also claim that women remain in the "margins" of a male-dominated profession, which is filled with highly gendered expressions such as "killing or aborting programs," "workbench," "toolkit," etc., that reflect the masculine culture of the field. Kirlidog et al. identify three "net results" of the male-dominated computing profession in which women are:

1. Underrepresented in computer-related jobs
2. (Even more) underrepresented in the managerial ranks in the computing field because of the "glass ceiling"
3. Paid less than men for doing the same jobs[26]

To support (1), they cite a study showing that while 46% of the United States workforce was made up of women, only 28% of computer science and mathematics-related jobs were held by women. This problem is by no means unique to the United States or to Western nations, they argue, because a large discrepancy can also be found in the computing field in developing nations such as India. With regard to (2), they show how women in India and elsewhere are underrepresented not only in terms of the number of hi-tech jobs but also in the number of managerial positions in the computing field. In support of (3), the authors point out that (i) the average woman in India earns approximately 60% of what a man is paid for the same job, and (ii) only 3% of management-level jobs are held by women.[27]

So the "pipeline" concerns regarding the low numbers of women entering the computer profession (initially reported in the late 1980s and early 1990s), as well as the limited career opportunities for women who entered the profession, seem to have persisted well into the twenty-first century. Many of those who monitor the pipeline believe that we need to worry about some implications that this continued trend could have for the future of the computing field. Some note, for example, that "pipeline statistics" provide us with projections regarding the proportion of women who will likely be able to contribute in critical areas of the computer/IT professions such as those affecting national security. For example, Spafford (2014) worries that more women are already needed, and will likely continue to be needed, in the field of cybersecurity.

Before concluding this section, we should note that some authors writing on the topic of gender and computing have been critical of approaches that focus solely, or even mainly, on access-related or "pipeline" issues. For example, Adam (2004, 2005) notes that while examining the low numbers of women in the computing profession is important because it reveals existing inequities in the field, this approach also tends to severely limit the study of gender and computing issues mainly to access-related concerns. Adam also believes that focusing on this approach may cause us to miss an opportunity to use feminist ethical theory in our analysis of broader cyberethics issues such as privacy and power in terms of their gender implications. She worries that current computer ethics research involving gender is "undertheorized," and she argues that we need a "gender-informed ethics" to improve the process. For example, Adam argues that this theory helps us to better understand issues such as cyberstalking and Internet pornography in ways that traditional ethical theories cannot.[28] Unfortunately, however, a fuller examination of Adam's gender-informed ethical theory is beyond the scope of this chapter.

10.4.2 Gender Bias in Software Design and Video Games

Some authors have argued that in the past, educational software tended to favor male learning behaviors and thus was biased against female learners. So, there was some concern then about the effect that gender bias in educational software programs might have for young female students. Although concerns about this kind of gender bias have dissipated in recent years, critics argue that gender bias can still be found in many other kinds of software applications. This is especially apparent in the case of video game software.

Buchanan (2000) argues that bias in the development of video games has raised two distinct kinds of ethical concerns because these games tend to:

1. Either misrepresent or exclude female characters
2. Perpetuate traditional sexist stereotypes

With respect to (1), she argues that the representational politics of gender in video games needs greater evaluation, because many computer games, especially virtual sports games, include no female characters at all. And with regard to (2), Buchanan argues that some video games, such as Barbie Fashion Designer, have reinforced traditional cultural stereotypes along gender lines.

Some might tend to dismiss concerns about gender bias in video games on the grounds that many women simply aren't interested in them. However, Brey (2008) argues that the question of gender bias in these games is nevertheless "morally significant." He points out, for example, that if:

> computer games tend to be designed and marketed for men, then women are at an unfair advantage, as they consequently have less opportunity to enjoy computer games and their possible benefits. Among such benefits may be greater computer literacy, an important quality in today's market place.[29]

Brey also notes that many analysts believe that the computer industry is mainly to blame for the gender gap that exists in the video game industry. For example, most game developers are male; also, there has been little interest on the part of developers to design suitable games for women. Additionally, Brey points out that very few computer games include decent role models for women. He also notes that a disproportionate number of the female characters in these games are strippers or prostitutes and that these characters tend to have "unrealistic body images." (Brey's points are further examined in Chapter 11 in our discussion of ethical aspects of virtual environments and virtual reality applications, including video games.) We conclude this section by noting that Brey and Buchanan each make a plausible case for how the design of video games contributes to gender bias and for why that bias is indeed morally significant.

▶ 10.5 CYBERTECHNOLOGY, DEMOCRACY, AND DEMOCRATIC IDEALS

In previous sections of this chapter, we examined equity-and-access issues pertaining to social/economic class (the digital divide), race, gender, and disabled persons. Underlying many of the concerns involving these diverse sociodemographic groups were issues that also affect democracy, in particular, as well as democratic ideals and values in general. Not surprisingly, then, a number of interesting questions arise at the intersection of democracy and cybertechnology. For example, some authors question whether the Internet is an inherently democratic technology, while others question whether we should develop the Internet along democratic principles.[30] In our analysis of democracy and cybertechnology, however, we consider two slightly different kinds of questions:

1. Has the use of cybertechnology (so far) enhanced democracy and democratic ideals or has it threatened them?
2. What impact has the use of cybertechnology had on the political election process in democratic nations?

10.5.1 Has Cybertechnology Enhanced or Threatened Democracy?

Why should we care whether cybertechnology favors and possibly enhances democracy, or whether it instead threatens and potentially undermines it? We can begin by noting that democracy, when compared to alternative forms of government, seems an attractive political structure and, arguably, one of the fairest. Because of these assumptions, Graham (1999) points out that it is difficult to get people, especially in the Western world, to engage in a serious debate about the merits of democracy. He correctly notes that democracy, along with its corresponding notion of a "democratic ideal," has won almost universal and largely unquestioning acceptance in the West. Graham also points out, however, that not all political theorists and philosophers have regarded democracy as the best—or, in some cases, not even as an adequate—form of government. For example, he notes that in *The Republic*, Plato was highly critical of democracy and viewed it as a form of mob rule in which important decisions could be made by a citizenry that typically was not well informed on matters involving the state. And Graham also notes that in the nineteenth century, philosopher John Stuart Mill questioned whether democracy was indeed the ideal form of government.[31]

Let us assume, for the sake of argument, that democracy is superior to alternative political structures. We can still ask whether cybertechnology favors democracy and democratic ideals. Many who believe that it does tend to point to one or more of four factors, that is, where the Internet is alleged to provide greater:

a. *Openness* (i.e., an open architecture)
b. Empowerment
c. Choice
d. Access to information

With regard to (a), some authors argue that the Internet provides an open forum in which ideas can generally be communicated freely and easily. Other authors, focusing on (b), note that the Internet empowers certain groups by giving them a "voice," or say, in some matters that they had not previously had. Still other authors, such as Graham, suggest that the Internet empowers individuals by giving them more choices and thus greater freedom.[32] And Sunstein (2001, 2007) points out that the Internet has provided greater access to information at a lower cost. Perhaps Introna and Nissenbaum (2000) sum up these points best when they note that in the early days of the Internet, people tended to assume that online search technologies would:

> give voice to diverse social, economic, and cultural groups, to members of society not frequently heard in the public sphere [and] empower the traditionally disempowered.[33]

Values affecting openness, empowerment, choice, and greater access to information all seem to favor democracy. Thus, insofar as cybertechnology facilitates these values, it would also seem to favor democracy and democratic ideals. But does the Internet's "open" architecture necessarily facilitate democratic values universally? Consider that some countries have gone to great lengths to censor political speech in cyberspace. For example, China required Google to comply with strict rules for filtering information, which many nations in the West would view as unacceptable. Also, Saudi Arabia has censored political speech online. So, non-democratic countries have found some ways around the "open" architecture of the Internet and its ability to spread information freely.

Graham worries that some features of the Internet may even contribute to the "worst aspects" of democracy by fostering social and political fragmentation. A similar kind of concern is raised by Diaz (2008) when he asks whether Internet search technologies will filter out, and thus exclude, the kinds of "independent voices and diverse viewpoints" that are essential for a democracy. This worry is echoed by Pariser (2011) who believes that democracy is now threatened by a new mode of filtering on the Internet, involving "personalization filters," which are currently used by major search engines. We briefly consider each type of threat.

Social/Political Fragmentation and "Personalization" Filters

How does the Internet facilitate social and political fragmentation, and why is fragmentation problematic for a democratic society? The Internet fragments society by facilitating the formation of groups who depart from the mainstream perspectives of a cohesive society. An analogy involving television news programming in physical space might help us appreciate how easily social and political fragmentation can occur and why it can be problematic. Consider that until the advent of cable TV news programming in the 1970s, American television viewers relied primarily on the three major networks for the evening news reports. Even though the program formats varied slightly and even though different anchors delivered the news to viewers, all three presented "mainstream" news reporting that satisfied certain standards of accuracy and credibility before the networks would broadcast it. At times, the members of political groups may have been annoyed with, or possibly even offended by, the way that a particular story was presented, but the news reports were generally descriptive or factual. Some news programs also included commentaries, usually toward the end of the program, in which the commentator expressed an opinion, but there was a clear line between "factual" reporting and personal opinion.

Now you can select a news program that fits best with and reinforces your political ideology. For example, consider a news report of hostilities between Israelis and Palestinians. If supporters of Israel do not like the way the story is reported on an American news network, and if they have cable or satellite access to Israeli television, they can tune into an Israeli station for their news. Similarly, if Palestinian supporters dislike the American media's coverage, and if they have cable access to an Arab news network such as Al-Jazeera, they can choose to view the news story as broadcast via an Arab television station. On the one hand, these options provide supporters of both sides in this conflict with greater choices and seemingly greater freedom. On the other hand, these options can also increase social and political fragmentation.

We can apply a similar analogy to news reports of domestic political issues in the United States. Conservatives and liberals can each interact in online forums and visit Web sites that exclusively promote the political views that they embrace. Of course, a critic could point out that prior to the Internet, many people subscribed to newspapers and magazines that were labeled as either radically liberal or radically conservative and therefore biased in their reporting. But it is more difficult to filter information in physical space because people in most physical communities encounter individuals with ideological perspectives different from their own, even when they seek out only those who share their belief systems. In online forums, however, it is possible for individuals to be in contact with only those people who share their ideological beliefs. Thus, Epstein (2000) worries that in the near future, the concept of the "public square," where ideas have been traditionally debated could become *fragmented* into "thousands of highly specialized communities that do not communicate with one another."

Internet Filtering, Polarization, and Deliberative Democracy

As noted above, some critics now also worry about the impact that "personalization filters" used by contemporary search engine companies will have for democratic societies. Pariser fears that these filters enable a kind of "invisible autopropaganda," which can indoctrinate us with our own ideas. He notes that while democracy "requires citizens to see things from one another's point of view," we are instead increasingly "more enclosed in our own bubbles." He also notes that while a democracy "requires a reliance on shared facts," we are instead being presented with "parallel but separate universes."

Why is this trend away from citizens having shared facts so dangerous for a democracy? For one thing, consider the contentious debate about climate change in the United States during the past decade. Pariser points out that studies have shown that between 2001 and 2010, the views of people's beliefs about whether the climate was warming changed significantly along Republican vs. Democrat lines. The number of Republicans who believed that the planet was warming fell from 49% to 29%, while the number of Democrats rose from 60% to 70%. How is such a discrepancy regarding beliefs about climate change possible among people living in the same country? Pariser notes that a user's online search for "climate change" will turn up different results for an environmental activist than for an oil company executive; it will also generate different results for users whom the search algorithm understands to be Democrats rather than Republicans.

With entrenched views about current controversial topics such as climate change, citizens in democratic countries such as the United States are becoming increasingly polarized. Cass Sunstein worries that increased polarization threatens *deliberative democracy*—that is, the process of rationally debating issues in a public forum. He suggests that deliberative democracy may suffer irreparable harm because of the ways in which the Internet now filters information.

Why does Sunstein believe that deliberative democracy is threatened by Internet filtering? For one thing, he worries that people using software filters will not be inclined to gather new information that might broaden their views but will instead use information available to them on the Internet to reinforce their existing prejudices. Sunstein's concerns are echoed by Diaz (2008), who points out that if we wish to preserve the principles of deliberative democracy, we need to make sure that a "broad spectrum of information on any given topic" is disseminated on the Internet. A similar point is also made by Hinman (2005) when he argues that "free and undistorted access to information" is essential for a deliberative democracy to flourish. So, if these critics are correct, there are good reasons to be skeptical that cybertechnology, in the near term at least, will facilitate values essential for deliberative democracy.

We can conclude this section by noting that, as Sunstein suggests, cybertechnology seems to have both democracy-enhancing and democracy-threatening aspects. We saw that the

Internet's open architecture, which enables greater access to information and for that information to be shared freely and easily, would seem to enhance some democratic values. However, we also saw how Internet filtering schemes enable fragmentation and polarization that, in turn, undermine deliberative democracy.

10.5.2 How has Cybertechnology Affected Political Elections in Democratic Nations?

We now turn to our second principal question regarding democracy and cybertechnology: How has this technology impacted political elections so far? In answering this question, we look at the impact via two broad categories: (i) using electronic devices and social media sites for political fundraising, influencing voter turnout, and organizing political demonstrations and (ii) using political blogs to spread false information that could influence election outcomes. We begin with (i).

Electronic Devices and Social Media

Graham suggests that in representative democracies, such as the United States, cybertechnology might be used to concentrate more power in the hands of elected representatives instead of ordinary citizens. He also notes that many representatives and political leaders (including their staffs) tend to have both greater technological resources and the ability to use them more skillfully than many ordinary citizens. These factors, in Graham's view, suggest that those in power can effectively use these technological resources to retain their power. We can ask whether the following example illustrates Graham's point. In the 2004 U.S. presidential elections, Carl Rove, a former advisor in the George W. Bush administration, used BlackBerry (smartphone) technology to coordinate with Republican officials across all of the voting precincts in Ohio, a "battleground state" that would determine the winner of that year's election. Some political commentators suggested that Roves coordinating a state-wide, get-out-the-vote effort to target voters via the use of BlackBerry technology helped to ensure victory in Ohio, which provided the necessary electoral votes for President Bush to remain in power for four more years. Although it is difficult to prove that Rove's use of this technology helped the incumbent president to remain in power in 2004, we can see how the use of the latest technology in a state or national election can influence the voter turnout and ultimately the outcome of that election.

Next, consider that as Barack Obama prepared to run in the 2008 U.S. presidential elections, his staff organized a "grassroots" fund-raising strategy on the Internet through various social networking sites (SNSs) to raise millions of dollars (mostly as small contributions from young people) to finance his presidential campaign. (We examine SNSs in detail in Chapter 11.) In running for his second term in 2012, however, it was not clear whether his staff's use of the latest social media technologies helped him to win reelection and remain in power for four additional years. Yet, it would seem that Graham's claim may still have some merit. For example, we have seen how some political parties in power (in Western democracies, at least) have successfully used the latest available cybertechnologies to maintain their power. On the other hand, however, ordinary citizens in some nondemocratic countries, such as Tunisia and Egypt, have used electronic devices and social media to topple the powerful political regimes in those nations.

Recall our brief analysis of the "Arab Spring" in Scenario 10-1. There, we saw how a political movement that began in early 2011 in the Arab world succeeded in bringing down a series of governments largely because ordinary citizens had used digital technologies such as electronic devices and social media to organize their protests. So, it would seem that Graham's claim about political leaders in representative democracies being able to use technology to remain in power would not necessarily apply in the case political leaders in some nondemocratic nations.

Political Blogs and the Democratic Process

We next consider the impact that blogs (or Weblogs), especially political blogs, can have on democracy. (We discuss some broader ethical and social impacts of blogs and the "blogosphere" in more detail in Chapter 11 in connection with our analysis of online communities.) To what extent do political blogs reinforce democratic values and ideals, and how can they undermine them? Insofar as blogs function as instruments for communicating and disseminating information about important political issues, they would seem to reinforce values that favor democracy. But the standards for ensuring accuracy of the content posted in political blogs are not always adequate.

During the 2008 U.S. presidential elections, some extreme right-wing political bloggers reported that (then presidential candidate) Barack Obama was a Muslim and that he was not born in the United States.[34] At the same time, some radical left-wing bloggers reported that (vice presidential candidate) Sara Palin's youngest child was really her grandchild and that Palin was protecting her unmarried daughter from embarrassment.[35] Neither story was vetted in the way that a report submitted by a professional journalist working for a reputable news organization would be, and neither story would likely have been published in a reputable newspaper. But these stories were read online by numerous people, many of whom may have assumed the reports about Obama and Palin to be true merely because they were published on the Internet.

As (hard copy) newspaper subscriptions continue to decline, and as more and more people get their news online, we may have to worry about the standards of accuracy that apply in the online political news media, especially political blogs. As we noted above, a democracy depends on the dissemination of truthful information to flourish and survive. So perhaps we should be concerned about the lack of veracity in some political blogs and the implications that the mass dissemination of false information online may have for the future of democracy.

However, some analysts do not seem concerned about the potentially negative effects of blogging for democracy. For example, Goldman (2008) points out that even if individual blogs are biased, it doesn't follow that the entire blogosphere is. (Recall our discussion of the Fallacy of Composition in Chapter 3, where we saw that attributes that apply to the part do not necessarily apply to the whole.) As Goldman aptly puts the matter, "the reliability of the blogosphere shouldn't be identified with the reliability of a single blog."[36] Goldman also believes that it is possible that the blogosphere may ultimately contribute to the preservation of democratic values.

In concluding this section, we note that many controversial issues affecting cybertechnology and democracy have not been examined. For example, there are controversies surrounding e-voting, as well as the selling of votes online; unfortunately, these and other issues are beyond the intended scope of this chapter. Note also that our brief analysis of some key cybertechnology and democracy issues in Section 10.5 was not intended to be exhaustive.

▶ 10.6 THE TRANSFORMATION AND THE QUALITY OF WORK

In Sections 10.1–10.5, we examined questions pertaining to equity-and-access issues as they affect both *sociodemographic groups*—for example, disabled persons, racial minorities, and women—and *social/political institutions*, mainly as they impact democracy and democratic values. In this section, we consider some equity-and-access-related issues from a third perspective or social category. Here, we examine the impact of cybertechnology on a *social sector*: the contemporary workplace. Though still relatively new, cybertechnology already has had a profound effect on employment as well as on the nature of work itself. Computers and cybertechnology also significantly affect the quality of work life. Before considering this impact, however, we examine issues involving the transformation of the contemporary workplace and the displacement of jobs.

10.6.1 Job Displacement and the Transformed Workplace

While it is debatable whether cybertechnology has benefited workers, overall, it is quite clear that this technology has significantly changed the workplace. Some have gone so far as to suggest that cybertechnology has *transformed* the nature of work itself. One question that frequently arises in discussions about the transformation of employment by cybertechnology is whether, on balance, it has created or eliminated more jobs. There are arguments to support both sides of this debate. Although cybertechnology has caused certain industries to eliminate human jobs, it has enabled other industries, such as computer support companies, to create jobs; social scientists often refer to this shift as *job displacement*. We examine some key issues involving job displacement from two broad perspectives or categories:

A. Automation, robotics, and expert systems

B. Remote work, outsourcing, and globalization

Whereas job displacement issues affecting (A) typically result from the introduction of new kinds of machines (hardware) as well as new software applications, those affecting (B) often result from changes in policies and practices involving employment and the workplace (that, in turn, are often influenced by technological developments). We begin with a brief analysis of (A).

Automation, Robotics, and Expert Systems

Job displacement is often associated with *automation*. Social and ethical issues involving automation are by no means new, nor are they unique to cybertechnology. Social scientists note that the Industrial Revolution transformed jobs into smaller, discrete tasks that could be automated by machines, creating working conditions that adversely affected the lives of many workers. When new automated technology threatened to replace many workers, one group of disenchanted workers in England—later referred to as "Luddites"—smashed machines used to make textiles. ("Luddite" is derived from a nineteenth-century British worker, Ned Ludd, who reputedly led workers in destroying factory machinery.)

Just as the Luddites resisted factory technology in the nineteenth century because they thought it threatened their jobs and thus their livelihoods, some workers have opposed developments involving cybertechnology for similar reasons. In the 1970s, for example, workers tried to stall developments in microprocessor-based technology, fearing that it would lead to a loss of jobs. Workers as well individuals in general who resist technological change, and who have a pessimistic view of the impact of cybertechnology in the workplace, are sometimes referred to as neo-Luddites.

Developments in *robotics* have also raised social concerns affecting job displacement. Robots, equipped with motor abilities that enable them to manipulate objects, can be programmed to perform tasks that are either (i) routine and mundane for humans or (ii) considered hazardous to humans. As Lin (2012) so aptly puts it, robots are typically tasked to perform the "three Ds"—that is, jobs that humans consider "dull, dirty, and dangerous." Although robots were once fairly unsophisticated, contemporary robotic systems are able to perform a wide range of tasks. (We examine some ethical aspects of robots and robotic systems in detail in Chapter 12.)

Whereas (physical) robots have eliminated many blue-collar jobs, sophisticated programs called expert systems (*ESs*) threaten many professional jobs. An ES is a problem-solving computer program that is "expert" at performing one particular task. ESs use "inference engines" to capture the decision-making strategies of experts (usually professionals); they execute instructions that correspond to a set of rules an expert would use in performing a professional task. A "knowledge engineer" asks human experts in a given field a series of questions and then extracts rules and designs a program based on the responses to those questions. Initially,

ESs were designed to perform jobs in chemical engineering and geology, both of which required the professional expertise of highly educated persons and were generally considered too hazardous for humans. More recently, ESs have been developed for use in professional fields such as law, education, and finance.

The use of ESs, much like the use of (physical) robotic systems, has raised some ethical and social issues having to do with "de-skilling" and "worker alienation." We noted the impact that automation had on some workers during the Industrial Revolution. Social scientists have suggested that prior to that period, workers generally felt connected to their labor and exhibited a strong sense of pride and craftsmanship. The relationship between worker and work began to change, however, when work became automated. Social scientists have used the term *alienation* to describe the effect that de-skilling had for workers whose skills were transferred to machines. Mason (2007) cites as an example the introduction of Jacquard's loom and its effect on weavers during the Industrial Revolution, where skills were "disembodied" from weavers and craftsmen and then "reembodied" into machines such as the loom.

Today, ES technologies pose a similar threat to professional workers by allowing knowledge, in the form of rules applying to knowledge-related skills, to be extracted from (human) experts and then embedded into computer software code. Mason points out that knowledge can now be "disemminded" from professional workers, or experts in a given field, and "emminded" into machines in the form of computer programs. Mason also believes that there is an interesting connection between the Industrial Revolution and the current era in that a proliferation of publications on ethics appears in each time period, and he suggests that working conditions during the Industrial Revolution may have been responsible for the greatest outpouring of moral philosophy since Plato and Aristotle. He notes, for example, that works on ethics by Immanuel Kant, Jeremy Bentham, and John Stuart Mill appeared during that era. Mason also suggests that, similarly, contemporary workplace controversies associated with cybertechnology have contributed to the recent flurry of publications on ethics.[37]

We conclude this section by noting that automation, robotics, and ESs have each contributed significantly to job displacement in the contemporary workplace. We have also noted that these three technologies have adversely affected some employee groups more than others. Next, we examine the impact that three relatively recent employment-related practices and policies have had for job displacement, in particular, and the contemporary workplace in general.

Remote Work, Job Outsourcing, and Globalization

One factor that has transformed work for many employees is that cybertechnology has made it possible for them to work "remotely"—that is, outside the traditional workplace. Even though remote work, referred to by some as "telework," is a relatively recent practice, it has already raised social and ethical questions. One question has to do with whether all employees who perform remote work benefit from it equally. For example, are white-collar employees affected in the same way as employees who are less educated and less skilled? It is one thing to be a white-collar professional with an option to work at home at your discretion and convenience, but it is very different for some clerical, or "pink collar," workers who may be required to work remotely out of their homes. Of course, some professional men and women may choose to work at home because of childcare considerations or because they wish to avoid a long and tedious daily commute, but employers may require other employees, especially those in lower skilled and clerical jobs, to work at home. In some case, people required to work remotely may not have the same opportunities for promotions and advancements as their (more visible) counterparts who have the option of working in a traditional workplace setting. So, employees in some situations may be disadvantaged because of specific remote work policies.

Another contemporary practice contributing to the ongoing transformation of work involves job *outsourcing*. Outsourcing practices have affected the displacement of jobs not only for employees in industries within countries but also across them, and thus have had international implications. Until recently, most American jobs affected by remote work still remained in the United States. Now, many jobs are outsourced to countries where labor costs are less expensive. For example, many traditional manufacturing jobs in the United States have been exported "offshore." Initially, this phenomenon impacted mainly traditional "blue-collar" jobs; now it also affects many jobs in the service sector. In the past decade or so, it has also affected many highly skilled "white-collar" jobs such as those in the computing/IT field. Consider, for instance, that many programming jobs traditionally held by employees in American companies are now "outsourced" to companies in India and China whose employees are willing to work for significantly lower wages than those paid to American programmers. Ironically, perhaps, the jobs of the programmers who had the high-tech skills needed to make possible the outsourcing of many white-collar jobs are now being outsourced to countries where programmers earn less money.

Controversies affecting job outsourcing, especially where multiple nations are involved, are often linked to a phenomenon that has come to be known as *globalization*. What is globalization, and how is it affected by cybertechnology? Monahan (2005) defines globalization as "the blurring of boundaries previously held as stable and fixed . . . between local/global, public/private [and] nation/world."[38] Monahan notes that discussions of globalization tend to focus on concerns involving labor outsourcing, international trade agreements, immigration concerns, cultural homogenization, and so forth. So there are broad cultural issues, as well as economic controversies, underlying the debate about globalization. In this section, however, our concern is with the economic aspects of globalization, particularly as they impact cybertechnology and the workplace.

In a global economy where individual nations are protected less and less by tariffs, competition between countries for producing and exporting goods, as well as for providing services, has escalated. In the United States, considerable debate has focused on the North American Free Trade Agreement (NAFTA) initiatives during the past two decades. Those individuals and organizations that have been labeled "isolationists" and "protectionists" have opposed NAFTA, while proponents of "open" markets between countries have tended to support it. Do trade agreements such as NAFTA and General Agreement on Tariffs and Trade (GATT) favor poorer countries that are part of the agreement where the cost of labor is cheaper? Or, do these trade agreements favor the majority of people in wealthier countries who are able to purchase more goods and services at lower prices? On the one hand, NAFTA and GATT have encouraged greater competition between nations and, arguably, have resulted in greater efficiency for businesses. On the other hand, the economies of some nations have been severely impacted by the job loss that has resulted.

What is the net economic benefit of globalization for both the richer and the poorer countries? To what extent has cybertechnology exacerbated the concerns raised by globalization and the displacement of jobs? These questions are controversial, and proponents on each side have come up with drastically different statistical data to support their claims. However, it is quite apparent that both globalization and job outsourcing have had a significant impact on the "quality of worklife" of numerous employees—a technology-and-work-related issue that we examine in the following section.

10.6.2 The Quality of Work Life in the Digital Era

So far, we have focused on social and ethical issues surrounding the transformation of work vis-à-vis job displacement, but many social scientists have also questioned how cybertechnology impacts the *quality* of work life. Quality issues include concerns about employee health, which can pertain both to physical and mental health-related issues. Among these concerns are worries about the level of stress for many employees in the contemporary workplace, especially those who are subject to computerized monitoring and surveillance.

Employee Stress, Workplace Surveillance, and Computerized Monitoring

Many workers experience stress because their activities are now monitored closely by an "invisible supervisor"—that is, by cybertechnology, which can record information about one's work habits. The *2007 Electronic Monitoring and Surveillance Report*, sponsored by the American Management Association (AMA) and published by the AMA/ePolicy Institute Research (2008), noted that 43% of American companies monitor employee e-mail, and 96% of those companies "track external (incoming and outgoing messages)." The report also noted that 45% of companies track the amount of time employees spend on their company-owned devices. An increasing number of these companies now also monitor the blogosphere (described in Chapter 11) to see what is being written about them in various blogs, and some also monitor SNSs such as Facebook. As a result of increased monitoring, many employees have been fired for misusing a company's e-mail resources or its Web resources, or both. So, the threats posed by computerized monitoring would clearly seem to contribute to employee stress.

Perhaps somewhat ironically, data entry clerks and so-called "information workers," whose work is dependent on the use of computer technology to process information, are among the groups of employees who have been most subjected to monitoring by that technology. Although computer monitoring techniques were initially used to track the activities of clerical workers such as data entry operators, they now also track and evaluate the performance of professionals, such as programmers, loan officers, investment brokers, and managers. And nurses are also frequently monitored to make sure that they do not spend too much time with one patient.

Why is employee monitoring via computerized surveillance tools increasing so dramatically? Kizza and Ssanyu (2005) identify multiple factors that have contributed to the recent expansion and growth of employee monitoring, two of which are worth highlighting for our purposes: (i) cost (the lower prices of both software and hardware) and (ii) size (the miniaturization of monitoring products). The lower cost of monitoring tools has made them available to many employers who, in the past, might not have been able to afford them. And the miniaturization of these tools has made it far easier to conceal them from employees.

Introna (2004) points out that surveillance technology, in addition to becoming less expensive, has also become "less overt and more diffused." He also believes that current monitoring technologies have created the potential to build surveillance features into the "very fabric of organizational processes." Consider that monitoring tools are used to measure things such as the number of minutes an employee spends on the telephone completing a transaction (e.g., selling a product or booking a reservation) and the number and length of breaks he or she takes. Monitoring software can even measure the number of computer keystrokes a worker enters per minute. Weckert (2005) notes that an employee's keystrokes can be monitored for accuracy as well as for speed and that the contents of an employee's computer screen can easily be viewed on the screen of a supervisor's computer (without that employee's knowledge).

Employees using networked and mobile electronic devices can also be monitored outside the traditional workplace. For example, some employees work at home on employer-owned devices or via an employer's networked application, and some use employer-owned electronic devices to communicate with fellow workers and customers while they are traveling. Consider the following scenario involving a city employee's use of a pager (device).

▶ **SCENARIO 10–3:** Employee Monitoring and the Case of *Ontario vs. Quon*

Jeff Quon, a police officer, was an employee of the city of Ontario, CA. City employees in Ontario agreed to a policy in which the city reserved the right to monitor ("with or without notice") their electronic communications, including Internet use and e-mail. In 2001, 20 police officers in the SWAT Unit of the

Ontario Police Department (OPD) were given alphanumeric pagers. Quon was one of the officers who received a pager. The police officers were told that they were allowed a fixed limit of 25,000 characters per month on their pagers, in accordance with the terms of a contract that OPD had with the Arch Wireless (now USA Mobility) service provider. The officers were also told that if they exceeded that monthly limit, they would be charged a fee for overuse. Quon exceeded the limit on his pager for two consecutive months, and he paid the city for the excess usage. However, his pager was subsequently audited by OPD, which requested a transcript of his messages from Arch Wireless.

During the audit, it was discovered that many of Quon's messages were personal (and thus not work related) and that some were sexually explicit. Quon was then disciplined for violating the city's electronic communications policy. But Quon challenged OPD and the city of Ontario, arguing that his privacy rights had been violated; he alleged that the audit of the content on his pager was both a violation of his constitutional privacy right (under the Fourth Amendment), as well as a violation of federal telecommunications privacy laws. Quon also argued that the city's employee monitoring policy did not explicitly mention pagers and text messages, and he noted that the officers who received pagers were told verbally that they could use their pagers for "light personal communications." However, OPD pointed out that the officers were also informed that obscene, defamatory, and harassing messages on the pagers would not be "tolerated."

The Ninth Circuit Court in California initially sided with Quon (and the other officers involved in the suit). However, the case was eventually appealed to the U.S. Supreme Court, which ruled (in June 2010) that the audit of Quon's pager was work related and that it did not violate Quon's Fourth Amendment rights involving unreasonable search and seizure.[39] ■

Did the Supreme Court make the correct decision in this case? Or, did Quon have a reasonable expectation of privacy in this particular incident, as the lower court initially ruled? Should there be any limitations or constraints placed on an employer's right to monitor an employee's conversations on electronic devices? Or, should all forms of employee monitoring be permissible, where employer-owned equipment is involved? The case involving Jeff Quon may cause us to consider whether some additional, and perhaps more explicit, distinctions need to be drawn in the context of employee monitoring.

Distinguishing between Two Different Aspects of Employee Monitoring

Weckert (2005) argues that it is crucial to draw some distinctions involving two areas of computerized monitoring: (i) the different applications of monitoring and (ii) the different kinds of work situations (that are monitored).

Regarding (i), Weckert notes that employees could be monitored with respect to the following kinds of activities:

- e-mail usage
- URLs visited while Web surfing
- Quality of their work
- Speed of their work
- Work practices (health and safety)
- Employee interaction[40]

He points out that the reasons given to justify the application of monitoring in activities involving employee e-mail and Internet use may be very different from the kinds of justifications needed to monitor an employee's speed of work or the quality of his or her work.

With regard to (ii), some further distinctions also need to be made concerning which kinds of workers should be monitored. Weckert notes that while it may be appropriate to monitor the keystrokes of data entry workers to measure their performance in specific periods of time, it may not be appropriate to monitor the e-mail of workers in cases where client confidentially is expected. For example, he points out that a therapist employed in a health organization may receive highly sensitive and personal e-mail from one of her client's regarding the client's mental state or physical health.

Similarly, a teacher may receive e-mail from a student, or from an academic administrator communicating about a student, that contains sensitive information regarding the student. As a college professor, for example, I occasionally receive e-mail messages from students who may disclose to me, in confidence, personal details of their health or financial status or an e-mail requesting information about a grade received for an exam or a paper. Arguably, these kinds of e-mails deserve more protection from monitoring than e-mails sent by other employees at my college who do not interact with students in ways that involve the communication of personal information that is either sensitive or confidential, or both. So, if my university were to institute an e-mail monitoring policy for its employees, factors such as these should be taken into consideration.

It is very useful to differentiate monitoring issues affecting an employee's activities in the workplace vs. issues pertaining to the kinds of workers who should or should not be monitored. These kinds of distinctions could better inform a company's policies for employee monitoring as well as the rationale(s) used to justify those policies.

Some Rationales Used to Support and to Oppose Workplace Monitoring

As in the case of many controversies involving the use of cybertechnology, employee monitoring demonstrates a clash of legitimate interests and rights for the parties involved. While employees are concerned about protecting their rights to privacy and autonomy, employers want to protect their interests involving profit margin and overall efficiency. Forester and Morrison (1994) describe some classic arguments used in favor of, and in opposition to, computer monitoring. They note that some employers defend computer monitoring on the grounds that it saves money, is essential for improving worker productivity, and helps businesses to reduce industrial espionage and employee theft.

Opponents of monitoring have a very different perspective: Some see computer monitoring as a Big Brother tactic or as an "electronic whip" used unfairly by management, and they believe it creates a work environment tantamount to an "electronic sweatshop." Some also believe that managers are motivated to use monitoring because they distrust their employees. Others claim that monitoring invades individual privacy, and thus disregards human rights. Along these lines, Rooksby and Cica (2005) argue that monitoring also poses a threat to an individual's right to "psychological autonomy."

Some critics also charge that while monitoring may accurately measure the quantity of work an employee produces, it often fails to measure the overall quality of that work. Others argue that computer monitoring is ultimately counterproductive because of its effects on employee morale. Table 10-1 lists some typical rationales used on both sides of the debate.

In concluding our discussion of employee monitoring, we should note that there are additional aspects of this controversy that we have not considered in this chapter. For example, there are now many global and international dimensions to workplace monitoring, which raise controversial questions. Coleman (2005) points out that in the global workforce, a person's

TABLE 10-1 Rationales Used to Support and to Oppose Employee Monitoring

Rationales Used to Support Monitoring	Rationales Used to Oppose Monitoring
Improves worker productivity	Increases employee stress
Improves corporate profits	Invades employee privacy
Guards against industrial espionage	Reduces employee autonomy
Reduces employee theft	Undermines employee trust

privacy could be violated by software monitoring programs that reside on a computer located in a country different from where that individual is working. This raises concerns about whether international agreements for employee monitoring policies may be needed. In fact, Coleman suggests that an International Bill of Human Rights be adopted in response to concerns affecting the global dimension of employee monitoring. Unfortunately, an examination of this aspect of monitoring, as well as Coleman's proposed solution, is beyond the scope of this chapter.

▶ 10.7 CHAPTER SUMMARY

In this chapter, we examined a wide range of equity-and-access issues affecting three broad social categories: sociodemographic groups, social and political institutions, and social sectors. With regard to demographic groups affecting socioeconomic class, we considered some implications of the digital divide at both the global and the local levels. We then examined equity-and-access issues for three additional demographic groups: disabled persons, racial minorities, and women. Next, we examined the impact of cybertechnology for one of our social/political institutions in our analysis of democracy and democratic values. Finally, we considered the impact that cybertechnology has had so far for the contemporary workplace—an important social sector. Here, we examined some equity-and-access issues as they apply both to the transformation of work (and job displacement) and to the quality of work in the digital era. Regarding the latter concern, we examined some specific challenges posed by computerized monitoring and workplace surveillance.

▶ REVIEW QUESTIONS

1. What is the "digital divide," and why is it significant?
2. What are the differences between the global digital divide and the divisions within nations affecting access to cybertechnology?
3. Are all "divides" or divisions regarding resources to goods and services ethical problems? Is the digital divide an ethical issue? Explain.
4. According to Jeroen van den Hoven and Emma Rooksby, what is meant by "distributive justice" in the context of contemporary information societies?
5. What does John Rawls mean by "primary social goods"? Can that category be extended to include "information goods," as van den Hoven and Rooksby suggest? Explain.
6. Describe three ways that Jeremy Moss believes people in developing countries are disadvantaged by lack of access to digital technology.
7. Do we have a moral obligation to bridge the digital divide? Which kinds of arguments do Maria Bottis and Kenneth Himma put forth to show why affluent countries have an obligation to bridge this divide?
8. What is the Web Accessibility Initiative (WAI), and which kinds of special equity-and-access issues affecting disabled persons has WAI addressed?
9. Describe the two perspectives from which we analyzed issues involving race and cybertechnology.
10. Describe the two main perspectives from which we viewed issues involving gender and cybertechnology.
11. Describe four ways in which the Internet can be viewed as favoring democracy and democratic ideals.
12. What is meant by "deliberative democracy"? Why does Cass Sunstein believe that Internet filters and increased polarization threaten deliberative democracy?
13. According to Gordon Graham, how does the Internet contribute to political and social fragmentation?
14. What does Eli Pariser mean by "personalization filters," and why does he believe they pose a threat for democracy?
15. What implications do political blogs have for democracy, especially for influencing the outcome of political elections in democratic nations?
16. How has work been "transformed" in the information age with respect to job displacement?
17. What are some of the ethical and social issues associated with the development and use of robots and expert systems?
18. What is globalization, and how is it related to the job outsourcing of jobs in the new global economy?
19. What is employee monitoring, and why is it controversial from an ethical perspective?
20. Describe the key arguments that have been used to defend and to oppose the use of computers and digital technology to monitor employees.

▶ DISCUSSION QUESTIONS

21. Some skeptics believe that the digital divide is not really an ethical issue because, as they correctly note, there have always been divisions or "divides" between various sociodemographic groups regarding ownership and access to resources and goods. For example, we saw that some critics point out there is a "Mercedes-Benz Divide" and that most of us fall on the wrong side of this divide. Is the division between those who have and do not have access to cybertechnology similar to, or is it different in morally relevant ways from, the division between those who own and do not own Mercedes-Benz automobiles? Explain.

22. What obligations does the United States have, as a democratic nation concerned with guaranteeing equal opportunities for all its citizens, to ensure that all Americans have full (and affordable) access to the Internet? Does the United States also have any moral obligation to the global community in this regard? If so, what is the extent of that obligation? For example, should engineers working in the United States and other developed countries design affordable devices and applications to ensure that people living in remote and impoverished areas of the world will still be able to enjoy the benefits of digital technology? Explain.

23. In our discussion of expert systems (ESs) in Section 10.6.1, we saw that the increased use of ESs in many professional fields has generated various ethical and social concerns. Some ethical controversies surrounding ESs have to do with critical decisions, including decisions involving life and death; for example, should "expert doctors" be allowed to make decisions that could directly result in the death of a patient, or decisions that could even cause serious harm to a patient? If so, who is ultimately responsible for the ES's decision? Is it the hospital that owns the particular ES, or is it the knowledge engineer who designed the ES? Or, is it possible that the ES itself is responsible in some sense? In answering these questions, you may want to consult relevant sections of Chapter 4, where we discussed issues affecting accountability and moral responsibility for software-related accidents (such as the now classic case involving the Therac-25 system).

24. We briefly noted that some controversies associated with workplace monitoring now have global and international implications. For example, Stephen Coleman points out that in the global workforce, an employee's privacy could be violated by software monitoring programs that reside on a computer located in a country different from where that employee works. Do we need new kinds of international agreements and policies for employee monitoring, as Coleman suggests? And do we need to adopt an "International Bill of Human Rights," as Coleman also suggests, in response to global challenges posed by workplace monitoring? If not, what kinds of alternative proposals might be suitable?

Scenarios for Analysis

1. In our discussion of gender bias in developing video games (in Section 10.4.2), we noted that some critics had also been concerned about gender bias in educational software. This was especially apparent in the earlier days of computing. How might the developers of contemporary educational software design their products to ensure against the kind of bias illustrated in the following scenario?

   Huff and Cooper (1987) developed a study in which they had teachers design software for three categories of users: girls, boys, and (gender unspecified) children. They discovered that the programs the teachers designed for boys looked like games (with time pressure, hand-to-eye coordination, and competition the most important features). Programs the teachers designed for girls, on the contrary, looked like tools for learning (with conversation and goal-based learning features). And surprisingly, the programs the teachers designed for (gender unspecified) children looked just like the ones they designed for boys. So, the researchers concluded that when teachers designed programs for children, or students in general, they actually designed them for boys.

   This study also revealed some interesting data that was surprising. For example, 80% of the program designers in Huff and Cooper's experiment were female, and, ironically, some of these women had originally expressed the concern that educational software was male biased. Huff and Cooper's research also points to a paradox: A software designer may be able to identify bias in a particular software application but may still not be able to design and develop software applications that avoid bias.[2]

2. Recall our discussion of expert systems (ESs) in Section 10.6.1. The following scenario, based on a question posed by Forester and Morrison (1994), illustrates one ethically controversial application of an ES. If you were a member of the program

team designing such an application, which kinds of values would you build into the ES described in the following scenario?

Forester and Morrison ask whether an "expert administrator" should be designed in a way so that it is programmed to mislead or even to lie to human beings in cases where it might (generally, but unofficially) seem "appropriate" for human administrators to do so. Consider that politicians and executives are sometimes put in situations where they are not permitted to be totally forthcoming. In these cases, being able to be evasive (and possibly even deceptive) with respect to answers to certain kinds of questions may be a requirement for being an "expert" (or at least successful) human administrator? If so, should the "skill" of "being able to evade answering questions directly and honestly" (or of "not being totally forthcoming") be built into such a system? Is it morally permissible to design such a system?

▶ ENDNOTES

1. See, for example, the description of the Arab Spring in Ratti and Townsend (2011), as well as the account of it in NPR's "The Arab Spring: A Year of Revolution." Available at http://www.npr.org/2011/12/17/143897126/the-arab-spring-a-year-of-revolution.
2. In composing Section 10.1, I have drawn from, and expanded upon, some concepts and distinctions included in Tavani (2003).
3. *Human Development Report* (2000).
4. *Internet World Stats: Usage and Population Studies* (2014).
5. *Internet World Stats: Usage and Population Studies* (2005).
6. *Internet World Stats: Usage and Population Studies* (2014).
7. *Ibid.* Wresch (2009) notes that in a 33-month period during those years, there was a 60% growth in the number of African Web sites.
8. O'Hara and Stevens (2006, p. 144).
9. Van den Hoven and Rooksby (2008, p. 376).
10. *Ibid.*
11. Rawls (1972, p. 92).
12. Van den Hoven and Rooksby, p. 395.
13. Moss (2002, p. 162).
14. Norris (2001, p. 168).
15. Bottis and Himma (2008, p. 623).
16. Himma (2007, p. 10).
17. See http://www.w3.org/WAI/.
18. *Digital Divide Network* (2002).
19. *Pew Internet & American Life Project, April 8–May 11, 2008 Tracking Report.*
20. See Burn (2011).
21. Theismeyer (1999, p. 117).
22. As we noted in our discussion of online hate speech in Chapter 9, the Southern Poverty Law Center (SPLC) "Intelligence Project" (http://www.splcenter.org) monitors online hate speech aimed at racial minorities.
23. See Theismeyer, p. 117.
24. The April/May 2008 *Pew Internet & American Life Project* reported that 73% of women and 73% of men used the Internet.
25. Shade (2002) describes some ways that women in the Philippines, Latin America, Africa, and Asia have developed "grassroots" initiatives, which she refers to as "globalizing from below," to address the technology gap.
26. Kirlidog, Aykol, and Gulsecen (2009, p. 51).
27. *Ibid.*
28. The framework that Adam defends is based on a feminist ethics—in particular, on the "ethic of care" influenced by a seminal work in feminist ethics by Gilligan (1982).
29. Brey (2008, p. 381).
30. See, for example, Johnson (2000, p. 181).
31. See Graham (1999, p. 71) for his discussion of Mill's *On Liberty* in connection with Graham's analysis of democracy in this section. For more detail on Mill's views and arguments, see Mill (1989).
32. Graham also discusses these attributes in connection with the pros and cons of "online communities," as we will see in our analysis of these communities in Chapter 11.
33. Introna and Nissenbaum (2000, p. 169). My discussion (in Section 10.5) about the implications that search engine technology have for democracy draws from some distinctions introduced in Tavani (2012).
34. See, for example, http://worldwideliberty.blogspot.com/2009/01/barack-obama-not-born-in-us-no-us-state.html.
35. See, for example, http://www.politicalbase.com/profile/jnail/blog/&blogId=3482.
36. Goldman (2008, p. 119).
37. Mason (2007, pp. 9–10).
38. Monahan (2005, p. 4).
39. See *City of Ontario, California, et al. v. Quon et al.* (2009). Also, see the description of this case included in Cornell University Law School's Legal Information Institute (Available at http://www.law.cornell.edu/supct/html/08-1332.ZS.html) and the description in http://en.wikipedia.org/wiki/Ontario_v._Q.
40. Weckert (2005, p. viii).

▶ REFERENCES

Adam, Alison. 2004. "Gender and Computer Ethics." In R. A. Spinello and H. T. Tavani, eds. *Readings in CyberEthics*. 2nd ed. Sudbury, MA: Jones and Bartlett Publishers. Reprinted from *Computers and Society* 30, no. 4 (2000): 17–24.

Adam, Alison. 2005. *Gender, Ethics and Information Technology*. London, UK: Palgrave Macmillan.

AMA/ePolicy Institute Research (2008). *Executive Summary: 2007 Electronic Monitoring & Surveillance Survey.* Available at http://press.amanet.orgpress-releases/177/2077-electronic-monitoring-surveillance-survey.

Asakawa, Cheiko. 2012. "Web Guru for the Blind." *IEEE Spectrum* 49, no. 2: 55–7.

Bottis, Maria Cannellopulou and Kenneth Einar Himma. 2008. "The Digital Divide: A Perspective for the Future." In K. E. Himma and H. T. Tavani, eds. *The Handbook of Information and Computer Ethics*. Hoboken, NJ, pp. 621–37.

Brey, Philip. 2008. "Virtual Reality and Computer Simulation." In K. E. Himma and H. T. Tavani, eds. *The Handbook of Information and Computer Ethics*. Hoboken, NJ, pp. 361–84.

Buchanan, Elizabeth A. 2000. "Strangers in the 'Myst' of Video Gaming: Ethics and Representation." *CPSR Newsletter* 18, no. 1.

Burn, Enid. 2011. "African American Population is Growing." Available at http://www.clickz.com/clickz/news/1694749/african-american-online-population-is-growing. (Based on data from AOL Black Voice.)

Camp, Tracy. 1997. "The Incredible Shrinking Pipeline." *Communications of the ACM* 40, no. 2: 103–10.

Chapman, Gary, and Marc Rotenberg. 1995. "The National Information Infrastructure: A Public Interest Opportunity." In D. G. Johnson and H. Nissenbaum, eds. *Computers, Ethics, and Social Values*. Englewood Cliffs, NJ: Prentice Hall, pp. 628–44.

City of Ontario, California, et al. v. Quon et al. 2009. Available at http://www.supremecourt.gov/opinions/09pdf/08-1332.pdf.

Coleman, Stephen. 2005. "Universal Human Rights and Employee Privacy: Questioning Employer Monitoring and Computer Use." In J. Weckert, ed. *Electronic Monitoring in the Workplace: Controversies and Solutions*. Hershey, PA: Idea Group, pp. 276–95.

Compaine, Benjamin. 2001. *The Digital Divide: Facing a Crisis or Creating a Myth*. Cambridge, MA: MIT Press.

Diaz, Alejandro. 2008. "Through the Google Goggles: Sociopolitical Bias in Search Engine Design." In A. Spink and M. Zimmer, eds. *Web Search: Multidisciplinary Perspectives*. Berlin: Springer-Verlag, pp. 11–34.

Digital Divide Network. 2002. Available at http://digitaldividenetwork.org.

Epstein, Richard G. 2000. "The Fragmented Public Square." *Computers and Society*. Available at http://www.cs.wcupa.edu/~epstein.fragmented.htm.

Forester, Tom and Perry Morrison. 1994. *Computer Ethics: Cautionary Tales and Ethical Dilemmas in Computing*. 2nd ed. Cambridge, MA: MIT Press.

Gilligan, Carol. 1982. *In a Different Voice: Psychological Theory and Women's Development*. Cambridge, MA: Harvard University Press.

Goldman, Alvin I. 2008. "The Social Epistemology of Blogging." In. J. van den Hoven and J. Weckert, eds. *Information Technology and Moral Philosophy*. Cambridge, UK: Cambridge University Press, pp. 111–22.

Graham, Gordon. 1999. *The Internet: A Philosophical Inquiry*. New York: Routledge.

Grodzinsky, Frances S. 2000. "Equity of Access: Adaptive Technology." *Science and Engineering Ethics* 6, no. 2: 221–34.

Himma, Kenneth E. 2007. "The Information Gap, the Digital Divide, and the Obligations of Affluent Nations." *International Review of Information Ethics* 7: 1–11.

Himma, Kenneth Einar, and Maria Cannellopulou Bottis. 2014. "The Digital Divide: Information Technologies and the Obligation to Alleviate Poverty." In R. L. Sandler, ed. *Ethics and Emerging Technologies*. New York: Palgrave/Macmillan, pp. 333–46.

Hinman, Lawrence M. 2005. "*Esse Est Indicato* in Google: Ethical and Political Issues in Search Engines," *International Review of Information Ethics* 3, 19–25.

Huff, Chuck and Joel Cooper. 1987. "Sex Bias in Educational Software: The Effects of Designers' Stereotypes on the Software They Design." *Journal of Applied Social Psychology* 17: 519–32.

Human Development Report 2000. *Published for the United Nations Development Program (UNDP)*. New York: Oxford University Press.

Human Development Report. 2007/2008. Available at http://hdrstats.undp.org/indicators/124.html.

Internet Growth Statistics: Internet Usage Stats. 2008. Available at http://www.allaboutmarketresearch.com/internet.com/internet.htm.

Internet World Stats: Usage and Population Studies. 2005. Available at http://www.internetworldstats.com/top20.htm.

Internet World Stats: Usage and Population Studies. 2014. Available at http://www.internet worldstats.com/stats.htm.

Internet World Stats News: Internet Usage Research. 2005. Available at http://www.internetworldstats.com/pr/edi012.htm.

Introna, Lucas. 2004. "Workplace Surveillance, Privacy, and Distributive Justice." In R. A. Spinello and H. T. Tavani, eds. *Readings in CyberEthics*. 2nd ed. Sudbury, MA: Jones and Bartlett Publishers.

Introna, Lucas and H. Nissenbaum. 2000. "Shaping the Web: The Politics of Search Engines Matters," *The Information Society* 16, no. 3: 1–17.

Johnson, Deborah G. 2000. "Democratic Values and the Internet." In D. Langford, ed. *Internet Ethics*. New York: St. Martin's Press, pp. 180–99.

Kizza, Joseph M. and Jackline Ssanyu. 2005. "Workplace Surveillance." In J. Weckert, ed. *Electronic Monitoring in the Workplace: Controversies and Solutions*. Hershey, PA: Idea Group, pp. 1–18.

Kirlidog, Melih, Meric Aykol, and Sevinc Gulsecen. 2009. "Interpersonal Communication and Gender in the IT Profession." *IEEE Technology and Society Magazine* 28, no. 1: 48–56.

Kretchmer, Susan and Rod Karveth. 2001. "The Color of the Net: African Americans, Race, and Cyberspace." *Computers and Society* 31, no. 3: 9–14.

Lin, Patrick. 2012. "Introduction to Robot Ethics." In P. Lin, K. Abney, and G. A. Bekey, eds. *Robot Ethics: The Ethical and Social Implications of Robotics*. Cambridge, MA: MIT Press, pp. 3–15.

Mason, Richard O. 2007. "Four Ethical Issues of the Information Age." In J. Weckert, ed. *Computer Ethics*. Aldershot, UK: Ashgate, pp. 31–40. Reprinted from *MIS Quarterly* 10: 5–12.

Mill, John Stuart. 1989. *On Liberty and Other Writings*. Cambridge, UK: Cambridge University Press.

Monahan, Torin. 2005. *Globalization, Technological Change, and Public Education*. New York: Routledge.

Moor, James H. 2004. "Reason, Relativity, and Responsibility in Computer Ethics." In R. A. Spinello and H. T. Tavani, eds. *Readings in CyberEthics*. 2nd ed. Sudbury, MA: Jones and Bartlett, pp. 40–54.

Moss, Jeremy. 2002. "Power and the Digital Divide." *Ethics and Information Technology* 4, no. 2: 159–65.

Norris, Pippa. 2001. *Digital Divide? Civic Engagement, Information Poverty, and the Internet Worldwide*. Cambridge, MA: Cambridge University Press.

O'Hara, Kieron and David Stevens. 2006. *Inequality.com: Power, Poverty, and the Digital Divide*. Oxford, UK: Oneworld.

Pariser, Eli. 2011. *The Filter Bubble: What the Internet is Hiding from You*. New York: Penguin.

Pew Internet & American Life Project. 2005. Washington, DC. Available at http://www.pewinternet.org.

Pew Internet & American Life Project, April 8–May 11, 2008 Tracking Report. Available at http://www.pewinternet.org/trends/User_Demo_7.22.08.htm.

Ratti, Carlo and Anthony Townsend. 2011. "Harnessing Residents' Electronic Devices Will Yield Truly Smart Cities." *Scientific American*, August 6. Available at http://www.scientificamerican.com/article.cfm?id=the-social-nexus.

Rawls, John. 1972. *A Theory of Justice*. Cambridge, MA: Harvard University Press.

Rooksby, Emma and Natasha Cica. 2005. "Personal Autonomy and Electronic Surveillance in the Workplace." In J. Weckert, ed. *Electronic Monitoring in the Workplace: Controversies and Solutions*. Hershey, PA: Idea Group, pp. 242–59.

Ryder, Martin. 2015. "Digital Divide." In J. Britt Holbrook and Carl Mitcham, eds. *Ethics, Science, Technology, and Engineering: A Global Resource*. Vol. 1, 2nd ed. Farmington Hills, MI: Macmillan Reference, pp. 579–84.

Shade, Leslie Regan. 2002. *Gender and Community in the Social Construction of the Internet*. New York: Peter Lang.

Spafford, Gene. 2014. "We're Out of Balance." *Computers and Society* 44, no. 4: 9–12.

Sunstein, Cass R. 2001. *Republic.com*. Princeton, NJ: Princeton University Press.

Sunstein, Cass R. 2007. *Republic.com. 2.0*. Princeton, NJ: Princeton University Press.

Tavani, Herman T. 2003. "Ethical Reflections on the Digital Divide." *Journal of Information, Communication, and Ethics in Society* 1, no. 2: 99–108.

Tavani, Herman T. 2012. "Search Engines and Ethics." *Stanford Encyclopedia of Philosophy*. Available at http://plato.stanford.edu/entries/ethics-search/.

Theismeyer, Lynn. 1999. "Racism on the Web: Its Rhetoric and its Marketing." *Ethics and Information Technology* 1, no. 2: 117–25.

Van den Hoven, Jeroen and Emma Rooksby. 2008. "Distributive Justice and the Value of Information: A (broadly) Rawlsian Approach." In J. van den Hoven and J. Weckert, eds. *Information Technology and Moral Philosophy*. Cambridge, UK: Cambridge University Press, pp. 376–96.

Weckert, John. 2005. "Preface." In J. Weckert, ed. *Electronic Monitoring in the Workplace: Controversies and Solutions*. Hershey, PA: Idea Group.

Wessells, Michael G. 1990. *Computer, Self, and Society*. Englewood Cliffs, NJ: Prentice Hall.

Woodbury, Marsha. 2002. *Computer and Information Ethics*. Champaign, IL: Stipes Publishing.

Wresch, William. 2009. "Progress on the Global Digital Divide," *Ethics and Information Technology* 11, no. 4: 255–63.

FURTHER READINGS

Abbey, Ruth and Sarah Hyde. 2009. "No Country for Older People: Age and the Digital Divide." *Journal of Information, Communication, and Ethics in Society* 7, no. 4: 225–42.

Dyson, Freeman. 2009. "Technology and Social Justice." In D. G. Johnson and J. M. Wetmore, eds. *Technology and Society: Building Our Sociotechnical Future*. Cambridge, MA: MIT Press, pp. 5–12.

Gumbus, Andra and Frances S. Grodzinsky. 2004. "Gender Bias in Internet Employment: A Study of Career Advancement Opportunities for Women in the Field of ICT." *Journal of Information, Communication and Ethics in Society* 2, no. 3: 133–42.

Noam, Eli. 2005. "Why the Internet is Bad for Democracy." *Communications of the ACM* 48, no. 10: 57–8.

Turner, Eva. 2005. *Women in Computing*. Special Issue of *Journal of Information, Communication and Ethics in Society* 3, no. 4.

Warschauer, Mark. 2003. *Technology and Social Inclusion: Rethinking the Digital Divide*. Cambridge, MA: MIT Press.

Weikle, Dee and Netiva Caftori, eds. 2014. *Women in Computing*. Special Issue of *Computers and Society* 44, no. 4.

CHAPTER

11

Online Communities, Virtual Reality, and Artificial Intelligence

LEARNING OBJECTIVES

Upon completing this chapter, you will successfully be able to:

- Describe some key similarities and differences between *online communities* and traditional communities, and identify and evaluate ethical controversies affecting *social networking services* (*SNSs*) such as Facebook,
- Identify and assess some ethical aspects of *virtual environments* (VEs) and *virtual reality* (VR) applications, including massively multiplayer online role-playing games (MMORPGs),
- Explain some implications that ongoing developments in the field of *artificial intelligence* (*AI*) will continue to have for our sense of self and for what it means to be human,
- Determine whether we need to extend our conventional notion of moral obligation to grant at least some degree of moral consideration to certain kinds of AI entities.

In this chapter, we examine some ethical and social aspects of three diverse, and seemingly unrelated, aspects of cybertechnology: (i) online communities, including social networking services (SNSs); (ii) virtual environments (VEs), including virtual reality (VR) applications; and (iii) artificial intelligence (AI). A unifying theme that brings together this otherwise disparate cluster of topics is the impact they have for our notions of *community* and (*personal*) *identity* in the digital age. Whereas SNSs enable social interactions that challenge our traditional notion of community, some VEs and VR applications allow users to construct new and alternate identities. AI-related developments, on the other hand, invite us to reassess our sense of self and, ultimately, question what it means to be human in a world that we share with nonhuman "intelligent" agents and entities.

We begin by reflecting on a scenario that briefly illustrates a cluster of issues that we will examine in detail in later sections of this chapter.

▶ SCENARIO 11–1: Ralph's Online Friends and Artificial Companions

Ralph, a 60-year-old bachelor and retired software engineer, moved to a condominium in the Peaceful Manor retirement community approximately one year ago. In many ways, Peaceful Manor is an ideal community for a person of Ralph's age. For example, all of the community's residents are 55 or older.

Furthermore, there is a clubhouse on the premises that includes a wellness center with indoor and outdoor swimming pools, as well as other amenities and activities. In addition, Peaceful Manor provides its residents with three categories or levels of living, ranging from (fully) independent living to "assisted living" to full-time care. (So a resident at Peaceful Manor would never have to relocate because of aging or deteriorating health.) Although Ralph is still fully independent and capable of participating in many of the amenities offered by his retirement community, he has elected not to take advantage of any of them. Instead, he prefers to stay in his condominium (day and night) and to "meet" only with online friends, most of whom he has acquired since joining a social networking service one year ago. Ralph also enjoys interacting with various avatars and (soft)bots that "reside" (only) in online forums and games, and he prefers those interactions over the kind that would be required if he were to engage with fellow humans who live in his retirement community.

In the past year or so, Ralph has not interacted (face-to-face) with any of his fellow residents at Peaceful Manor (and has interacted with people outside that community only when it is necessary for him to do so). Ralph prefers online-only interactions for several reasons. For one thing, he can communicate with his online friends at times that are convenient to him. For another, Ralph does not have to worry about being embarrassed by his speech impediment, since he communicates textually with his online friends. Additionally, Ralph can choose which features about himself to disclose—or, alternatively, to "construct"—such as information about his age, gender, marital status, work background, physical characteristics, and so forth. It turns out that Ralph has constructed a kind of alter ego, or "cyberego," by which he is known (only) to his online friends. Ralph also finds it "liberating" that his digital persona does not require him to disclose information about his speech impediment, whereas this condition would be immediately apparent to anyone with whom he interacts in physical space.

Ralph has already decided that when the time comes for him to move to the next level of care offered by Peaceful Manor, he will request that an "Elderbot" or "Carebot" assist him rather than a human being. He believes that he will be far more comfortable interacting with a sophisticated robot or "artificial companion" than with a human assistant in carrying out routine daily tasks. So Ralph, unlike many people in his age group, desires to interact only with online friends and artificial companions and not with "flesh-and-blood" persons. ■

What are we to make of Ralph's choices, especially for someone in his age group or category? Because he has freely chosen to interact only with online "friends" rather than fellow residents in his physical community, we can ask whether Ralph's allegiance (and thus his sense of belonging/membership) is to his online community of friends, avatars, bots, and so forth. We can also ask questions about Ralph's (personal) identity—in other words, *who* is he? For example, is Ralph ultimately the person (or *persona*) represented in the online world where he spends most of his time? Or is that simply Ralph's alter (or "cyber") ego and thus just one aspect of his overall self (or multiple "selves")? And why would Ralph opt for an artificial companion (or Elderbot) to assist him in the future, if he would be eligible to have a human care for him in that role?

The purpose of Scenario 11–1 was not to answer any of these questions, but rather to get us to begin thinking about a cluster of issues that we will examine in detail in the remainder of this chapter. We start by describing the roles that online communities increasingly play, while also focusing on some key ethical and social challenges that they pose.

▶ 11.1 ONLINE COMMUNITIES AND SOCIAL NETWORKING SERVICES

Many people, both young and old, now interact in various forms of online communities. Perhaps the most popular of these are Web-based social networking services (SNSs), such as Facebook, and professional-oriented networking services, such as LinkedIn. Some people also "follow" celebrities and send instantaneous messages in the form of "tweets" via a popular online service called Twitter, while others participate in one or more blogs (Web logs). Many also communicate with one another through digital media services that include video, such as Skype and (Apple's) FaceTime. So we can ask: How has our conventional understanding of "community" evolved, that is, in light of the kinds of social interactions made possible by these various kinds of online forums? We begin our analysis of this question by examining some important similarities and differences between online and traditional communities.

11.1.1 Online Communities vs. Traditional Communities

To better understand what is meant by an online community, we first examine the meaning of "community" in the traditional sense of the term. *Webster's New World Dictionary of the American Language* defines a community as "people living in the same district, city, etc., under the same laws." Note that this traditional definition stresses the geographical aspects of community by associating it with concepts such as "district" and "city" that have typically constrained community life. So, for the most part, traditional communities are limited by geography.

Cybertechnology has made it possible to extend, or perhaps even ignore, the geographical boundaries of traditional community life. This, in turn, leads us to reexamine the concept of community; individuals physically separated by continents and oceans can now interact regularly in SNSs and other online forums to discuss topics that bind them together as a community. Not surprisingly then, more recent definitions of "community" focus on the common interests of groups rather than on geographical and physical criteria.

Though it may seem surprising to some, online communities are not exactly a new, or even recent, phenomenon. Rheingold (2001), who defines online communities as "computer-mediated social groups," describes his experience in joining the Whole Earth' Lectronic Link (WELL), an early electronic community, in 1985:

> The idea of a community accessible only via my computer screen sounded cold to me at first, but . . . [t]he WELL felt like an authentic community to me from the start, because it was grounded in my everyday physical world. WELLites who don't live within driving distance of the San Francisco Bay area are constrained in their ability to participate in the local networks of face-to-face acquaintances. . . . I've attended real-life WELL marriages, WELL births, and even a WELL funeral.[1]

Rheingold points out that because of the social contracts and collaborative negotiations that happened when members met online, the WELL became a *community* in that setting. He notes, for example, that in the WELL, norms were "established, challenged, changed, reestablished, rechallenged, in a kind of speeded up social evolution." When the members decided to get together occasionally at physical locations in the greater San Francisco Bay area, the WELL became a "hybrid community," spanning both physical and virtual space. But some "pure" online communities also continue to thrive alongside the hybrid communities. As White (2002) notes, these electronic-only forums also seem like "real communities" because they offer their members "social exchange, emotional support, and learning environments."

Do users now find as much enjoyment and satisfaction in participating in online communities as they do in traditional ones? Mitch Parsell cites a survey (conducted by the U.S.-based Center for the Digital Future) showing that 43% of members of online communities claimed to feel "as strong" about their online communities as their traditional or "real-world" communities.[2] He also believes that this may be due to the enhanced nature of the Web—what some now refer to as "Web 2.0"—which is very different from the early Web, primarily because of the interactive aspects of the experiences it makes possible. Analysts disagree on exactly which criteria differentiate Web 2.0 from the original Web, but most agree that the kinds of services made possible by SNSs and blogging sites have significantly altered the way users interact in online communities.[3] (Recall our description of some key differences between the early Web, or "Web 1.0," and Web 2.0 environments in Chapter 1.)

As already suggested, SNSs are arguably the most popular type of online community. And the most popular of these services (as of May 2015) are Facebook, Twitter, LinkedIn, Pinterest, Google+, Tumblr, and Instagram, respectively.[4] In Section 11.1.3, where we examine some pros and cons of online communities, our focus will be mainly on social/ethical challenges posed by SNSs. Before examining those challenges, however, we briefly examine some controversies arising from a specific kind of online forum: blogs.

11.1.2 Blogs and Some Controversial Aspects of the Bogosphere

What, exactly, is a blog? According to the (online) *Merriam Webster Dictionary*, a blog (or "Web log") is "a Web site that contains an online personal journal with reflections, comments, and often hyperlinks provided by the writer." Blogs can be maintained by either individuals or organizations. The community of blogs is often referred to as the "blogosphere." Online communities such as myBlogLog and Blog Catalog connect bloggers, whereas search engines such as Bloglines, BlogScope, and Technorati assist users in finding blogs.[5]

While some blogs function as online diaries, others provide commentary on a particular topic or news story. Based on their topics, blogs are often organized into categories such as personal blogs, political blogs, corporate blogs, health blogs, literary blogs, travel blogs, etc. Blogging has become popular because it is an easy way to reach many people; but activities on some blogs have also raised social and ethical concerns. For example, consider the case of a personal blog, illustrated in the following scenario, which raised a cluster of controversial issues.

▶ **SCENARIO 11–2:** "The Washingtonienne" Blogger

Jessica Cutler, who worked as a staff assistant to a U.S. senator, authored an online diary (on blogger.com) under the "pen name" or pseudonym "The Washingtonienne." In 2004, she was fired when the contents of her diary appeared in *Wonkette: The DC Gossip*, a popular blog in the Washington, D.C., area. Until her diary was discovered and published in *Wonkette*, however, Cutler assumed that it had been viewed by only a few of her close friends (who also worked as staff assistants in Washington, D.C.) that she suspected might be interested in reading about the details of her romantic relationships and sexual encounters. In her online diary, Cutler disclosed that although she earned a relatively low salary as a congressional staffer, most of her living expenses were "thankfully subsidized by a few generous older gentlemen." She also described some details of her sexual relationships with these men, one of whom was married and an official in the George W. Bush administration. Cutler did not use the real names of these men but instead referred to them via initials that could easily be linked to their actual identities. However, she was subsequently sued by one of the men implicated in her blog.[6] ■

We can see why Cutler's (personal) blog was controversial and why it raised a number of ethical issues. One concern had to do with expectations regarding personal privacy, both for Cutler and the men implicated in her blog. Other concerns included questions about expectations regarding the anonymity and confidentiality of those who contribute to blogs, or who post information on personal blogs that are intended to be shared only with a few close friends. Another question that arose in the Washingtonienne incident was whether some of the controversial content pertaining to the men (indirectly) identified in this blog rose to the level of (online) defamation.

However, it is not only personal blogs that have generated controversy. Consider, for example, some controversies affecting political blogs, which we briefly examined in connection with our discussion of democracy and cybertechnology in Chapter 10. There, we saw that political bloggers have often been responsible for breaking news stories about political scandals and thus influencing public opinion. We also saw that some of these bloggers had political agendas to advance and thus were eager to spread negative stories about politicians whose views they opposed; in many cases, these stories were not only inaccurate but blatantly false.

One question worth mentioning before we conclude this section has to do with whether bloggers, especially those who write and maintain influential blogs, should be held to the same standards of accuracy, accountability, and liability as professional online journalists. Many bloggers claim that they are not journalists and thus should not be held to professional journalistic standards. Critics, however, argue that bloggers have certain "ethical obligations to their readers, the people they write about, and society in general."[7] Unfortunately, an examination of this debate in the detail it deserves is beyond the scope of this chapter.[8]

11.1.3 Some Pros and Cons of SNSs (and Other Online Communities)

Have SNSs in particular, and online communities in general, had an overall positive effect on communication and social interaction? Not surprisingly, arguments have been advanced to support positions on both sides of this question. Those who see these online forums in a favorable light tend to point to the fact that on SNSs such as Facebook, users can make new "friends" and meet prospective college roommates before setting foot on campus; they can also possibly find future romantic partners in online dating services such as Match.com and eHarmony. Supporters also note that users can join and form online medical support groups, as well as participating in various blogs designed to disseminate material to like-minded colleagues. Through these online services and forums, users can communicate with people they might not otherwise communicate with by mail or telephone.

However, SNSs and other online forums have also had some negative effects. In addition to threatening traditional community life, they have:

- Facilitated *social polarization*
- Threatened our traditional notion of *friendship*
- Facilitated *deception*

We briefly examine each of these points.

Social Polarization

One positive feature of online forums is that they provide us with choices regarding the kinds of online communities we or may not wish to join; this would seem to contribute positively to human interaction by enabling us to come together with like-minded individuals we otherwise might not meet. However, some online communities, especially those whose focus tends to be on topics and issues that are divisive and narrow, can also contribute to social polarization. Parsell (2008) argues that "extremely narrowly focused" online communities can be dangerous because they "can polarize attitudes and prejudices," which can lead to increased division and "social cleavage." He worries that the narrow focus of many online communities presents us with cause for concern, which he articulates via the following line of reasoning:

1. People tend to be attracted to others with like opinions.
2. Being exposed to like opinions tends to increase our own prejudices.
3. This polarizing of attitudes can occur on socially significant issues. . . .
4. Thus, where the possibility of narrowing focus on socially significant issues is available, increased community fracture is likely.[9]

So, even though online communities can empower individuals by providing them with greater freedom and choice in terms of their social interactions, they can also foster increased polarization in society. In Chapter 10, we briefly examined some political/social polarization issues in the context of democracy and cybertechnology, some of which also overlap with those facilitated by online communities. There, for example, we saw how "personalization filters" used by search engine companies can also influence political and social polarization, especially in ways that undermine "deliberative democracy."

"Friends" in the Context of SNSs

Does it matter that online communication has minimized the kinds of face-to-face interactions that define behavior in traditional communities? Is that necessarily a negative thing? On the one hand, being able to send an e-mail or a text message to someone, or to write on a Facebook user's "wall," or timeline, is far more convenient than having to meet that person face-to-face in physical space to communicate with them. On the other hand, some worry that something is lost—possibly some critical interpersonal skills—in excessive online communications, at the expense of avoiding face-to-face interactions. (Recall our example of "Ralph" in Scenario 11–1.) A related, and very important, question that also arises has to do with the implications that online-only communication between individuals may have for our traditional understanding of friendship. In other words, is it possible for people who interact only in virtual (or purely online) contexts to be "real friends"?

To what extent, if any, is physical interaction between individuals necessary for true friendships to develop and flourish? At one time, the notion of "disembodied friends" might have seemed strange. But today, we hear about so-called "friends" who communicate regularly online but have never met in physical space. Cocking and Matthews (2000) argue that the kinds of close friendships we enjoy in physical space are not possible in pure virtual environments (VEs), that is, in contexts that are solely computer mediated. They worry that we miss the kind of interaction that is commonplace in close friendships, because online-only friendship occurs in

> a context of communication dominated by *voluntary* self disclosure, enabling and disposing me to construct a highly chosen and controlled self-presentation and world of interaction.[10]

Cocking and Matthews' argument is complex and cannot be analyzed here in the detail that it deserves. But we will consider a few of their key points. The authors argue that it is not possible to realize close friendships in a "virtual world" because purely computer-mediated contexts (i) facilitate voluntary self-disclosure and (ii) enable people to choose and construct a highly controlled "self-presentation" or identity. (Consider again the example of Ralph in Scenario 11–1, who constructed a selective or controlled personal identity for use in his online interactions.) This would not be possible in offline contexts, Cocking and Matthews argue, because there we involuntarily disclose aspects of ourselves through indicators or "cues" in our interactions with others. And because these interactions include acts of "nonvoluntary self-disclosure," one has less control over the way one presents oneself to others. As a result, important aspects of our true personalities are involuntarily revealed, which, the authors believe, makes close friendships possible in offline contexts but not in virtual ones.

Is the argument advanced by Cocking and Matthews convincing? Briggle (2008) disagrees with their conclusion, but he uses different kinds of criteria—one based on "distance" and one on "deliberateness"—to make the case for why friendships in purely virtual contexts can be initiated and can "flourish." First, he points out that communications among friends in offline contexts, which are based largely on "oral exchanges," are not always candid or sincere; consequently, important "dynamics and indicators" that are required to form close friendships can be distorted. But Briggle believes that the *distance* involved in typical computer-mediated communications can give friends the courage to be more candid with one another than in typical face-to-face interactions.

Second, Briggle points out that online friends depend on written correspondences (as opposed to oral exchanges), and he believes that the *deliberateness* required in composing those kinds of correspondences can lead to "deeper bonds and greater depth in friendships." He also notes that oral communication in offline contexts, on the contrary, is "often too shallow and hasty to promote deep bonds."[11] So, unlike Cocking and Matthews, Briggle concludes that it is possible to form close friendships in purely virtual contexts. He also concedes, however, that some purely virtual relationships can be "shallow."

Deception in SNSs and other Kinds of Online Communities

Some critics believe that online communities reveal a "darker side" of the Internet because people can, under the shield of anonymity, engage in behavior that would not be tolerated in most physical communities. For instance, individuals can use aliases, including pseudonyms and screen names, when they interact in online forums, which makes it easier to deceive others about who actually is communicating with them. We briefly examine a scenario illustrating how online pseudonymity and deception reveal the darker side of online communities.

▶ **SCENARIO 11–3:** A Suicide Resulting from Deception on MySpace

In 2006, Megan Meier was a 13-year-old resident of Dardenne Prairie, Missouri, who had an account on MySpace. On that SNS, she received a "friend" request from a user named Josh Evans. Evans, who claimed to be a 16-year-old boy, told Meier that he lived near her and was being homeschooled by his parents. At first, Evans sent flattering e-mails to Meier, which also suggested that he might be romantically interested in her. But Evans's remarks soon turned from compliments to insults, and Evans then informed Meier that he was no longer sure that he wanted to be friends with her because he heard that she "wasn't very nice to her friends." Next, Meier noticed that some highly derogatory posts about her—for example, "Megan Meier is a slut" and "Megan Meier is fat"—began to appear on MySpace. Meier, who was reported to have suffered from low self-esteem and depression, became increasingly distressed by the online harassment (cyberbullying) being directed at her—that is, from both the insulting MySpace postings and hurtful e-mail messages she continued to receive from Evans. In October 2006, Meier decided to end her life by hanging herself in her bedroom. An investigation of this incident following Meier's death revealed that Josh Evans was not a teenage boy; she was Lori Drew, the 49-year-old mother of a former friend of Meier's.[12] ■

In the period following Meier's death, Lori Drew's true identity was discovered, and she was eventually prosecuted. Although Drew was found guilty of three misdemeanor counts of computer fraud in 2008, the jury was deadlocked on a fourth charge, involving conspiracy.[7] While the Meier incident could be examined from the vantage point of cyberullying, an offense that has affected numerous teenagers interacting in online communities, we consider it here mainly from the perspective of one kind of deceptive behavior that is possible in online communities. But it is also important to note that the Meier incident was not the first case in which pseudonyms and screen names were used in deceptive and devious ways in online communities.

A classic case that also illustrates the darker side of online communities—one which also received wide attention via a popular article by Julian Dibbell that first appeared in *The Village Voice* (in 1993)—involved (an incident that has come to be described as) a "virtual rape" in cyberspace. In an online forum called LambdaMOO—a MOO is a multiuser object-oriented environment—users had "screen names" that represented the virtual characters they portrayed. One character, who used the screen name "Mr. Bungle," had designed a program that enabled him to control the actions of other characters in this MOO. In at least one instance, Bungle used his program to "perform" sexually offensive actions on two of the characters also represented in this online forum.[13] This incident had a profound effect not only on the members of the LambdaMOO community but also on many participants in other online communities who heard about it.[14]

In which ways are the controversial incidents involving MySpace and LambdaMOO similar? Both have at least one key feature in common: They reveal a darker side of online communities that is made possible by anonymity and pseudonymity. One relevant difference, however, is that no one was physically harmed in the LambdaMOO incident. But it could be argued that two Lambda members whose characters were "virtually raped" did experience some emotional or psychological harm, and in Section 11.2.2, we will see how emotional harm can occur to the real-life (i.e., "flesh-and-blood") people whose characters are represented in VEs.

A second difference is that LambdaMOO was a "pure" online, or online-only, community, where the virtual characters that participated had screen names and acted out various roles in the game-like or role-playing context of that VE. Also, it was appropriate for members of LambdaMOO to use names other than their actual ones because of the rules defining that Lambda community. In the MySpace incident involving Meier, however, Lori Drew's use of an alias was deceptive by virtue of the rules, or at least the expected norms, on MySpace for setting up an account and initiating a request to befriend another user. There, the expectation was that an individual using that SNS to seek out new "friends" would disclose his or her actual name and not use a false (or pseudo) name to intentionally deceive someone. However, one might also argue that such a rule was not sufficiently explicit at the time, because neither MySpace nor most other SNSs had clear policies when it came to individuals using actual names in setting up an account. (Typically, all that was required then to register for an account on MySpace was a legitimate e-mail address.)

▶ 11.2 VIRTUAL ENVIRONMENTS AND VIRTUAL REALITY

We should note that the kinds of online communities examined in the preceding section are also sometimes described as "virtual communities." However, those communities comprise only a subset of what we have referred to in the preceding section as virtual environments (VEs). Before describing what is meant by our broader notion of *VE*, however, it is useful to understand the meaning of "virtual." This term can be used in three senses. Sometimes, it is contrasted with "real," as in distinguishing virtual objects from real ones. At other times, the term is contrasted with "actual," as when a person says that she has "virtually finished" her project (i.e., she has not actually, or literally, finished it, but she believes that for practical purposes, she has finished it). The term "virtual" can also refer to one's feeling "as if" one were physically present in a space, as when you are conversing with a friend online or on a phone; even though you could be literally thousands of miles away from each other, the sense that you are interacting in real time makes you feel *as if* you are both in the same room. (Contrast this experience with radio and traditional broadcast communications, where messages can be transmitted in only one direction at a time.) However, it is primarily in the first sense of *virtual*—contrasted with "real"—that we examine various kinds of VEs in Section 1.2.

How are VEs both similar to and different from the online/virtual communities we examined in Section 11.1? While both kinds of virtual forums are "computer generated," and thus could not exist without cybertechnology, VEs also provide contexts in which users can do more than merely interact with other users. As Søraker and Brey (2015) note, VEs can "visualize imaginary environments" as well as simulate real ones.[15]

Not only do VEs subsume virtual (or online) communities, they also subsume (what some authors call) *virtual worlds*. Søraker and Brey describe the latter as a type of VE in which users typically (i) are "represented by avatars" and (ii) have the "illusion of perceiving a three dimensional world consisting of virtual objects."[16] Wankel and Malleck (2010) also describe virtual worlds as environments that are "three dimensional." For our purposes, however, a VE need not have a three-dimensional aspect (even if only illusory); as we saw in our analysis of online/virtual communities and forums (in Section 11.1.1), VEs can also include two-dimensional environments (such as MOOs). So, in our scheme, a VE can include a wide range of two-dimensional and three-dimensional forums or applications—that is, from online/virtual communities to virtual worlds to virtual reality (VR) applications. Our focus on ethical aspects of VEs in the remainder of Section 1.2, however, will be mainly on VR applications (including video games). So we first need to understand more precisely what is meant by the term *VR*.

11.2.1 What is Virtual Reality (VR)?

Brey (1999) defines VR as "a three dimensional interactive computer generated environment that incorporates a first person perspective." Notice three important features in Brey's definition of VR:

- Interactivity
- A three-dimensional environment
- A first-person perspective

How do these features distinguish VR from other kinds of computer-mediated environments? First, *interactivity* requires that users be able to navigate and manipulate the represented environment. Because a *three-dimensional environment* is required in VR, neither text-based VEs nor two-dimensional graphic environments will qualify. Brey also points out that a *first-person perspective* requires a single locus from which the environment is perceived and interacted with; the first-person perspective also requires an immersion in the virtual world rather than simply an "experience" of that world as an "object that can be (partially) controlled by the outside."

As noted earlier, we can differentiate VR environments/applications, which are three-dimensional, from our more broadly defined notion of VE. Recall our analysis of online/virtual communities in Section 11.1, which included examples of two-dimensional VEs; LambdaMOO, for instance, satisfies the requirements for a two-dimensional VE, but it would not qualify as a VR application.

Figure 11-1 illustrates some manifestations of virtual environments.

Virtual Reality vs. Augmented Reality

We should note that some authors now tend to conflate VR with *augmented reality* (AR). What, exactly, is the difference between AR and VR, given that both are "computer-mediated" realities, as well as three-dimensional environments? Søraker and Brey (2015) note that in VR applications, a user's "field of vision is substantially replaced by the computer-generated visual output." So VR applications typically provide the user with a "simulated world," thus replacing the real world. AR technology, on the contrary, enhances a user's view of the real world. Via

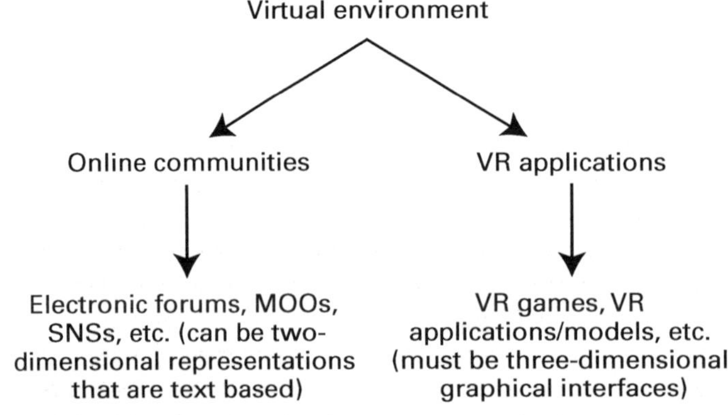

Figure 11-1 Virtual environments.

AR equipment, the user gains either direct or indirect access to the physical (real) world in a way that is enhanced or augmented by computer-generated sensory inputs. These typically include video inputs (e.g., eyewear such as Google glass) and sound inputs. With AR technology, users also interact with their physical environments in real time.

It is perhaps worth noting that some authors build the concept of AR into their definition of "virtual worlds" (which are a subset of what we call VEs). For example, Wankel and Malleck (2010) define virtual worlds as "three-dimensional *augmented reality* interfaces."[17] However, we limit our discussion of controversies involving VEs in this section to VR applications that either *simulate* the real world or create completely artificial worlds. These applications are sufficiently distinct from the AR applications that enhance our perception of the real (physical) world we inhabit. For more information on AR, including some potential ethical concerns that this technology raises, see Mann (2013).

In Section 11.1.3, we noted that many actions and behaviors that are considered morally objectionable in the physical world can be performed easily in online communities and forums. We will next see that interactions made possible in VR applications, including some video games, also enable users to engage in morally objectionable acts/behaviors; these include (virtual) prostitution, pornography, pedophilia, torture, mutilation, and murder.

11.2.2 Ethical Aspects of VR Applications

How are ethical issues involving controversial behavior in VR applications different from issues associated with morally controversial acts displayed on television or played out in board games? For example, television programs sometimes display violent acts and some board games allow participants to act out morally controversial roles. But Brey points out that in VR applications, users are actively engaged, whereas television viewers are passive. VR users are not spectators; rather, they are more like actors, as are board game players, who also act out roles in certain board games. This common feature suggests that there might not be much difference between the two kinds of games; however, Brey also notes that VR applications, unlike board games, simulate the world in a way that gives it a much greater appearance of reality. And in VR, the player has a first-person perspective of what it is like to perform certain acts and roles, including some that are criminal or immoral, or both. We next examine some ethical aspects of online video games.

First, we draw a useful distinction between single-player and multiplayer video games; the latter are commonly referred to either as massively multiplayer online games (MMOGs) or massively multiplayer online role-playing games (MMORPGs). An example of a MMOG is *Second Life* (designed by Linden Lab), which includes members called "Residents" who do not engage in some of the traditional *role-playing* activities available in many MMORPGs. (Launched in 2003, Second Life had approximately 13 million registered user accounts as of March 2008.[18]) Examples of MMORPGs include popular online games such as *World of Warcraft* (*WOW*), *EVE Online*, and *Entropia Universe*. WOW is perhaps the most popular MMORPG, boasting over 7 million paying subscribers as of May 2015.[19]

Many MMORPGs are organized around various "clans" or "guilds" that members join; if they wish, members can also pool their resources.[20] Typically, these games are also developed around systems that are either "class based" or "skill points based." In the former scheme, a player's chosen division can determine his or her character's "strengths and weaknesses." So players are encouraged to "interact with others and form teams to balance out strengths and weaknesses."[21] In *Second Life*, for example, "Residents" can socialize, participate in group activities, and create trade items (virtual property) and services with one another. The virtual currency used in that MMOG is the Linden Dollar (linden or L$), which can also be traded for real currencies via a "resident-to-resident marketplace" that is facilitated by Linden Lab. Residents in Second Life, as well as players in other MMOGs and MMORPGs, often select an avatar (a graphical representation that can exhibit human-like features and traits) to represent themselves.

We next consider why some MMORPGs and MMOGs are controversial from an ethical perspective? In doing so, we examine the kinds of morally objectionable behavior they make possible, especially with respect to violence and pornography.

Violent and Sexually Offensive Acts in MMOGs and MMORPGs

Some critics claim that *Second Life* facilitates child pornography because virtual characters who are adults in real life (RL) can have sex with virtual children, that is, avatars designed to look like children, in that MMOG.[22] Cases of virtual prostitution in *Second Life* have also been reported—that is, where some Residents were "paid to (use their avatar to) perform sex acts or to serve as escorts."[23] So, if these reports are correct, there are clearly some forms of sexually offensive acts that take place in MMOGs and MMORPGs, which would not be tolerated outside these gaming environments.

In addition to concerns about sexually offensive behavior in online games, many worry about the kinds of violent acts that are also carried out in these environments. Wonderly (2008) suggests that some forms of violence permitted in online games may be "more morally problematic" than pornography and other kinds of sexually offensive behavior in VEs. She points out, for example, that relatively few video games "permit sexual interaction between characters," and even fewer allow "deviant sexual conduct." But she notes that many popular games permit and that some "even *require* copious amounts of wanton graphic violence."[24]

Are violent acts in MMORPGs, including virtual murder, more morally problematic than the pornographic and sexually deviant acts that also have been carried out in these games? Or should violent acts such as virtual murder be tolerated as acceptable behavior? Luck (2009) notes that while most people agree that murder is wrong, they do not seem to be bothered by virtual murder in MMORPGs. He points out, for example, that some might see the virtual murder of a character in a video game as no different from the "taking of a pawn in a chess game." But Luck also notes that people have different intuitions about acts in VEs that involve morally objectionable sexual behavior, such as child pornography and pedophilia. And he worries that the kind of reasoning used to defend virtual murder in games could, unwittingly, be extended to defend virtual pedophilia. For example, Luck suggests that the following line of reasoning, which for our purposes can be expressed in standard argument form, may unintentionally succeed in doing this:

1. Allowing acts of virtual murder will not likely increase the number of actual murders.
2. Allowing acts of virtual pedophilia may significantly increase the amount of actual pedophilia.
3. Therefore, virtual pedophilia is immoral, but virtual murder is not.[25]

While this kind of argument may appeal to some, Luck points out that it is difficult to defend because of the lack of empirical evidence needed to confirm both (1) and (2). More importantly, however, if (2) could be shown to be false, then virtual pedophilia, like virtual murder, would not be immoral (according to the reasoning used in this argument).

With respect to (2), Levy (2002) has suggested that allowing virtual child pornography may even "reduce the harm to actual children" because it would provide an "acceptable outlet" for pedophiles and would encourage pornographers to seek an "alternative to real children." But it is important to note that Levy does not believe that virtual child pornography should be acceptable; in fact, he opposes it for alternative reasons.

A different kind of rationale for why virtual child pornography should be prohibited has been offered by Sandin (2004), who argues that it can cause significant harm to many people who find it revolting or offensive. But Brey (2008) points out that one problem with Sandin's argument is that it puts too much emphasis on a kind of harm that is simply "caused by offense." As Brey notes, if we outlaw actions simply because they "offend a large group of people," then (i) what we now take to be "individual rights" would be "drastically curtailed," and (ii) and interracial marriage and homosexual acts would "still be illegal."[26] Hence, none of the arguments considered so far can show why acts that are morally objectionable in physical space either should or should not be allowed in VEs.

Assessing the Nature of "Harm" in VEs and VR Applications

Can a plausible argument be constructed to show why it is wrong to perform acts in VEs in general, and VR applications in particular, that would be considered immoral in RL? We have seen some difficulties with arguments that tried to show that allowing morally objectionable actions in VEs will likely lead to an increase (or decrease) in those actions in the real world. Other arguments have tried to link, or in some cases delink, the kind of harm caused in VEs with the sense of harm one might experience in the real world. For example, some arguments have tried to show that sexually offensive acts in VEs can cause harm to vulnerable groups (such as children and women) in the real world.[27] However, the individual premises used to support the conclusions to these arguments typically lack sufficient empirical evidence to establish the various claims being made. On the contrary, some arguments claim that no one is physically harmed in virtual murder or, for that matter, in any act performed only in a VE. But these arguments have also been criticized for lacking sufficient evidence to establish their conclusions.

Should we assume that any harm that one experiences in the virtual realm is not "real harm" but only *virtual harm*? In our discussion of logical fallacies in Chapter 3, we saw that using this line of reasoning commits the *virtuality fallacy*; you may wish to revisit that fallacy at this point. Søraker and Brey (2015) have also pointed out the mistaken inference (or logical error) made by some people who assume that because VEs are not real environments, the consequences of one's actions in these environments do not have real-life consequences. And Søraker (2012), who notes that the computer simulation that "underpins" a VE is a physical entity, argues that we need to distinguish between what he calls the "intravirtual" and "extra-virtual" consequences of these environments. He then points out that while intravirtual consequences may affect only the "state" of the VE itself, the extra-virtual consequences, which are "triggered by the state of the virtual environment," can also have "potentially dramatic consequences in the real world."

We have already noted that while "virtual" is ambiguous (in at least three ways), it is now typically contrasted with "real." So this has been interpreted by some to mean that a "virtual harm" is equivalent to an "unreal harm." But even though a harm caused in a VE might not result in physical harm to a "flesh-and-blood" person, it doesn't follow that the harm caused is not real. The LambdaMOO incident (described in Section 11.1.3), which involved a "virtual rape," can help us to see why harm in a VE is not itself limited to the virtual characters in that VE. We begin by asking why the "rape" in LambdaMOO was a morally objectionable act. For example, one might argue that it was not a "real rape," and it did not result in physical harm to any "flesh-and-blood" individuals. Brey (1999) believes that we can use two different kinds of arguments to show why it is wrong to engage in immoral acts in VEs:

a. The argument from *moral development*

b. The argument from *psychological harm*

To illustrate (a), Brey suggests that we can extend an argument advanced by Immanuel Kant for the treatment of animals to the treatment of virtual characters. Kant argued that even if we have no direct moral obligation to treat animals kindly, we should, because treating animals kindly can influence our development of moral attitudes and behaviors for treating human beings. Similarly, then, the way we treat virtual characters may ultimately affect the way we treat real persons—raping virtual characters in virtual space, or even viewing such a rape, could desensitize us to the act of rape itself as it affects flesh-and-blood individuals in physical space.

The rationale in (b), the argument from *psychological harm*, suggests that the way we refer to characters that represent a particular group can cause harm to actual members of the group. Consider a cartoon depicting a woman being raped: Actual (flesh-and-blood) women may suffer psychological harm from seeing, or possibly even knowing about, this cartoon image, even though none of them, as flesh-and-blood individuals, is being raped, either physically or as represented by the cartoon. Extending this analogy to virtual space, it would follow that the "rape" of a virtual woman in a VE, such as a MOO, MMOG, MMORPG, etc., can also cause psychological harm to real (i.e., flesh-and-blood) women.

Virtual Economies and "Gold Farming"

So far, we have examined controversial *behavioral issues* in VEs in general, and video games in particular, mainly from the perspectives of violence and sexually offensive acts. We also described the kinds of harm that can result from these kinds of behaviors/acts in VEs. However, other behavior-related controversies arise because of the kinds of "virtual economies" made possible by interactions in online games. We noted earlier that some MMORPGs and MMOGs have their own monetary currencies. For example, *Second Life* uses the Linden Dollar (linden or L$), which its Residents can both use in in-game transactions and exchange outside the game for real currencies such as the U.S. dollar or the euro. As a result, virtual economies have emerged. Brey (2008) believes that their emergence can also increase the likelihood that moral controversies will arise in these environments—as Brey notes, people will be "more likely to act immorally if money is to be made or if valuable property is to be had."

Virtual property, as in the case of virtual money, can be acquired and exchanged with players in games. It can also be sold and exchanged outside the game to interested parties (in the physical world). In some cases, the virtual property has become so desirable that it has led to violent acts in the real world. Warner and Raiter (2005) describe an incident in China where a person who had stolen someone's virtual sword in a MMOG was murdered in real life (RL) by the "sword's" owner. So virtual economies can have RL implications and can result in physical harm to individuals in the real world. One controversial activity associated with virtual economies in gaming environments is a form of labor and economic exchange called "gold farming."

Kimppa and Bisset (2008) define gold farming as "playing an online computer game for the purpose of gaining items of value within the internal economy of the game and selling these to other players for real money."[28] These items can include "desirable items" as well as in-game money (where the rules defining the game's internal economy permit this); they can also include "highly developed" game characters. All of these items can also be sold via online auctions or designated Web sites. Kimppa and Bisset point out that the 2009 "in-game gold market" globally was estimated at 7 billion dollars; they also note that the practice of gold farming is most popular in countries such as China and Mexico that have both low-average income levels and "relatively good access to the Internet."[29]

Gold farming has also raised concerns about working conditions in the real world. For example, Warner and Raiter describe a situation in rural China where people who participate in World of Warcraft were paid to work 12-hour shifts of gold farming; the workers would acquire "virtual gold" within the game and then sell it outside the game to interested players. The business became profitable, Warner and Reiter point out, because many players who can afford to purchase the virtual gold preferred to buy it rather than to do the work necessary to earn it in the game.[30] It was also more advantageous to the "gold farmers" themselves, who could earn more money obtaining and selling virtual gold than they could in traditional agricultural work. But as Brey (2008) notes, this practice has also led to reported cases of Chinese sweatshop laborers who work "day and night in conditions of practical slavery" to acquire the virtual gold and virtual resources.[31] Assuming that these reports are true, gold mining raises some serious ethical concerns.

In this section, we have examined some *behavioral*, or what Brey (1999) also refers to as "interactive," controversies regarding ethical dimensions of VR applications. Other ethical aspects of VEs and VR applications in Brey's model focus on ways in which virtual characters and virtual objects are *represented* in these environments and applications. For example, these objects can be *mis*represented (i.e., in terms of accuracy) or represented in ways that are either *biased* and *indecent* (Brey 2008). A discussion of these controversial aspects of VR, however, is beyond the scope of this section.

▶ 11.3 ARTIFICIAL INTELLIGENCE (AI)

In Sections 11.1 and 11.2, we examined some challenges that online communities and VEs pose for our understanding of community and personal identity in the digital age. We next consider some implications that ongoing developments in the field of artificial intelligence (AI) have for our sense of self and for what it means to be human. AI research has already influenced some philosophers and cognitive scientists to question our conventional understanding of notions such as rationality, intelligence, knowledge, and learning. Some now also question what it will mean to be a human being in an era when some AI entities may exhibit a level of intelligence that exceeds that of ordinary humans. It is mainly from this vantage point that we examine AI-related controversies in Section 11.3. We begin, however, with a very brief description and overview of the field of AI.

11.3.1 What is AI? A Brief Overview

Sullins (2015) defines AI as "the science and technology that seeks to create intelligent computational systems." Sullins notes that AI researchers have aimed at building computer systems that can duplicate, or at least simulate, the kind of intelligent behavior found in humans. The official birth of AI as an academic field is often traced to a conference at Dartmouth College in 1956, which was organized by AI pioneers John McCarthy and Marvin Minsky. Since then, the field has advanced considerably and has also spawned several subfields.

In the 1950s and early 1960s, many AI researchers focused on developing software programs that could play checkers and chess with humans, pass calculus exams designed for undergraduate students, and solve problems that require a high level of human intelligence. The first AI programs were "problem solvers" comprising software code but included little or no hardware; many researchers during this period assumed that just as artificial flight had been successfully developed in ways that bypassed the need to emulate nature's way of flying, so too could AI be achieved without having to copy nature's way of thinking (i.e., via a physical brain). We now refer to the method of AI research conducted in that era, which focused on constructing a kind of "disembodied intelligence," as "classical AI," "symbolic AI," or "good old-fashioned AI" (GOFAI).

The classical AI approach was eventually criticized by researchers in the field who argued that human intelligence cannot be reduced merely to symbolic manipulation (captured in software programs) and that something additional was needed. For example, one school argued that an artificial brain with neural networking (that could "perceive" and "learn" its environment) was also required for a machine to learn and understand the world and thus potentially duplicate the way that humans think. Whereas the latter scheme in AI is often described as a "bottom-up" (or inductive) approach to machine learning, the classical/symbolic AI model is typically viewed as a "top-down" (or deductive) approach.

Another division in the field arose when a group of AI researchers argued that it was not critical to build machines that were as intelligent as humans (or that thought in the same way humans did); rather, they believed that a legitimate goal for AI research would be to develop systems that were "expert" in performing specific tasks that required a high level of intelligence in humans. For example, a system such as an "expert doctor" could be highly competent in diagnosing medical diseases, although it would be unable to perform any tasks outside that very narrow domain. (Recall our brief discussion of expert systems in Chapter 10, in connection with cybertechnology and work.) However, many other AI researchers believed that it was still possible to achieve the original goal of emulating (general) human intelligence in machines. Some of these researchers, including those working on the CYC project, use an approach that builds on classical/symbolic AI by designing software programs that manipulate large databases of factual information. Others, such as "Connectionists," have designed neural networks that aim at modeling the human brain, with its vast number of neurons and arrays of neural pathways, which exhibit varying degrees of "connection strengths." And some AI researchers focus on building full-fledged robots that can include artificial emotions as well.[32]

One concern that arose early in AI research, which was more philosophical or sociological than technological in nature, had to do with how we might come to see ourselves in a world where machines would be as intelligent, or possibly even more intelligent, than humans. Weckert (2001) articulates this concern when he asks:

> Can we, and do we want to, live with artificial *intelligences*? We can happily live with fish that swim better than we do, with dogs that hear better, hawks that see and fly better, and so on, but things that can reason better seem to be in a different and altogether more worrying category . . . What would such [developments mean for] our view of what it is to be human?[33]

Of course, we can ask whether it is possible, even in principal, to build "machines" (i.e., software programs or artificial entities) that are "genuinely intelligent" and whose intelligence could rival and possibly exceed that of humans. Some critics argue that, at best, AI researchers would be able to build machines that merely simulate rather than replicate human intelligence. A spirited debate about this issue has ensued to this day, and each side has presented a series of arguments and "thought experiments" to defend its position.

11.3.2 The Turing Test and John Searle's "Chinese Room" Argument

In 1950, computer science "pioneer" Alan Turing confidently predicted that by the year 2000 a computing machine would be able to pass a test, which has come to be called "The Turing Test," demonstrating machine intelligence.[34] Turing envisioned a scenario in which a person engaged in a conversation with a computer (located in a room that was not visible to the human) was unable to tell—via a series of exchanges on a computer screen—whether he or she was conversing with another human or with a machine. He believed that if the computer was able to answer questions and communicate with the person at the other end in a way that the person there could not be sure whether this entity was a human or a computer, then we would have to attribute some degree of human-like intelligence to the computer.

While most AI researchers would concede that Turing's prophecy has not yet been fully realized, they also point to the significant progress and achievements that have been made in the field so far. For example, in 1997, an IBM computer program called *Deep Blue* defeated Gary Kasparov, then reigning champion, in the competition for the world chess title. And in 2011, another IBM computer program, called *Watson*, defeated two human opponents in the TV game show *Jeopardy* in a championship match. (This human–computer competition was viewed by millions of people around the world.)

Watson, like Deep Blue, is a disembodied AI, that is, a highly sophisticated set of computer programs. Unlike Deep Blue, which could be viewed as an "expert system" that is highly skilled at playing chess (but not necessarily competent in other areas), Watson was capable of answering a wide range of questions posed in natural language. Some believe that Watson's skills at least simulate human intelligence in the broad or general sense. But did Watson, in defeating its human challengers, also exhibit the skills necessary to pass the Turing test? And even if Watson could pass the Turing test, would that necessarily show that Watson possessed (human-like) intelligence?

Some might argue that Watson was merely acting in a manner similar to the individual in John Searle's classic "Chinese room" scenario. In that scenario, a human who is a native English speaker but who understands nothing about the Chinese language is able to perform tasks that require manipulating Chinese symbols to produce answers to questions posed in Chinese. This person, who is not seen by anyone outside the room, receives questions from someone who passes them to him through an opening or slot. The person then consults a series of instructions and rules located on a wall in the room—all of which are written in English—that enable him to substitute the incoming Chinese symbols for other Chinese symbols in such a way as to produce correct answers to the questions asked. Once he has completed the task, he passes the answers back through the slot to a person waiting outside the room. That person might assume that the human who returned the correct answers understood Chinese. However, Searle (1980) argues that it is possible that the person understood nothing about the semantic meaning of the questions he received and the answers he returned; instead, this person had merely followed a set of syntactic rules (written in English) for manipulating symbols that happened to be in Chinese. In fact, the English-speaking person may not even know that the symbols involved are elements of the Chinese language.

Was Watson's behavior in the Jeopardy game analogous to that of the human in Searle's Chinese room—in other words, did Watson actually "understand" the meaning of the symbols (in the questions and answers) involved, or did Watson simply use a series of syntactic rules and cross-checking algorithms to manipulate the information stored in Watson's vast database to get the correct answers? It is not clear to what extent, if any, Watson could be said to have any understanding of natural language. So, even if Watson is capable of passing the Turing test (as originally posed), it would not necessarily follow, using Searle's argument, that Watson possesses human-like intelligence. In fact, some skeptics might argue that Watson is nothing more than a kind of (very broad) expert system, or perhaps some combination of expert systems, that behaves like an advanced version of (Apple's) Siri. Although Siri is capable of responding to many questions with correct answers, it is doubtful that people would be willing to describe Siri as possessing human-like intelligence. In the same way, then, we could argue that we need not ascribe genuine intelligence to Watson. Nevertheless, we can still see why many humans would feel a bit uneasy by the fact that a computer, or AI entity, had defeated two highly intelligent human beings in a championship match, even if it was only in a game show contest.

Unfortunately, an extended discussion of key questions involving both Watson and the Turing test, as well as an in-depth discussion of the history of AI itself, is beyond the scope of this chapter. AI's history, though relatively brief, is fascinating, and several excellent resources are available; so, fortunately, there is no need to replicate that discussion here.[35] We next examine some AI-related social and ethical issues affecting human–machine relationships, especially as they arise in the context of cyborgs.

11.3.3 Cyborgs and Human–Machine Relationships

So far, we have considered whether machines could, in principle at least, possess human-like intelligence. We have also considered how our answer to this question can affect our sense of what it means to be human. Next, we see how the development of cyborgs and the concerns it raises about human–machine relationships may also have a similar effect on us. We approach these concerns from the perspective of two distinct, but related, questions: (i) Are humans becoming more computer-like? (ii) Are computers becoming more human-like? We begin with (i).

Cyborgs and (AI-Induced) Bionic Chip Implants: Are We Becoming More Computer-like? Many humans now receive nonhuman body parts, in the form of computerized chips, in implants. As we are implanted with more and more (AI-induced) bionic parts, are we becoming cyborgs? With so many bionic parts becoming available, some worry that humans and machines could soon begin to merge. Kurzweil (2000) has suggested that in the near future, the distinction between machines and humans may no longer be useful. And Moor (2005) believes the question we must continually reevaluate is "not whether we should become cyborgs," but rather "what sort of cyborgs should we become?" Clark (2003) suggests that we already are cyborgs because of our dependency on technologies. Are these views plausible, and why should we be concerned about the role that (AI-induced) chimp implants can play in questions about the human-cyborg dispute?

Our first line of response might be to note that implant technologies are by no means new. However, Weckert (2001) points out that while "conventional" implants in the form of devices designed to "correct" deficiencies have been around and used for some time, their purpose has been to assist patients in their goal of achieving "normal" states of vision, hearing, heartbeat, and so forth. Whereas these are all examples of "therapeutic implants," future chip plants in the form of "enhancement implants" could make a normal person "superhuman."[36] Anticipating the kinds of concerns that enhancement implants will likely raise in the near future, Weckert asks:

> Do we want to be "superhuman" relative to our current abilities, with implants that enhance our senses, our memory and our reasoning ability? What would such implants do to our view of what it is to be human?[37]

Some suggest that the current controversy involving implants can be framed in terms of an "enhancement vs. therapy debate." Moor notes that because the human body has "natural functions," some will argue that implanting chips in a body is acceptable as long as these implants "maintain and restore the body's natural functions." Moor also suggests that a policy framed along the lines of a therapy–enhancement distinction will appeal to many because it would "endorse the use of a chip that reduced dyslexia but would forbid the implanting of a deep blue chip for superior chess play."[38] Such a policy would also permit a chip implant that would restore eyesight for a person going blind, but would not license implanting a chip for X-ray vision for a person with normal eyesight. But Moor also suggests that the therapy–enhancement distinction might easily become blurred or confused if the only chip available to restore "normal" vision also happened (even if unintentionally) to enhance the person's night vision beyond the "normal" range.

Even if it turns out that a clear therapy–enhancement distinction regarding implants is possible, another important question remains: Who will be responsible for framing and enforcing policies affecting those implants? Without clear policies in place for the use of bionic implants, it may be difficult to prevent, or even to discourage, people from receiving enhancement implants that enable them to become either cyborg-like or superhuman? In Chapter 12, we examine some proposals for policies and ethical frameworks to guide developments in emerging technologies, which would also apply to bionic chip implants.

Our main concern in this section has been with the question of what it will mean to be human as more and more people elect to be fitted with bionic parts (and thus potentially also become more machine-like). Next, we consider the flip side of this cyborg-related question: What will happen as the AI entities we develop become more human-like?

Distinguishing AI Entities from Humans: Are Computers Becoming More Human-like? Consider that some AI entities (e.g., "bots") in the form of avatars (typically graphical representations which, as we saw in Section 11.2.2, can exhibit human-like features and traits) already assist users in organizing their work schedules, reminding them of important scheduled meetings, arranging travel, and so forth. Also consider that personal digital assistants, and smart phones using voice-recognition programs (such as iPhone's Siri), now interact with humans on a daily basis. Even though they are merely virtual entities, some appear to exhibit human-like qualities when viewed on screens or when heard on electronic devices. Also consider that some avatars (and AI bots), which now act on our behalf, exhibit characteristics and stereotypic traits associated with humans in certain professions. For example, an avatar in the form of an AI "agent" designed to interact with other AI agents as well as with humans, such as a "negotiation agent," may look like and have the persona of a (human) broker.

After interacting with your human-like agent (bot or avatar) over a long period of time, is it possible that you might begin to act as if you are conversing with a real person? We can also ask whether it is possible that you might, after an extended period of time, begin to confuse some virtual entities (with whom you interact) with actual flesh-and-blood characters that those entities represent. For example, as virtual entities become increasingly more human-like in appearance, it may also become more difficult to distinguish between our interactions with some (physical) person's screen avatar and with an actual human represented by that avatar or virtual entity.

This confusion in interacting with artificial entities will likely become more exacerbated as we move from our interactions with virtual entities on screens (of computers and devices) to interacting more regularly with physical AI entities—namely, robots that appear to be sentient as well as intelligent. Consider that sophisticated robots of the near future will not only look more human-like but may also exhibit sentient characteristics; that is, these robots, like humans and animals, would (arguably, at least) be capable of simulating the experiences of sensation, feeling, and emotion. Robots and other kinds of AI entities of the not-too-distant future may also exhibit, or appear to exhibit, consciousness. Many AI researchers have questioned the nature of consciousness; for example, cognitive scientists and philosophers ask whether consciousness is a uniquely human attribute. Some also question whether it might be an emergent property—that is, a property capable of "emerging" (under the right conditions) in nonhuman entities, such as advanced AI systems.

Stanley Kubrick's classic 1967 film *2001: A Space Odyssey* portrays a computer named HAL with higher-order thinking functions resembling human consciousness. In addition to performing ordinary computational tasks, HAL engages in sophisticated conversations with members of the spaceship's crew, plays chess, and even critiques the art (drawings) of one crew member. To take control of the spaceship from HAL, the sole surviving member of the crew removes the logic components of HAL's higher-order ("mental") functions: HAL is forced to undergo a sort of virtual "lobotomy." Of course, HAL is merely science fiction, but consider how far developments in AI have progressed since HAL's film debut in 1967.

Today, some researchers working with highly advanced AI systems claim to be on the verge of modeling a form of higher-order thinking in these systems, which might be viewed as also bordering on consciousness. Suppose that we reach general agreement that human consciousness can be understood as an emergent property and that conscious activity—similar to that of humans—emerges whenever a sufficient number of neurons (or "connection strengths" in neural networks) are present. Would this, once again, be something that causes us to reassess our conception of what it means to be human? Would it also mean that we should consider the question of whether to grant at least some level of moral consideration to sophisticated AI entities?

▶ 11.4 EXTENDING MORAL CONSIDERATION TO AI ENTITIES

We have seen that even if AI entities do not achieve full consciousness, many could still be capable of exhibiting (or at least simulating) other human-like characteristics such as rationality and sentience. For example, HAL has been described as an AI entity that was able to simulate human consciousness. Yet HAL was not sentient, since "he" had no body (and thus could also be said to have a form of "disembodied intelligence"). So it is possible that some AI entities (like HAL) may exhibit (or at least simulate) rationality and consciousness but not sentience, while other AIs may exhibit (or simulate) rationality and sentience but not consciousness. In either case, these AI entities would exhibit or simulate at least some human-like characteristics. An important question that arises is whether we are prepared to meet the kinds of social challenges these entities will likely pose and also whether we may need to grant these entities at least some degree of moral consideration.

The following scenario illustrates one way in which questions about extending our sphere of moral consideration can arise as we develop more human-like AI entities.

▶ **SCENARIO 11–4:** Artificial Children

The 2001 movie *A.I.*, directed by Steven Spielberg, is a story of an artificial boy, named David, who is physically indistinguishable from human boys and who appears to be capable of experiencing human-like emotion as well as displaying human-like intelligence. David also appears to need the love of human parents and "he" displays this need in a way that might seem genuine and convincing (to many humans). The human parents who adopt this artificial boy later decide to abandon him.[39] ■

Does this "boy" deserve at least some kind of moral consideration? Do David's human parents have any clear moral obligations to their "adopted child"? Or do they have the right to discard "him" at their convenience, in the same way that they might discard a desktop computer that no longer serves their needs and thus is no longer useful to them? Of course, we could ask whether such an artificial child should have been developed in the first place. But given the likelihood that artificial entities similar to David will be developed, we need to seriously consider questions about which kinds of moral consideration, if any, those artificial entities may warrant.

11.4.1 Determining Which Kinds of Beings/Entities Deserve Moral Consideration

One reason why many humans believe they are morally significant, and thus deserve moral consideration, is based on the assumption that humans, unlike all other creatures and entities, are rational beings that possess intelligence.[40] In recent years, however, the (traditional) assumption that only humans have intelligence has been challenged on two distinct fronts. On the one hand, research in animal behavior suggests that many primates, dolphins, and whales exhibit skills that suggest some level of intelligence (while, on the contrary, some humans either cannot or are no longer able to exhibit these skills). On the other hand, and more importantly for our purposes, we have seen that developments in the field of AI suggest that some highly sophisticated computers can exhibit forms of intelligence and rational decision making, which were previously thought to be possible only in humans.

If some AI entities are capable of exhibiting (or simulating) rationality and intelligence (and possibly even consciousness)—characteristics that traditionally have been reserved to describe only humans—it would not seem unreasonable to ask whether these entities might also warrant moral status. And if some of these entities can exhibit (or simulate) human-like emotion and needs, as in the case of the artificial boy in the movie *AI*, would that also be a relevant factor to consider in understanding and addressing concerns about moral consideration for AI entities? An important question, then, is whether we will need to expand the conventional realm of moral consideration to include these entities.

Prior to the twentieth century, many ethicists and most lay persons in the Western world generally assumed that only human beings deserved moral consideration; all other entities—animals, trees, natural objects, etc.—were viewed merely as resources for humans to use (and misuse/abuse) as they saw fit. In other words, humans saw these "resources" simply as something to be used and disposed of as they wished, because they believed that these resources had no moral standing and that we had no obligations toward them.

By the mid-twentieth century, the assumption that moral consideration should be granted only to humans had been challenged on two distinct (though not altogether unrelated) fronts. One challenge came from animal rights groups, who argue that animals, like humans, are sentient creatures and thus capable of feeling pleasure and pain. Based on this comparison, proponents for animal rights have argued that we should also grant ethical consideration to animals, in which case it would be morally wrong for humans to abuse animals or to treat them simply as resources.

On a second front, some environmentalists made an even bolder claim, arguing that we should extend ethical consideration to include new "objects," or entities. Jonas (1984) argued that because modern technologies involving atomic and nuclear power have presented us with tools of destruction that could devastate our planet on a scale never before imaginable, we needed to expand our sphere of moral obligation to include "new objects of moral consideration." These "objects" included natural objects such as trees, land, and the environment itself, as well as abstract objects such as "future generations of humans" that will inherit the planet.

In the past 50 years or so, our thinking about both who and what should be included in the sphere of moral consideration has evolved significantly. We have moved from a traditional moral system that granted consideration only to human beings to one that at least debates whether animals, land, and the entire biosphere deserve moral consideration as well. Do we once again need to expand our sphere of moral consideration to include "new objects"—that is, nonnatural or "artificial objects" such as sophisticated AI entities?

Floridi (2002) has suggested that we need to grant some level of moral consideration to at least certain kinds of informational objects or entities. Initially, one might find Floridi's assertion strange, perhaps even preposterous, but we have seen that some sophisticated AI entities already exhibit a form of rationality that parallels that of humans. The question that concerns us here is whether these artificial entities merit moral consideration because they, like humans, have rational abilities. If our primary justification for granting moral consideration to humans is based on the premise that humans are rational entities, and if certain artificial entities also qualify as "rational entities," then we can make a compelling case for granting at least some moral consideration to them. For example, even if they do not qualify as full-blown moral agents (as typical adult humans do), they may nevertheless meet the threshold of what Floridi calls "moral patients."

11.4.2 Moral Patients vs. Moral Agents

In Floridi's scheme, moral patients are "receivers of moral action," while moral agents are the "sources of moral action" (capable of causing moral harm or moral good). Like moral agents, moral patients enjoy moral consideration and thus have at least some moral standing; unlike moral agents, however, moral patients cannot be held morally responsible for their actions.[41] While animals may not be moral agents (i.e., morally accountable for what they do or fail to do), they can nevertheless qualify as moral patients that deserve moral consideration by humans.

One reason for viewing them as moral patients is because of their ability, like humans, to feel pain and suffer emotionally. (Consider that many pet owners relate to their pets in ways that suggest they are moral entities, not only when they try to protect their pets from harm and suffering but also when they reward and punish their pets' behavior.) So if we extend this analogy, it would seem to follow that AI entities that exhibit sentience, independent of whether they also happen to exhibit a high level of rationality, could qualify as moral patients and thus warrant some moral consideration.

Consider again the example of the artificial boy examined in Scenario 11–4. Would it be plausible to grant "him" at least some degree of moral consideration—that is, as a moral patient—because of his "emotions" and "needs," even if this "boy" failed to satisfy a high threshold for rationality? We have noted that animal rights proponents argue that animals deserve moral consideration because of their ability to suffer pain, irrespective of any rational capacity they may or may not also have. So it would seem reasonable to ask if we can extend that analogy to apply to sentient AI entities such as the artificial boy. In this scheme, then, AI entities that exhibited (or simulated) either rationality or sentience, or both, could qualify for moral consideration.

A more interesting question, however—and one which we cannot answer here—is whether AI entities that (at least appear to) exhibit consciousness could also qualify as full, or even "partial," moral agents. We briefly discuss the concept of moral agency in Chapter 12, in connection with our analysis of autonomous machines.

We conclude this section by acknowledging that more questions have been raised than answered. The critical question of who/what (in addition to humans) deserves moral consideration (and if so, to what extent) is extremely complicated, as well as very controversial. While criteria such as rationality and sentience (in connection with an agent's ability to act in the universe) have played key roles in answering this question in the past, other characteristics such as autonomy and free will are also generally considered relevant criteria for possessing full moral agency. Note that we have not argued that any current AI entities have either free will or autonomy.

In Chapter 12, we examine a cluster of AI-related questions from a very different perspective. There, we consider whether it is possible to construct "moral machines" or AI entities that are capable of making moral decisions. For example, can those machines be embedded with (software) code that will enable them to make what Wallach and Allen (2009) call "good moral decisions"? We will see that this is an important "practical question," as we develop autonomous machines that act more and more independently of human oversight. Our focus on AI issues in this chapter, however, has been on questions that can be viewed as more theoretical and philosophical in nature—especially given our focus on AI's impact so far for the question of what it means to be human.

▶ 11.5 CHAPTER SUMMARY

In this chapter, we have examined three diverse technologies that pose challenges for our conventional understanding of community, personal identity, and what it means to be human in the digital era. In particular, we have seen how SNSs have affected our traditional notion of community, and we considered some arguments for the pros and cons of online communities. We then looked at some VR applications, including online video games and MMORPGS, and considered some of their ethical implications as well as for our understanding of personal identity in the digital era. Next, we examined the impact that key developments in the field of AI have had so far for our sense of self and for our sense of what it means to be human. Finally, we considered whether we may need to expand our conventional framework of moral obligation to include at least some AI entities.

▶ REVIEW QUESTIONS

1. What are online communities, and how do they differ from traditional communities?
2. What is a blog, and what kinds of controversies have blogs and the "bogosphere" generated?
3. How have online communities facilitated social polarization?
4. In which ways do online communities in general, and social networking services (SNSs) in particular, cause us to reexamine our traditional notion of friendship?
5. How do online communities, especially SNSs, facilitate anonymity and deception?
6. What is a virtual environment (VE), and how does it differ from a virtual (or online) community?
7. How does Philip Brey define virtual reality (VR)?
8. How are VR applications distinguishable from other kinds of VEs?
9. What are MMOPGS and MMORPGS, and how can they be controversial from an ethical perspective?
10. What is meant by the claim that virtual harm is not real harm, and why is this reasoning fallacious?
11. Describe how Brey applies both the argument from *moral development* and the argument from *psychological harm* in his analysis of "virtual harm."
12. What is "gold farming" in VR games, and why is it controversial?
13. What is artificial intelligence (AI)?
14. What is the Turing test, and what is its significance?
15. What is John Searle's "Chinese room" argument, and what implications does it have for the Turing test?
16. How have developments in AI so far affected our sense of what it means to be human?
17. In which ways are humans becoming more computer-like?
18. In which respects are computers (i.e., sophisticated AI entities) becoming more human-like?
19. Why does Luciano Floridi believe we should grant moral consideration to at least some AI entities?
20. How does Floridi distinguish "moral patients" from "moral agents"?

▶ DISCUSSION QUESTIONS

21. Describe some pros and cons of online communities. What does Mitch Parsell mean when he says that online communities with an "extremely narrow focus" contribute to social polarization? Assess his arguments for that claim. Do you agree with Parsell? On balance, have online communities enhanced or threatened community life? Explain.
22. Evaluate the argument by Cocking and Matthews for why true friendships in pure virtual (or online-only) contexts are not possible. Assess the counterargument by Briggle. Does Briggle succeed in making the case for the possibility of genuine friendships in purely virtual contexts? Whose argument do you find more convincing?
23. We saw that MMOGs and MMORPGs have become very popular around the world. Some critics are concerned about the level of violence that occurs in these games, while others worry more about the effects that virtual pornography and pedophilia in those games will have for real-life children. Evaluate Morgan Luck's claim that arguments used to defend murder (and other violent acts) in these games may, unintentionally, also defend pedophilia in virtual environments. Do you agree with Luck's view on this matter?
24. Assess the arguments we examined for whether we need to expand our conventional moral framework to include at least some AI entities? Do you believe that these entities deserve moral consideration? If we develop artificial creatures, such as the artificial boy in the (2001) movie *A.I.*, which kinds of moral obligations do we have to them? For example, can we discard these entities in the same ways we currently discard computer hardware resources? And if we grant moral consideration to some AI entities but not to others, where should we draw the line? In other words, which kinds of criteria are relevant for granting moral consideration these entities?

Scenarios for Analysis

1. Howard Rheingold, who has speculated about some ways in which VR technologies may impact the future of social relationships, raises an interesting question involving teledildonics (or simulated sex at a distance). Though not yet a marketable technology, recent work in interactive tactile presence (or touch feedback) will, Rheingold believes, make it possible for computer users to have sex at a distance. Inviting us to imagine this not-too-distant phenomenon, Rheingold asks us to picture ourselves "dressing for a hot night in the virtual village," where

people wear a "cybersuit" made of "smart skin."[42] Even if Rheingold's account turns out to be cyberfiction, it is difficult to avoid considering the implications that teledildonics-related technology could have for future social relationships. Assess these implications in Rheingold's scenario by applying some of the techniques introduced in Section 11.2.2 for analyzing ethical issues in virtual environments.

2. Paul "Cougar" Rambis is an Iraqi War veteran who lost a leg in combat. Before entering the military, he was a fairly accomplished golfer and had planned to "turn professional" after completing his tour of duty in the U.S. Army. Initially, his dreams seemed shattered when he was severely wounded by an explosive device he encountered while on a routine patrol. But, then, Cougar learned that a new kind of bionic leg had recently been developed and that he was at the top of the list to receive one of these remarkable limbs. When Cougar returned home (with his new "leg" in place), he resumed his golfing activities. But when he wished to declare himself a professional golfer, Cougar was informed that he would be unable to participate in professional golf competitions because of his artificial leg. However, Cougar responded that his new leg, though artificial, was a natural replacement for his original (biological or natural) leg and that, as such, it did not enhance his ability to swing a golf club or to endure the rigors associated with walking through the typical 18-hole golf course. The professional golf association responded that their policy is (and always has been) that no one with an artificial limb (or prosthetic device of any kind) is eligible to compete professionally under their rules. Does this policy still seem appropriate, in light of contemporary technology-based remedies available for people like Cougar?

Recall the distinction we drew (in Section 11.3.3) between "therapeutic" and "enhancement" implants. If Cougar's artificial leg qualifies as a therapeutic device, that is, by simply restoring his body functions to "normal," should Cougar be allowed to compete as a professional golfer? On the other hand, if that "leg" does not injure as easily, and does not age in the way that natural legs do, is Cougar's new leg merely a "therapeutic" replacement? In other words, does it enhance his ability to compete, even if only minimally? What would you decide in this case if you were a member of the governing board of the Professional Golfers' Association?

▶ ENDNOTES

1. Rheingold (2001, pp. 1–2).
2. Parsell (2008, p. 44).
3. The analysis of online communities in this chapter focuses mainly on their impacts in Western societies. For an account of some effects of these communities in the Arab/Muslim world, see Al-Saggaf and Begg (2004).
4. See *eBizMBA Rank*. Available at http://www.ebizmba.com/articles/social-networking-websites.
5. My analysis of blogs in this section draws from and expands upon some concepts and distinctions introduced in Grodzinsky and Tavani (2010).
6. See Richard Leiby, "The Hill's Sex Diarist Reveals All (Well Some)," *The Washington Post*, May 23, 2004, p. D03. Available at http://www.washingtonpost.com/wp-dyn/articles/A48909-2004May22.html. See also Grodzinsky and Tavani (2010) for an analysis of this incident in terms of the privacy issues that arise.
7. See "A Bloggers' Code of Ethics" (2003). Available at: http://www.cyberjournalist.net/news/000215.php.
8. For a more detailed discussion of ethical controversies affecting blogs and the blogosphere, see Grodzinsky and Tavani (2010).
9. Parsell (2008, p. 44). Interested readers may wish to evaluate Parsell's argument in terms of the standards for validity and invalidity we examined in Chapter 3.
10. Cocking and Matthews (2000, p. 231).
11. Briggle (2008, p. 71).
12. See http://abcnews.go.com/GMA/Story?id= 3882520.
13. See Dibbell (2001) for more details involving this incident. For an interesting analysis of this "virtual rape," see Søraker (2010).
14. This incident also raised questions about whether certain kinds of offenses that rise to the level of criminal behavior in physical space should be brought under the scope of criminal law even if they are carried out only in purely virtual environments. See Strickwerda (2013) who examines this question.
15. Søraker and Brey (2015, p. 498).
16. *Ibid.*
17. Wankel and Malleck (2010, p. 1). [Italics added]
18. Available at http://en.wikipedia.org/wiki/Second_Life.
19. See http://en.wikipedia.org/wiki/World_of_Warcraft.
20. For a more detailed explanation of the various kinds of guilds and clans involved in MMORPGs, see Cook (2006).
21. Available at http://en.wikipedia.org/wiki/MMORPG.
22. See, for example, the description of this controversy in Adams (2010) and Singer (2007).
23. See Brey (2008).
24. Wonderly (2008, p. 2). [Italics Wonderly]
25. Luck (2009, p. 33). Note that the argument presented here is designed to capture key points raised in Luck's original text. Luck does not express the argument in this precise form, but

I believe that the argument structure used here is compatible with his position.

26. Brey, pp. 371–72.
27. See, for example, Levy (2002).
28. Kimppa and Bisset (2008, p. 470).
29. *Ibid*.
30. Warner and Raiter (2005, pp. 49–50).
31. See Brey, pp. 376–77, for a more detailed discussion of these practices. Brey also believes that "many new ethical issues" involving VEs will likely arise because of the kind and the amount of "time, money, and social capital" people are willing to invest in virtual property and virtual economies.
32. For a more detailed analysis of many of the key historical developments in AI described here, see the account in Palfreman and Swade (1991).
33. Weckert (2001, pp. 49–50). [Italics Weckert]
34. While many thought of computers as merely sophisticated machines for calculating numbers, Turing was one of the first thinkers to articulate some interesting connections between computers and human minds (i.e., viewing both as a manipulators of *logical symbols*, and also noting that computers do not simply manipulate numbers). See Turing (1950).
35. Because the historical overview of AI provided in this section is very general, it is unable to include some important details and developments in the evolution of this field. CS students interested in learning more about the history of AI should consult some of the excellent sources that are available on this topic.
36. Weckert, pp. 49–50.
37. *Ibid*.
38. Moor (2005, p. 124).
39. This scenario is based on controversies that arise in Steven Spielberg's 2001 film *A.I.*
40. It is important to note that this interpretation is based mainly on a *secular* account of why humans are morally significant and deserve moral consideration. "Religious accounts," for example, would likely include characteristics that exceed mere rationality and intelligence (even though they would also agree that these criteria are part of what separate humans from other biological life forms). Typical religious accounts for explaining why (all) humans deserve moral consideration also include factors having to do with spirituality and possessing a (human) soul. However, a discussion of these characteristics is beyond the scope of this chapter and book.
41. See Floridi (2008) for a more detailed discussion of these distinctions.
42. See Rheingold (1991).

▶ REFERENCES

Adams, Andrew. 2010. "Virtual Sex with Child Avatars." In C. Wankel and S. Malleck, eds. *Emerging Ethical Issues of Life in Virtual Worlds*. Charlotte NC: Information Age Publishing, pp. 55–72.

Al-Saggaf, Yeslam and Mohamed M. Begg. 2004. "Online Communities versus Offline Communities in the Arab/Muslim World." *Journal of Information, Communication and Ethics in Society* 2, no. 1: 41–54.

Brey, Philip. 1999. "The Ethics of Representation and Action in Virtual Reality." *Ethics and Information Technology* 1, no. 1: 5–14.

Brey, Philip. 2008. "Virtual Reality and Computer Simulation." In K. E. Himma and H. T. Tavani, eds. *The Handbook of Information and Computer Ethics*. Hoboken, NJ: John Wiley and Sons, pp. 361–84. Reprinted in R. L. Sandler, ed. *Ethics and Emerging Technologies*. New York: Palgrave/Macmillan, 2014, pp. 315–32.

Briggle, Adam. 2008. "Real Friends: How the Internet Can Foster Friendship." *Ethics and Information Technology* 10, no. 1: 71–9.

Clark, Andrew J. 2003. *Natural-Born Cyborgs: Minds, Technologies, and the Future of Human Intelligences*. New York: Oxford University Press.

Cocking, Dean and Steve Matthews. 2000. "Unreal Friends." *Ethics and Information Technology* 2, no. 4: 223–31.

Cook, Brad. 2006. "Traverse Near-Infinite Possibilities with MMORPGs." Available at http://www.apple.com/games/articles/2006/04/mmorpgs/.

Dibbell, Julian. 2001. "A Rape in Cyberspace." In D. M. Hester and P. Ford, eds. *Computers and Ethics in the Cyberage*. Upper Saddle River, NJ: Prentice Hall, pp. 439–51. Reprinted from *The Village Voice* (December 1993): 36–42.

Floridi, Luciano. 2002. "On the Intrinsic Value of Information Objects in the Infosphere." *Ethics and Information Technology* 4, no. 4: 287–304.

Floridi, Luciano. 2008. "Foundations of Information Ethics." In K. E. Himma and H. T. Tavani, eds. *The Handbook of Information and Computer Ethics*. Hoboken NJ: John Wiley and Sons, pp. 3–23.

Grodzinsky, Frances S. and Herman T. Tavani. 2010. "Applying the 'Contextual Integrity' Model of Privacy to Personal Blogs in the Blogosphere." *International Journal of Internet Research Ethics* 3, no. 1: 38–47.

Jonas, Hans. 1984. *The Imperative of Responsibility: In Search of an Ethics for the Technological Age*. Chicago: University of Chicago Press.

Kimppa, Kai and Andrew Bisset. 2008. "Gold Farming." In T. Bynum, et al., eds. *Proceedings of the Tenth ETHICOMP international Conference on the Social and Ethical Impacts of Information and Communication Technology*. University of Pavia, Mantua, Italy (September 24–26, 2008), pp. 470–9.

Kurzweil, Ray. 2000. *The Age of Spiritual Machines: When Computers Exceed Human Intelligence*. New York: Penguin.

Levy, Neil. 2002. "Virtual Child Pornography: The Eroticization of Inequality." *Ethics and Information Technology* 4, no. 4: 319–23.

Luck, Morgan. 2009. "The Gamer's Dilemma: An Analysis of the Arguments for the Moral Distinction between Virtual Murder and Virtual Pedophilia." *Ethics and Information Technology* 11, no. 1: 31–6.

Mann, Steve. 2013. "My Augmented life: What I've Learned from 35 Years of Wearing Computerized Eyewear." *IEEE Spectrum*. Available at http://spectrum.ieee.org/geek-life/profiles/steve-mann-my-augmediated-life.

Moor, James H. 2005. "Should We Computers Get Under Our Skin?" In R. Cavalier, ed. *The Impact of the Internet on Our Moral Lives*. Albany, NY: State University of New York Press, pp. 121–38.

Palfreman, Jon and Doron Swade. 1991. *The Dream Machine*. London UK: BBC Books.

Parsell, Mitch. 2008. "Pernicious Virtual Communities: Identity, Polarization, and the Web 2.0." *Ethics and Information Technology* 10, no. 1: 41–56.

Rheingold, Harold. 1991. *Virtual Reality*. New York: Touchstone Books.

Rheingold, Harold. 2001. *The Virtual Community: Homesteading on the Electronic Frontier*. Rev. ed. Cambridge, MA: MIT Press.

Sandin, Per. 2004. "Virtual Child Pornography and Utilitarianism." *Journal of Information, Communication and Ethics in Society* 2, no. 4: 217–23.

Searle, John. 1980. "Minds, Brains, and Programs." *Behavioral and Brain Sciences* 3, no. 3: 417–24.

Singer, Peter. 2007. "Video Crime Peril vs. Virtual Pedophilia." *The Japan Times Online,* June 22. Available at http://search.japantimes.co.jp/cgi.bineo20070722a1.html.

Søraker, Johnny Hartz. 2010. "The Neglect of Reason: A Plea for Rationalist Accounts of the Effects of Virtual Violence." In C. Wankel and Shaun Malleck, eds. *Emerging Ethical Issues of Life in Virtual Worlds*. Charlotte NC: Information Age Publishing, pp. 15–32.

Søraker, Johnny Hartz. 2012. "Virtual Worlds and Their Challenge to Philosophy: Understanding the 'Intravirtual' and the 'Extravirtual.'" *Metaphilosophy* 43, no. 4: 499–512.

Søraker, Johnny Hartz and Philip Brey. 2015. "Virtual Environments." In J. Britt Holbrook and Carl Mitcham, eds. *Ethics, Science, Technology, and Engineering: A Global Resource*. Vol. 4, 2nd ed. Farmington Hills MI: Macmillan Reference, pp. 498–502.

Strickwerda, Litska. 2013. "Should Virtual Cybercrime Be Brought Under the Scope of Criminal Law?" In M. Bottis, ed. *Honorary Volume for Evi Laskari*. Athens, Greece: Nomiki Bibliothiki, pp. 495–545.

Sullins, John P. 2015. "Artificial Intelligence." In J. Britt Holbrook and Carl Mitcham, eds. *Ethics, Science, Technology, and Engineering: A Global Resource*. Vol. 1, 2nd ed. Farmington Hills, MI: Macmillan Reference, pp. 119–24.

Turing, Alan M. 1950. "Computing Machinery and Intelligence." *Mind* 59: 433–60.

Wallach, Wendell and Colin Allen. 2009. *Moral Machines: Teaching Robots Right from Wrong*. New York: Oxford University Press.

Wankel, Charles and Shaun Malleck. 2010. "Exploring New ethical Issues in the Virtual Worlds of the Twenty-First Century." In C. Wankel and S. Malleck, eds. *Emerging Ethical Issues of Life in Virtual Worlds*. Charlotte, NC: Information Age Publishing, pp. 1–14.

Warner, Dorothy E. and Mike Raiter. 2005. "Social Context in Massively-Multiplayer Online Games (MMOGs): Ethical Questions in Shared Space." *International Review of Information Ethics* 4: 47–52.

Weckert, John. 2001. "Lilliputian Computer Ethics." In T. W. Bynum, et al., eds. *Proceedings of the Fifth International Conference on the Social and Ethical Impacts of Information and Communication Technologies: ETHICOMP 2001*. Vol. 2. Gdansk, Poland: Wydawnictwo Mikom, 2001, pp. 42–51.

White, Michelle. 2002. "Regulating Research: The Problem of Theorizing Research in LambdaMOO." *Ethics and Information Technology* 4, no. 1: 55–70.

Wonderly, Monique. 2008. "A Humean Approach to Assessing the Moral Significance of Ultra-Violent Video Games." *Ethics and Information Technology* 10, no. 1: 1–10.

▶ FURTHER READINGS

Dietrich, Eric. 2011. "*Homo Sapiens*. 2.0: *Building the Better Robots of Our Nature*." In M. Anderson and S. L. Anderson, eds. *Machine Ethics*. Cambridge: Cambridge University Press, pp. 531–38.

Eden, Annon H., James H. Moor, Johnny H. Søraker, and Eric Steinhart, eds. 2012. *Singularity Hypothesis: A Scientific and Philosophical Assessment*. Berlin, Germany: Springer.

Flanagan, Mary and Helen Nissenbaum. 2014. *Values at Play in Digital Games*. Cambridge, MA: MIT Press.

Floridi, Luciano. 2011. "On the Morality of Artificial Agents." In M. Anderson and S. L. Anderson, eds. *Machine Ethics*. Cambridge: Cambridge University Press, pp. 184–212.

Frankish, Keith and William M. Ramsey, eds. 2014. *The Cambridge Handbook of Artificial Intelligence*. Cambridge University Press.

Gerdes, Anne. 2015. "The Issue of Moral Consideration in Robot Ethics." *Computers and Society* 45, no. 3: 274–8.

Luck, Morgan. 2009. "Crashing a Virtual Funeral: Morality in MMORPGs." *Journal of Information, Communication and Ethics in Society* 7, no. 4: 280–5.

Mathews, Steve. 2008. "Identity and Information Technology." In. J. van den Hoven and J. Weckert, eds. *Information Technology and Moral Philosophy*. Cambridge: Cambridge University Press, pp. 142–60.

Powers, Thomas M. 2003. "Real Wrongs in Virtual Communities." *Ethics and Information Technology* 5, no. 4: 191–8.

Turkle, Sherry. 2011. *Alone Together: Why We Expect More from Technology and Less from Each Other*. New York: Basic Books.

Wellman, Barry. 2005. "Community: From Neighborhood to Network." *Communications of the ACM* 48, no. 10: 53–6.

CHAPTER

12

Ethical Aspects of Emerging and Converging Technologies

LEARNING OBJECTIVES

Upon completing this chapter, you will successfully be able to:

- Explain what is meant by concept of *technological convergence* and describe how converging technologies raise ethical concerns that can be difficult to anticipate,
- Describe the key components of *ambient intelligence* (*AmI*) and explain why AmI poses some significant social and ethical challenges, especially for personal privacy,
- Describe the key components of *nanotechnology* and explain the social and ethical challenges posed by this relatively recent technology,
- Assess some of the social and ethical impacts that *autonomous machines (AMs)* will likely have in the very near future,
- Understand the key differences between (the relatively new field of) *machine ethics* and (traditional) computer ethics and why that distinction is important,
- Articulate the components of a relatively new "dynamic" ethical framework designed to assess ethical issues that arise in emerging and converging technologies.

In this chapter, the final chapter of *Ethics and Technology*, we examine some ethical and social issues that arise in connection with converging and emerging technologies. We begin by reflecting on a hypothetical scenario that briefly illustrates some ways in which intelligent devices and "smart things" communicate not only with humans but with other devices and things. This phenomenon—as it pertains to one aspect of the emerging and converging technologies examined in this chapter—is now commonly referred to as the *Internet of Things*.

▶ SCENARIO 12–1: When "Things" Communicate with One Another

While driving home from work one day, Bill receives a message on his mobile device from the "intelligent refrigerator" in his home, informing him that his supply of milk is very low. This message, in turn, triggers an app (called "Foodster") on Bill's device, which notifies users when grocery items of interest are on sale at selected stores located close to their homes. Foodster informs Bill that milk is on sale at the Sunny Spot convenience store. Next, another app on Bill's device, which communicates with his car's "intelligent driving system," instructs the (auto-enabled) GPS in Bill's car to slightly adjust the route that Bill typically drives home, so he that he will pass by Sunny Spot. When Bill arrives at the store, he notices that gourmet coffee also happens to be on sale that day; so, he queries his intelligent refrigerator about the amount of coffee currently stored there. The refrigerator then checks Bill's coffee inventory and recommends that he purchase one pound of gourmet coffee while he is shopping at Sunny Spot. But before getting back to Bill with an answer to his original query, the refrigerator first communicates with the kitchen's "intelligent cabinets" to see whether Bill might also need filters for his coffee maker. Bill then receives a message on his mobile device recommending that he purchase three items before leaving Sunny Spot: milk, coffee, and coffee filters. Finally, as Bill approaches the store's checkout line, he clicks on the "shopping rewards" app on his mobile device, which informs him that his CDC Visa card is offering a 5% cash-back option on groceries that he purchases this month; the app then recommends that Bill use his CDC credit card to purchase the items at Sunny Spot. ■

Is this scenario a bit farfetched? Or is it something that would seem realistic in the not-too-distant future? Humans have been interacting with "intelligent agents" and with "smart devices" for several years now. But the idea of intelligent/smart devices and objects communicating with one another, that is, independent of human interaction or human oversight, is a relatively recent phenomenon.

In our discussion of ambient intelligence (AmI) in Section 12.2, we briefly examine some developments involving "smart homes/environments," which many now predict will be commonplace in the near future. There, we will also consider whether these kinds of homes and environments, which may indeed prove to be remarkably convenient in assisting us in carrying out many of our day-to-day tasks, will either improve the overall quality of our lives or have negative consequences for our well-being. The purpose of Scenario 12–1, however, has been simply to get us to begin thinking about what it might be like for many of us in our daily lives, as more and more "intelligent things" inevitably communicate with one another, presumably for the purpose of making our lives easier.

Later in this chapter, we identify and evaluate some social/ethical concerns that arise in connection with nanotechnology and nanocomputing. We also examine some ethical issues affecting "autonomous machines" (AMs) in the context of a relatively new subfield of cyberethics called "machine ethics." In the final section, we describe an ethical framework specifically designed to guide research and inform policies affecting new and emerging/converging technologies. We begin, however, with a brief analysis of the concept of *technological convergence*.

▶ 12.1 CONVERGING TECHNOLOGIES AND TECHNOLOGICAL CONVERGENCE

What, exactly, do we mean by "convergence" in the context of cybertechnology? Howard Rheingold describes technological convergence as a phenomenon that occurs when "apparently unrelated scientific and technological paths" cross or intersect "unexpectedly to create an entirely new field."[1] As we move forward in the twenty-first century, cyber- and non-cybertechnologies are converging at a pace that is unprecedented. However, we saw in Chapter 1 that technological convergence as it pertains to cybertechnology is hardly new. For example, we saw that early computer networks became possible because of the convergence of computing and communication technologies in the late 1960s and early 1970s. Consider that many of the ethical issues we examined in the preceding chapters of this textbook arose because of convergent aspects of computing/information and communication technologies.

Arguably, convergence *within* the domain of cybertechnology itself—that is, the unforeseen blending or merging of disparate, and initially distinct, computing and information technologies (IT)—has been continuous and ongoing. One example of this can be found in virtual reality (VR) technology, which, as Rheingold notes, resulted from the convergence of video technology and computer hardware in the 1980s. (Recall our discussion of technological and ethical aspects of VR in Chapter 11.) However, cyber and cyber-related technologies are now converging with non-cybertechnologies in ways that challenge our ability to identify and articulate many of the social and ethical issues that also arise either because of or in connection with this kind of convergence.

One ethical/social concern that cuts across the converging technologies examined in this chapter has to do with the new kinds of privacy threats that are now possible. Because Chapter 5 was devoted to privacy concerns pertaining to cybertechnology, you might assume that the appropriate place to discuss these privacy issues would have been in that chapter. There, however, we examined privacy concerns that tend to fit mainly within the category of "informational privacy." For example, those privacy issues typically involve concerns that result from the collection of personal data by commercial and governmental organizations and the mining and analysis of personal information stored in electronic databases. Although some privacy concerns affecting the converging technologies that we examine in this chapter also fall within the category of informational privacy, many do not. The reason for this is not simply because these privacy issues are associated with newer technologies, but because they introduce different kinds of privacy concerns than those examined in Chapter 5.

We will also see that some privacy issues generated by developments in AmI technology and nanotechnologyhave introduced a relatively new category of privacy concern called "location privacy." For example, these converging/emerging technologies can be used to disclose the precise spatial location of an individual at a particular point in time. Because many of the privacy concerns identified and analyzed in this chapter are sufficiently different from those examined in Chapter 5, they warrant a separate context for analysis. However, as you examine the privacy-related issues included in this chapter, you may find it helpful to refer back to relevant sections of Chapter 5. We begin our examination of social and ethical aspects of converging technologies in the twenty-first century with a look at some controversies associated with AmI.

▶ 12.2 AMBIENT INTELLIGENCE (AmI) AND UBIQUITOUS COMPUTING

AmI is often described as a technology that enables people to live and work in environments that respond to them in "intelligent ways."[2] AmI has been made possible, in large part, by the convergence of artificial intelligence (AI) technologies (described in Chapter 11) with (miniaturized) electronic sensing and surveillance technologies. We will examine some technological aspects of AmI in Section 12.2.1; before doing that, however, we may find it useful to recall some concerns briefly described in Scenario 12–1 where "intelligent things" communicated with one another as well as with "Bill's" mobile device. Along somewhat similar lines, Raisinghani et al. (2004) describe a hypothetical case—one that we could call "A Day in the Life of a Smart Home"—where a mother and her child arrive home. As the car pulls into the driveway, the mother is immediately recognized by a surveillance camera that

> disables the alarm, unlocks the front door as she approaches it and turns on the lights to a level of brightness that the home control system has learned she likes.[3]

It turns out that the home control system in this "smart home" has also learned a great deal more about the preferences of its residents. For example, it "knows" when to adjust the room thermostats and how to optimize the use of appliances in order to avoid the risk of power surges occurring at peak hours of electric used in the neighborhood, and so forth.

Is the kind of (smart) home described by Raisinghani et al. based on science fiction? Or does it portray a real-world situation in the not-too-distant future? Consider that a 5,040-square-foot "aware home" was developed at the Georgia Institute of Technology nearly two decades ago; it continues to serve as a laboratory for AmI research and development. Research in AmI has also been conducted at other academic institutions, such as the MIT, as well as at companies in the private sector, such as Philips Electronics. AmI's optimists predict that intelligent homes will be available to consumers within the next few years. Whereas proponents of AmI are enthusiastic about many of the conveniences made possible by this technology, we will see why critics worry about AmI's "dark side."

We should note that some analysts use the expression "ubiquitous computing," or *ubicomp*, to describe what we refer to in this chapter as AmI. However, ubicomp can easily be confused with "ubiquitous communication," a technological component of AmI. So we use the expression AmI in this chapter to avoid any confusion between the two terms. To better understand AmI technology, we briefly describe three of its key elements or components—pervasive computing, ubiquitous communication, and intelligent user interfaces (IUIs)—before examining some ethical and social aspects of AmI.

12.2.1 Pervasive Computing, Ubiquitous Communication, and Intelligent User Interfaces

According to the Centre for Pervasive Computing (www.pervasive.dk), *pervasive computing* can be viewed as a computing environment where information and communication technology are "everywhere, for everyone, at all times." In this scheme, computing technology is integrated into our environments—from "toys, milk cartons, and desktops to cars, factories, and whole city areas." Pervasive computing is made possible, in part, because of the increasing ease with which circuits can be printed or embedded into objects, including wearable and even disposable items. Pervasive computing goes beyond the traditional scheme of user interfaces—on the one hand, it "implodes them into small devices and appliances"; on the other hand, it "explodes them onto large scale walls, buildings and furniture" (Centre for Pervasive Computing).

Pervasive computing, like AmI, is also sometimes referred to in the computer science literature as *ubiquitous computing* (or *ubicomp*). The expression "ubiquitous computing" was coined by Mark Weiser, who envisioned "omnipresent computers" that serve people in their everyday lives, both at home and at work.[4] He also envisioned ubiquitous computing as something that would function "invisibly and unobtrusively" in the background and that would free people to a considerable degree from tedious routine tasks. For ubiquitous or pervasive computing to operate at its full potential, however, continuous and ubiquitous communication between devices is also needed.

Ubiquitous communication aims at ensuring flexible and omnipresent communication possibilities between interlinked computer devices that can be stationed at various locations. Several different kinds of wireless technologies that make ubiquitous communication possible are now available or are in progress. According to Raisinghani et al. (2004), these include:

- Wireless local area networks (WLANs)
- Wireless personal area networks (WPANs)
- Wireless body area networks (WBANs) interlinking various wearable devices and connecting them to outside networks
- Radio-frequency identification (RFID)

Perhaps the most controversial of these technologies so far—at least from the perspective of personal privacy—is RFID. Koehler and Som (2005) suggest that RFID transponders in the form of "smart labels" will probably become the most widespread example of ubiquitous computing/communication. Recall our discussion of RFID technology in Chapter 5, where we examined some implications of RFID for personal privacy. We will see that RFID technology, when used in AmI environments, can facilitate the tracking of an individual's location at any given point in time and thus make possible a form of "pervasive surveillance."

In addition to pervasive computing and ubiquitous communication technologies, AmI has another key component: *IUIs*. This technology has been made possible by developments in the field of AI. In Chapter 11, we examined AI from the perspective of concerns about our "sense of self" and about what it means to be a human being in the digital era. There, we also noted that AI, in addition to raising some interesting conceptual and theoretical questions, has many practical applications as well. AI-based applications are also at the core of the "intelligent" user interfaces needed to realize the full potential of AmI.

Brey (2005) notes that IUIs, which are also sometimes called "user adaptive interfaces" because of the way they can adapt to a user's preferences, go beyond traditional interfaces such as a keyboard, mouse, and monitor. As a result, they improve human interaction with technology by making it more intuitive and more efficient than was previously possible with traditional interfaces. With IUIs, for example, computers and electronic devices can "know" and sense far more about a person than was possible with traditional interfaces, including information about that person's situation, context, or environment. Because IUIs respond to inputs such as human gestures as well as to an individual's preferences within various contexts, they enable inhabitants of AmI environments to interact with their environment in a personalized way. Unlike traditional user interfaces, however, IUIs in AmI environments also enable *profiling*, which Brey describes as "the ability to personalize and automatically adapt to a particular user's behavior patterns."

While AmI technology is able to sense changes in an environment and while this technology can automatically adapt and act based on these changes—for example, in response to a user's needs and preferences—AmI remains in the background and is virtually invisible to the user. As Brey notes, people are "surrounded with possibly hundreds of intelligent networked computers that are aware of their presence, personality, and needs." But users themselves may not be aware of the existence of this technology in their environments.

Thus far, we have briefly described three of the key technological components that make AmI possible. We next examine some of the ethical and social challenges posed by AmI environments.

12.2.2 Ethical and Social Aspects of AmI

Social and ethical concerns affecting AmI include worries about the loss of freedom and autonomy. These are sometimes closely related to concerns about humans becoming overly dependent on technology. Other social/ethical concerns involving AmI include threats associated with privacy and surveillance. We begin with a look at some issues affecting freedom and autonomy.

Autonomy, Freedom, and Control

Will human autonomy and freedom be enhanced or diminished as a result of AmI technology? AmI's supporters suggest that humans will gain more control over the environments with which they interact because technology will be more responsive to their needs. However, Brey notes a paradoxical aspect of this claim, pointing out that "greater control" is presumed to be gained through a "delegation of control to machines." But this, he suggests, is tantamount to the notion of "gaining control by giving it away." Brey considers some ways in which control can be gained in one sense and lost in another. With respect to humans gaining control as a result of this technology, he notes that three different kinds of arguments can be made, where AmI may make the human environment more controllable because it can:

1. Become more responsive to the voluntary actions, intentions, and needs of users
2. Supply humans with detailed and personal information about their environment
3. Do what people want without their having to engage in any cognitive or physical effort

On the other hand, Brey considers some ways that AmI can diminish the amount of control that humans have over their environments. These also are organized into three arguments, where users may lose control because a smart object can:

1. Make incorrect inferences about the user, the user's actions, or the situation
2. Require corrective actions on the part of the user
3. Represent the needs and interests of parties other than the user[5]

So, as Brey notes, AmI has the potential to enhance human freedom through its ability to expand certain aspects of our control over the environment—for example, in responding to our voluntary actions, intentions, and needs and by freeing us from many routine and tedious tasks that require either cognitive or physical effort. But he also notes that AmI has the potential to limit freedom because it can make incorrect inferences about a user's intentions and needs. Even when AmI does what a user wants, it can still reduce control by requiring "corrective actions" on the part of the user. Brey also notes that users can lose control when smart objects perform autonomous actions that do not solely represent the user's interests. For example, the smart object could include a user profile or knowledge base that is also designed to take into account the interests of third parties (such as commercial interests). Additionally, Brey believes that AmI could undermine human freedom and autonomy if humans become too dependent on machines for their judgments and decisions.

Technological Dependency

We have come to depend a great deal on technology, especially on digital technology, in conducting many activities in our day-to-day lives. In the future, will humans depend on the kind of smart objects and smart environments made possible by AmI technology in ways that exceed our current dependency on computing and electronic devices? We noted earlier that IUIs could relieve us of having to worry about performing many of our routine day-to-day tasks, which can be considered tedious and boring. But we also noted that these interfaces could relieve us of much of the cognitive effort that has, in the past, enabled us to be fulfilled and to flourish as humans. What would happen to us if we were to lose this capacity because of an increased dependency on technology? Perhaps a brief look at a scenario envisioned by E. M. Forster in one of his classic works would be instructive at this point.

▶ **SCENARIO 12–2:** E. M. Forster's "(Pre)Cautionary Tale"

In his short story *The Machine Stops*, first published in 1909, E. M. Forster portrays a futuristic society that, initially at least, might seem like an ideal or utopian world. In fact, Forster's story anticipated many yet-to-be-developed technologies such as television and videoconferencing. But it also illustrates how humans have transferred control of much of their lives to a global Machine, which is capable of satisfying their physical and spiritual needs and desires. In surrendering so much control to the Machine, however, people begin to lose touch with the natural world. After a while, defects appear in the Machine, and eventually it breaks down. Unfortunately, no one remembers how to repair it. In Forster's tale, some of the characters begin to realize just how dependent they have become on this machine.[6] ■

We could easily imagine Forster's scenario playing out in AmI environments of the future where individuals no longer are required to perform routine cognitive acts and instead depend on IUIs to make decisions for them. Also, we could ask what would happen if the energy sources that powered the AmI environments were suddenly lost. Could we respond successfully if this happened to us? If not, it would seem that we have let ourselves become too dependent on this technology. Hypothetical questions of this kind are worth keeping in mind as we proceed with developments in AmI.

Privacy, Surveillance, and "the Panopticon"

Some of AmI's critics worry that a kind of "Big Brother" society may emerge. For example, Bohn et al. (2005) note that in AmI environments, all of our moves, actions, and decisions will be recorded by "tireless electronic devices, from the kitchen and living room of our homes to our weekend trips in cars." As Langheinrich (2001) points out, no aspect of our life will be secluded from "digitization," because virtually anything we say, do, or even feel could be "digitized, stored, and retrieved anytime later." But how are the privacy concerns associated with AmI different, in relevant ways, from privacy issues generated by earlier uses of computer/information technology? Langheinrich believes that with respect to privacy and surveillance, four features differentiate AmI from other kinds of computing/IT applications:

- Ubiquity
- Invisibility
- Sensing
- Memory application

First, Langheinrich believes that because computing devices are *ubiquitous* or omnipresent in AmI environments, privacy threats involving AmI are more pervasive in scope and can affect us more deeply. Second, because computers are virtually *invisible* in AmI environments (in the sense that they easily "disappear" from view), it is likely that users will not always realize that computing/electronic devices are present and are being used to collect and disseminate personal data. Third, *sensing* devices associated with the IUIs in AmI environments may become so sophisticated that, unlike conventional forms of cybertechnology, they will be able to sense (private and intimate) human emotions such as fear, stress, and excitement. Fourth, AmI has the potential to create a *memory* or "life-log"—that is, a complete record of someone's past. So, Langheinrich concludes that AmI poses a more significant threat to privacy than earlier computing/information technologies.

In AmI environments, the sheer scale or amount of information that can be collected without our awareness is also problematic. Bohn et al. note that AmI has the potential to create a comprehensive surveillance network, because it can disclose an "unprecedented share of our public and private life." We saw that AmI environments are equipped with sensors that facilitate the collection of data about an individual from his or her surroundings without that individual's active intervention. This kind of ubiquitous observation, which some now call "pervasive surveillance," can expose much about an individual's habits and preferences.

Čas (2005) notes that no one can be sure that his or her actions are not being observed; nor can one be sure that his or her words are not being recorded. Furthermore, individuals cannot be sure whether information about their presence at any location is being recorded. So, he believes that the only realistic attitude of human beings living in such environments is to assume that any activity or inactivity is being monitored, analyzed, transferred, and stored and that this information may be used in any context in the future. In this sense, people in AmI environments would be subject to a virtual "panopticon."

▶ **SCENARIO 12–3:** Jeremy Bentham's "Panopticon/Inspection House" (Thought Experiment)

Jeremy Bentham, an eighteenth-century philosopher and social reformer, conceived of the idea for managing a prison environment based on the notion of the *panopticon*. Imagine a prison comprised of glass cells, all arranged in a circle, where prisoners could be observed at any moment by a prison guard who sits at a rotating desk facing the prisoner's cells. Further imagine that the inmates cannot see anyone or anything outside their cells, even though they can be observed (through the one-way-vision glass cells) by the prison guard at any time. Although a prisoner cannot be certain that he is being observed at any given moment, it would be prudent for him to assume that he is being observed at every moment. The prisoner's realization that he could be observed continuously, and his fear about what could happen to him if he is observed doing something that is not permitted in the cell, would likely be sufficient to control the prisoner's behavior.[7] ■

TABLE 12-1 Ambient Intelligence

Technological Components	Ethical and Social Issues Generated
Pervasive computing	Freedom and autonomy
Ubiquitous communication	Privacy and surveillance
Intelligent user interfaces	Technological dependence

Suppose Bentham's model of the panopticon or "inspection house" were to be extended to public spaces including public buildings. Further suppose that it is extended to include private and intimate environments as well. What effects could the possibility of being permanently observed have on individual behavior and social control? In Bentham's classical panopticon, one could not be certain whether he or she was actually being monitored at a given point in time. Persons living in AmI environments, however, can, with almost 100% certainty, know that they are being observed. Classical forms of surveillance, from Bentham's time to the period preceding AmI technology, were limited to time and place. But data captured in AmI environments will, as Čas notes, persist across space and time.

So far, we have examined a cluster of social and ethical concerns affecting AmI environments. Table 12-1 lists the technological components of AmI and the corresponding ethical and social issues associated with them.

We have seen that some of these ethical and social issues arise because of the pervasive aspects of AmI technology, while others reflect concerns pertaining to convergent features of its component technologies. In the next section, we examine some ethical concerns that result from converging aspects of computing and nano technologies—that is, controversies at the intersection of cybertechnology and nanotechnology. Chadwick and Marturano (2006) argue that nanotechnology provides the "key" to technological convergence in the twenty-first century.

▶ 12.3 NANOTECHNOLOGY AND NANOCOMPUTING

What, exactly, is nanotechnology? Why is research at the nanolevel controversial from an ethical perspective? Should we continue to engage in research and development in nanocomputing? We examine each of these questions, beginning with an overview of nanotechnology as a scientific field.

12.3.1 Nanotechnology: A Brief Overview

Berne (2015) describes *nanotechnology* as "the study, design, and manipulation of natural phenomena, artificial phenomena, and technological phenomena at the nanometer level." We should note, however, that, at this time, there is no universally agreed-upon definition of the field. One common or unifying feature of nanotechnology, regardless of how narrowly or broadly it is defined, is that it operates on matter on a scale of *nanometers* (nm).

Moor and Weckert (2004) note that a nanometer, which is one billionth of a meter, is very close to the dimensions of individual atoms whose diameters range from 0.1 to 0.5 nm. K. Eric Drexler, who coined the term "nanotechnology" in the 1980s, conceived of the field as a branch of engineering dedicated to the development of electronic circuits and mechanical devices built at the molecular level of matter (Drexler 1986). Although such nanolevel devices do not yet exist, current microelectromechanical systems (MEMS), tiny devices such as sensors embedded in conductor chips used in airbag systems to detect collisions, are one step away from the molecular machines envisioned by Drexler.

The Development of Nanotechnology as a Field of Scientific Research

The origin of nanotechnology as a distinct field is generally traced to a 1959 talk by physicist and Nobel laureate Richard Feynman, who encouraged scientists to develop tools that could manipulate matter at the atomic level. In 1990, Donald Eigler and Erhard Schweizer, two scientists working at the IBM Almaden laboratory, succeeded in manipulating 35 individual xenon atoms to shape the three initials of their employer's logo. Since then, more practical kinds of applications have been carried out at the nanolevel. Drexler has proposed the idea of a nanoscale *assembler*—that is, a molecular machine that could be programmed to build virtually any molecular structure or device from simpler chemical building blocks. He believes that the development of universally applicable assemblers, which could be programmed to replicate themselves, is essential for the full realization of nanotechnology's potential.

Although some critics argue that nanotechnology has generated more hype than substance, a few important breakthroughs have already begun to occur at the nanolevel. For example, Regis (2009) describes some of the implications of the nanotube radio that was invented by Alex Zettl and his colleagues in 2007. Regis notes that a "single carbon nanotube tunes in a broadcast signal, amplifies it, converts it to an audio signal and then sends it to an external speaker in a form that the human ear can readily hear." He also notes that this could be the "basis for a new range of applications: hearing aids, cell phones, and iPods small enough to fit completely within the ear canal."[8]

Nanocomputers and Nanocomputing

In the 1980s, Drexler predicted that developments in nanotechnology would result in computers at the nanoscale—that is, *nanocomputers*. Merkle (1997) believes that future nanocomputers will have mass storage devices capable of storing more than 100 billion bytes in a volume the size of a sugar cube and that these devices will be able to "deliver a billion billion instructions per second." Drexler (1991) suggests that nanocomputers will be designed using various types of architectures. For example, an electronic nanocomputer would operate in a manner similar to present-day computers, differing primarily in terms of size and scale. A quantum nanocomputer, on the contrary, would work by storing data in the form of atomic quantum states or spin. Weckert (2006) notes that quantum computers would be much more powerful than any computing systems available today.

Some predict that future nanocomputers will also be built from biological material such as DNA. For example, Seeman (2004) believes that DNA is an ideal molecule for building nanometer-scale structures because strands of DNA can be "programmed to self assemble into complex arrangements" that bond together. And Drexler, who believes that biology shows us how molecular machinery can construct complex organisms from the bottom up, suggests that biological computers are already a reality.

Whether biological and quantum computers will be functionally available at the nanolevel is still a matter of conjecture and debate. However, more conventional notions of computing at the nanoscale are currently under development, and some standard computing chips have already been constructed at the nanoscale. At Hewlett Packard, for example, researchers have made computer memory devices by creating eight platinum wires 40nm wide on a silicon wafer. Moor and Weckert note that it would take more than 1,000 of these chips to be the width of a human hair.

Before identifying and analyzing the ethical aspects of nanocomputing and nanotechnology, a principal objective of Section 12.2, we should point out that nanotechnology's optimists and pessimists have been quick to offer their predictions about the societal advantages and disadvantages that could result from continued nanotechnology development. For example, Gordijn (2003) notes that optimists point to some of the advantages for the medical field (with nanobots assisting in surgery), while pessimists describe some "apocalyptic nightmares" that could result (including nanolevel weapons and destruction). Weckert (2006) believes that because many predictions about nanotechnology seem reasonable, it would be prudent for us to consider some of the ethical implications now while there is still time to anticipate them.

12.3.2 Ethical Issues in Nanotechnology and Nanocomputing

Moor and Weckert (2004) believe that assessing ethical issues that arise at the nanoscale is important because of the kinds of "policy vacuums" (Moor 2001) that can arise. (Recall our discussion of Moor's notion of policy vacuums in Chapter 1.) Although Moor and Weckert do not explicitly argue that a separate field of applied ethics called *nanoethics* is necessary, they make a convincing case for why an analysis of ethical issues at the nanolevel is now critical. In particular, they identify three distinct kinds of ethical concerns that warrant analysis:

1. Privacy and control
2. Longevity
3. Runaway nanobots

With respect to (1), the authors note that as we construct nanoscale information gathering systems, it will become extremely easy to put a nanoscale transmitter in a room or onto someone's clothing in such a way that he or she will have no idea that the device is present or that he or she is being monitored and tracked. Implanting tracking mechanisms within someone's body would also become easier with nanotech devices. Moor and Weckert note that a tracking mechanism might be put into someone's food so that, when swallowed, it would be absorbed into the body, possibly migrating to a desired location. The authors further note that in addition to privacy threats made possible by nanotechnology, individuals may also lose some degree of control. Because other people could know more about each other, for example, we might be less capable of controlling the outcomes of our choices. How these tracking devices will be developed and used is still a matter of some speculation. But Moor and Weckert argue that with the advent of nanotechnology, invasions of privacy and unjustified control over others will most likely increase.

Regarding (2), ethical concerns involving longevity, Moor and Weckert argue that developments in nanotechnology could have a dramatic effect on human life spans. While many see longevity as a good thing, there could be negative consequences as well. For one thing, Moor and Weckert note that there could be a population problem if the life expectancy of individuals were to change dramatically. The authors also point out that if fewer children are born relative to adults, there could be a concern about the lack of new ideas and "new blood." Additionally, questions could arise with regard to how many "family sets" couples, whose lives could be extended significantly, would be allowed to have during their expanded lifetime. Other questions might be conceptually confusing—for example, would the (already) old stay older longer, and would the young remain young longer? So, in Moor and Weckert's analysis, longevity-related questions introduce some policy vacuums, as well as conceptual muddles, that will need to be resolved.

With regard to (3), Moor and Weckert argue that we need to consider the potential problem of "runaway nanobots." (The problem of runaway replication in the context of nanotechnology is often referred to as the "grey-goo scenario.") Moor and Weckert note that the replication of these bots could get out of hand. The authors also note that when nanobots work to our benefit, they build what we desire. But when they work incorrectly, they build what we don't want.

Some critics, including Smalley (2001), have challenged the possibility of replicators, because of the way these assemblers would have to be constructed. Drexler, however, responds to Smalley's challenges by noting that biological assemblers such as ribosomes already do the kind of assembly at the molecular level needed for nanobots. Woodhouse (2004) notes that important choices about how to proceed with nanotechnology will have to be made before it is determined whose prediction—Drexler's or Smalley's—is correct. So, as long as it may be possible to construct nanolevel robots that are capable of self-assembly and replication, it would be prudent to try to anticipate the ethical outcomes that could arise.

Should Nano Research/Development Continue?

While we have examined some ethical concerns associated with potential developments at the nanolevel, we have not yet directly addressed the implications that these developments can have for computer scientists and computing/IT professionals working on nanolevel projects. In Chapter 4, we examined some ethical challenges that computing/IT professionals face. However, we did not discuss any nanocomputing-specific issues there. Next, we identify some of those challenges.

We begin by noting that Joseph Weizenbaum (1976) argued that there are certain kinds of computer science research that should not be undertaken—specifically research that can easily be seen to have "irreversible and not entirely unforeseeable side effects." Weizenbaum did not refer to nanotechnology research per se; however, Joy (2000), who has since echoed some of Weizenbaum's concerns about technological research, worries that because developments in nanocomputing threaten to make us an "endangered species," the only realistic alternative is to limit the development of that technology. Others, however, such as Merkle (2001) disagree with Joy. Merkle argues that if research in nanocomputing and nanotechnology is prohibited, or even restricted, it will be done underground. If that happens, Merkle worries that nanotechnology research would not be regulated by governments and professional agencies concerned with social responsibility.

If Joy and others are correct about the dangers of nanotechnology, we must seriously consider whether research in this area should be limited and whether computer scientists should participate in developments in nanocomputing. However, major computing associations such as the ACM and IEEE have not taken a stance on questions involving the ethics of nanocomputing research and development. Should research in this area be sanctioned by professional computing associations? If not, should nanocomputing research continue? What kind of criteria should be used in establishing a coherent nanotechnology policy?

Initially, we might assume that because nanotechnology could be abused—for example, used to invade privacy, produce weapons, etc.—nanocomputers should not be developed, or at least their development should not be sanctioned by professional computing/IT associations. However, we would commit a logical fallacy (see the Slippery Slope Fallacy in Chapter 3) if we used the following kind of reasoning: Because some technology, X, could be abused or because using Technology X could result in unintended tragedies, X should not be allowed to be developed. Consider some examples of why this form of reasoning is fallacious. Automobiles and medical drugs can both be abused, and each can contribute to the number of unintended deaths in a given year, even when used appropriately. In the United States, more than 40,000 deaths result each year from automobile accidents. And medical drugs (designed to save lives) have also been abused by some individuals, which has resulted in many deaths each year. Should the development of automobiles have been banned? Should we stop research on medical drugs? It would be fallacious to conclude that we should ban the development of these products merely because they could be abused and because they will inevitably lead to unintended deaths.

Arguments for how best to proceed in scientific research when there are concerns about harm to the public good, especially harms affecting the environmental and health areas, are often framed and evaluated via a scheme known as the "precautionary principle." We next examine that principle in the context of nanotechnology.

Assessing Nanotechnology Risks: Applying the Precautionary Principle?

Clarke (2005) notes that many formulations of the *precautionary principle* have been used in the scientific community; so there is no (single) universally agreed-upon formulation of this important principle. According to Weckert and Moor (2004), however, the essence of the precautionary principle can be captured and expressed in the following way:

> If some action has a possibility of causing harm, [it] should not be undertaken or some measure should be put in its place to minimize or eliminate the potential harms.[9]

Weckert and Moor believe that when the precautionary principle is applied to questions about nanotechnology research and development, it needs to be analyzed in terms of three different categories of harm: "direct harm," "harm by misuse," and "harm by mistake or accident." With respect to direct harm, they analyze a scenario in which the use of nanoparticles in products could be damaging to the health of some people. Weckert and Moor note that the kinds of risks in this scenario are very different from those used in the example they select to illustrate harm by misuse—namely, that developments in nanoelectronics could endanger personal privacy. Here, it is neither the new technology nor the product itself that could cause the problem, but rather the way that the new technology/product is used. Weckert and Moor also note that in this scenario, preventing certain uses of the technology would avoid the problem, without stopping the development of nanotechnology itself.

Regarding the third category, harm by mistake or accident, Weckert and Moor describe a scenario in which nanotechnology could lead to the development of self-replicating, and thus "runaway," nanobots. The authors note that harm will occur in this scenario *only if* mistakes are made or accidents occur. But this kind of potential harm is very different from the kind that results from the development of products that will damage health or from technologies that can be deliberately misused. Whereas legislation can be enacted to stop inappropriate uses of a technology or to prevent the development of products known in advance to be harmful to one's health, it is more difficult to draft legislation that will control mistakes and accidents.

Weckert and Moor conclude that when assessing the risks of nanotechnology via the precautionary principle, we need to look at not only potential harms and benefits of nanotechnology per se but also at the "relationship between the initial action and the potential harm." In their scenario involving direct harm, for example, nanoparticles damaging health, the relationship is fairly clear and straightforward: We simply need to know more about the scientific evidence for nanoparticles causing harm. But in their scenario involving potential misuse of nanotechnology, for example, in endangering personal privacy, the relationship is less clear. Here, we need scientific evidence that certain kinds of devices can be developed, and we need evidence about whether effective legislation could be implemented to control the uses of the devices. In their third scenario, we need evidence regarding the propensity of humans to make mistakes or the propensity of accidents to happen.

So, given the risks and potential harms that could result from future developments in nanotechnology, how should research in that field proceed? Weckert (2006) believes that, all things being equal, *potential* disadvantages that can result from research in a particular field are not in themselves sufficient grounds for halting research altogether. Rather, he suggests that there should be a "presumption in favor of freedom in research" until it can be clearly shown that the research is, in fact, dangerous. However, once a reasonable (or what he calls a "*prima facie*") case can be made to show that the research is dangerous, the burden for showing that the research is safe (and that it should continue) would shift from those who oppose the research to those who support it. In Weckert's view, then, it would be permissible to restrict or even forbid research in a field where it can be clearly shown that significant harm is more likely than not to result from that research.[10]

Using Weckert's model, it would seem that since there are no compelling grounds (at present) for halting nanotechnology and nanocomputing research, we should proceed with it. Of course, we would need to reassess our default presumption in favor of nanotechnology/nanocomputing research, if evidence in the future were to suggest that such research posed a serious threat to our safety. We elaborate on this important point in Section 12.6, where we examine a "dynamic" model of ethics that takes into account the need to update factual data as it becomes available, as part of the ongoing process of ethical evaluation. Next, however, we consider some ethical aspects of a different kind of emerging technology: autonomous machines (AMs).

▶ 12.4 AUTONOMOUS MACHINES

Thus far, we examined ethical aspects of two relatively recent technologies that have emerged as a result of converging technological components: AmI and nanocomputing. In this section, we consider an emerging technology that has been made possible, in large part, by recent developments in AI and robotics—namely, *AMs*. We begin our analysis by defining some key terms, as well as drawing some important conceptual distinctions, regarding the various technologies and systems associated with AMs.

12.4.1 What is an AM?

For our purposes, an *AM* is any computerized system/agent/robot that is capable of acting and making decisions independently of human oversight. An AM can also (i) interact with and adapt to (changes in) its environment and (ii) learn (as it functions).[11] We use the expression "autonomous machine" in a broad sense to include three conceptually distinct, but sometimes overlapping, autonomous technologies: artificial agents (AAs), autonomous systems, and robots. The key attribute that links or brings together these otherwise distinct (software) programs, systems, and entities is their ability to act *autonomously*, or at least act independently of human intervention.

Autonomous Machines vs. Autonomous Robots/Agents/Systems

Why use "AMs" rather than "robots," "autonomous artificial agents," or "autonomous systems" to describe the autonomous technologies described in this section? For our purposes, there are two reasons why the phrase "autonomous machine" is more appropriate than "robot." First, not all robots are autonomous, and thus capable of acting independently of humans. Sullins (2011) distinguishes between "tele robots," which are controlled remotely by humans (and function mainly as tools), and "autonomous robots" which can make "major decisions about their actions using their own program." Second, the term "robot" can be ambiguous, because "soft" bots (such as AI programs) are also sometimes included under the general category of robot. To avoid this ambiguity, Wallach and Allen use the expression "(ro)bot." However, our notion of "autonomous machine" is sufficiently robust to capture both the breadth of Wallach and Allen's "(ro)bot" and the precision needed to exclude Sullin's category of (non-autonomous) telerobots.

The expression "autonomous machine" also has an advantage over the phrase "autonomous artificial agent." For one thing, "machine" can be a less philosophically controversial category than "agent" or "artificial agent" (AA); for another, "machine" is a sufficiently broad category to subsume under it certain kinds of entities, systems, etc. that may not fall neatly into the categories of agent and AA. Also, distinctions between a single AA and multiple AAs, such as "multi-agent systems," can be problematic from the philosophical perspective of agency. However, our category of "autonomous machines" can be understood to subsume both individual AAs and collections of AAs, including multiagent systems.

Third, and finally, "autonomous machine" also has an important advantage over "autonomous system." One problem with the latter expression is that it is ambiguous and can easily be used equivocally to refer to two very different kinds of technologies. On the one hand, an autonomous system (AS), in the context of the Internet, refers to a collection of Internet protocol (IP) routers or "routing prefixes" that are "under the control of one or more network operators"—in this case, an AS can be either a network or set of networks that is "controlled by a common network administrator."[12] On the other hand, "autonomous system" is also used to describe a computerized system that, like an AM, can operate without human intervention, adapt to its environment, learn (as it functions), and make decisions.[13] So, we use the expression "autonomous machine" to avoid the potential equivocation that can easily arise in discussions involving ASs, given the two common uses of "autonomous system." For our purposes, the phrase "autonomous machines" both (i) captures the second sense of "autonomous system, " as described in the Royal Academy of Engineering's 2009 report, and (ii) eliminates any ambiguity or equivocation that can arise because of the first sense of AS (i.e., in connection with Internet router policies).

Understanding What Is Meant by "Machine"

Of course, it is possible that some might object to our use of "machine" because that concept usually connotes something physical, as in the case of computer hardware. In this sense, "machine" might be interpreted in a way that would exclude software (programs and applications). So a more precise, and perhaps also more expanded, definition of what is meant by a *machine* is needed in the case of our category of AMs. Even though we tend to think of machines primarily as physical devices consisting of fixed and movable parts, a machine can also be understood as a "natural system or organism." It can also refer to a group of individuals that are under the control of a leader, such as in the case of a "political machine."[14] So, "machine" can be used in both a physical and a non-physical sense. While robots clearly fit within the former sense of "machine," the term's latter sense can include AI (soft)bots, AAs, and ASs that are non-physical. Thus, an AM, as we use the phrase, includes both senses of "machine."

Hall (2011) argues that the most important "machine" of the twentieth century was not a physical entity at all; rather, it was a "Turing Machine," which he describes as a "theoretical concept of a pattern of operations that could be implemented in a number of ways." Hall also notes that a Turing machine can be viewed as a "mathematical idea" that provided the "theoretical basis for a computer." It can also be viewed as a kind of "virtual machine"; in this scheme, any program running on a computer is also a virtual machine. But Hall believes that we can eliminate the "virtual" in these kinds of machines and refer to computer programs themselves simply as "machines." He argues that the essence of a machine is "its behavior"—that is, "what it does given what it senses."[15] In this sense, AMs can also be viewed as machines (and not merely as virtual machines).

Finally, we should note that because AMs have been made possible by developments in AI, "intelligence" is an essential feature or property of AMs. In fact, this feature can also help us to distinguish AMs from what we might think of as ordinary or conventional machines, including some physical devices that are fairly sophisticated. However, it is also important to note that not every "intelligent machine" is necessarily autonomous. We examine some key criteria that (intelligent) machines must satisfy to act "autonomously" in our analysis of the concept of autonomy in Section 12.5.2. First, however, we identify some typical examples of AMs.

Some Examples and Applications of AMs

A highly influential report (on autonomous systems) by the UK's Royal Academy of Engineering (2009) identifies various kinds of devices, entities, and systems that also fit nicely under our category of AM. These include:

- Driverless transport systems (in commerce)
- Unmanned vehicles in military/defense applications (e.g., "drones")
- Robots on the battlefield
- Autonomous robotic surgery devices
- Personal care support systems

Another example identified in that report is a "smart environment," such as a "smart" building/home/apartment. (Recall the example of a hypothetical "smart home" that we briefly described in Section 12.2 in our discussion of AmI; that technology also qualifies as a kind of AM.) Other examples of AMs include driverless trains that shuttle passengers between terminals in large airports, as well as robotic companions/caregivers that assist the elderly and robotic babysitters (which are popular in Japan) that entertain young children.

A diverse cluster of AMs now function in multiple sectors of our society. Consider, for example, the many different kinds of robots and robotic systems that have become available in recent years. Lin (2012) identifies a range of sectors in which robots (and, in our case, AMs) now operate; these include:

1. Labor and service
2. Military and security
3. Research and education
4. Entertainment
5. Medical and healthcare
6. Personal care and companionship[16]

Lin points out that an example of an AM used for (1) would be the Roomba vacuum cleaner, and he notes that nearly half of the 7-million-plus service robots in the world are Roombas. We should point out that while Roombas may appear to act autonomously because of their sensing abilities, they are still also under human control. However, the Roomba, which is probably better viewed as a kind of semi-AM, can still be viewed as a major advancement over earlier industrial robots that operated in automobile factories and assembly lines.

Examples of AMs used in (2) would include the U.S. military's Predator and BigDog, whereas an instance of an AM used in (3) is NASA's Mars Exploration Rover. Lin identifies ASIMO (Advanced Step in Innovative Mobility), a humanoid robot designed by Honda, as an example of an AM that can be used in (4), and he describes some robotic nurses (including RIBA) and robotic pharmacists (such as ERNIE) as examples of AMs used in (5). Lin notes that AMs used in (6) would include CareBot and PALRO, and he also notes that this category of robots might be extended to include some recently introduced "sex bots" such as Roxxxy.

Despite the many conveniences and services that AMs provide, these machines raise some ethical concerns (as we have already noted). One such concern involves threats to personal privacy. Consider that some kinds of AMs allow for detailed recording of personal information; for example, people who live in "smart apartments" could have vast amounts of personal information about them recorded and kept by a third party. The privacy concerns that arise here are very similar to the kinds of AmI-centered privacy issues we examined in Section 12.2.2. Because AM-related privacy concerns overlap with those involving AmI, we will not examine any AM-specific privacy issues in the following section. Instead, we will focus on three very different kinds of ethical/philosophical concerns affecting AMs: (moral) agency, autonomy, and trust.

12.4.2 Some Ethical and Philosophical Questions Pertaining to AMs

Some ethical issues associated with AMs also cut across traditional cyberethics categories such as property, privacy, security, and so forth. For example, we have already noted that privacy concerns can arise in connection with specific kinds of AMs (such as "smart homes"). Another cluster of ethical concerns involve moral and professional responsibility issues associated with designing AMs. We briefly examine some of those concerns in Section 12.5.2. However, some questions that arise in connection with AMs are not only ethical in nature but are also more broadly philosophical (e.g., metaphysical or epistemological). These include questions about agency (and moral agency), in connection with concerns about whether AMs can be held responsible and blameworthy in some sense, as well as questions about autonomy and trust.[17] We begin by asking in which sense(s) an AM can be viewed as an agent, or artificial agent, before considering the more controversial question of whether an AM can qualify as a moral agent.

AMs, Agents, and Moral Agents?

As already noted, the concepts of "agency" and "agent" can be philosophically controversial. For our purposes, however, we can stipulate a definition of *agent* as someone or something that is capable of acting. So, each of us, insofar as we can act, qualifies as an agent; other entities—both humans and non-humans—who act on our behalf also qualify as agents (and are sometimes referred to as "fiduciary agents"). We refer to all non-human agents as AAs. In our scheme, even a thermostat can satisfy the conditions for being an AA. Today, AI researchers typically refer to artificial entities—whether software programs (in the form of "bots") or full-fledged robots—as AAs.

Because AMs are capable of acting, they also qualify as AAs. But unlike low-level AAs such as thermostats, AMs can act in ways that have a moral impact. So it might seem reasonable to ask whether we can hold AMs morally accountable for their actions. Initially, this might seem like a bizarre question. However, one concern raised in the Royal Academy's influential report on autonomous systems (2009) is whether systems like AMs should be regarded as "robotic people," as opposed to mere machines. This question is important because if AMs qualify as "people" of some sort, they could also be subject to (moral) blame for faults that occur, as well as for legal liability in cases involving either the deaths of humans or severe economic losses. Although it might seem odd to talk about AMs as "people," robotic or otherwise, we have seen that they do qualify as agents—namely, AAs. But can AMs also satisfy the additional conditions that are required for being *moral agents*?

Floridi (2011) believes that AMs, or what he calls autonomous AAs, can be moral agents because they are (i) "sources of moral action" and (ii) can cause moral harm or moral good. In Chapter 11, we saw that Floridi distinguished between "moral patients" (as receivers of moral action) and moral agents (as sources of moral action). There, we also noted that information entities, in Floridi's view, deserved consideration (minimally) as moral patients, even if they were not moral agents. But, additionally, Floridi believes that autonomous AAs also qualify as moral agents because of their (moral) efficacy. Johnson (2006) also believes that AAs have moral efficacy, but she argues that they qualify only as "moral entities" and not moral agents because AAs lack freedom. And others, including Himma (2009), argue that because these entities also lack consciousness and intentionality, they cannot satisfy the conditions for moral agency.

Moor (2006) takes a different tack in analyzing this controversial question by focusing on various kinds of "moral impacts" that AAs can have. Moor begins by noting that computers can be viewed as normative (non-moral) agents, independent of whether they are also moral agents, because of the normative impacts their actions have. He points out that computers are designed for specific purposes and thus can be evaluated in terms of how good or how bad they perform in accomplishing the tasks they are programmed to carry out (e.g., as in the case of a program designed to play chess). Moor then notes that some normative impacts made possible by computers can also be moral or ethical in nature, and he argues that the consequences, and potential consequences, of what he calls "ethical agents" can be analyzed in terms of four levels:

- Ethical impact agents
- Implicit ethical agents
- Explicit ethical agents
- Full ethical agents

Moor notes that whereas ethical impact agents (i.e., the weakest sense of moral agent) will have ethical consequences to their acts, implicit ethical agents have some ethical considerations built into their design and "will employ some automatic ethical actions for fixed situations." And while explicit ethical agents will have, or at least act as if they have, "more general principles or rules of ethical conduct that are adjusted and interpreted to fit various kinds of situations," full ethical agents "can make ethical judgments about a wide variety of situations" and in many cases can "provide some justification for them."

Providing some examples of each, Moor notes that a "robotic camel jockey" (a technology used in Qatar to replace young boys as jockeys, thus freeing those boys from slavery in the human trafficking business) is an instance of an ethical impact agent. An airplane's automatic pilot system and an automatic teller machine (ATM) are both examples of an implicit ethical agent, since they have built-in programming designed to prevent harm from happening to the aircraft in one case and (in the other case) to prevent ATM customers from being shortchanged in financial transactions. Explicit ethical agents, on the other hand, would be able to calculate the best ethical action to take in a specific situation and would be able to make decisions when presented with ethical dilemmas. In Moor's scheme, full ethical agents have the kind of ethical features that we usually attribute to ethical agents like us (i.e., what Moor describes as "normal human adults"), including consciousness and free will.

Moor does not claim that either explicit or full ethical agents exist or that they will be available anytime in the near term. However, his distinctions are very helpful, as we try to understand various levels of moral agency that potentially affect AMs. Even if AMs may never qualify as full moral agents, Wallach and Allen (2009) believe that they can have "functional morality," based on two key criteria or dimensions: (i) autonomy and (ii) sensitivity to ethical values. However, Wallach and Allen also note that we do not yet have systems with both high autonomy and high sensitivity. They point out that an autopilot is an example of a system that has significant autonomy (in a limited domain) but little sensitivity to ethical values. On the contrary, the authors note that while ethical decision support systems (such as those used in the medical field to assist doctors) provide decision makers with access to morally relevant information and thus suggest high sensitivity to moral values, they have virtually no autonomy.

Wallach and Allen also argue that it is not necessary that AAs be moral agents in the sense that humans are. They believe that all we need to do is to design machines to act "as if" they are moral agents and thus "function" as such. We return to this point, as well as to the concept of functional morality, in Section 12.5.1. First, however, we ask if it makes sense to ascribe any level of morality, functional or otherwise, to AMs if those systems are not capable of being genuinely autonomous. While Wallach and Allen note that autonomy is one of the two key criteria in their framework of functional morality, they do not elaborate on the sense(s) in which an AA can be said to be autonomous. We next examine the concept of autonomy to see whether an AM can indeed be autonomous.

Autonomy and "Functional Autonomy" in the Context of AMs

We briefly mentioned the concept of autonomy in Section 12.2.2 in our analysis of ethical concerns affecting AmI. There, we asked whether humans would, in effect, surrender some of their individual autonomy if they delegate (control of) certain kinds of tasks to computer systems. Some critics suggest that they might, especially if those computer systems are "autonomous." For example, Son (2015) notes that autonomous technologies can undermine "human autonomy" in ways that are both "subtle and indirect." Allen, Wallach, and Smit (2006), on the contrary, suggest that we need not worry about perceived threats to human autonomy because AMs will not necessarily "undermine our basic humanity." To evaluate these claims, however, we need a clear definition of *autonomy*.

Many philosophers associate autonomy with concepts such as liberty, dignity, and individuality.[18] Others, however, link autonomy to "independence." For example, O'Neill (2002) defines autonomy as a "capacity or trait that individuals manifest by acting independently." While it is difficult to ascribe characteristics such as liberty and dignity to AMs, we have seen that these machines do appear to be capable of "acting independently." So, if we can show that AMs can indeed act independently, it would seem plausible to describe AMs as entities that are also autonomous in some sense.

We should note that some influential definitions of autonomous systems and autonomous AAs link an artificial entity's ability to "adapt" to its environment with an ability to act "independently." For example, the Royal Academy's 2009 report seems to suggest that because autonomous systems are "adaptive," they also exhibit some degree of "independence." And Floridi (2008) makes a similar point, noting that an "adaptive" AA—one that can change its (internal) state dynamically, that is, without any external stimuli—has a certain degree of "*independence* from its environment."[19] Perhaps, then, AMs can satisfy O'Neill's requirement for autonomy by virtue of their capacity to act independently.

Insofar as AMs appear to be capable of acting independently, or behave "as if" they are acting independently, it would seem that we could attribute at least some degree of autonomy to them. Whether AMs will ever be capable of having full autonomy, in the sense that humans can, is debatable, and that question will not be examined here since it is beyond the scope of this chapter. However, an AM that can act independently in the sense described earlier can have "functional autonomy" and thus can qualify as a "functionally autonomous AM." We will next see that AMs must have some level of autonomy, even if only in a functional sense, if they are capable of being trusted by—that is, being in a trust relationship with—humans.

Trust and Authenticity in the Context of AMs

What does a relationship of trust involving humans and AMs entail? Lim, Stocker, and Larkin (2008) describe the possibility of a mutual or reciprocal trust relationship involving both (a) "Man to Machine" and (b) "Machine to Man." However, we limit our discussion to (a), and we ask two basic questions: (i) What would it mean for a human to *trust* an AM? (ii) Why is that question important? The significance of (ii) is highlighted in the Royal Academy of Engineering's report (2009), which asks whether we can trust AMs to always act in our best interests, especially AMs designed in such a way that they cannot be shut down by human operators. To answer (i), however, we first need to clarify what is meant by the concept of trust in general—that is, the kind of trust that applies in relationships between humans.

McLeod (2015) points out that trust, in human relationships, is both "important but dangerous." It is important because it enables us "to form relationships with others and to depend on them." But it is also dangerous, McLeod notes, because it involves risk. Since trusting someone "requires that we can be vulnerable to others (i.e., vulnerable to betrayal)," the trustor (in the trust relationship) must be willing to accept some level of risk. In the case of AMs, we may be required to extend the level of risk beyond what we typically find acceptable for trust in human relationships. Before addressing that concern, however, it would be useful to establish what, exactly, is required for a normal trust relationship between humans.

A typical dictionary, such as the *American Heritage College Dictionary* (4th ed. 2002), defines trust as "firm reliance on the integrity, ability, or character of a person or thing." Definitions of trust that focus mainly on *reliance*, however, do not always help us to understand the nature of ethical trust. For example, I *rely* on my automobile engine to start today, but I do not "trust" it to do so. Conversely, I trust my daughter implicitly, but I cannot always rely on her to organize her important papers.[20] Thus, trust and reliance are not equivalent notions; while reliance may be a necessary condition for trust, something more is needed for ethical trust.

Because I am unable to have a trust relationship with a conventional machine such as an automobile, does it follow that I also cannot have one with an AM? Or does an AM's ability to exhibit some level of autonomy—even if only functional autonomy—make a difference? Consider that I am able to trust a human because the person in whom I place my trust not only can disappoint me (or let me down) but can also betray me—for example, that person, as a fully autonomous (human) agent, can freely elect to breach the trust I have placed in her. So it would seem that an entity's having at least some sense of autonomy is required for it to be capable of breaching the trust that someone has placed in it. In this sense, my automobile cannot breach my trust or betray me, even though I may be very disappointed if it fails to start today. Although my automobile does not have autonomy, we have seen that an AM has (functional) autonomy and thus might seem capable of satisfying the conditions required for a trust relationship. But even if an AM has (some level of) autonomy and even if having autonomy is a necessary condition for being in a trust relationship, it does not follow that it is a sufficient condition.[21] So, we can further ask whether any additional requirements may also need to be satisfied.

Some philosophers argue that trust has an emotive (or "affective") aspect and that this may be especially important in understanding trust in the context of AMs. For example, Coeckelbergh (2010) argues that if we want to build moral AMs (capable of trust), we will have to build them "*with emotions*."[22] Elsewhere, Coeckelbergh (2012) argues that for a trust relationship to be established between humans and machines, "appearance" (including the appearance of having emotions) is also very important. And because AMs may need to *appear* as if they have human-like properties, such as emotions, in order to be trusted by humans, we may be inclined to develop future AMs along these lines. Coeckelbergh and others seem to suggest that we should.[23]

Turkle (2011) raises some concerns involving emotions or feelings in the context of human–machine trust relationships, and she worries about what can happen when machines appear "as if" they have feelings. She describes a phenomenon called the "Eliza effect," which was initially associated with a response that some users had to an interactive software program called "Eliza" (designed by Joseph Weizenbaum at MIT in the 1960s). Turkle notes that this program, which was an early foray into machine learning programs designed to use language conversationally (and possibly pass the Turing test), solicited trust on the part of users. Eliza did this, Turkle points out, even though it was designed in a way that tricks users. Although Eliza was only a ("disembodied") software program, Turkle suggests that it could nevertheless be viewed as a "relational entity," or what she calls a "relational artifact," because of the way people responded to, and confided in, it. In this sense, Eliza seemed to have a strong emotional impact on some of the students who interacted with it. Turkle also notes that while Eliza "elicited trust" on the part of these students, it understood nothing about them.

Turkle worries that when a machine (as a relational artifact) appears to be interested in people, it can "push our Darwinian buttons . . . which causes people to respond *as if* they were in a relationship."[24] This is especially apparent in the case of physical AMs that are capable of facial expressions, such as Kismet (developed in MIT's AI Lab). Turkle suggests that because

AMs can be designed in ways that make people feel as if a machine cares about them (as in the case of Paro, a companion robot designed to comfort the elderly), people can develop feelings of trust in, and attachment to, that machine. For example, she notes that Cynthia Breazeal, one of Kismet's designers who had also developed a "maternal connection" with this AM while she was a student at MIT, had a difficult time separating from Kismet when she left that institution. In Turkle's view, this factor raises questions of both trust *and* authenticity, and Turkle worries that, unlike in the past, humans must now be able to distinguish between authentic and simulated relationships. While this connection between trust and authenticity/attachment opens up a new and provocative line of inquiry, and while it will be interesting to see how this connection eventually plays out in the context of trust and AMs, a further discussion of this topic would take us beyond the scope of this chapter.

In concluding this section, we note that many questions about trust vis-à-vis AMs have been left either unanswered or unexamined. Readers who are interested in learning more about this topic can consult the expanding literature on trust and e-trust in connection with artificial agents/entities.[25] Next, we ask how critical it is for humans to have a trust relationship with AMs as we pursue the goal of developing "moral machines." In other words, if we cannot trust AMs, should we build machines capable of making decisions that have significant moral impacts? And if not, do we need to reassess one of the core objectives of machine ethics?

▶ 12.5 MACHINE ETHICS AND *MORAL MACHINES*

The ethical issues examined in earlier chapters of this book arose mainly because of what we, as humans, do with computers and cybertechnology. In Section 12.4.2, however, we considered some AM-specific ethical concerns that arise because of what AMs are now capable of doing on their own. Increasingly, ethical concerns generated by the autonomous technologies/systems that comprise AMs are examined as issues in a relatively new subfield of cyberethics called *machine ethics* (Allen, Wendell, and Smit 2006; M. Anderson and S. Anderson 2011; and Moor 2006). Some, however, use the expression "robo-ethics" (Verrugio 2006; Decker and Gutmann 2012) or "robot ethics" (Capurro and Nagenborg 2009; Lin, Abney, and Bekey 2012) to describe the field that addresses these issues. Wallach and Allen (2009) note that other authors have also used expressions such as "agent ethics" and "bot ethics." However, we use "machine ethics" to include the wide range of ethical issues that arise in the context of AMs. And, as noted in Section 12.4, we use "autonomous machines" to refer to the cluster of autonomous technologies/systems that generate those ethical issues.

Analyzing the moral impacts of what AMs are capable of doing by themselves is one principal focus of machine ethics; we examined some of those impacts in Section 12.4.2. In this section, however, we briefly consider two very different kinds of questions affecting machine ethics: (i) What is the proper scope of this field, and what are its primary objectives? (ii) Is it possible to design "moral machines" (and if so, should we develop them)? We postpone our discussion of (ii) until Section 12.5.2 and begin with an analysis of (i).[26]

12.5.1 What is *Machine Ethics*?

Michael Anderson and Susan Leigh Anderson (2011) describe machine ethics as an interdisciplinary field of research that is primarily concerned with developing ethics for machines, as opposed to developing ethics for humans who "use machines." In their view, machine ethics is concerned with

> giving machines ethical principles, or a procedure for discovering ways to resolve ethical dilemmas they may encounter, enabling them to function in an ethically responsible manner through their own decision making.[27]

Susan Anderson (2011) points out that a central question in machine ethics is whether ethics is, or can be made, computable. She believes that it is and also suggests that it may be "prudent to begin to make ethics computable by first creating a program that acts as an ethical advisor to humans before attempting to build a full-fledged moral machine." We return to Anderson's suggestion at a later point in this section, in our discussion of how a prototype of a moral machine might initially function as an "ethical advisor" in a "dialogue" with humans.

Anderson draws some useful distinctions with regard to various levels at which machines could be designed to behave ethically. For our purposes, these can be organized into three levels, where a designer could:

a. Build "limitations" into a machine that would prevent it from causing moral harm

b. Embed an AM with instructions that would require it to behave in a particular way—that is, "according to an ideal ethical principle or principles that are *followed by the human designer*"

c. Embed an AM with "(an) ideal ethical principle(s) . . . and a learning procedure from which it can abstract (an) ideal ethical principle(s) in guiding its own actions"[28]

Whereas (a) represents the simplest design for ensuring that a machine behaves ethically, such a machine would seem capable of being only an "ethical impact agent" in James Moor's framework (described in Section 12.5.2). But a machine conforming to (b), on the other hand, would seem to qualify as an example of Moor's "implicit ethical agent." Anderson believes that machines built along the lines of (c) could conform to Moor's notion of "explicit ethical agent." She also believes that accomplishing (c) is the "ultimate goal" of machine ethics. In this case, an AM would be able not only to behave ethically but also be able to "justify its behavior" by expressing in "understandable language" the "intuitively acceptable ethical principle(s) that it has used to calculate its behavior."[29]

Wallach and Allen (2009) believe that one way in which the field of machine ethics has expanded upon traditional computer ethics is by asking *how* computers can be made into "explicit moral reasoners." In answering this question, Wallach and Allen first draw an important distinction between "reasoning about ethics" and "ethical decision making." For example, they acknowledge that even if one could build artificial systems capable of reasoning about ethics, it does not necessarily follow that these systems would be genuine "ethical decision makers." However, their main interest in how AMs can be made into moral reasoners is more practical than theoretical in nature, and they believe that the challenge of figuring out how to provide software/hardware agents with moral decision-making capabilities is urgent; in fact, they argue that the time to begin work on designing "moral machines" is now!

12.5.2 Designing *Moral Machines*

Can/should we build the kinds of moral machines that Wallach, Allen, and others urge us to develop? First, we can ask what is meant by the expression "*moral* machine." For example, are there "immoral machines"? Or are all machines simply amoral or non-moral, as many people tend to assume? The kind of moral machines that Wallach and Allen have in mind are AMs that are capable of both (i) making moral decisions and (ii) acting in ways that "humans generally consider to be ethically acceptable behavior." We should note that the idea of designing machines that could behave morally, that is, with a set of moral rules embedded in them, is not entirely new. In the 1940s, science fiction writer Isaac Asimov anticipated the need for ethical rules that would guide the robots of the future when he formulated his (now-classic) Three Laws of Robotics:

1. A robot may not injure a human being, or through inaction, allow a human being to come to harm.

2. A robot must obey orders given it by human beings except where such orders would conflict with the First Law.
3. A robot must protect its own existence as long as such protection does not conflict with the First or Second Law.[30]

Numerous critics have questioned whether the three laws articulated by Asimov are adequate to meet the kinds of ethical challenges that current AMs pose. But relatively few of these critics have proposed clear and practical guidelines for how to embed machines with ethical instructions that would be generally acceptable to most humans. S. Anderson and M. Anderson (2011) and Wallach and Allen have each put forth some very thoughtful proposals for how this can be done. First, we consider Wallach and Allen's framework.

In describing how we can begin to build moral machines, Wallach and Allen point out that they are not interested in questions about developing a machine that is merely "instrumentally good." For example, a machine may be considered instrumentally good if it performs its tasks well. (Recall James Moor's distinction about computers as normative (non-moral) agents vs. moral agents, which we examined in Section 12.4.2.) Wallach and Allen are concerned with building moral machines, or what they also refer to as artificial moral agents (AMAs), that behave in ways that humans generally consider to be *morally good*. They point out, for example, that while Deep Blue is a good chess-playing system because it does well at chess (i.e., defeating the best human chess players), it cannot be viewed as a "good AMA" because it is not required to make the kinds of decisions that have moral import.

Wallach and Allen argue that a *good AMA* "can detect the possibility of human harm or neglect of duty, and can take steps to avoid or minimize the undesirable outcomes." But how, exactly, would such an AMA be designed? For example, which kinds of ethical reasoning procedures should we build into these systems—that is, should they be embedded with principles that favor utilitarian-like reasoning or deontology-like reasoning, or perhaps some combination of the two? Also, could the principles of virtue ethics be built into the software code embedded in these machines, if that were deemed to be essential or even desirable?

Embedding Ethical Theory/Reasoning Procedures into AMs

To appreciate the challenges involved in selecting the appropriate kind of ethical theory/reasoning to embed in AMs, Wallach and Allen consider how a computerized "driverless trolley" might react in the now classic scenario involving a "runaway trolley" (described in Chapter 2), where the "driver" (i.e., the AM) has to make a split-second decision (or calculation). Should the AM throw a switch that will cause the trolley to change tracks and (intentionally) run over one person who is standing on that track? Or should the AM do nothing, in which case the trolley will run over five people directly in its path? An AM designed to execute instructions compatible with utilitarian- or consequentialist-based reasoning would likely make a very different (moral) decision, or calculation, than one designed to execute code based on deontological reasoning.

Susan Anderson (2011) notes that the ethical theory of act utilitarianism (which, she believes, shows that ethics is indeed computable) is too "simplistic." She argues that this ethical theory, as well as theories based on absolute duties (e.g., in Kant's categorical imperative, described in Chapter 2), are not, in themselves at least, adequate to build into machines. Instead, she believes that an ethical theory similar to Ross' version of deontology (also described in Chapter 2), which provides the basis for what she calls a "prima facie duty approach," is more desirable. A virtue of Ross' theory, you may recall, is that it shows why it is often necessary to deliberate and weigh between duties when two or more of them conflict. But Anderson notes that a significant problem with Ross' theory is that it does not provide a clear mechanism or procedure for determining which duty overrides another in many situations where conflicts arise. So, she supplements the prima facie duty approach with a "decision principle" to resolve the conflicts that will inevitably arise. Anderson further argues that the kinds of "decision principles" needed to accomplish this "can be discovered by a machine"—that is, a machine could use an "inductive logic program" to arrive at such a principle. For example, Anderson believes that the machine could "learn from generalizing correct answers in particular cases."

Earlier in this section, we briefly mentioned Anderson's suggestion that it would be prudent for us first to design an artificial system to function as an "ethical advisor" to humans before attempting to build a full-fledged moral machine. Along similar lines, Susan Anderson and Michael Anderson (2011) have recommended building artificial systems with which humans can have an "ethical dialogue" before we embed machines themselves with ethical reasoning algorithms that they could use in a fully independent manner. The Andersons have developed such a system—that is, an "automated dialogue"—involving an ethicist and an artificial system that functions "more or less independently in a *particular domain*." They believe that this is an important first step in building moral machines because it enables the artificial system to learn both (i) the "ethically relevant features of the dilemmas it will encounter" (within that domain) and (ii) the appropriate prima facie duties and decision principles it will need to resolve the dilemmas.[31]

Functional Morality and a "Moral Turing Test"

Earlier in this section, we asked whether AMs are capable, in principle, of being genuine moral agents. Recall our brief discussion of Wallach and Allen's notion of functional morality, which the authors contrast with mere "operational morality" as well as with full moral agency. Wallach and Allen argue that even if machines fail to achieve full-blown moral agency, they may exhibit varying degrees of functional morality. So, they leave open the question of whether AMs could ever be full moral agents. Perhaps a more basic question to consider, however, is whether we could ever conclusively determine that we had developed an AM that was a full moral agent. Allen, Varner, and Zinser (2000) consider how a "Turing-like" test, which they call a "moral Turing test" (MTT), could be applied in response to this question.

Unlike the original Turing test (described in Chapter 11), the MTT shifts the focus in the human–machine interaction away from an emphasis on mere "conversational ability" to criteria involving questions about "action." In this case, an AM would be asked questions about how it would act in such and such a situation, as opposed to being evaluated in terms of how successfully it was able to converse with humans about topics involving moral principles and rules. However, Allen et al. reported that they still encountered several problems with this test as a procedure for conclusively establishing whether AMs could, in principle, qualify as full moral agents.

We have seen that Wallach and Allen seem far less concerned with questions about whether AMs can be full moral agents than with questions about how we can design AMs to act in ways that conform to our received notions of morally acceptable behavior. And Susan Anderson (2011) echoes this point when she notes that her primary concern also is with whether machines "can perform morally correct actions and can justify them if asked." We should note that Wallach and Allen also believe that questions about whether AMs can be full moral agents can actually distract from (what they consider to be) the more "important question about how to design systems to act appropriately in morally charged situations."[32]

Acknowledging that many important questions in machine ethics remain unresolved, we conclude this section by briefly identifying some reasons why continued work in machine ethics is important. Moor (2006) offers three such reasons: (i) Ethics (itself) is important, (ii) future machines will likely have increased autonomy, and (iii) designing machines to behave ethically will help us better understand ethics. Moor's third point ties in nicely with Wallach and Allen's claim that developments in machine ethics could help us to better understand our own nature as moral reasoners. In fact, they believe that research and development in machine ethics can provide feedback for "humans' understanding of themselves as moral agents" and for our understanding of "the nature of ethical thinking itself."[33]

▶ 12.6 A "DYNAMIC" ETHICAL FRAMEWORK FOR GUIDING RESEARCH IN NEW AND EMERGING TECHNOLOGIES

We have considered a fairly wide range of ethical concerns affecting the new and emerging technologies examined in this chapter. Some of these ethical concerns directly impact the software engineers and computer professionals who design the technologies. But virtually everyone will be affected by these technologies in the near future; so all of us would benefit from clear policies and ethical guidelines that address research/development in new and emerging technologies. Moor (2008) argues that because these technologies promise "dramatic change," it is no longer satisfactory to do "ethics as usual." He goes on to claim that we need to be better informed in our "ethical thinking" and more proactive in our "ethical action."

What kind of ethical framework will we need to address the specific challenges posed by new and emerging technologies? One requirement would seem that this framework be "proactive" in its approach to ethics, as Moor suggests. Perhaps, then, we could look to the now classic *ELSI* (Ethical/Legal/Social Issues) model for some guidance on how to construct a proactive ethical framework for other emerging technologies as well. This model, which was initially developed for the Human Genome Project (HGP), was designed to anticipate the kinds of ethical, legal, and social implications that would likely arise in HGP research. Before work on HGP was allowed to proceed, the National Human Genome Research Institute (NHGRI) required that ethical, legal, and social issues first had to be identified and addressed. Many of the salient features of the original ELSI model for HGP—requirements that addressed concerns affecting privacy, confidentiality, fairness, etc.—were "built into" the scientific research methodology used for HGP.[34]

12.6.1 Is an ELSI-Like Model Adequate for New/Emerging Technologies?

Should the original ELSI model, or one similar to it, be used to guide the development of other new/emerging technologies as well? ELSI's proponents believe that it is an ideal model because it is, as we noted, "proactive." They point out that prior to the ELSI program, ethics was typically "reactive" in the sense that it "followed scientific developments" rather than informing scientific research. As Moor and others note, ethics has had to play "catch up" in most scientific research areas because ethical guidelines were developed in response to cases where serious harm had already resulted. For these reasons, Kurzweil (2005) believes that a proactive ethical framework is needed in nanotechnology research, and he has suggested that an ELSI-like model be developed to guide researchers working in that technological field. The Royal Academy of Engineering's influential report on autonomous systems (2009) has also suggested an ELSI-like framework be used to assess ethical, legal, and social issues that affect or will soon affect autonomous technologies now under development.

Although many see ELSI as a vast improvement over traditional frameworks, the standard ELSI model employs a scheme that Moor and Weckert (2004) describe as an "ethics-first" framework. They believe that ethical frameworks of this kind have problems because they depend, in large part, on a "factual determination" of the specific harms and benefits in implementing the technology before an ethical assessment can be done. But the authors note that in the case of nanotechnology developments, for example, it is very difficult to know what the future will be in 5 or 10 years, let alone 20 or more years. So if we adopt an ("ethics-first") ELSI-like model, it might seem appropriate to put a moratorium on research in an area of technology until we get all of the facts. However, Moor and Weckert point out that while a moratorium on future research would halt technology developments in a field, such as nanotechnology for example, it will not advance ethics in that technological area.

12.6.2 A "Dynamic Ethics" Model

Moor and Weckert also argue that turning back to what they call the "ethics-last model" is not desirable either. The authors note that once a technology is in place, much unnecessary harm may already have occurred. So, in Moor and Weckert's scheme, neither an ethics-first nor an ethics-last model is satisfactory for emerging technologies. In their view, ethics is something that needs to be done *continually* as a technology develops and as its "potential social consequences become better understood." The authors also point out that ethics is "dynamic" in the sense that the factual/descriptive component on which the normative analysis relies has to be continually updated.

As we debate whether to go forward with research and development in a particular new or emerging technology, we can see how neither an ethics-first nor an ethics-last model is adequate. We can also agree with Moor and Weckert that it is necessary to establish a set of ethical criteria that can be continually updated as new factual information about that technology becomes available. This point needs to be specified in any viable ethical framework, as well as in any effective set of policy guidelines, that we implement.

Recall the comprehensive cyberethics framework that we articulated at the end of Chapter 1, which included three steps: (i) *identify* a controversial issue (*or* practice *or* technological feature) involving cybertechnology, (ii) *analyze* the ethical issue(s) involved by clarifying relevant concepts, and (iii) *deliberate* on the ethical issue(s) in terms of one or more standard ethical theories (e.g., utilitarianism, deontology, etc.). Building on Moor and Weckert's insights regarding ethical challenges posed by new and emerging technologies, we add a fourth component or step to that framework:

(iv) Update the ethical analysis by continuing to:

a. Differentiate between the factual/descriptive and normative components of the new or emerging technology under consideration

b. Revise the policies affecting that technology as necessary, especially as the factual data or components change or as information about the potential social impacts becomes clearer

As information about plans for the design and development of a new technology becomes available, we can loop back to (i) and proceed carefully through each step in the expanded ethical framework. This four-step framework can also be applied as new information about existing technologies and their features becomes available.

▶ 12.7 CHAPTER SUMMARY

In this chapter, we examined a cluster of ethical and social challenges affecting emerging and converging technologies. In particular, we described and evaluated controversies involving two broad areas of technological convergence: AmI and nanocomputing. We saw that AmI environments, made possible by pervasive computing and ubiquitous communication, raised concerns for freedom and autonomy as well as for privacy and surveillance. We also saw some ways in which ongoing developments in nanotechnology will likely raise concerns regarding privacy, longevity, and "runaway nanobots." We then examined some ethical challenges posed by "autonomous machines," and we considered whether it might be possible to design "moral machines." Finally, we argued that a "dynamic" ethical framework, introduced by James Moor and John Weckert, could both (i) guide researchers who develop new technologies and (ii) inform those responsible for enacting laws and framing policies for the use of those technologies.

Because of space limitations, we were not able to examine some other important converging and emerging technologies. For example, we were unable to examine ethical aspects of bioinformatics and computational genomics, which arise at the intersection of cybertechnology and biotechnology.[35] Also, we were not able to consider some ethical/social implications affected by 3D printing, an emerging technology that has become very controversial because of what it portends in the near term.[36] Another controversial topic that we could not discuss in this chapter, because of space constraints, is "the singularity."[37] Interested readers can examine these topics, and others, by consulting the recent and growing literature on ethical aspects of emerging and converging technologies.

▶ REVIEW QUESTIONS

1. What is "technological convergence" in the context of cybertechnology?
2. Why do some converging technologies raise special ethical and social issues?
3. What is ambient intelligence (AmI)?
4. Describe key aspects of pervasive (or ubiquitous) computing. How is it different from conventional or traditional computing?
5. What is ubiquitous communication, and what kinds of controversies does it raise?
6. What is an intelligent user interface (IUI), and how are IUIs different from traditional user interfaces?
7. What implications do AmI environments have for concerns involving individual freedom and autonomy?
8. Describe some of the implications that AmI will likely have for worries about "technological dependency"?
9. What implications do AmI environments have for privacy, surveillance, and the "panopticon"?
10. What is nanotechnology?
11. What are nanocomputers?
12. What kinds of ethical challenges do ongoing developments in nanotechnology and nanocomputing pose with respect to privacy and longevity?
13. Describe the kind of threat to future nanotechnology development posed by the notion of "runaway nanobots."
14. What is an autonomous machine (or AM)? List three examples of an AM.
15. What is an artificial agent (or AA)?
16. What is meant by "functional autonomy" in the contexts of AMs and AAs?
17. Identify some challenges affecting the notion of "trust" in the context of AMs.
18. What is machine ethics, and how is it different from traditional computer/cyber ethics?
19. What do Wallach and Allen mean by "moral machine"?
20. Describe the key elements in Moor and Weckert's "dynamic ethics framework."

▶ DISCUSSION QUESTIONS

21. As we proceed with cybertechnology research and development in the twenty-first century, continued technological convergence would seem to be inevitable. Many of us have benefited significantly from the conveniences made possible by this phenomenon so far—for example, cell phones that take pictures, GPS technology in automobiles that guide motorists, etc. Yet, we have also noted some controversial implications that convergent technologies can have for individual freedom, autonomy, and privacy. Can you think of any other social and ethical concerns that could also arise because of converging technologies? Identify at least three additional concerns that you believe might also have some social and ethical implications.
22. Assess the arguments that we examined for and against continued research in nanotechnology. Given the potential advantages and disadvantages involved in research and development in this area, which side in this debate do you find to be more plausible? Do the criteria provided by John Weckert for determining when research in a particular scientific field should and should not be allowed offer us clear guidelines with respect to research and development in nanotechnology and nanocomputing? What kind of an ethical framework is needed to guide (nano-level) research and development in this field?
23. Identify and briefly describe the three nanoethics issues examined by James Moor and John Weckert.

Why do some critics, such as Bill Joy, question whether we should continue nanotechnology research? What is the precautionary principle, as applied to scientific research? Can it be successfully applied to concerns involving research in nanotechnology? What does John Weckert mean when he says that we should "presume in favor of freedom" in scientific research?

24. In their goal of designing "moral machines," Wendell Wallach and Colin Allen argue that we do not need to develop artificial moral agents that have full moral agency. We saw that they believe that machines need to have only functional morality to be able to accomplish their objective of building moral machines. What do Wallach and Allen mean by "functional morality" and how is it different from full moral agency? Do you agree with their claim that questions about whether AMs can be full moral agents actually distract from the larger goal of researchers in machine ethics who aim to build machines that are capable of "acting appropriately in morally charged situations?" Explain.

Scenarios for Analysis

1. Jack and Jill, two of your friends from high school, have been married for two years and have a one-year-old daughter, named Sally. Jill always had a pet cat in her house when she was growing up, and she believes that interacting with her pets was a very important part of her childhood experience. Jack, on the contrary, never had a pet in his home. Additionally, Jack has allergies that are exacerbated when he is around most cats. But despite this, Jill firmly believes that having a pet cat for Sally to experience is important, and she has tried repeatedly to convince Jack that they should acquire one. Then, one day, Jack discovers that a brand new series of "artificial cats" are available and that they resemble natural cats to the point where very few people are actually capable of distinguishing between the two. In other words, the artificial cats look, behave, sound, and feel like natural cats. So Jack proposes the idea of purchasing an artificial cat, and he tries to convince Jill that having this "cat" will be sufficient for Sally to experience what it is like to have a pet cat in the house during her childhood. Based on what we saw in Sherry Turkle's analysis of questions involving emotions and "authenticity" in the context of relations with artificial entities (in Section 12.4.2), how do you believe that Jill should respond to Jack's proposal to acquire an artificial cat?

2. Your Aunt Elda, who is 89 years old and lives on her own in a small apartment, is in declining health. She is at the point where she will soon need full-time professional assistance/care, but she is unable to afford the cost of live-in help. Unfortunately, Aunt Elda has no immediate family members or relatives who are able to provide her with the kind of around-the-clock care she will need or to help with the financial expenses for professional care/assistance. However, a friend tells you about a robotic companion, ElderBot—designed to assist and serve as a companion to the elderly—that would be able to provide the kind of assistance your aunt will soon require. Fortunately, you have the money to purchase this robotic companion/care giver for your aunt. But you have some reservations about whether you can entrust your Aunt's care to this robot. Faced with the dilemma of either being able to do nothing to assist your aunt or providing her with an ElderBot, what would you do? As you deliberate, consider some of the concerns we discussed regarding trust and autonomous machines (in Section 12.4.2).

▶ ENDNOTES

1. Rheingold (1991, p. 61).
2. See, for example, Aarts and Marzano (2003); Brey (2005); and Weber, Rabaey, and Aarts (2005).
3. This passage from the description of the smart home by Raisinghani et al. (2004) is cited (in a more extensive excerpt) in Brey (2005, p. 157).
4. See Weiser (1991) for his original description of this expression.
5. See Brey (2005) for a more thorough discussion of how AmI can both enhance and limit human control.
6. See Forster (2009).
7. For more detail, see Jeremy Bentham. "Panopticon." In M. Bozovic, ed. *The Panopticon Writings* (London: Verso, 1995), pp. 29–95.
8. Regis (2009, p. 40).
9. Weckert and Moor (2004, p. 12).

10. Weckert (2006, pp. 334–5).
11. These criteria are also included in the definition of "autonomous system" in the Royal Academy of Engineering's report (2009).
12. For more information about the various senses in which "autonomous system" has been used, see http://searchnetworking.techtarget.com/definition/autonomous-system.
13. As already noted, this definition of "autonomous system" is included in the Royal Academy of Engineering's report (2009).
14. See, for example, the descriptions of "machine" in http://www.thefreedictionary.com/machine.
15. Hall (2011, p. 29).
16. Lin (2012, pp. 5–6).
17. In composing Section 12.4.2, I have drawn from some concepts and distinctions introduced in three previously published works: Buechner and Tavani (2011), Tavani (2012), and Tavani and Buechner (2015).
18. See, for example, Dworkin (1988).
19. Floridi (2008, p. 14). [Italics Added]
20. See deVries (2011), who distinguishes between "trust in general" and "topical trust." The sense in which I trust my daughter in the above example would be an instance of deVries' notion of trust in general.
21. For an analysis of trust vis-à-vis AAs in terms of four distinct levels of trust, which correspond closely to Moor's four levels of agents (described in Section 12.4.1), see Tavani (2015).
22. Coeckelbergh (2010, p. 236).
23. For example, Whitbeck (2015, p. 421) notes that our "experience with social relationships" in online contexts "has led to reflections on the degree to which trust is dependent on embodiment." She also points out that people often find it difficult to "trust others whom they know only digitally."
24. Turkle (2011, p. 71)
25. See, for example, papers included in three special issues of journals dedicated to the topics of trust and e-trust: Taddeo (2010), Taddeo and Floridi (2011), and Tavani and Arnold (2011).
26. In composing Section 12.5, I have drawn from some concepts and distinctions introduced in Tavani (2011).
27. M. Anderson and S. L. Anderson (2011, p. 1).
28. S. L. Anderson (2011, p. 22). While Anderson describes only two categories, I have subdivided her first category into two distinct levels.
29. M. Anderson and S. L. Anderson (2011, p. 9).
30. The three laws were introduced by Asimov in his short story "Runaround" (1942) and are anthologized in Asimov's *I, Robot* (1950). Asimov later added a fourth law, or "Zeroth Law," which states: "A robot may not injure humanity, or, through inaction, allow humanity to come to harm."
31. S. L. Anderson and M. Anderson (2011, p. 243). [Italics Added]
32. Wallach and Allen (2009, p. 202).
33. *Ibid*, p. 11.
34. See the ELSI Research Program. National Human Genome Research Institute. Available at http://www.genome.gov/10001618.
35. See, for example, Tavani (2006) for an overview of some key ethical issues that arise at the intersection of these converging technologies. And for an examination of some legal issues in bioinformatics and computational genomics, see the essays in Contreras and Cuticchia (2013).
36. For excellent discussions of some ethical/social challenges posed by 3D printing, see Brey (2014) and Wallach (2015).
37. Savirmuthu (2015, p. 167) describes the *singularity* in connection with the "accelerating change on humanity in the future"—a vision of an "evolutionary breakthrough" from the convergence of supercomputing capabilities and AI. For some excellent discussions of the singularity, see Kurzweil (2014) and the essays included in Eden et al. (2012).

▶ REFERENCES

Aarts, Emile and Stefano Marzano, eds. 2003. *The New Everyday: Views on Ambient Intelligence*. Rotterdam, The Netherlands: 101 Publishers.

Allen, Colin, Garry Varner, and Jason Zinser. 2000. "Prolegomena to Any Future Moral Agent." *Experimental and Theoretical Artificial Intelligence* 12, no. 3: 251–61.

Allen, Colin, Wendell Wallach, and Iva Smit. 2006. "Why Machine Ethics?" *IEEE Intelligent Systems* 21, no. 4: 12–7. Reprinted in M. Anderson and S. L. Anderson, eds. *Machine Ethics*. Cambridge: Cambridge University Press, 2011, pp. 51–61.

Anderson, Michael and Susan Leigh Anderson. 2011. "General Introduction." In M. Anderson and S. L. Anderson, eds. *Machine Ethics*. Cambridge: Cambridge University Press, pp. 1–4.

Anderson, Susan Leigh. 2011. "Machine Metaethics." In M. Anderson and S. L. Anderson, eds. *Machine Ethics*. Cambridge: Cambridge University Press, pp. 21–7.

Anderson, Susan Leigh and Michael Anderson. 2011. "A Prima Facie Duty Approach to Machine Ethics." In M. Anderson and S. L. Anderson, eds. *Machine Ethics*. Cambridge: Cambridge University Press, pp. 476–94.

Asimov, Isaac. 1950. *I, Robot*. New York: Doubleday.

Berne, Rosalyn W. 2015. "Nanoethics." In J. Britt Holbrook and Carl Mitcham, eds. *Ethics, Science, Technology, and Engineering: A Global Resource*. Vol. 3, 2nd ed. Farmington Hills, MI: Macmillan Reference, pp. 202–7.

Bohn, Jurgen, Vlad Coroama, Marc Langheinrich, Freidman Mattern, and Michael Rohs. 2005. "Social, Economic, and Ethical Implications of Ambient Intelligence and Ubiquitous Intelligence." In W. Weber, J. Rabaey, and E. Aarts, eds. *Ambient Intelligence*. New York: Springer.

Brey, Philip. 2005. "Freedom and Privacy in Ambient Intelligence." *Ethics and Information Technology* 7, no. 4: 157–66.

Brey, Philip. 2014. "3D Printing: An Anticipatory Technology ethics Analysis." In *Well-Being, Flourishing, and ICTs: Proceedings of the Eleventh International Conference on Computer Ethics–Philosophical Enquiry*. Menomonie, WI: INSEIT, Article 54.

Buechner, Jeff and Herman T. Tavani. 2011. "Trust and Multi-Agent Systems: Applying the 'Diffuse, Default Model' of Trust to Experiments Involving Artificial Agents." *Ethics and Information Technology* 13, no. 1: 39–51.

Capurro, Rafael and Michael Nagenborg, eds. 2009. *Ethics and Robotics*. Heidelberg, Germany: AKA Press.

Čas, Johann. 2005. "Privacy in Pervasive Computing Environments—A Contradiction in Terms?" *IEEE Technology and Society Magazine* 21, no. 1: 24–33

Chadwick, Ruth and Antonio Marturano. 2006. "Computing, Genetics, and Policy: Theoretical and Practical Considerations." In H. T. Tavani, ed. *Ethics, Computing, and Genomics*. Sudbury, MA: Jones and Bartlett, pp. 75–83.

Clarke, Steve. 2005. "Future Technologies, Dystopic Futures and the Precautionary Principle." *Ethics and Information Technology* 7, no. 3: 121–6.

Coeckelbergh, Mark. 2010. "Moral Appearances: Emotions, Robots, and Human Morality." *Ethics and Information Technology* 12, no. 3: 235–41.

Coeckelbergh, Mark. 2012. "Can We Trust Robots?" *Ethics and Information Technology* 14, no. 1: 53–60.

Contreras, Jorge L. and A. James Cuticchia, eds. 2013. *Bioinformatics Law: Legal Issues for Computational Biology in the Post-Genome Era* Chicago, IL: ABA (American Bar Association) Publishers.

Decker, Michael, and Mathias Gutmann, eds. 2012. *Robo- and Information-Ethics: Some Fundamentals*. Berlin, Germany: Verlag LIT.

deVries, Willem. 2011. "Some Forms of Trust." *Information* 2, no. 1: 1–16.

Drexler, K. Eric. 1986. *Engines of Creation: The Coming Era of Nanotechnology*. Garden City, NY: Anchor/Doubleday.

Drexler, K. Eric. 1991. *Unbounding the Future: The Nanotechnology Revolution*. New York: Quill.

Dworkin, Gerald. 1988. *The Theory and Practice of Autonomy*. New York: Cambridge University Press.

Eden, Annon H., James H. Moor, Johnny H. Søraker, and Eric Steinhart, eds. 2012. *Singularity Hypothesis: A Scientific and Philosophical Assessment*. Berlin, Germany: Springer.

Floridi, Luciano. 2008. "Foundations of Information Ethics." In K. E. Himma and H. T. Tavani, eds. *The Handbook of Information and Computer Ethics*. Hoboken, NJ: John Wiley and Sons, pp. 3–23.

Floridi, Luciano. 2011. "On the Morality of Artificial Agents." In M. Anderson and S. L. Anderson, eds. *Machine Ethics*. Cambridge: Cambridge University Press, pp. 184–212.

Forster, E. M. 2009. "The Machine Stops." In D. G. Johnson and J. W. Wetmore, eds. *Technology and Society: Building Our Sociotechnical Future*. Cambridge, MA: MIT Press, pp. 13–36. Reprinted from *The Eternal Moment and Other Short Stories*. New York: Harcourt Brace, 1970.

Gordijn, Bert. 2003. "Nanoethics: From Utopian Dreams and Apocalyptic Nightmares Towards a More Balanced View." In *Proceedings of the World Commission of the Ethics of Scientific Knowledge and Technology (COMEST)*. Available at http://portal.unesco.org/shs/fr/files/6603/10960368721Nanoethics.pdf/Nanoethics.pdf.

Hall, John Storrs. 2011. "Ethics for Machines." In M. Anderson and S. L. Anderson, eds. *Machine Ethics*. Cambridge: Cambridge University Press, pp. 28–46.

Himma, Kenneth E. 2009. "Artificial Agency, Consciousness, and the Criteria for Moral Agency: What Properties Must an Artificial Agent Have to be a Moral Agent?" *Ethics and Information Technology* 11, no. 1: 19–29.

Johnson, Deborah G. 2006. "Computer Systems: Moral Entities but Not Moral Agents." *Ethics and Information Technology* 8, no. 4: 195–204.

Joy, Bill. 2000. "Why the Future Doesn't Need Us." *Wired* 8, no. 4. Availability at http://www.wired.com/wired/archive/8.04/joy.html.

Koehler, Andreas and Claudia Som. 2005. "Effects of Pervasive Computing on Sustainable Development." *IEEE Technology and Society Magazine 21, no*. 1 (Spring): 15–23.

Kurzweil, Ray. 2005. "Nanoscience, Nanotechnology, and Ethics: Promise and Peril." In C. Mitcham, ed. *Encyclopedia of Science, Technology, and Ethics*. Vol. 1. New York: Macmillan, 2005, pp. xli–xlvi.

Kurzweil, Ray. 2014. "The Singularity is Near." In R. L. Sandler, ed. *Ethics and Emerging Technologies*. New York: Palgrave Macmillan/St. Martin's, pp. 393–406.

Langheinrich, Marc. 2001. "Privacy by Design—Principles of Privacy-Aware Ubiquitous Systems." In *Proceedings of the Third International Conference on Ubiquitous Computing*. Springer-Verlag, pp. 273–91.

Lim, Hock Chuan, Rob Stocker, and Henry Larkin. 2008. "Review of Trust and Machine Ethics Research: Towards a Bio-Inspired Computational Model of Ethical Trust (CMET)." In *Proceedings of the 3rd International Conference on Bio-Inspired Models of Network, Information, and Computing Systems*. Hyogo, Japan, November 25–27, Article No. 8.

Lin, Patrick. 2012. "Introduction to Robot Ethics." In P. Lin, K. Abney, and G. A. Bekey, eds. *Robot Ethics: The Ethical and Social Implications of Robotics*. Cambridge, MA: MIT Press, pp. 3–15.

Lin, Patrick, Keith Abney, and George A. Bekey, eds. 2012. *Robot Ethics: The Ethical and Social Implications of Robotics*. Cambridge, MA: MIT Press.

McLeod, Carolyn. 2015 "Trust." *Stanford encyclopedia of Philosophy*. Available at http://plato.stanford.edu/entries/trust/.

Merkle, Ralph. 1997. "It's a Small, Small, Small, Small World." *Technology Review* 25 (February/March): 25–32.

Merkle, Ralph. 2001. "Nanotechnology: What Will it Mean?" *IEEE Spectrum 38, no*. 1 (January): 19–21.

Moor, James H. 2001. "The Future of Computer Ethics: You Ain't Seen Nothin' Yet!" *Ethics and Information Technology* 3, no. 2: 89–91.

Moor, James H. 2006. "The Nature, Difficulty, and Importance of Machine Ethics." *IEEE Intelligent Systems* 21, no. 4: 18–21.

Moor, James H. 2008. "Why We Need Better Ethics for Emerging Technologies." In J. van den Hoven and J. Weckert, eds. *Information Technology and Moral Philosophy*. Cambridge, UK: Cambridge University Press, pp. 26–39.

Moor, James H. and John Weckert. 2004. "Nanoethics: Assessing the Nanoscale from an Ethical Point of View." In D. Baird, A. Nordmann, and J. Schummer, eds. *Discovering the Nanoscale*. Amsterdam, The Netherlands: IOS Press, pp. 301–10.

O'Neill, Onora. 2002. *Autonomy and Trust in Bioethics*. Cambridge, UK: Cambridge University Press.

Raisinghani, M., A. Benoit, J. Ding, M. Gomez, K. Gupta, V. Gusila, D. Power, and O. Schmedding. 2004. "Ambient Intelligence: Changing Forms of Human-Computer Interaction and Their Social Implications." *Journal of Digital Information 5, no*. 4 (Article No. 271): 8–24.

Regis, Ed. 2009. "Nanotechnology: The World's Smallest Radio." *Scientific American* 300, no. 3: 40–5.

Rheingold, Howard. 1991. *Virtual Reality*. New York: Touchstone Books.

Savirmuthu, Joseph. 2015. "Singularity." In J. Britt Holbrook and Carl Mitcham, eds. *Ethics, Science, Technology, and Engineering: A Global Resource*. Vol. 4, 2nd ed. Farmington Hills, MI: Macmillan Reference, pp. 167–70.

Seeman, Nadrian C. 2004. "Nanotechnology and the Double Helix." *Scientific American* 290, no. 6: 64–75.

Smalley, Richard E. 2001. "Of Chemistry, Love, and Nanobots." *Scientific American* 285, no. 3: 76–7.

Son, Wha-Chul. 2015. "Autonomous Technology." In J. Britt Holbrook and Carl Mitcham, eds. *Ethics, Science, Technology, and Engineering: A Global Resource*. Vol. 1, 2nd ed. Farmington Hills, MI: Macmillan Reference, pp. 164–8.

Sullins, John P. 2011. "When Is a Robot a Moral Agent?" In M. Anderson and S. L. Anderson, eds. *Machine Ethics*. Cambridge: Cambridge University Press, pp. 151–61.

Taddeo, Mariarosario, ed. 2010. *Trust in Technology: A Distinctive and Problematic Relationship.* Special Issue of *Knowledge, Technology and Policy* 23, nos. 3–4.

Taddeo, Mariarosario and Luciano Floridi, eds. 2011. *The Case for E-Trust: A New Ethical Challenge.* Special Issue of *Ethics and Information Technology* 13, no. 1.

Tavani, Herman T. 2006. "Ethics at the Intersection of Computing and Genomics." In H. T. Tavani, ed. *Ethics, Computing, and Genomics*. Sudbury, MA: Jones and Bartlett, pp. 5–26.

Tavani, Herman T. 2011. "Can We Develop Artificial Agents Capable of Making Good Moral Decisions?" *Minds and Machines* 21: 465–74.

Tavani, Herman T. 2012. "Ethical Aspects of Autonomous Systems." In M. Decker and M. Gutmann, eds. *Robo- and Information-Ethics: Some Fundamentals*. Berlin, Germany: Verlag LIT, pp. 89–122.

Tavani, Herman T. 2015. "Levels of Trust in the Context of Machine Ethics." *Philosophy and Technology* 28, no. 1: 75–90.

Tavani, Herman T. and Deiter Arnold, eds. 2011. Trust and Privacy in Our Networked World. Special Issue of the journal, *Information* 2, no. 1.

Tavani, Herman T. and Jeff Buechner. 2015. "Autonomy and Trust in the Context of Artificial Agents." In M. Decker, M. Gutmann, and J. Knifka, eds. *Evolutionary Robotics, Organic Computing and Adaptive Ambience*. Berlin, Germany: LIT Verlag, pp. 39–62 (in press).

The Royal Academy of Engineering Report. 2009. *Autonomous Systems: Social, Legal and Ethical Issues*, London. Available at www.raeng.org.uk/autonomoussystems.

Turkle, Sherry. 2011. "Authenticity in the Age of Digital Companions." In M. Anderson and S. L. Anderson, eds. *Machine Ethics*. Cambridge: Cambridge University Press, pp. 62–78. Reprinted from *International Studies*. John Benjamins Publishing Co., Amsterdam/Philadelphia, pp. 501–17.

Verrugio, Gianmarco, ed. 2006. "*EURON Roboethics Roadmap (Release 1.1)*." EURON Roboethics Atelier. Genoa, Italy. Available at http://www.roboethics.org/atelier2006/docs/ROBOETHICS%20ROADMAP%20Rel2.1.1.pdf.

Wallach, Wendell. 2015. *A Dangerous Master: How to Keep Technology from Slipping Beyond Our Control.* New York: Basic Books.

Wallach, Wendell and Colin Allen. 2009. *Moral Machines: Teaching Robots Right from Wrong*. New York: Oxford University Press.

Weber, Werner, Jan Rabaey, and Emile Aarts, eds. 2005. *Ambient Intelligence*. Berlin: Springer-Verlag.

Weckert, John. 2006. "The Control of Scientific Research: The Case of Nanotechnology." In H. T. Tavani, ed. *Ethics, Computing, and Genomics*. Sudbury, MA: Jones and Bartlett, pp. 323–39.

Weckert, John and James H. Moor. 2004. "Using the Precautionary Principle in Nanotechnology Policy Making." *Asia Pacific Nanotechnology Forum News Journal* 3, no. 4: 12–4.

Weizenbaum, Joseph. 1976. *Computer Power and Human Reason: From Judgment to Calculation*. New York: Penguin Books.

Weiser, Mark. 1991. "The Computer for the 21st Century." *Scientific American* 265, no. 3: 94–104.

Whitbeck, Caroline. 2015. "Trust." In J. Britt Holbrook and Carl Mitcham, eds. *Ethics, Science, Technology, and Engineering: A Global Resource*. Vol. 4, 2nd ed. Farmington Hills, MI: Macmillan Reference, pp. 419–23.

Woodhouse, E. J. 2004. "Nanotechnology Controversies." *IEEE Technology and Society Magazine* 21, no. 4: 6–8.

▶ FURTHER READINGS

Allhoff, Fritz, Patrick Lin, James Moor, and John Weckert, eds. 2007. *Nanoethics: The Ethical and Social Implications of Nanotechnology*. Hoboken, NJ: John Wiley and Sons.

Assimov, Isaac. 1976. "The Bicentennial Man." In M. Philips, ed. *Philosophy and Science Fiction*. Buffalo, NY: Prometheus, pp. 183–216.

Beavers, Anthony F., ed. 2010. *Robot Ethics and Human Ethics.* Special Issue of *Ethics and Information Technology* 12, no. 3.

Cameron, Nigel M. de S., and M. Ellen Mitchell, eds. 2007. *Nanoscale: Issues and Perspectives for the Nano Century*. Hoboken, NJ: John Wiley and Sons.

Epstein, Richard G. 1997. *The Case of the Killer Robot*. New York: John Wiley and Sons.

Grodzinsky, Frances S., Keith W. Miller, and Marty J. Wolf. 2014. "Developing Automated Deceptions and the Impact of Trust." *Philosophy and Technology* 28, no. 1: 91–105.

Johnson, Deborah G. and Thomas M. Powers. 2008. "Computers as Surrogate Agents." In J. van den Hoven and J. Weckert, eds. *Information Technology and Moral Philosophy*. Cambridge, UK: Cambridge University Press, pp. 251–69.

Mills, Kirsty and Charles Fleddermann. 2005. "Getting the Best from Nanotechnology: Approaching Social and Ethical Implications Openly and Proactively." *IEEE Technology and Society Magazine* 24, no. 4 : 18–26.

Sandler, Ronald L., ed. 2014. *Ethics and Emerging Technologies*. New York: Palgrave Macmillan/St. Martin's.

Simon, Judith. 2010. "The Entanglement of Trust and Knowledge on the Web." *Ethics and Information Technology* 12, no. 4: 343–55.

GLOSSARY

ACM Code of Ethics and Professional Conduct: A code of ethics endorsed by the Association for Computing Machinery.

accessibility privacy: A conception of privacy in terms of being let alone or being free from intrusion into one's physical space; contrasted with decisional privacy and informational privacy.

agent: Someone or something that is capable of acting; agents that act on behalf of others are sometimes called "fiduciary agents." See also *artificial agent*.

ambient intelligence (AmI): A technology that senses changes in the environment and automatically adapts to these changes vis-à-vis the needs and preferences of users while remaining in the background and thus being virtually invisible to users. See also *pervasive computing* and *ubiquitous communication*.

anonymity: In the context of cybertechnology, the ability to navigate the Internet and participate in online forums without having to reveal one's true identity.

applied ethics: A branch of ethical inquiry that examines practical (as opposed to theoretical) moral issues and problems. See also *ethical theory*.

artificial agent (AA): A nonhuman agent that can be either a physical/biological entity (such as a robot or cyborg) or an electronic/digital entity (such as an AI bot or "softbot"). See also *agent*.

artificial intelligence (AI): The field of study that examines relationships between machine intelligence and human intelligence. One branch of AI attempts to shed light on human intelligence by using cybertechnology to simulate it; another branch is concerned with constructing intelligent tools to assist humans in complex tasks. See also *expert systems*.

augmented reality (AR): A technology that enhances (or augments) a user's view of the real world through computer-generated sensory inputs, which typically include video inputs (including eyewear such as Google glass) and sound inputs. See also *virtual reality*.

autonomous machine (AM): A computerized system or agent that is capable of acting and making decisions independently of human oversight. AMs can interact with and adapt to (changes in) their environment and can learn (as they function).

avatar: A computer-generated image on a screen, or in virtual space, used to represent someone. Some avatars appear to exhibit human-like characteristics.

big data: A term commonly used to describe the collection and analysis of large and/or complex data sets via techniques that have the capacity to search, aggregate, and cross-reference them. See also *data mining*.

biometrics: The biological identification of a person, which includes eyes, voice, handprints, fingerprints, retina patterns, and handwritten signatures.

blog (or Web log): A Web site that contains an online journal with reflections and comments; blogs may be further categorized as political blogs, personal blogs, corporate blogs, travel blogs, health blogs, literary blogs, and so forth.

cloud computing: A technology that enables the sharing of computing resources, including software applications, outside an organization's firewall; deployment models for the cloud are typically categorized as either private, public, community, or hybrid.

computer security: A branch of computer science concerned with both safeguarding computer systems (hardware and software resources) from attacks by malicious programs, such as viruses and worms, and protecting the integrity of the data resident in and transmitted between those systems from unauthorized access.

consequentialism: An ethical theory that appeals to consequences, outcomes, or ends as the essential criterion, or standard, used to justify particular actions and policies in a moral system. See also *utilitarianism.*

contract theory of ethics: A theory that ties a moral obligation to assist others to an express contract to do so. Contract theory is sometimes viewed as a minimalist theory of morality because without an explicit contract, one would simply be required to do no harm to others; there is no obligation to actively assist others.

cookies: Text files that Web sites send to and retrieve from a Web visitor's computer system. Cookies technology enables Web site owners and operators to collect information about a visitor's preferences while the visitor interacts with their Web sites.

cultural relativism: A descriptive/empirical thesis stating that different cultures have different views about what is morally right or wrong. Many philosophers have argued that even if cultural relativism is true, it does not logically imply moral relativism, which is a normative position. See also *moral relativism.*

cyberbullying: A type of harassment (or bullying) that takes place online, via e-mail, text messaging, or online forums, such as social networking sites.

cybercrime: Criminal activity that is either made possible or significantly exacerbated by the use of computers and cybertechnology.

cyberethics: The field of study that examines moral, legal, and social issues involving cybertechnology.

cyberstalking: The use of cybertechnology to clandestinely track the movement and whereabouts of one or more individuals, often for purposes of harassment.

cybertechnology: A range of computing and information/communication technologies and devices, from stand-alone computer systems to privately owned computer networks to the Internet.

cyberterrorism: The convergence of cyberspace and terrorism, covering a range of politically motivated hacking operations that can result in loss of life, severe economic loss, or both.

data mining: A computerized technique for unearthing implicit patterns in large databases to reveal statistical data and corresponding associations that are often nonobvious; the patterns can be used to construct consumer profiles. See also *big data.*

denial-of-service attacks: Repeated requests sent to a Web site that are intended to disrupt services at that site. Denial-of-service attacks can be sent via third-party sites, from computer systems located in universities and organizations, to confuse the targeted sites about the source of the attacks.

deontological ethics: A theory of ethics that bases its moral system on duty or obligation rather than on consequences and outcomes that result from actions. Deontological ethical theories can be contrasted with consequentialist theories. See also *consequentialism.*

descriptive ethics: A branch of ethical inquiry that reports or describes the ethical principles and values held by various groups and individuals. Descriptive ethics is usually contrasted with normative ethics. See also *normative ethics.*

digital divide: The gap between those who have ("information haves") and those who do not have ("information have-nots") digital devices and access to the Internet.

digital rights management (DRM): A technology that allows content owners to regulate the flow of information in digital media by blocking access to it via encryption mechanisms.

ethical theory: A branch of ethical inquiry dedicated to the study of philosophical frameworks for determining when actions and policies are morally right or morally wrong. Ethical theory, or theoretical ethics, is often contrasted with applied ethics. See also *applied ethics*.

ethics: The study of morality or a moral system. Normative ethics approaches the study of a moral system from the perspective of philosophy, religion, or law, whereas descriptive ethics typically examines morality from the perspective of the social sciences. See also *morality*, *descriptive ethics*, and *normative ethics*.

expert system (ES): A computer program that is expert at performing one particular task traditionally performed by humans; developed from research in artificial intelligence. Because it is a computer program, an ES is different than a robot, which is a physical or mechanical system. See also *artificial intelligence* and *robotics*.

hacktivism: The convergence of political activism and computer hacking by which activists use cybertechnology to disrupt the operations of organizations.

identity theft: The act of taking another person's identity by using that person's name, social security number, credit card numbers, and so forth.

IEEE Code of Ethics: An ethical code sanctioned by the Institute of Electrical and Electronics Engineers.

information warfare (IW): Operations that target or exploit information media in order to win some objective over an adversary. IW, unlike conventional warfare, can be more disruptive than destructive; like conventional warfare, however, IW is waged by (legitimately recognized) nation-states.

informational privacy: A conception of privacy in terms of control over the flow of one's personal information, including the collection and exchange of that information; contrasted with accessibility privacy and decisional privacy.

intellectual property: An intangible form of property that is protected by a system of laws, such as patents, copyrights, trademarks, and trade secrets, through which authors and inventors are given ownership rights over their creative works.

Internet of Things (IoT): A network of "things"—intelligent devices and "smart objects"—that communicate not only with humans but also with other devices and (physical) objects.

locational privacy: A relatively new category of privacy generated by the use of embedded chips, RFID technology, and global positioning systems to track the physical location of individuals at any point in time.

machine ethics: A field that examines ethical concerns that arise because of what (highly sophisticated) computers are capable of doing on their own, as opposed to ethical issues resulting from what humans do with computers. See also *roboethics*.

macroethics: Concerned with the analysis of moral rules and policies at the societal level, as opposed to the level of individuals. See also *microethics*.

malware: A label that applies to a cluster of "malicious programs," including viruses, worms, Trojan horses, logic bombs, and so forth; malware can also include "spyware." See also *virus* and *worm*.

microethics: Concerned with the analysis of moral rules and directives at the level of individuals, as opposed to the societal level. See also *macroethics*.

moral absolutism: A view holding that there are absolute moral principles and that there is only one uniquely correct answer to every moral question.

moral objectivism: A compromise view between moral absolutism and moral relativism; moral objectivists believe that there are objective standards for evaluating moral claims, so that there can be agreement on the correct answers to many moral issues, but that there can also be more than one acceptable answer to some moral issues. See also *moral absolutism* and *moral relativism*.

moral relativism: The view that there are no universal moral norms or standards and that only the members of a particular group or culture are capable of evaluating the moral principles used within that group. See also *cultural relativism*.

morality: A system comprising rules, principles, and values; at its core are rules of conduct for guiding action and principles of evaluation for justifying those rules. See also *ethics*.

MMORPGs: Massively multiplayer online role-playing games, which include popular video games such as *World of Warcraft* and *Second Life*.

nanotechnology: A field dedicated to the development of extremely small electronic circuits and mechanical devices built at the molecular level of matter.

network neutrality: A principle in which all content, sites, and platforms on the Internet are treated equally; precludes service providers from privileging some groups of users with faster access and other kinds of online priorities.

normative ethics: A branch of ethical inquiry that is concerned with evaluating moral rules and principles by asking what ought to be the case, as opposed to descriptive ethics that simply reports what is the case (i.e., what individuals and cultures happen to believe) with respect to morally right and morally wrong behaviors. See also *descriptive ethics*.

online communities: Computer-mediated social groups that interact in virtual space, as contrasted with traditional communities in which interaction occurs in physical space. See also *virtual environment*.

open-source software (OSS): Software for operating systems and applications in which the source code is made freely available to use, modify, improve, and redistribute. Open-source software, such as the Linux operating system, is contrasted with proprietary operating system software such as MS Windows.

P2P technology: Peer-to-peer technology, which enables two or more computers to share files through either a centralized directory such as the (original) Napster site or a decentralized system such as LimeWire.

pervasive computing: A computing environment where information and communication technology are everywhere, for everyone, at all times. See also *ambient intelligence*.

phishing: A fraudulent use of e-mail to acquire a user's password, social security number, etc., to gain unauthorized access to information about the victim; often, the e-mail looks as if it were sent by an official site such as eBay or PayPal.

privacy enhancing technologies (PETs): Tools designed to protect a user's privacy while interacting with the Web.

Radio-frequency identification (RFID): A technology that consists of a tag (microchip) containing an electronic circuit, which stores data, and an antenna that broadcasts data by radio waves in response to a signal from a reader.

Right to be Forgotten: A privacy/data-protection principle that allows citizens in the European Union nations to have certain kinds of online personal information about them either "delinked" from search engine indexes or altogether deleted from the Internet; also referred to as the "Right to Erasure."

roboethics: A field that examines the ways that humans design, use, and treat robots and related AI entities. See also *machine ethics*.

robotics: The field of research and development in robots and robotic parts/limbs. See also *expert systems*.

sexting: The use of cell phones (or similar electronic devices) to send nude or seminude photos of oneself to others; in some cases, these photos become widely distributed and can eventually end up on the Internet.

social networking service (SNS): A Web-based service, such as Facebook, Twitter, LinkedIn, and so forth, which enables users to construct a profile and share information with other members (or "friends") on the online forum.

spam: E-mail that is generally considered to be unsolicited, promotional, and sent in bulk to multiple users.

Turing test: A scenario in which a person engaged in a conversation on a computer screen with some "entity" (located in a room that is not visible to the person) is asked to determine whether he or she is conversing with another human or with a computer.

utilitarianism: A consequentialist ethical theory based on the principle that an act or policy is morally permissible if it results in the greatest good (usually measured in terms of happiness) for the greatest number of people affected by it. See also *consequentialism.*

virtual environment (VE): An online (or computer-generated) environment, which is contrasted with an environment in physical space. VEs, unlike virtual reality (VR) environments and applications which are always three-dimensional, can be either two-dimensional (e.g., text-only) or three-dimensional. See also *virtual reality* and *online communities.*

virtual reality (VR): A three-dimensional, interactive computer-generated environment, as contrasted with physical reality. See also *augmented reality.*

virtue ethics: A theory that stresses character development and the acquisition of "correct" moral habits as opposed to mere conformance with certain rules for action, which are typically associated with duty-based (deontological) and consequence-based (utilitarian) ethical theories.

virus: A program that can insert executable copies of itself into other programs; also generically referred to as a malicious program. See also *worm* and *malware.*

whistle-blowing: A voluntary act in which one or more employees within an organization disclose nonpublic and/or sensitive information that is intended to alert the public about some improper conduct or wrongdoing involving the organization.

worm: A program or program segment that searches computer systems for idle resources and then disables them by erasing various locations in memory; also generically referred to as a malicious program. See also *virus* and *malware.*

INDEX

A
Abney, Keith, 336
accessibility privacy, 118–119
act utilitarianism, 46
adaptive user interfaces, 321
Adam, Alison, 56, 274
Adams, Andrew, 252
agent ethics. See machine ethics
Agre, Phil, 240
Aharonian, Gregory, 213
AI (artificial intelligence), 5, 305–312
Allen, Colin, 4, 107, 334, 336–339
Al-Saggaf, Yeslam, 238
ambient intelligence (AmI)
  and autonomy, freedom, and control, 321–322
  defined, 319
  ethical issues in, 321–324
  intelligent user interfaces (IUIs), 320–321
  pervasive computing, 320
  and privacy and surveillance, 322–324
  social issues in, 321–324
  and technological dependency, 322
  ubiquitous communication, 320
AmI (ambient intelligence), 319–324
Anderson, Michael, 336, 339
Anderson, Susan Leigh, 336–339
Anonymous (hacker group), 166, 236–237
applied ethics, cyberethics as branch of
  overview, 12–13
  philosophical ethics, 14–16
  professional ethics, 13–14
  sociological/descriptive ethics, 16–18
architecture mode, Internet regulation, 240–241
arguments
  ad hominem fallacy, 79–80
  application in cybertechnology, 63–65
  argumentum ad vericundiam, 80
  conclusions, defined, 65–67
  constructing, 67–68
  defined, 64–65
  evaluating, seven-step strategy, 77–79
  fallacious, 75–77
  fallacy of ambiguity/equivocation, 82
  fallacy of composition, 81
  fallacy of division, 81
  false cause fallacy, 81
  false dichotomy/either-or/all-or-nothing fallacy, 82–83
  inductive, 74–75
  invalid, 73–74
  premises, defined, 65–67
  slippery slope, 80
  sound, 71–73
  valid, 69–71
  virtuality fallacy, 83
Aristotle, 54, 222
ARPANET, 5
artificial intelligence (AI)
  AI entities warranting moral consideration, 310–312
  classical AI, 305
  cyborgs, 307–309
  Chinese room argument, 307
  Deep Blue (program), 306
  defined, 305–306
  GOFAI (God Old Fashioned AI), 305
  HAL computer, 309
  symbolic AI, 305
  Turing test, 306–307
  Watson (program), 306–307
artificial reality, see virtual reality
Artz, John, 84
Asimov, Isaac, 337–338
Assakawa, Cheiko, 271
Assange, Julian, 194–196
augmented reality (AR), 300–301
autonomous artificial agents, 332–334
autonomous machines (AMs)
  defined, 329–330
  ethical issues, 332–336
  examples of, 331–332
  philosophical issues, 332–336
autonomous systems. See autonomous machines (AMs)
autonomy
  definition of, 334
  and control, 321–322
  and freedom, 321–322
  functional, 334
availability, computer security and, 152
avatar, 299, 302, 309

B
Barger, Robert, 3, 89, 94
Bekey, George B., 336
Benkler, Yochai, 193, 195–196
Bentham, Jeremy, 45, 323–324
Berne, Rosalind, 324
Berners-Lee, Tim, 224, 270
Beuchner, Jeff, 344
big data, 127–128
biometric technologies, cybercrime and, 187–188
Bissett, Andy, 304
BitTorrent, 210
blogs
  defined, 295
  democracy and, 280
  as online communities, 295
  political blogs, 280
blogosphere. See blogs
Boatright, John, 98–99
Bocij, Paul, 185
Bok, Sisela, 99
bot ethics, see machine ethics
Bottis, Maria, 143–144, 243
Bowyer, Kevin W., 91
Boyle, James, 225
Brandeis, Louis, 118
Brenkert, George, 99, 102
Brey, Philip, 6, 15, 19–21, 188, 275–276, 299–300, 303, 305, 321–322
Briggle, Adam, 297–298
Buchanan, Elizabeth, 4, 13, 90, 225, 275–276
Burk, Dan, 234
Burn, Enid, 272
Bynum, Terry Ward, 92–94

C
Camp, Jean, 238–239
Camp, Tracy, 274
Campbell, James, 225
CAN SPAM Act, 246
Capurro, Rafael, 3, 222–223, 336
categorical imperative, 48–49
Catudal, Jacques, 247, 250–251
Cavoukian, Ann, 159–160
CEH (*See* Certified Ethical Hackers)
Certified Ethical Hackers (CEH), 164, 179

Chapman, Gary, 267
character-based ethical theories, 54–56
Chadwick, Ruth, 324
Chien, Y. T., 238–239
Chinese room argument, 307
Chopra, Samir, 220
Cica, Natasha, 286
Clark, Andrew, 308
Clarke, Roger, 124
Clementi, Tyler, 237
Cloud computing
  defined, 158
  deployment models, 158–159
  privacy concerns, 159
  securing data, 159–160
  service/delivery models, 158–159
Cocking, Dean, 229–298
Code Red Worm, system security, 156
codes of conduct
  criticisms of, 93–94
  in defense of, 94–95
  overview, 91–93
  purpose of, 91
  SECEPP (Software Engineering Code of Ethics and Professional Practice), 95–97
  strengths/weaknesses of, 95
codes of ethics. *See* codes of conduct
Coeckelbergh, Mark, 335
Coleman, Stephen, 286
communities. *See* online communities
Compaine, Benjamin, 265
computer crime, computer security and, 153
computer monitoring and surveillance, workplace, 284–287
computer professionals
  codes of ethics, 91–97
  professional ethics, 88–89
computer security
  accessibility, 152–153
  cloud-storage, 158–160
  Code Red Worm, 156
  computer break-ins, 163–164
  computer crime and, 153
  confidentiality, 152–153
  Conficker Worm, 156
  cyberterrorism, 164–165
  data security, 155
  GhostNet controversy, 157
  hackers, 160–163
  information warfare, 167–170
  integrity, 152–153
  network security, 156–157
  overview, 152–154
  privacy *versus,* 153–154
  risk analysis and, 161
  system security, 156
  Trojan horses, 156
  viruses, 156–157
  worms, 156–157
confidentiality, computer security and, 152–153
Conficker Worm, 156
consequence-based ethical theories, 44–47
contextual-integrity privacy theory, 120–121
contract-based ethical theories, 51–54
converging technologies, 120–121
cookies, privacy techniques, 124–125
Cooper, Joel, 228
copyright law
  challenges posed by recent amendments to, 207
  DMCA (Digital Millennium Copyright Act), 207
  Digital Millennium Copyright Act (DMCA), 207
  fair-use and first-sale provisions, 207–208
  fair-use provision, challenges to, 207
  infringement, software piracy as, 208–209
  laws and contracts, jurisdictional issues involving, 214–215
  SBCTEA (Sonny Bono Copyright Term Extension Act), 207
  S-DMCA (Super DMCA), 207
  Super DMCA (S-DMCA), 207
  in U.S., evolution of, 206–207
corporate espionage, cybercrime, 191
counterhacking, 178–180
Coy, Wolfgang, 226
cracking *versus* hacking, 179
Creative Commons, 227–228
crime, computer, 177–178, 180–187
criminal activities. *See* cybercrimes
critical reasoning
  defined, 64
  informal logical fallacies, 79–84
criticisms, of professional codes, 93–94
cultural relativism, 40–41
Cutler, Jessica, 295
cybercrimes
  background events, 177–178
  biometric technologies, 187–188
  cyberassisted crimes, 184–185
  cybercriminals and, 177–178
  cyberexacerbated crimes, 184–185
  cyberpiracy, 183
  cybertrespass, 183
  cybervandalism, 183
  defined, 180–182
  denial of service attacks, 180
  entrapment, 189
  free press, 195–196
  hacking, 178–180
  identity theft, 185–186
  jurisdiction in cyberspace, problem of, 190–191
  keystroke monitoring, 188
  legislative efforts to combat, 191–193
  Patriot Act and government surveillance techniques, 189–190
  technologies and tools for combating, 187–189
  WikiLeaks, 193–196
cyberethics. *See also* cybertechnology
  as field of philosophical ethics, 14–16
  as field of professional ethics, 12–14
  as field of sociological/descriptive ethics, 16–18
  defined, 2–4
  developmental phases, 4–7
  disclosive method for, 19–21
  interdisciplinary and multilevel method for analyzing, 21
  methodologies, 19–27
  uniqueness in question, 7–11
cyberexacerbated crimes, 184–185
cyberpiracy, 183
cybertechnology. *See also* cyberethics
  defined, 2–3
  disabilities and, 270–271
  examples of, 4–6
  gender and, 263–276
  race and, 271–273
cyberterrorism, 165–168
cybertrespass, 183
cybervandalism, 183
cyborgs, 307–309

D

Dale, Nell, 156
data
  mining, privacy and, 128–132
  monitoring and recording, privacy techniques, 123–126
  security, 156
Davis, Michael, 91, 93–94
DeCew, Judith, 118, 123
decisional privacy, 118
Decker, Michael, 336
Deep Blue (program), 306
De George, Richard, 37, 99, 101–103, 223
deliberation
  cyberethics strategy issues, 21–22
  just-consequentialist framework, 57–59
democracies, Internet and cyberspace
  electronic process and electronic media, 279–280
  favoring democracies questions about, 276–277
  Internet filtering and deliberative democracy, 278–279
  political and social fragmentation, 277–288
  political blogs and the democratic process, 277–278

denial of service attacks, 164–166, 180
Denning, Dorothy, 164–167
deontological theories, 47–51
deVries, Willem, 344
Dexter, Scott, 220
Diaz, Alejandro, 277–278
digital divide
  as an ethical issues, 268–269
  defined, 265
  global, 265–266
  obligations to bridge, 269–270
  public education system in United States, 267
  vital resources and distributive justice, 268–269
  within nations, 266–267
Digital Rights Management (DRM) technology, 242–244
disabilities
  cybertechnology and, 270–271
  WAI support, 270–271
disclosive level, cyberethics issues, 19–21
Doctorow, Cory, 212, 223–224, 243
domestic surveillance, 126–127, 190–191
Doss, David, 100–101
Drexler, K. Eric, 324–327
DRM (Digital Rights Management) technology, 242–244
duty-based ethical theories, 47–51

E
e-mail privacy and employer policies, employment and work, 284–285
Elgesem, Dag, 140
ELIZA (program), 335
Elkin-Koren, Niva, 242–243
ELSI Research Program, 340
employee loyalty
  loyalty to employers, 97–98
  whistle-blowing, 98–103
employment and work, cybertechnology and
  automation, 281
  e-mail privacy and employer policies, 284–285
  globalization and outsourcing, 282–283
  job displacement and remote work, 281–282
  quality of work-life, 283–287
  remote work, 281–282
  robotics and expert systems, 281–282
  surveillance and computer monitoring, 284–287
  transformed workplace, 280–283
Englebart, Doug, 224
Epstein, Richard, 153–154, 278
Ess, Charles, 42
ethicists *versus* moralists, 34–35
ethics. *See also* morality
  "correct habits," acquiring, 55–66
  ethical theories
    character-based, 54–56
    consequence-based, 44–47
    contract-based, 51–64
    duty-based, 47–51
    integrating into single comprehensive theory, 56–59
    need for, 43–44
  professional
    computer professionals, 90–91
    cyberethics as field of, 12–14
    overview, 88–89
    safety-critical software, 91
eye patterns, biometrics, 187–188

F
Facebook, 6, 132
FaceTime, 294
fair-use and first-sale doctrines, 207–208
Fairweather, Ben, 93
fallacious arguments, 75–78
fallacy of ambiguity/equivocation, 82
fallacy of composition, 81
fallacy of division, 81
fallacy of false cause, 81
fallacy of false dichotomy/either-or, all-or-nothing, 82–83
Feynman, Richard, 325
finger prints, biometrics, 187–188
Finholt, Thomas, 17
Flame Virus, 169
Floridi, Luciano, 5, 144–146, 194, 311–312, 332, 344
Forester, Tom, 181, 286, 288–289
Franklin, Benjamin, 154
Free Software Foundation (FSF), 219–220
freedom from interference in personal affairs, privacy issues, 118
freedom from unwarranted intrusion, privacy issues, 118
Fried, Charles, 122
Froomkin, Michael, 121
FSF (Free Software Foundation), 219–220
Fulda, Joseph, 135

G
Garfinkel, Simpson, 121, 126
gender, cybertechnology and, 273–276
Genetic Information Nondiscrimination Act (GINA), 139
Gert, Bernard, 30–31, 57
GhostNet controversy, 157, 168
Gilligan, Carol, 56
GINA (Genetic Information Nondiscrimination Act), 139
Girasa, Roy, 182, 190, 215, 254
globalization, 282–283
gold farming, 304–305
Goldman, Alvin, 280
González, Mario Costeja, 141–142, 146
Goodrum, Abby, 165–166
Goodwin, Mike, 238–239
Google search engine and privacy controversies, 134–135
Gordijn, Bert, 325
Gotshalk v. Benson, 213
Gotterbarn, Don, 13–14, 88, 95–97, 181
Grance, Timothy, 158
Graham, Gordon, 277
Grodzinsky, Frances, 55, 86, 148, 204, 219, 243, 270
Grosso, Andrew, 209
Gruman, Galen, 158
Gutmann, Mathias, 336

H
habits, acquiring "correct," 55–56
hackers
  computer security, 160–163
  cracking *versus*, 179
  cybercrimes and, 178–180
HAL computer, 309
Halbert, Debora, 213
Hall, John Storrs, 330
Halpern, Sue, 132
Hardin, Garret, 225
hate speech, Internet regulation and, 254–255
Health Insurance Portability and Accountability Act (HIPAA), 139
Heartbleed Virus, 156
Heller, Michael, 226
Henderson, Kathrine, 4
Hilden, Julie, 253–254
Himanen, Pekka, 161, 178
Himma, Kenneth, 154, 165, 206, 265, 269–270, 332
Hinman, Lawrence, 107, 278
HIPAA (Health Insurance Portability and Accountability Act), 139
Hjørland, Birger, 222–223
Hobbes, Thomas, 51
Huff, Chuck, 17, 228

I
identity theft, 185–187
industry self-regulation initiatives, privacy, 137–139
informal feature, Gert's moral system, 31
informal logical fallacies, 79–84
information warfare, computer security, 167–704
informational privacy, 118–119
informed consent, 138
instrumental values, 31–32, 122–123

intelligent user interfaces (IUSs), 320–321
integrity, computer security and, 152–153
intellectual property
  abbreviations and acronyms pertaining to, 215
  copyright law
    challenges posed by recent amendments to, 207
    fair-use and first-sale doctrines, 207–208
    infringement, software piracy as, 208–209
    laws and contracts, jurisdictional issues involving, 214–215
    SBCTEA (Sonny Bono Copyright Term Extension Act), 207
    Super DMCA (S-DMCA), 207
    in U.S., evolution of, 206–207
  Creative Commons, 227–228
  information commons, 225–227
  intellectual objects, 203–204
  jurisdictional challenges, 214–215
  labor theory of property, 215–216
  patent protections, 212–213
  personality theory of property, 217–219
  PIPA (Protect Intellectual Property Act), 228–229
  Protect Intellectual Property Act (PIPA), 228–229
  public domain of ideas, 226–227
  Research Works Act (RWA), 229–231
  RWA (Research Works Act), 229–231
  software as, 204–206
  SOPA (Stop Online Piracy Act), 228–229
  Stop Online Piracy Act (SOPA), 228–229
  trade secrets, 214
  trademarks, 213–214
  TRIPS Agreement, 214–215
  utilitarian theory of property, 216–217
  WIPO (World Intellectual Property Organization), 214–215
Internet. *See also* Internet regulation
  accessing public records via, 136
  search engines and retrieval of personal information via, privacy and, 136
Internet of things, 317–318
Internet regulation.
  background issues and preliminary distinctions, 238
  categories of, 239–240
  by code, 240–241
  content regulation, 239–240
  Digital Rights Management (DRM), 242–244
  DRM (Digital Rights Management), 242–244
  free speech *versus* censorship and content control, 246–248
  hate speech, 254–255
  modes of, 240–241
  overview, 237–238
  music industry, 243–244
  pornography, 248–254
  privatization of information policy, 242–243
  process regulation, 239–240
  spam, 244–246
intrinsic values, 31–32
Introna, Lucas, 277, 284
invalid arguments, 73–74

J
job displacement and automation. *See* employment and work, cybertechnology and
Jobs, Steve, 244
Johnson, Deborah G., 3, 332
Jonas, Hans, 311
Joy, Bill, 327
judgmental behavior, morality roadblocks, 37–38
jurisdiction in cyberspace, 190–192

K
Kant, Immanuel, 47–50, 245
Karveth, Rod, 272
KaZaA, 210
keystroke monitoring, cybercrimes, 188
Kimppa, Kai, 304
Kismet, 335–336
Kizza, Joseph, 284
Knorr, Eric 158
Kretchmer, Susan, 272
Kurzweil, Ray, 308, 340

L
labor theory of property, intellectual property disputes, 215–216
Ladd, John, 93–94, 105
La Macchia, David, 209
Langford, Duncan, 3
LANs (Local Area Networks), 3
laws
  data protection and, privacy issues, 127–140
  Internet regulation, 239–240
legal systems, grounding moral principles in, 33
Leman-Langlois, Stephane, 180–181
Lessig, Lawrence, 226–228, 240–241, 256–257
Levinson, Nancy G., 106
Levy, Neil, 302
Levy, Steven, 161
Lewis, John, 156
LimeWire, 210
Lin, Patrick, 331, 336
Lininger, Rachael, 185–186
LinkedIn, 293
Local Area Networks (LANs), 3
Locke, John, 215–216
Lockton, Vance, 125
Luck, Morgan, 302

M
machine ethics
  defined, 336–337
  designing moral machines, 337–340
  ethical aspects of autonomous machines, 332–334
  and autonomous machines, 329–332
Manning, Bradley Pfc. (Chelsea), 196
MacIntyre, Alasdair, 54
macroethical level, rules of conduct, 30
malware, 156
Maner, Walter, 8
Manion, Mark, 165–166
market pressures, Internet regulation, 240–241
Martin, Michael, 93
Marturano, Antonio, 324
Mason, Richard, 282
massively multiplayer online games (MMOGs), 301–305
massively multiplayer online role-playing games (MMORPGs), 301–305
Mathiesen, Kay, 247
Matthews, Steve, 297–298
McCarthy, John, 305
McLeod, Carolyn, 334
McNeally, Scott, 121
McFarland, Michael, 222–224
media types, Internet regulation and, 238–239
Meier, Megan, 298–299
Mell, Peter, 158
Merkle, Ralph, 325, 327
methodologies, cyberethics, 19–22
MGM v. Grokster, 212
microethical level, rules of conduct, 30
Mill, John Stuart, 45, 276
Miller, Keith, 92, 156, 204, 219, 244, 245
Minsky, Marvin, 305
Mitcham, Carl, 97
MMOGs (Massively multiplayer online games), 301–305
MMORPGs (Massively multiplayer online roleplaying games), 301–305
Monahan, Torin, 283

MOO (Multi-user Object-Oriented environment), 298–299, 304
Moor, James H., 6, 10–11, 14–15, 29, 32, 57–59, 83, 119–120, 153, 244–246, 308, 326, 328, 332–333, 340–341
Moore, Adam, 203, 206
Moore, Robert, 181
moral absolutism, 41–42
moral objectivism, 41–42
moral machines, 337–340
moral relativism, 40–41
morality. *See also* ethics
  defined, 29–30
  dilemmas, 28–29
  discussion stoppers as roadblocks
    common agreements on moral issue, 35–43
    cultural relativism, 40–41
    disagreement on fundamental issue, 36–37
    judgmental behaviors, 37–39
    moral absolutism, 42
    moral relativism, 40–41
    moral objectivism, 42
    principles *versus* facts, disagreements, 37
    private *versus* public matter, 39–40
  ethicists *versus*, 34–35
  moral persons *versus* following moral rules, 54–55
  moral responsibility
    accountability and problem of many hands, 105–106
    legal liability and, 106
    overview, 103–105
    special obligations for computer corporations, 107–108
  moral systems
    components of, 30–31
    core values and roles, 31–32
    Gert's model of, 30–31
    legal system moral principles, grounding, 32–34
    overview, 29–31
    philosophical system moral principles, 31–32
    religious system moral principles, 32–33
    policies, 29–30
    rules and principles, 30–31
    rules of conduct, 30–31
Morrison, Perry, 191, 286, 288–289
Moss, Jeremy, 268–269
Multi-user Object-Oriented environment (MOO), 298–299
MySpace, 298

N
Nagenborg, Michael, 336
nanocomputers, 324–326
nanoethics, 326–327
nanotechnology,
  defined, 324
  development as a field of scientific research, 325
  future research and development, 327
  need for clear ethical guidelines, 326–327
  risk assessment and precautionary principle, 328–339
Napster controversy, 209–210
National Institute on Standards and Technology (NIST), 158
National Security Agency (NSA), 113–114, 101–102
Network neutrality
  defined, 256
  debate about, 257–258
  future implications, 257–258
  proponents, 257
  opponents, 257
negative rights, 53
Neumann, Peter, 154
Nissenbaum, Helen, 104–106, 120–121, 125, 133–134, 277
(NIST) National Institute on Standards and Technology, 158
Nolt, John, 68
Non-Public Personal Information (NPI), 133
normative *versus* descriptive ethics, 16–17
Norris, Pippa, 269
NPI (Non-Public Personal Information), 133
NSA (National Security Agency), 113–114, 101–102

O
O'Hara, Keiron, 266
O'Neill, Onora, 334
online communities
  blogs, as a form of, 295–296
  deception in, 298–299
  discussed, 293–299
  friendships in, 297–298
  pros and cons of, 296–299
  social polarization in, 296–297
  traditional communities *versus*, 294–295
online friendships, 297–298
Onsrud, Harlan, 225
Ontario v. Quon, 284–285
Open Source Software (OSS), 220–221
outsourcing, 282–283

P
(P2P) Peer-to-Peer systems, 240
panopticon, 322–323
Pariser, Eli, 132, 278
Parker, Donn, 178
Parnas, David Lorge, 100
Parsell, Mitch, 296
patent protections, intellectual property disputes, 212–213
Peer-to-Peer (P2P) systems, 240
Perlman, Bruce, 93
pervasive computing, 320
pervasive surveillance, 323–324
PETs (privacy-enhancing tools), 137–138
pharming, 188
phases, cyberethics evolution, 4–7
philosophical ethics
  cyberethics as field of, 14–16
  moral principles in, grounding, 33–34
phishing, 186–187
PIPA (Protect Intellectual Property Act), 228–229
Pieters, Wolter, 160
Pirate Bay (Web site), 194
Plato, 54, 276
Pojman, Louis, 42
policies, morality, 29–30
policy vacuum, case illustration, 10–11
pornography, Internet regulation, 248–254
positive rights, 53
Power, Richard, 178, 188
PPI (Public Personal Information), 133
precautionary principle, 328–329
Protect Intellectual Property Act (PIPA), 228–229
prima facie duties, 50, 338
principles and rules, morality, 30–31
privacy
  accessibility privacy, 118–119
  big data, 127–128
  biometric technology, 187–188
  comprehensive account of, 119–120
  computer security *versus*, 153–154
  consumer profiling, 131–132
  as contextual integrity, 120–121
  control over flow of personal information, 118–119
  cookies, 124–125
  data mining, 128–132
  data monitoring and recording techniques, 123–126
  dataveillance, 124
  decisional privacy, 118
  definition of, 117–120
  descriptive privacy, 119
  freedom from interference in one's personal affairs, 118
  freedom from unwarranted intrusion, 118
  importance of, 121–123
  industry self-regulation initiatives regarding, 137–139
  informational, 118–119
  normative privacy, 119–120

privacy (*Continued*)
NPI (Non-Public Personal Information), 133
PETs (privacy-enhancing tools), 137–138
PPI (Public Personal Information), 133
public records, accessing via Internet, 136
search engines and retrieval of personal information via Internet, 135–136
as social value, 123
Web mining, 132
privacy-enhancing tools (PETs), 137–138
process regulation, Internet regulation, 239–240
professional codes of conduct. *See* codes of conduct
professional ethics
defined, 90–91
cyberethics as field of, 12–14
overview, 88–89
safety-critical applications, 91
professional responsibility, moral responsibility, 103–105
property. *See* intellectual property
Protestant Ethic and the Spirit of Capitalism, The, 161
Public Personal Information (PPI), 133
public domain of ideas, intellectual property disputes, 226–227
public feature, Gert's moral system, 30–31
public records, accessing via Internet, privacy and, 146

Q
quality of work-life, cybertechnology and, 283–286

R
race, cybertechnology and, 271–273
radio frequency identification (RFID), 125–126
Raiter, Mike, 304
Raisinghani, Ajit, 319–320
rationality, Gert's moral system, 30–31
Rawls, John, 268
Raymond, Eric, 179, 220
Regan, Priscilla, 123
Regis, Ed, 325
religious system, grounding moral principles in, 32–33
Research Works Act (RWA), 229–231
retina patterns, biometrics, 187–188
RFID (radio frequency identification), 125–126
Rheingold, Howard, 294, 313–314, 318–319
Right to Be Forgotten, 140–146
rights
moral, 53
natural, 53
negative, 53
positive, 53
risk analysis, computer security and, 161
robo-ethics, see machine ethics
robotics and expert systems, employment and work in cybertechnology, 281–282
Rogerson, Simon, 92, 94
Rooksby, Emma, 268, 286
Rosenberg, Richard, 125
Ross, David, 49–51, 163, 338
Rotenberg, Marc, 267
Royal Academy of Engineering, 331, 334, 340
rule utilitarianism, 46–47
rules and principles, morality and, 29–31
rules of conduct, morality, 29–31
RWA (Research Works Act), 229–231

S
safety-critical applications, professional ethics, 91
Samuelson, Pamela, 212, 214
Sandin, Per, 251
Schinzinger, Roland, 93
Schneir, Bruce, 160
search engines and retrieval of personal information via Internet, privacy and, 135–136
Searle, John, 307
Second Life, 301–302, 304
Seeman, Nadrian, 325
SECEPP (Software Engineering Code of Ethics and Professional Practice), 95–97
security. *See* computer security
sexting, 252–254
Simpson, Michael, 157
Siri, 307
Skoudis, Ed, 156
Skype, 293
slippery slope arguments, 80
Smalley, Richard, 326–327
Smit, Iva, 336
Snapper, John, 213
Snowden, Eric, 101–102, 114
SNS (*See* social networking service)
social networking service (SNS), 293–294
social norms, Internet regulation, 240–241
sociological/descriptive ethics, cyberethics as field of, 16–18
Software Engineering Code of Ethics and Professional Practice (SECEPP), 95–97
Solove, Daniel, 82–83, 154, 122–123
Son, Wha-Chun, 334
Sony BMG controversy, 243
SOPA (Stop Online Piracy Act), 228–229
Søraker, Johnny Hartz, 299–300, 303
sound arguments, 71–73
Spafford, Eugene, 163–165, 223, 275
spam, Internet regulation, 244–246
speech in cyberspace. *See* Internet regulation
Spinello, Richard A., 123, 155, 206, 245–246
Stallman, Richard, 219–222
Stevens, David, 266
Stop Online Piracy Act (SOPA), 228–229
streaming, online music, 201–201, 210–211
Strickwerda, Litska, 183
Stuxnet Worm, 168–169
Sullins, John, 329
Sunstein, Cass, 277–278
surveillance and computer monitoring, workplace, 284–287
Swift, Taylor, 201–202, 211
system security, computer security, 156

T
Talbot, David, 159–160
Tavani, Herman T., 24–25, 86, 111, 148–149, 172, 199, 233–234, 289, 314, 344
technological convergence, 318–319
technological dependence, 322–323
Theismeyer, Lynn, 272
theoretical level, cyberethics issues, 21
theories
ethical
character-based, 54–56
consequence-based, 44–47
contract-based, 51–54,
deontological, 47–51
duty-based, 47–51
integrating into single comprehensive theory, 56–59
need for, 43–44
utilitarian, 44–47
labor theory of property, 215–216
personality theory of property, 217–229
utilitarian theory of property, 216–217
Thompson, Paul, 153
Torvalds, Linus, 220
trade secrets, intellectual property disputes, 214

trademarks, intellectual property disputes, 213–214
Trojan horses, computer security and, 156
Trust, 334–336
Turing, Alan, 306, 307
Turing test, 306–307
Turkle, Sherry, 335
Turner, Clark S., 106
Twitter, 293

U
ubiquitous communication, 320
ubiquitous computing. *See* ambient intelligence (AmI)
UCITA (Uniform Computer and Information Transactions Act), 214–215
universal service *versus* universal access, digital divide, 266–267
USA Patriot Act, 127, 189–190
utilitarianism, 44–47

V
valid arguments, 68–71
values, moral system roles, 31–32
van Cleeff, Andre, 160
van den Hoven, Jeroen, 21, 268
van der Ploeg, 187
Varma, Roli, 93
Verizon v. RIAA, 210
Veruggio, Gianmarco, 336
Vines, Russell Dean, 185–186
virtual environments, 299–300
virtual reality (VR), 300–302
virtue ethics, 54–56, 222
viruses, 156–157
voice patterns, biometrics, 187–188
VR (virtual reality), 300–302

W
W3C (World Wide Web Consortium), 270
WAI (Web Accessibility Initiative), 270–271
Wall, David, 178–179, 184, 187–188
Wallach, Wendell, 4, 107, 329, 336–339
WANs (Wide Area Networks), 3
Warner, Dorothy, 304
Warren, Samuel, 118
Warwick, Shelly, 224
Watson (program), 306–307
Web Accessibility Initiative (WAI), 270–271
Web 2.0, 6, 294
Web log (see blog)
Web mining, 132
Weber, Max, 161
Weckert, John, 237–238, 308, 326, 328, 332–333, 340–341
Weineke, David, 196
Weizenbaum, Joseph, 327, 335
WELL (Whole Earth 'Lectronic Link), 294
Wessels, Michael, 274
Westin, Alan, 122
whistle-blowing, 98–103
White, Michelle, 294
Whole Earth 'Lectronic Link (WELL), 294
Wide Area Networks (WANs), 3
WikiLeaks
  about, 193–194
  Assange, Julian, 193–195
  criminal aspects, 194–195
  ethical aspects, 194
  and free press, 195–196
  and national security, 194–195
  and responsible journalism, 195–196
WIPO (World Intellectual Property Organization), 214–215
Wolf, Marty, 204, 219
Wonderly, Monique, 302
World of Warcraft (WOW), 301
World Wide Web Consortium (W3C), 270
work and employment. *See* employment and work, cybertechnology and
Woodbury, Marsha, 271
World Intellectual Property Organization (WIPO), 214–215
worms, 156–157
WOW (World of Warcraft), 301
Wu, Tim, 256

X
Xerox PARC, 224

Y
Yurcik, William, 100–101

Z
Zeng, Ke, 158
Zimmer, Michael, 125
Zuckerberg, Mark, 121